The Newgate Calendar: Comprising Interesting Memoirs of the Most Notorious Characters Who Have Been Convicted of Outrages On the Laws of England Since the Commencement of the Eighteenth Century; with Occasional Anecdotes and Observations, Speeches, Confes

Andrew Knapp

Nabu Public Domain Reprints:

You are holding a reproduction of an original work published before 1923 that is in the public domain in the United States of America, and possibly other countries. You may freely copy and distribute this work as no entity (individual or corporate) has a copyright on the body of the work. This book may contain prior copyright references, and library stamps (as most of these works were scanned from library copies). These have been scanned and retained as part of the historical artifact.

This book may have occasional imperfections such as missing or blurred pages, poor pictures, errant marks, etc. that were either part of the original artifact, or were introduced by the scanning process. We believe this work is culturally important, and despite the imperfections, have elected to bring it back into print as part of our continuing commitment to the preservation of printed works worldwide. We appreciate your understanding of the imperfections in the preservation process, and hope you enjoy this valuable book.

THE
NEWGATE CALENDAR;

COMPRISING

INTERESTING MEMOIRS

OF

THE MOST NOTORIOUS CHARACTERS

WHO HAVE BEEN CONVICTED OF OUTRAGES ON

The Laws of England

SINCE THE COMMENCEMENT OF THE EIGHTEENTH CENTURY;

WITH

OCCASIONAL ANECDOTES AND OBSERVATIONS,
SPEECHES, CONFESSIONS, AND LAST EXCLAMATIONS OF SUFFERERS.

BY

ANDREW KNAPP AND WILLIAM BALDWIN,

ATTORNEYS AT LAW.

Tower of London.

VOL. IV.

London:
J. ROBINS AND CO. IVY LANE, PATERNOSTER ROW.
1828.

KNAPP AND BALDWIN'S
NEWGATE CALENDAR,
AND
Criminal Recorder.

The Affray in which Bolding was killed.

JAMES SWEENY, RICHARD PEARCE, EDMUND BUCKLEY, PATRICK FLEMING, MAURICE BRENWICK, AND JOHN SULLIVAN,
CONVICTED OF MURDER.

These unhappy men were natives of Ireland, and belonged to that numerous class who resort to England in search of employment; but whose conduct is too often a disgrace to their own country, and a demoralizing example for this. The murder, for which these malefactors justly forfeited their lives, originated in that vulgar antipathy which the lower orders of one nation feel for their brethren of another; forgetful that all men should be brothers in distress.

On their trial, which took place at Chelmsford, on the 16th of August, 1810, it appeared in evidence that John Bolding, for whose murder they were arraigned, kept the Eagle and Child public house, at Forest Gate, in the parish of West Ham, and that on Sunday evening, the 20th of May preceding, a dispute took place in the kitchen, between one Morrisy, an Irish labourer, and one Thomas, an English carter. There was present another Irishman, named Scandling, and an officer's servant, of the Cornish militia.

These silly representations of their respective countries kept up a boisterous debate for a considerable time, during which challenges to fight were given, and Morrisy and the officer's servant were proceeding to blows, when the housekeeper, Sarah Cumber, interfered, and succeeded in pacifying them for a moment. Morrisy then proposed to depart; but the landlord, suspecting that he wanted only to collect his countrymen, prevented him at first, though it appears he afterwards permitted him to withdraw, and then bolted the doors. The landlord's conjecture was right; Morrisy returned with a mob of followers, but was refused admittance. Soon after a man named Daniel Mahony knocked, when Scandling, who had remained within, opened the door, contrary to the wishes and in spite of the remonstrance of the proprietor. Mahony, in an outrageous manner, stormed, swore, and brandished his stick over his head. He had not continued long in this violent manner, when a gang of thirty of his countrymen demanded admittance. This being refused, they proceeded to break the windows and window-shutters, and Scandling, once more, in defiance of the opposition of the landlord, unbolted the door. As the band of ruffians rushed in, the carter and the officer's servant escaped through the back door; and fortunately for them, as otherwise, in all probability, they would have met the fate of their host. Mahony demanded the cause of the uproar, and was answered by a ferocious Hibernian that the English had insulted an Irishman. 'That's enough,' he returned, leaping into the bar, and, knocking down the landlord, continued to beat him till his head was much bruised, his arms broken, and his body greatly wounded. A female interfering, a blow was made at her, and she was obliged to fly and hide herself. The ruffians next proceeded to search for the carter and the servant; but, not finding them, they swore they would murder some one before they departed, and actually beat an old man, who was running away, who had three of his teeth knocked out, and his thigh dislocated from the kicks he received. These sanguinary brutes next demanded some gin, which was given them, and they departed, exclaiming, 'Who will insult an Irishman?'

Bolding, the landlord, languished seven days, and then expired, in consequence of the wounds he received. These six men were then taken up, all the others having absconded, and being sworn to as implicated in the riot, they were found guilty as accessaries to the murder, being associated for illegal purposes, which, according to Lord Hale, makes each accomplice responsible for the conduct of a part, or whole.

Sullivan, who was guilty of nothing except being present, was respited, but the other five unfortunate men were executed on Saturday morning, August the 18th, 1810.

JOHN LUMLEY,
WHIPPED FOR POT-STEALING

THERE is no petty thieving which has so much increased as stealing the pewter wherein London publicans serve their customers with porter. Even families have been detected in disgracefully withholding and denying their having publicans' pots in their possession, while proof has been offered that they had not returned them to the owner. Such people are worse than the petty thief who more daringly robs; and pity 'tis that the law could not reach them as far as the punishment inflicted on Lumley.

To check the severe and increasing losses arising from pot-stealing, which is nearly incredible, the publicans, who now form a respectable association in London, as Licensed Victuallers, brought a bill into parliament for the better protection of their property; but the Commons conceiving, perhaps, the complaint not to be of sufficient magnitude for the interference of the legislative body, threw out the bill; so that their remedy remains upon the law of indictments for petty larceny, which, from being troublesome and expensive, these meanest of thieves are but seldom prosecuted to conviction.

The publicans attribute the opposition made to their bill to the pewterers;—what envy even in these grades of society!—and, by way of revenge, the former have entered into a resolution to manufacture their own pots!

John Lumley was indicted at the Westminster sessions, 1810, for stealing a pewter pint pot, the property of the landlord of the Cart and Horse public house, Tooley Street: there was also another charge against him for a similar offence, namely, having in his possession a pot belonging to the landlord of the Black Lion; and a third for stealing two pewter pots, the property of the landlord of the Green Dragon, Bermondsey Street.

It appeared in evidence that the prisoner was passing along Ratcliff Highway on Wednesday evening, when he was observed to drop a pot from under his coat, which a person near him instantly picked up; and perceiving it to belong to a public house, and a publican in the neighbourhood having recently lost several pots, the man followed the prisoner, secured him, and took him to the house in question; and, sending for a constable, they proceeded to search him, when no less than six pint pots were found concealed about his person, none of which, however, belonged to the landlord of the house where he then was, but to several public houses in the Borough, amongst which were the Black Lion and the Cart and Horse public houses in Tooley Street, and the Green Dragon, in Bermondsey Street. Upon discovering from what neighbourhood the pots came, the constable brought the prisoner to Union Hall, where the landlords of the above and other public houses attended, and swore to the pots being their property.

The prisoner, when called on for his defence, said he was going from the Borough to Ratcliff Highway on business; and, having occasion to turn up a court near London Bridge, he found the pots standing there: he picked them up, and it was his intention, on his return home from where he was going, to have returned them to their respective owners.

The jury found him Guilty.

The chairman observed that the offence of which the prisoner had been convicted was one of so great magnitude as to call for the severest punishment. It would scarcely be credited, but it had been ascertained, that the depredations of this sort committed on the property of publicans, in and around the metropolis, amounted to the enormous sum of one hundred thousand pounds per annum. The prisoner had been convicted on the clearest evidence, and the Court felt itself bound to inflict a punishment which might operate to put a stop, if possible, to this evil. The sentence of the Court then was, that he should be confined to hard labour three months in the House of Correction, and once during that time to be publicly whipped from the end of Horsemonger Lane to the end of Lant Street, in the Borough; which was severely inflicted.

WILLIAM MOULDS
EXECUTED FOR THE MURDER OF WILLIAM TURNER.

THIS case exhibits a most cruel and treacherous crime—the assassination of a fellow-creature, at the very moment when the murderer had been proffered his assistance.

William Moulds was indicted for the wilful murder of William Turner, by shooting him on the king's highway, near Farnham, on the 18th of May, 1810. The prisoner was a soldier in the 52d regiment, from which he deserted from Winchester, accompanied by two females, of the names of Elizabeth Roper and Mary Fisher.—As he was on the road, he declared to them that he must have some man's clothes, to prevent his being taken as a deserter, and he would shoot some one to get them. As they went along they were joined by the deceased; and, after some conversation about a bed, he told them they should have some straw in his brother's barn at Farnham. The deceased was walking a few yards before with Elizabeth Roper, when the prisoner fired at him with his musket, and the ball entered his back. He had, however, strength enough to run to Farnham, when he reached the house of a Mr. Bott, a surgeon; he lived two days, and then expired. A party of soldiers were sent out in pursuit of the prisoner, and he was apprehended. The deceased saw him, and identified his person, before he died. After he had shot the deceased, one of the girls fainted, and he and the other took her into an adjoining clover field. Here he declared he was sure that the ball must have entered the man's body, and he could not have run above twenty yards, and he wished he had gone back to have had his money and clothes.

The jury found no hesitation in finding him guilty; and the judge immediately passed on him the sentence of the law. He was executed at the New Prison, Horsemonger Lane, August the 16th, 1810.

RICHARD VALENTINE THOMAS,
EXECUTED FOR FORGERY.

THIS youthful malefactor evinced an extraordinary propensity for that species of crime which at length brought him to a premature and ignominious death. He was the son of a respectable tradesman of the city of London, who placed him, at the age of sixteen, in the counting-house of an opulent bargemaster near Blackfriars. He had not been long here when he forged a check on his employer's bankers, for one thousand pounds, and obtained the money. The fact was discovered; but his master, in pity to his youth, and from respect to his family, declined to prosecute, in consideration of being reimbursed. The father of the guilty youth paid the thousand pounds, and sent the boy to Portsmouth, where he entered him on board a ship of war then bound for the West Indies, thinking such a course most likely to prevent him from the commission of future crimes.

He went the voyage, but on his return he deserted from the ship, and again bent his course to London, where he renewed his former habits. From his knowledge of many commercial houses, and of the bankers with whom they did business, he contrived to acquire large sums through the means of blank checks, which he filled up, and committed forgeries to a vast extent, there being no less than thirteen indictments against him, at the time of his conviction.

During the month of July, 1810, he frequented the Surrey Theatre, and the Equestrian Coffee-house, contiguous to it, the waiter of which he sent to Messrs. Smith and Co. to get the banking book of Messrs. Diffell. This enabled him to ascertain the balance of money which Messrs. Diffell had in the hands of their banker. He then sent back the book by the same person, with a request to have a check-book, upon receiving which he filled up a check for four hundred pounds, eight shillings, and delivered it to Mr. Johnson, the box and house keeper of the Surrey Theatre, with whom he appeared to be on intimate terms, telling him he had some custom and excise duties to pay, requesting him to get payment of the check in notes of ten and twenty pounds.

Johnson went to Messrs. Smith's; but, as they could not pay him as he wished, he received from them two notes of two hundred pounds each, which he immediately took to the Bank, and exchanged for the notes Thomas wanted. The forgery being soon detected, Thomas was taken into custody, in company with a woman with whom he cohabited. Upon searching her, a twenty-pound note was found, which was identified by a clerk of the Bank as one of those paid to Johnson in exchange for the two-hundred-pound notes. The woman, being asked where she got it, answered Thomas gave it her; when he, being locked up in an adjoining room, called out ' No, you got it from a gentleman.'.

In a privy which communicated with Thomas's room fragments of ten-pound and twenty-pound notes were found, and upon several of the pieces the date corresponded with the entry in the Bank.

In addition to this, Mrs. Johnson, mistress of the Equestrian Coffee-house, produced a twenty-pound note which she had received from Thomas on the same day the check was presented; and which, with the fragments, &c. made up exactly the sum of four hundred pounds. These facts being proved on his trial, and the forgery established, he was found Guilty, and sentenced to be hanged on Monday, September 3, 1810.

From the day of his conviction, August the 20th, until the Saturday preceding his execution, notwithstanding the zealous exhortation of the chaplain, who daily attended him, he could scarcely be aroused from an apathetic indifference to his fate, or to a penitent sense of the crime for which he was to suffer. On Sunday he attended divine service in the chapel of the gaol, where near three hundred persons of respectable appearance were also present, most of whom appeared to be more deeply affected by the situation of the prisoner than he himself.

He was attired in a fashionable and gentlemanly style. His dress consisted of a blue coat with gilt buttons, lined through with black silk; white waistcoat, with black silk breeches, and stockings; his hair unpowdered, and his upper lip adorned with Hussar mustachios. His coffin, covered with black, was placed before him; and when the chaplain stated that the unfortunate youth, who had now but a few hours to live, was a veteran in the species of crime for which he was convicted, although he had not yet completed his nineteenth year, the whole auditory were dissolved in tears; not excepting the gaoler, who sat by him, though familiar with such scenes; while the youth himself manifested a pensive firmness, and was the only person present who appeared indifferent to his fate.

Next morning, September 3, 1810, he was brought to the top of Horsemonger Lane gaol. His dress was precisely the same as that already described; and he met his fate with decorous resignation.

JOHN WHITMORE, ALIAS OLD DASH,
EXECUTED FOR A RAPE.

THE summary punishment of a ravisher, by a conscientious Emperor of the Turks, in days of old, if now, perchance, inflicted, might more tend to check the inordinate, unlawful, lust of men, than all the public executions of such destroyers of the peace of females.

Our laws, and certainly wisely too, restrain us from seeking redress at our own hands, except in case of self-defence: but where is the man, witnessing a brutal attack upon his wife or daughter, that would, by a jury of his fellow-men, be convicted of a deadly crime, in searching the heart's blood of their ravisher upon the guilty spot of his atrocity?

Mahmoud, Sultan of Damascus, one night while he was going to bed, was addressed by a poor villager, who complained that a young Turk of distinction had broken into his apartment, and forced him to abandon his wife and family to his abuses. The good sultan charged that, if the Turk returned, he should immediately give him notice of it. Three days after the poor man came again with the same complaint. Mahmoud took a few attendants with him, and, being arrived at the complainant's, commanded the lights to be extinguished, and, rushing in, cut the ravisher to pieces. He then ordered a light, to see whom he had killed, and, being satisfied, he fell on his knees, and returned God thanks; after which he ate heartily of the poor man's bread, and gave him a purse of gold. Being asked the reason of this extraordinary behaviour, he replied, 'I concluded this ravisher was one who might fancy himself entitled to my protection, and consequently might be no other than my son: therefore, lest the tenderness of nature should enervate the arm of justice, I resolved to give it scope in the dark. But, when I saw that it was only an officer of my guards, I joyfully returned God thanks. Then I asked the injured man for food to satisfy my hunger, having had neither sleep nor sustenance from the moment I heard the accusation till I had thus punished the author of the wrong, and showed myself worthy of my people's obedience.'

Princes, nobles, men of fortune— 'read, mark, learn, and inwardly digest.' The hut of the meanest peasant, by the law of Britain, is sacred as your own gorgeous palaces and castles; and, should you dare to violate his female relative therein, each injured owner may prove a Sultan Mahmoud.

John Whitmore was capitally indicted for a rape on the person of Mary, the wife of Thomas Brown, on the 24th of October, 1810, on the Common between Hayes and West Bedford. The prisoner was a labourer in the powder-mills at Harlington Common; and the prosecutrix, who lives at Hayes, having one of her sons by a former husband living as servant with Mr. Potts, a farmer, at West Bedford, had gone thither about twelve o'clock with some clean linen for her son. She stopped at a public house in the neighbourhood whilst he changed his linen, and there saw the prisoner, who, after asking her several questions, told her she had come much the longest way about, on her way from Hayes, and offered to show her a much shorter cut over the heath on her return. The prosecutrix thanked him, and accepted his offer. He accompanied her as if for that purpose, decoyed her two miles out of her way to an unfrequented part of the heath, amongst some bushes, under pretence of looking after a stray horse, and there brutally violated her person.

The poor woman, who was forty-seven years of age, as soon as she could, ran away from him, over the heath, and again lost her way; by accident she met a gentleman, who put her in the right road, and she reached her home about eight o'clock at night. She was afraid to tell her husband what had occurred till the following Sunday.

The husband next day set out with the constable in search of the prisoner, from the description given by his wife, and on Tuesday traced him to a public house at Twickenham, where he was known by the familiar appellation of 'Old Dasher;' and there, after a stout resistance, he was taken into custody. The facts were, on his trial, which took place at the Old Bailey, in October, 1810, clearly established by the poor woman, who evinced through the whole of her evidence traits of modesty and chastity of mind that would have reflected honour upon any character.

The prisoner, by the questions he asked her in making his defence, attempted to impeach her as consenting to his brutal purpose, and thereby only aggravated his crime.

The common-sergeant summed up the evidence for the jury; who, after a minute's consideration, found the prisoner Guilty—Death. The fate of this malefactor received no commiseration.

JAMES FALLAN,

EXECUTED FOR THE MURDER OF HIS WIFE.

Few actions can degrade the dignity of man more than that of striking a woman; and fewer still are more debasing to human nature than that of a husband striking his wife— one whom, before the altar, he had promised to love, cherish, and protect. The frequency of such deeds, however, have diminished their vileness and atrocity, in the common estimation of the world; but the brave and the virtuous still regard them with detestation and horror. Those who are dead to the feelings of manhood, and wanting in the Christian duties of life, may, however, be intimidated from such a practice by the following particulars of a man, who, perhaps, thought, like them, that he might with impunity wreak his passion on his defenceless companion, whose soothing exclamations of tenderness were poor protection against the brutal force of her inhuman husband, whose blows were followed by death, and for which he died upon the GALLOWS.

James Fallan bore, without deserving it, the name of soldier. He was a corporal in the guards, from which service he obtained his discharge, in consequence of a liver complaint, and was admitted a pensioner at Chelsea Hospital on the 8th of February, 1811, and took up his abode in a cellar in the Marketplace. The very next day, two of his comrades, also pensioners, with two servant-women, came to see him, and they drank pretty freely, until they had finished all the spirits then in the cellar. Fallan then desired his wife to go out for more; but she, perhaps, thinking that they had already drank enough, or that her pocket could not afford any more, refused, or, at least, did not obey; upon which the friends departed. Fallan then demanded of his wife why she did not do as he had desired her, upon which an altercation ensued, and the wife, by no means inclined to silence, bestowed upon her husband some abusive terms, when he struck her upon the face, which he repeated, knocking her down several times, though she cried out 'Dear Jemmy, don't murder me!' He, however, continued beating her with such violence, that a woman named Sarah Llewellyn, who lodged in the same cellar with him, attempted to interfere, when he threatened to serve her in the same manner, and then eturned, with renewed violence, to beat his unfortunate wife, who by this time had sat or fallen down on the bed. Llewellyn now attempted to get out, but he prevented her. As his fury had not been yet exhausted, he returned to renew his blows on his wife; and the woman availed herself of the opportunity to run out for assistance. She found three women listening at the cellar door, who went with her up stairs to request a man to come down; but he refused, and on their return they distinctly heard the continuance of the blows, the poor woman all the time crying out, ' Oh! dear Jemmy, don't kill me!' till her groans grew fainter and fainter.

Llewellyn, afraid to venture down, remained on the stairs all night, and next morning she found Fallan and his wife in bed together, upon which she expressed her satisfaction. The unfortunate woman appeared shockingly bruised, and complained very much of a pain in her side.

' Cut my head, and then give me a plaster,' is very applicable to the conduct of such husbands as Fallan. He now sent for a surgeon, and had some blood taken from his wife, who did not appear to get better on that account. On Tuesday morning Fallan went out for the avowed purpose of procuring another lodging, but did not return until the Saturday following, when he saw his wife, and then went away again. The unfortunate woman languished till next day, Sunday, when she died, in consequence of which her brutal husband was taken into custody.

His trial came on at the Old Bailey, April the 5th, when, in addition to these facts, it was proved by a surgeon, who opened the body of the deceased, that she came by her death in consequence of the four false ribs, on the left side, being broken, two of which were forced into the *pleura*, and had wounded several of the vessels, and occasioned a great effusion of blood, which was the immediate cause of her death.

Fallan, in his defence, produced a long written statement, imputing the quarrel to the ill temper of the deceased, and alleged that he had only struck her with his open hand and the whalebone of a woman's stays; and that, if her ribs were broken, it must have been in consequence of her falling over a deal box in the cellar. He concluded by saying, so far from having any malice towards his wife, he loved her tenderly.

Lord Ellenborough summed up the evidence, and the jury, after a short consultation, found him Guilty, when the recorder proceeded to pass on him the awful sentence of execution and dissection on the Monday following.

Accordingly, on Monday, April 8th, 1811, he was executed in front of Newgate. He was only twenty-nine years of age, and had seen much service. He was attended by a Roman-Catholic priest; but appeared quite indifferent to his fate, and kicked off his shoes when he got upon the platform. After hanging the usual time, his body was taken to Bartholomew Hospital for dissection.

AGNES ADAMS,
IMPRISONED FOR UTTERING A FALSE NOTE.

For three or four years previous to this trial, numberless impositions had been practised upon the unwary in the metropolis, in passing paper manufactured in imitation of the notes of the Bank of England. These have been traced to have originated in the Fleet prison, a receptacle for debtors only; through whose iron bars next the street the passenger is eternally importuned by some of its inhabitants with 'Pray remember the poor debtors!'

These notes were printed on paper similar to those of the Bank of England; but upon the slightest inspection they were easily detected; which creates surprise at so many having been imposed upon. The great success of sharpers passing them chiefly arose from the hurry of business, and from the novelty of the fraud. The shopkeeper would see the word one, two, three, &c. an exact imitation, but did not examine farther, or he would have found, instead of pounds, the counterfeit expressed pence; and this, with all the wisdom of our laws, was found not to be forgery. Instead of 'Governor and Company of the Bank of England,' the worthless paper substituted 'Governor and Company of the Bank of Fleet.' Such a gross deception we may be sure could no tlong be practised, and now every tradesman, who has dearly been taught precaution, in taking a bank-note, will be convinced that it is not a 'Fleet.'

The circulation of Fleet paper was generally intrusted to profligate women, who cohabited with the men who made them. This mode was less suspicious, and in a single year had been carried on to a considerable amount.

Of this description, and we could adduce many such, was Agnes Adams; who, in passing one of such notes, denominating two pence, as a two-pound Bank of England note, to Mr. Spratz, a publican of St. John Street, Clerkenwell, was by him detected, seized, prosecuted and convicted at the Middlesex Sessions, 1811. The punishment could only be extended to six months' hard labour in the House of Correction.

The fraternity of thieves about London have fabricated or cant names for the different articles which they steal. The Fleet notes they called '*Flash Screens*.'

EDWARD BEAZLEY,
WHIPPED FOR DESTROYING WOMEN'S APPAREL.

UNTIL the severe examples made of this boy, females often found their clothes drop to tatters, and such as restricted themselves to mere muslin and chemise were frequently dreadfully burnt, in a way invisible, and almost unaccountable. A set of urchins, neither men nor boys, by way of a 'high game,' procured aqua-fortis, vitriol, and other corrosive liquids, and, filling therewith a syringe, or bottle, would sally forth to give the girls ' *a squirt*.'

Of this mischievous description we find Edward Beazley, who was convicted of this unpardonable offence at the Old Bailey, the 11th of March, 1811.

He was indicted for wilfully and maliciously injuring and destroying the apparel of Anne Parker, which she was wearing, by feloniously throwing upon the same a certain poisonous substance, called aqua-fortis, whereby the same was so injured as to be rendered useless and of no value.

He was also charged upon two other indictments for the like offence, on the prosecution of two other women.

It appeared that the prisoner, a little boy about thirteen years old, took it into his head to sally into Fleet Street, on the night of Saturday, February 16, and there threw the same upon the clothes of several of the Cyprians who parade up and down there. He was caught, carried before the sitting magistrate at Guildhall, and fully committed on three several charges.

Three ladies appeared, and proved the facts stated in the indictments, and exhibited their burnt garments, such as pelisses, gowns, and other articles, which were literally burnt to riddles.

He was found Guilty.

His master, Mr. Blades, and an eminent chymist on Ludgate Hill, gave him a good character for honesty; he never knew any thing wrong of him before; but he acknowledged that he had access to both vitriol and aqua-fortis.

The Court having a discretionary power under the act of parliament, instead of transporting him for seven years, only ordered him to be well whipped in the gaol, after which he was returned to his friends.

MARY GREEN,
CONVICTED OF PUTTING OFF BASE COIN.

COINERS of base money employ low people to go from shop to shop to put off their counterfeits; and in doing this every stratagem that can be devised is employed. One of these tricks is to ask change for a good dollar; and, in counting the shillings given for it, they secrete one or more of them, and substitute counterfeits. Then they pretend that part of their change is bad; and the tradesman, unconscious of the deception, takes their base coin, and gives them good money in return. This the rogues, among each other, call ' ringing the changes.'

At the Sessions for Middlesex, held the 5th of April, 1811, Mary Green, a decent-looking girl, was found guilty of putting off two bad shillings to Mr. Harris, a linen-draper, in Pickett Street, Temple Bar.

She went into Mr. Harris's shop, and asked for small silver for a dollar; Mr. Harris gave it her. She walked two or three yards up the shop, and, addressing herself to the shopman, told him that his master had given her two bad shillings. This Mr. Harris denied, and refused to take them. She then conducted herself most rudely; whereupon a constable was sent for. Before he arrived, she still persisted in her impudent behaviour, saying that she had no more money about her but the dollar. Lack, the officer, soon arrived, and searched her, and there were found concealed about her twelve shillings and four six-pences, all in good silver, besides the change of the dollar.

The jury, after a charge from Mr. Mainwaring, found her Guilty.

As soon as the verdict was pronounced, the counsel for the prosecution acquainted the Court, that as the punishment was pointed out by the act of parliament, from which they could not deviate, the prisoner's case could not be affected by the profligacy of her character. He thought it right to mention that this was the second time she had been brought into that court (first with her mother) for this kind of crime; that her father was transported; and her younger sister was then in confinement under the sentence of the Court for the same kind of offence. She was sentenced to six months' imprisonment.

RICHARD ARMITAGE AND C. THOMAS,
EXECUTED FOR FORGERY.

FORGERY, from the accumulating number of instances the farther we proceed in our work, is manifestly a crime which increases with the certainty of punishment. Murderers, if aught of palliation can be offered for the frailty of human nature, may indulge a distant hope of the extension of the royal mercy. Forgery is now never pardoned—a determination on the part of the crown, laid down in the cases of the Perreaus and of Doctor Dodd, whom no interest could save from an ignominious death. Thus excluded from all hope of pardon, it is daily becoming more common; and the alteration in the law, from the pillory and corporal punishment to death, has no terrifying influence. The ancient punishment for this crime we find thus minutely described in a London periodical publication for the year 1731:—

'*June 9th.*—This day, about noon, Japhet Crook, *alias* St. Peter Stranger, was brought to the pillory at Charing Cross, according to his sentence for forgery. He stood an hour thereon; after which a chair was set on the pillory; and he being put therein, the hangman with a sort of pruning-knife cut off both his ears, and immediately a surgeon clapt a styptic thereon. Then the executioner, with a pair of scissors, cut his left nostril twice before it was quite through, and afterwards cut through the right nostril at once. He bore all this with great patience; but when, in pursuance of his sentence, his right nostril was seared with a red-hot iron, he was in such violent pain that his left nostril was let alone, and he went from the pillory bleeding. He was conveyed from thence to the King's Bench Prison, there to remain for life. He died in confinement about three years after.'

The crime for which Armitage and Thomas so very justly suffered was of the very worst description of forgery—a scandalous breach of public trust—a robbery upon the very corporation they were bound to protect from the nefarious attempts of others. Like Aslett, their former head of department, they long had practised impositions on the Bank of England, unsuspected; and in the mean time maintained the show of integrity. Aslett was detected by Bish, the lottery-office keeper, wherein he performed a public service—Armitage and Thomas by Robert Roberts, the notorious swindler, to save the halter's noose being affixed round his own neck.

The circumstances which led to the detection more excited public interest than the frauds of Walsh and Hunt, two members of the House of Commons,—more than Chinnery's flight or Davison's incarceration—for who can bring back to mind any public act of delinquency that more excited the astonishment of the individual, or alarmed the mercantile interest of the country, than the result of this Roberts's escape from that strong and dread prison, the House of Correction, Coldbath Fields? Hence the history of the accomplice in this case becomes more interesting, than any other particulars which can be brought forward respecting the sufferers.

'Robert Roberts,' say the London newspapers of the day, 'who has made his escape from Coldbath Fields Prison, is one of the most expert swindlers of the present day. He must have made a large sum by personating Earl Percy, for it does not appear that he returned all the money he obtained by that fraudulent transaction; he also stands charged with committing forgeries to a large amount, and consequently has sufficient means to facilitate his escape out of the country, if unfortunately he should not be speedily arrested.'

Towards the latter end of August, 1810, Robert Roberts was apprehended for being concerned in the many forgeries which for some time had been practised on the Bank of England and the commercial part of the metropolis. He was brought to one of the public offices, and from thence remanded to the House of Correction in Coldbath Fields. In a few days, in company with another prisoner, of the name of Harper, he effected his escape, and the public were surprised at seeing large printed sheets of paper, pasted on the walls of the city, announcing this extraordinary circumstance, and offering a large reward for their apprehension, but particularly for the discovery of Roberts, the other belonging merely to the gangs of smaller rogues.

Mean time strict inquiry was made into the manner of this singular escape. The prison was searched; and Aris the gaoler,* or governor, as such fellows style themselves, and his sons acting as turnkeys, were brought before a bench of Middlesex magistrates, on the 31st August, 1810, on a charge of conniving thereat.

Mr. Aris, senior, his four sons, and the whole of the servants of the prison, were closely examined. It appeared that the two prisoners, Roberts and Harper, were not supposed to know each other; and that the whole of the gates leading from

* This is the gaoler who persecuted a reputable tradesman in the Strand, for defamation of his character; and a jury actually gave him large damages! This was not the heaviest punishment which awaited the convicted; as will be seen by the following obituary, of the 24th of September, 1808:—

'Died, on Saturday morning, Mr. Dickie, late stationer in the Strand, who has been confined nearly five years in the Fleet Prison, in consequence of a verdict given against him for seven hundred pounds damages for uttering defamatory words against Mr. Aris, the Governor of Coldbath Fields Prison. He has left a distressed widow and four children still to lament his unfortunate offence and unhappy death.'

the confinement of Roberts, six in number, were found open in the morning, they having been made fast at locking-up time on the preceding night. The prisoners then made their escape over the wall, by ascending a new lodge in the prison, not then finished; and when at the top of the wall they were supposed to have let themselves down by a rope, as a hook was found in the morning by Daniel Aris, the gaoler's son.

The investigation closed with the suspending of Aris, the gaol-keeper, the committal of Daniel Aris, his son, for felony, and the dismissal of another of Aris's sons, who was a turnkey.

No clue had then been had of Roberts or Harper. The evidence against Roberts, relative to the forgery upon the Bank, was quite conclusive, and a woman he cohabited with was admitted an evidence.

At a second examination the testimony went still further to criminate the son of Aris, who was fully committed; but the method of escape remained then a secret, and was not disclosed until some time after. The facts were these:—Roberts bribed a person, employed to sweep the cells, to get him impressions of the keys, by which he procured some to be made; and the same person instructed Harper how to open the gates, and secure his own and Roberts's escape. Much mystery, however, was thrown over the whole case, and it evidently appeared that Roberts had a friend, besides the sweeper, within the prison, but who he was remained a secret. Aris's son was subsequently acquitted.

During these long examinations, and notwithstanding a large reward was offered for his apprehension, Roberts evaded the strict search of justice. It was known that he had carried off a considerable sum of money, his proportion of the success of the forgeries wherein he was implicated, and for which the unfortunate subjects of this case only suffered. At length he was identified at a tavern at Vauxhall, where he had taken up his lodgings as a country attorney detained in town on his own concerns.

The remaining part of this singular case is short. Roberts, to save his own life, impeached Armitage and Thomas, two clerks filling places of great trust in the Bank of England, as the immediate agents of the many forgeries which had been of late committed on that corporation; and he was admitted evidence against them on the part of the crown.

Richard Armitage was first apprehended. He was brought to the public office in Marlborough Street on the 8th April, 1810; and, after a short examination, was committed to the New Prison for trial at the next Old Bailey sessions. Among the witnesses bound over to give evidence against him was Mrs. Roberts, the mistress of his base accuser. His forgeries of dividend warrants were to the amount of two thousand four hundred pounds.

On the 2d of May following, C. Thomas was apprehended, and brought to the same office, on a charge of having forged several dividend warrants; and, after three separate examinations, was also committed for trial.

The prisoner was a Bank clerk in the Imperial Annuity Office, and the warrants forged were to obtain the dividends of a person who had been dead about three years, and whose executors had not applied for his property. It appeared that three hundred and sixty pounds had been paid out of the Bank, and the prisoner's name was signed as an attesting witness. It was also proved that bank-notes, with which the dividends were paid, were found in the prisoner's possession. Under these circumstances the prisoner was fully committed for trial. This is one of the cases disclosed by Roberts.

Armitage was fully committed, and Roberts and his wife were the principal witnesses against him.

The trials of these unfortunate men were unattended by any other circumstance worthy noticing, farther than, independent of the evidence of Roberts and his wife, which, unsupported, would have received little credit, full proof was adduced of their guilt; —they were consequently found guilty, and received sentence of death.

On the 24th of June, 1811, Richard Armitage and C. Thomas, late clerks in the Bank, were executed in the Old Bailey, pursuant to their sentence, for repeated forgeries on that corporation. The former, from severe illness, was under the necessity of being supported by a friend while ascending, and during his continuance on the scaffold. He was attended by a clergyman, to whose pious admonitions he appeared to pay becoming attention. The latter, who was a Catholic, was attended by a priest of that persuasion, and conducted himself with apparent fortitude.

JANE COX,
EXECUTED FOR MURDER.

WE have already reprobated the constant practice of country apothecaries, and even their apprentices, selling poison to any one who offers the stale pretext of killing rats. The lust of lucre, even in the pennyworth, induces these underlings of the disciples of Esculapius to supply the means of death to the lowest order of the community—even to women—when they might often perceive that it was craved for diabolical purposes. There ought to be a law, as from Shakspeare we learn was in Mantua of old, against such practices; for the Apothecary in *Romeo and Juliet* says:—

'Such mortal drugs I have, but Mantua's law
Is DEATH to any he that utters them.'

The world, it appears, since the days of Shakspeare, has become more corrupt, for crimes have greatly accumulated. On the subject of selling poison for the purpose of committing murder, which of old was punished with death, we find, rom 'Hill's Journey through Sicily and Calabria,' that in the year 1791, at Palermo, a city not far distant from Mantua, an old woman was executed for dealing out such mortal drugs.

'Many people in this town and neighbourhood,'(Palermo,) says this author, 'died in a sudden and extraordinary manner; they were generally seized with vomiting, and expired in a few hours. A young woman went to an officer of justice to make some complaints concerning her husband; he desired her to be reconciled, and refused to proceed against him, upon which she turned away in a rage, muttering that she knew how to be revenged. The magistrate paid attention to what she said, and gave orders for her being arrested; when, upon strict inquiry concerning the meaning of her word, she confessed that it was her intention to poison her husband, by purchasing a bottle of vinegar from an old woman, who prepared it for that purpose. In order to ascertain the truth of this story, another woman was sent to the old jade, to demand some of the vinegar, which was sold for about ten pence a bottle. "What do you want with it?" said the vender: "Why," (replied the other,) "I have a very bad husband, and I want to get rid of him." Hereupon the old woman, seventy-two years of age, produced the fatal dose; upon which she was immediately seized, and conducted to prison, where she confessed that she had sold forty-five or forty-six bottles. Many people were taken up; but as, upon further inquiry, it was discovered that several of the nobility had been purchasers, the affair was dropped, and the old woman alone suffered death.'

Jane Cox was indicted on the 9th August, 1811, for the wilful murder of one John Trenaman, an infant, sixteen months old; and Arthur Tucker, as an accessary before the fact. The latter was a respectable farmer, living at Hatherleigh, in Devonshire; and the infant was his natural child. It appeared that Jane Cox had, on the 25th of May, 1811, administered to the child a quantity of arsenic, by putting it into the child's hands, and which it put into its mouth, and ate it; in consequence of which it died in about two hours. The prisoner, in her written confession, had implicated Tucker, as having persuaded her to do the fact, and stated his having taken the arsenic from under the roof of a cottage, and given it to her, and promised her a one-pound note if she would administer it to the child. This was not believed.

The prisoner, Jane Cox, after a trial of seven hours, was convicted. Tucker was acquitted. He called a number of respectable witnesses, who gave him a very high character.

On Monday the 12th of August, 1811, pursuant to her sentence, this unfortunate woman was brought to the 'new drop,' the place of execution, and underwent the dread sentence of the law.

She addressed the spectators at some length, and in a very audible manner; she repeated her former confession, with some further particulars respecting the means used by Tucker to prevail on her to commit the horrid deed, for which she acknowledged she ought to die; but lamented that the person who had instigated her to the commission of it was not also to suffer with her.

FREDERIC BARDIE, ALIAS PETER WOOD,
INDICTED FOR CUTTING AND MAIMING.

This unfortunate man, who fell a victim to his ungovernable passions, was a native of Falaize, in Normandy. His parents were respectable, and he traded in his own vessel to the West Indies, where he had a wife and two children at the time of his death. His little bark being taken in 1803, by the 'John Bull' letter of marque, he was carried to Liverpool, and from thence to Chatham, where he was put on board the Canada prison-ship, in the Medway, along with his captive countrymen.

During the *eight* years of his sorrowful captivity his conduct was exemplary; but it appears he was subject to sudden gusts of passion. On the 12th of March he wanted to go into the cooking-room; but was prevented by Ebenezer Alexander, a private marine, who was on duty there, and whose orders were to that effect. The sentinel desired him to get leave from the sergeant, which he pretended to go for, and returned, saying he had obtained it. This Alexander refused to credit, as he knew in that case a corporal would have come to inform him, and therefore persisted in his refusal. Upon this Wood drew a knife from his pocket, and, calling the sentinel some vulgar names, said he would kill him. Alexander, who was not apprehensive of danger, paid no attention to the threat; but several fellow-prisoners, who knew their countryman's failing, ran to prevent him. Wood, however, before they could secure him, came up to the sentinel, and, seizing him round the neck with his left arm, inflicted with his knife two dreadful wounds in the left breast. The marine fell, and was carried to the hospital, where he was confined thirty-one days. Wood was secured, and brought to trial at the following assizes at Maidstone, when he was found Guilty, and received sentence of death.

Thursday, September the 5th, 1811, was the day appointed for carrying his sentence into execution, on Penenden Heath. He was escorted by the usual retinue, and a vast concourse of people, who sincerely lamented his fate. A Catholic confessor attended to prepare him for the awful moment, assisted by the chaplain and Mr. Shelton. He appeared penitent and resigned; and before he ascended the scaffold he requested of Mr. Shelton to say something for him to the people who surrounded him, which he did, as follows:—

'Good people! the poor unfortunate man who is about to suffer the dreadful sentence of the law desires me, as he cannot speak our language, to tell you that he is sincerely sorry for having committed the crime which has brought him to this miserable and untimely end; and that he trusts, through the prevailing influence of the venerable priest who attends him, he has made his peace with his God, and rests with full confidence of forgiveness at his dread tribunal. He also directs me to warn you against the violence of vindictive passion, by which alone he was actuated to commit this dreadful crime. He truly forgives every one, and hopes, in his last moments, you will offer up your prayers for him; this I am confident you will do, in consequence of his deep contrition, and the circumstance of his being a stranger in this country.'

After this he was supported to the platform, and an end was put to his sufferings.

ARTHUR BAILY,
EXECUTED FOR STEALING A LETTER OUT OF THE POST-OFFICE.

BAILY was a native of Ashburton, in Devonshire, and came early to Bath, where he lived in some respectable places, as servant, from which he was strongly recommended to Mr. Price, postmaster at Bath. In this employ he conducted himself, for seven years, with great assiduity, and to the complete satisfaction of his master. About nine years before he committed the fatal act for which he suffered, he married an amiable woman, by whom he had several children, and took a public house near the bottom of St. James Street, Bath, but afterwards removed to the Fox Inn, at Mitford, on the Frome and Warminster road, which premises he purchased.

As Mr. Price always esteemed him a faithful servant, he was, during the busy season at Bath, called on to lend assistance in the post-office, such as making up the mails, sorting letters, &c. and here he was tempted to commit the fatal act for which he died an ignominious death. Among other letters he secreted one belonging to Messrs. Slack, linen-drapers, containing bills of exchange, on one of which he forged an endorsement. For this offence he was tried at the assizes for Somersetshire, and found Guilty. He was sentenced to be executed at Ilchester, September 11, 1811.

Scene in a Slave Market, described by Dr. Pinckard.

THE HONORABLE ARTHUR WILLIAM HODGE,
EXECUTED FOR THE MURDER OF HIS NEGRO SLAVE.

As the circumstances attending this case happened in one of our West-India colonies, we feel no apology necessary for introducing it into our pages, particularly as it affords us an opportunity for making a few remarks on that abominable traffic, the SLAVE TRADE, which, to the disgrace of Europe, has not yet ceased to exist, although the efforts of England have been so long directed to its abolition.

We think there is no human being—we know there is no real Englishman—who does not sympathize with the suffering African, when dragged from his parent soil, and all the associates he had formed there. A friend, a parent, a wife, or child, may each and all combine in imbittering the hour of separation, when the chains and whips of the tyrants who buy and sell him are less galling than the uncontrollable anguish of his soul. This is a picture which gains ready admission to the human breast, and needs no evidence to make it appalling. There can be no fear of exaggeration, for description must fall short of reality, as the painter and the poet are alike unable to depict the revolting horrors of such a scene.

Let us turn from the cries, the tears, the lamentations of Africa, where rum is bartered for blood, and the inhuman contract made between two of the greatest ruffians that curse the earth—a slave-captain and a barbarian prince;—let us turn from these to our West-India islands, and see how the poor untutored negro, who differs from ourselves only in education and colour, is treated by men descended from Englishmen, and some of whom were born in England. We shall not trust our feelings on the subject, but give plain facts, such as we find them in official papers transmitted to Lord Liverpool by Governor Elliot, and which were afterwards laid before a committee of the House of Commons. We select the deposition of the deputy secretary of the island of Nevis, because it was subsequently supported by others, and because it embraced the revolting particulars of the conduct of the cruel Huggins. The examination took place before the Assembly of the Island of Nevis.

'John Burke, junior, deputy secretary of the said island, upon oath saith, that on Tuesday, the 23d of January, 1810, he was standing in the street opposite the house of the Rev. William Green, when he saw Edward Huggins, sen. Esq. and his two sons, Edward and Peter Thomas Huggins, ride by, with a gang of negroes, to the public market-place; from whence the deponent heard the noise of the cart-whip; that deponent walked up the street, and saw Mr. Huggins, senior, standing by, with two drivers flogging a negro-man, whose name deponent understood to be Yellow Quashy. That deponent went into Dr. Crosse's gallery, and sat down; that two drivers continued flogging the said negro-man for about fifteen minutes, that, as he appeared to be severely whipped, deponent was induced to count the lashes given the other negroes, being under an impression that the country would take up the business. That deponent heard Mr. George Abbot declare, at Dr. Crosse's steps, near the market-place, that the first negro had received three hundred and sixty-five lashes: deponent saith that Mr. Huggins, senior, gave another negro-man one hundred and fifteen lashes; to another negro-man sixty-five lashes; to another negro-man forty-seven lashes; to another negro-man one hundred and sixty-five lashes; to another negro-man two hundred and twelve lashes; to another negro-man one hundred and eighty-one lashes; to another negro-man fifty-nine lashes; to another negro-man one hundred and eighty-seven lashes; to a woman one hundred and ten lashes; to another woman fifty-eight lashes; to another woman ninety-seven lashes; to another woman two hundred and twelve lashes; to another woman two hundred and ninety-one lashes; to another woman eighty-three lashes; to another woman forty-nine lashes; to another woman sixty-eight lashes; to another woman eighty-nine lashes; and to another woman fifty-six lashes; and that the woman who received two hundred and ninety-one lashes appeared young, and was most cruelly flogged. That all the negroes were flogged by two expert whippers; that Mr. Edward Huggins, junior, and Mr. Peter Huggins, were present at the time the negroes were punished: that Dr. Cassin was present when some of the negroes were whipped, and when a man received two hundred and forty-two lashes. That deponent understood that Dr. Cassin was sent for by Mr. Huggins, senior; that Edward Harris, Esq. Mr. Peter Butler, and Dr. Crosse, were present at Dr. Crosse's house a part of the time during the punishment; and that Mr. Joseph Nicholson, Mr. Joseph Laurence, and Mr. William Keepe, were present all the time.   JOHN BURKE, JUN.

'Sworn before me, this 31st of January, 1810, at the Secretary's office.—WILLIAM LAURENCE.'

A bill of indictment having been preferred against the said Mr. Huggins, in consequence of one of the female slaves dying, he was acquitted, on which occasion Mr. J. W. Tobin addressed an animated letter to the governor, asserting that the jury was packed, and that their verdict excited the surprise and indignation of the respectable part of the community.

In justice to our government at home, we think it right to state that, in the letter of Lord Liverpool to the governor, after adverting to the heinousness of the transaction, he says, 'I am commanded by his Royal Highness the Prince Regent to direct that you will remove from that honorable situation any magistrate or magistrates who actually witnessed the infliction of the punishment without interference; and that he cannot receive from the council and assembly of the Virgin Islands a more flattering assurance of their regard to the wishes of their sovereign, and of the interest they feel in supporting the honour of the British name, than their anxious endeavours to ameliorate the condition of that class of beings, whose bitter and dependent lot entitles them to every protection and support.'

Let us now bring forward the evidence of an individual, whose testimony has never been impugned, on the sufferings of African slaves in the British West-India Islands.

We make the following extracts from a work published by Dr Pinckard, inspector-general of hospitals, and physician to the Bloomsbury Dispensary, entitled 'Notes on the West Indies.'—The facts took place at an English plantation in Demerara, where the doctor was stationed himself at the time.

'Two unhappy negroes, a man and a woman, having been driven by cruel treatment to abscond from the plantation of Lancaster, were taken a few days since, and brought back to the estate, when the manager, whose inhuman severity had caused them to fly from his tyrannic government, dealt out to them his avenging despotism with more than savage brutality. Taking with him two of the strongest drivers, armed with the heaviest whips, he led these trembling and wretched Africans, early in the morning, to a remote part of the estate, too distant for the officers to hear their cries; and there tying down first the man, he stood by, and made the drivers flog him with many hundred lashes, until, on releasing him from the ground, it was discovered that he was nearly exhausted; and in this state the inhuman monster struck him with the butt-end of a large whip, and felled him to the earth; when the poor negro, escaping at once from his slavery and his sufferings, expired at the murderer's feet. But, not satisfied with blood, this savage tyrant next tied down the naked woman on the spot by the dead body of her husband, and with the whips, already deep in gore, compelled the drivers to inflict a punishment of several hundred lashes, which had nearly released her also from a life of toil and torture.

'Hearing of these acts of cruelty on my return from the hospital, and scarcely believing it possible that they could have been committed, I went immediately to the sick-house to satisfy myself by ocular testimony; when, alas! I discovered that all I had heard was too fatally true; for, shocking to relate, I found the wretched and almost murdered woman lying stark naked on her belly upon the dirty boards, without any covering to the horrid wounds which had been cut by the whips, with the still warm and bloody corpse of the man extended at her side, upon the neck of which was an iron collar, and a long heavy chain, which the now murdered negro had been made to wear from the time of his return to the estate.

'The flesh of the woman was so torn as to exhibit one extensive sore from the loins almost down to her hams; nor had humanity administered even a drop of oil to soften her wounds. The only relief she knew was that of extending her feeble arm in order to beat off the tormenting flies with a small green bough, which had been put into her hand for that purpose by the sympathizing kindness of a fellow-slave. A more shocking or distressing spectacle can scarcely be conceived. The dead man, and the almost expiring woman, had been brought home from the place of punishment, and thrown into the negro hospital, amidst the crowd of sick, with cruel unconcern. Lying on the opposite side of the corpse was a fellow-sufferer in similar condition to the poor woman. His buttocks, thighs, and part of his back, had been flogged into one large sore, which was still raw, although he had been punished a fortnight before.

'A few days after the funeral, the attorney of the estate happened to call at Lancaster, to visit the officers; and the conversation naturally turning upon the cruelty of the manager, and the consequent injury derived to the proprietors, we asked him what punishment the laws of the colony had provided for such horrid and barbarous crimes; expressing our hope that the manager would suffer the disgrace he so justly merited; when, to our great surprise, the attorney smiled, and treated our remarks only as the dreams of men unpractised in the ways of slavery. He spoke of the murder with as little feeling as the manager who had perpetrated it, and seemed to be amused at our visionary ideas of punishing a white man for his cruel treatment of slaves.

'To the question, whether the manager would not be dismissed from the estate? he replied, "Certainly not;" adding, "that if the negro had been treated as he deserved, he would have been flogged to death long before." Such was the amount of his sympathy and concern! "The laws of the country," he said, "were intended to punish any person for punishing a slave with more than thirty-nine lashes for the same offence; but by incurring only a small fine he could at any time punish a negro with as many hundred lashes as he might wish, although the governor and the fiscal were standing at his elbow."

That the slaves universally believe in transmigration to Africa after their decease, and that this renders them often desirous to terminate their miseries by suicide, which masters have the greatest difficulty in preventing, are statements pointedly made by Dr. Pinckard. But his account of two negro funerals, which he witnessed himself, are still more striking, as evidence of the *humanity* of planters, and the *happiness* of their slaves. At both these solemnities the most unbounded marks of joy, and, as it were, congratulation, formed the rude ceremonial. The corpse of the happy negro, now rescued from his chains by a Power against which not even white men could contend, was followed by his surviving comrades, singing and capering for joy; not asking him, like the barbarians of the polar circles, why he died, or lamenting that he had left them, but addressing him in exclamations of envy; of hope that they should speedily follow him, and of confidence that the moment of their death would prove also the signal of relief from their miserable state.

Great wretchedness is occasioned at slave sales, by the separation of their friends and relatives. This dreadful and inherent feature of the traffic has not, perhaps, been sufficiently attended to. The following description of a mother who was exhibited at a sale, with her son and three daughters, furnishes an instance:—

'The fears of the parent, lest she should be separated from her children, or these from each other, were anxious and watchful, beyond all that imagination could paint, or the most vivid fancy portray. When any one approached their little group, or advanced to look towards them with the attentive eye of a purchaser, the children, in broken sobs, crouched nearer together, and the fearful mother, in agonizing impulse, instantly fell down before the spectator, bowed herself to the earth, and kissed his feet; then alternately clinging to his legs, and pressing her children to her bosom, she fixed herself upon her knees, clasped her hands together, and in anguish cast up a look of humble petition, which might have found its way even to the heart of a Caligula;—and thus, in Nature's truest language, did the afflicted parent urge the strongest appeal to his compassion, while she implored the purchaser, in dealing out to her the hard lot of slavery, to spare her the additional pang of being torn from her children.'

Though Dr. Pinckard was always well received by the planters—lived in their society on a footing of the closest intimacy—was a witness of all the good, as well as the evil, of their manners—and was, in every respect, most naturally and properly inclined to vindicate them, where truth will permit; yet his whole volumes, abounding in every species of information, containing all the results of his attentive unwearied observations on the state of the slaves, as well as of the colonies in general, do not offer to the most attentive perusal one single fact or circumstance approaching to a defence of the evil so often imputed to the slave trade. Their whole compass offers not a line to contradict, nor even in any degree to weaken, the mass of evidence upon which former writers on colonial affairs have long denounced that detestable enormity. On the contrary, he furnishes, almost in every page, new examples of its evils, and new grounds for its abolition.

It is a humiliating and melancholy fact, that the more despotic the government the happier the slave. We never hear of the magistrates of Rome interfering to protect the defenceless children of sorrow until the times of the emperors, when one of them ordered an imperious master to be punished, and his slaves to be liberated. In free states the limited authority of magistrates prevents them from interfering in individual concerns; and it frequently happens that the slave-owners are also magistrates. Under despotisms this is not always the case. Human feelings are not there controlled by laws, and the cruel master cannot escape the laudable indignation which his conduct excites when the executive punishes in accordance with the feelings of the moment, and not by the directions of legislative statutes, previously enacted. For these reasons we find the slaves in the French and Spanish colonies much better treated than in our own. There are one or two exceptions; but, generally speaking, this is the case; and we blush for our country while we acknowledge the fact. As a further proof of our remarks, we shall exhibit the state of slavery in Republican America, and see whether tyranny ever inflicted greater tortures than take place in that land of freedom.

Mr. John Parrish, an American-born citizen, and an enlightened Quaker, in a pamphlet published in Philadelphia, 1806, by Kimber, Conrad, and Co. says:—

'There is a species of slave-trade carried on in the United States, which in cruelty equals that in the West Indies. A class of men, whose minds seem to have become almost callous to every tender feeling, have agents in various places suited to their purpose, who travel through different states, and by purchase, or otherwise, procure considerable numbers of these people, which consequently occasions a separation of the nearest connexions in life. Husbands from wives, and parents from children—the poignant sensations marked on their mournful countenances disregarded—are taken in droves through the country like herds of cattle, but with less commiseration; for, being chained, or otherwise fettered, the weight and friction of their shackles naturally producing much soreness and pain, they are greatly incommoded in their travel. Gaols, designed for the security of such as have forfeited their liberty by a breach of the laws, are, through the countenance of some of the magistracy, made receptacles for this kind of merchandise; and, when opportunity presents for moving them further, it is generally in the dead of night, that their cries might not be heard, nor legal methods pursued for the liberation of such as have been kidnapped. Others are chained in the garrets or cellars of private houses, till the numbers becoming nearly equal to the success which may have been expected, they are then conveyed on board, and crowded under the hatches of vessels secretly stationed for that purpose, and thus transported to Petersburg, in Virginia, or such other parts as will insure the best market; and many are marched by land to unknown destined places.

'Is it not a melancholy circumstance that such an abominable trade should be suffered in a land boasting of liberty?—While I was waiting with others on the legislature of Maryland, at their session in 1803, it was well known that a vessel lay in the river below Baltimore, to take in slaves—a practice frequent on the waters of Maryland, Delaware, and many other places.

'The evidence of a free African will not be taken against a white man; and, therefore, he may go unpunished.

'Many of the people of colour, who had fled to prevent their being sold to southern traders, have, by authority of the fugitive law, been pursued, brought back, and sold to men of this description; and, as government has refused to afford them any redress, to God only could they look for support. Thus this law is put in force against an unoffending helpless people, while of the fugitive for murder or theft little or no notice is taken; so that the true spirit of judgment is turned backward.

'In some places, cognizance is

taken of murder, long after the perpetration. In Great Britain, the Governor of Goree, in Africa, for ordering a soldier to be illegally whipped, which occasioned his death, was tried and executed fifteen or twenty years afterwards.* How have the coloured people's lives been sported with in some parts of the United States! Numbers have been whipped to death, and otherwise murdered, and little or no notice taken, in a judicial capacity. It was reported, from good authority, that a black man who was sold from near Snow Hill, in Maryland, to a distant part of the Continent, returned back, and lay out of doors. Being accused of stealing from his neighbours, he was pursued, taken, and brought into the village one morning, and there hung without judge or jury; of which no more notice was taken than if they hung a dog!

'It was a just observation of Thomas Jefferson (late President of the United States), "that the whole commerce between master and slave is one perpetual exercise of the most boisterous passions on the one part, and degrading submission on the other." Many instances have occurred, and some of a recent date, where the slaves have rather chosen death, than to remain in a state of bondage, liable to be separated from all that is dear to them. Some have plunged into the water, and drowned themselves; others have cut their throats—one in particular, lately in Delaware county gaol, and another on the pavement in Philadelphia, finding they were about to be sent from their relatives to the West Indies. Others, in attempting to make their escape, have resorted to desperate means for accomplishing it. A number of these unhappy people were taken from the eastern shore of Maryland, by two of the southern slave-traders, called Georgiamen—by name Henry Spiers and Joshua Butts, who being concerned with the treasurer of the state of Georgia, were furnished by him with eight or ten thousand dollars out of the treasury, to speculate on; but as they were returning with their purchases through Virginia, they were exterminated by their prisoners; who were afterwards apprehended, and several of them executed.

'When I was travelling through North Carolina, a black man, who was outlawed, being shot by one of his pursuers, and left wounded in the woods, they came to the ordinary where I had stopped to bait my horse, in order to procure a cart to bring the poor wretched object in. Another, I was credibly informed, was shot, his head cut off, and carried in a bag by the perpetrators of the murder, who received the reward,† which was said to have been two hundred dollars, and that the head was stuck on a coal-house at an iron-works in Virginia. His crime was going, without leave, to visit his wife, who was in slavery at some distance. One Crawford gives an account of a black man being gibbetted alive in South Carolina, and the buzzards came and picked out his eyes. Another was burnt at the stake in Charlestown,

* See the case of Governor Wall, here alluded to.
† Advertisement from the Edenton newspaper:—'North Carolina, Oct. 29, 1795. 'Ten Dollars' Reward will be paid for apprehending and delivering to me my negro-man, named Moses, who, after being detected in some villainy, ran away this morning about four o'clock; or I will give five times the sum to any person that will give due proof of his being killed, and never ask a question to know by whom it was done. 'W. SKINNER.
This Skinner was a general in the American army, and a great *stickler* for liberty!

in the same state, surrounded by a multitude of spectators, some of whom were people of the first rank. The poor object was heard to cry "Not guilty! not guilty!"

'A judge on the eastern shore of Maryland sold thirteen of his slaves to a southern trader, among whom was a man who was sent to gather oysters, while his wife was taken away: when he returned, and found his wife was gone, he expostulated with his learned master, asking "Whether he had not been a faithful slave for more than twenty years, and requesting he might go after his wife:" but this boon of mercy was refused. A man by the name of Black, in Cedar Creek Neck, the latter end of April, 1805, in the state of Delaware and county of Sussex, suspended a black lad; and, tying three fence-rails to his feet, beat him to death, and then buried the body in the night. On discovery of the fact, the corpse was taken up, and, by the coroner's inquest, he was found guilty of wilful murder. It further appeared that Black had been the death of two unhappy victims before, which was kept secret. What made the former murder more lamentable was, the lad was innocent of the crime he was charged with, viz. taking leather for a pair of shoe soles, which Black's son afterwards acknowledged he had taken. The murderer escaped justice.

'From an account, published in the "American Daily Advertiser," by a person who had taken a tour along the eastern shore of Maryland, it appears that from that side of the bay only there were not less than six hundred blacks carried off in six months by the Georgiamen, or southern traders.* Some of the agents of those southern traders are so hardy as to publish advertisements of their readiness to purchase these kinds of cargo, which they effect in various ways; frequently by purchases made so secretly, that the poor blacks, when engaged at their meals, or occupied in some domestic concerns, not having the least intimation of the design, are suddenly seized, bound, and carried off, either to some place provided for the purpose, or immediately on board the vessel. Many are obtained by kidnapping, until the whole supply is completed.

'I have heard some men in eminent stations say, "the country must be thinned of these people (the blacks)—they must be got rid of at any rate." Some from embarrassed circumstances have made sale of these wretched objects, who, being fallen upon unawares, were handcuffed, and sent afar off, which has struck such a terror to other slaves, who would otherwise have remained with their masters, that they have run away. A man and his wife on the same shore of Maryland, being thus circumstanced, fled under such alarm, that the woman left behind her sucking child.† After they were taken, I met them, coupled together in irons, and drove along the road like brute beasts, by two rough unfeeling white men. About sixty in one drove of these poor men, women, and children, were lately driven through Pennsylvania; and not only the males, but the women, were so iron-bound, that

---

* This may be called the very heart of the United States. The spot whereon the city of Washington, the seat of government, stands, was chosen for no other reason but that of being exactly the centre of the Union. It belonged, formerly, partly to Maryland, and partly to Virginia; being upon the boundary lines of those two states.

† No mothers, in the most polished nations, are more tender and affectionate to eir offspring than negro-women. What, then, must have been the horrors of the le, in a case like this?

it was with great difficulty the latter suckled their children.

'It has been asked, what can be said in favour of emancipation, when so many that are free are crowded into gaol for dishonesty? I am not disposed to countenance wrong things, but they may plead the example of the whites. That disposition for theft which they have been branded with must be ascribed to their situation, and not to any depravity in a moral sense. The man in whose favour no laws of property exist probably feels himself less bound to respect those made in favour of others. When arguing for ourselves, we say, "that laws, to be just, must give a reciprocation of right;" that, without this, they are mere arbitrary rules of conduct founded in force, and not in conscience; and it is a problem, which I give the master to solve, whether religious precepts against the violation of property were not framed for him as well as his slave; and whether the slave may not as justifiably take a little from one who has taken all from him, as he may slay one who may slay him; that a change in relation, in which a man is placed, should change his ideas of moral right or wrong, is neither new, nor peculiar to the colour of blacks. Homer tells us it was so upwards of two thousand six hundred years ago:—

"Jove fixed it certain that whatever day
Makes man a slave takes half his worth away."
'JEFFERSON'S NOTES ON VIRGINIA.'

This wretched race of men, both in the West India Islands and United States of America, are bought and sold, exactly as we sell our horses, oxen, sheep, and swine. Planters, who are to a man gamblers, will stake a negro on the turn of a card, or the cast of the dice; or barter them for a horse, cattle, or a piece of land. They are put up in lots at auction, as we sell horses, and carried hundreds of miles from the place where they were born. On the death of their master they are sold, along with the quadruped stock of the estate, to the best bidder, as the following advertisement, taken from a paper printed in the very town where General Washington was born, will fully prove:—

'To be sold at auction, pursuant to the last will and testament of Mann Page, deceased, all the personal property belonging to his estate; consisting of about one hundred and sixty negroes, together with all the stock of horses, three mules, cattle, sheep, plantation utensils, and about one thousand barrels of corn. Amongst the negroes are seven very valuable carpenters, three excellent blacksmiths, two millers, and some other tradesmen. The greater part, if not the whole, of this valuable property, will be sold on a credit of twelve months; the purchaser giving bond with approved security, to bear interest from the date, if not punctually paid. All sums under twenty dollars must be paid in money.'

Were we to extract, from more recent publications, the many cases of cruelty lately exercised upon the unhappy children of Africa, we should fill a volume; but we trust that we have said enough to make the reader exclaim, with Cowper,

'I would not have a slave to till my ground,
To fan me when I sleep, and tremble when
I wake, for all that human sinews, bought and sold,
Have ever earned.'

Strange that men professing to be followers of the mild and merciful Jesus should inflict such tortures as we have already described, and stranger still that interest should not predominate in their cruel and selfish minds; recent experiments having clearly demonstrated that it would be much more advantageous for the planter to have his ground cultivated by freemen than slaves; for one manumitted negro will do more work than three bondsmen; so much better a stimulant to industry are wages than the whip. But the planters cannot be brought to believe in a fact which Nature herself, providing against slavery, has established throughout the world; for her laws have ordained that nine men out of every ten must endure the penalty of Adam—live by labour; and labour, in all climes, is only adequate to the support of life. The negroes in the West Indies, if free tomorrow, would labour to support themselves; and would certainly work harder than they do now, even to do that. Consequently the planter would have his ground tilled for less than what the support of his slaves costs him, and thereby save the money he must pay to keep up his *live stock*. This should be an inducement, even overlooking the other circumstances which would attend a consummation so devoutly to be wished as the abolition of slavery.

But the curse of commerce is on the whole West India proprietors. They bought the blacks as slaves, and slaves they will retain them, unless they get not only their money, but the interest of it, back. Traders like what is tangible, and despise the promise of advantages so remote as those depending on the abolition of slavery, and we fear the whip and the driver will still continue to be in request. Yet, with all our abhorrence of this cruel system, a moment's reflection will show us that it is supported and perpetuated by our own idle and pernicious habits. The tap-room might justly be called the tomb of the poor negro's liberty; for it is the vicious and thoughtless consumers of poisonous rum and unwholesome tobacco which enable their task-master to keep them in degradation. Little does the affected beau think, while he is extending his nostrils, by filling them with 'pungent grains of tittilating dust,' or the young miss, while she is sipping her tea, that the snuff and sugar, which they are so wantonly wasting, are not only in themselves useless, but manufactured by the labour of slaves, and not unfrequently tinged with their actual blood.* But the lower classes are most culpable. The consumption of rum and tobacco is not only an idle, fulsome, and vicious habit, but extremely expensive, and could be dispensed with by the poor, their greatest admirers, with advantage to their health, morals, and pockets; while their useful abstinence would be contributing to put a stop to the sufferings of their African fellow-creatures.

But our admonition, we fear, is as vain as our lamentations. The community will continue consuming the produce of the West Indies, and the task-master to inflict his torture; while the poor negro, in the words of the poet, may justly reproach us:—

THE NEGRO'S COMPLAINT.

'Forced from home and all its pleasures,
  Afric's coast I left forlorn;
To increase a stranger's treasures,
  O'er the raging billows borne.
Men from England bought and sold me,
  Paid my price in paltry gold;
But, though slave they have enrolled me,
  Minds are never to be sold.

'Still in thought as free as ever,
  What are England's rights, I ask,
Me from my delights to sever,
  Me to torture, me to task?

---

* The writer of this was present in a grocer's shop when a negro child, apparently a year old, was taken out of a sugar-hogshead, having been smothered there either by carelessness or design.—The descendant of Ishmael was consigned to the silent grave, and the grocer served his customers with the sugar that preserved the little black.

Fleecy locks and black complexion
  Cannot forfeit Nature's claim;
Skins may differ, but affection
  Dwells in white and black the same.

' Why did all-creating Nature
  Make the plant for which we toil?
Sighs must fan it, tears must water,
  Sweat of ours must dress the soil.
Think, ye masters, iron-hearted,
  Lolling at your jovial boards;
Think how many backs have smarted
  For the sweets your cane affords.

' Is there, as ye sometimes tell us,
  Is there One who reigns on high?
Has He bid you buy and sell us,
  Speaking from his throne, the sky?
Ask him if your knotted scourges,
  Matches, blood-extorting screws,
Are the means that duty urges
  Agents of his will to use?

' Hark! he answers!—wild tornadoes,
  Strewing yonder sea with wrecks,
Wasting towns, plantations, meadows,
  Are the voice with which he speaks.
He, foreseeing what vexations
  Afric's sons should undergo,
Fixed their tyrant's habitations
  Where his whirlwinds answer—No!

' By our blood in Afric wasted,
  Ere our necks received the chain;
By the miseries that we tasted,
  Crossing in your barks the main;
By our sufferings, since ye brought us
  To the man-degrading mart;
All sustained by patience, taught us
  Only by a broken heart;

' Deem our nation brutes no longer,
  Till some reason ye shall find
Worthier of regard, and stronger
  Than the colour of our kind.
Slaves of gold, whose sordid dealings
  Tarnish all your boasted powers,
Prove that you have human feelings,
  Ere you proudly question ours!'
            COWPER.

The sum of these doleful tales is the case of Hodge, who, for his wickedness to his slaves, expiated his crimes by the hands of the executioner, unpitied by the whites, and execrated by the blacks.

The Hon. Arthur Wm. Hodge, proprietor, and one of the members of his majesty's council in the island of Tortola, was indicted for the murder of one of his own negroes, of the name of Prosper.

The prisoner, on his trial, being put to the bar, pleaded Not Guilty. The first witness called to prove the charge was a free woman of colour, of the name of Pareen Georges. She stated that she was in the habit of attending at Mr. Hodge's estate to wash linen; that one day Prosper came to her to borrow six shillings, being the sum that his master required of him, because a mango had fallen from a tree, which he (Prosper) was set to watch. He told the witness that he must either find the six shillings or be flogged; that the witness had only three shillings, which she gave him, but that it did not appease Mr. Hodge: that Prosper was flogged for upwards of an hour, receiving more than one hundred lashes, and threatened by his master that, if he did not bring the remaining three shillings on the next day, the flogging should be repeated; that the next day he was tied to a tree, and flogged for such a length of time, with the thong of the whip doubled, that his head fell back, and that he could bawl no more.—From thence he was carried to the sick-house, and chained to two other negroes: that he remained in this confinement during five days, at the end of which time his companions broke away; and thereby released him; that he was unable to abscond; that he went to the negro-houses, and shut himself up; that he was found there dead, and in a state of putrefaction, some days afterwards; that crawlers were found in his wounds, and not a piece of black flesh was to be seen on the hinder part of his body where he had been flogged.

Stephen M'Keogh, a white man, who had lived as manager on Mr. Hodge's estate, deposed that he saw the deceased, Prosper, after he had been so severely flogged; that he could put his finger in his side;

he saw him some days before his death in a cruel state; he could not go near him for the blue flies. Mr. Hodge had told the witness, while he was in his employ, that, if the work of the estate was not done, he was satisfied if he heard the whip.

This was the evidence against the prisoner. His counsel, in their attempt to impeach the veracity of the witnesses, called evidence as to his general character, which disclosed instances of still greater barbarity on the part of Mr. Hodge. Among other examples, the witness, Pureen Georges, swore that he had occasioned the death of his cook, named Margaret, by pouring boiling water down her throat.

Before the jury retired, the prisoner addressed them as follows:—

'Gentlemen, as bad as I have been represented, or as bad as you may think me, I assure you that I feel support in my affliction from entertaining a proper sense of religion. As all men are subject to wrong, I cannot but say that that principle is likewise inherent in me. I acknowledge myself guilty in regard to many of my slaves; but I call God to witness my innocence in respect to the murder of Prosper. I am sensible that the country thirsts for my blood, and I am ready to sacrifice it.'

The jury, after some deliberation, brought in a verdict of Guilty.

There were six other indictments on similar charges against the prisoner.

After, as well as previous to, his condemnation, and to the last moment of his life, Mr. Hodge persisted in his innocence of the crime for which he was about to suffer. He acknowledged that he had been a cruel master (which, as he afterwards said, was all he meant, in his admission to the jury, of his guilt in regard to others of the slaves); that he had repeatedly flogged his negroes; that they had then run away, when, by their own neglect, and the consequent exposure of their wounds, the death of some of them had possibly ensued. He denied all intentions of causing the death of any one, and pleaded the unruly and insubordinate disposition of his whole gang as the motive for his severity. These were the sentiments in which he died.

Governor Elliott sent to Lord Liverpool the depositions of the witnesses who were examined on this trial. The deposition of Mr. Robertson states that he has every reason to suspect Mr. Hodge of having murdered five of his slaves!

The governor then mentions the proceedings he had thought proper to adopt; gives an account of the trial and conviction of Mr. Hodge —the majority of the petit jury recommended him to mercy!! but none of the judges seconded the recommendation.

From the period of his condemnation to his execution, which took place May the 8th, 1811, Governor Elliott thought it expedient to proclaim martial law and to embody the militia; but, fortunately, no disturbance took place. However, the governor added, that 'the state of irritation, nay, I had almost said, of anarchy, in which I have found this colony, rendered the above measures indispensable for the preservation of tranquillity, and for ensuring the due execution of the sentence against Arthur W. Hodge. Indeed, it is but too probable that without my presence, in a conjuncture so replete with party animosity, unpleasant occurrences might have ensued.'

The evidence adduced during this trial shows to what an alarming height cruelty is still practised in the West Indies. The legislature of this country, or the crown, is imperiously called upon to interfere, and put a final check to atrocities which inflict a deep wound upon the character of the nation. If the colonial assemblies have not hitherto evinced an inclination to stop these proceedings, they are unfit and unworthy to legislate; and the parent state should resume an authority which has been so feebly exercised for the protection of the weak.

ANTONIO CARDOZA,
EXECUTED FOR THE MURDER OF THOMAS DAVIS.

THIS malefactor was a sailor, and a native of Portugal. He was indicted at the Old Bailey, January 11, 1811, along with Sarah Brown, *alias* Golz, a Jewess, and Mary Rogers, both women of the town, for the wilful murder of Thomas Davis, a British seaman, in Nightingale Lane, on the night of the 12th of December, 1810.

The facts of the case were these:—The deceased, somewhat tipsy, was on his way home, in company with his brother, James Davis, when, passing these girls in the street, he put his arm round the waist of Brown, which she resented by striking him several times on the head with her patten, which she held in her hand. James Davis desired her not to be angry, as his brother was tipsy, and that he would give her something to drink; upon which the other woman struck him in the face with her umbrella. A squabble ensued; Davis flung the umbrella into a green-grocer's shop, and in the struggle both fell to the ground, upon which the girl got up first, and, holding him down, called out 'Antonio! Antonio! why don't you fetch Antonio?' addressing the other girl, Rogers, who immediately ran to a public house, and called Antonio, when Cordoza, and three other Portuguese sailors, rushed out, and attacked the two brothers.

James Davis succeeded in repelling the ruffians, and was on the point of getting away, when, looking round, he saw the deceased knocked down by Cardoza, and, while he was down, the vindictive Portuguese took from his sleeve a knife, and stabbed his victim in the back, the infamous woman, Brown, all the time crying out to Antonio, 'Kill the b——r! don't leave a bit of life in him! it's the way all English b——rs should be served.'

The wounded man exclaimed, 'Brother, I'm killed!' and on being removed to the shop of Mr. King, a surgeon in the neighbourhood, he died in two minutes. These facts were substantiated by several witnesses who saw the transaction; and Cardoza was immediately found guilty of murder; but Mary Brown only of manslaughter, as there had been a quarrel between her and the deceased; whereas Cardoza, without any personal provocation, inflicted the deadly wound. Rogers was acquitted, as there was no evidence affecting her, except that of standing by.

Sentence was immediately passed on this desperate foreigner, and he was ordered for execution on the Monday morning following, January 14, 1811, which was accordingly carried into effect opposite Newgate.

From the time of his trial to the last moment of his existence he persisted in his assertion of innocence, and was heard to say that, during his trial, the man who actually committed the murder was in court. If he was innocent, which we by no means take upon ourselves to advocate, his fate inculcates an important lesson on the evil of keeping bad company; and, if not actually guilty of the murder, his conduct was little less criminal for joining with those that did it, in defence of prostitutes, for whom he must have been a *bully*, as they called individually on him by name when insulted by the deceased.

Previous to his being brought from the Press-yard he cried bitterly; but on mounting the scaffold he acted with becoming fortitude. He was attended by a Portuguese clergyman, with whom he joined in fervent prayer, and a few minutes after eight o'clock he was launched into eternity. The concourse of spectators was immense, and among the crowd were several of his countrymen, who seemed much affected at the melancholy scene. After being suspended for the usual time, his body was cut down, and conveyed to Bartholomew's Hospital for dissection, where it was exposed to public view during the day.

Some doubts were entertained by the public as to the power vested in the judges of ordering the execution of this man during the indisposition of his majesty, George III. and the consequent deficiency in the executive power, as the regent was not then appointed, from a feeling that it would be unjust to deprive a human being of life, however enormous his crime, while the fountain of mercy was closed. Mr. Sheridan mentioned this case in the House of Commons the Thursday after the execution, and was answered by the secretary of state for the home department that, according to the statute respecting conviction for murder, it is enacted that the judge, before whom a murderer is convicted, shall, in passing sentence, direct him to be executed the next day but one after his being found guilty, (unless the same shall be Sunday, and then on the Monday following,) and that his body be delivered to the surgeons to be dissected and anatomized. The judge may likewise direct his body to be afterwards hung in chains, but in no wise to be buried without dissection. In the case of this malefactor, the secretary stated that the judges who tried him had no doubt of his guilt; and that, as no application came from the unfortunate man himself, it was deemed advisable to let the law take its course, otherwise he would have been respited.

Our readers will please to recollect that we have already stated the law upon this head, by which they will see that in all cases of capital conviction, within the city of London, it is necessary that a regular report of the prisoners should be made to his majesty, or, in the event of his indisposition, as in the present case, to his representative, of the respective cases, and his sanction must be obtained before execution can take place. This rule, however, only applies to the city of London, as the judges going circuit act under a special commission, which empowers them to pass sentence of death, and to direct its execution in all cases, as well as to respite it, and relax the other restraints upon sufficient cause, without the direct authority of the king

WILLIAM TOWNLEY,
EXECUTED FOR BURGLARY.

WILLIAM TOWNLEY was a native of Winchcomb and at the age of twenty-nine exhibited a remarkable instance to what extent human depravity may be carried. In 1779, when only seventeen years of age, he was, with an elder brother, convicted of burglary, and sentenced to two years' imprisonment in the Penitentiary House. He had not long regained his liberty when he was brought a second time to the gaol, charged with a capital offence, found guilty, and sentenced to transportation for seven years, which period he served on board the hulks at Woolwich; from whence he was only discharged three months when he was a third time committed for the crime for which he justly suffered.

In the last interval he had entered as a substitute in the Worcestershire militia, for forty guineas, ten of which he had received: he soon squandered the money, and then perpetrated a burglary, for which he was tried at Gloucester, and received sentence of death.

He persisted in declaring the witnesses against him perjurers, until within a short time of the execution, when, it is said, just before he received the sacrament, he admitted his full share in the crime for which his life became forfeited to the offended laws of his country.

Saturday, the 23d of March, 1811, he was executed at the new drop before Gloucester gaol, and had been suspended about twenty minutes when a reprieve arrived! Is the life of man of so little value, that those intrusted with important power will not study correctness? Some stupid clerk in office directed it to the sheriff of Herefordshire instead of Gloucestershire, by *mistake!* On Friday night it arrived, but was not opened till next morning, when immediately the importance of its contents to the wretched object of intended mercy was ascertained, and an express sent off, by Mr. Bennett, of the hotel, at his own expence; but, alas! the messenger was twenty minutes too late to arrest the fatal hand of the executioner; and he whom he came to save was gone to that 'bourn from whence no traveller returns.' What must have been the feelings of the clerk who misdirected the letter?

RICHARD ANDREWS AND ALEXANDER HALL,

TRANSPORTED FOR FRAUD.

ANDREWS had been long a depredator upon the public; and though he had not, like Roberts, the advantage of being a counsellor-at-law, yet he well knew how to 'keep his neck out of the halter:' he would not, in fact, touch upon what might amount to a felony; but, with all their art and knowledge, we are always finding swindlers stumbling upon the pillory, or strolling on board a transport.

The first public examination of Andrews, of any moment, was at the Police-office, in Queen Square, Westminster, on the 31st of March, 1807; when Colonel Davison (not of St. James's Square) stated that he became acquainted with the prisoner in the King's Bench. It was very material for the colonel to get a seat in parliament; and, as the prisoner had often represented himself as intimately connected with some of the first characters in the country, the colonel disclosed his affairs to him, who undertook to forward his intention. He described himself as the intimate acquaintance of the Earl of Besborough, Lord Fitzwilliam, and R. Spencer, Esq. from whom he received contributions while in prison. After the colonel had left the Bench, he frequently relieved him with pecuniary trifles, till he was liberated by the Insolvent Act; and he then carried his pretensions to the extreme, by observing that he had been offered a seat in parliament by Earl Fitzwilliam, but it would ill become him to accept it, having been so recently liberated; and he could, by the interest of the Earl of Besborough, have the honour conferred on the colonel, as it was by the interest of that earl that Lord Fitzwilliam's promise was to be realized. The colonel went to dine with B. Goldsmid, Esq. at Roehampton, and the prisoner accompanied him in his carriage to the Earl of Besborough's house, at the same place; but the earl was from home. He saw the prisoner again in a day or two, when he informed him that he had conversed with the Earl of Besborough on the subject of a seat in parliament; and the earl jocosely remarked, 'I should conceive you to be a Don Quixote to want a seat, after taking the benefit of the Insolvent Act.' The conversation then became more serious; and the colonel, as his friend, was to have the seat promised by Earl Fitzwilliam. The prisoner went on to state that he was connected with the noble earl, who had four boroughs in Ireland, and who would dispose of them at four thousand pounds each; and, if the colonel should have other friends to accommodate, he might have the preference, as the noble earl had authorized him to find candidates. The colonel found candidates for all the boroughs the prisoner had talked of, and by his desire the money was deposited in the hands of a banker. The candidates, when they became members, were to retain their seats for five years, in case of a dissolution of parliament. The colonel here observed that he had such full confidence in the prisoner as by his artifices to have been led away in a manner that made him look more like an accomplice than a dupe. He had been so deceived by the plausible pretences and the solemnity of the prisoner's conduct, that his mind was tranquillized: thus he had obtained of him (the colonel), and his friends, by his recommendation, four thousand pounds, he having got two thousand pounds in two payments, as he said, for the Earl of Besborough, as part of the consideration for the boroughs in Ireland. The other money consisted in relieving the temporary embarrassments of the prisoner, and accepting his bills. The colonel had accepted bills for a carriage, which the prisoner had made in Poland Street; also for his stud, &c. besides those of different tradespeople. The colonel, having at length entertained some suspicion of the prisoner, waited on the Earl of Besborough, when he found his suspicions realized.

The Earl of Besborough stated that he knew no more of the prisoner than having received letters from him while in prison, asking relief, which he granted to him in trifles. He knew nothing of what had been related respecting the boroughs; and the other noblemen who had been talked of knew no more of the prisoner than having afforded relief to his distresses.

A gentleman, who had agreed to purchase one of the boroughs, proved that he had paid the prisoner four hundred pounds, as part of the consideration, and had been completely misled. The prisoner was committed for re-examination.

He formerly kept his carriage, and a dashing equipage, in Half-Moon Street, Piccadilly; but he was apprehended in an obscure lodging in Westminster.

In a few days Andrews was again brought to the same office for a further examination. On this occasion the principal evidence against him was Mr. Harris, an aged gentleman, a surgeon and man-midwife in the Strand, whose ruin had been the consequence of the conduct of the prisoner.

It appeared, by the statement of this gentleman, that he accidentally met with a lady, (who turned out to be the wife of the prisoner,) in 1800. It being late at night, he offered to see the lady home; and he did so, to Edward Street, Cavendish Square. The prisoner expressed his warmest acknowledgments for the trouble Mr. Harris had taken, and invited him to dine, &c. at his table.

A mutual intimacy now subsisted between the parties, and Mr. Harris attended professionally at the accouchement of Mrs. Andrews, in February, 1801. In April the prisoner took apartments at the house of Mr. Harris, and remained there above twelve months; but never paid board or lodging. The prisoner kept his carriage at the time. He used to represent himself as a man of fortune, and the brother of the person who was the proprietor of the Dartford powder-mills. Mr. Harris was employed by the prisoner to inspect jesuit barks, opium, &c. which he (the prisoner) used to purchase in considerable quantities. The complainant, on a certain day in April, 1801, supped with the prisoner, and others; and, after having drank freely, and reduced himself to a state of stupefaction, the party retired, and shortly after returned with a bundle of papers, which he signed, as a witness, without knowing what they were. The complainant stated that he believed opium had been mixed with his wine, for he felt himself very ill the next day. Mr. Harris had not signed these papers many days, when he was arrested at the suit of Mr. Barron, druggist, in the Strand, though unconscious of having contracted a debt with that gentleman; but the business was settled by the attorney, whilst Mr. Harris was in a lock-up-house. He was released, and returned to his house, which was then in Theobald's Road. He used to ride with the prisoner in his carriage; and on a certain day, when at the foot of Westminster Bridge, the prisoner alighted, and observed that he was going for a gentleman; and he, in a few minutes, brought a sheriff's officer, who served a writ on the complainant, who knew of no debt he owed, and he was hurried away in the carriage to the King's Bench prison, where he remained until October, 1804, when he was cleared by the Insolvent Act. He could get no redress for this cruel treatment, and he reflected with horror on the conduct of Andrews, who called on him again after his release. At this time a cupboard door was standing open in Mr. Harris's house, and the prisoner reached a box from off a shelf, and rattled it. The complainant was at this moment sent for into his shop, and the prisoner went up stairs with the box, which contained plate to the amount of two hundred pounds. The complainant returned, and followed the prisoner up stairs; but he had gone off with the box and plate. Mr. Harris saw the prisoner again in the evening, when he said that he had made a temporary use of the plate, to save himself from being arrested, but he would return it in a day or two; but he ultimately absconded. The plate was the property of a West-India merchant, who had married the daughter of Mr. Harris, and it was left in his possession for safety, whilst the merchant was gone abroad.

Another charge was exhibited against the prisoner by a young man, in whose mother's house the prisoner lodged in 1797. He had obtained twenty-one pounds of the woman, which was chiefly expended in clothing a female with whom he had cohabited. The prisoner had given the young man two letters to take to the Duke of Devonshire and Earl Spencer, which were, according to his account, recommendations for the father of the youth to get a comfortable place; but whilst he was gone the prisoner decamped from the house. The young man had seen the prisoner with Sir Watkin Lewes, who had informed him he would pay the debt; but he (the witness) had very recently seen Sir Watkin, who said he had also a charge to institute against the prisoner.

William Brown, late coachman to the prisoner, appeared in his old master's livery, blue and silver lace, to answer interrogatories respecting goods which had been obtained by the prisoner from Mr. Asser, chinaman; but Mr. Asser was not present, and the testimony was of no avail.

The magistrate informed the prisoner that his situation wore a serious aspect, for he stood charged with felony. The prisoner observed that he had been advised to say nothing until he came before a jury; but he had feelings which, irritated by an abominable conspiracy, compelled him to speak. He then entered into a long vindication of his conduct in a firm manner, and protested his innocence. He also begged of the persons present to suspend their judgment till the hour of trial. The magistrate replied that it was astonishing the prisoner should make solemn asseverations of his innocence, when it was palpable that, without fortune, or any visible means of obtaining support, he had been enabled to keep a carriage and sumptuous equipage—that there had been a multiplicity of persons at the office to substantiate charges against him; and he (the magistrate) considered it the duty of his official situation to remand the prisoner, for the further investigation of his conduct. He was therefore remanded accordingly.

On the 10th of April following, Andrews underwent a fourth examination. The first witness called was Mrs. Harris, the wife of the merchant who had lost his plate, and the daughter of Harris, from whose house it was said to have been stolen. This lady corroborated what had been advanced by Mr. Young, who redeemed the plate.

Mr. Brown, who resides in the neighbourhood of Bedford Square, stated that he lived on an independent property, and first became acquainted with the prisoner in the King's Bench, a few months since. He (Mr. Brown) was discharged by the Insolvent Act as well as the prisoner, and about the same time; they had become the most intimate friends; and Mr. Andrews, after his release, lived in Great Russell Street, Bloomsbury, where he kept his chariot and a livery servant, which was afterwards replaced by a family coach and two livery servants. Mr. Andrews had given this witness to understand that he was on the eve of coming to an unlimited fortune, as the heir of Bishop Andrews; and Mr. Brown and his lady used frequently to dine with the prisoner, as did he and his lady with them. At Mr. Andrews's dinner party Colonel Davison, Maltby, M'Cullum, and others, used to be present; but these persons were never invited to Mr

Brown's table. In a conversation with a Mrs. Roberts, who used to dine at the prisoner's table, that lady, in the presence of Mrs. Brown, felt herself surprised at seeing Mrs. Andrews pay some tradesmen's bills, and publicly deprecated so mistaken an idea! This witness had subscribed four hundred pounds to Mr. Andrews's system of finance, besides having done him some little favours while he was in the King's Bench. He had also some bills of Colonel Davison's acceptance, which were not yet due. Mr. Brown had also received a letter from the prisoner, addressed to the Earl of Besborough, which was to procure him (Mr. Brown) a place of four or five hundred a year under government, which he delivered to the earl. Mr. Brown had received this mark of kindness from the prisoner, after he had lent him four hundred pounds; and he needed no promise for that advance, for Mr. Andrews, by his open conduct, had completely got the better of his purse, which he felt no hesitation in opening to him.

A poor man of the name of Newcombe, at whose house the prisoner lodged, lost twenty-five pounds by him, by paying chandler's shop and other little scores, and gave a very singular description of the prisoner's conduct. He acted the part of an embarrassed gentleman, and one day read a printed speech, which he said he made from the hustings at Ipswich, when he was a candidate for the representation of that borough in parliament.

Andrews complained of the unfair conduct of the magistrate during the inquiry, and again denied ever having had an intention of injuring any one. A committee, he said, sat daily at Fishmongers' Hall, to carry on this foul conspiracy against him; and, however his feelings might be tortured by being made a ridicule in that office, a jury would convince the world of his innocence.

Again he was brought up, and fresh charges exhibited against him; but so artfully had he gone about the commission of the different frauds, that he evaded the full punishment due to his crimes, for near five years, though during that long period he lived, to use an old saying, 'by his wits.' But justice, though sometimes tardy, will surely at length overtake the most artful and hardened offender. Andrews, after this long course of infamy—he who had duped nobles, and deceived men of all grades in society—was at length caught in swindling a tavern-keeper out of a dinner!

He was at length committed, upon seven different indictments, to take his trial. It appeared in the course of his various examinations that he committed depredations on all ranks, from the rich and fashionable down to a poor washerwoman, in whose house, when closely pursued, he took lodgings, borrowed money of her, and even defrauded her of the articles that she received in the way of her occupation.

At the Middlesex quarter sessions, on Tuesday, September the 24th, 1811, Richard Andrews and Alexander Hall were put to the bar, charged upon an indictment with defrauding Isaac Kendall, by means of certain false pretences, of the sum of thirteen pounds, five shillings, against the form of the statute in that case made and provided.

When the indictment was about to be read, and the prisoners called upon to plead, Andrews addressed the Court, and repeated his application to have the trial postponed, being quite unable, for the want of pecuniary assistance, to have the professional aid of those who were competent to support him on so severe an occasion. He said, also, that the want of money prevented him from procuring the necessary witnesses, whose evidence could alone prove his innocence, and convince the world that he was not the man whom newspaper report had so branded; for there was not a journal published in the nation that did not impose upon him an assumed characteristic. In some he was called 'Parson Andrews,' in others 'Captain Andrews;' many had the good nature to dub him 'Doctor Andrews;' but they all agreed in one point, namely, that of giving him every name but that which belonged to him. He called God to witness that in the whole course of his life he never arrogated to himself any characteristic that did not belong to him, or assume any other description than that of plain 'Richard Andrews.' Yet he was persecuted beyond example. He entreated of the Court, he supplicated the Bench, that he might be allowed a month to prepare himself; that he might have the benefit of counsel, and be provided with the necessary instructions for his counsel, as he was convinced, if that indulgence should be allowed to him, that he would make his innocence, as far as the intent of wronging the prosecutor, perfectly manifest; at present he could neither obtain the support of witnesses and proofs, the assistance of solicitor, nor the aid of counsel. He submitted to the Court that the prosecutor had two indictments for the one offence against him, and he begged to know upon which of them he intended to try him, as he understood that he had preferred another bill against him.

Mr. Alley, for the prosecution, here interfered, and observed, that the defendant well knew, that although there were two indictments, that yet there was but one charge, and that was a charge for an offence committed so far back as the 12th February last, and therefore he could not complain of surprise; and as to the fact of preferring another bill, in point of substantial truth it was no such thing. It was no more nor no less than merely amending a clerical error in the first bill—the introduction of a single word instead of another. Therefore the defendant had not to take this for a bill of the present sessions.

Several observations were made by Andrews, and the counsel for the prosecution severally replied to them.

At length Mr. Mainwaring stated the sentiments of the Court, the substance whereof was, that, although they were disposed to give every reasonable and humane assistance that they could to all persons in the predicament of the prisoner, yet that they actually did not perceive that satisfactory grounds were adduced for postponing this trial any longer. The circumstance of deficiency of pecuniary means was not a reason why the public justice of the country was to be delayed; but the prisoner, as in such cases, would find counsel in the Court themselves—the judges would be his counsel, as in humanity they ought.

The trial then proceeded. Mr. Alley stated the case, that it was an indictment under the 30th of Geo. III. commonly called 'the Swindling Act,' and, after expatiating on the enormity of offences such as the prisoner was accused of, proceeded to call his witnesses.

Isaac Kendall stated himself to be the proprietor of the coffee-house situate in St. Clement's Churchyard. He said, that on the 12th of February last, the two prisoners, Andrews and Hall, came to his house, and ordered dinner.

Mr. Kendall continued — The coffee-room was very full, and I was busy attending the company. Before they finished their dinner they called for a bottle of wine. There was another gentleman in the coffee-room, who spoke to Mr. Hall. This gentleman was invited to join them after dinner

Q. By Mr. Alley—Is not the person you speak of a most respectable man? do you not know him very well?—A. Beyond a doubt.

Kendall—After dinner they called to me and asked for their bill; I made it out; it amounted to one pound, seven shillings, and sixpence. They offered me a check on Drummond and Co.

Q. By the Chairman.—Who do you mean by they?—A. Hall offered me the check; on looking at it I saw an informality, and would not take it. I then returned it to Hall; Andrews said he would draw another, and they begged pardon for the mistake; the check had thirteen on it instead of thirteen pounds; I saw Andrews draw another for thirteen pounds, five shillings.

Q. By the Chairman—Was the first check in the name of Andrews, though offered by Hall?—A. Yes.

Q. Did you see Andrews draw it?—A. I was rather busy at the moment, but he called for pen and ink, and he had a book of checks by his side. The draft was for thirteen pounds, five shillings, on Drummond and Co. While Andrews was doing something with it, I took Hall aside, and asked him was all right; he answered, 'O! yes! my dear fellow, don't be afraid;' and, speaking of Andrews, he said, ' He was a rich uncle of his, who had been very kind to him on various occasions, and that I need not fear.'. The opinion I formerly entertained of Hall was so high that I would have given him forty pounds, instead of the balance of the draft, had he asked it.

Q. Was any thing said to the gentleman who had joined the prisoners' company, about going to the theatre?—A. It was agreed that he should accompany them there; they did not go out together. It was proposed by them (the prisoners) to dine at my house on the Wednesday or Thursday following, when they would bring a party of friends, and the gentleman was also invited. When the prisoners left the house, the gentleman stopped at the bar to inquire whether the dinner would be on the Wednesday or Thursday. In the mean time they went away. I went to the door along with the gentleman, but they were gone. We looked both to the right and left, but they were not to be seen. I then suspected something was wrong. I sent my son next morning to Drummond's, but there were no effects to pay the draft. In a day or two after, I went, accompanied by my son, to the bankers'; but it was useless: the draft has never been paid.

Mr. Heald, from the house of Messrs. Drummond, proved that Andrews had not, at the time of the drawing the said draft, any cash whatever in their hands; that the last money which lay in their hands, belonging to him, was three shillings and sixpence, which was paid to his messenger three years ago; but he admitted that there was a cash account with the prisoner Andrews, in their house, and that, within three years previous to the year 1808, his account exceeded six thousand pounds. It was, however, all drawn out in January, 1808.

The prosecution on the part of the crown being finished, the prisoners were called on their defence, when Andrews asked a few questions of Mr. Kendall and Mr. Heald, and then addressed the Court, admitting that he drew the draft, and that the money was given to his unfortunate friend, the other prisoner; but he submitted, that as he had kept an account in the banking-house, even had that account been over-drawn, yet that he did not consider himself, much less did he consider Hall, as guilty of any violation of the law. He glanced at the effects which prejudice must have upon a man so miserably situated as he was, and concluded with a strong appeal to the merciful consideration of the Court and of the jury.

Mr. Mainwaring recapitulated the whole of the evidence, making suitable comments upon it, and upon the law of the case, as far as regarded the offence charged against both the prisoners, and left it with the jury to say whether they were guilty or not; and the jury, after a very short consultation, brought in a verdict of Guilty.

They were both again tried, upon a second indictment, for a like offence, in defrauding a person of the name of Brundell, who keeps a tavern at Blackwall, of thirty pounds.

The prisoners went to Mr. Brundell's house and dined; after dinner they got him to sit down and drink a glass of wine with them, and in the course of the conversation they signified that a party of twenty would dine there on the Thursday following, and bespoke a turtle dinner accordingly for that number, at the rate of twenty shillings a head. In a little time after dinner, a letter was received by Mr. Brundell at his bar, and on opening it he found another directed 'To Richard Andrews, Esq.' which letter was instantly handed up stairs to Mr. Andrews. Mr. Andrews no sooner received it than a conversation took place respecting the sale and purchase of an estate; at length the prisoners again got into a conversation with Mr. Brundell; and, in short, they tendered to him a draft for fifty pounds on Messrs. Biddulph and Co. and, desiring him to stop twenty pounds on account of the intended turtle dinner, got the difference, which was thirty pounds, from him; and, after finishing two or three bottles, they walked off. When the draft was presented the next day at Messrs. Biddulph's the fraud was discovered, for he had no account there, and Mr. Brundell saw no more of his guests till they were in custody. They were both found Guilty on this indictment.

Mr. Mainwaring passed the sentence of the Court, which was, that, for the first offence, they should be imprisoned in Newgate six months, and, for the second, that they should be transported for seven years.

MICHAEL WHITING,
EXECUTED FOR POISONING HIS TWO BROTHERS-IN-LAW.

CRIME has different shades; but a deeper dye cannot be given to it, than when one in the assumed robe of sanctity attempts to dip his hands in human blood, particularly when that blood is united to him by ties of consanguinity.

Michael Whiting lived at Downam, where he occasionally preached, being a methodist parson, but as the bounty of those who listened to his pious exhortations was not very large, he endeavoured to add to his resources by keeping a shop in which he sold bread, meal, &c. and, what must surprise our London readers, he also vended drugs, being at once a comforter of the soul and body.

This arch hypocrite had two brothers-in-law, named George and Joseph Langman, who resided on a small farm near Downham. They were both under age, and had two sisters, one of whom was married to Whiting, and the other, aged ten years, lived with her brothers. To possess himself of the small estate of these youths Whiting had recourse to a most diabolical plan.

The little sister was sent to his shop for some bread, and, learning from her that the housekeeper of the brothers was about going from home for a few days, he affected much kindness, and promised paying them a visit. He did so, and with unusual liberality brought with him materials for making a pudding or two, observing to the housekeeper, 'Catherine, be sure you make the boys a pudding before you go.'

After doleing out a few texts of Scripture, which he had ready on all occasions, and which, to use a profane comparison, he applied with as much judgment as Sancho Panza did his proverbs, he departed, taking with him the little girl, tenderly remarking that her sister would take better care of her than her brothers, during the housekeeper's absence.

Catharine made the puddings; but remarked, during the process, that the dough would not properly adhere, and when she departed she left them in a kneading-trough. The brothers, not suspecting that any mischief was intended, boiled one of the puddings for dinner, and, when properly done, sat down to partake of it; but, before they had swallowed three mouthfuls, they were seized with violent vomitings. Suspecting that the pudding was poisoned, they threw a small piece of it to a sow in the yard, which she had scarcely swallowed when the poor animal was taken sick, and, after lingering a short time, died.

The eldest brother, by the application of proper medicine, soon recovered; but the youngest lingered for a long time ere he regained his health. The pudding was now analyzed by an university professor of chymistry, who found it to contain a large quantity of corrosive sublimate of mercury, and no other poisonous ingredient,—a fact which destroyed the defence set up by Whiting, that he had laid some *nux vomica* for rats, some of which he supposed had got among the meal. On examining his bins, however, it appeared that he had evaded investigation by previously throwing the meal into the privy.

For this offence Whiting was indicted at the Isle of Ely assizes, on Thursday the 5th of March, 1811; when, in addition to the above facts, it was proved that, in the event of the Langmans' death, he would come in for their property, in right of his wife, as the next heiress of her brothers.

The trial lasted till six o'clock in the evening, when the jury retired; and, after a deliberation of ten minutes, found the prisoner Guilty, when he was immediately sentenced to be hanged.

LORD LOUTH,
CONVICTED FOR ABUSE OF HIS AUTHORITY AS A MAGISTRATE.

WE have already recorded some desperate and foolish acts of the Irish peasantry; but, if crime ever admits of palliation, much may be advanced in apology for the illegal conduct of that oppressed people. Apprehensive that the laws of the realm are unfavourable to them, they lie at the mercy of every tyrant who may choose to gratify caprice or promote his own interest. Driven thus by oppression, can it be wondered at that they take upon themselves to do what they erroneously suppose the law will not do for them, and plunge into acts that make them amenable to justice? The weak and the defenceless are soon overpowered by legal authority; but their lordly and imperious tyrants, who goaded them to deeds of blood, are applauded for their loyalty, while their poor tenantry are suspended upon the gibbet as examples to scare the million, who return from the sight strengthened in their hereditary opinion that there is "no law for an Irishman." Let them, however, undeceive themselves, and learn, from the following case, that the impartial omnipotence of British laws is able to protect the poorest peasant and punish the most lordly villain.

Lord Louth disgraced at once the peerage and the magistracy*

* A memorable reproof of a magistrate occurred at Cardiff this year, 1811, upon the circuit there. A gentleman of opulence, a magistrate, and of undoubted repute, addressed a letter to one of the judges, in which his object was, not only to accuse a culprit (committed for manslaughter upon a coroner's inquest) of a deliberate and savage murder, but also, upon the evidence of assertion alone, to inflame the judicial mind of his correspondent against that prisoner, by persuading the judge, before-hand, that unless the accused should be cut off by the law, not a life near him, or within his reach, could be safe. He represented this man as a conspirator in a desperate clan of miscreants, who were men of sanguinary habits and passions.

He told the judge that all the witnesses who were to be heard were partial to the accused, and would suppress the facts they knew, unless his lordship would make them speak out; and he desired him to keep the secret of these hints, for which he gave this reason, that every thing valuable to him was at stake in withholding from this clan a knowledge of the part he took against them.

When the judge had read this letter, which he received in court, the bar and grand jury attending, he told them a letter had been just put into his hand, and he named the writer of it; he added, that circumstances of peculiar delicacy respecting the subject of that letter imposed upon his feelings the painful necessity of deferring to publish the contents till the gaol had been delivered; but that he should then direct his principal officer to read it aloud, and should pass a marked and public censure upon it, after delivering which he should command the deposit of the letter upon the files of the court, for safe custody, accompanied by a note of its doom, that if the writer chose to appear he would be in time, and would be heard. When the man accused of the manslaughter had been tried, and had received sentence of imprisonment for three months, he was remanded. The writer of the letter did not appear, and the judge delivered himself nearly as follows to a numerous audience:—

'You have heard this letter, and your looks were eloquent. They reprobated this tampering and cruel artifice.

'A magistrate of the county, at whose mercy, in some degree, are the lives and liberties of men, writes to me for the single purpose of insinuating and whispering away a man's life, by undue influence upon the judgment or the feelings of his correspondent.

'His object is, to invert the habit and principle of a judicial trust, which is that of being counsel for the prisoners, into the new and sanguinary department of a suborned advocate against them. His letter prompts me to goad the witnesses into evidence more hostile to the culprit than it was their intention to give—advice to me, insinuated behind the back of the accused, and just before his trial, upon evidence of assertion alone, unduly and surreptitiously communicated!

'But what heightens the depravity of this insult upon the Court, and the cruelty of it, as it has taken aim at the parties who are implicated, is the confidence proposed and claimed.

'My God!' said the judge, 'is it in 1811 that any man breathing, a subject of this realm, could think a judge base enough to be an accomplice in this fraud upon the sacred honour of his covenant upon oath; of his dignified indifference to parties; and, above all, of his presumptions, which are those of the law, that up to the moment of conviction, by authentic and sworn proof, the accused are innocent?

by an act of oppression which, alas! is too frequent in Ireland. His lordship had a tenant, named Matthews, who occupied four acres of land, and was employed us a labourer, by his lordship, from 1801 to 1809, without ever incurring the displeasure of this stem of aristocracy. But the noble peer thought his tenant too happy, and resolved upon diminishing his enjoyments, by converting his four acres of poor land to his own use. Perhaps his lordship wanted to try upon this *mighty farm* some new system of agriculture; but Paddy thought his lordship might put his theory into practice in some corner of his large domain, and bluntly refused to surrender his little field to the rapacious nobleman, who, it appeared, wanted it only because he thought, by sowing turnips in it, he could make it more productive than by leaving it at a moderate rent with poor Matthews.

'Provoke not the mighty,' said the moralist; but Paddy did not understand, or at least did not act upon this maxim, and from that hour forward he experienced nothing from his lordship but repeated acts of vexatious oppression. But the Irish are an enduring people, and from long habit are regardless of such trifling acts of cruelty from their betters. His lordship was no philosopher, and he was indignant at finding Paddy a stoic, when he had not the honour himself of belonging to any fraternity of sages, although his economical propensities entitled him to be classed with the respectable followers of the elder Cato, and the turnip-loving Fabius, whose attachment to cheap diet was equalled, if not surpassed, by this Irish nobleman.

Paddy had his full share of that shrewd sagacity which Providence has, for wise reasons, no doubt, so amply dispensed to his countrymen, and defeated, for a while, by his cunning, the anger of his landlord. But what can wisdom do, when opposed to power without principle? His lordship caused Matthews to be summoned before him on an alleged charge of cutting down some trees of his lordship's between *sun-rise* and *sun-set*; but the wisdom of Providence has wonderfully qualified all things in nature. Where it has given the poisonous sting, it has denied the members of progression,—wings or feet. In the moral world, where we find a bad man we generally find a great deficiency of intellect. It appeared, that where his lordship accused Matthews of cutting down the timber, a tree had not grown for centuries; and consequently the hearing of the case was postponed from that day, Monday, to the following Saturday.

Matthews thought the charge abandoned; but no! on the following Thursday his lordship, accom-

'What can be said for the writer?
'Even to him I would be merciful. Is it an error of judgment? Is it ignorance? But can we forget that he is a *magistrate*, and that he is a *man?* Shall a magistrate be indemnified, or dismissed with a gentle rebuke, who is ignorant of the judicial honour imposed upon him by his peculiar office? Is he a man so unenlightened as to be unapprised of those feelings which tell every honourable mind that no man is to be condemned unheard, and whispered out of the world by a secret between his accuser and his judge?
'As a memorial to after-ages of the disgrace inseparable from attempts like these, I direct the officer to file this letter upon the records of the Court, accompanied by a note of the fact that it was read aloud in open Court, and severely censured by the judge to whom it was addressed.'
The other judge assenting, it was made a rule of the Court.

panied by several constables, beset his house and made him prisoner. In vain the poor man declared his wife was dying! In vain he pointed to his dead infant, that required to be interred! In vain he protested his innocence, and beseeched his landlord to allow him to remain at home for another day to perform the last melancholy office for his child. But the peer was inexorable, and, without either oath, information, or document whatever, to substantiate the charge, committed the poor man to gaol for a felony. Here he remained twenty-four days, and was not discharged until the assizes, when there was no prosecution.

For this conduct a criminal information was filed against his lordship in the Court of King's Bench; and, it appearing that he was actuated by malicious motives, and a vile spirit of revenge, he was found guilty of abuse in his office of magistrate. The Court recommended him to make adequate compensation to the injured man, and, to afford him time to do so, protracted the period of declaring his sentence.

On the 19th of June, 1811, his lordship was brought up to receive sentence, and, it appearing that he had paid Matthews three hundred pounds, Judge Day sentenced him to three months' confinement in Newgate.

During his lordship's sojourn in durance, his parsimonious habits attracted the notice of Watty Cox, the editor of the Irish Magazine, who was confined for a libel. Accordingly Watty honoured his lordship with a place in his publication, and gave an engraving of the degraded nobleman in the act of blowing his fire with a mutilated pair of bellows, insinuating that his parsimony would not allow him to purchase a good one.

HARRIET MAGNIS,
TRIED FOR STEALING A CHILD.

IN this very singular and mysterious affair, suspicion first fell upon an innocent lady, the wife of a surgeon in the navy, and, after two examinations of several witnesses, all of whom mistook her person, she was committed for trial at the Old Bailey. It is true she was acquitted; but what alleviation could be offered to her feelings—what reparation made to an injured husband and distressed relatives?

At length the mystery began to develope itself. The first information received in London, was from a magistrate in Gosport, acquainting Mr. and Mrs. Dellow of the discovery that their child was safe there, and ready to be delivered to its parents. The father instantly set off, and soon after returned home with his son, when he was required to appear before the Lord-Mayor of London, where he found William Barber, the keeper of the Gosport Prison, ready to give evidence against a woman of that town of the name of Harriet Magnis, in whose possession the child was found.

This man, having seen a handbill describing the child, got information that it was at Gosport, and went to the lodgings of Mrs. Magnis, who lived in a very respectable way. He asked her if she had a child, and if it was her own; to which she replied, rather faintly, that it was; but upon his saying that he doubted it, and desiring to see the child, she took him very readily to the room where it was in bed, and confessed to him that she had found the boy in London

The keeper handed a copy of her confession and examination at Gosport to his lordship. Mrs. Dellow said that her husband had brought her child home alive and well, though not quite so lusty. The lord-mayor remanded the prisoner for further examination, when it appeared that a woman at Gosport observed a neighbour of hers in possession of a boy, bearing the marks described, and answering to the age. She immediately thought it was Thomas Dellow, who had been so long missing; the more so, as she had reason to believe that the pretended mother had never borne a child. She communicated her suspicions to the gaoler, when Mrs. Magnis confessed the whole affair, and her motive for the robbery; that her husband, who was a gunner on board one of his majesty's ships, and had saved a considerable sum of money for a man in his station of life, was extremely partial to children, and had often expressed his most anxious wish to have a little darling, as he used to term it. His wife, not less anxious to gratify him in this respect, wrote to him while at sea, that she was in the family way. The gunner, highly delighted that he had obtained his desired object, sent home the earnings of many a cruise, amounting to three hundred pounds, with a particular charge that the infant should be well rigged, and want for nothing: if a boy, so much the better.

The next letter from his hopeful wife announced the happy tidings that his first-born was a son; and that she would name him Richard, after his father.—The husband expressed his joy at the news, and counted the tedious hours until he should be permitted to come home to his wife and child.

At home he at length arrived, but at an unfortunate time, when the dear Richard was out at nurse, at a considerable distance; change of air being necessary to the easy cutting of his teeth. The husband's time being short, he left his home with a heavy heart, without being able to see his offspring; but he was assured that on his next trip to Gosport he should have the felicity he had so often pined for, of clasping his darling to his bosom. It was not until November last that he was at liberty to revisit home, when he had again the mortification to find that his son, whom he expected to see a fine boy of three years old, had not yet cut his teeth, or that he was from home on some other pretence. The husband, however, was not to be pacified thus: he would go and see his son, or his son should come to him. Mrs. Magnis, finding him determined, thought the latter much the best way; and accordingly set off to fetch the boy. The metropolis occurred to her as the market best calculated to afford her a choice of children; and, passing down Martin's Lane, she was struck with the rosy little citizen, Tommy Dellow, and at once determined to make him her prize. He was playing with his sister at the green-grocer's shop-door, into which Mrs. Magnis went, with the double view of purchasing some apples, and carrying off the boy.—She made much of the sister, caressed the boy, and gave him an apple. The children being pleased with her attention, she asked the little girl to shew her to a pastry-cook's shop to buy some cakes, when she got clear off with the boy, and left the girl behind.

Poor Magnis felt a parental affection for the boy; and, when the imposition was discovered before the magistrate, he was grieved to the heart at being obliged to part with him under all the circumstances the transaction. The little fellow himself seemed highly pleased with all the work he occasioned.

Harriet Magnis was committed to Winchester gaol;* and, when she was brought to trial at the assizes for Hampshire, it was agreed, after many arguments urged by counsel on both sides, that the offence was committed in London, and not in Hampshire, and that consequently she must be acquitted.

BENJAMIN WALSH, ESQ. M.P.
CONVICTED OF FELONIOUSLY STEALING.

MR. WALSH had long been known in the city of London as a dashing mercantile character. In copartnership with a Mr. Nisbett, he contracted with the chancellor of the exchequer for a lottery of fifty thousand tickets. This proved, to such a man, a very lucky speculation. He rubbed off his debts by a statute of bankruptcy; and he soon procured for himself a seat in the Parliament of his country!

The meeting of the creditors under the commission against Walsh and Nisbett brought to light some of the finesse practised by lottery contractors and by lottery-office-keepers. The first meeting took place on the 12th of November, 1808, when Mr. Montague, as counsel for Mr. Whiting, the printer, stated that he should object to persons who were subscribers in Walsh and Nisbett's list proving, under the idea of their being partners; and as he conceived Mr. Bish was not only a great person in this business, but also a great creditor, he should like to try his strength with him first. Mr. Bish was on oath, and Mr. Montague put several questions to him, chiefly whether he conceived himself as a partner with Messrs. Walsh and Nisbett.—Mr. Bish answered, that he conceived that, if there really was a profit on the lottery, he was entitled to a share on eight hundred and fifty-four (the number of tickets he was a subscriber for) as that here to fifty thousand, the number of tickets which the two lotteries consisted of. Mr. Burroughs then asked a variety of questions of Mr. Bish, as to the nature of the contract for a lottery, and whether he did not know, of his own knowledge, that the most gross, infamous, and scandalous practices had been used to make false sales, and thereby raise the price of the transfer of tickets from the original subscribers to other persons. Mr. Bish answered that such practices had been used, but that he was no ways privy to them, but was the instrument in detecting them. After debating a variety of intricate points for upwards of three hours, the commissioners being divided two and two, a petition seemed to be generally recommended to the chancellor on this unprecedented and important business.

Notwithstanding all this clamour of creditors, Walsh and Nisbett bustled through their broken fortunes; and, from the counting-house desk, the former, as we have already observed, was placed in the seat of a legislator for his country. There, among 'the great men, the grave men, and the sage men of the land,' he beheld a fair field for the exercise of his talents. Elevation to rank and power soon wipes away every former stain of reputation, and effaces each blot of character.

* This we thought at the time a strange kind of commitment—a prisoner to be tried in Hampshire for an offence committed in the city of London.

Among the dignified of the House of Commons, Sir Thomas Plomer, it seemed, had not a whit worse opinion of his brother member Walsh than if no lottery contract had been made, or any bankruptcy against him issued forth. In short, Sir Thomas intrusted him with a very large sum of money to purchase government securities; but Walsh laid it out in the stocks of the United States of America in his own name, and endeavoured to fly to that land of refuge to the guilty; but was overtaken by the arm of justice, at the port from whence he intended to quit his native country.

Walsh was pursued by the solicitor of the duped knight and a Bow Street runner, to Falmouth; to which port it was discovered he had fled by stopping his letters, under a government order, at the General Post-Office. Young members of parliament are fond of franking the letters of their friends; and it appeared that Walsh was no very tenacious of his prerogative, that, in an ignominious concealed flight, he must still indorse upon his letters, "Free, B. Walsh."

This degenerate legislator was arraigned at the bar of the Old Bailey, charged with feloniously stealing twenty-two bank-notes of one thousand pounds each, and one bank-note for two hundred pounds, the property of Sir Thomas Plomer, Knt. with intent to defraud him of the said sum of money: in other counts of the indictment the offence was variously charged, to which the prisoner pleaded Not Guilty.

Mr. Garrow observed, that, if it had been possible for the prosecutor in this action to have extended indulgence or commiseration towards the unfortunate prisoner at the bar, his honourable and humane feelings and character would have most willingly abstained from the present prosecution; but, from the nature of the case, he was called upon to discharge an important public duty, which was indispensable. The prosecutor was his majesty's solicitor-general, and had long been acquainted with the gentleman whom he had now the painful duty to prosecute. His father had been a director of the Bank of England, and from this the prosecutor was induced to intrust the prisoner as a stock-broker. He then proceeded to state the case, as it appeared in evidence, from which he concluded that, at the time of the prisoner's getting the means into his power, it was his intention to perpetrate the felony. As to the question of law, he took it from the oldest authorities, that the crime of larceny was imputable to the prisoner. The crime of simple larceny was sufficiently known and well defined; it was feloniously taking the personal chattels against the will, and without the knowledge, of the owner, with intent to convert them to his own use, and upon the evidence it would appear that the prisoner at the bar had taken this money with no other intent.

Sir Thomas Plomer stated that he had for many years employed the prisoner as a stock-broker, and in the month of August last apprized him that he had made a contract for the purchase of an estate, for which he was to pay at Michaelmas, and it would be necessary for him to sell out stock to a considerable amount. The prisoner advised, at that time, to postpone selling out, as he expected a considerable rise in stock, and the longer he postponed it the better; but in November the prisoner urged him strongly to sell out, as stock would fall considerably, saying, he had consulted the most intelligent persons upon the subject; and, in consequence of this, he gave him authority to sell out stock to the amount of thirteen thousand four hundred pounds, three per cent. and eighteen thousand six hundred pounds, reduced consols. On the following day he called at the prisoner's office in the city, who told him he had made the contract for the sale, and it was agreed to be transferred on the Wednesday or Thursday following, which accordingly took place; and he then consulted the prisoner on the best way of disposing of the money until he should want it, and he advised the purchase of exchequer bills; but it was then, he said, too late in the day for that purpose. The next day the prisoner called at his chambers at Lincoln's Inn, and he gave him a check on Messrs. Goslings, his bankers, for twenty-two thousand pounds, for the purpose of purchasing those exchequer bills, and he promised to return with them that day at four o'clock; this was Thursday, the 5th December. He returned about half-past four, appeared agitated, and complained of an asthma; and after a little pause told him he had made the contract with Mr. Trotter, Mr. Coutts's broker; but the exchequer bills could not be delivered until Saturday, as they were locked up in the Bank, and Mr. Coutts was not in town; and that he should call on that day at three o'clock. At that time he produced six thousand pounds exchequer bills, which he said he would lodge with his bankers, along with the receipt for the balance. He afterwards inquired at his bankers', and found the exchequer bills for six thousand pounds were lodged, but no receipt, and he never saw the prisoner after until he saw him in Bow Street.

Upon his cross-examination by Mr. Scarlett, he admitted he had given the check for twenty-two thousand pounds for the express purpose of purchasing exchequer bills, as his stock-broker: he did not give any particular injunction as to the mode of obtaining the money for the check, but left it to his own discretion.

William Ewins, clerk at Goslings and Co.'s, proved the payment of the check for twenty-two thousand pounds to the prisoner in person; and Mr. William Hannan proved the purchase of six thousand five hundred pounds in exchequer bills, by order of the prisoner; and George Hankley, his clerk, proved the delivery of them to the prisoner.

Mr. Ennis De Berdt, a broker of American stock, proved the prisoner having commissioned him, on the 29th of November, to purchase ten or eleven thousand pounds American stock, for a gentleman going to that country. The purchase was completed; and on Thursday, the 5th of December, about twelve o'clock in the forenoon, the prisoner paid him in eleven bank-notes of one thousand pounds each, for ten thousand four hundred and fifty-nine pounds, nineteen shillings, American stock; and the witness gave him a check on his bankers for the balance.

Mr Joseph Walsh, brother of the prisoner, proved a payment to him of one thousand and ninety-nine pounds odd, on the 5th of December, due to him by his brother some time.

Thomas Clark, the brother-in-law of the prisoner, also proved a payment to him by the prisoner, on the same day, of one one-thousand-pounds' bank-note, and he gave him a check on his banker for six hundred pounds, leaving in his hands four hundred pounds.

Henry Atwright, clerk of the prisoner, proved his having changed a bank-note for one thousand pounds given to him by the prisoner on that same day.

Here Mr. Garrow took occasion to observe, that there was not the slightest ground of suspicion that any of the witnesses had any previous knowledge of the prisoner's intention.

Mr. Charles, of the Bank of England, proved his having made the contract with the prisoner for the purchase of the stock sold out by Sir Thomas Plomer.

Joseph Hearn, a silversmith, proved the purchase of three hundred pounds in Portuguese doubloons from him by the prisoner on the 5th of December.

Mr. Scarlett, in addressing the Court for the defence, hoped he should not be understood to entertain any other sentiments of this offence than a conviction of the moral turpitude of the prisoner; and he was satisfied the prisoner himself entertained no other sentiment, and felt all the contrition belonging to such a crime; but it now became his duty to make such objections as occurred to him:—First, there could be no charge of this sort for stealing the check, for it was in evidence that the prosecutor had given it the prisoner for a specific purpose; and it was not altogether misapplied, for he had purchased some exchequer bills, and the law did not allow the act of felony to be in part separated. The second objection was under the statute of the second year of the reign of George II. by which the security intended by the legislature was to such property as was still available to the party himself. In this case the prosecutor had parted with all control over the check by delivering it to the prisoner. Thirdly, the felonious intent of the party taking was not in itself sufficient to constitute a felony when the party to whom the property belonged had relinquished his control over it; and, in support of these objections, he referred to several cases in point.

After some observations by Mr. Garrow, Mr. Scarlett, and Mr. Alley, it was agreed that the jury should find a verdict subject to the future judgment of the twelve judges upon the chief baron's report.

The chief baron acquiesced in this arrangement, and then adverted to that part of the evidence which went to show the previous intent of the prisoner to commit the felony; observing, at the same time, that it was impossible, upon such evidence, not to find the prisoner guilty; who, in consequence of the objections made by his counsel, would have all the benefit of the judgment of the twelve judges hereafter.

The jury immediately returned a verdict of—Guilty.

During the whole of the trial the prisoner was much affected; but particularly when that part of the letters was read relative to the situation of his wife and children.

The result of the argument before the judges was, that the facts proved did not, in estimation of law, amount to felony, and as Walsh had been convicted of that offence he received a free pardon.

The Commons expelled him from his seat in their house; and he was again made a bankrupt, whereupon Sir Thomas found himself entitled only to a pitiful dividend under the second commission.

WILLIAM HEBBERFIELD,
EXECUTED FOR FORGERY.*

WILLIAM HEBBERFIELD stood capitally indicted for feloniously forging, and, in a second count, for uttering, knowing it to be forged, a certain two-pound note, with intent to defraud the Governor and Company of the Bank of England. Forgeries of their notes to a most enormous amount had been for a considerable time going on, the authors of which the company were not able to discover. The prisoner was confined in Newgate under a sentence of two years' imprisonment, by the Court of King's Bench, on a conviction for conspiracy in aiding the escape of the French General Austin, a prisoner of war in this country upon his parole. There was also a prisoner named Barry, confined in the House of Correction at Clerkenwell, on a sentence of six months' imprisonment, for uttering counterfeit dollars. Mr. Weston, the principal clerk of Messrs. Kaye and Freshfield, solicitors of the Bank, went to Barry in prison on Monday, the 23d September; and, in consequence of a plan then concerted, he gave Barry eight pounds in Bank of England notes, which he previously marked with the letter W; he then accompanied Barry in a coach, together with one of the turnkeys, named Beckett, to Newgate, where Barry went in, and directly, without communicating his purpose to any one, to the room of the prisoner, where there were a number of persons with him. He went up to the prisoner, gave him six one-pound notes of the marked ones he had received from Mr. Weston, of which the prisoner returned him three, saying he had not enough of the other notes ready until to-morrow, and then gave him, in lieu of the three notes he kept, forged notes to the nominal value of six pounds. With these Barry immediately returned to Mr. Weston who waited in the street, and immediately Beckett went in, accompanied by Brown and another officer, to the prisoner's chamber where Beckett asked him to produce what property he had about him. Upon which the prisoner produced from one pocket a handful of gold, from another a pocket-book filled with bank-notes, from another a quantity of loose bank-notes, and he also produced a stocking stuffed with the like currency. Beckett, on examining these notes, and not perceiving amongst them any of the marked ones he sought for, told the prisoner he had some more, and desired him to produce them. Upon which the prisoner took some other notes from his side-pocket, and laid them on the bed where he was sitting.—Beckett took those up. They were the marked notes; he said these were what he wanted, and returned the prisoner the rest. Upon which the prisoner, probably prophesying his purpose, snatched the notes, and thrust them into the fire. Beckett's assistant, however, rescued them from the flames, and they were proved to be the same which Barry had paid him just before; and the notes Barry received

* The number of persons prosecuted for forged notes of the Bank of England, and for uttering, or having them in their possession, knowing them to be forged, from the year 1797 to 1811 inclusive, amounted to no less than four hundred and seventy-one. The number of persons prosecuted for counterfeiting the tokens issued by the Bank of England, or for uttering the same, was, in 1804, eight persons; 1805, none; 1806, two; 1807, none; 1808, one; 1809, nine; 1810, six; and 1811, twenty three.

in lieu were also proved to be forgeries.

The prisoner was found Guilty—Death. He suffered before Newgate on the 29th of January, 1812, with Paul Whitehead, a man of genteel appearance, who was tried at the same sessions for forging the name of Thomas Gullan, an acceptor of a bill of eighty-seven pounds, ten shillings, and thereby defrauding Messrs. Robarts, Curtis, and Co. They met their fate with decent fortitude, and when on the fatal scaffold shook hands, after which they were launched into eternity.—The crowd was immense.

Tucker fraudulently performing the Marriage Ceremony.

JOHN TUCKER,

TRANSPORTED FOR OBTAINING MONEY UNDER FALSE PRETENCES.

THIS impostor's career in villainy, though short, was notorious; or few swindlers ever contrived to arrest so much of public attention, with so little advantage to themselves; as it must be admitted his gains bore no proportion to the address with which he imposed upon a *learned* profession.

John Tucker was the son of a poor man who resided in a village near Exeter, and got his living by carrying vegetables for sale to that city. His son, entertaining higher notions than the father, procured as much education as qualified him for the situation of a teacher of writing and arithmetic in schools, and in this profession he spent a few years of his life, until some misconduct of his caused his dismissal from an academy at Hammersmith.

While engaged as an usher, he

contrived to get into the society of many students of Oxford, from whom he learned numerous particulars of the college, the fellows, the degrees, &c. and with this information he determined to assume the character of a *master of arts*, and commence *parson*.

He represented himself as just come from college, and waiting for church preferment, which he expected quickly to take place, in consequence of his connexion with a great man, whose letters in corroboration he always carried about him, unless when in company with those who might know the writing, and then the original he stated was at home; but the copy he had with him. In this way he practised his deceptions to a great extent, assuming different names, saying at one time that his father was Recorder of Exeter, and at another that he was himself Rector of Frome, but uniformly asserting that he was in holy orders, and thereby succeeded in perpetrating his depredations on the clergy, whom he generally contrived to dupe.

He got a pretty good footing at St. Clement's Church, in the Strand, by merely calling there, sometimes, in a curricle, gig, or on horseback, pretending he was just come from the country; and, under pretence of being familiar with several gentlemen at Oxford, he imposed upon Mr. Gurney, the rector, and Mr. Shepherd, his assistant, with whose connexions he got acquainted. He frequently dined with them, and often did duty at the church.

One day Mr. Shepherd had to bury a corpse, and about the same hour was engaged out to dine; when Tucker, being there, offered his service, and he actually performed the burial ceremony. Dr. Hawker was engaged to preach a charity-sermon at that church. Tucker made his appearance in the vestry at an early hour; and, although Mr. Shepherd had promised to read the prayers for the doctor, this fellow got possession of the surplice against the consent of the clerk and sexton, and went into the desk, where he remained, though, on Mr. Shepherd's arrival, the sexton offered to pull him out. This and some other circumstances exciting suspicions against him, he was refused permission to officiate there in future.

One Sunday morning he went to Hammersmith, before the commencement of the church service, and introduced himself to the rector as the Rev. Mr. Tucker, just arrived from Oxford, &c. and that he was engaged to dine with the master of Hammersmith academy. He offered his service to the rector, who politely accepted it, observing, 'Probably you could give us a sermon.' Tucker replied that he was not exactly prepared; but that he would read prayers in the morning and preach in the afternoon. The rector lent him his best gown; and, when the service was over, Tucker strutted through the town with it on his back, and went to the academy, where he had formerly lived as usher. The master and family were much surprised to see him, especially in a clerical dress, as his conduct was not the most proper when last at Hammersmith. But he had a ready tale; and, deceived by his false representations, they invited him to dinner. In the mean time the rector received information that Tucker was an impostor, and accordingly went to the academy, where he found him swaggering away in his gown. Tucker affected to be greatly hurt at the charge; and, on a constable being sent for, he pretended sudden illness, and retired to the garden; and, the better to conceal his design of running away, left his hat behind; but he supplied its place by borrowing one from the biggest boy, and made good his retreat.

Tucker also officiated at Park Street Chapel, read prayers, preached, and administered the sacrament; and so powerful had the impression been that he was a *parson*, that the clerk of this chapel, on being applied to by a tavern-keeper respecting Tucker, went security for his bill.

To detail the impositions of this vile swindler would be nearly impossible, so various were his schemes, and so many were his dupes. He not only baptized and buried, but actually performed the marriage ceremony; and when, in St. Martin's Church, he published the banns of matrimony, it is said the ladies were delighted with his fine audible voice. Tavern and coffee-house keepers were his dupes, and there were few he came in contact with from whom he did not contrive to borrow a few shillings or a few pounds.

Such a course of fraud could not continue. On the 29th of July, 1811, application was made at the police office, Bow Street, by a clergyman belonging to a man-of-war, in consequence of Tucker having imposed on him, and got from him, at various times, to the amount of thirty pounds. This being borrowed money, no warrant could be granted. But in the evening a very different charge was made by Thomas Edbrook, of the City of Quebec public house, in Oxford Street, from whom he had received money and wine on false pretences. An officer being dispatched in pursuit of Tucker, he was found to have enlisted in the 21st regiment, representing himself as a young man of family, who would quickly buy him off when they heard of his situation. In consequence of this representation, he was living at the sergeant's expense. When brought before the magistrates he candidly acknowledged that he had frequently performed all the duties of a clergyman without being in orders. It was no sooner known that Tucker was in custody than hundreds flocked to make their charges; but the greater number, ashamed of their credulous simplicity, shrunk back when they had heard that enough was deposed to criminate him. He was tried at the Middlesex sessions for obtaining three bottles of wine, and five shillings and sixpence in money, on false pretences. The evidence being gone through, he made the following speech in his defence:—" Your worship, and gentlemen of the jury—In this age of curiosity, when matters, however trifling in their nature, usurp as much the attention of mankind as the high concerns of empires, it is not wonderful that a being, humble as myself, should obtain some portion of that attention. It is the less wonderful, gentlemen, as I have been considered fair game by the whole pack of those who live by poisoning the public mind. The editors of newspapers, and the tribe of caricaturists, have contributed all in their power to misrepresent me. I have filled the columns of their journals and their shops; but I blame them not—I have been to them a profitable concern, and they must write and paint to be able to eat. In order, however, to stem in some degree the torrent of misrepresentation, although very unwilling to obtrude myself upon the public, I determined to sell my likeness, thinking that its exhibition might in some measure tend to correct the mistaken ideas entertained of me.' [The chairman here interrupted the prisoner, and begged him to confine himself to the matter of the indictment. It was better for him to deny or to disprove what had been alleged against him.] The prisoner in continuation—'Language, then, sir, could not speak louder in behalf of the knavery than the testimony of that first witness.—I know not what to say,—I stand here as a wretched example of human infirmity. I made my entrance into human life friendless and unassisted, without one fostering hand to cherish or direct me, and depending solely on the exertion of my talents for my progress through the world. I had, perhaps, too much confidence in my own powers; and, unfortified by religion, I may have little suspected the deceitfulness of my own heart.—I am now fallen,—I am borne down by my own follies, as well as by the calumnies of a merciless world. My reputation gone, —poverty and scorn heavy upon me; my name and my crime filling the papers of the day, and sung even in ballads through the streets. Coming from the gloom of a prison, and torn by those anxieties which loss of character, more than fear of punishment, is able to excite, am I not, gentlemen, a young man most deserving of your pity? Am I not an object that must raise in your bosoms every emotion of tenderness and compassion? I once was fair in reputation, and my morning life was without a cloud; I now feel the value of the one, and all is darkness before me. Should you, gentlemen, restore me to the walks of life, I can only say, most sincerely, that my future conduct will be such as to prove that your clemency shall not have been thrown away.'

The jury found him Guilty, and the chairman sentenced him to transportation for seven years.

JOHN WILLIAMS,
MURDERER AND SUICIDE.

THE metropolis—indeed the whole nation—was never before so completely horror-struck, at any private calamity, as at the daring and inhuman murders perpetrated in the very heart of the city of London, on the close of the year 1811.

On a dark evening in the beginning of the month of December, about the time when tradesmen are shutting up their shops, Mr. Marr, a respectable draper, sent his servant-maid to purchase some oysters for the family supper. Mr. Marr was in the act of placing goods, which had been exposed to the view of customers on the counter, upon their shelves. The girl left the shop door a-jar, expecting to return in a very few minutes; but unfortunately the nearest place of sale for oysters had disposed of the whole, and she therefore went farther on her errand. Mean time two or more ruffians entered the shop, shut the door, knocked down Mr. Marr, and cut his throat. They next seized his shop-boy, and murdered him. Mrs. Marr was in the kitchen, hushing her babe to sleep. Hearing an extraordinary noise and scuffling above, as was supposed, she hastily laid the child in the cradle, and ran up stairs, where she was met by the blood-thirsty monsters, and instantly murdered in the same way they had dispatched Mr. Marr and the boy.

The child, disturbed with being hastily laid down, cried aloud, and the villains, doubtless apprehensive that it would cause an alarm— more horrible still to relate—descended, and cut its innocent throat so as nearly to sever its tender head from the body.

By this time the girl returned with the oysters, and finding the shop door shut, rang the bell; but no person answered. At this instant a watchman, passing on his round, asked what she did there; and he pulled the bell with violence, which so much alarmed the villains that they made a precipitate retreat through a window of the back part of the house, across some mud, and along an intricate way, which no one that had not previously reconnoitered the situation, could have readily found.

The watchman, finding the bell still unanswered, went to the next door neighbour, and gave an alarm. Some three or four men collecting together, it was determined to scale the wall which divided Mr. Marr's back premises from those of the adjoining house. This was done without much loss of time, and there was presented one of the most woeful scenes that ever disgraced human nature. The body of Mr. Marr and his shop-boy, the latter of whom appeared, from evident marks, to have struggled for life with the assassins, near each other; that of Mrs. Marr in the passage, and the infant in its cradle, all dead, but yet warm and weltering in their blood. The horrible scene for a moment petrified those who first entered, and they naturally feared the murderers might still be in the house, plundering the property therein. They opened the street door, and called out an alarm of ' Murder!' which spread with such rapidity that the neighbourhood was very soon in an alarm. The nightly watch mustered, and the drum of the melancholy beat to arms— in fine, though now near midnight, so great a crowd assembled that it was necessary to shut the doors, while some one explained the cause of the alarm to those in the street.

The coroner's jury of course brought in the verdict. ' Guilty of wilful murder against some person or persons unknown!'

' In murder's annals shall we find
A deed so savage in its kind,
So formed to rend the feeling heart,
And bid the soul with horror start;
Yet force that very heart to own
'Twas well that neither fell alone?
Yes, it was well—the husband's bier
Drank not his widow's frenzied tear:
Nor did her blood-stained beauty crave
Like anguish o'er her early grave :
Nor were their mingled sorrows shed
On their sweet babe's ensanguin'd head.
One doleful moment's matchless woe,
One dire unutterable blow,
And all was past—concerted there
Fled the last sighs of sorrow and despair.
Trust we, in that tremendous hour,
Almighty Mercy's soothing power
O'er the pale victims shed a ray,
The harbinger of endless day :
Then bade the unfettered spirits rise
To sudden glory to the skies.'

Scarce had the horror excited by the fate of these unfortunate persons subsided, when the neighbourhood in which they resided became again a scene of confusion, horror, and dismay; and, by the spectacle which was presented on Thursday night, the 19th of December, 1811, a new and irresistible feeling of alarm pervaded all the inhabitants, lest some of their domestic circles should next become the objects of midnight assassination.

Shortly after eleven o'clock, the neighbourhood of New Gravel Lane was alarmed by the most dreadful cries of ' Murder!' Crowds of individuals resident on the spot soon collected around the house whence proceeded the appalling sounds (the King's Arms public house, No. 81, Gravel Lane,) and it was immediately ascertained that the cries which excited such general alarm came from a man who was seen descending, almost in a state of nudity, by a line formed by the junction of two sheets, from the two-pair-of-stairs' window of the house in question. On reaching the extremity of the sheets, which was nearly eight feet from the ground, he was assisted by the watchman, who caught him in his arms, when he cried out, in the greatest agitation, ' They are murdering the people in the house !' These words were no sooner uttered than a short consultation was held by the people assembled, and it was at once resolved that an entry should be forced into the house through the cellar flap, which was shortly accomplished. On looking round the cellar, the first object that attracted attention was the body of Mr. Williamson, which lay at the foot of the stairs, with a violent contusion on the head, his throat dreadfully cut, and an iron crow by his side; they then proceeded up stairs into the parlour, where they found Mrs. Williamson also dead, with her skull and her throat cut, blood still issuing from the wound; and near her lay the body of the servant woman, whose head was also horribly bruised, and her throat cut in the most shocking manner.

During the examination before the magistrates of the Shadwell Police-office, Mr. Anderson deposed that he was a constable: he knew Mr. and Mrs. Williamson; they were highly respected in the neighbourhood, and for the space of fifteen years kept the King's Arms public house, which was the resort of foreigners of every description. At eleven o'clock every night they invariably closed their house. On Thursday night, the 19th of December, 1811, Mr. Williamson adopted the same plan. Ten minutes before eleven witness called for a pot of beer. During the time Mrs. Williamson was drawing the beer, Mr. Williamson, who was sitting by the fire, said to him, ' You are an officer—there has been a fellow listening at my door, with a brown coat on; if you should see him take him into custody, or tell me.' Mr. Anderson answered ' He certainly would, for his and his own safety.' These were the last words Mr. Anderson mentioned, and then retired. Witness lived next door but one to the deceased; between twenty and thirty minutes after he left the King's Arms he intended to go for another pot of beer; as soon as he got out of his house he heard a noise, when he saw the lodger lowering himself down into the street by the sheets. He ran into the house for his staff, and proceeded to the spot. The watchman caught the lodger in his arms, when witness and others broke the cellar flap open, and began to look round the cellar; on coming to the staircase, they saw Mr. Williamson lying on his back, with his legs upon the stairs, his head downwards: by his side was an iron instrument, similar to a stone-mason's crow, about three feet long, in diameter three quarters of an inch: it was much stained with blood. Mr. Williamson had received a wound on the head, his throat was dreadfully cut, his right leg was broken by a blow, and his hand severely cut. From these marks of violence witness supposed Mr. Williamson made great resistance, being a very powerful man. They then proceeded up into the sitting-room, when they saw Mrs. Williamson lying on her left side; her skull was fractured, and her throat cut and bleeding most profusely; near to Mrs. Williamson was the servant woman, lying on her back, with her head under the grate; her skull was more dreadfully fractured than that of her mistress, her throat most inhumanly cut, and none of the bodies were cold. Witness then stated that the premises were afterwards examined, and it was discovered that the murderers had made their escape from a back window looking into a piece of waste ground belonging to the London Dock Company. The sill of the window was stained with blood, and the sash remained thrown up. The distance which the villains had to jump did not exceed eight feet, and the ground beneath was soft clay; so that they could sustain no injury even had they fallen. From the waste ground in question there was no difficulty whatever in escaping, as it communicated with several by-streets.

John Turner, the man who escaped from the window, and who was a lodger in the house, deposed as follows:—

'I went to bed about five minutes before eleven o'clock; I had not been in bed more than five or ten minutes before I heard the cry of "We shall all be murdered!" which I suppose was the cry of the woman servant. I went down stairs, and saw one of the villains cutting Mrs. Williamson's throat, and rifling her pockets.

'I immediately ran up stairs, took up the sheets from my bed, fastened them together, and lashed them to the bed-posts; I called to the watchman to give the alarm; I was hanging out of the front window by the sheets; the watchman received me in his arms, naked as I was; a great mob had then assembled opposite the door: as soon as I got upon my legs the door was forced open; I entered, and found the bodies lying as described. There was nobody lodged in the house but myself, except a grand-daughter of Mrs. Williamson. I have lived in the house about eight months, and during that time I have found them to be the most peaceable people that could keep a public house. The man whom I saw rifling Mrs. Williamson's pocket, as far as I could see by the light in the room, was about six feet in height, dressed in a genteel style, with a long dark loose coat on. I said nothing to him; but, terrified, I ran up stairs, and made my escape as already mentioned. When I was down stairs, I heard two or three very great sighs; and when I was first alarmed, I heard distinctly the words, "We shall all be murdered." Turner farther deposed that, at the time he went to bed, Mrs. Williamson was on the stairs, taking up a silver punch-ladle and watch, which were to be raffled for on the following Monday, into her bed-room for security.'

The wounds on the heads of the unfortunate sufferers were evidently inflicted by an iron bar; and from their position, as well as from the cuts on the throat, one of the murderers would appear to have been left-handed. The under part of the house was a skittle-ground, next to the entrance of which was the cellar door, by both of which entries it seemed that the villains attempted to escape, as marks of blood were discovered upon them. During the time the horrid deed was perpetrating, a public house, almost adjoining, was filled with people drinking, and a few doors on the other side was a rendezvous for seamen, all of which looked into the waste ground alluded to.

Of the many examinations which took place at the Shadwell Police office, the investigations of Mr. Graham, of the Bow Street office and many other active magistrates we shall select such as fix these most dreadful crimes upon a man of the name of John Williams, who evaded justice by committing the additional crime of suicide.

This man at length was apprehended as one of the murderers; and on his examination, John Frederic Ritchen, a Dane, also a prisoner, under suspicion of being an accomplice, stated that he lodged in the same house with Williams for about twelve weeks and three or four days, but knew little of him, except as a fellow-lodger. On being minutely questioned respecting his knowledge of two persons—a carpenter and a joiner, (whose names, though known at the office, were, for obvious reasons, suppressed,) as acquaintances of Williams—he said that, about three or four weeks ago, he saw them drinking at the Pear Tree public house with Williams, and since that time had seen them there without Williams. On the night of the murder of the Marr family, a few minutes before Williams came home, there was a knock at the door, and he, the examinant, went down to open it, when he found the key had been taken from the inside of the lock, and he called to the mother of Mrs. Vermillee, the landlady, to come down and open the door. Hearing her coming down, he went up to his own room; and, when there, heard her in conversation with a man, whose voice resembled that of one of the two men before mentioned. A few minutes afterwards Williams himself came in. This was almost half past one o'clock. Three or four days before Williams was taken up he observed that the large sandy-coloured whiskers, which had before formed a striking feature of Williams's appearance, had been cut off. About eleven o'clock on the day after the murder of the Marr family, the examinant went from curiosity to examine the premises, which he entered, and saw the dead bodies. From thence he returned to the Pear Tree, where he found Williams in the back yard, washing out his stockings, but he did not tell Williams where he had been. Being questioned respecting his knowledge of the maul, and also the iron instrument, which was a round bar, about an inch in diameter, between two and three feet in length, flattened at the end into the shape of a chisel, but not with a cutting edge, being apparently a tool for caulking, he said the maul resembled one he had seen about the Pear Tree public house, but he could not identify it. A pair of blue woollen trowsers, and also a pair of canvass trowsers, were then produced, which had been found between the mattrass and the bed-clothes of the hammock in which the examinant slept at the Pear Tree. The legs of the blue trowsers had evidently been washed, for the purpose of cleaning them from mud, of which the appearance was still perfectly visible in the creases, that had not been effectually cleansed. These trowsers were damp at the time of the examination; the canvass trowsers were also damp, but they presented no particular appearance. The examinant stated that both these pairs of trowsers had formerly belonged to a person since gone to sea, and he had since worn them himself.

Mrs. Orr stated that, on the Saturday before Marrs' murder, about half past one o'clock in the morning, she was getting up linen, when she heard a noise about the house, as if a man was attempting to break into the house. She was frightened, and asked 'Who is there?' A voice answered, which she knew to be Williams's, 'I am a robber!' She answered, 'Whether you are a robber or not, I will let you in, and am glad to see you.' Williams entered, seating himself down till the watchman was calling the hour of past two o'clock; Williams got up from his chair, and asked the landlady if she would have a glass. She assented; but, as he would not go for it, she went to the Pear Tree public house, and could gain no admittance. She returned, when Williams inquired how many rooms there were in her house, and the situation of her back premises. She replied there were three rooms, and that her back yard communicated with Mrs. Vermillee's house. The watchman came into Mrs. Orr's house, which Williams resisted for some time. The watchman told Mrs. Orr that he had picked up a chisel by the side of her window. Williams ran out, unobserved, at this information; soon afterwards he returned; the watchman was going, when Williams stopped him, and desired him to go to the Pear Tree, and get some liquor. The house was then open. While the watchman was gone for the liquor Williams took up the chisel, and inquired where she got it. Mrs. Orr retained the instrument till the Monday following. Hearing that Williams was examined, she went to Mrs. Vermillee's, and showed her the chisel. Mrs. Vermillee compared it with the tools in Peterson's chest, when it was found to bear the same marks, and declared that it was taken out of her house. Mrs. Orr instantly delivered the chisel to the magistrates of Shadwell-Street office, as being a further trace to the villainy. Mrs. Orr said she knew Williams for eleven weeks; he frequently nursed her child, and used to joke with her daughter. They both thought him an agreeable young man, and of a most insinuating address, and never thought he could be the man who would attempt to rob or murder.

The ripping-chisel which was found in Mr. Marr's house was conveyed to Newgate, in order to be identified by Mr. Vermillee. The conference was private, and continued until four o'clock in the evening. Mr. Vermillee gave testimony to the instrument, called a ripping-hook, being among the chest of tools deposited in his house. We must here remind our readers that the said ripping-hook, about two feet in length, was found by the side of Mrs. Marr, and the same which Mr. Vermillee deposed that he knew perfectly well.

For a considerable time after the perpetration of these sanguinary atrocities, the police devoted, without intermission, the whole of their time, from an early hour every morning till midnight, to the incessant pursuit of the murderers.

When the gaoler went to the room in the House of Correction in Coldbath Fields, where Williams was confined, in order to call him to his last examination before the magistrates, his body was found dead, hanging to a beam; thus adding to his manifold crimes that of self-murder!

'Those only wish to die who fear to live,
Fettered with guilt, reflection, and remorse;
Made cowards by an age of former crimes:
Hence this distaste of life.'

Of all the sins of mankind we are taught to believe suicide the most offensive to the Creator. It is a crime engendered by cowardice, and its commission rests in those hands alone whose hearts can no longer bear against the stings of conscience, the torments of jealousy, the fear of exposure, or the idea of being curtailed of accustomed luxury, rank, or power. The canon law assures us that Judas committed a greater crime in hanging himself than in betraying Jesus Christ.

Hence such law denies Christian burial to those who are guilty of suicide, concluding thence that it is not lawful to inherit on earth from one who hath himself no inheritance in heaven.

On the last day of this fatal year the remains of this sanguinary assassin (for, from the circumstances which had been developed, not a doubt can exist but that he was a principal, if not the only actor, in the horrible massacres) were privately removed, at eleven o'clock at night, from the cell in Coldbath-fields' prison, where he committed suicide, and conveyed to St. George's watch-house, near the London Docks, preparatory to interment. Mr. Capper, the magistrate, had an interview with the secretary for the home department, for the purpose of considering with what propriety the usual practice of burying suicides in the nearest cross-roads might be departed from in the present instance, and it was then determined that a public exhibition should be made of the body through the neighbourhood which had been the scene of the monster's crimes. In conformity with this decision, the following procession moved from the watch-house, about half past ten o'clock on Tuesday morning:—

Several hundred constables, with their staves, clearing the way.
The newly-formed patrole, with drawn cutlasses.
Another body of constables.
Parish officers of St. George's, St. Paul's, and Shadwell, on horseback.
Peace-officers, on horseback.
Constables.
The high constable of the County of Middlesex, on horseback.

The Body of Williams,
Extended at full length on an inclined platform, erected on the cart, about four feet high at the head, and gradually sloping towards the horse, giving a full view of the body, which was dressed in blue trowsers and a white and blue striped waistcoat, but without a coat, as when found in the cell. On the left side of the head the fatal maul, and on the right the ripping-chisel, with which the murders were perpetrated, were exposed to view. The countenance of Williams was ghastly in the extreme, and the whole had an appearance too horrible for description.

A strong body of constables brought up the rear.

The procession advanced slowly up Ratcliffe Highway, accompanied by an immense concourse of persons, eager to get a sight of the murderer's remains. When the cart came opposite to the late Mr. Marr's house, a halt was made for near a quarter of an hour. The procession then moved down Old Gravel Lane, along Wapping, up New Crane Lane, and into New Gravel Lane. When the platform arrived at Mr. Williamson's late house, a second halt took place. It then proceeded up the hill, and again entered Ratcliffe Highway, down which it moved into Cannon Street, and advanced to St. George's turnpike, where the New Road is intersected by Cannon Street. There a grave, about six feet deep, had been prepared, immediately over which the main water-pipe runs. Between twelve and one o'clock the body was taken from the platform, and lowered into the grave, immediately after which a stake was driven through it; and, the pit being covered, this solemn ceremony concluded.

During the last half-hour the crowd had increased immensely—they poured in from all parts, but their demeanour was perfectly quiet. All the shops in the neighbourhood were shut, and the windows and tops of the houses were crowded with spectators. On every side, mingled with execrations of the murderer, were heard fervent prayers for the speedy detection of his accomplice or accomplices; but from subsequent discoveries, there is reason to think he perpetrated the foul deed without assistance. Of his guilt there does not remain a doubt; for the knife which he always carried about him was found concealed in a hole in the room where he slept, incrusted with blood!

The sensation produced by these horrid murders awakened the apprehensions of several parishes for individual safety. Meetings were held, and resolutions passed with a view to establish a more vigilant system of police, and many useful plans were adopted and carried into practice, which we hope will prevent the recurrence of such diabolical deeds.

JOHN CLAYTON AND WILLIAM JENKINS,
EXECUTED FOR BURGLARY.

WE have now to record one of the most daring robberies that was ever committed, as well as the greatest perseverance and exertions by police-officers, to detect and apprehend robbers. Reid, belonging to Perry's party of the patrole, received information that the house, No. 4, in Bury Street, St. James's, kept by Mrs. Martin, was marked to be robbed by a gang of thieves, who had got to the knowledge that she in general went out every evening, principally to the play, through the thoughtless and imprudent conduct of her female servant, Mary Wakelin, who had admitted one of them, named Clayton, to visit her as a sweetheart; having got acquainted with her under a false representation that he was a trunk-maker, living in Oxford Street. Monday se'nnight was the time fixed on for the perpetration of the robbery. Perry, Reid, Limbrick, and others, applied to a neighbour residing opposite to Mrs. Martin's house, to accommodate them with a room, to watch the proceedings of the night. They went there about half past seven o'clock, and in about three quarters of an hour after, three or four men and two women came and walked up and down in the front of Mrs. Martin's house; and, after some time, one of the men knocked at Mrs. Martin's door. The servant girl answered it. The man who knocked at the door proved to be Clayton, who pretended to be the girl's sweetheart; they crossed over the way talking together, he kissing and squeezing her. Clayton expected to be admitted that night, but the girl was not able to fulfil her promise, owing to her mistress being unwell, and consequently not going out.

On the following Tuesday night, about eight, or half past eight o'clock, the officers, being at their usual place to watch, observed Clayton knock at Mrs. Martin's door. The servant came to the door; they walked away together, and went to a liquor-shop, and had some gin. When they were separating, he professed such strong love for her, that he was nearly broken-hearted at parting with her, and kissed her at least a dozen times. On Wednesday night, about the same time, Clayton and two other men appeared before Mrs. Martin's house. They threw stones against the kitchen window, which not answering the purpose of bringing out the girl, they threw some halfpence, which had the desired effect. She came out, and went and had some liquor with them. Clayton kissed and courted the girl for some time in the street. During all these visits, Clayton wished very much to go into the house; but the girl told him she dared not, her mistress being still ill, and remaining confined in the house. On Thursday night Clayton attended alone; but his companions were supposed to be at an adjoining house. The girl came out, and they went and drank together. On Friday night Clayton was accompanied by two or three more men: they walked up and down in front of the house, while Clayton knocked at the door. The girl answered it, and came out to him, and they talked together for some time; the whole gang was very eager to get into the house that night. On Saturday, Sunday, Monday, and Tuesday nights, Clayton pursued similar conduct, going with the girl on her errands, drinking together, &c. On Tuesday night, the girl told Clayton that her mistress was so much recovered, that she expected she would be well enough to go the following night to the play.

On Wednesday night, about eight o'clock, Mrs. Martin, accompanied by a male and female friend, went in a coach to the theatre. In a few minutes after, the servant girl came out, and returned shortly with Clayton, arm in arm together. They talked together several minutes at the door, and then went in. In about a quarter of an hour after, Clayton came out, and returned in about five minutes, accompanied by another man. Clayton knocked at the door, and the girl opened it. She appeared to refuse letting the other man in; but Clayton forced open the door, and the other man rushed in. The officers, who had been upon the close watch every night, then went over to the house, and heard all three talking very loud in the kitchen. From the noise, and what they saw through a key-hole, they ascertained that the two men were dragging the girl up stairs against her will, and she was exclaiming, "Lord have mercy upon me! what shall I do?" One of the men told her, if she made such a noise he would blow her brains out, and presented a pistol to her head, and kept it there. They forced her up stairs, she continuing the above exclamation in defiance of their threat. The officers heard doors being broken open, &c. and, in a few minutes after, the other man came down stairs, and returned with the kitchen poker: they then heard other doors break open, but not hearing the noise of the girl continued, the officers were afraid she was being murdered, and were proceeding to force the street-door with an iron crow, which the girl hearing, exclaimed it was her mistress, gave a sudden spring, released herself from them, ran down stairs, and the robbers after her: they got into the passage just as the officers had got into the passage.—Clayton and Jenkins appeared as if nothing had happened, and wanted to get out. Perry and Reid seized them: the villains made a most desperate resistance, which they were enabled to do, being very tall, stout, powerful men: the officers, however, soon secured them. On searching Clayton, a large clasp knife and a bad dollar were found. On Jenkins were found a pistol, two bad dollars, &c. On examining the house, the officers discovered that a large quantity of property had been packed up, ready to be carried off. Several rooms and closets were broken open, and they were in the act of breaking open a chest when they were disturbed.

The trial of these desperadoes came on at the Old Bailey, the

15th of January, when Mary Wakelin, before named, deposed that she first became acquainted with the prisoner Clayton about eight or ten days before the 1st of January; he then came to her mistress's house, when she answered the door, and told her his name was Wilson, and that he had a letter for Mrs. Martin, which was the name her mistress went by. A night or two afterwards, he threw things down the area. Her mistress sent her out with a message, and she then saw Clayton, who asked her to take something to drink, which she at first refused; but upon his insisting they went and had something to drink. She saw him a night or two afterwards in the streets, as she went out on an errand, and frequently after that; but she never saw the prisoner Jenkins till the night of the first of January.

The jury found both the prisoners Guilty.

The fearful sentence was carried into effect on the scaffold before the debtors' door, Newgate, at the usual hour, and with the accustomed solemnity. Clayton was twenty-eight years of age, and Jenkins thirty-five.

After the culprits had been divested of their irons, Clayton observed to Jenkins it was an awful moment, and he exhorted him to cheer his spirits, and die with manly fortitude—adding that the sentence was just, and trusting their example would warn others against keeping bad company.

A servant, who had formerly lived with Mrs. Martin, informed a man with whom she lived, that there was always money in the house. This was communicated to others, and seven persons had beset the house several nights—but one of the gang, who had squabbled about the division of other spoil, gave information at Bow Street of their intention.

WILLIAM JEMMET,
EXECUTED FOR ROBBERY ON THE HIGH SEAS.

THIS malefactor had been purser on board his majesty's ship Amphitrite, and from some unsuccessful speculations had got himself into embarrassed circumstances. In 1809 he entered into a concern, with some others, to ship goods for the Brazils. Jemmet, accompanied by a mariner, named Moore, went to Mr. White, a ship-broker, in London, and entered into negotiation for the purchase of a Portuguese vessel then lying in the Thames. They professed to treat on behalf of the house of Lazarus and Cohen, and purchased the ship for seven hundred pounds, which was paid for at two payments. They then employed Mr. White to procure them freight for Pernambuco. The vessel, which they called the Maria, was then advertised as ready to receive goods, and vast quantities were shipped; among other things, seven casks of dollars, containing thirty-two thousand ounces of silver. The cargo was estimated at eighty or ninety thousand pounds; and the freight, amounting to eight hundred and eighty-six pounds, six shillings, was paid in advance.

In April, 1810, the Maria, Captain da Sylva, sailed from the Downs, where Jemmet went on board; but, instead of proceeding to the Brazils, they shaped their course for the West Indies. On their way from Teneriffe to Porto Rico the vessel's sides were painted yellow, and her name changed from Maria to the Columbia, of New York. The first mate took the command. They were not suffered to break bulk at Porto Rico, and in consequence they proceeded to Porto Plato, in St. Domingo, where they freighted a schooner with part of the cargo, and then sailed to St. Jago, in the Isle of Cuba, where the dollars were landed by Jemmet. They then steered for the Havannah, where the crew was discharged, and the vessel dismantled. Neither the owners of the ship nor the cargo ever heard how either was disposed of.

Jemmet, being dishonestly possessed of property, proceeded to Philadelphia, where he procured bills on England for six thousand pounds, with which he returned home. But an account of his villainy had preceded him, and on his appearance in London he was taken into custody, and committed to prison. His trial came on at the Old Bailey, February 28, 1812, when these facts were proved against him by some of his crew, and he was accordingly found Guilty—Death.

WILLIAM CUNDELL AND JOHN SMITH,
EXECUTED FOR HIGH TREASON.

Repentance and a corresponding conduct are sure of forgiveness, for the past, before Heaven; but earthly tribunals differ from those above; and it is supposed that occasional examples of capital punishment are necessary for the good of society, though the victims of penal laws may have ceased to offend, and consequently, from them individually, there is nothing more to apprehend. In hanging one man, and acquitting another guilty of the same crime, there may be policy; but there certainly is not justice; and he that suffers may reasonably accuse his judges of vindictiveness and partiality. There are, however, shades of criminality which would warrant a difference of punishment, and we hope that, in the present case, these shades were found by the attorney-general, who conducted the prosecution, and we have no reason to suspect he did not.

In 1808, a number of British sailors and mariners were confined, as prisoners of war, in the Isle of France. The prison, being much crowded, was greatly incommoded with dirt and vermin, and, there being no way of escaping from such inconvenience but that of desertion, every art was practiced by their keepers to induce the unhappy prisoners to enter the French service. Fifty men, among whom were Cundell and Smith, had not virtue enough to resist the temptations on one hand, and the hope of escaping from distress and filth on the other. They forgot their country and allegiance, and put on the enemy's uniform, acting as sentinels over those who were so recently their companions in captivity.

These traitors continued to do duty with the French until the surrender of the island to the British forces, when Cundell and Smith, with ten others, positively refused to accompany the enemy, and threw themselves upon the mercy of their country, having immediately surrendered to the English, while the thirty-eight others marched off to old France.

These culprits were now transmitted to England, and a special commission was issued for their trial, which took place at the Surrey Court House, February the 6th, 1812.

Cundell, Smith, and five others, were found guilty of adhering to his majesty's enemies, when the attorney-general stated that he thought the ends of justice obtained, and that he would not press the conviction of the remaining five, who were discharged, not for any want of proof of their guilt, but through the clemency of the government. He pitied the situation of the unfortunate men at the bar; but as an example, to deter others from forsaking their duty, it was necessary that the law should take its course, in order that those engaged in the service of their country might be impressed with the conviction, that such offenders could not expect to escape the hands of justice. There were reasons for selecting the men who had been tried, as well as those who were acquitted, and, from his official knowledge of the particulars, he thought the ends of justice obtained.

The lord chief baron then proceeded to pass sentence, after a suitable address—'That you, and each of you, be taken to the place from whence you came, and thence be drawn on a hurdle to the place of execution, where you shall be hanged by the necks, but not till you are dead: that you be severally taken down, while yet alive, and your bowels taken out, and burnt before your faces; that your heads be then cut off, and your bodies cut in four quarters, to be at the king's disposal.'

The prisoners were then, after again crying for mercy, re-conducted to their cells. Almost every individual in court was dissolved in tears during the melancholy scene.

On Monday morning, the 16th of March, 1812, William Cundell and John Smith, pursuant to their sentence, were hung, and afterwards beheaded, at Horsemonger Lane, in the presence of some thousands of spectators, and their remains then delivered over to their respective friends for interment. During this melancholy occasion the sight was distressing. At eight o'clock, these two young men were conducted from their cells to chapel, from whence, after remaining some time, they were drawn on a hurdle to the place of execution, and having with becoming fortitude ascended the scaffold, attended by the clergyman, they again spent a short period in prayer, seemingly thoroughly sensible of that fate fast approaching them. The dreadful moment having at length arrived, they were launched off, and their bodies, after hanging nearly half an hour, were taken down. The scene then, while the executioner was performing that part of the remaining sentence, in severing off their heads, and alternately with his right hand presenting each to the surrounding spectators, exclaiming, 'Behold the head of a traitor!' became truly awful, and apparently dissolved in tears each individual who beheld the fate of two men, who thus, in the bloom of life, suffered death, according to the laws of their country.

The remaining five were pardoned on condition of serving in colonies beyond the seas.

GEORGE SKENE, ESQ.
EXECUTED FOR FORGERY.

In our long catalogue of crimes we have not presented a malefactor of the description of Mr. Skene,— a man who held an office, the duties of which, one would imagine might have fully guarded him against the commission of a crime which reduced him to a level with the unfortunate creatures whose cases came daily before him. Yet such is the weakness of human nature, and so uncontrollable our propensities, created by unbounded appetite, or cursed avarice, that this man committed a forgery on the very office in which he held a confidential situation.

George Skene was of a most respectable family in the north of Scotland; where he received a liberal education. He was possessed of considerable mental acquirements, pleasing manners, and an amiable disposition; and received a character, on his trial, such as is seldom bestowed on a criminal in a court of justice. At an early age he removed to London, where he obtained a situation in the Shadwell Police Office, and subsequently in that of Queen Square as chief clerk, with a salary of two hundred pounds a year.

The duties which devolved upon him consisted of receiving all fees and fines, and disbursing all demands on the office. The latter being generally greater than the former, he had to apply to the receiver-general at the secretary of state's office for such sums as the receipts of the office were inadequate to discharge.

How many are virtuous, because they are precluded from temptation! Mr. Skene, being in the constant habit of receiving money for all tradesmen's bills presented by him, foolishly thought that fictitious accounts, when vouched in the usual way, would pass undiscovered and enable him to add to the other emoluments of his office by an act which was at once a breach of trust and an unpardonable crime.

In pursuance of this design he presented and obtained money for four receipts, purporting to be from four different persons; but, suspicion arising, the case was investigated; when it appeared that the receipts were forgeries, considerable additions being made to each account.

For this offence he was committed to prison, and brought to trial at the Old Bailey on the 15th of January, 1812. The facts being proved he was called upon for his defence, when he declared to God and his conscience that he had no intention of committing any fraud, and attributed the errors in his accounts to the circumstance of his being absent five hundred miles from London, on professional business, a short time previous to the commission of the deed for which he was indicted.

The Marquis of Huntley, and above a dozen magistrates, gave testimony as to his character, and the chief baron in summing up observed that the character of a well-spent life had its weight in cases of doubt; but, where the evidence was conclusive, it was much to be lamented that character was forfeited. The jury, after a short consultation, returned a verdict of Guilty, and he was ordered for execution.

From the moment of his conviction to a few days previous to his execution, this young man was buoyed up with the hope of the royal mercy; and a paragraph appeared in some of the newspapers, stating that he had received the royal pardon. This hope, however, as well as those arising from a scheme formed for his escape, were dissipated, and he was given to understand that he had no mercy to expect. He expressed his perfect resignation to his fate, and took leave of his friends with becoming fortitude. On Tuesday, about four o'clock, he, in company with Lord Robert Seymour, took the sacrament; and next morning, March the 18th, 1812, he was attended by

Ordinary, until summoned to the Press-yard; from whence at eight o'clock he proceeded to the scaffold. Previous to ascending the platform, he was considerably affected; but in a few seconds he resumed his fortitude, and, taking off his hat, submitted himself to the executioner, who, having performed his melancholy office, retired, leaving Dr. Ford with Mr. Skene in prayer. In two minutes afterwards the platform fell, and he was launched into eternity. Having been suspended the usual time, the body was cut down and carried within the prison, where it remained until eight o'clock, when it was delivered to his friends.

Mr. Skene's wife, who had been previously the wife of the Earl of Fife, was burnt to death about four years before the ignominious termination of her husband's life.

'I never see a criminal carried to execution,' says the learned and benevolent Boerhaave, 'without asking myself whether I may not be more guilty than this man.' It might not be unproductive of good if every person in this vast metropolis would put the same interrogation to himself on those mornings when the prisons of this city are emptied in the grave. Perhaps those who witness such melancholy exhibitions might then return home, with a conviction of the necessity of reforming their own lives: for how many are there whose conscience must accuse them of a greater crime than that of defrauding government of a small sum of money; and how many greater offences are there for which the law has not provided so severe a punishment as that inflicted on George Skene.

THOMAS BOWLER,

EXECUTED FOR MALICIOUSLY FIRING AT MR. BURROWES.

An unprovoked and foul spirit of revenge, indulged in to excess, precipitated this hoary sinner on the commission of a crime for which he forfeited his life to the injured laws of his country. The motives which prompt other men to deeds of blood were wanting here; plunder was not the object; nor was there a single worldly advantage which this desperate man could promise himself from the premature death of his neighbour; nor does it appear that he received a provocation from his intended victim that would justify the slightest act of hostility, much less a premeditated attempt on his life.

Thomas Bowler was a wealthy farmer, who resided near Harrow, and had for his neighbour another farmer named Burrowes, who was also a hay-salesman in St. James's, Haymarket. These men had a trifling dispute about some trees; but which was amicably adjusted without any application to lawyers. Notwithstanding this apparent conciliation Bowler from that moment nourished a spirit of revenge, and about the middle of March, 1812, in the presence of one Sheppard, in St. James's Market, said 'Damn that Burrowes's eyes, I'll Burrowes him before long; he shan't live to the end of June, if I was to be hanged the next moment.' Sheppard remonstrated, and Bowler replied, 'I'll be d——d if I don't be the death of him.' This was communicated to Burrowes, who took no farther notice of it than just to observe 'I don't fear him; he is too fond of his own life to take away mine.'

Bowler, being a man who never put any restraint on his violent passions, indulged his evil propensity for better than two months, and on the 30th of May prepared to carry into execution his foul design, as he knew his unsuspecting neighbour would be on his way to London at a certain hour, to attend his duty in the Haymarket.

His preparations were all coolly and deliberately arranged. He provided a boy to keep a swift horse to carry him out of danger in case of pursuit; and, as the pan of his blunderbuss lost the priming, he carried it on that very morning to a blacksmith for repair, telling him he wanted it to shoot a mad dog. While the smith was employed on the lock he went out, and kept walking up and down; and, as he saw Burrowes coming up the road in his chaise-cart, he returned into the smith's shop, took up the blunderbuss, and stationed himself behind an elm-tree, which concealed him all but his feet from Mr. Burrowes. Where Bowler stood was about fifteen yards from the canal bridge, at Alperton; and, just as the chaise-cart gained the bridge, the assassin took a deliberate aim, when Burrowes exclaimed 'Don't fire!' and stooped down in the cart. 'Damn your eyes, take that!' said Bowler, firing, and wounded Mr. Burrowes in the neck and back. At the report of the blunderbuss the horse ran away, and the assassin mounted his horse, and galloped off, leaving his hat behind him, and throwing the blunderbuss into the ditch.

What added to the atrocity of this act was the age of the perpetrator, which at the time was more than sixty years. Besides, he was immensely rich, and had a respectable family to suffer disgrace by his unprincipled wickedness.

Happily Mr. Burrowes' wounds were not mortal; he gradually recovered, and diligent pursuit was made after the hoary fugitive. For a week he avoided the vigilance of Mr. Burrowes' friends; but on the 6th of June he was apprehended at his own house. To the person who took him into custody he offered ten, twenty, and, lastly, thirty thousand pounds, to be allowed his liberty; but his offers were rejected, and he was carried to the police-office, from which he was fully committed to Newgate. He thought bail would be accepted, and offered to deposit ten thousand pounds.

Bowler's friends now began to prepare for his defence; and, knowing there was no possibility of controverting the fact, endeavoured 'to establish a case of lunacy. For this purpose a commission was sued out, and a jury gave a verdict that he was insane from the preceding March, in consequence of a fracture in his skull, occasioned by a fall from his horse.

His trial came on at the Old Bailey, July the 3d, 1812, when the case of the prosecution being gone through, several witnesses were examined to establish his insanity. Among these were three or four medical men, who gave it as their decided opinion that he was in an unsound state of mind; and various acts of eccentricity and extravagant passion were adduced in support of the defence. But as his conduct at the time of the dreadful act, in preparing the means of escape, argued a conviction of a knowledge of right and wrong, the jury found him Guilty, and he was sentenced to be hanged.

For some time he supported himself with the hope of royal mercy, till Thursday, August the 20th, when he was given to understand that his execution was appointed to take place the ensuing day. He met his fate with pious firmness, on Friday, August the 21st, 1812.

DANIEL DAWSON,
EXECUTED FOR POISONING RACE-HORSES.

To that useless, and, we fear, vicious race of men denominated the *sporting* world, this malefactor belonged. He had, for many years, made Newmarket his residence, and was variously employed by the frequenters of that mart of folly and dissipation. His principal occupation was that of *toulter*, a name given to those who conceal themselves among the furzes on the heath, to see the trials of horses, and make reports to the *betters*. Dawson, though perfectly illiterate, had a comprehensive mind, and on these occasions his judgment and integrity gave great satisfaction; for he was able to determine, with great accuracy, the superior powers of one horse over another.

Seeing his judgment so beneficial to others, he resolved to make it more useful to himself, and commenced *better;* but Newmarket was not the school for morality or honour, and Dawson had none. Gamblers do not wish to trust entirely to chance, and generally contrive some method to influence the issue in their own favour. This dishonest man had recourse to a practice which terminated in an ignominious death; and, though he protested not having intended the mischief that occurred, still it did not prove less fatal.

Dawson had been long in the habit, in imitation of his betters, of conveying deleterious drugs into the drink of race-horses, for the purpose of disqualifying them for the course, and consequently enabling those who knew the cause to stake their money on the safe side. In this practice he continued for some time without detection, until April, 1811, when he conveyed into a watering-trough a large quantity of the solution of arsenic, out of which two horses, the property of Lord Foley and Sir F. Standish, had to drink. The drug was too powerful, and the horses died. Suspicion fell upon Dawson, and a man named Cecil Bishop, an accomplice, when they were taken into custody. Bishop, on apprehension, made a full confession, and accused Dawson of having poisoned another horse in 1809, belonging to Mr. Adams, of Royston, Herts; and established a chain of conclusive evidence against his companion in iniquity, for which he was admitted an evidence.

For this offence Dawson was indicted at the Lent assizes at Cambridge, as a principal; and it appearing he was only an accessary, he was acquitted, but was detained on a charge of poisoning race-horses in 1809. His second trial, which took place in August, 1812, proved fatal to him. He was found Guilty, to the satisfaction of a crowded court, and had sentence of death passed on him.

For some time after conviction he had hopes of mercy. Lord Foley, for some communication made by Dawson, was disposed to save his life; but all his efforts proved unavailing, and he was left to his fate. Disappointed in the hopes of the royal clemency, he resolved to attempt securing his own liberty; by what means will best appear from the following letter:—

' DEAR WIFE,—I learn by yours I am in danger; by that I have another way to escape without fear of being discovered.—You go to a tool-shop, and get a small hack saw, as the watchmakers use, the smaller the better, to convey to me; the best way you can get it in will be between some turf, with some black thread; if you can find a better way, do it; but be careful, for all the danger is to get that to me, for I have but one bar to cut, and I am in town by four o'clock in the morning.—They will not miss me till eight, when they come to unlock us. I shall be by that out of their reach. Dear girl, bring me the turf six pieces at a time. When I have got the saw, I must have some friend come round to see the Castle, but take no notice of me, but to see the situation; I am in full north; and come again in one hour after we lock up; bring rope enough to reach over the wall, and he stand on the other side, and hold it till I am up the wall. Fasten a large spike to the end of the rope, and throw it over the wall, and tie knots about nine inches asunder, to hold by, and about twenty-five feet long. There is no danger in this, for there is nobody inside, after we come to bed. A rainy night will be best; but I will let you know the night by another line. Mr. Prince says he has got a very respectable man, who will come forward and swear to every thing of the concern, all but seeing it put in. If any body can be found to write to Lord F. O. (alluding to a threat,) it will have great effect. Mr. J. B. South Street, Grosvenor Square, Mr. B. King's Mews, Elbs (meaning Theobald's) Road, Gray's-Inn Lane, have a good look out, if there is any danger. I shall soon be along with you, with a little of your assistance; by applying to the people above mentioned you will get good intelligence. When you write, direct your letters to Mrs. Howell's sister. When you come, ask me for my pocket-book, and I can give you all at once. I shall call them things breeches and coat, so you will know.'

This letter was detected in the hand of his wife, by the gaoler, whose suspicions were excited by the circumstance of their parting on this occasion with more than usual emotion. Baffled in all his schemes, he for a time indulged the criminal design of taking away his own life; but from which he was persuaded by the pious exhortations of the chaplain.

Seeing no hopes of either mercy or escape, he resigned himself to his fate, but persisted in denying having intended to destroy the horses, as he only wanted to incapacitate them from winning. Of the frequenters of Newmarket he gave an appalling picture, and alleged that many gentlemen of turf notoriety deserved, as much as he did, the punishment that awaited him; for that there were not three fair betters amongst them, and that one nobleman, in particular, would cheat his Creator if his lordship had a match with him.

Dawson spent his last days in all the fervency of prayer, and expressed his pious hope in the forgiveness of the Almighty. The last parting from his wife was truly affecting, and he described it as worse than death. The night before his execution he slept sound, and ate, next morning, a hearty breakfast. Previous to his receiving the sacrament he tied a yard of black riband round his neck, which, at his dying request, was conveyed to his afflicted wife. At twelve o'clock he was led to the platform, on the top of Cambridge Castle, and was turned off amidst an immense concourse of spectators, it being market day. He died without a struggle.

LIEUTENANT GAMAGE,
EXECUTED FOR MURDER.

This unfortunate young officer fell a victim to ungovernable passions. He had ordered a sergeant of marines upon some duty, which the sergeant, conceiving it incompatible with his situation, refused performing; and was, withal, insolent in his replies. The lieutenant burst into a violent passion, ran to his cabin, seized his dirk, returned, and stabbed the sergeant to the heart. For this crime he was tried by a court martial, and sentenced to death.

The execution took place on board the Griffon, in November, 1812. He bore his fate with manly fortitude. About eight o'clock he was attended by the clergyman, and remained with him till about half past nine, when the procession began from his cabin to the platform, from whence he was to be launched into eternity. The clergyman walked first; then Lieutenant Gamage, attended on each side by two friends, officers; several officers followed afterwards; every one present was deeply affected at the unfortunate fate of this young gentleman, the ship's company particularly. Boats from the different ships attended, as usual, round the execution, and 'God receive his soul' frequently burst forth from different seamen. He bowed and thanked them three times, and seemed deeply affected with the sympathy he excited. He spoke shortly to his own crew, warning them to beware of giving way to sudden passion. As soon as he reached the platform, he prayed again with the clergyman, and precisely at ten o'clock, the signal gun being fired, he was run up to the yard-arm, amidst the repeated exclamations from the seamen of 'God bless and receive him!' He appeared to suffer but little.

Previous to the execution, the following circular address was sent by Admiral Foley to every ship in his fleet:—

'The commander-in-chief most earnestly desires to direct the particular attention of the fleet to the melancholy scene they are now called to attend—a scene which offers a strong, and much he hopes, an impressive lesson to every person in it—a lesson to all who are to command, to all who are to obey.—Lieutenant Gamage is represented by every person who knew him, and by the unanimous voice of the Griffon's ship's company, as a humane compassionate man—a kind indulgent officer; yet, for want of that guard which every man should keep over his passions, this kind, humane, compassionate man commits the dreadful crime of murder!

'Let his example strike deep into the minds of all who witness his unhappy end; and, whatever their general disposition may be, let them learn from him, that, if they are not always watchful to restrain their passions within their proper bounds, one moment of intemperate anger may destroy the hopes of a well-spent honourable life, and bring them to an untimely and disgraceful death. And let those who are to obey learn from the conduct of the sergeant the fatal effects which may result from contempt and insolent conduct towards their superiors.—By repeated insolence the sergeant overcame the kind and gentle disposition of Lieutenant Gamage; and, by irritating and inflaming his passion, occasioned his own death.

'The commander-in-chief hopes

that this afflicting lesson may not be offered in vain; but, seriously contemplating the awful example before them, every officer and every man will learn from it, never to suffer himself to be driven by ill-governed passion to treat with cruelty or violence those over whom he is to command, nor by disobedience or disrespect to rouse the passions of those whom it is his duty to obey and respect.

(Signed) 'THOMAS FOLEY.'

The body was brought on shore for interment at two o'clock, and was received at landing by Perrer Dower, Esq. governor of the naval hospital, who, with a number of naval and military officers, attended this unfortunate young gentleman's remains to the burial-ground at the naval hospital, where they were deposited. General Trollope, and the officers of the Griffon, with several of the crew, were present.

It might have been hoped that his untimely fate would have served to check the passions of young officers in dispensing their orders to those under their command. We are, therefore, sorry to find a case nearly similar, and immediately after that of Lieutenant Gamage.

A court martial was held on Tuesday, 24th of November, 1812, in Plymouth harbour, on Mr. Paul Walker, late midshipman of his majesty's cutter Sylvia, on charges of drunkenness, contempt, disobedience of orders, and for stabbing Isaac Smith, corporal of marines, in several places with a dirk; which being clearly proved, the Court adjudged the said Walker to forfeit the whole of his time as midshipman, and to serve before the mast of such of his majesty's ships as the commander-in-chief shall direct; and, as a further disgrace, ordered him to be taken alongside every ship and vessel in the said harbour, where the sentence was publicly read.

JOACHIM, MARTIN, MILLINGTON, AND WILLIAMS,
EXECUTED FOR THE MURDER OF THEIR OFFICERS.

AT a court martial held on board his majesty's ship Salvador del Mundo, in the Hamoaze at Plymouth, in December 1812, these inhuman seamen were tried for one of the most foul, unprovoked, and desperate murders which ever disgraced the British navy.

It appeared in evidence that Joachim, a Portuguese; Martin, a black, belonging to the Diana; Millington, an Irishman; and Williams, an Englishman, belonging to the Growler gun-brig; Baptist, another black, concerned in the murder, drowned, with two other seamen, named Boyd and Grant, admitted as evidence against them, were put on board the French prize-brig Le Suir Maree, along with the three persons they murdered, viz. Mr. Andrews, master's mate; Mr. Bolen, quarter-master; and Mr. Winsland Steward, a passenger; and that, after in vain attempting to carry the vessel into an enemy's port, they were again fallen in with by the Diana and Aquilon frigates, and brought to Plymouth in irons.

The first witness, Boyd, deposed that, on the 25th of November, himself, with Grant, the prisoners, the black since drowned, and the three missing people, were put on board the brig, and directed to proceed to Plymouth, which they did, until the night of the 29th, or morning of the 30th; when, off Scilly, the diabolical plan was put in execution. That he and Grant had the first watch, from eight to twelve, and were relieved at twelve by some of the prisoners. That at about three o'clock he was called by Joachim, but he did not then attend to him;—that he was called the second time, when he went upon deck, where he was told by Joachim and Baptist they had taken the vessel, and intended to take her to France, and if he would join them he might;—this offer he peremptorily refused, and called for Bolen, who did not answer; he called again, and was answered by one of the prisoners that he was dead. Horror instantly struck him to the soul: he, however, called for Grant, who answered very low; on which Joachim told him, as he was a poor seaman like himself, he might go below, and they should not hurt him: that he then went down the steerage into the cable-tier, where he found Grant, who had been previously called up, and asked the same questions. Here their situation must have been truly dismal, expecting every moment to be murdered also. They were kept as prisoners by the negro, Martin, who stood over them with Mr. Andrews's sword. Boyd farther stated that there was only a sliding door which parted them and the cabin, where they saw a body covered over with a quilt, and lying on the floor, which was afterwards removed on deck, and thrown overboard. That in the morning, at day-light, they heard a voice on deck say 'Two sail in chase;' and about eight o'clock they heard the boat lowered from the stern, and row off. That, after the boat was gone, Boyd looked on deck, and, perceiving only Baptist, Millington, and Williams, he said to Grant, 'Now is our time to go on deck, and throw the black (Baptist) overboard, and secure the other two;' with which Grant complied, and they both went up:—by this time the vessels were near them, and they were about seven miles from the Saints Island, standing quite on upon the land. For some time they (the witnesses) appeared to take no notice; but, on Boyd observing the force-top bowline loose, he desired the black to haul it taught, and he went to assist, hoping to get an opportunity to throw him overboard; but, not finding an advantageous opportunity then, he walked behind him towards the stern, and, observing the main-mast topsail-sheet gone, he desired him to haul that taught. When the desired moment arrived, he seized the black, and threw him outside the bulwark, where the fellow clung with his hands to the rigging, and with his teeth almost bit off Boyd's thumb. On Grant observing this, he ran to Boyd's assistance, and struck the black on the head with a stick, and knocked him overboard. That he (Boyd) then went to the helm, seized Millington, tied his hands, and set him on the deck;—that Grant, at the same time, seized Williams, and set them side by side on the deck, when they stood the vessel off the land, to near the frigate, and to avoid the black, who was still swimming. That the Aquilon's boat boarded them soon after, when he related to the lieutenant what had happened, and was then taken on board the Diana.

Grant deposed exactly to the same effect, and both of them gave their evidence in the most clear and steady manner.

The prisoners stated no cause that led them to commit this diabolical act. They were sentenced to suffer death on board such ships, and at such time, as the lords commissioners of the admiralty should be pleased to direct.

The awful sentence, although

read in the most impressive manner by the judge-advocate, had not the smallest effect on any one but Millington, who cried much, for which he was jeered by Williams, who told him that hanging was nothing but choking!

The president, before dismissing the Court, took the opportunity of returning thanks to Boyd and Grant for their brave and seaman-like conduct while in such a perilous situation; and said he hoped it would never be forgotten by those present, and that their high and meritorious behaviour deserved the greatest praise.

They were hanged from the yard-arm of a vessel of war.

THE MARQUIS OF SLIGO,

FINED AND IMPRISONED FOR ENTICING SEAMEN TO DESERT HIS MAJESTY'S NAVY.

In 1810 the noble marquis, then a very thoughtless young man, quitted college, and proceeded on his travels, visiting those places in person, of whose ancient fame and greatness he had read so much. Being partial to marine excursions, and willing to indulge himself in one in the Mediterranean, he hired, at Malta, a brig called the Pylades; and, having been introduced to Captain Sprainger, of the Warrior, then on that station, he received from that naval officer much information and kindness.

The noble marquis, being frequently rowed to and from the Warrior by some of her athletic crew, seems to have thought the addition of a few of these fine fellows a desirable acquisition to his handful of Italians. Accordingly it appears he succeeded in enticing two of them, upon which suspicion fell upon his lordship; for it was supposed no ordinary inducement had been held out to them, as they were men of tried fidelity, long standing, and had then three years' arrears of wages due to them. Captain Sprainger paid the marquis a visit on board the Pylades; and, on hinting his suspicions, his lordship appeared greatly hurt; upon which the captain, from their intimacy, contented himself with cautioning his noble friend upon the danger of having deserters on board, as the navy was then very low, being nearly two thousand under its complement. He then left the marquis, and from his own ship sent him a description of the men missing, requesting that, if they offered themselves to his lordship, they might be sent to some of his majesty's ships at Malta.

It must be admitted, we fear, that British seamen are generally too much disposed to leave the service, and probably, in the present instance, did not require much pressing: but still we cannot acquit his lordship of something worse than ingratitude; for he kept the men concealed on board, and pledged his word of honour that he had them not.

Next day the Warrior sailed; and the noble marquis, fired with the fame of his grandfather, Lord Howe, resolved that his brig should be a letter of marque, for the purpose of upholding the honour of the British flag. For the business of navigation, a comparatively few men would have done; but in this new capacity he required at least forty. To procure these was no very difficult task on a station where men were hourly in the habit of quitting their ships; and his lordship's servant, in the course of an evening or two, added fourteen brave fellows to their complement.

On the 13th of May his lordship sailed to Palermo, and from thence to Messina, where, on pledging his word of honour that he had no deserters on board, he received a six months' protection for forty men, having inserted false names for the men-of-war's men. The Pylades then proceeded on her course, and on the 30th of May she was chased by the Active, an officer of that ship having heard that deserters were on board. Ere the boat came alongside, his lordship ordered the men-of-war's men below, and, though a search took place, they escaped detection.

The marquis next sailed to Patmos, where ten of the men were allowed to go on shore, and that evening the vessel sailed without them. On this transaction so much contrary evidence was given on the trial, that we are at a loss which side to credit. The men on shore said that his lordship proposed stopping for a fortnight, and that no signal for sailing was made. The reverse of this was sworn by others of the crew, and we leave the reader to form his own opinion. The abandoned men, however, appear to have suffered great hardship; and at Scio, when accompanied by the British consul to the Pylades, his lordship refused to receive any of them except four, who were useful in the management of the vessel.

Some of the men returned to their duty, and, were tried by a court martial. From Constantinople the marquis wrote to Captain Strainger, stating that he found he had some of his men on board, and that he was determined to send them on shore the first opportunity; that, if the business was brought into a Court, he would do the best to defend himself; and that, at the worst, he had an ample fortune, and could pay the fines.

Tired with travelling, his lordship returned home, and soon after his arrival in England he was indicted for enticing British seamen from their duty. The trial came on at the Old Bailey, December 16th, 1812, when, after a protracted inquiry, his lordship was found Guilty, and sentenced to pay a fine of five thousand pounds, and be imprisoned four months in Newgate.

On this case it is unnecessary for us to make any observation. Unfortunately, in the folly and indiscretion of youth, this young nobleman was betrayed into a forgetfulness of what he owed to his country and to himself, and descended from those pure principles which high rank ought to generate. He had perverted the great advantages which he possessed to draw his inferiors from their duty, and thereby exposed them to ignominy and punishment, as well as serving, in a slight degree, to weaken the defence of the kingdom. However, it is a source of consolation, that his lordship's aberration from duty afforded another instance of the impartiality of British laws, which have a like punishment for similar offences for the high and the low.

Perhaps it is not the least curious particular attending this case, that his lordship's mother, the Dowager Marchioness of Sligo, soon after her son's trial, was married to Sir William Scott, the judge who passed sentence on the youthful marquis.

JOHN LOMAS AND EDITH MORREY,
EXECUTED FOR THE MURDER OF MR. MORREY.

'MY son, learn to say No,' was the dying injunction of a pious mother to a beloved youth; and, though the advice was concise, it is one of the most sage that ever was delivered from mortal lips. He that learns to say 'No' to the first invitation to crime will never become guilty; for the climax of iniquity is never attained at once, but must be approached through all the progressive ways of vice. Reader! peruse the atrocious narrative we are about to relate; and, while you mourn for the weakness and wickedness of your species, commune with yourself on the importance of learning to say 'No,' an ignorance of which brought this guilty pair to an ignominious death.

John Lomas lived as servant with a farmer named Morrey, who resided in Cheshire, and by whom he was treated with great kindness. Lomas, not being more than twenty years of age, attracted the notice of his mistress; and, though she was the mother of five children, she admitted a criminal passion for her servant boy. Some acts of kindness on her part conciliated the youth, and the condescension of the mistress emboldened him to familiarity. The wholesome barriers of respect and deference being once broken through, modesty was left without a protector, and the guilty pair plunged into all the excesses of forbidden enjoyment. Henious as was their conduct, had it stopped here, they would have escaped the miserable condition to which they reduced themselves. But the guidance of virtue once forsaken, the progress of guilt is rapid.

This atrocious pair, either apprehensive of discovery, or wishing to perpetuate their guilty connexion, resolved on removing the unsuspicious husband, whose existence they thought a drawback on their mutual happiness.

Various attempts to murder the unfortunate man proved abortive, until the night of the 11th of April, 1812. Morrey had been out at a cocking, and returned home at the usual hour. He spoke with his usual kindness to Lomas, and laughed and joked with his wife as they were going to bed, little suspecting the dreadful intentions which that barbarous woman harboured towards the father of her children. Between one and two o'clock Mrs. Morrey got up and went to Lomas's room, desiring him to get up, and murder her husband. The infatuated youth obeyed the horrid summons, and, ascending, had an axe put into his hands; while his mistress held the candle, Lomas struck his master three blows on the head, and as the unfortunate man moaned, he was heard by a servant-maid in an adjoining apartment, who, making a noise, alarmed the murderers, when they ran out of the room, Mrs. Morrey extinguishing, at the same time, the candle.

Morrey continuing to moan, Lomas was sent in again to dispatch him; but, after giving several blows, came out without having effected his horrid purpose. At this Mrs. Morrey said, 'John, he is alive; go in and kill him;' and put a razor into his hand for the purpose. On his entering a third time, their miserable victim was yet alive, and seemed to recognise Lomas, whom he caught by the shirt, and laid his head down on his breast, in a supplicating manner; but at this moment the monster drew the razor twice across his throat, and terminated his struggles for existence.

Mrs. Morrey now went into the servant-maid's room, and prevented her from escaping through the window, telling her to remain quiet, as there were murderers in the house.

To save appearances, Lomas ran through the neighbourhood, lamenting and proclaiming that some villains had murdered his master. Several people attended, and blood being found on Lomas, and traced to his room, he was accused of the murder, when he unhesitatingly confessed it, and implicated his mistress. When the constable came to take her into custody, she drew from her pocket a razor, and inflicted a deep wound in her throat; but it did not prove mortal. The razor was found in a pond, where Lomas had thrown it; and his bloody shirt was taken out of his trunk, where he had concealed it.

So great was the sensation produced in the country by the perpetration of this horrid murder, that when the trial of these malefactors came on at Chester, July 21st, 1812, the court was crowded to excess, it being computed that four thousand persons attended to hear the verdict. The facts of the case being proved, the jury, without retiring, pronounced them Guilty, and they were ordered for execution the ensuing Monday. When sentence was passed, Lomas stretched out his hands and exclaimed, 'I deserve it all—I don't wish to live; but I hope for mercy.' His more miserable companion pleaded pregnancy; and, a jury of matrons proving this to be case, she was respited.

The trial continued six hours. Edith Morrey wore a veil when she was put to the bar; but this being ordered to be removed, she held her handkerchief to her face, and preserved, throughout the awful investigation, a sullen, unmoved, hardness. From the time of her imprisonment, she protested her innocence; and, thinking that there was not a sufficient evidence to criminate her, she spoke with confidence of acquittal. On the other hand, Lomas all along confessed his crime in all its horrid circumstances.

On Sunday, the day before execution, Edith Morrey acknowledged her guilt, and desired to speak with Lomas. This was granted, and they partook of the sacrament together, previous to which they had some mutual recrimination, Morrey being unwilling to acknowledge the minute particulars of her atrocious conduct. But they parted in friendship; and, praying for each other, acknowledged their sins.

On Monday, according to his sentence, Lomas was removed from Chester Castle to the New City Gaol. The sheriffs received him at the boundaries, and, on being placed in a cart, he fell on his knees, and continued in prayer till he arrived at the gaol, in front of which the drop was erected. He declared he would rather die than live, and every part of his deportment evinced the sincerity of his professions. When the rope was placed round his neck, he addressed a few words to the surrounding multitude, observing that he had made his peace with God, and warned them to take example by his present awful situation. Soon after he was launched into eternity; but, being in the vigour of youth and health, he struggled violently before he quitted this mortal state.

The miserable Edith Morrey having given birth to an infant, and the time of parturition over, she prepared to meet the fate of her paramour. On the 7th of February, 1813, she was conducted to the place of execution, and it is some alleviation to our feelings that she died a penitent. She was dressed in widow's weeds, and, when placed upon the platform, she advanced to the front and addressed the multitude. 'My dear Christians, I hope you will take warning by my melancholy situation. My crime has been of a double nature. In the first place I have broken one of God's commandments, by committing adultery, and defiling the marriage bed; and, in the next, I have committed a most inhuman murder, imbruing my hands in the blood of an affectionate and most indulgent husband.'—Then clasping her hands, she exclaimed, 'Lord, unto thee I commend my spirit,' and in a moment after she was launched into eternity.

JOSEPH SIMMONS WINTER, BENJAMIN ALLEN, WILLIAM TAYLOR, JOHN IVEY, & ROBERT COOPER,

THE THREE FIRST EXECUTED FOR STEALING SILK, AND THE TWO LATTER TRANSPORTED FOR RECEIVING IT, KNOWING IT TO BE STOLEN.

These men belonged to a gang of desperate villains who frequently committed depredations on the River Thames; but all their previous acts of dishonesty were lost in the enormity of the one we are about recording, which, at the time of perpetration, created a greater notoriety than any case of felony we remember to have heard of.

The brig 'Velocity,' laden with silk and ostrich feathers, sailed in the month of May, 1812, from Gibraltar to London. Coming from a country afflicted with a pestilential disease, the ship was obliged to perform quarantine on her arrival in the mouth of the Thames. Of this circumstance the band of pirates got notice, and having ascertained that a man named Banton, master of the 'Sisters' hoy, was to go down to Stangate Creek to fetch up the silk and feathers, they engaged him—nothing loath—to aid them in making away with the cargo. His mate, named Knox, was also in the secret, and approved of the scheme. Winter was also the master of a hoy, and engaged to carry the robbery into execution; for which purpose he followed with his hoy, that when Banton should purposely run his vessel aground, he was to come alongside, and carry off the silk, &c.

Thieves cannot exist without receivers; and these villains had more than one. Cooper, who kept three public houses, and was turning at the rate of seventeen thousand pounds a year, agreed to purchase the silk at a certain price; a man named Ingram was also to receive it; and Ivey, who was a toy-chandler in Artillery Lane, agreed to make sales for them. Cooper and Ingram went down to Dagenham to receive the goods, where it was expected they would have been landed.

On the 14th of July the hoy received the goods, and sailed. Winter followed; but in consequence of Banton having a Custom-house officer on board, who was well acquainted with the river, he refused to fulfil his promise. Thus disappointed, they execrated Banton, and for this time abandoned their intentions; but on the 'Sisters' coming up to the Custom House on Saturday, they entered into a new conspiracy to steal the silk and feathers, there being ten bales of the first, and two of the latter, on board. Allen and Taylor, who were working men on the river, were two of those concerned. On Tuesday night they went on board, when one of the thieves imitated Banton's voice, and told the officers that he should move out in the river, to be ready for the morning's tide, as he wanted to get in the London Docks, and requested of them to go below, and get into bed. The stupid fellows did so, and the villains carried the hoy into a wharf above Blackfriars Bridge, on the Surrey side, where they quickly carried off the cargo. When the officers awoke next morning they found themselves confined; and when, with great difficulty, they broke through the skylight, they found the goods in which they were in charge had been carried off.

The silk and feathers were first removed to a stable in Woolpack Yard, Gravel Lane. The parties afterwards met at several public houses, to concert means to dispose of the property. Ivey refused to be immediately concerned, but promised to sell the feathers when the alarm excited was allayed, and received payment for the part he had already taken. Cooper then agreed to pay for the silk nine hundred pounds, and actually sold a part of it to a Mr. Gibbs, of Cumberland Street, Shoreditch. He then employed one Harris, a clerk, and brother to an attorney, to dispose of more of it; and this man negotiated with some of the trade, pretending that he was employed by men of character, but whose names, from motives of delicacy, he was not at liberty to disclose. The silk being of a peculiar nature, and sent to the purchaser in an unusual state of package, he indignantly rejected it, suspecting that it was part of the stolen silk, then universally advertised.

Several of the party were apprehended on suspicion; but there being no evidence against them, they were acquitted. Harris acted as their professional agent, and supplied them with money. At length a new light was thrown on the affair. A silk-thrower, whose mills were at Bruton, was sent some of this silk to prepare; and suspecting, from its state, that it belonged to that stolen, informed the parties concerned of the circumstance, upon which several of the villains were taken into custody; but the affair being of a complicated nature, it was found necessary to admit some of the accomplices as evidence against the others. For this purpose three men, named Brown, Fenwick, and Banton, were admitted as approvers; and Winter, Allen, Taylor, Ivey, Knox, Cooper, and Harris, were indicted at the Old Bailey, October the 30th, 1812.

Their trial occupied the Court three days, during which time the jury were not permitted to separate. The facts being deposed against them, several witnesses were called as to character; and Cooper had the solicitor of the Customs and Excise examined, to show that he had been frequently prosecuted as a smuggler, with a view to persuade the jury, by inference, that he bought the silk, with the idea that it was smuggled.

The jury, having been charged, retired at twelve o'clock at night, and soon returned with a verdict of Guilty — Death — against Winter, Taylor, and Allen:—Ivey and Cooper Guilty—transportation; and acquitting Harris and Knox.

Knox, it appeared, knew nothing of the last transaction; and no evidence went to show that Harris was otherwise employed than as a professional agent.

After their conviction several instruments were conveyed to Winter and Allen, with a view to enable them to make their escape; and a similar attempt was made a few days before their final one upon earth. The three unfortunate men suffered the sentence of the law, January 25, 1813.

CHARLES FREDERICK PALM AND SAMUEL TILLING,
EXECUTED FOR MUTINY AND MURDER.

These sanguinary men were indicted at the Sessions of the High Court of Admiralty, at the Old Bailey, on Friday the 18th December, 1812, for the murder of James Keith, master of a trading vessel, called 'The Adventure.'— There were other counts in the said indictment against the prisoners, charging them with the murder of William Smith, the first mate of the said vessel, and two black men belonging thereto, called, the one Joe, and the other John.*

From the evidence adduced on the trial it appeared that the deceased, James Keith, was master and sole owner of the vessel in question; and that, having embarked the whole of his property therein, to the extent of nearly two thousand pounds, he resolved to make a voyage to the South Seas upon a fishing concern; and for that purpose engaged a crew, which, with himself and three boys, amounted altogether to fourteen persons. Palm was a Swede, an experienced seaman, by his commander appointed to the post of second mate.

'The Adventure' sailed from Portsmouth in the month of November, 1811, and for a part of the time had a prosperous voyage; but one of the crew becoming sickly, and eventually dying, the captain put into the Island of St. Thomas's, and took on board the two black men, Joe and John, already mentioned. He then shaped his course towards Congar, upon the coast of Africa, intending thus to make his voyage to the South Seas; but, whilst an hundred leagues off that place, the crew began to show strong symptoms of mutiny; and, on a morning in April, about four o'clock, a boy named George, who was at the helm, called to the captain, saying there was something bad going on upon deck. The unfortunate Keith, who had already in vain attempted to conciliate his crew, instantly arose from his bed, and, without putting on his clothes, hurried to the deck, where he saw Palm, the second mate, in the act of striking a light.

The captain asked what he was about, when Palm struck him with the cooper's hammer, which he had ready in his hand. In the mean time, another man, since dead, attacked the chief mate, who had come on deck immediately after the captain, and struck him repeatedly with the cook's axe, and Palm, and two other Swedes (both since dead), took an active part in throwing the captain and chief mate overboard.

After this all hands went below, except the boy at the helm. Palm produced a Bible, and they all took an oath upon it, wishing they might never see the light of heaven if they divulged what had passed.

The boy left at the helm was

* The prisoner, Palm, being an alien, was asked, in the usual manner, whether he would be tried by a jury composed of half Englishmen, and the other half foreigners. He hesitated; but answered that he would rather trust himself to Englishmen, than have a single Swede on the jury.

afterwards sworn; and, after the bodies of the captain and chief mate had been thrown overboard, the two Swedes provided themselves each with a pistol and a glass of rum: the rum they offered to the blacks; and, whilst in the act of drinking it, each shot his man; when both were immediately thrown overboard by Palm and the two Swedes.

After this they plundered the captain's property, and Palm had a five-pound note out of it. Palm then took charge of the vessel; but it was afterwards determined to scuttle the ship, and take to the boats, and steer for the coast of Guinea.

Two boats were prepared, and provisions put into them with the crew, eleven in number; they were three days and three nights before they reached land, and then one of the boats was swamped, and a boy was drowned; they then walked along the beach till night, when they lay down on the sand to sleep, and next day went into the country. The moment, however, they were discovered, the black natives rushed upon them, seized, plundered, and stripped them naked, and led them off through the country, to be sold as white slaves.

In this deplorable state they remained several weeks, traversing a vast extent of country, during which all of them died through disease, cruelty of the negroes, or fatigue, except Palm, Tilling, William Wright, not yet apprehended, and Henry Madis. The survivors were marched, or rather driven, to Cape Lopez, a southern promontory of Africa, where the black chief released them, supposing they were shipwrecked mariners, and, after a short time, a Portuguese vessel touching there, Palm and Wright took their voyage to Europe in her, and in a few days, a Liverpool ship also touching there, Tilling and Madis got a passage in her, and they were landed at Liverpool in September.

Tilling, appearing an object of charity, was admitted a patient in the hospital; and Mr. Capper, the first mate of the ship which brought them back to their native country, humanely took the boy, Madis, to his own home. In about a week after their arrival, when Madis went to see Tilling at the hospital, he was greatly surprised to see Palm at the same place, having, on the morning of that same day, been taken in as a patient from the ship that brought him over.

The day on which young Madis landed in Liverpool he wrote the outlines of the above sad story to his mother in London; and urged her to send him money to defray travelling charges, that he might lay the whole before a London magistrate.

Such was the evidence against the prisoners. The impulse which appeared principally to occupy the mind of Palm was that of criminating his fellow-prisoner, whom he laboured to make appear to have acted an equal part in the bloody scene with himself; which by no means came out in evidence: on the contrary the work of death seemed to have been done by Palm and his brother Swedes, of which country the greater part of the crew were composed.

Witnesses were called to the character of Tilling, among whom was his sister; who all spoke highly of his former conduct in life. This might have had some weight in his behalf; indeed nothing vindictive was proved against him, and those charitably inclined believed that he took the forced oath, and appeared, after the murderous deeds were done, as indeed any one would, to retain the blessing of life;—but Tilling did not act like Madis, who gave information of the horrid transaction on his return to his native country. They were both found Guilty, and suffered at Execution Dock on the 21st December, 1812.

Palm appeared to be about fifty years of age; but the hardships he had undergone among the negroes in Africa might have had a premature effect upon his appearance. Tilling bore the marks of youth, not more than twenty-five years. They were placed in the cart which led them to Execution Dock without betraying those emotions natural to men in their unfortunate situation. Palm, soon as seated, put a quid of tobacco into his mouth, and offered another to his wretched companion, who refused it with indignation. Some indications of pity were offered for the fate of Tilling; Palm, execrations alone.

WILLIAM BROWN,
EXECUTED FOR THE MURDER OF A CHILD.

WILLIAM BROWN was a private in the royal artillery, and lived as servant with Lieutenant Webber. He bore a most exemplary character in the regiment; though, a short time before the commission of the crime for which he suffered, some articles were missing from his master's lodgings, which it was suspected he had stolen; and, as he got some intimation of the charge against him, he absented himself on the night of the 4th of April, 1812, from the barrack, and this circumstance seems to have led to the fatal deed.

The circumstances of the case were of an extraordinary nature. On the morning of the 5th, he returned to the barrack as early as between five and six, and called up a person of the name of Jeffecot, with whom he had lived. After some preliminary conversation, he told him he had committed a crime for which he must be hanged, and desired that he might be taken to the guard-house, where he was received by the sergeant-major. When in custody, he requested to speak with the sergeant in private. This being granted, he told him that, being walking in the country the preceding evening, he was going over a stile, which led into a lane, where a little girl was at play. The child, alarmed at his sudden appearance, cried, when he seized her in his arms, and with his finger and thumb strangled her. As soon as she was dead, he carried her under his arm to some distance, and then laid her on some stone steps which he described, and where the body was subsequently found, and, from the marks on its little throat, it was evidently killed as the monster described. The name of the child was Isabella M'Guire, aged seven years. Brown could ascribe no motive for the perpetration of the dreadful act, and, as he had no malice against the child, he could not tell how he came to do it. We are, therefore, either to suspect that he had a disposition habituated to cruelty, or was stimulated to the deed by temporary insanity; for human nature, thank God, is not altogether so sanguinary, as deliberately to shed innocent blood, without any provocation whatever.

For this offence he was indicted at Maidstone on the 7th of August, 1812, when he was found Guilty, and underwent, according to his sentence, the dreadful fiat of the law on the following Monday.

Bellingham shooting Mr. Perceval.

JOHN BELLINGHAM,

EXECUTED FOR THE MURDER OF THE RIGHT HON. MR. PERCEVAL.

THERE are some crimes linked to immortality by the very atrocity which accompanies them. The incendiary who 'fired the Ephesian fane' will live as long as literature endures; and, like Felton, who assassinated the Duke of Buckingham, the name of Bellingham is a subject of English history, made more conspicuous than his predecessor in guilt by the circumstances which attended the commission of his premeditated crime.

John Bellingham was brought up in a counting-house in London, and afterwards went to Archangel, where he lived three years with a Russian merchant. Having returned to his native country, he married an amiable young woman—a Miss Nevill, the daughter of a respectable merchant and ship-broker, who, at the time of Bellingham's union with his family, lived at Newry, but who subsequently removed to Dublin. Bellingham, being a man of activity and intelligence, was now employed by some northern merchants to pay another visit to Russia, on commercial affairs. This was in 1804, and he went accompanied by his wife. At Archangel he engaged in some transactions with the house of Dorbecker and Co.; and before the expiration of a twelvemonth a quarrel took place, when each party made a pecuniary claim upon the other. The subject was referred, by the governor-general, to the decision of four merchants, two of whom Bellingham was allowed to select from his countrymen resident at Archangel. By the award of these arbitrators Bellingham was found to be indebted to the house of Dorbecker and Co. in the sum of two thousand roubles; but this sum he refused to pay, and appealed to the senate against the decision.

In the mean time a criminal suit had been instituted against him, by the owners of a Russian ship which had been lost in the White Sea. They accused him of having written an anonymous letter to the underwriters in London, stating that the insurances of that ship were fraudulent transactions; in consequence of which the payment for her loss was resisted. No satisfactory proof being adduced, Bellingham was acquitted: but before the termination of the suit he attempted to quit Archangel; and being stopped by the police, whom he resisted, he was taken to prison; but was soon after liberated, through the influence of the British consul, Sir Stephen Shairp, to whom Bellingham had made application, requesting to be protected from what he considered the injustice of the Russian authorities.

Soon after this the senate confirmed the award of the arbitrators, and Bellingham was delivered over to the college of commerce, a tribunal established, and acknowledged by treaty, for taking cognizance of commercial matters relating to British subjects. He was to remain in custody till he discharged the debt of the two thousand roubles; but his confinement was by no means severe; for he had permission to walk wherever he pleased, attended by an officer belonging to the college. Lord G. L. Gower being at this time ambassador at the Russian Court, Bellingham made frequent application, and, at various times, received from his secretary small sums of money to support him during his confinement. One night, in particular, he rushed into his lordship's house at St. Petersburgh, and requested permission to remain all night, to avoid being retaken by the police, whom he had escaped. This was granted, although Lord Gower had no authority to protect him from a legal arrest. It appears he was afterwards retaken, and, being confined by the authorities of the country, the British ambassador could have no pretence to solicit his release. His lordship, however, in a conversation with the minister for foreign affairs, expressed a personal wish that the Russian government, seeing no prospect of recovering the money from Bellingham, would liberate him, on condition of his immediately returning to England. What effect this had we are not told, as Lord Gower soon after quitted the Russian court.

The foregoing is taken from the statement published by Lord Granville Leveson Gower, in his own justification, against the charge made against him by Bellingham on his trial. We hope, for the honour of our country, that this statement is correct; and we must confess that a review of all the circumstances tends to confirm its accuracy. Our ambassador, it is admitted, had the case investigated; and as his refusal to interfere was subsequently confirmed by that of the English government, it is evident that Bellingham must have had no just cause of complaint, or, at least, not of a nature that called for diplomatic negotiation or pecuniary recompense. In justice, however, to the unfortunate man, we shall, when we come to his trial, give his own statement, and leave the reader to draw his own conclusion.

Bellingham having, by some means or other, procured his liberation, returned to England, and at Liverpool commenced the business of an insurance-broker; and as his wife kept a milliner's shop, he might have done well, had not the Russian business impressed itself on his mind to that degree of fervency, that his friends regarded him, on this topic, as in a state of insanity. From continually talking of this affair he soon came to expect redress; and, having made application to the Marquis Wellesley, he was referred to the privy council, and from the privy council to the Treasury. Not receiving redress, he applied to the chancellor of the exchequer, who refused to support his claims. He was then advised to petition parliament; but, as it was too late in the session of 1811 to receive private petitions, he was obliged to have recourse to other remedies; and he accordingly, in the Christmas of this year, came to London, and memorialized his royal highness the prince regent, who referred it to the Treasury, from the secretary of which he received a letter, stating that he had nothing to expect from government.

This denial was subsequently repeated, in consequence of another memorial; and nothing shows more the delusion under which he laboured, on this business, than his persisting to seek redress for his real or imaginary grievances, after being repeatedly denied. On one occasion he carried his wife, who in vain endeavoured to divert him from his Russian malady, with another lady, to the secretary of state's office, for the purpose of convincing her that the business was in a train of settlement; and though he was there verbally informed that he had nothing to expect, he renewed, on their way home, the subject, and expressed his conviction of having all his losses made good in a very short time.

He continued in London from Christmas to March, prosecuting his claims; but being every way rejected, he had recourse to a novel mode of seeking redress, which was nothing less than soliciting the aid of the police. The following singular letter he transmitted to the magistrates of Bow Street:—

'*To their Worships the Police Magistrates of the Public Office, in Bow Street.*

'SIRS,—I much regret its being my lot to have to apply to your worships under most peculiar and novel circumstances.—For the particulars of the case, I refer to the enclosed letter of Mr. Secretary Ryder, the notification from Mr. Perceval, and my petition to parliament, together with the printed papers herewith. The affair requires no further remark, than that I consider his majesty's government to have completely endeavoured to close the door of justice, in declining to have, or even to permit, my grievances to be brought before parliament for redress, which privilege is the birthright of every individual. The purport of the present is, therefore, once more to solicit his majesty's ministers, through your medium, to let what is right and proper be done in my instance, which is all I require. Should this reasonable request be finally denied, I shall then feel justified in executing justice myself—in which case I shall be ready to argue the merits of so reluctant a measure with his majesty's attorney-general, wherever and whenever I may be called upon so to do. In the hopes of averting so abhorrent, but compulsive an alternative, I have the honour to be, Sirs, your very humble and obedient servant,

'JOHN BELLINGHAM.
'*No. 9, New Millman Street, March 23, 1812.*'

This letter was submitted to the government, but excited no alarm; and an answer was returned by Mr. Read, stating that the office could not interfere. This is the first intimation we have of the diabolical design which entered his head, and which he afterwards so fatally carried into execution. Once more he applied to the Treasury, and again was told he had nothing to expect, and that he might resort to whatever measures he thought fit. This he considered, as he expressed it, a *carte blanche* to take justice into his own hands; and as Mr. Perceval refused to sanction his application to parliament, he resolved to make him a sacrifice to his revenge, that he might thereby have an opportunity of arguing the merits of his case;—thinking, from an infatuation perfectly unaccountable, that his wrongs, or what he considered such, would be ample justification of so foul a deed; for all along he anticipated acquittal for the murder he premeditated, and afterwards committed.

This determination having unhappily entered his mind, he began to prepare for putting it into execution. He purchased a pair of pistols, powder, and a bullet-mould; had an additional pocket made for conveniently carrying them; and nightly took his stand in the lobby of the House of Commons, through which the members had to pass. On the 11th of May, 1812, he took his station, as usual, behind the folding door; and at five o'clock in the evening, as the Right Honorable Spencer Perceval, chancellor of the exchequer, passed in, Bellingham presented his pistol, and fired. The unfortunate gentleman received the ball in his left breast, which passed through his heart. He reeled to a short distance, and, exclaiming 'Oh, murder!' fell upon his face, and instantly expired. Loud cries of 'Shut the door, let no one out!' now resounded through the hall; and, when some one asked 'Where's the murderer?' Bellingham, who still held the pistol in his hand, answered 'I am the unfortunate man.' Being interrogated as to his motives for committing such an act, he replied 'Want of redress, and denial of justice.'

During the momentary confusion which followed the firing of the pistol, he made no attempt to escape; and though when taken into custody he betrayed some agitation, he soon recovered his self-possession, and with great calmness answered every question, and corrected one of the witnesses in an omission in his evidence against him. During his examination before the magistrates up stairs, in the House of Commons, he persisted in denying any personal enmity to Mr. Perceval, for whose death he expressed the greatest sorrow, separating, by a confusion of ideas, the man from the minister; and seemed to think he had not injured the individual, though he had taken away the life of the chancellor of the exchequer.

This event excited the greatest sensation. A cabinet council was called, and the mails were stopped, until instructions were prepared to secure tranquillity in the districts; for at first it was apprehended that the assassin was instigated by political motives, and that he was connected with some treasonable association.

Measures being provided for securing order through the country and the metropolis, Bellingham was removed, about one o'clock in the morning, to Newgate, and conducted to a room adjoining the chapel. One of the head turnkeys, and two other persons, sat up with him all night. He retired to bed soon after his arrival, but had no sound sleep during the night. He arose soon after seven o'clock, and requested some tea for breakfast, of which he took but little. No private persons were allowed to see him; but he was visited by the sheriffs, and a few other public characters. He conversed very cheerfully, and expressed no regret for the deed he had perpetrated, conceiving himself justified in what he had done, and did not seem to view it in a criminal light; for, he said, the government had given him a *carte blanche* to do his worst, which he had done.

Alderman Combe, one of the committing magistrates, in endeavouring to learn the habits and associates of Bellingham, called on the woman at whose house he lodged; but could learn nothing from her but that her lodger was a quiet inoffensive man, of a religious turn, and, though somewhat eccentric, a great favorite in the family. On being told of the deed he had perpetrated, she expressed her incredulity; for she had met him, a few minutes before five o'clock on the fatal evening, when he told her that he had just been buying a prayer-book.

The morning of his committal Bellingham wrote a letter to this woman; and as it exhibits the state of his mind, in his miserable situation, we shall give it entire.

' Tuesday Morning, Old Bailey.

' DEAR MADAM,—Yesterday midnight I was escorted to this neighbourhood by a noble troop of light horse, and delivered into the care of Mr. Newman, (by Mr. Taylor, the magistrate, and M. P.) as a state prisoner of the first class. For eight years I have never found my mind so tranquil as since this melancholy, but necessary, catastrophe. As the merits or demerits of my peculiar case must be regularly unfolded in a criminal court of justice, to ascertain the guilty party, by a jury of my country: I have to request the favour of you to send me three or four shirts, some cravats, handkerchiefs, night-caps, stockings, &c. out of my drawers, together with comb, soap, tooth-brush, with any other trifle that presents itself, which you think I may have occasion for, and enclose them in my leather trunk, and the key please to send sealed, per bearer; also my great coat, flannel gown, and black waistcoat, which will much oblige,

' Dear Madam,

' Your very obedient servant,

' JOHN BELLINGHAM.'

' To the above please to add the prayer-book.

' To Mrs. Roberts.'

At two o'clock he ate a hasty dinner, and requested to dine at the same hour in future. After passing the day in a tranquil manner, he retired to bed at twelve, slept till seven next morning, and breakfasted about nine. He appeared quite composed, talked with apparent indifference about his trial, and repeated his former statement. The sheriffs, with several other gentlemen, paid him another visit, and, entering on the subject of Mr. Perceval's death, Bellingham became less tranquil, vindicated the act, and declared that, had he a thousand lives to lose, they would not have prevented him from pursuing his object in the same way.

Notwithstanding the unpardonable crime for which he was about to be tried, he anticipated acquittal; and when asked by a friend if he had any commands for his wife, he said not, as in a day or two he should be himself in Liverpool.

On May the 15th, 1812, four days after the death of Mr. Perceval, came on, at the Old Bailey, the trial of this assassin. The judges, at ten o'clock, took their seats on each side of the lord-mayor; and the recorder, the Duke of Clarence, the Marquis Wellesley, and almost all the aldermen of the city of London, occupied the Bench. The court was crowded to excess, and no distinction of rank was observed; so that members of the House of Commons were forced to mingle in the throng. There were also present a great number of ladies, all led by the most intense curiosity to behold the assassin, and to hear what he might urge in defence or in palliation of his atrocious act.

At length Bellingham appeared, and advanced to the bar with a firm step, and quite undismayed. He bowed to the Court most respectfully, and even gracefully. The impression which his appearance made, accompanied by this unexpected fortitude, it is impossible to describe. A mute horror sat upon every countenance, while the miserable cause seemed unconscious of the effect he had produced. He was dressed in a light brown surtout coat, and striped yellow waistcoat; his hair plainly dressed, and without powder.

Before Bellingham was called on regularly to plead, Mr. Alley, his counsel, made application to have the trial postponed, for the purpose of procuring proofs of his client's insanity, which was alleged in two affidavits he held; and had no doubt, if time was allowed, that the prisoner could be proved insane. Mr. Alley was here interrupted, as the Court could not hear him until the prisoner had first pleaded.

When the indictment was read, the usual question, 'Guilty or not guilty?' was put to Bellingham, when he addressed the Court:—
'My lords,—Before I can plead to this indictment, I must state, in justice to myself, that by hurrying on my trial I am placed in a most remarkable situation. It so happens that my prosecutors are actually the witnesses against me. All the documents, on which alone I could rest my defence, have been taken from me, and are now in possession of the crown. It is only two days since I was told to prepare for my defence; and when I asked for my papers, I was told they could not be given up. It is, therefore, my lords, rendered utterly impossible for me to go into my justification; and, under the circumstances in which I find myself, a trial is absolutely useless. The papers are to be given to me after the trial, but how can that avail me for my defence? I am, therefore, not ready for my trial.'

The Court, however, insisted that he should plead to the indictment; and then, in a subdued tone of voice, he said 'Not guilty: I put myself upon God and my country.' The attorney-general then rose, in explanation of the papers, which he said should be given to the prisoner when he came to make his defence. Mr. Alley here rose, to urge his former plea for the postponement of the trial, but was overruled by the Court; and the jury being sworn, the trial proceeded. The evidence being gone through, Bellingham was called on for his defence; and understanding that his counsel could not speak for him, he demanded his papers, and, having arranged them, he addressed the Court in a speech of two hours' length. He began by thanking the attorney-general for opposing the defence set by his counsel, which went to prove that he was insane; but he expressed his obligations for the zeal shown by his counsel, and their intention in setting up such a plea at the desire of his friends. He then spoke nearly as follows:—

'I beg to assure you that the crime which I have committed has arisen from compulsion rather than from any hostility to the man whom it has been my fate to destroy. Considering the amiable character and universally admitted virtues of Mr. Perceval, I feel, if I could murder him in a cool and unjustifiable manner, I should not deserve to live another moment in this world. Conscious, however, that I shall be able to justify every thing which I have done, I feel some degree of confidence in meeting the storm which assails me, and shall now proceed to unfold a catalogue of circumstances which, while they harrow up my own soul, will, I am sure, tend to the extenuation of my conduct in this honorable court. This, as has already been candidly stated by the attorney-general, is the first instance in which any the slightest imputation has been cast upon my moral character. Until this fatal catastrophe, which no one can more heartily regret than I do, not excepting even the family of Mr. Perceval himself, I have stood alike pure in the minds of those who have known me, and in the judgment of my own heart. I hope I see this affair in the true light. For eight years, gentlemen of the jury, have I been exposed to all the miseries which it is possible for human nature to endure.—Driven almost to despair, I sought for redress in vain. For this affair I had the *carte blanche* of government, as I will prove by the most incontestable evidence, namely, the writing of the secretary of state himself. I come before you under peculiar disadvantages. Many of my most material papers are now at Liverpool, for which I have written, but have been called upon my trial before it was possible to obtain an answer to my letter.—Without witnesses, therefore, and in the absence of many papers necessary to my justification, I am sure you will admit I have just grounds for claiming some indulgence. I must state that, after my return from my voyage to Archangel, I transmitted to his royal highness the prince regent, through my solicitor, Mr. Windle, a petition; and, in consequence of there being no reply, I came to London to see the result. Surprised at the delay, and conceiving that the interests of my country were at stake, I considered this step as essential, as well for the assertion of my own right, as for the vindication of the national honour. I waited upon Colonel M'Mahon, who stated that my petition had been received; but, owing to some accident, had been mislaid. Under these circumstances, I drew out another account of the particulars of the Russian affair, and this may be considered the commencement of that train of events, which led to the afflicting and unhappy fate of Mr. Perceval.'

He then read various documents, containing a statement of the whole of his affairs in Russia; and, in the course of narrating these hardships, took occasion to explain several points, adverting, with great feeling, to the unhappy situation in which he was placed, from the circumstance of his having been but lately married to his wife, then about twenty years of age, with an infant at her breast, and who had been waiting for him at St. Petersburgh, in order that she might accompany him to England—a prey to all those anxieties which the unexpected and cruel incarceration of her husband, without any just grounds, was calculated to excite.—He also described his feelings at a subsequent period, when his wife, from an anxiety to reach her native country (England) when in a state of pregnancy, and looking to the improbability of his liberation, was obliged to quit Petersburgh unprotected, and undertake the voyage at the peril of her life; while Lord L. Gower and Sir S. Shairp suffered him to remain in a situation worse than death. 'My God! my God!' he exclaimed, 'what heart could bear such excruciating tortures, without bursting with indignation at conduct so diametrically opposite to justice and to humanity. I appeal to you, gentlemen of the jury, as men—I appeal to you as brothers—I appeal to you as Christians—when, under such circumstances of persecution, it was possible to regard the actions of the ambassador and consul of my own country with any other feelings but those of detestation and horror! In using language thus strong, I feel that I commit an error; yet does my heart tell me, that towards men who lent themselves thus to bolster up the basest acts of persecution, there are no observations, however strong, which the strict justice of the case would not excuse my using. Had I been so fortunate as to have met Lord Levison Gower instead of that truly amiable and highly lamented individual, Mr. Perceval, he is the man who should have received the ball!'

After reading several other papers, he thus proceeded:—' If, whenever I am called before the tribunal of God, I can appear with as clear a conscience as I now possess, in regard to the alleged charge of the wilful murder of the unfortunate gentleman, the investigation of whose death has occupied your attention, it would be happy for me, as essentially securing to me eternal salvation;—but that is impossible. That my arm has been the means of his melancholy and lamented exit, I am ready to allow. But, to constitute murder, it must clearly and absolutely be proved to have arisen from malice prepense, and with a malicious design, as I have no doubt the learned judge will shortly lay down, in explaining the law on the subject. If such is the case, I am guilty—if not, I look forward with confidence to your acquittal.

'That the contrary is the case has been most clearly and irrefutably proved; no doubt can rest upon your minds, as my uniform and undeviating object has been an endeavour to obtain justice, according to law, for a series of the most long-continued and unmerited sufferings that were ever submitted to a court of law, without having been guilty of any other crime than an appeal for redress for a most flagrant injury offered to my sovereign and my country, wherein my liberty and property have fallen a sacrifice for the continued period of eight years, to the total ruin of myself and family (with authenticated documents of the truth of the allegations), merely because it was Mr. Perceval's pleasure that justice should not be granted, sheltering himself with the idea of there being no alternative remaining, as my petition to parliament for redress could not be brought (as having a pecuniary tendency) without the sanction of his majesty's ministers, and that he was determined to oppose, by trampling both on law and right.

'Gentlemen, where a man has so strong and serious a criminal case to bring forward as mine has been, the nature of which was purely national, it is the bounden duty of government to attend to it; for justice is a matter of right, and not of favour. And when a minister is so unprincipled and presumptuous at any time, but especially in a case of such urgent necessity, as to set himself above both the sovereign and the laws, as has been the case with Mr. Perceval, he must do it at his personal risk; for by the law he cannot be protected.

'Gentlemen, if this is not fact, the mere will of a minister would be law; it would be this thing to-day and the other to-morrow, as either interest or caprice might dictate.—What would become of our liberties? where would be the purity and the impartiality of the justice we so much boast of?—To government's non-attendance to the dictates of justice is solely to be attributed the melancholy catastrophe of the unfortunate gentleman, as any malicious intention to his injury was the most remote from my heart. Justice, and justice only, was my object, which government uniformly objected to grant; and the distress it reduced me to drove me to despair in consequence; and, purely for the purpose of having this singular affair legally investigated, I gave notice at the Public Office, Bow Street, requesting the magistrates to acquaint his majesty's ministers, that if they persisted in refusing justice, or even to permit me to bring my just petition into parliament for redress, I should be under the imperious necessity of executing justice myself, solely for the purpose of ascertaining, through a criminal court, whether his majesty's ministers have the power to refuse justice to a well-authenticated and irrefutable act of oppression, committed by the consul and ambassador abroad, whereby my sovereign's and country's honour were materially tarnished, by my person endeavoring to be made the stalking-horse of justification, to one of the greatest insults that could be offered to the Crown.

'But, in order to avoid so reluctant and abhorrent an alternative, I hoped to be allowed to bring my petition to the House of Commons —or that they would do what was right and proper themselves.

'On my return home from Russia, I brought most serious charges to the privy council, both against Sir Stephen Shairp and Lord Granville Levison Gower, when the affair was determined to be purely national, and consequently it was the duty of his majesty's ministers to arraign it by acting on the resolution of the council. Suppose, for instance, the charge I brought could have been proved to be erroneous, should I not have been called to a severe account for my conduct? but, being true, ought I not to have been redressed?

'After the notice from the police to government, Mr. Ryder, conscious of the truth and cruelty of the case, transmitted the affair to the Treasury, referring me there for a final result. After a delay of some weeks the Treasury came to the resolution of sending the affair back to the secretary of state's office; at the same time I was told by a Mr. Hill, he thought it would be useless my making further application to government, and that I was at liberty to take such measures as I thought proper for redress.

'Mr. Beckett, the under secretary of state, confirmed the same, adding that Mr. Perceval had been consulted, and could not allow my petition to come forward. Thus, by a direct refusal of justice, with a *carte blanche*, to act in whatever manner I thought proper, were the sole causes of the fatal catastrophe —and they have now to reflect on their own impure conduct for what has happened.

'It is a melancholy fact, that the warping of justice, including all the various ramifications in which it operates, occasions more misery in the world, in a moral sense, than all the acts of God in a physical one, with which he punishes mankind for their transgressions; a confirmation of which, the single, but strong, instance before you is one remarkable proof.

'If a poor unfortunate man stops another upon the highway, and robs him of but a few shillings, he may be called upon to forfeit his life. But I have been robbed of my liberty for years, ill treated beyond precedent, torn from my wife and family, bereaved of all my property to make good the consequences of such irregularities, deprived and bereaved of every thing that makes life valuable, and then called upon to forfeit it, because Mr. Perceval has been pleased to patronize iniquity that ought to have been punished, for the sake of a vote or two in the House of Commons, with, perhaps, a similar good turn elsewhere.

'Is there, gentlemen, any comparison between the enormity of these two offenders? No more than a mite to a mountain. Yet the one is carried to the gallows, while the other stalks in security, fancying himself beyond the reach of law or justice: the most honest man suffers, while the other goes forward in triumph to new and more extended enormities.

'We have had a recent and striking instance of some unfortunate men, who have been called upon to pay their lives as the forfeit of their allegiance, in endeavoring to mitigate the rigours of a prison.—(Alluding to the trials of Cundell and others, for high treason, at Horsemonger Lane,)— But, gentlemen, where is the proportion between the crimes for which they suffered, and what government has been guilty of, in withholding its protection from me? Even in a Crown case, after the years of sufferings, I have been called upon to sacrifice all my property, and the welfare of my family, to bolster up the iniquities of the Crown, and then am prosecuted for my life, because I have taken the only possible alternative to bring the affair to a public investigation, for the purpose of being enabled to return to the bosom of my family with some degree of comfort and honour. Every man within the sound of my voice must feel for my situation; but by you, gentlemen of the jury, it must be felt in a peculiar degree, who are husbands and fathers, and can fancy yourselves in my situation.—I trust that this serious lesson will operate as a warning to all future ministers, and lead them to do the thing that is right, as an unerring rule of conduct; for, if the superior classes were more correct in their proceedings, the extensive ramifications of evil would, in a great measure, be hemmed up—and a notable proof of the fact is, that this Court would never have been troubled with the case before it, had their conduct been guided by these principles.

'I have now occupied the attention of the Court for a period much longer than I intended; yet, I trust, they will consider the awfulness of my situation to be a sufficient ground for a trespass, which, under other circumstances, would be inexcusable. Sooner than suffer what I have suffered for the last eight years, however, I should consider five hundred deaths, if it were possible for human nature to endure them, a fate far more preferable. Lost so long to all the endearments of my family, bereaved of all the blessings of life, and deprived of its greatest sweet, liberty, as the weary traveller, who has long been pelted by the pitiless storm, welcomes the much-desired inn, I shall receive death as the relief of all my sorrows. I shall not occupy your attention longer; but, relying on the justice of God, and submitting myself to the dictates of your consciences, I submit to the fiat of my fate, firmly anticipating an acquittal from a charge so abhorrent to every feeling of my soul.'

Here the prisoner bowed, and his counsel immediately called several witnesses, who deposed to their belief in his insanity: but as he always conducted his own affairs, and was never under restraint, this defence could not legally avail, and the judge having charged the jury, a verdict of Guilty was returned. The Recorder then passed on him the awful sentence of the law, and he was ordered for execution on Monday, and his body to be anatomized—a sentence which Bellingham heard with the utmost composure.

The trial lasted eight hours. The Horse Guards were stationed near Blackfriars' Bridge during that period, ready to act in preservation of order, if called on. Other precautions were taken in the city; but, happily, the public peace remained undisturbed; and this assassin was tried and condemned, to the satisfaction of the friends of justice, without creating any emotion throughout the kingdom.

Bellingham, from his condemnation, was fed upon bread and water. All means of suicide were removed, and he was not allowed to be shaved; a prohibition which gave him much concern, as he feared he should not appear as a gentleman. He was visited by the Ordinary on Saturday, and some religious gentlemen called on him on Sunday, with whose conversation he seemed greatly pleased. He appeared naturally depressed by his situation; but persisted in a resolute denial of any guilt in his crime. He frequently said that he had prepared himself to go to his Father, and that he should be pleased when the hour arrived. He seemed to rejoice as the fatal hour drew nearer, and, on Sunday morning, received the sacrament with great devotion, making the responses in an audible and correct manner.

Being informed, by Mr. Newman, that two gentlemen from Liverpool had called, and left word that his wife and children would be provided for, he seemed but little affected; but, having requested pen, ink, and paper, he wrote the following letter to his wife:—

'My blessed Mary,—It rejoiced me beyond measure to hear you are likely to be well provided for. I am sure the public at large will participate in, and mitigate, your sorrows; I assure you, my love, my sincerest endeavours have ever been directed to your welfare.—As we shall not meet any more in this world, I sincerely hope we shall do so in the world to come. My blessing to the boys, with kind remembrance to Miss Stephens, for whom I have the greatest regard, in consequence of her uniform affection for them. With the purest intentions, it has always been my misfortune to be thwarted, misrepresented, and ill-used in life; but, however, we feel a happy prospect of compensation in a speedy translation to life eternal.—It's not possible to be more calm or placid than I feel, and nine hours more will waft me to those happy shores where bliss is without alloy. Your's ever affectionate,—'JOHN BELLINGHAM.'

That this man was afflicted with a strange malady, which occasionally rendered him incapable of correct conclusions, must be evident from the following note, which he wrote the night preceding his execution:—'I lost my suit solely through the improper conduct of my attorney and counsel, Mr. Alley, in not bringing my witnesses forward, (of which there were more than twenty): in consequence, the judge took advantage of the circumstance, and I went of [on] the defence without having brought forward a single friend—otherwise I must inevitably have been acquitted.'

On Monday morning, at the usual hour, the execution took place, in the accustomed manner, and unattended by any circumstance distinguishing it from similar exhibitions. In all the conversations he had with the Ordinary, Dr. Ford, Bellingham, so far from exhibiting any thing like contrition, continued to glory in the act for which he was about to suffer. He talked incessantly of the non-redress of his alleged grievances, nor would he listen to any of the suggestions of Dr. Ford on the impossibility of any government interfering to prevent the regular course of the laws in another country. He constantly wound up his answers by expressing a hope that the fate of Mr. Perceval would prove a warning to men in power not to neglect the claims of injured individuals, and he continued to the last to exult in the success of his efforts to revenge his own injuries.

Bellingham was, in his person, tall and raw-boned, with a thin long visage, and aquiline nose: his eyes were sunken and his complexion sallow. His age was forty-two; and, as he was grossly misrepresented at the time of his committing the horrid act, we think it but justice, revolting as was his turpitude, to state that his widow and friends all bear testimony that his general character was that of strict integrity—a kind husband and father—loyal in his political opinions—and punctual in the observance of religious duties; and the whole tenor of his life, with the exception of the Russian affair, on which it was supposed he was insane, proves him to have been a well-intentioned man. It may not be unnecessary to observe, in reference to the effect which he supposed might be produced by the death of Mr. Perceval—that other ministers would pay more attention to the complaints of oppressed individuals, we must express a hope that his fate will operate as a warning to others, not to cherish and ripen in their bosoms the seeds of hatred and vengeance, till they grow up and break forth in acts of bloodshed and murder.

ROBERT TOWERS,

IMPRISONED FOR ENDEAVOURING TO BRIBE A TURNKEY OF NEWGATE.

There is something in the human breast which endures us to favour the efforts of mistaken generosity, and disposes us to regard with forgiveness those departures from rigid justice which take place in behalf of friendship. The following case is one of those where justice is opposed to feeling; and, though we do not find fault with the sentence, we cannot refuse our sympathy to the sufferer.

Robert Towers was a warm-hearted sailor who felt acutely, and whose actions emanated from his feelings. Allied by blood and friendship to the unfortunate George Skene, whose case we have already given, he forgot his crime in the contemplation of the punishment that awaited his offence; and, with a precipitancy that did more honour to his heart than his head, he meditated effecting the escape of his friend from Newgate, about a fortnight after his committal.

For this purpose he invited a turnkey, named Samuel Davis, to drink with him. They went to the New Inn, where Towers inquired of Davis what family he had; and then hinted that it was in his power to procure for himself the means of making them all comfortable for life. Davis, thinking that the favour required of him related to Mr. Skene's accommodation, promised to do every thing in his power; but this not amounting to Towers's expectations, he gave him clearly to understand that he expected nothing less than Mr. Skene's escape, promising to release Davis from the necessity of continuing turnkey, and that his reward should be paid, not in bank-notes, but in gold. The turnkey refusing to accede to these terms, nothing further passed until Mr. Towers's next visit to his friend, when Mr. Newman called him into a private room, and confronted him with Davis, who had told his employer what had passed.—Towers did not deny the charge; but contented himself with stating that he offered Davis no specific sum.

Mr. Towers was now taken into custody, and brought to trial at the Old Bailey, April the 6th, 1812, when, the charge being proved, he was found Guilty, and sentenced to pay a fine of fifty pounds, and be imprisoned for twelve calendar months in the gaol of Newgate.

WILLIAM BOOTH,
EXECUTED FOR FORGERY.

THIS malefactor was not impelled by poverty or distress to the commission of the crime for which he lost his life. He lived near Birmingham, and occupied two hundred acres of land; but, being desirous of acquiring wealth by speedier means than the produce of honest industry afforded, he resorted to the culpable and dangerous practice of fabricating notes, purporting to be of the Bank of England. Unlike other criminals, he was not seduced into the act by design or ignorance; he entered upon it with the full knowledge of the consequence of detection; and, as he knew that no device or stratagem could evade discovery, he resolved to bid defiance to the minions of law, and oppose force to force.

For this purpose he had his house barricaded, the windows secured by strong iron bars, and the approach to the place of illegal manufacture secured by three doors, well and studiously fastened with bolts, &c.

Thus shut up, as he thought, in his impregnable fortress, he considered himself out of danger; but all his precaution could not avail. It was discovered that he had issued forged notes to a large amount, and the police of Birmingham were on the alert to apprehend him. For a while he kept them at defiance; but, at length, the whole posse laid regular siege to his invulnerable castle. Various modes were devised for gaining admittance; but all proved fruitless, until one of the constables procured a ladder, which reached to one of the upper windows. As he was ascending he saw Booth run to the middle of a room over the parlour, and take some papers, of the size of bank-notes, from a rolling-press, and put them into the fire. By breaking open the attic window the constable procured an entrance, through which he was followed by several of his comrades. The interior of the house displayed not less industry to baffle assailants than the exterior. Trap-doors were ingeniously contrived for opposing an enemy or facilitating escape; but the activity of the officers of justice rendered all his precautions of no avail. They jumped through one trap-door while Booth was escaping by another; and, having pursued him from concealment to concealment he was apprehended. Part of the papers were taken out of the fire, and found to have the Bank mark in them.

Booth was fully committed for trial, and a workman of his, being apprehended, gave information of a trunk of forged notes, which he had buried by his master's orders. These were produced on his trial, which took place at the Stafford assizes, and along with other corroborating circumstances established his guilt to the satisfaction of the jury, and he was sentenced to be hanged.

The 15th of August, 1812, was the day appointed for the final suffering of this unfortunate man. A most distressing occurrence took place at the time of his execution—the rope slipping, he fell to the ground, and many people thought that he was dead; but he got up, and fell upon his knees, praying to the Almighty for mercy. The scaffold was again prepared; but, owing to a mistake the drop remained fast when Booth gave the signal for it to fall; and it was not until much force was applied that it gave way, and the miserable criminal was launched into eternity.

THOMAS NUGENT, & JOHN & WILLIAM FOLKARD,
PILLORED FOR ATTEMPTING TO DEFRAUD THE CREDITORS OF JOHN FOLKARD.

Among all the frauds of London none are more frequent, or more extensive, than those practised by dishonest bankrupts on their unsuspicious creditors.

John Folkard carried on business, as a silversmith and jeweller, in the Surrey Road, between four and five years, and was in good credit; a character he might have retained, had he not entered into a scheme for enriching himself by speedier means than the profits of his business afforded. He became acquainted with a money-lender, named Thomas Nugent, and, in conjunction with him, and his own brother, William Folkard, he resolved to become a bankrupt; but, that he might do so advantageously, they fabricated bills, purporting to be drawn on them by different men, whom they got to swear to their fictitious debts for a few shillings. Debts, too, were entered on the books, pretended to be due by men either no longer in existence, or no longer in the country; and, when all things were prepared, John Folkard's name appeared in the Gazette, to the great astonishment of his creditors. His object was to take them by surprise, and to have one of his friends appointed assignee before they were aware of his design.

From some circumstances of a suspicious nature, the *bona fide* creditors saw it was necessary to unite, and get some of themselves chosen assignee, instead of those proposed by the bankrupt. After a severe struggle they were successful, and Messrs. Powis, Hemming, and Taylor, were chosen. On inspecting the list of debts, several appeared fictitious. One man, who was described as a bullion-dealer on Ludgate Hill, whose debt appeared to be one hundred and thirty-eight pounds, was no where to be found, and many others, with demands equally as large, were only just emerged from prison, through the mercy of the Insolvent Act, and, so far from being able to lend money, were objects of charity.

The assignees waiting on these people, and insisting on having the particulars of their accounts, under the threat of prosecution, so alarmed a woman, who called herself Baroness Minkwitz, that she disclosed the premeditated fraud.

In consequence of her testimony Thomas Nugent and the two brothers were taken into custody. On Friday, September the 25th, 1812, their trial came on at the Old Bailey, when the whole transaction was satisfactorily proved by parties concerned, and numerous corroborating facts. After an investigation of ten hours they were found Guilty, and the Common Sergeant sentenced John Folkard to be imprisoned two years, and stand twice in the pillory; Thomas Nugent to be imprisoned eighteen months, and stand once in the pillory; and William Folkard to be imprisoned one year, and to stand once in the pillory.

JOHN DAVISON, ESQ.
TRANSPORTED FOR FELONIOUSLY STEALING.

THE station of life of this offender, a captain in the royal marines, and his being twice brought before our notice, give him some notoriety. He was first indicted on the 13th of November, 1810, at the assizes for the county of Somerset, for stealing a piece of muslin, value thirty shillings, the property of James Bunter, mercer, of Taunton.

The counsel for the prosecution stated that the facts were few and short, but cogent and irresistible. Alexander Baller, apprentice to Mr. Bunter, deposed that Captain Davison came to his master's house on the 25th July, when he alone was in the shop, and asked to look at some muslins he had seen the night before. After looking at them some time he went towards the door; but, before that, he had thrown his handkerchief upon four or five of the pieces, which he had folded up: he then sat down in a chair rather below where the muslin was, and asked to look at some stockings; there was at this time a piece under his handkerchief, and, whilst taking out some stockings, the witness observed him draw his handkerchief from the counter into his lap with both his hands, the muslin being still under the handkerchief. He then asked for some fashionable waistcoat patterns, and took up the handkerchief and squeezed it together, put it under his coat, and walked out of the shop. On searching the captain's lodgings, the piece of muslin was found, and clearly identified.

Several persons of the first respectability gave the prisoner an excellent character.

The judge told the jury, however they might lament that a gentleman of the prisoner's condition in life, who had borne so honourable a character till the present time, should on this occasion have forfeited that character, that it was their duty, if they were satisfied with the evidence they had heard, to find him guilty, however painful the discharge of that duty might be. In cases where a fair doubt could be entertained, character ought to have considerable weight with a jury; but where the facts were clear, and established by credible witnesses, however good the character of the prisoner might have been up to the time of committing the felony, it was no excuse for the commission of it. And unless they could say that the prisoner, at the time of drawing the handkerchief from the counter with both his hands, as the witness Baller stated, was ignorant that the muslin was contained in it, he did not know how to state to them a ground of doubt; the muslin, as they saw, was of considerable bulk, and not likely to be contained in a silk handkerchief, without its being perceived by the prisoner; and if they thought so, it was their duty to say that he was guilty.

The jury, after a few seconds' consideration, returned a verdict of Guilty, and he was sentenced to transportation for seven years; but was afterwards pardoned on condition of quitting the country for that period.

The base are never honourable. This malefactor continued, contrary to promise, in England, and had recourse to a practice more highly criminal than even stealing; for he was convicted at Oxford, on the 18th January, 1813, for having in his custody one ten-pound, two five-pound, and two one-pound, forged Bank of England notes, without being able to assign or prove any lawful cause or excuse. He was charged with the offence at Birmingham, but escaped, and was pursued to Oxford, where they traced him to the Cross Inn, and took him into custody. On searching him, they found the forged notes wrapped up in a brown paper parcel, with two blank forged Leicester bank-notes for one pound each, not filled up or signed; and also several counterfeit three-shilling tokens.

The charges being satisfactorily proved, the Court sentenced him to transportation for fourteen years.

THE LUDDITES,
GUILTY OF RIOTING AND ADMINISTERING UNLAWFUL OATHS.

The cotton manufacturers of Nottinghamshire, Derbyshire, Leicestershire, and some parts of Yorkshire, having suffered under a considerable reduction of wages and scarcity of work, which they attributed to the very extensive introduction of machinery, associated in such numbers for the destruction of frames and looms, and the annoyance of those manufacturers who had been most forward in introducing the machines, that those counties became the seat of the most serious tumults, not unattended with murder. They pretended to be followers of a leader whom they called General Ludd, and hence arose the term Luddites. A considerable number of those misguided men were at length brought to condign punishment.

A special commission was issued for their trial, and was opened by Baron Thompson at the city of York, on Monday the 4th January, 1813, in a most impressive charge to the grand jury.

On Tuesday, the 5th, the business of the Court commenced with the trial of John Swallow, John Batley, Joseph Fletcher, and John Lamb, for a burglary and felony in the house of Mr. Samuel Moxon, at Whitley Upper: the jury pronounced them all Guilty.

Throughout the whole of these important trials the evidence was nearly to the same effect—administering unlawful oaths—riotously assembling

—destroying the frames and looms of manufacturers of cloth—breaking into houses—robbery, and murder. We shall, however, proceed more particularly to state the cases marked with blood.

On Wednesday, George Mellor, of Longroyd Bridge, William Thorp, and Thomas Smith of Huddersfield, were indicted for the wilful murder of William Horsfall, of Marsden, merchant and manufacturer, at Lockwood, in the West Riding of the county of York.

It appeared from the evidence of John Armitage, who kept a public house at Crossland Moor, called the Warren House, that Mr. Horsfall had, on the 28th of April, been at Huddersfield market, and on his return called at witness's house about a quarter past six in the evening, and got a glass of rum and water, treated two persons who were there, paid his reckoning, and rode away:—did not stop twenty minutes at witness's; nor did he get off his horse. Between witness's house and Marsden, there is a plantation belonging to Mr. Ratcliffe, and about a quarter of a mile from Warren House. About seven o'clock, witness heard that Mr. Horsfall had been shot. Witness and the two persons whom the deceased had been treating went out together, and found Mr. Horsfall about twenty or thirty yards below the plantation, sitting on the road-side, bleeding very much. They got him down to Warren House as soon as they could. Mr. Horsfall died there.

Henry Parr was at Huddersfield on the 28th of April last; was upon the road between Huddersfield and Marsden; and, after he had passed the Warren House, heard the report of fire-arms—saw a person riding before him — report seemed to come from Mr. Ratcliffe's plantation—saw smoke arising at the same time, and four persons were in the plantation in dark-coloured clothes; the person who was before witness on horseback, after the report, fell down on the horse's chine, and the horse turned round as quick as possible; Mr. Horsfall raised himself by the horse's mane, and called 'Murder!' As soon as he called out murder, one of the four men got on the wall with one hand and two feet, and Parr called out, 'Have you got enough yet?' and he (Parr) set off to Mr. Horsfall at full gallop. Mr. H. said, 'Good man, you are a stranger to me; I'm shot.' Mr. Horsfall grew sick, and blood began to flow from his side. Mr. H. desired witness to go to Mrs. Horsfall's.

Bannister, a clothier, met Parr on the road, who told witness that Mr. Horsfall was shot. Witness found Mr. H. on the road-side very bloody.

Mr. Horton, surgeon, gave his testimony professionally. He extracted a ball from the deceased, and found several wounds in his body, and had no doubt they were the cause of his death.

Benjamin Walker, an accomplice, stated that the prisoners, George Mellor and Thomas Smith, worked with him at Wood's; and, in a conversation about the attack on Mr. Cartwright's mill, Mellor said there was no way to break the shears—but shoot the master. Mellor had a loaded pistol, and said he must go with him to shoot Mr. Horsfall. The pistol was loaded. Witness and the three prisoners went to the plantation. Smith and Walker went together, and got to the plantation first—Thorp and Mellor came afterwards. George Mellor ordered witness and Smith to fire, if they missed Mr. Horsfall; witness did not fire, but heard Mellor say Mr. Horsfall was coming, and soon after heard the report of a pistol; they waited at a short distance till the job was done.

The prisoners attempted to prove an *alibi*.

The jury withdrew about twenty minutes, and returned a verdict of Guilty against all the prisoners.

On Friday these wretched men were brought to the place of execution, behind the Castle at York. Every precaution had been taken to render a rescue impracticable. Two troops of cavalry were drawn up near the front of the platform, and the avenues to the Castle were guarded by infantry.

A few minutes before nine o'clock the prisoners came upon the platform. After the Ordinary had read the accustomed forms of prayer, George Mellor prayed for about ten minutes. William Thorp also prayed; but his voice was not so well heard. Smith said but little, but seemed to join in the devotions with great seriousness.

The prisoners were then moved to the front of the platform; and, after saying a few words, the executioner proceeded to perform his fatal office, and the drop fell.

On the 8th John Baines the elder, John Baines the younger, Zachary Baines, of the same family, the elder near seventy years of age, and the latter scarce sixteen, John Eadon, Charles Milnes, William Blakeborough, and George Duckworth, all of Halifax, were tried for administering an unlawful oath to John Macdonald; and all, except the boy, were found Guilty.

On the 9th January, James Haigh, of Dalton, Jonathan Deane, of Huddersfield, John Ogden, James Brook, Thomas Brook, John Walker, of Longroyd Bridge, and John Hirst, of Liversedge, were tried for attacking the mill of Mr. William Cartwright, at Rawfolds. Mr. C. being apprehensive of an attack being made upon his mill, procured the assistance of five soldiers, and retired to rest about twelve o'clock, and soon afterwards heard the barking of a dog. Mr. C. arose; and, while opening the door, heard a breaking of windows, and also a firing in the upper and lower windows, and a violent hammering at the door. Mr. C. and his men flew to their arms; a bell placed at the top of the mill, for the purpose of alarming the neighbours, being rung by one of his men, the persons inside the mill discharged their pieces from loop-holes. The fire was returned regularly on both sides. The mob called, 'Bang up, lads! in with you! keep close! damn that bell! get to it! damn 'em, kill 'em all!' The numbers assembled were considerable. The attack continued about twenty minutes. The fire slackened from without; and they heard the cries of the wounded. The men that were wounded were taken care of. They afterwards died. One of the accomplices, W. Hall, was one of those connected with Mellor and Thorp, and assembled with many other persons, by the desire of Mellor, in a field belonging to Sir George Armitage, Bart. on the night of the 11th of April. They called their numbers, remained there some time, and then marched off: Hall's number was seven. Mellor commanded the musket company, another the pistol company, and another the hatchet company: they were formed in lines of ten each. Two of the men were to go last, and drive up the rear.— Some had hatchets, some hammers, some sticks, and others had nothing.

Another accomplice gave a similar testimony.

The jury found James Haigh, J.

Dean, John Ogden, Thomas Brook, and John Walker, Guilty—James Brook, John Brook, and John Hirst, Not Guilty.

Jan. 11.—J. Hay, John Hill, and William Hartley, were next tried, for a burglary in the house of Mr. George Haigh, of Sculcoates; and found Guilty.

On Thursday the grand jury, after stating they had no more bills before them, inquired if any more were prepared.—Mr. Parke said—'I shall, with leave of the Court, answer the question put by the grand jury.' Their lordships intimated assent, and Mr. Parke proceeded:—' My learned friends and myself have examined the different cases which have been presented to you; and, considering that many of these people have acted under the influence of other persons, we have, in the exercise of that discretion confided to us by the Crown, declined, at present, to present any other bills before you; and I hope this lenity will produce its proper effects, and that the persons on whom it is exercised will prove themselves, by their future good conduct, deserving of it. But, if it be abused, proceedings against them can be resumed.'

Jan. 12.—James Hay, Joseph Crowther, and N. Hayle, were found guilty of taking from James Brook a promissory note of one pound, and some silver and copper coin.

Several prisoners were, through the lenity of government, admitted to bail, on their entering into recognizances, the prisoners in two hundred pounds each, and their bail in one hundred pounds each.

Mr. Baron Thompson then passed sentence on the prisoners.—Ffteen were sentenced to death; six to be transported for seven years; sixteen were discharged on bail; and sixteen were discharged without bail.

On Satuardy the following malefactors convicted before mentioned were also brought to the same place of execution, at different times, viz. at eleven in the forenoon, John Hill, Joseph Crowther, N. Hayle, Jonathan Dean, John Ogden, Thomas Brook, and John Walker, were placed upon the scaffold. Many of them, after the clergyman had repeated 'The Lord have mercy upon you!' in a very audible voice articulated 'I hope he will.' The bodies, after hanging till twelve o'clock, were then cut down.

At half past one o'clock, John Swallow, John Batley, Joseph Fisher, William Hartley, James Haigh, James Hey, and Job Hay, were also executed. The conduct of the prisoners was becoming their awful situation.

HUFFUM (ALIAS HUFFEY) WHITE, AND RICHARD KENDALL,

EXECUTED FOR ROBBING THE MAIL.

HUFFEY WHITE was a more expert and notorious housebreaker, and perpetrated more adroit burglaries, than any malefactor who has suffered during the last fifty years. He was totally illiterate, yet contrived to convey information to his wife by means of holographs, which could not be deciphered by any, but the initiated. When in prison he drew a hand manacled with iron; and when conviction was likely to follow, he portrayed a gallows: similar designs gave his accomplices, when at a distance, notice of his various proceedings; and thus his ingenuity obviated the defects of his education.

In 1809 he was sentenced, for a burglary, to transportation for life, preparatory to which he was sent on board the hulks at Woolwich. Not liking the treatment he experienced there, he contrived to make his escape, and once more visited the scenes of his former crimes in London. At this time he became acquainted with the notorious Jem Mackcoull, whose case we shall hereafter give, and agreed to accompany him to Chester, for the purpose of robbing the bank there.

White lodged in the house of a blacksmith, named Scottock, who supplied him with the necessary implements. The pair of villains, having directed the smith to forward them the keys, &c. to Chester, set off for that place early in 1810; and, having made their observations, called at the coach-office for the box of implements. Fortunately the friction of the coach had broken one corner of the box, through which a skeleton key suspiciously obtruded. An officer was sent for, and, being concealed when White and Mackcoull came to demand the box, he secured them both, on which they were committed to the house of correction as rogues and vagabonds.

Mackcoull went by the name of Martin, and White assumed that of Evans; but a description of their persons being transmitted to Bow Street, an officer was sent for, who quickly recognised them both. White was brought to trial at the next assizes, and received sentence of death, for being at large before the expiration of his period of transportation; but this sentence was afterwards commuted to transportation for life, and he was once more sent to his former station in the hulks, Mackcoull remaining in Chester gaol, to which he was sentenced six months for being a rogue and a vagabond.

At the expiration of six months Mackcoull returned to London, and, agreeing with one French to rob the Glasgow bank, they wished for the assistance of Huffey White, and actually contrived to liberate him from the hulks, after which they set off for Scotland. For the particulars of the robbery which they committed there we must refer the reader to the case of Mackcoull; it being only necessary to state here that the amount of their booty was the enormous sum of twenty thousand pounds.

Immediately after their return to London, however, White was apprehended; but, through the agency of Mrs. Mackcoull, and part of the money being restored to the bank, White was not prosecuted; his former sentence, however, being still in force, he was again sent to the hulks, from which he once more escaped, but confined his depredations to the country, where he committed various burglaries. A short time before his apprehension, he contrived, by skeleton keys, &c. to open the doors of the Kettering bank; and such was the masterly manner in which he effected his entrance, and conducted the business altogether, that the bankers, Messrs. Keep and Gotch, remained ignorant of the robbery, until an accomplice, on White's trial, detailed the transaction. They conceived it impossible for such a thing to take place without their knowledge, or, at least, without exciting suspicion; and, accordingly, treated the information as fabulous, until told the number of the page in which their London banking account was kept, and which could only have been obtained by an inspection of their private ledger. It was fortunate, however, that the bankers had not more cause to know of their nocturnal visitors, which was owing to their meeting with an iron chest that they could not open; and, fearful of creating suspicion, they removed nothing, intending, on a future night, to make another visit, and come provided with proper keys.

The crime for which White was at length executed was the robbery of the Leeds mail, on the 29th of October, 1812, near to Higham-Ferrers, in Northamptonshire. The guard having gone over the top of the coach to the front seat, the robbers contrived, during his short absence, to open the lock and extract the mail-bags, which they carried off.

Information of the robbery being given at the General Post-office, two officers of Bow Street, Richard and John Limbrick, were dismissed in pursuit of the villains. White was the man suspected; and they, hearing that he was seen at Bristol, proceeded thither. On their arrival there they learned that Ned Burkitt and John Goodman, two well-known thieves, were living there, and they had no doubt but White resided with them. Burkitt had passed himself off as a captain, and had taken a house, the front of which was towards the fields, in consequence of which the officers had much trouble in watching it for four days, being obliged to go round, about a quarter of a mile, for fear of creating alarm. At length they saw Goodman and his wife go into Bristol, where they took him into custody, on suspicion of being concerned in the robbery of the Canterbury bank.

Having secured their prisoner, they returned to the house, and gave a double knock at the door, which was answered by Burkitt; the officers rushed upon him, but he made a violent resistance, and was secured with great difficulty. In the mean time White effected his escape over a shed, and through an adjoining house.

His career, however, was drawing to a close. It was intimated that he, and one Haywood, intended paying Liverpool a visit, in consequence of which the police were every where on the alert. Early in April, 1813, they were traced to a house in the Scotland Road, which was immediately surrounded by constables and assistants. An old woman, for some time, refused their admittance; but, as they were preparing to force the door, it was opened. Two officers rushed down to the cellar; one of them seized Haywood, at which White struck him a dreadful blow, and pushed past him. The other officer, however, seized him, and a severe struggle ensued. A pistol was fired by a constable, and, after a desperate resistance, they were secured. Under the flags in the cellar were found all the implements of housebreaking, skeleton-keys in abundance, with matches, tapers, &c. &c. The woman was also taken into custody.

At the ensuing summer assizes at Northampton, Huffey White, Richard Kendall, and Mary Howes, *alias* Taylor, were arraigned for the robbery of the Leeds mail. The evidence against White and Kendall was circumstantial. They were seen on the road, the evening of the robbery, in a gig, and subsequently at the house of Mary Howes, who lived not far from the spot where the mail was robbed; and, what was not a little singular, theirs was the only gig which passed through the turnpike on that evening. Next morning White and Kendall were seen together, and were traced, without a chasm, to London, where White offered to negotiate some of the bills and notes with Richardson, who had been before this time convicted of robbing the house of the Marchioness of Downshire.

Forty witnesses were examined on this trial, which lasted fourteen hours; and such was the interest produced, that the court was crowded to excess. The judge having charged the jury, they retired, and soon after returned, finding White and Kendall Guilty, but acquitted the woman, in accordance with the direction of the judge; it appearing that her offence did not take place in the county she was arraigned in. This informality, and not her innocence, saved her life.*

The night preceding their execution, White attempted to make his escape, and had succeeded so far as to cut off his irons, and break through several doors; but he was stopped at the outward gate, and reconducted to his cell. At nine o'clock, August the 13th, 1813, the procession approached the place of execution at Northampton. Kendall appeared deeply impressed with a sense of the awful fate that awaited him; but uniformly persisted in declaring his innocence, and said that he fell a victim in consequence of having the misfortune to be in company with his fellow-sufferer the night of the robbery. He declared, on the gallows, that he was a murdered man; he appealed to the populace, which was immense, in a speech of some length, in which he endeavoured to convince them of his perfect innocence.

White's deportment was such as to convince the surrounding multitude that he was not impressed with the fear of death. Hardihood never forsook him, and he more than once found fault with the manner in which the chaplain performed his duty. From the time of his conviction he disregarded the gallows; and, being humanely asked by a clergyman if he could administer any sort of comfort to him, answered—' Only by getting some other man to be hanged for me.' He declared Kendall innocent, a few minutes before they were launched into eternity.

White was a man whose face did not indicate his profession. He was remarkable for his silence and easy manner, temperate in his habits, and never known to injure any one in their person; on the contrary, he always refused to be concerned with those who indulged in violence.

PHILIP NICHOLSON,
EXECUTED FOR MURDER.

From the assault of an external enemy precaution may secure us; but against the midnight visit of the domestic assassin no foresight can provide. Hence the universal abhorrence with which a traitorous servant is viewed, when he, unmindful of the laws of nature and society, attacks those whom he was paid to protect. Murder in any case is a crime of great magnitude, but it becomes doubly revolting

* While White was in prison his wife applied to Mackcoull for the means of going down to him; but that villain, fearing that White might disclose some important secrets, amused the unfortunate woman with promises, which he broke from day to day, in the hope that her husband might be hanged before she could see him. Another person supplied her with the means; and, in 1820, Mrs. White went down to Scotland, to give evidence against Mackcoull. This woman led an abandoned life, and resided chiefly in a brothel.

when committed by a dependant on a kind benefactor.

Among those whose crimes have acquired for them a detestable immortality Philip Nicholson stands conspicuous—we might almost say alone—for he was an isolated monster of atrocity, whose case admits not a single palliative to detract from the naked wickedness of his barbarous and wanton cruelty. He was not prompted to the deed of blood by any of those causes which usually precipitate men into crime: plunder was not his object; and it could not be revenge, for he received no provocation. In fact he was a murderer without a motive; and the victims of his satanic turpitude were the last in the world whom he should have injured—the best of masters and mistresses.

Mr. and Mrs. Bonar were an aged, happy, and respectable couple, who resided at a mansion called Camden Place, in the village of Chiselhurst, Kent, where they had lived about eight or nine years, in all the enjoyments which attend upon virtue and affluence. Their decline of life was serene and cloudless; they looked back without regret, and regarded the future devoid of apprehension. Their children were good and prosperous; and every thing around indicated tranquillity and happiness. But, alas! terrene possessions are insecure, and no man can say to-morrow shall be at his own disposal.

On Sunday night, May the 30th, 1813, Mr. Bonar went to bed at his usual hour of twelve o'clock, and his wife followed at two. Her maid undressed her in the ante-room, and, having disposed of every thing in their own places, retired to bed. During the night no noise was heard by any of the domestics. The two maids slept in rooms situate in the rear of the house, the groom and the coachman over the stable, and Philip Nicholson, the footman, had his bed in the hall, being the only male servant who slept in the house.

At half past six o'clock next morning one of the garden labourers came to call up Nicholson, and remarked to him that the hall-door and windows-shutters were open; when he answered that he was not aware of their being so. At seven the maids were called up by one of the under servants, who told them that a bad smell came from the mistress's bed-room, and that footmarks of blood were visible in the ante-room; something dreadful was immediately apprehended, and one of the maids exclaimed that there had been murder. In great agitation she then ran down stairs, where, horrid to relate, she found her master and mistress were weltering in their blood; the old lady lying on the bed, while the corpse of her husband was stretched upon the floor, literally swimming in gore. The instrument with which the diabolical act was perpetrated, a kitchen poker, lay bent near the head of the bed.

In the confusion and dismay which followed the discovery of the appalling spectacle, Nicholson was observed to take the sheets from his master's bed, and, in spite of the remonstrance of the maid, to wrap them up in his own, after which he threw a blanket over the corpse. He looked much agitated; but they were all greatly alarmed, and took no particular notice of his conduct. He roused one of the maids, who had swooned away in the hall, and told her to go to her mistress, for that she was still alive. This was found to be the case, as she breathed softly, but made no attempt to speak.

Nicholson now insisted on going to town for a surgeon, and, in attempting to saddle a horse, betrayed so much agitation that the groom was obliged to assist him: when mounted, he seemed incapable of keeping his seat, which surprised the groom, as he had served in the dragoons.

On the road he was seen to drink copiously of brandy, and a little after eight o'clock he arrived at the house of Mr. Astley Cooper, who instantly set off for Camden Place, in the hope of affording surgical assistance to the murdered lady. Nicholson went next to the Red Lion, near Bedlam, where he saw a man named Dale, who had been only a few weeks discharged for improper conduct from Mr. Bonar's service; and to whom he used this remarkable expression: 'The deed is done, and you are suspected; but you are not in it.' He then proceeded to the office at Bow Street, in a state of intoxication, to give information of the murder. Having mentioned his interview with Dale, that person was brought to the office; but he established a most satisfactory *alibi*, and was discharged. Three officers immediately set off for Chiselhurst.

Mr. (afterwards, Sir Astley) Cooper arrived with all possible dispatch at Camden Place, but was too late; the wound was mortal, and Mrs. Bonar expired at eleven minutes past one o'clock, having been through the whole previous time insensible, and only once uttering the exclamation of ' Oh dear !'

'We never witnessed,' says one who saw it, ' such a scene of horror as the bed-room presented. Almost the first object which met the eye on entering was the dead body of Mr. Bonar, with the head and hands steeped in blood: the skull was literally broken into fragments in two or three places; and there was a dreadful laceration across the nose, as if effected by the edge of a poker. His hands were mangled in several places, apparently by the same instrument: there was also a severe wound on the right knee. From the numerous wounds on the body of Mr. Bonar, the swollen state of his mouth, and the convulsive adhesion of his hands and knees, it is clear that he had struggled with all his force against his horrid murderer. The most shocking circumstance connected with this spectacle was the appearance of the night-cap, which lay a few paces from the head, drenched in blood, with a lock of grey hair sticking to it, which seemed to have been struck from the skull by the violence of the blow of the poker. The pillows of his bed lay at his feet, completely dyed in blood. The manly athletic person of Mr. Bonar—for, though advanced in life, he seems to have been a powerful man—gave an increase of horror to this afflicting sight. The view of Mrs. Bonar, though equally distressing, excited more pity than terror: though her head had been fractured in a dreadful manner, yet there was a calm softness in her countenance, more resembling a healthy sleep than a violent death; it might have been supposed that her life had parted from her without one painful effort. The linen and pillow of the bed in which she lay were covered with blood, as was also the bed of Mr. Bonar. They slept in small separate beds, but placed so close together that there was scarce room for a person to pass between them. The interval of floor between the beds was almost a stream of blood. No slight additional horror arose from the contrast of the spacious handsome apartment in which this scene of death was exhibited. The most heart-moving spectacle yet remained. About seven o'clock in the evening, Mr. Bonar, jun. arrived from Faversham, where he was on duty as Colonel of the Kent local militia. In spite of the efforts of Mr. Angerstein, jun. and some other gentlemen, he rushed up stairs, exclaiming, 'Let me see my father! indeed I must see him.' It was impossible to detain him: he burst into the bed-chamber, and immediately locked the door after him. Apprehensions were entertained for his safety, and the door was broken open, when he was seen kneeling with clasped hands over the body of his father. His friends bore him away, and hurried him, tottering and fainting, into an adjoining chamber.'

The officers were now busy in investigating the scene of murder. There was no appearance of any one having broken into the house, nor was there any attempt at robbery; for the bureau remained locked, and the watches of the deceased were found in their usual places.—Of the perpetrator or perpetrators of the murder nothing had transpired for some time but suspicion and surmise; and no motive could be assigned for the assassination of two persons, who were not only inoffensive, but universally beloved for their kindness and benevolence. It was at first supposed the instrument of murder, the poker, did not belong to the house; but this was subsequently proved to be the case, and the error originated from the circumstance of its having been recently repaired, by order of a servant who had just left Mr. Bonar's service.

The mystery soon began to develop itself. It was observed that, though the room was covered with blood, there were no bloody footsteps in the hall, nor in the anteroom; and, though the hall-door was found open, there was no appearance of the assassins having passed through it. A pair of Nicholson's shoes were found in a closet, stained with blood, and on applying them, as well as another pair, to the bloody footsteps in the bedroom, they were found exactly to correspond. His night-cap was also discovered to have marks of blood on it; but the sanguinary marks could be traced no farther, as he had artfully confounded his own linen with the bloody sheeting which he had taken from his master's bed.

The suspicion thus excited gradually received confirmation from the unfeeling conduct of Nicholson himself, which tended, more than the above circumstances, to fix upon him the charge of murder. In place of following the officers to the house of his late master, he contrived to get from their sight in Brydges Street, and proceeded through town drinking with his acquaintances wherever he met them.

In the mean time his room was searched, and, there being no sign of his returning, a warrant was issued for his apprehension.

Forrester, one of the city officers, was sent in pursuit of him, and, after diligent inquiry, he was traced to Whitechapel, where he found him on horseback, drinking at the inn-door of the Three Nuns with an old acquaintance. Forrester laid hold of the bridle of the horse, and, after a smart scuffle, in which Nicholson received some slight bruises, he was secured, and conveyed to Giltspur Street Compter. He was then in a state of intoxication approaching to insanity. Some gentlemen questioned him; but no admission of guilt could be drawn from him. He was carried before the lord mayor, and examined; but such was drunken state that no rational answer could be extracted.

The next day, Tuesday, he was again brought to the Mansion-house; he denied all knowledge of the perpetrators of the murder, and when reprimanded for removing the sheets, as well as calling upon Dale before he called at the Police Office, he pleaded ignorance.

It appeared, from the account he gave of himself, that he was a native of Ireland, and had been discharged from the thirteenth dragoons in consequence of a broken wrist. He subsequently lived three years with the city remembrancer, and had been only three weeks in the employ of his late master, Mr. Bonar. Among the servants at Camden Place he was looked upon as a man of harmless disposition and good nature, with no discernible failing but one, drunkenness, to which he was greatly addicted, being seldom sober when he could procure any spirits.

All questions which were deemed necessary having been put to him, he was sent, in custody of Adkins and another officer, to Chiselhurst, to give evidence before the coroner's jury, who were to sit that evening on the bodies of the deceased.

The evidence being gone through before the coroner, Mr. Martyr, he was reading over the depositions of the several witnesses for their assent and signature, when an alarm was given that Nicholson had attempted his own life. He had been in custody of two officers, and requested leave to go into the yard, which was refused; but he was permitted to enter a water-closet in the passage leading to the servants' hall; while here he cut his throat with a razor, which, it appeared, he had concealed in the front of his breeches. The gash was so deep, and it bled so profusely, that it was supposed he could not live many minutes. The head seemed almost severed from the body, and a large hand might have been inserted in the wound. Fortunately two surgeons of Bromley were in attendance, one of whom, Mr. Holt, immediately rushed forward, and, with great presence of mind, seized with both his hands the gushing arteries, which he stopped from bleeding until the application of more regular means.

An express was instantly dispatched for Mr. Astley Cooper, who arrived in three hours, and, having dressed the wound, declared Nicholson out of danger. To prevent a hemorrhage, every precaution was taken; his head was placed in a fixed position, and two attendants constantly held his hands. Being a Roman Catholic, a priest was sent for; but he made no declaration, and, in the few words he spoke, persisted in declaring his innocence.

The coroner's jury, after a long and patient investigation, returned a verdict of 'wilful murder against Philip Nicholson.'

The sensation which the murder produced throughout the country was amazing. Nicholson's attempt at suicide seemed to confirm the suspicion of his guilt; and every one was anxious to see the monster who was charged with so foul a crime.

On Monday, June the 7th, he was visited by several of the nobility, among whom were Lord Castlereagh, Lord Camden, and Lord Robert Seymour. During their presence he showed repeated symptoms of annoyance and agitation; this circumstance, together with an attempt to make him look more cleanly, caused his wound to bleed afresh. This happened about seven o'clock in the evening; and, as the hemorrhage was of an alarming nature, a dispatch was sent off for Mr. Astley Cooper, who arrived about eleven o'clock. Mr. Bramston, the priest, with Mr. Bonar, came about the same time; and great apprehensions were entertained for the life of the unfortunate wretch.

At six o'clock next morning he requested Mr. Bramston to send for Mr. Bonar immediately. When this gentleman entered, Nicholson burst into tears, and, begging pardon of Mr. Bonar, expressed his wish to make a full confession. A neighbouring magistrate, and other gentlemen, having been sent for, Nicholson, in their presence, made and afterwards signed a voluntary confession that the murder was committed by him, but it did not appear that he had any motive whatever for the perpetration of the dreadful deed.

In consequence of assertions contained in this confession, search was made for the linen, when it was found in a laurel bush. The stockings were very bloody, and the shirt was rent almost to rags about the neck and front, in consequence of the opposition made by Mr. Bonar.

Nicholson, who, before his confession, looked gloomy, fierce, and malicious, afterwards became perfectly calm, and had even an air of satisfaction. He repented his attempt at suicide; and, as much apprehension was entertained for his recovery, every thing that could disturb him was studiously kept out of sight.

When Nicholson was considered out of danger, he was removed to the House of Correction, Coldbath Fields, where he remained until the 17th of August, when he was carried to Maidstone to take his trial; and on the 20th, at eight o'clock, he was placed at the bar. His looks were gloomy and sad; but, on the whole, he appeared firm and collected. He pleaded 'Not Guilty,' in consequence, he said, of the persuasions of several persons.

The case was fully made out by the witnesses, independently of the confession; and, when called on for his defence, he merely inquired if the truth of his declaration was at all doubted. The son of the city remembrancer appeared to give testimony to his character, which he described as humane and gentle, there being never any complaint made against him for the three years he lived with his father, except for frequent intoxication.

The judge having charged the jury, they immediately returned a verdict of 'Guilty;' after which he was asked, in the usual form, if he had any thing to say, when he replied, 'Nothing.'

Mr. Justice Heath then proceeded to pass sentence nearly in the following terms:—' Prisoner, after a minute trial, you have been convicted by a jury of your country of traitorously murdering your master; whom, instead of attacking, it was your duty to protect, at the peril of your life. What was your motive for so atrocious a crime does not appear: it does not seem to have been revenge; you were not intoxicated, nor offended at your master, against whom it was impossible to feel resentment, for his whole life was a series of kindness and beneficences, for which he is now gone to receive his reward. You, Nicholson, must soon appear before a tribunal more awful than this, and I solemnly recommend you to employ the short interval which remains to you in making your peace with Heaven. Nothing that I can say can aggravate the sense of your guilt in the minds of this assembly: I shall, therefore, proceed to discharge my duty in passing upon you the sentence of the law, which is, that you be taken hence to the place from whence you came, and on Monday next be drawn on a sledge to the place of execution, and there hanged till you are dead, and then your body shall be given to be dissected and anatomized.'

Immediately after the sentence, the prisoner put in a paper, and desired it to be read. The judge said this was irregular, but looked at the paper, and told the jury that it contained a confession of crime, which was imputed to excessive drinking.

The paper which he put in and desired to be read was as follows:—

'I acknowledge, with the deepest contrition, the justice of the sentence unto death which has been just passed upon me. My crimes are, indeed, most heavy; I feel their weight, but I do not despair; nay, I humbly hope for mercy, through the infinite mercy of my Lord and Saviour Jesus Christ, who bled and died for me. In order to have a well-grounded hope in him, my all-merciful Redeemer, I know that it is my bounden duty not only to grieve from my heart for my dire offences, but also to do my utmost to make satisfaction for them. Yet, alas! what satisfaction can I make to the afflicted family of my master and mistress, whom, without any provocation, I so barbarously murdered? I can make none beyond the declaration of my guilt and horror of soul that I could perpetrate deeds so shocking to human nature, and so agonizing to the feelings of that worthy family. I implore their forgiveness, for God's sake; and, fully sensible of their great goodness, I do hope that, for his sake, they will forgive me.—I freely give up my life as a just forfeit to my country, whose laws I have scandalously outraged. Departing this tribunal, I shall soon appear before another tribunal, where an eternal sentence will be passed upon me. With this dread sentence full in my view, I do most solemnly declare, and I desire this declaration to be taken as my dying words, that I alone was the base and cruel murderer of my master and mistress; that I had no accomplice; that no one knew or possibly could suspect that I intended to perpetrate those barbarities; that I myself had no intention of committing those horrid deeds, save for a short time, so short as scarcely to be computed, before I actually committed them; that booty was not the motive of my fatal cruelties; I am sure the idea of plunder never presented itself to my mind: I can attribute those unnatural murders to no other cause than, at the time of their commission, a temporary fury from excessive drinking; and, before that time, to the habitual forgetfulness, for many years, of the great God and his judgments; and the too natural consequence of such forgetfulness, the habitual yielding to the worst passions of corrupted nature; so that the evil that I was tempted to do, that I did: the Lord in his mercy has, nevertheless, spared until now my life—that life which I, in an agony of horror and despair, once most wickedly attempted to destroy: he has most graciously allowed me time for repentance; an humble and contrite heart must be his gift; that gift I hope he has granted to my most ardent supplications: in that hope, and bearing in mind his promise that an humble and contrite heart he will not despise, I, freely offering up to him my sufferings, and my life itself, look forward, through his most precious blood, to the pardon of all my crimes, my manifold and most enormous crimes, and most humbly trust that the same mercy which he showed to the penitent thief who was crucified with him he will show to me: thus meekly confiding in thee, O Jesus! into thy hands I commend my spirit. Amen.

'PHILIP NICHOLSON.'
'This 20th August, 1813.'

The signature was in Nicholson's own handwriting: the rest appeared written by another hand.

After sentence of death was passed, Nicholson was placed in the condemned cell, which in the Maidstone gaol is under ground, and the approach to it is dark and dreary, down many steps. In this cell Mr. Bonar had an interview with the prisoner, at half past five on Monday morning. On his approaching the cell, he found Nicholson on his knees at prayer.

At about twelve o'clock, the preparations for the removal of Nicholson being nearly completed, Mr. Bonar, accompanied by his brother, and Mr. Bramston, the Catholic clergyman, had another interview with the unfortunate man, soon after which the hurdle or sledge, which was in the shape of a shallow box, about six feet by three, was drawn up to the gaol door; at each end was a seat just capable of holding two persons. Nicholson, double ironed, was first placed in it, with his back to the horses; he was also pinioned with ropes, and round his shoulders was coiled the fatal cord; by his side sat the executioner; opposite to the prisoner the Rev. Mr. Bramston took his seat, and by his side sat one of the Maidstone gaolers with a loaded blunderbuss. Every thing being in readiness, the procession advanced at a very slow pace towards Pennenden Heath, which is distant from Maidstone nearly a mile and a half, on which was erected a temporary new drop, which had a platform raised seven feet from the ground, and was large enough to contain about a dozen persons. A little before two o'clock the hurdle arrived, and stopped immediately under the gallows, when Mr. Bramston and Nicholson knelt down on it, and remained for some time in prayer. Some time previous to this Mr. Bonar arrived on the ground in a post-chaise, and took his stand within twelve yards of the fatal spot, with the front windows full on the gallows, and which he kept open during the whole time; but each of the side windows was closed by blinds. So anxious was Mr. Bonar to get from the unfortunate wretch his very dying words, as to whether he had either motive or accomplice, that a person was deputed to ascend the platform after the cord was round the prisoner's neck, and to ask him the following questions:—

Q. 'Now that you have not many moments to live, is all that you have stated, namely, that you had no motive that you can tell of, nor had you any accomplice, true?'—A. 'All that I have stated is true.'

'Then there is no creature living on earth who had any thing to do with the murder but yourself?'—'No, no one.'

'You had no accomplices?'—'None.'

'Had you any antipathy to either your master or mistress, before you committed the horrid murder?'—Clasping his hands together as well as his heavy irons would permit him, 'As God is in Heaven it was a momentary thought, as I have repeatedly declared before.'

The above were the last words of this unhappy man; in a few minutes after they were uttered, the bottom of the platform, which, we have before stated, was constructed like one of the new drops, was let fall, and Nicholson was launched into eternity. He died unusually hard, being greatly convulsed.

Nicholson's parents were Irish, his father a Protestant, his mother a Catholic; but he was doubtful of the place of his birth, though he had a complete Irish accent. He was a man about the middle height, not bulky, but well fixed and muscular; his countenance bore evidence of a decided resolute character, but his features were neither unfavourable nor unpleasing; his age was twenty-nine years.

His acknowledgment of his guilt and its causes relieves us from the necessity of comment upon his case. To irreligion and habitual drunkenness he rightly ascribed the momentary infatuation which preceded the dreadful crime, for which he was afterwards exhibited as a warning spectacle to others; for, it is to be observed that, the day before the murder, he had been frequently seen in the beer-cellar, and no doubt the effects of intoxication might have produced a paroxysm approaching to temporary insanity. What an example! Let others learn from it that the habitual drunkard can never account for his own actions; but let him also learn, from the fate of Nicholson, that intoxication is no excuse for crime.

WILLIAM HOWE, ALIAS JOHN WOOD,
EXECUTED FOR THE MURDER OF MR. ROBINS.

THE following case, while it exhibits the utmost depravity and wickedness, affords a consolatory instance of the persevering industry of two officers of justice, whose conduct merits the highest praise, and well deserved whatever reward had been offered for the apprehension of the murderer.

On the evening of the 18th of December, 1812, as Mr. Benjamin Robins, a farmer of Dunsley, near Stourbridge, was returning home from market on foot, he was overtaken by a man, who, under pretence of inquiring his way, walked with him for a mile, when he suddenly fired a pistol at him, and robbed him of twenty-six pounds and his watch. Mr. Robins reached home in great agony, when the wound was found to be so serious, that, after languishing eight days, he expired.

The alarm caused by this atrocity induced the magistrates of Bow Street to send down Adkins and Taunton, two most active officers, by whose extraordinary exertions the wretch was traced to London, where, after a patient watch of many days and nights, they at length succeeded in securing him. He was conveyed directly to Stourbridge, where he was identified by those who saw him on the day of the murder. At the Stafford assizes, March the 17th, 1813, he was put upon his trial, when, in addition to other facts, it was proved that after his apprehension he had sent a letter to his wife, directed Mrs. Howe, wherein he told her to go to a rick near Stourbridge, to search for something. Vickers and Aston went to the rick, and in a hole, apparently made by a hand, they found three bullets and a pistol, a fellow to the one found in the box.

A watch, which proved to have belonged to Mr. Robins, was also found to have been sold by Howe; and, after a trial of ten hours, his guilt was fully established by the corroborating testimony of between thirty and forty witnesses. The judge passed on him the awful sentence of the law; after which Howe, who did not call a single witness, exclaimed, 'My heart is innocent!'

He appeared quite indifferent during his trial; but at the time of his execution, Monday, the 20th of March, he seemed to be impressed with the awfulness of his situation, and manifested corresponding symptoms of repentance.

ANTONIO TARDIT,
EXECUTED FOR THE MURDER OF A FELLOW-PRISONER.

WE have, in the progress of our work, exhibited many a monster of atrocity; but it was reserved for us to crown the climax of wickedness with the case of Antonio Tardit, the deliberate murderer of his countryman, his fellow-soldier, his fellow-prisoner, in a strange country, where both endured all the privations of captivity; and for what? because he suspected the victim of his long-cherished vengeance to have supplied materials for a satire, in which Tardit considered himself ridiculed!

In the year 1811, a French prisoner in Porchester depot composed some verses; and, among the characters introduced in the poem, one, very unfortunately, struck Tardit, who was also a prisoner of war, as expressly written to satirize him. This idea, whether erroneous or not, invariably operated upon the demoniac spirit of the wretch, who sought numerous opportunities to glut his vengeance on another prisoner, named Leguey, who, he imagined, had given the hints to the writer of the verses, enabling him to delineate the characteristic traits in question.

Fifteen long months, with all the irksomeness of a prison, were unable to cool the fiery vengeance which burned within his breast; and, early in the year 1813, he prepared to sacrifice his victim. In order to render his weapon, a large sharp knife, more certain in its operation, he first sharpened it, and then bound the handle with a thick cord, that the grasp might be more firm. This knife he denominated his 'guardian angel,' and slept every night with it under his pillow. The dreams of this monster so much disturbed a fellow-prisoner; who slept in an adjoining hammock, that he asked Tardit if he should not awaken him whenever he became so dreadfully agitated. 'No!' replied this demon of vengeance, 'for I am then dreaming of a deadly enemy who has dishonoured me; and, although he appears to conquer for a time, yet the vision always terminates by giving me his blood.'

On Monday evening, March the 1st, 1813, about eight o'clock, Tardit found the long-wished for opportunity; when rushing upon his victim in the privy, he literally ripped him open, when the bowels, in consequence, obtruded themselves, and the unfortunate man bent forward to receive his entrails, exclaiming, 'I am murdered!' 'Oh, no!' cried the murderer, ironically, 'it is merely a scratch;' then twice plunged his knife in the back of Leguey, exclaiming, 'Take that—and that!' He was proceeding thus to inflict additional wounds, when his murderous arm was arrested; on which the villain exclaimed, 'I have now completed my work, and am content; you may take the weapon and me where you like!'

While they were binding his arms, he desired those around him to stand aside, that he might glut his vengeance by looking on his immolated victim, remarking ironically, 'I have sent you before me on your journey, that you may provide me a lodging.' One of the prisoners then inquired why he did not prove that he, at least, possessed one noble sentiment, by plunging the weapon in his own breast after the perpetration of the deed, in order to escape the gallows. 'It was,' replied the wretch, 'originally my intention; but it afterwards struck me that I might expire first, and then the certainty of taking away his life would not have been known to me, and nothing less would have gratified my heart.'

Soon after the villain was ironed he fell into a sound and tranquil sleep, from which he did not awake until late the following morning, when he said he had not had so undisturbed a repose for the last twelve months.

Tardit was tried at the ensuing summer assizes for Hampshire, and found Guilty. In his defence he said Legney had dishonoured him, and reduced him to despair. Sentence was immediately passed on him, and the next day but one he suffered the penalty of his diabolical crime.

AZUBAH FOUNTAIN AND GEORGE TURNER ROWELL,
EXECUTED FOR MURDER.

WE should readily admit that some men are naturally depraved, did we not know the power of habit, whether good or bad; and this should be an inducement to parents to impress upon the minds of their children those principles of moral rectitude, which are generally found to lead the mind from such actions as bring in their train ignominy and disgrace.

We are persuaded that neither of these malefactors, whose case is before us, heard in their youth many useful lessons, or received, before their minds were depraved, much wholesome advice. We allude particularly to Rowell, who seems to have been habitually vicious; but the unhappy woman who shared his ignominious fate appears more imbecile than wicked, more weak than criminal; her conduct was perfectly unaccountable; and, though we must execrate her crime, we can scarcely refrain from pitying her; for she appears to have fallen a victim to the arts of Rowell, working on a weak mind, irritated by the brutal conduct of an unfeeling husband.

At the Lincoln assizes, on the 3d of August, 1813, Azubah Fountain, aged thirty-six, and George Turner Rowell, aged twenty-three, were indicted for the wilful murder of Robert Fountain, the husband of Azubah, by administering four ounces of laudanum in some elderberry-wine; and, thinking this quantity insufficient, a further dose of two ounces was given him in a cup of ale, of which he died.

Rowell, who at the time of the murder was, as we have observed, only twenty-three years of age, was a native of Melton-Mowbray, at which place he bore a very bad character. From 1807 to 1809 he worked, being a cooper, with Mr. Skinner, of Bingham, who frequently told him, when reproving him for his evil practices, 'that he was fearful, when he left his employ, it would be his lot to suffer the vengeance of the laws;' a prediction which was too truly fulfilled, for this vicious and irreclaimable young man was not to be advised.

In 1813 he went to lodge with Robert Fountain at Lincoln, and had not been in the house more than twelve weeks when the act for which he suffered took place, and in which the wife was deeply implicated. Of their guilt there cannot be a doubt; and what makes Rowell doubly culpable is the fact that he was about to be married to the daughter of his host, having received his consent to that effect a day or two before the murder.

On the ensuing Friday they were both taken to the place of execution near Lincoln, where they were launched into eternity. Rowell persisted to the last in denying that he knew to what purpose the laudanum was to be applied; whilst his partner in guilt continued to assert that they both had frequent conversations on the subject, and that he knew, when he got it, that it was to poison her husband.

The distraction of one of Morris's wives on his Conviction.

HENRY MORRIS,
TRANSPORTED FOR BIGAMY.

'FRAILTY, thy name is Woman,' says Shakspeare. The immortal bard is right; or how could we find them, in spite of precept and example, still the victims of the dissolute and designing; clinging to their destroyers with a devotional tenacity, which, like their beauty, almost makes us pardon their indiscretion; so accustomed are we to expect virtue where appearances promise all that is commendable. But, if we must lament the infatuation of the frailer sex, in what terms can we express our detestation of the villain who calculates on their weakness and simplicity; and, like the veiled prophet of Korassan, exhibits not the hideousness of his natural character until the victim is secured? But, alas! not even then has infatuated woman resolution enough to evince the dignity of insulted virtue; for we too often find them, as in the present instance, become more attached, as their destroyer becomes more worthless.

Henry Morris, in 1813, was indicted at Green Street, Dublin, for marrying Mary Anne Murphy, on the 15th of May, 1811, having previously been married to Maria Fontaine, on the 7th of August, 1805, who was alive at the time of his second marriage.

Both marriages being proved, Dennis Murphy, the afflicted father of the last of the prisoner's wives, (for he had several,) came forward, and detailed a narrative of wrongs, that sensibly affected the Court. He first knew the prisoner on the 15th of October twelvemonth, at a billiard-room, in Dame Street. He told him of his being deeply in love with his daughter, who was then only fifteen years of age; and represented himself as a teacher, of great respectability. Morris was then introduced to Mr. Murphy's family, and continued his visits for five or six months; at the expiration of which period he persuaded the credulous girl to elope with him.

Two months after, the villain Morris wrote the unfortunate father a letter; expressed much contrition for what had occurred; and attributed it to the violence of his love, 'which would not brook delay.' He begged God's and Murphy's pardon; and requested a meeting. A meeting accordingly took place; the parties were reconciled; and Morris and Miss Murphy were legally married. But, before the wounded feelings of the father had been healed, he accidentally acquired information which caused them to bleed afresh. He learned, too surely, that his hopeful son-in-law had several wives; and that he had abandoned four young girls whom he had successively married. The poor man, with tears which bespoke the anguish of his heart, here mentioned that Maria Fontaine had died of a broken heart three weeks before the trial; and said that his unfortunate daughter still continued so attached to her destroyer, that she spent the whole of her time with him in Newgate, coming home occasionally for support, which was given to her; for the unhappy parents could not bring themselves to desert their poor child, under any circumstance; and, if they were to do so, would consider themselves accountable in the eye of Heaven for the crimes she should fall into; as, in case of being turned from the paternal door, she had no alternative but street prostitution.

This wretched girl, lovely as unfortunate, was in court during the trial, and remained close to the prisoner. When the verdict was pronounced, she burst into the most outrageous expressions of grief; cried out most violently to save him; tore her hair, and clung round his neck, declaring that she would not be separated from him. The judges, however, ordered her to be removed, but directed that it should be done as gently as possible; and she was accordingly carried out of court in a state of utter distraction. Morris was then sentenced to transportation for seven years; the judge remarking that he had often ordered a man to be hanged for an offence much less heinous.

We cannot omit this opportunity of saying a few words respecting the virtue of prudence, which may be called the guardian of all the other domestic virtues. Without expatiating on its general importance, perhaps, it may be sufficient to remark that the affliction of Murphy's family, and the ruin of his miserable child, proceeded directly from the total absence of prudence in the old man. He introduces a stranger; encourages his addresses to his daughter, only fifteen years of age; and then permits them to go out alone; for under pretence of going to prayers they had eloped! Surely he who took such little precaution to guard his child from error deserved to suffer for that child's impropriety. This case, however, we hope will not be unproductive of public benefit. Parents may learn from it to guard their children from the arts of strangers; and young women may be taught that to trust their ears to the tongue of men, whose character they know not, is to invite the seducer to spread his snares for their ruin.

ROBERT KENNETT,
EXECUTED FOR FORGERY.

A LONG course of iniquity brought this malefactor to the gallows. The first mention we hear of him was in the debates in the House of Commons on the conduct of the Duke of York; where it appeared Kennett, though not worth a shilling, proposed lending his royal highness seventy thousand pounds upon annuity, with the additional consideration of a place to be obtained for him under government, through the interest of the royal duke.

The address with which Kennett imposed on his royal highness may be inferred from the several letters* which were made public, and strongly evinced the zeal and per-

* 'Lieutenant-Colonel Taylor presents his compliments to Mr. Kennett, and is directed by the Duke of York to transmit to him a copy of a letter from Mr. Pitt's private secretary, in reply to the application which his Royal Highness made in Mr. Kennett's favour for the Collectorship of the Customs of Surinam; which answer, his Royal Highness regrets, is not conformable to his wishes. Colonel Taylor would have sent it earlier, had he not been absent from London when it was sent to the Horse Guards.
'August 7th, 1804.'

'Downing Street, Friday, 3d August, 1804.
'MY DEAR SIR,—I have not failed to state to Mr. Pitt the wishes of his Royal Highness the Duke of York, communicated through you, that he would nominate Mr. Kennett to the office of Collector of his Majesty's Customs at Surinam; and I am directed to request that you will submit to his Royal Highness, that, desirous as Mr. Pitt must at all times be to attend to his Royal Highness's commands, he is fearful that, from prior engagements, he is so circumstanced, as not to have it in his power to do so on the present occasion.
'I am, &c.   (Signed)   'W. D. ADAMS.'
ADDRESSED—'Lieut.-Colonel Taylor.'

'Colonel Taylor presents his compliments to Mr. Kennett, and is extremely sorry that he could not wait, as the Duke's carriage was waiting for him. He is directed by his Royal Highness to say, that he will apply for the situation of Assistant Commissary-General, &c. &c. at Surinam; but that he will be able to do it with more effect, if Sir H. Mann will write to his Royal Highness, recommending Mr. Kennett.
'Robert Kennett, Esq. &c. &c. &c
'Horse Guards, Aug. 15.'

'Bromley Hill, Kent, Aug 30th.
'SIR,—I am sure Mr. Pitt would have been very happy to have attended to your request, respecting Mr. Kennett; but I know, upon the application of the Duke of York, he was informed that the office of collector had been appointed to. As to the other office, having received a letter, written by the desire of his Royal Highness the Duke, I made the inquiries respecting it, and I do not find that there is any such

tinacity with which situations were solicited for him, in return for the supposed accommodation he was to afford the royal duke.

Before Kennett, however, succeeded in effectually imposing upon his royal highness, his character was discovered, and consequently all correspondence ceased. From that time he subsisted on ways and means; which, as they were practised in private, it is impossible for us to be acquainted with.

In 1812 he became acquainted with Richardson and Cooke, the two accomplices, who discovered the villainy of Badcock and others, whose case will be next given. With these men he planned and forged a bill of exchange on an unwary tradesman, for the sum of one hundred and sixty pounds, which they too securely obtained without detection or prosecution, and lodged in the funds. Having obtained this sum, they found access to Messrs. Trowers and Co. stock-brokers, who sold for them the stock they had so recently lodged, and paid them with a draft on Messrs. Glyn and Co.

Possessing this draft, they forged one like it for two thousand pounds, and Kennett obtained cash for it in the following manner:—He took a lodging in Frances Street; and a young man, having advertised for a clerkship, was engaged by Kennett. This lad he sent with the check, which was paid in two large notes; after which he went, as directed, to the Bank, and obtained small notes for them in exchange. He then went to Moorgate Coffee House, where Kennett, who had assumed the name of Blunt, promised to meet him. He was not there, but a note was left appointing another place of meeting, where he did not attend; but the young man at length met him in Warwick Court, Holborn, where he delivered him the money. At this time he was concealed in a strange dress—having on a large wig, brown great coat, top boots, &c.

Richardson and Cooke having informed against all those with whom they were connected, Kennett was amongst the number; and accordingly he was apprehended, and brought to trial at the Old Bailey; when he was found Guilty on the evidence of his accomplices, which was fully corroborated by the testimony of other witnesses.

When brought up to receive sen-

office as Assistant-Commissary and Agent for Prisoners, (or Commissary-General, as it was called in the Duke's letter,) to be appointed from hence: the Commissary-General in the West Indies, Mr. Glassford, recommends such deputies as he finds necessary for conducting the business of his department; and they are usually appointed by the Treasury in consequence. The office of Agent for prisoners I conceive to be under the direction of the Transport Board.

'Believe me, Sir, most faithfully yours, 'C. Lone.'

'Lieutenant-Colonel Taylor encloses, for Mr. Kennett's perusal, a letter from Mr. Chapman, and is very sorry to find from it that the situation of Vendue Master is disposed of. Mr. Chapman has been out of town, which accounts for the delay in regard to the receipt of the information now given. Should Mr. Kennett wish to see Colonel Taylor, he will be here to-morrow, between three and five o'clock.

'Horse Guards, 22d Nov. 1804.'

(Private.)

'*Downing Street, 22d Nov. 1804.*

'Dear Taylor,—Lord Camden desires me to request you will express to the Duke of York his great regret that the office of Vendue Master of Surinam was disposed of before you communicated his Royal Highness's wish in favour of Mr. Kennett.

'Believe me, very sincerely yours, 'Jas. Chapman.

'I should have give you an earlier answer, but have been out of town.'

Addressed—'Lieut.-Colonel Taylor,' in an envelope, 'To Mr. Kennett, &c.'

tence, and asked the usual question what he had to say why sentence of death should not be passed on him, he addressed the Court, saying that he was convicted on the testimony of those who, he urged, were not entitled to credit. He then adverted to the deplorable state of his family, consisting of a wife and four children; and added, that his eldest son died fighting for his king and country; a circumstance for which he thanked God, as he was thereby saved from the horror of witnessing the ignominious fate of his miserable father. He then remarked that some of his ancestors had obtained the highest honours which the city of London had to bestow; and that his uncle (Alderman Kennett) had filled that chair, as chief magistrate, from whence sentence of death was about to be passed on him. He concluded by imploring mercy. After which the Recorder passed sentence in the usual form.

On Wednesday, June the 16th, 1813, this unhappy man was executed in front of Newgate. He was brought upon the scaffold at eight o'clock, dressed in a plain suit of mourning, and attended by the Ordinary of Newgate, with whom he remained some time in prayer During this short and awful period he appeared to be perfectly resigned to his fate, which he met with becoming fortitude.

WILLIAM BADCOCK, R. BRADY, ALIAS OXFORD BOB, AND S. HILL,

EXECUTED FOR FORGERY.

THESE offenders were brought to justice through the information of two accomplices, Richardson and Cooke. They all met at the Horns Tavern, Doctors' Commons, where they agreed to commit forgeries on some banking house in the city.

It was agreed that Hill was to procure genuine checks, from which Cooke was to execute the forgeries. Badcock was then to procure porters to carry the forged checks, that they might be cashed; and Richardson was to watch the porters, to see that the checks were paid without hesitation, and to return and inform Badcock 'that all was right.'

On the 4th of September, 1812, Hill received three checks from Parsons, a hay-salesman, in Whitechapel, who did not know for what purpose they were wanted. From one of these Cooke forged, in the the name of Burchell and Co. to the amount of seven hundred and sixty pounds on the house of Robarts, Curtis, and Co. The first check being paid, they forged the two others; and, in two days they robbed the one banking house of three thousand and eight hundred pounds which these worthies divided among them at the Moorgate Coffee House.

The notes were then sold at twenty per cent. discount to one Edmund Birkett, who was subsequently brought to justice.

These facts were fully corroborated by other witnesses in addition to the evidence of the accomplices, Richardson and Cooke; and the prisoners were found Guilty— Death, at the Old Bailey, July 17th, 1813.

On Thursday, July 29th, Badcock was executed in the front of Newgate; Birkett, already mentioned, suffered also with him; as well as one Ennis, for forgery, and William Smith, for taking money out of a letter in the Post Office.

These unhappy men were brought upon the scaffold a few minutes before eight o'clock; and, after Ennis had remained in prayer some time with a Catholic clergyman, and the three others with the Ordinary of Newgate, they met their fate with becoming fortitude. Smith and Ennis evinced great penitence. Birkett had contrived to secrete a pistol, with so much address as to evade detection upon the search which took place the night before the execution; and about eleven o'clock, although a fellow-prisoner and one of the turnkeys were in the cell with him, he discharged a ball into his left side. He failed, however, in his object of destroying himself, and only inflicted a wound which caused much pain. He ascended the scaffold without assistance, and submitted to his fate with the others.

Brady and Hill subsequently underwent the sentence of the law in the same place.

DAVID SPREADBURY,
EXECUTED FOR FORGERY.

THIS case illustrates the remark we have often made, that crime, however ingeniously committed, cannot escape detection—nay, the very solicitude to avoid suspicion is frequently the cause of creating it; and it generally so happens; that, while the depredator thinks he is flying from danger, he is only plunging into the coils of justice.

David Spreadbury arrived in the dress of a gentleman at Deeping, on the 26th of March, 1813, in the Peterborough coach, and ordered a chaise from the New Inn, saying he was going to Lincoln. Before he took his departure, however, he got the proprietor of the inn to change for him a note for ten pounds, which afterwards turned out to be a forgery: it purported to be of the bank of Johnson and Eaton, of Stamford. He was next found on the road from Newark to Grantham, having hired a chaise at the Kingston Arms, where he got another ten-pound note exchanged. He said, at Newark, that his luggage had gone on by the coach, and that he was anxious to overtake it. He accordingly set off in the chaise; but suspicion arising, the note was shown to some person, who pronounced it to be a forgery. One of the waiters now mounted a swift horse, and pursued the villain, of whom he got information at Foston toll-bar, where he had received good notes for another forgery for ten pounds. The waiter, hearing this, continued the pursuit.

The post-boy suspected that all was not right, in consequence of Spreadbury saying at each turnpike that he had no change, and presenting a ten-pound note in payment, and actually passed through one without paying, though the post-boy knew he had abundance of change in his pocket.

The post-boy at length observed that they were pursued; and, suspecting that it was some one from his master, he slackened his pace. Spreadbury observed this, and urged the boy to proceed, but without effect; for he refused to use the whip, and kept moving slowly.

Near Grantham Spreadbury expressed his apprehensions that their pursuer was a highwayman; and, as the post-boy continued obstinate, he thought it better to trust to his heels, and accordingly jumped out of the chaise. He ran forward to Grantham; but the post-boy and waiter did not lose sight of him, and he was apprehended in a little lane, which he thought to make his way through, but was disappointed, as there was no egress at the extremity.

On searching him, there were found on his person about forty pounds in good notes, and some silver; and, in the passage where he thought to secrete himself, were discovered seven ten-pound notes, forgeries, and one blank-note, unsigned, rolled up. There was no doubt but he had dropped these when he found there was no hope of eluding his pursuers.

At the summer assizes, at Lincolnshire, he was capitally indicted for uttering forged notes, knowing them to be such. Of his guilt there could not be a doubt, and he was accordingly convicted. The judge passed on him the awful sentence of the law, and the unfortunate man suffered, on Friday, Aug. the 13th, 1813.

WILLIAM CORNWELL,
EXECUTED FOR THE MURDER OF MRS. STEVENS.

This malefactor was a native of Cambridgeshire, and was born, in 1789, within about six miles of Cambridge. His employment was that of an hostler, and, having lived two years at the Axe and Gate Inn, Holborn, he removed to the Red Lion Inn, in the same street. While in this last employment, he contracted several small debts in the neighbourhood, to avoid which he ultimately left London, and in April, 1813, he was employed at Woodford by a coach-keeper. He had not continued here more than six weeks, when it is supposed he committed the murder for which he suffered. When we shall make the reader acquainted with the unfeeling levity of his conduct, we think there will be little disposition to give much credit to his dying declaration of innocence.

On Monday, the 7th of June, 1813, a decent poor woman, named Stevens, who kept a little chandler's shop at Woodford, was found murdered, her throat having been cut by the shop-knife, and her head dreadfully bruised by a mallet, which she kept for the purpose of breaking sugar.

Mrs. Stevens had been seen on the Saturday night, on which it is supposed the murder took place, at ten o'clock; and her door was heard to slam, at eleven o'clock, as if some persons had come out of the shop, and pulled it violently after them. It had a spring latch, and could be fastened in that manner. On Sunday her next door neighbour tapped at her window, as if to awaken her, about ten o'clock; but, though he did not see her stirring, he took no further notice till the next morning, when it was obvious from the circumstance of her shop remaining shut, that something serious was the matter. A ladder was procured, and access to her apartment was gained, through a back window. Her bed was seen undisturbed; but, on descending into the shop, the poor woman was found murdered, as we have already described, her pockets turned inside out, and her till emptied of its contents.

The sensation produced by this dreadful and mysterious murder was intense. Search was every where made, but no clue was found that might lead to a detection of the perpetrator. But murder cannot be concealed, and the incaution of the guilty generally leads to their own apprehension.

It was ascertained that Mrs. Stevens, previous to her murder, had been in possession of a new silver watch, made by Ridley, of Woodford, and numbered 1,544. This had been carried off; and, as a likely means of discovering the murder, it had been pretty generally advertised.

On Sunday Cornwell purchased a hat, and some other articles, in Woodford, with a one-pound note; and on Wednesday came into London on his master's coach. Going to the Sun public house, in Gate Street, Lincoln's Inn Fields, the landlady, Mrs. Davis, upbraided him for leaving the neighbourhood without paying a score he owed her; shortly after which, he discharged it, by giving Mr. Davis a watch worth five pounds for an old one of little value, and receiving half a crown. The watch answering the description of Mrs. Stevens's, Davis gave information of the circumstance, and Cornwell was apprehended, and underwent an examination of three hours. He gave an account of himself up to nine o'clock on the Saturday evening previous to the murder, when he stopped short, and refused to answer any more questions.

On the day appointed for his next examination, he swore he would not walk to the office, and he was, therefore, brought up doubly ironed, and strongly hand-cuffed. During the examination, he exhibited a continued laugh, or sneering grin, and behaved in the most hardened manner, and with the most indecorous levity, though every thing in the proceedings was solemn and awful. He heard the evidence in support of the charge with contemptuous indifference; and his unfeeling and brutal conduct served to add additional horror to the crime imputed to him.

In addition to the facts already detailed, Cornwell's employer deposed that he never knew him to have a one-pound note by him; for his wages were only fifteen shillings a week, and every week he partly anticipated his pay by borrowing. But this witness confirmed some part of Cornwell's statement on his examination.

Cornwell himself said he had nothing more to say, and that they might hang him if they pleased. The churchwardens were then bound over to prosecute, and Cornwell was fully committed.

The trial of this malefactor came on at Chelmsford, August the 6th, when, after a patient investigation of six hours, he was found Guilty. The evidence against him was circumstantial; but, as detailed by eighteen witnesses, it was so conclusive, that the jury had not a moment's hesitation in returning their verdict. Lord Ellenborough passed sentence on him in a most feeling manner, which affected every one in court, except the prisoner himself.

Cornwell exhibited the same unbecoming levity and hardihood during the progress of the trial which he had shown at his previous examinations and ever since he had been in custody, always persisting in his innocence. Upon the judge pronouncing on him the dreadful sentence of the law, he said, with a convulsive grin, 'Thank you, my lord and gentlemen;' after which he was removed from the bar.

Cornwell having complained, the preceding day, that he was poor and friendless, one of the magistrates humanely ordered him a counsel at his own expense.

The magistrates, in order to produce the greater horror in the public mind, requested of the judge that, in this instance, the ordinary place of execution might be departed from, and that the criminal might be hung at Woodford instead of Chelmsford. This being complied with, Cornwall was removed in the gaol caravan at nine o'clock on Monday to the place of execution.

Upwards of three thousand of the inhabitants of Woodford, and its vicinity, were collected on the occasion. He not only declined making any confession, but refused to join in prayer; declaring that he had nothing to say, but was innocent of the crime for which he was going to suffer; and, repeating this assertion, he was launched into eternity.

JOHN BRITAIN,
EXECUTED FOR THE MURDER OF HIS WIFE.

THIS is a melancholy case; and the victim of offended laws excites our pity, though we must approve his punishment.

John Britain was indicted at the Warwick assizes, August the 18th, 1813, for the wilful murder of his own wife. On his trial the principal evidence against him was his own son, who, on the sight of his father, was scarcely able to sustain the shock. His countenance betrayed his horror at the painful part he was called on to act: nor were his feelings confined to himself: judges, counsel, jury, and spectators, were alike affected at the scene. After some time had been allowed the witness to recover himself, the judge (Sir S. Le Blanc) told him that the task was, indeed, a painful one; but that it was a duty he owed to his God, his country, and the memory of his deceased mother, to relate to the Court such circumstances of the murder of his deceased parent as were within the compass of his knowledge, recollecting that his father had broken the chain that binds society together. After repeated encouragement from the counsel, he proceeded in his testimony, with but little interruption, and in the course of it stated the following facts:—

The witness was sleeping, on the morning of the 5th of April, in the same room with his father, mother, and a younger brother; about six o'clock, on being suddenly disturbed by a noise which proceeded from that part of the room where his parents slept, he rose and went to the spot, and there found his father standing in a threatening attitude over the bed in which his mother lay. On examining the bed, he found his mother weltering in her blood, which flowed from a wound she had received from a bar of iron which his father held in his hand. The prisoner was again in the act of raising his hand to strike the deceased, when witness rushed up to him, and wrested the bar from his grasp, exclaiming at the same time, 'O, my dear father, have mercy!' and, in his endeavours to obtain the murderous weapon, received a violent blow on one of his arms. On his father becoming cooler, witness went again to his mother, and saw that she was much bruised about the head and face, her blood flowing very fast: her speech was gone, and she appeared to be in extreme agony. He wiped the blood from her face with some water, and his father in a short time came to the bed and assisted him. Witness left the room to call for the assistance of his neighbours, and then proceeded in search of medical aid. The witness further stated, that he had often been disturbed in his rest, during the last six or seven months previous to the murder, by his father's singular behaviour; as, for instance, by getting out of bed at night, going down stairs, and misplacing the furniture, and by his use of strange expressions. He was convinced that his father laboured, at times, under mental derangement, but nothing had occurred of that description within a month previous to the murder.

Some other evidence, in corroboration of the facts above stated, was gone through, when the prisoner was called upon for his defence. He accordingly uttered a long and unconnected address, partaking more of a soliloquy than of any thing else. He seemed to rely on his insanity at the time the fatal deed was committed, and on the act being voluntary and unpremeditated.

The learned judge, in summing up, stated to the jury that they had to confine themselves to the question, whether the prisoner was sane at the time of committing the deed, the fact of the deceased having met her death at his hands being indisputable.

The jury in ten minutes returned their verdict—Guilty.

On the following Friday he was executed in front of Warwick gaol, in the presence of a large concourse of spectators. He declared that he had no animosity against his wife the time he went to bed on the night of the murder; but that, on a sudden and irresistible impulse, and without any provocation, he jumped out of bed, and perpetrated the horrid crime with a bar of iron. After condemnation he manifested an appearance of calmness and serenity. He left three children to lament his shocking end, and bewail the fate of their mother.

JOSEPH RICHARDSON, JAMES SYMONS, AND NATHAN SYMONS;

THE TWO FIRST CONVICTED OF STEALING, THE LAST FOR RECEIVING STOLEN GOODS.

On the night of the 29th of March, 1813, the house of the Marchioness of Downshire, in Hanover Square, was broken into, and robbed of plate, jewels, &c. to the amount of four thousand pounds. The villains effected their entrance by means of a lamplighter's ladder, which they had released from the place where it had been lodged behind the marchioness's stables.

For several days they escaped the most diligent pursuit of the police, but were at length brought to justice through the information of their accomplice, Richardson, who, it appeared, had been the principal executer of this robbery, though not the planner of it.

Richardson, although but a young man, is supposed to have committed a number of daring robberies, and had broken out of two of the strongest prisons in the kingdom. Being suspected of this robbery, he was apprehended by Becket, an officer, who, on searching him, found banknotes to the amount of five hundred and twenty-three pounds, which he offered to give Becket if he would let him go; he was, however, conveyed to the House of Correction, where he disclosed the circumstances of the marchioness's robbery, and accompanied the officers to various places in search of the parties concerned.

At No. 4, Seymour Court, they found Old Symons in bed, and took him into custody. He at first denied that his name was Symons, but Adkins knew him when he had put on his clothes. Under the bed, in a box, they found a large quantity of the marchioness's property. Next day more rings and jewellery were given up by Richardson; and Harry Adkins found young Symons locked up in a cupboard in the house of one Levi, a Jew.

The family of the Symons' were a notorious set of cheats and robbers, and on this occasion planned the robbery which the young Symons and Richardson executed. The mother and daughter, having shared in the plunder, were also apprehended, as well as one Frankill, a well-known character.

The parties were indicted at the Old Bailey, June the 5th, 1813, when, after a protracted trial, young Symons and Richardson were found Guilty—Death; and Old Nathan Symons guilty of receiving the property, knowing it to be stolen. The others were acquitted for want of evidence, and Richardson, in consequence of his timely information, was considered a fit object for a commutation of punishment. He was subsequently pardoned, and became an useful spy for the police.

The trial excited great interest; and the Duke of Sussex, Marchioness of Downshire, and several of the nobility, were present the whole time.

LUKE HEATH,
EXECUTED FOR MURDER.

WE have thought it our duty, frequently, to remark upon the evil consequences of excessive drinking, as we find it, too often, the immediate cause of many of those crimes which bring ruin upon families, and disgrace and ignominious death upon individuals. Yet, fraught as intoxication is with evil, we still hesitate to pronounce it as productive of crime in its consequence as that demoralizing vice—seduction. The case we are about to detail saves us from the necessity of comment, as it fearfully illustrates the fatal tendency of this too common sin; and holds out an important lesson to the youth of both sexes, in which they may learn that forbidden enjoyments, and honourable fidelity, are as opposite to each other as light and darkness.

Luke Heath was the son of a respectable farmer, who lived in the parish of Cow-Honeybourne, Gloucestershire. In the same parish, and within a quarter of a mile of Heath's residence, dwelt a poor man, named James Harris, the father of three daughters, two of whom were married, and the youngest, Sarah, lived in the house with him.

Unfortunately, Luke Heath formed an acquaintance with this girl, and, dreading that the old man would not sanction his addresses, he prevailed on her to permit him to visit her without her father's knowledge. Unhappily, she consented, and, from meeting him in the pent-house, she agreed to admit him to her bed-room, after the old man had retired to rest.

The better to prevent a discovery of their stolen hours, they oiled the hinges of the doors which led to their apartment, lest their creaking might create suspicion in the father, who, thus undisturbed, slept soundly, nor dreamed of the destroyer of his child being under one roof with him.

In unhallowed love, the birth of the enjoyment is the death of the passion; and the woman who complies with the lover's importunities soon witnesses a termination of his attentions. Heath and his mistress soon repented of their criminal intercourse; for appearances were beginning openly to declare that she was about to become a dishonoured mother. Their meetings were no longer attended with impatient rapture. Reproach was all on one side, and repentance on the other, while the intervals were spent in fruitless conjectures about what should be done. No doubt she requested of him to blot disgrace from her character by marriage, and the sequel seems to imply that he must have consented.

On the night of the 22d of June, 1809, James Harris and his daughter retired to rest. Next morning the old man arose; but, as he could not go to the kitchen without passing through his daughter's room, he was somewhat alarmed at finding her door open, and herself not in bed, which, at the hour, was rather an unusual thing. Suspecting that she had gone into the garden, he went to look for her, and on his way found the back door ajar, a pitchfork thrown across the path, but no appearance of his daughter. He then proceeded into the village, and, at the house of one of his married daughters, learned, for the first time, that Sarah was with child by Luke Heath.

This information increased the poor man's apprehension for the safety of his child; and, after going to the house of his third daughter to inquire for her, he returned home, and was told that Sarah was found in the pond into which it had been thrown after it was murdered. There was a scar on the left temple, and a hole in the back part of the head; the fork was found bloody, which the old man had not observed before, and blood was also scattered about the pent-house and the path adjoining. The pond where the body had been found was about sixty yards from the house.

The village was now alarmed, and suspicion instantly fell upon Heath, who was apprehended on his father's farm, dressed in a dirty smock frock. He denied all knowledge of the murder, and, when asked where was his other frock, he said he had no other. He attended the coroner's inquest; but there being no evidence to implicate him, he was acquitted.

In a few days, however, circumstances arose to increase the suspicion against him, in consequence of which a warrant was granted, but he could not be found, neither could any thing be discovered in his father's house which might throw light on the mysterious affair. But his sudden flight was presumptive evidence of his guilt; and accordingly every exertion was used to apprehend him. The officers of justice were dispatched throughout the kingdom in pursuit of him; and, after a diligent search of three months, they returned unsuccessful.

Near four years had elapsed, when Heath was discovered to have been living, during the two preceding years, in the neighbourhood of Kidderminster, as a farm servant, where he went under the name of Farmer John. Information was given to a magistrate, and he was taken into custody. He denied he knew Sarah Harris, that he ever heard of her mother, or that he ever lived in Gloucestershire; but, on Cow-Honeybourne being mentioned, he hid his face in his hands, became greatly agitated, and shed tears. When asked where he had spent the two intervening years between his departure from Gloucestershire and his visit to Kidderminster, he said he was on board a man of war; but an officer of marines, being present, questioned him, and, from his answers, inferred that he had never been on board ship in his life.

While Heath remained in Kidderminster gaol, he confessed to a fellow-prisoner that Sarah Harris had been pregnant by him, that she was murdered with a pitchfork, and he was the man; but hoped he would not tell.

Heath was now removed to Gloucester, where his trial came on at the summer assizes, when the evidence of his guilt was conclusive. The jury found him guilty, and the judge passed on him the awful sentence of the law.

On Heath's return to prison, after his condemnation, he made a full confession of his guilt, and appeared truly penitent. On Monday, August 30, 1813, he was executed. The multitude who witnessed his sufferings were immense; but he did not address them. After a short ejaculation he was turned off; and, having hung the usual time, his body was given to the surgeons for dissection.

JOHN HANNAH,
EXECUTED FOR THE MURDER OF HIS WIFE.

THIS case exhibits so much brutal insensibility, that we shall give it in the words of the witnesses on whose testimony he was convicted. He was indicted at the general sessions for Yarmouth, September the 3d, 1813, for the wilful murder of his wife. His age was sixty-seven years.

On the trial, Elizabeth Betts deposed that she rented a room directly over the one in which the prisoner lived; that on the morning of the 15th of April she was alarmed about three o'clock with a dreadful cry of murder; she went down stairs and called out, 'You old rogue, you are murdering your wife;'—she heard Elizabeth Hannah say, 'For God's sake come in, for my husband is murdering me!' but witness, knowing the violence of the prisoner's temper, was afraid, and said she dare not go in, but went up stairs to dress herself, with a view of procuring assistance; she went out and told a neighbour, of the name of Thomson, that Hannah and his wife were quarrelling, and was going to the watch-house to procure some assistance; she, however, did not succeed, the watch being off duty; on her return her children were crying and out of bed, which obliged her to remain with them; she called frequently to the prisoner to come out of his room, or he would be the death of his wife; she heard the cries of the deceased about a quarter of an hour after her return from the watch-house; she distinctly heard three heavy groans, after which all was silent, and she went to bed; she got up about six o'clock, and did not leave the door of the prisoner till it was opened by the constable.

James Storey, a constable, deposed that he broke open the door of the house, and entered the room with several neighbours, when he saw Elizabeth Hannah lying on the bed, dead, with her arms by her side, as if laid out, and the bed-clothes covered smoothly over her; the bed-clothes were removed, and he saw the deceased had apparently a bruise on the front of her neck he saw the prisoner sitting near the bed-side, smoking a pipe, and looking at the bed. He said to him, 'Why, John, surely you have murdered your wife:' to which he replied, 'She was always quarrelling with me.' Witness said there were other means of getting rid of her than killing her. The prisoner made no reply.

The prisoner made no defence, and the jury brought in their verdict, Guilty. The trial lasted five hours, during which the prisoner, who was represented of a most ungovernable temper, remained entirely unmoved. He behaved likewise with the same brutal insensibility at the place of execution on Monday, September 6th, 1813. On ascending the gallows he confessed 'That he was the murderer of his wife, by strangling her with his hands, and not with a rope, as had been stated; he said they had lived a very uncomfortable life for many years past, owing to his wife giving her company to other men, which was the cause of his committing the murder.' The instant before being turned off, he particularly requested to see his daughter, when he was informed it was not possible, as she was confined in Bedlam; he also desired the gaoler to look under the step of the cell, and he would there find four shillings and sixpence. He had disposed by will of some little property, the joint savings of himself and his wife. A signal was then given, and the unfeeling man was immediately launched into eternity. The body, after hanging the usual time, was delivered to the surgeons for dissection. The gaoler, on his return, found the money, as described, in the cell.

MICHAEL M'ILVENA,

EXECUTED FOR CELEBRATING A MARRIAGE, HE BEING A LAYMAN.

THE happiness of the greater portion of mankind may be said to be domestic; and, as this depends entirely upon the female part of the community, any thing which tends to destroy their character, and consequently their peace of mind, should be guarded against as a direct attack upon the happiness of society in general. Woman, deprived of her maiden innocence in civilized countries, may be said to be an outcast from society—deserted by her own sex, and insulted by that of her destroyer; abandoned to despair, or plunged into prostitution, where the excess of crime may cause a momentary forgetfulness of her miserable condition. The man who prevails upon her to make the first fatal step toward such a vicious course deserves the universal execration of his species; but the villain who steals her virtue under the sanction of apparent matrimony, and, when she fondly imagines she is an honoured wife, finds herself a forlorn object for the finger of Scorn to point at, deserves what befell Michael M'Ilvena—the gallows.

This villain was an impostor, who aspired to no greater notoriety than that which he acquired by cheating the credulous and simple inhabitants of a village. He was a native of Ireland; and, in his migrations through the northern part of that kingdom, personated, successively, the characters of a Catholic priest, a Protestant minister, and a lawyer. The last place we find him in was the village of Ballinahinch, where he went under the appellation of The Counsellor.

While here he became acquainted with a man of the name of Christopher Jennings, with whom he conspired to debauch a young girl, named Mary Hair.

This unsuspecting creature was

only seventeen years of age; and had been servant, a year and a half, with Mr. Knox, of Drumanockan, near Dromore. Having spent the Christmas of 1812 with her father and mother, she was returning to her master's house, when she met Jennings on the road, with whom she had been acquainted. He took her into a public house, and made, as he had often done before, proposals of marriage to her. The artless girl consented; and both proceeded to Ballinahinch, with the intention of procuring a clergyman.

Jennings took her into a public house, where M'Ilvena was sitting, and to whom she was introduced by her intended husband; who said, 'There is the minister who will marry us.' It must be observed that Mary Hair was a Protestant and Jennings a Catholic; consequently it was necessary the ceremony should be performed by a Protestant clergyman; for a Catholic is prohibited marrying a Protestant subject under any circumstance; and Jennings might have suspected that Mary, simple as she was, would have declined the union, had M'Ilvena professed himself any thing but a Protestant clergyman.

M'Ilvena, with assumed sanctity, pulled out his book, and went through, what Mary thought, a ceremony; joining their hands, and interrogating the parties in the usual form. After the ceremony the poor girl asked for a certificate. This at first was refused; but, as she insisted on it, he took pen and ink, and wrote the following:—

'These are to certify that Mary Hair is this day joined in marriage to Christopher Jennings, of Drumara. As given under my hand, this 26th December, 1812.
'W. M'G.'

This scrawl contented the deluded girl; and the mock parson intimated that he was always paid for such duties. Mary then gave him ten tenpennies, which he threw on the table in an indignant manner; saying, 'Am I to be college-bred, and learned, and not receive my just dues?' To carry on the farce, Jennings said, 'And please your reverence, Mr. Gawdy, whatever is your demand I'll pay.' The parson then took up the tenpennies, and put them in his pocket; after which he went out to procure the new-married couple a lodging.

In a short time he returned, saying he had engaged lodgings for them; and, after partaking of another jug of punch, he conducted them to the house of a poor woman, named M'Kee; who, hesitating to admit them, M'Ilvena declared they were man and wife, lawfully married; which the old woman still seeming to doubt, he said, 'Blud and ounze, won't you believe my word of honour?' This succeeded; and the unfortunate girl admitted the villain, Jennings, to the rights of a husband.

Next morning Jennings directed her to give notice to her master; and he undertook to break the business to her father and mother. The poor girl was parting from him with reluctance, when he told her unblushingly that she was not his wife, and that she was deceived.

The unhappy girl was awakened to all the misery of her situation; and ran, in a state of distraction, to her parents, to whom she related all that had occurred. The necessary proceedings were immediately taken, and the *counsellor* and Jennings were committed to prison. At the summer assizes for Downpatrick, August the 17th, 1813, they were brought up for trial. M'Ilvena was first indicted; and, Mary Hair having deposed to the foregoing facts, she was cross examined, with a view to affect her testimony, by endeavouring to make her acknowledge a former connexion with Jennings. This she indignantly denied; and, when asked if she had had any objections to be treated by Jennings, she replied to the counsel, 'I suppose you have treated a girl before now yourself.'

M'Ilvena, in his defence, produced Jennings, who swore to palpable falsehoods. First, that he had an intimate knowledge of the prosecutrix long before the time mentioned in the indictment; next, that she never represented herself as his wife; and that M'Ilvena never pretended to join their hands together, or otherwise unite them in marriage.

Jennings, having given his evidence, was ordered back into the dock from whence he had come, and M'Ilvena was found guilty: after which he was called on, in the usual form, why sentence of death should not be passed on him. He appeared quite unmoved; and said he was not guilty of the crime imputed to him. The judge then proceeded to pass sentence on him; which he did in a very impressive manner, though frequently interrupted by exclamations of innocence from the prisoner. The offence being made by a particular act of parliament a capital felony, he was sentenced to be hanged. He asked for a long day, which was humanely granted, and his execution was deferred to the 18th of September, on which day it took place, in the midst of a vast concourse of spectators.

The day after M'Ilvena's trial, Jennings was placed at the bar, on an indictment for conspiring to debauch Mary Hair. He was almost instantly found Guilty; when the judge told him his crime was much enhanced by the attempt he made to screen his accomplice from punishment, in which he committed wilful and corrupt perjury. The sentence of the Court was, that he should stand for an hour on the pillory, be imprisoned for one year, and pay a fine of fifty pounds.

JAMES LEARY,

EXECUTED FOR THE MURDER OF EDWARD CLIFFORD.

It has, no doubt, been observed by our readers, that no small part of our Calendar has been occupied with details of atrocities, in which the natives of the sister island have been concerned. There are causes which tend to demoralize and deprave the lower orders of that unfortunate country,—their local insurrections, and continual migrations. The first, in addition to its evil tendency, subjects them to the vengeance of penal laws; and the latter exposes them to all the temptations to which poverty is subject, when released from those wholesome restraints which keep poor men temperate and honest.

The nominally high wages in this country, when contrasted with the low price of labour in Ireland, induce many of that kingdom to emigrate to England, where they find, too late, that the poor man may change his master, but not his condition; for he that has to live by labour must labour whilst he lives. By far the greater portion of them, however, like birds of passage, pay us only periodical visits; and these, whose strange manners and singular dress make them little less remarkable than the cuckoo, are mostly natives of the barren mountains of Connaught, which they desert, in summer, for the fertile plains of England.*

But there is another race of Hibernians, very different from these—natives of the south of Ireland, who are either obliged to fly from the violated laws of their country, or desert it in the hopes of bettering their condition. Liverpool, Bristol, and London, are the scenes where they play their part, and where, it must be admitted, they exhibit the degrading vices of human nature in the utmost perfection. This does not arise from any innate depravity, or national propensity to vice: it proceeds directly from circumstances. Speaking a different dialect, frequently a different language, and professing a proscribed religion, they encounter every where prejudice and reproach; to fly from which they are compelled to associate with each other, and drown their misfortunes in gin and brandy: vice follows as a thing of course, and crime too often ensues. The poor man, thus, who, in his native village, was sober and industrious, because he had a character to lose, is gradually initiated into vice, because he has no longer a character to sustain. Such a man has no sufficient inducement to be moral—and soon learns that, where so many are otherwise, individual wickedness is likely to pass undiscovered. Add to this the influence of bad example, and it can be no longer surprising that the labouring Irish in London are brutal, drunken, and vicious.

These observations have been

* We take the following description of Irish *cottiers* from the '*Dublin and London Magazine*,' for 1825:—

'The word *cottier*, in Ireland, is synonymous with *labourer* in all other countries; and those who come under the denomination are composed of that class of society who are doomed, by a wise Providence, literally to earn their bread by the "sweat of their brow." We have no right, therefore, to expect in these any thing not found in the major part of the population of all kingdoms—any thing but a perpetual necessity to toil and economise—any thing but what are the associates of a poor man—want, worldly want, and a long train of what many will consider privations. Nine-tenths of mankind are necessarily reduced to this condition; and, whatever theorists may say, in this condition they must continue while the economy of this world prevails.

'An Irish cottier is to be looked upon as the poorest man in the kingdom; one who, if he was not entitled to the appellation he bears, would be called a labourer, depending on his daily toil for support. At present he enjoys a portion of independence, which he would then lose; and cannot be under the apprehensions of him who has to provide for the day that is passing over him, because he can, if the fault is not his own, always possess an annual supply of provisions which habit has reconciled him to, that places him beyond the reach of absolute want, pauperism, and hunger.

'A cottier in Ireland is a poor man, who possesses from one to ten acres of land, upon which stands his habitation—mean, to be sure; but in what country do the poor possess splendid dwellings? For this holding he is generally obliged to work for his landlord—sometimes all, and sometimes half his time, according to the quantity of ground he occupies; but he frequently pays a certain rent, and employs his time in whatever way he thinks fit. Those who pay in labour are small cottiers, who have not more than two or three acres, which supply them with oats and potatoes; their employers, in almost every instance, being bound to give them feeding for a cow, and one or more sheep.

'The nominal price of labourers—six or eight pence a day—sounds low; but it should be recollected that, in Ireland, the farm-servants are all boarded; and that those who are thus paid are constantly employed—in their own words—wet and dry. The cottier has his work always provided for him: and for this, if he has common industry, his family are put in possession of absolute abundance; for a single acre of land, properly cultivated, will produce him at least sixty pounds of potatoes for every day in the year, while his cow supplies him with milk; and, as he can keep a pig, a goat, sheep, poultry, &c. he can have meat, drink, and clothes.'

drawn from us in consequence of the case we are about to narrate, and in the hope that it may be read by some of the Irish themselves. From it they may learn to refrain from transmitting false intelligence to their countrymen at home, whom, instead of deluding to quit Ireland,* they should deter from visiting London, where they are sure to encounter misery; and that too often leads to those crimes, for which many, who, like them, were once innocent, have suffered an ignominious death.

James Leary, whose case is now before us, was a native of Ireland, and, in addition to the shrewdness and cunning of his countrymen, possessed that persevering and concealed wickedness which belongs to criminals of all nations. Of his guilt there does not remain a doubt; yet the deliberate and hardened cunning of the man has thrown such a mystery over the whole case, that no one can pronounce with certainty who actually perpetrated the murder. There is, however, a melancholy consolation in knowing that Leary deservedly suffered; for, if he did not strike the blow, he confessed he was a spectator, and might have prevented it.

Edward Clifford was a native of Cahir, in the county of Tipperary, Ireland. He there became acquainted with a woman, named Burke, whose husband had deserted her. She was the mother of four children, and, in 1813, was pregnant of another, of whom Clifford was the father. To avoid the disgrace which the publicity of their criminal intercourse would surely bring upon them, they resolved to quit Ireland, and remove to London, where Clifford promised to support Mrs. Burke and her children by his labour.

Clifford had saved, by his earnings, sixteen or seventeen pounds, and Mrs. Burke's effects produced thirty pounds. With this sum they set off for the British metropolis, where they arrived early in the July of 1813. Clifford could not speak a word of English; but Mrs. Burke, who now assumed the name of Clifford, could, as she had been in London when a child. When they alighted from the waggon, at Fleet Market, they sat down on the flags, and were addressed by one

* As late as 1824, near two hundred Irish peasants were literally kidnapped by an unprincipled master of a steam packet, which sailed between Cork and Bristol. He sent his agents through the country, to the distance of twenty miles, to inform the peasantry that thousands of hands were wanted in London, where men received six and women four shillings a day, and that there was a certainty of constant employ for five years. The credulous people, who were only paid sixpence a day, and board, at home, immediately began to prepare for their journey, and, to provide for the expenses, sold their pig, pot, and every thing else they were possessed of. They paid sixteen shillings for their passage; yet the unfeeling wretch who commanded the packet, and whose conduct deserves execration more than half the depredators recorded in this work, refused to let them either boil a kettle, or have boiling water, without sixpence for every time they wanted it, so that, on their arrival in London, they had not a farthing in their pockets. Finding that they had been cruelly deceived, they wandered through the streets, not knowing what to do. Information being given at Marylebone Street Police-office, they were brought up, when an old woman, named Eleanor Walsh, with much feeling detailed the above particulars. She implored, above all things, that they might be sent home; for, though their cabins and every thing else were gone, still they would be able to make out something to eat in their own country, which they could not hope to do in this. The magistrate expressed his indignation at the supineness of the authorities in Cork in permitting such an exportation, and wrote concerning it to the Home department, in consequence of which instructions were given to provide against a repetition of such a transaction. The poor people were sent home.

of their countrywomen, who turned out to be the wife of Leary. She affected much kindness, and they were happy in meeting with one so cordial in a strange place. They inquired for lodgings, and Mrs. Leary invited them to her own room, in a lane that led into the market, to which they instantly removed, and where they passed for man and wife.

They continued four days with Leary, who was a bricklayer's labourer, and were charged two shillings and sixpence a night for their bed, which they were told was too much by one Slattery, whom they had known in Ireland, as he had only left it three months before. Slattery recommended them to a room in Church Lane, St. Giles's, to which they removed, and he went to lodge with them.

Here they continued for three weeks, without any hope of procuring employment, and Clifford seemed anxious to return to Ireland. On Saturday night, July the 24th, Leary, for the first time, paid them a visit, at eleven o'clock, and, being asked what brought him so late, answered he came to let Clifford know he had procured him work. Next morning Clifford went to Leary's lodgings about the work; and his wife, or rather she who assumed the title, followed him. They appeared to have been quarrelling, and, Leary saying Clifford was to dine with him, she insisted he should not. During the time they remained in the room Leary contrived to whisper in Mrs. Clifford's ear that her husband was determined to set off for Ireland, but charged her, for her life, not to mention who told her. She, notwithstanding, accused Clifford with intending to desert her; but he denied it, and inquired who told her, which she refused to answer.

Clifford and his wife, after this, returned to their own lodgings, where they remained until five o'clock, at which hour, just as they were sitting down to dinner, Leary and his wife, unexpected and uninvited, came in. Mrs. Clifford was much displeased, as Mrs. Leary was very drunk, though her husband was quite sober. Some beer was sent for, and about eight o'clock they stood up to go home. Previous, however, to doing so, Leary had drawn from Mrs. Clifford the particulars of how they kept their money; for she had imprudently told Mrs. Leary, on her first coming to town, that they had a trifle. On this occasion she acted with similar incaution, and informed Leary that her husband kept his own money about him, and that she had also a small sum, about which he knew nothing.

On Leary's going down stairs he called Clifford, and took him off with him. The poor unfortunate woman, apprehensive, from what she heard in the morning, that herself and children would be deserted, went out in search of her husband. She found, at nine o'clock, that he was drunk in Leary's room, and insisted on his going home with her. He complied, and in their way was overtaken by Leary, who took them into a public house, and made Clifford drink a glass of gin. After coming out of this one, he wheeled them into another, where they had some beer. Here he promised Mrs. Clifford that her husband should be in work on the morrow.

On their way up Holborn Hill, they walked too quick for Mrs. Clifford, who was far advanced in pregnancy. She requested they would wait for her; but Leary said they were going to his employer. She remonstrated against it, as it was too late to call on any gentleman particularly as it was Sunday evening. 'Never fear, Mrs. Clifford,' said Leary; 'do you take your time, and we shall be home before you, and have half a gallon of beer on the table.' They then left her, it being near ten o'clock.

The unfortunate woman then made the best of her way home; and, seeing her husband had not arrived, she sat up smoking the pipe—no uncommon amusement with her countrywomen—until the clock struck twelve. Slattery was in bed, and bore evidence to this fact. Being uneasy about Clifford, she arose about two, and between three and four went to Leary's lodgings. The door was locked on the outside, and Mrs. Leary said her husband was not within; for he had concealed himself when he heard the knock at the door. She then returned home, with intention to follow Clifford, who, she supposed, had set off for Ireland, and requested of her brother, who lived in Parker Street, Drury Lane, to procure her a pass from the parish. Between seven and eight o'clock, however, she heard of the murder of Clifford; and being taken to a public house in Gray's Inn Lane, where the body was, she recognised it.

The remains of this unfortunate man were found in a pond at the bottom of Gray's Inn Lane, into which he had been thrown, after being murdered: his brains had been knocked out with, as was supposed, a hammer, and one of his pockets was turned inside out: in the other were found only three halfpence, although it appeared he had, the preceding evening, thirteen or fourteen pounds about him.

Suspicion immediately fell upon Leary. Two officers went to his lodgings, at which his wife appeared greatly alarmed, and refused to tell where her husband worked. They, however, discovered; and, on going there, they saw him descending a ladder, with a hod on his shoulder. Unwilling to surprise him, they inquired for his master, when he replied, 'It is not my master you want; it is me.' They said it was, and apprehended him. On their way to the office, Leary said, 'I have heard of this poor man who has been killed.' On being asked how he heard, he said, 'Never mind how; I have heard.' On his person was found only one shilling and sixpence; nor was any money found in his room, though it was searched. A hammer, which seemed to correspond with the cuts in the hat of the deceased, was found buried in some coals.

After Leary was put in the strong room, he wished to see a person named Macarthy, a shoemaker, to whom he said, 'What do you think of this job of mine?' Macarthy replied, 'I think it a very bad case, and that the evidence brought against you will hang you;' and pressed him to acknowledge his guilt. Leary then hinted that, if he could get a person to prove that he was at home at ten o'clock, it would set all right. Macarthy said, 'Suppose you could do that, where were you between the time you left Mrs. Clifford and ten o'clock?' Leary said, 'There is where I shall fail.' Macarthy said he thought there was nothing would get him through it. 'Nothing,' said Leary, 'but one thing; and that is, to fix it upon somebody else.' Macarthy replied, 'If that is what you wanted me for, I will leave you to your fate, and you will be hung like a dog, and not one of your countrymen shall come forward to give one shilling.' On parting, Leary said, 'I know I shall be hanged: may I go to hell if I have any more to do with the murder than you.'

The coroner's inquest having sat on the body of the unfortunate Edward Clifford, it was removed, on Monday evening, to a public house in St. Giles's, there to be waked after the manner of his country. Several hundred persons went to see the remains of the unfortunate man, and on Thursday Leary was brought from the House of Correction, Coldbath Fields, in a hackney coach, heavily ironed, and well guarded, in order that he might see the body he was charged with so cruelly mangling. On entering the room, the lid of the coffin was removed, and his motions were watched. He took the hand of the deceased, declared his innocence of his blood, and said he should not know the man. He was certainly much altered. Leary trembled exceedingly; but, on going down stairs, he resumed his fortitude, and drank a pint of porter in the parlour: after which he was removed to Hatton Garden for further examination. On Friday evening the remains of poor Clifford were buried in St. George's burying-ground, attended by multitudes of his country-people.

From the time Leary beheld the mangled remains of Clifford he laboured under great agitation of mind, and was troubled with frightful dreams—the midnight testimonies of a guilty conscience. He appeared horror-struck; and parted, at night, with reluctance from the turnkey. On Sunday he wished to see the gaoler; and, after confessing that he knew of the murder, signed a long statement, in which he attempted to throw the charge upon the miserable widow—we call her widow, as we have called her wife, to prevent confusion in our narrative.

In consequence of this pretended confession, Mrs. Clifford, or rather Mrs. Burke, was committed to Coldbath Fields' Prison, and her children were sent to St. Pancras Poor-house, although a benevolent lady, near Fitzroy Square, had undertaken to provide for them. So great was the interest excited in her behalf, that some gentlemen had subscribed fifty pounds; but, at the request of the magistrates, they held it over, until some light was thrown upon the mysterious affair.

Leary's statement displayed a mind of great acuteness and circumspection; but, as it was not founded on truth, his allegations were easily confuted. In minor points he strictly adhered to facts; but, in the most material, he evidently departed from truth: for it was proved, by more than one witness, that Slattery, whom he accused of throwing the body into the pond, stopped at home the whole evening, and that Mrs. Clifford purchased a candle, and lit it in the street where she lived, at eleven o'clock.

It is true, the unfortunate woman, Mrs. Clifford, or Mrs. Burke, as we shall call her in future, did not exactly communicate her situation to the magistrates at the first and second examination; but delicacy might, and no doubt did, restrain her from acknowledging that she was not married to the deceased, or that her husband, who had culpably deserted her, was still living. But, while we make this extenuation of her conduct, let us not be accounted advocates for its impropriety; on the contrary, we condemn her, not only for concealing these facts on so solemn an occasion, but also for alleging that she had no money, when she had placed six pounds in the hands of a chandler to keep for her, and which six pounds she had without Clifford's knowledge.

On the other hand, it must be admitted that Leary's statement evinced much cunning and wickedness; he took care to hint that Mrs. Burke had meditated the crime, as he said he felt a stick under her clothes, insinuating the hammer with which the deed was perpetrated; and, that the act might appear to have had a motive, he alleged that Slattery aided her, from which it might be implied that herself and Slattery made away with Clifford, that they might cohabit together. This was a deep-laid scheme to implicate them both; and, to qualify himself for a king's evidence, he stated that he was looking on while the bloody deed was doing. Luckily for the ends of justice, this statement was satisfactorily contradicted in evidence, by which it appeared he pursued his diabolical ends with the most cruel patience, inebriating his victim, and then, under pretence of taking him to his employer, way-laying him. Still it must be admitted that he could have no enmity to the man, and that, if plunder was his object, he could have robbed him, as he was drunk, without murdering him to prevent detection. These are considerations which superadd to his own declaration of not having actually perpetrated the deed, and which must for ever involve the case in mystery.

Mrs. Burke was delivered in prison of her fifth child, and, at the next examination, which, for her convenience, took place at the House of Correction, Coldbath Fields, her other four children, three girls and a boy, were also present, and the two eldest gave their testimony in a very correct and respectful manner, which interested all present, among whom were some of the royal family, and numbers of the nobility; so great an interest did the case excite.

After this examination Leary was committed to Newgate; and on Friday, September the 17th, he was arraigned at the Old Bailey. Mrs. Burke appeared as principal evidence against him, and her testimony was corroborated by that of several others.

Leary, in his defence, complained of misstatements in the newspapers, and charged several of the witnesses for the prosecution with perjury. He said he was the son of a schoolmaster—to show he was not ignorant; and that, unlike others in his station of life, he was not addicted to petty theft.

He received an excellent character from several persons; but the jury found him Guilty, and he was sentenced to be hanged the ensuing Monday. He now became visibly affected, burst into tears, and seemed lost in affliction. He shook his hand with bitterness at Macarthy; but, before his removal from the dock, he extended it to him with apparent forgiveness; but Macarthy refused to take, what he called, his blood-stained hand.

On Monday morning the platform was erected as early as five o'clock, with the railing round it. At six the circle was formed by the constables, and the crowd began to assemble from all quarters of the town. The day was remarkably fine, and every window, and all the tops of the houses that had any view of the gallows, were covered with spectators. The Rev. Mr. Devereux arrived about six o'clock, and was admitted to the unfortunate prisoner, whom he found walking about his cell with hurried steps, clenched hands, and his eyes turned

KNAPP & BALDWIN's NEWGATE CALENDAR. 133

The coroner's inquest having sat on the body of the unfortunate Edward Clifford, it was removed, on Monday evening, to a public house in St. Giles's, there to be waked, after the manner of his country. Several hundred persons went to see the remains of the unfortunate man, and on Thursday heavy was brought from the House of Correction, Coldbath Fields, in a hackney coach, heavily ironed, and well guarded, in order that she might see the body he was charged with so cruelly murdering. On entering the room, the lid of the coffin was removed, the face of the deceased disclosed, and the head of his infant, and she was desired to view them. She was much affected. She was observed to turn pale, but as innocent as she protested herself to be, the scene of which she was so prominent a feature, was too affecting to be looked at with composure. The jury on examining the body, found that the poor Clifford had been most inhumanly treated...

...confession, Mrs. Clifford, or rather Mrs. Burke, was committed to Coldbath Fields' Prison, and her children were sent to the Parish Poor-house, although a benevolent lady, near Fitzroy Square, had undertaken to provide for them. So great was the interest excited in her behalf, that some gentleman had subscribed fifty pounds; but they held some still more extensive views upon the mysterious affair.

Love's sister-in-law deposed... [remainder illegible]

...prayer

about seven minutes, Denton's cap being pulled over his face all the time. Leary appeared very penitent and attentive to Mr. Devereux. At seven minutes before eight his cap was pulled over his face, and they were both launched into eternity. After the bodies were cut down they were put into a cart, and conveyed to the dissecting room, St. Bartholomew's Hospital, escorted by the city marshals, and a large posse of constables, where they were delivered up to the surgeons. Leary was observed to be a full quarter of an hour in convulsive agony, but Denton was dead almost as soon as he was let drop.

We have used no common diligence in collecting the particulars of this mysterious case, and shall not protract it by any comments of our own. One thing, however, may not be unnecessary to state, as it holds out a forcible lesson to our readers. Drunkenness appears to have been the means by which the murder was perpetrated. Had the unfortunate Clifford continued sober, he had escaped assassination; and, though his former conduct in cohabiting with a married woman, and then bringing her from her own country, deserves loud condemnation, yet it produced less mischievous consequence than that of getting inebriated. May others learn, from this case, that the man who, under the mask of good fellowship, prevails on his friend to drink till he is intoxicated, is a concealed enemy, and should be studiously avoided.

JOHN DENTON,
EXECUTED FOR THE MURDER OF MRS. DENTON.

This unfortunate man, whose case becomes doubly notorious from the circumstance of his having suffered at the same time with Leary, fell a victim to passion, brought on by intoxication. It is a melancholy truth, and one which should be impressed on the mind of the reader, that the greater number of malefactors who fall victims to the violated laws may attribute their misfortunes to drunkenness, and its concomitants, poverty and debauchery.

The facts of this case are short. John Denton had been a sailor in the early part of his life, but latterly followed the trade of a rigger, and was accounted a good workman. He was acquainted with a man of his own name, and, after his death, became very attentive to his widow, who resided in Bow Lane Buildings, in the parish of Bromley. Denton sometimes lived in the house; but it does not appear that any improper connexion took place, though they were very intimate, and he was very partial to her.

On the 13th of June, 1813, Denton was somewhat outrageous in his manner, no doubt from frequent potations of gin and beer, as it was fair time; and he struck a woman named Mrs. Whitehead. The widow considered his conduct improper and unmanly; and desired him to leave her house, and never enter it again. He came, however, in the evening, about seven o'clock, manifestly for the purpose of having revenge for the supposed insult. Mrs. Denton had her daughter and female friend with her when he entered; he kept one hand in his breast, and held a pot of beer in the other. He wanted the widow to drink with him, but she refused, and took some liquor of her own, saying 'Get you gone, John; you are a disgrace to your sex.' He asked 'What do you say? am I disgrace to my sex?' She replied in the affirmative, and e started up, drew a knife from his breast, rushed upon her, and ran her through the arm, the point of the knife penetrating her side. He was immediately taken into custody; and, when asked what induced him to commit the crime, he answered 'It was all for love.'

The widow survived only a month; for the artery of her arm being divided, a mortification ensued, which terminated in death. Denton was brought to trial at the Old Bailey, September the 18th, 1813; and though several witnesses deposed to various acts of extravagance, with a view to prove him insane, he was found Guilty. The particulars of his execution we have already given in the preceding case.

THOMAS FOSS,
EXECUTED FOR FORGERY.

THE man who fabricates a single bill, or check, may say something in palliation of his crime; but the deliberate forger of a bank-note has nothing to advance in extenuation of his guilt. He goes systematically to work, procures agents, and deliberates upon the means of defrauding the public in a permanent manner.

Few forgers of a more dangerous character than Thomas Foss have ever committed depredations on the public. He had been long employed in the Bank of England as copper-plate printer; but left it to commence business on his own account. He joined another person; but kept a private press of his own, without the knowledge of his partner.

So persevering was his industry, that he learned the art of engraving, and invented a method for impressing the water-marks upon paper. Having thus arranged every thing necessary for his purpose, he struck off some notes, and gave them to two persons, named Norman and Gwyn, to pass. These fellows had not continued long in their nefarious traffic, when their career was stopped: they were detected, and committed to prison.

While in confinement each of them, unknown to the other, offered to become king's evidence, and they were both admitted. In consequence of their information Foss was taken into custody, and the whole apparatus for fabricating forged notes was discovered.

Foss was indicted at the Old Bailey, September 18th, 1813, when, in addition to these facts, the printer to the Bank swore that the signature to the notes was in Foss's handwriting. He was accordingly found Guilty, received sentence of death, and was executed in front of Newgate, November the 10th, 1813. He died penitent.

CHARLES CALLAGHAN,
EXECUTED FOR THE MURDER OF MISS GOMPERTZ'S BUTLER.

HARDENED depravity attended this unfortunate and guilty young man through his short and vicious life; for, though he was not more than nineteen years of age, he committed many depredations, and when justice overtook him he refused to repent. He died as he lived—without the fear of God in his heart.

About the middle of December, 1813, the Misses Gompertz, who lived in Vauxhall, were alarmed one night by the report of a pistol, and, on going down stairs, found that their butler had been murdered by some villains, who had effected their escape. Several articles of plate were missing, and information of the robbery and murder was given at the different police-offices.

Soon after, Callaghan, and one Hylas Parish, were apprehended on suspicion, as they were about leaving London, under very mysterious circumstances. No evidence, however, could be adduced against them, sufficient to detain them on that charge; but, fortunately for the ends of justice, there were found on Callaghan duplicates of pledged property, which warranted their committal for a burglary in the house of Mr. Taylor, of Chatham.

These youthful depredators had not remained long in prison when Parish was induced, in the hope of pardon, to make a full confession. He stated that himself and Callaghan became acquainted at Vauxhall Gardens, and that they subsequently lodged together in the London Road. Callaghan and he agreed to commit a robbery, in the hope of recruiting their exhausted finances; and Callaghan proposed the house of the Misses Gompertz as the object of attack, as he had lived there for some time in the capacity of footman. Having thus agreed on their plan, they went one evening, about dusk, to reconnoitre the premises; after which they went to the Surrey Theatre.

When the performance was over, they returned, and, having gained admission into the garden, they forced open the kitchen window-shutter; but could not open the window itself, in consequence of which they cut out a pane of glass, and, having disburdened themselves of their coats, they forced their way through. When they had got in, they were alarmed by a rustling noise, which soon ceased, and they supposed it was made by a cat. Parish struck a light, he having some tinder with him; and, observing the tea-things on the dresser, they took up six silver spoons and a pair of sugar-tongs. Before they proceeded any further they took off their shoes, and then went into the pantry, where they were surprised to find the butler asleep in bed. This caused them to retreat into the kitchen, where they found two silver waiters. Callaghan then recollected that the butler had a watch, which always hung at the head of his bed, and desired Parish to go and fetch it.

Parish accordingly went, and while he was feeling for the watch the unfortunate man awoke, and, thinking it was a cat that was annoying him, hissed it away; but immediately after he started up, and ran to the kitchen window; at which Callaghan exclaimed 'Give it him—give it him, Bill!' Parish accordingly, to intimidate the butler, fired his pistol into the ceiling; but Callaghan, coming up to him, placed the muzzle of his close to the unfortunate man's ear, and blew his brains out. In their flight Callaghan left his shoes behind him; but they carried off part of the silver, which they pledged next day in town, except a small portion, which they carried to Gravesend, where they sold it.

In consequence of this confession Parish was admitted king's evidence, and Callaghan was indicted at the Surrey assizes, March the 31st, 1814, when the testimony of his accomplice was fully corroborated by that of other witnesses. He made no defence, and was instantly found Guilty.

On the ensuing Saturday he was executed, at the top of Horsemonger Lane Prison. At half past nine o'clock he was removed to the chapel, from whence, after remaining a short time, he was brought out to have his irons knocked off, previous to his having the sacrament administered to him; in the course of which he was frequently exhorted to confess his guilt of the crime for which he was about to suffer. But the pious solicitude of the chaplain was of no avail; and in that state of obdurate hardihood which attended him throughout he was launched into eternity, after which his body was given to the surgeons.

JOHN DREW MAY,
EXECUTED FOR FORGERY.

THE advocates for the abolition of capital punishment might adduce this case as a further illustration of the principle, that hanging one man does not prevent another from falling into the same crime; otherwise we should not see, at each successive sessions, men arraigned for forgery whose situations in life warrant us in supposing that they were not ignorant of the consequence of detection when they committed the crime.

How many have suffered for forgery, who had not even a remote intention of fraud! A merchant's credit, like a woman's honour, (once suspected, it is lost,) is frequently at the mercy of an hour; and, to prevent the tottering reputation from falling, forgery, particularly of bills, is too often resorted to as the means of obviating a temporary embarrassment. It is, no doubt, a dangerous resource; but it is one which some, whose credit is yet high, have ventured to adopt, escaping detection by timely meeting their engagements; whilst others, incautious and unforfortunate, have been disappointed in their expectation. The bill has been dishonoured, the forgery has been discovered, and the miscalculating culprit has been suspended on the gallows, because he had not a few pounds to take up a fictitious endorsement.*

We do not think that the man on whose case we are now entering comes under the description of those whose crime admits of palliation. He pocketed the money, and could not possibly refund it; and therefore we must condemn him as the very worst of forgers, for he imposed upon those who confided in him, and defrauded those whom he could not afterwards remunerate, if his villainy passed undetected.

In October, 1813, Mr. John Drew May, a respectable bill-broker, was brought before the lord-mayor on a charge of altering and interlining a certain bill, which was originally drawn for twenty-eight pounds, eight shillings, and sixpence, but which Mr. May paid away to a Mr. Berry, for one thousand and twenty-eight pounds, eight shillings, and sixpence, an addition being made to it, while in his possession, of one thousand pounds.

The discovery was made by Mr. Berry carrying the bill, for discount,

* On Tuesday, June the 8th, 1813, Joseph Nash, a grocer, in Newgate Street, was found guilty of forging an endorsement on a bill for four hundred and eighty-nine pounds, and three shillings. It appeared that bills with the same name endorsed on them had been frequently passed and honoured; but, in consequence of temporary embarrassment, he was unable to meet this one when due; though his property was fully adequate to discharge all his debts, and, a few days after the bill became due, he offered the money at the Bank, which was refused. Here was absence of guilty intention, and Mr. Nash was afterwards pardoned.

to the house of Down, Thornton, and Co. where it was found to have been altered. May, on being questioned on the subject, said he received it from a person at the west end, whose name and residence he was entirely ignorant of.

May was remanded, to admit of further inquiry; and on the 12th of June he was brought up for final examination, when the prosecutor, Mr. Thornton, wished to decline proceeding, in consequence of two similar charges being about to be preferred against the prisoner by the admiralty; but the lord-mayor thought it was no longer optional with Mr. Thornton, and, therefore, bound him over to prosecute.

The next charge preferred against Mr. May was for altering a navy bill. The case was this:—The victualling board had various contracts, and these were uniformly paid by bills, at different dates, on the treasurer of the navy, and which bills passed, in the money market, with the facility of bank-notes. In the present instance a bill for seven hundred and thirty-two pounds, thirteen shillings, and eight pence, was paid to a Mr. Ringsford, payable in ninety days. This bill, after passing through several hands, came, at length, in its original state, to Mr. May, and he was charged with inserting the figure of one before the seven, making the bill appear to have been drawn for one thousand, seven hundred, and thirty-two pounds, thirteen shillings, and eight pence. Whether he actually did so himself, or not, it is impossible to say; but it was proved that he personally received that sum for it, from Bruce, Warren, and Co. bill-brokers. The bill continued in circulation until due, each succeeding hand taking it for the value of one thousand, seven hundred, and thirty-two pounds, thirteen shillings, and eight pence, without inspecting the body of the bill; and, what appears still stranger, it was actually paid at the navy board for that amount. At length the fraud was discovered, and Mr. May was charged with the forgery.

For this last offence he was indicted at the Old Bailey, December 2, 1813, when the bill was traced, in its original state, to his hands, and was proved to have been passed by him in its interpolated condition. His counsel exerted themselves much to throw the blame upon Mr. May's clerk, named Lacey, his brother-in-law, who was thoroughly in his confidence, but who had absconded. It was proved that Lacey carried Mr. May's check-book, which he occasionally filled up, Mr. May's signature being affixed to the blank check. But, on the other hand, it did not appear that Lacey had any benefit in interpolating the bills, supposing he had done so; nor did May show that Lacey had either defrauded him or others.

Mr. May, being called on for his defence, addressed the jury with much feeling, observing that not only his life, but, what was infinitely dearer to him than life, his character and honest fame, were now in their hands. He was one of eight children, and had received a liberal and virtuous education; and, till the moment of this accusation, had lived with credit and reputation. He was content that his life should be forfeited, if any man could say that he had been wronged by him. He had been bred to business, had a wife and three children, and, after the labour of the day, was wont to seek domestic enjoyment in the bosom of his family, where he was sure to find it. Was it probable that a man so circumstanced would resign his claim to these endearments by committing a crime which could not fail to bring ruin on himself, and disgrace on those who were nearest and dearest to his heart? There was no proof that he had forged the bill, none that he had uttered it, knowing it to be forged; the case rested upon mere suspicion; and upon that suspicion any man might be placed at that bar.

He had reposed unlimited confidence in his clerk, and had left blank checks with him to fill up. His clerk was now beyond his reach; nor, if he was present, could he be compelled to answer any question which might criminate himself. Should the jury entertain any doubts, (and he was convinced they must have insurmountable ones,) the judge would tell them that he, the prisoner, was entitled to the benefit of them. He made no complaint on the subject of the prosecution, nor of the manner in which it was conducted; and he was certain the public prosecutor, having discharged what he conceived to have been his duty, would be the first to rejoice at his acquittal.

Several witnesses were then called, who gave the prisoner an excellent character for integrity and honour in his commercial transactions; and, the judge having summed up the evidence, the jury retired, and continued in consultation for two hours—a dreadful interval of suspense to the unfortunate prisoner, who, on their returning with a verdict of Guilty, became so agitated that he was scarcely able to stand.

When brought up to receive sentence, Mr. May briefly addressed the Court. He stated that, though, on his own account, he had no wish to live, stripped of the unblemished reputation he had formerly enjoyed; yet, for the sake of his parents, and of near and dear connexions, he wished his life to be spared. He acknowledged he had been found guilty after a long and patient trial; and hoped that the long confinement he had undergone, and the anxiety of mind with which it had been accompanied, would be looked upon as some expiation, even upon the supposition that he had been guilty of the imputed crime. It had not been proved that the bill, in its original state, had ever been in his hands, or that he had either forged it himself, or had uttered it, knowing it to be forged. The forgery must have been by another, who entirely possessed his confidence, and who had left the country. Did he seek to elude justice? He had been seized in the bosom of his family, in all that security that was the attendant on innocence. The bill had passed undetected through the hands of others; in the same manner, also, it might have passed through his. From the pressure of extensive business, he had been unable to examine all the bills that had passed through his hands, and the examination of them had in consequence been frequently intrusted to his clerk, as also the filling up of checks. He hoped it would be stated to the prince regent, that the jury had taken three hours to consider their verdict, which showed that no common doubts hung over his case. At all events, he was confident that he was before a tribunal where any doubts on the side of justice would leave room for the voice of mercy to be heard, and to prevail.--The most profound silence obtained while Mr. May was addressing the Court.

Sentence of death was then passed on the unfortunate man in the usual form.

From the time of Mr. May's condemnation his friends spared no exertion in endeavouring to procure an extension of the royal mercy; and their hopes were alive until

Friday evening, April the 3d, 1814, when they were given to understand that the law should take its course. The unfortunate man took leave of his three brothers that afternoon, as his execution was appointed for the next morning. His unhappy wife, being confined by indisposition, was saved the misery of a last interview.

He suffered with four other unfortunate men for forgery, Sturman for setting fire to his house, and another man, for burglary. May, being asked how how he felt, answered 'Happy,' and requested that his friends might be assured of that fact. His last words were, parting at the scaffold, 'This is the worst part of the ceremony; to go forth thus, and to die in a manner which will cast reflections on my posterity—it is this only part which gives me pain.'

JOHN ASHTON,
EXECUTED FOR HIGHWAY ROBBERY.

THE circumstance which attended the execution of this unfortunate man alone entitles him to a place in our pages, for otherwise his case is void of interest.

He was apprehended for a highway robbery, and convicted at the Old Bailey, when he received sentence of death. From the time of his conviction, he either affected, or suffered, complete insanity; but this did not release him from the consequence of his sentence; and, on Monday, August 22d, 1814, he was executed in front of Newgate, along with William Henry Lye, for burglary; John Mitchell, for forgery; Francis Sturgess, and Michael Mahoney, for highway robbery; and John Field, *alias* Jonathan Wild, for burglary. By half past six o'clock the Old Bailey, and houses adjacent, were crowded to great excess. At half past seven Mahoney was brought forward, for the purpose of being disencumbered of his irons. While his irons were knocking off, it was found necessary to search for a knife to cut some part of the cordage, which confined the irons. Mahoney, seeing this, stooped, and, with an Herculean effort, tore it asunder. This being the only Catholic, the Rev. Mr. Devereux attended him in constant prayer, in which he joined most fervently. Sturgess, Field, and Mitchell, conducted themselves with great propriety. The unfortunate Ashton had been in a state of insanity since the receipt of the awful warrant for his execution. In the Press Yard he distorted his countenance horribly. He was the fifth who mounted the scaffold, and ran up the steps with great rapidity; and, having gained the summit of the platform, began to kick and dance, and often exclaimed, 'I'm Lord Wellington!' The Rev. Mr. Cotton, who officiated for the first time as Ordinary, enjoined him to prayer, to which he paid little attention, and continued to clap his hands as far as he was permitted by the extent of the cord. Mitchell often invited him to prayer. All that could be done was ineffectual, and it was necessary to have two men to hold him during the awful ceremony. When they released him for the purpose of the Lord's Prayer being said, he turned round, and began to dance, and vociferated, 'Look at me; I am Lord Wellington!' At twenty minutes past eight o'clock the signal was given, and the platform fell. Scarcely, however, had the sufferers dropped, before, to the awe and astonishment of every beholder, Ashton rebounded from the rope, and was instantaneously seen dancing near the Ordinary, and crying out very loudly, and apparently unhurt, 'What do ye think of me? am I not Lord Wellington now?' He then danced, clapped his hands, and huzzaed. At length the executioner was compelled to get upon the scaffold, and to push him forcibly from the place on which he stood.

JAMES MITCHELL,
EXECUTED FOR THE MURDER OF MISS WELCHMAN.

JAMES MITCHELL was a native of Salisbury, where he first lived with a farmer in the capacity of ploughboy. He afterwards removed to London, and became a gentleman's servant. While in this situation he got acquainted with Miss Mary Ann Welchman, to whom, for two years, he was in the habit of paying his addresses.

Miss Welchman was a ladies' dress-maker, and lived as forewoman with Miss Macey, who carried on that business in Mount Street. She was an elegant young woman, about four-and-twenty years of age, and of a most amiable disposition. To her, in an evil hour, Mitchell paid his addresses, under the name of Smith, and represented himself as purser on board some ship. The credulous girl believed him worthy and honourable, and permitted him to visit her, at the house of her employer, where he was, for some time, treated with politeness and friendship. At length his own conduct betrayed his deceptions; he obtruded himself at improper hours, and more than once offended the young ladies in the workroom by the coarseness and indelicacy of his conversation. This coming to the knowledge of Miss Welchman's brother, he prevailed, with some difficulty, on his sister, to forego the acquaintance of Smith, alias Mitchell.

In accordance with her brother's advice, Miss Welchman had several interviews on the subject with Mitchell; but still he continued coming to the house, notwithstanding her prohibition, and persevered in his visits, although she had repeatedly denied herself. On Friday, August the 5th, 1814, he called at Mount Street, and was ushered into the workroom, where Miss Welchman was sitting.

He continued in the room the whole of the evening, and was very abusive in his language. Miss Welchman desired him several times to leave the house; but he refused, unless a letter was returned to him, which Miss Welchman declared she had destroyed. He then wanted her to provide supper, which she refused; he next wished her to go out with him, which she also refused, and declined lending him some money which he requested of her.

About eleven o'clock Miss Macey and her work-people went down to supper. Miss Welchman followed, leaving Mitchell above, without any one with him; but, as if recollecting something, she returned, saying she wanted to be alone with him for about five minutes.

She had scarcely entered the room when a loud scream was heard, and presently the report of a pistol, which was instantly followed by another. The house and neighbourhood became greatly alarmed. The assassin was seen descending from the first-floor window, and running, without a hat, down the middle of the street. The people of the house, on entering the room, saw the once lovely Miss Welchman a lifeless corpse, a pair of pistols lying on the floor, which on inspection bore evident marks of being the instruments with which the murder had been perpetrated. There was also found in the room the hat of Mitchell; and it appeared that, during the time of Miss Welchman's absence, he had opened the window-shutters, as they had been previously closed, and could not have been opened in the interval between the firing of the pistols and the escape of the assassin.

On examination, it was found that Miss Welchman had been shot in the head; one bullet had entered her temple, and the other had been resisted by the substance of the forehead. She lived a few minutes, but was unable to speak. It was evident Mitchell was the assassin; for no other man had been in the house, and several persons proved that no one whatever went out through the hall from the time the report of the pistol had been heard till after the examination of the premises.

The apprehension of Mitchell was now desired by all. The officers of justice were dispatched in pursuit of him, but without effect; for, as he had been for a length of time out of place, a clue to his last residence was not easily found. At length word was brought to town that he was in custody at his native place, Salisbury, to which he had bent his steps, and where he had been recognised by his old master, the farmer, who, having heard of the murder, immediately had him secured.

On the 13th of August he was brought up to Bow Street, in the custody of Taunton, where he underwent an examination, after which he was fully committed to Newgate. Mitchell appeared very little affected at his situation, and preserved a sullen silence.

Friday, September the 16th, Mitchell was arraigned at the Old Bailey, for the murder of Miss Welchman. The evidence was circumstantial, but conclusive; and, when called on for his defence, he denied the crime with which he was charged, and said that it was not proved the pistols and hat were his. He called no witnesses, and the jury, having been charged, retired for a few minutes, and returned with a verdict of Guilty.

The Recorder, after silence had been proclaimed, then pronounced the dreadful sentence of the law, which was heard by the prisoner without the least apparent emotion. 'Odious,' said the Recorder, 'as the crime of murder always was, in this instance it was attended by every possible circumstance of aggravation. He had, in the gratification of his blood-thirsty vengeance, taken away the life of an unoffending female, with whom he had proposed to connect himself in marriage. Where Nature had called aloud for kindness, he had exhibited cruelty; where he should have appeared in the character of a protector, he stood her murderer. In relation to an offence of such enormity, human laws concurred with the divine precept, "Whoso shedddeth man's blood, by man shall his blood be shed." The sentence of the law was, that he shall be taken back to prison, and on Monday morning taken to some place of execution, there to be hanged until dead, and his body delivered to the surgeons for dissection.'

As this malefactor suffered along with Hollings, we shall give his case next; after which we shall give the particulars of the execution of these two atrocious monsters.

The superstitious Application of the dead Hand of Hollings.

W. H. HOLLINGS,
EXECUTED FOR THE MURDER OF ELIZABETH PITCHER.

THIS man's conduct was at once infamous and extravagant. He had been in the excise, where he became acquainted with one Pitcher, also an excise-officer, who on his death-bed recommended his wife and daughter, Elizabeth, to the care and protection of his friend Hollings.

The friend of the father was caressed by the mother and daughter. The latter lived servant with Mr. Cartwright, in Lower Grosvenor Street, where Hollings had been in the habit of calling on her. Notwithstanding that he had a wife of his own, who did not live with him, and was fifty years of age, without any personal recommendation whatever, he had the infamous audacity to annoy this poor girl with his fulsome addresses, which she appears to have rejected altogether, as an honest and virtuous young woman should do.

For refusing to entertain his abominable passion, Hollings meditated the ruin of this unfortunate girl, who was only in her twentieth year. On July the 4th he went in the evening to the house of her master, and asked for Betsy; she came out to him, and closed the door after her; they had continued together for a few minutes when the report of a pistol was heard, and the butler, running out, saw Hollings supporting the poor girl, who had been shot through the heart, a wound of immense size being made in her side, from which flowed a copious discharge of blood.

Hollings did not attempt to escape. He held another pistol in his hand, which was found loaded to the muzzle, and the other had burst into a thousand pieces, having been similarly charged. On the steps lay a broken phial, containing arsenic and water, which Hollings thought to have taken, but the explosion of the pistol had shattered it out of his hands. When the patrol came up, he said, 'Don't seize me; I shall not attempt to go away.' He also asked 'if Elizabeth was dead, and if he might be permitted to kiss her cold lips.'

When taken to the watch-house, he said that he was in love with the deceased; and that he had sacrificed her for refusing to comply with his wishes. Being asked what those wishes were, he refused to give any explanation. During the night he drank four or five quarts of water, and vomited very much, occasioned by the poison he had taken, which, not being sufficient to cause death, only made him sick. His intention was, having shot the unfortunate girl, to poison himself; but the explosion of the pistol defeated his intentions.

On Friday, September the 16th, he was indicted at the Old Bailey, and tried, after the diabolical murderer, Mitchell. The facts of the murder having been proved, several witnesses deposed to various acts of insanity committed by the prisoner, during the last twelve months. He had been discharged from the excise in consequence of his strange conduct; and certainly there appeared sufficient evidence to lead to an opinion that he was under the dominion of occasional insanity. But his whole conduct, with regard to the murder, was atrociously consistent. He had loaded the pistols on purpose, provided the poison, and procured the presence of his victim, by pretending that he had a message for her. All these, taken into account, left no room to doubt but that at the time of the horrid deed he was perfectly sane. He was accordingly found Guilty; after which Hollings addressed the Court. He acknowledged that he had been fairly tried, and justly convicted. He hoped his fate would be a warning to all who heard his case against the indulgence of violent passions: he had loved—fervently loved—the unhappy girl whose life he had taken away. His offence was great; but he hoped for mercy, through the Saviour of mankind.

On Monday morning, September 19th, 1814, Mitchell and Hollings were executed in front of Newgate. So great was the public curiosity to see the unfortunate malefactors, that at seven o'clock on Monday morning the Old Bailey and Giltspur Street were crowded to a degree almost unprecedented. Much money was given for indifferent seats at the top of the houses opposite the debtors' door; and carts, waggons, and other vehicles, were all in requisition. It appears that Mitchell had entertained some hopes of acquittal, as he was often heard to say, 'There was no corroborating proof of his having fired the pistol.' At a quarter before eight the prisoners were introduced to the Press Yard, for the purpose of having their irons knocked off, accompanied by the Reverend Mr. Cotton and the Reverend Mr. Frere, the latter of whom sat up in constant prayer all the night with Hollings, who joined most fervently in the devotion. Mitchell, who was dressed in black, was first brought out from the cell; he looked pale, and maintained a deportment of sullen resignation; he did not say a word, nor did he betray the slightest symptoms of feeling at his awful situation. He appeared regardless of any earthly transaction. The irons being knocked off, and the usual awful ceremony of tying the hands being executed, he lifted his hands as far as he was permitted, and, looking up, bowed, and appeared to be in prayer. Hollings stepped forward to the block with an activity which at first reminded us of the unhappy man, Ashton. He was, however, very tranquil; and, upon being disencumbered of his irons, addressed the persons around him in nearly the following words; 'Here, you see, I stand, a victim to passion and barbarity: my crime is great; and I acknowledge the justice of my sentence. But oh! the unfortunate girl I loved, I adored, as one of my own. I have made contrition, and prayed for forgiveness; I resign myself, under an impression that Almighty God has heard my prayers, and will forgive me: may you and the world take warning by my example; and here I confess the justice of my fate —receive my soul, O God!' At the last expression his feelings overcame him, and he wept.

The whole of the awful arrangements being complete, they were ushered to the fatal scaffold. Mitchell was until this time firm and unconcerned: he was prayed to by Mr. Cotton. He became much agitated, and the horrors of death were strongly portrayed in his countenance. Hollings shook hands with the officers of justice, declared to Mr. Frere that he was quite happy, and mounted the scaffold with great firmness and resignation. The clergymen continued to pray to them until the fatal signal was given, when the drop fell. Mitchell continued in the strongest convulsions for several minutes, and appeared to die very hard.

After they had hung some time, three females were introduced, for the application of the 'dead man's hand,' supposed to remove marks, wens, &c. The first was a young woman of interesting appearance, who was so much affected by the ceremony that she was obliged to be supported.

At nine the bodies were cut down, and sent to St. Bartholomew's Hospital for dissection.

JOHN JAMES,
EXECUTED FOR MURDER.

THIS unfortunate man was a farmer at West Witton, in the North Riding of Yorkshire, and the crime for which he suffered was the consequence of a litigation between him and his landlord.

In November, 1813, one William Ridley, a sheriff's officer and auctioneer, went to seize some hay of James's, under pretence that he was in arrears for rent, which it subsequently appeared was not legally due. James had several reasons for disliking Ridley, in addition to that arising from his officiousness on the present occasion. He had, not long before, seized some of his hay, and, being auctioneer at the sale, he knocked down to himself, at fifteen shillings, what was well worth five pounds, if fairly exhibited.

The unfortunate James, teazed by litigation, and naturally irritable, vowed vengeance on the present occasion against Ridley, if he attempted to distrain for rent which was not due. The bailiff, hardened in such scenes, treated the denunciation with contempt, and proceeded directly to the field where the hay-stack was situated. Just as he opened the gate to give admission to his followers, the revengeful and infatuated James rushed from behind a hedge, seized Ridley, and, in an instant, plunged a knife several times into his back and neck. The bailiff, without a groan, fell down and expired.

James was now taken into custody, and brought to trial at York, March the 28th, 1814, when he was found Guilty; for, though it was fully proved that he owed no rent, and that the conduct of the deceased was highly aggravating, still it did not justify the summary vengeance inflicted on him, or extenuate the crime of murder.

When asked what he had to say why sentence of death should not be passed on him, he briefly replied, 'That he submitted to the laws of his country, though he had no law shown to him.'

The judge then proceeded to animadvert on the enormity of his crime, and ordered him for execution the next day but one.

William, the brother of John James, was indicted for aiding and assisting; but the charge against him amounted only to some words subsequently spoken, expressive of his satisfaction at the death of Ridley; and these, though they evinced a malignant obduracy of heart, were not sufficient to implicate him in the crime of his brother; consequently he was acquitted.

On the fatal consequences of giving way to sudden bursts of passion we have frequently remarked; and we hope our readers have not forgotten the examples we have adduced: if they have, we can only recommend their reflecting for a few minutes on the fate of this unfortunate man—torn from home, and all the endearing associations which made home agreeable, and afterwards suspended an ignominious spectacle on the gallows, because he had not learned to curb the natural viciousness of his temper, and seek justice where it would not ultimately be denied him.

ADMIRAL BRADLEY,
TRANSPORTED FOR FORGERY.

HIGH and chivalrous honour has always characterized the British navy; but, as it is composed of several thousands, we cannot hope to see it entirely free from unworthy members, though we really did not expect to find a rear-admiral convicted of a petty fraud, in practising which he committed a deliberate forgery to obtain the *mighty* sum of three pounds, eight shillings, and sixpence.

All vessels which bring home foreign letters are entitled to two-pence for each, as a remuneration for their trouble, and this they are always paid by the postmaster of the port where they come to anchor. The gallant admiral availed himself of this circumstance to commit the fraud for which he was transported. On the 10th of March, 1814, he brought four hundred letters to the post-office at Gosport, and received two-pence for each letter. He subsequently repeated his visits, and on the 10th of the following month he brought one hundred and eleven letters, which he said had come in the Mary and Jane, then lying at Cowes. For these he was paid three pounds, eight shillings, and sixpence, for which he gave his receipt, and signed it with the name 'William Johnson.'

The postmaster's son, suspecting that all was not right, made inquiries about the Mary and Jane, and found that there was not, nor had been, any such vessel at Cowes.

in consequence of this, a constable was sent to where Admiral Bradley lodged at Southwich, for at this time he was on the retired list. The admiral was asked if his name was Johnson: he said no, but that he had a friend in Portugal of that name. He denied being at Gosport with the letters: but the postmaster, his son, and daughter, knew him quite well, having seen him frequently.

The admiral was now fully committed, and brought to trial at the summer assizes at Winchester, in 1814. The above facts were fully proved, and it appeared in evidence that the admiral's conduct, at times, was very eccentric. He received a very good character from several naval officers; but he was found Guilty, and received sentence of death, to be executed on Saturday, the 6th of August. His friends succeeded in averting such a disgrace, and had the sentence commuted to transportation for life.

WILLIAM QUIN,
IMPRISONED AND WHIPPED FOR A MALICIOUS ASSAULT.

THIS misguided man was a native of Dublin, where he worked in a coach-maker's yard. In 1814 there was what is called a turn-out amongst coach-builders for higher wages, and Quin was one of those who contended for the new regulations. On the 1st of September he met a man named Kelly, a blacksmith, who had come up from the country in the hope of getting employment. He asked Kelly what he was doing. 'Looking for work,' he replied. 'What hire did you ask?' inquired Quin. Kelly replied, 'Not any particular wages; but a gentleman told me there was a turn-out amongst the men, but that, if I chose to work for sixteen shillings and three-pence, he would employ me.' 'Don't go into any yard,' said Quin, 'under nineteen shillings and sixpence or a pound,' and then left him.

Kelly, driven by distress, did go into Mr. Long's yard, in Mary Street, for sixteen shillings and three-pence a week, where he had only worked a few days when the combinators resolved to *slate* him, the Dublin flash word for an unmerciful beating.

On the 15th of the same month they put their threat into practice, just as Kelly and two other men were going across the street to their work. The two men saw their danger, and ran; but Kelly, apprehending no danger, was proceeding regularly into Mr. Long's yard, when a man came up, and struck him in the eye with a stone. Kelly, being recently from the country, knew how to handle his limbs, and tripped up his assailant; another, who attacked him, he served in the same way; when four men, armed with clubs, ran across the street, and knocked him down; and, when down, pommelled his face against the pavement, until released from his perilous situation by Mr. Long's men. Kelly recognised Quin as being the first of the four men who beat him, and it was Quin who knocked him down with the new spoke of a coach-wheel.

For this barbarous attack upon an unprotected stranger Quin was apprehended, and indicted September the 24th, 1814, for the assault. The jury, without hesitation, found him Guilty; and the recorder, previous to pronouncing sentence, observed that, if the prisoner possessed any of the common feelings of humanity, he must perceive the wickedness of the act he had committed, from the situation in which he had left the unfortunate prosecutor. The Court were at a loss what punishment to inflict for a misdemeanor accompanied with such atrocities. There was no crime short of murder or high treason that called for a higher degree of punishment than that of which the prisoner had been convicted: yet he trusted that the sentence which he was about to pronounce would have a more salutary effect than that which was pronounced, not a fortnight ago, for a similar offence. If that sentence had had the desired effect, the prisoner would not now be standing at the bar of the Court, an atrocious offender against the peace of the country. There was, however, one consolation, that, under such circumstances of brutality, death did not ensue; for, if homicide had been the consequence, no power on earth would have prevented the prisoner from suffering an ignominious death. When men of the description of the prisoner enter into those illegal combinations, they do not see the fatal consequences likely to follow: they are as bitter enemies to themselves as to the man they attack—disgraceful to themselves, disgraceful to their families, and disgraceful to their country: and all this is done, and those atrocious acts committed, to prevent an innocent and unoffending man from earning an honest livelihood,—against a man guilty of no other crime—against whom there was no cause ever to harbour resentment: but it seemed to be the determination of such men as the prisoner to carry their rules and regulations into execution with more despotic sway than is practised in the most inflamed counties.

The prisoner was sentenced to be imprisoned for six months on each of the indictments; and, on the indictment for the assault with an intent to murder, to be publicly whipped twice, to be fined fifty marks, and to give security for good behaviour, himself in one hundred pounds, and two sureties in fifty pounds each.

On the 2d of November Quin underwent the first whipping; but it appeared the common executioner by no means did his duty, and for this purpose another was provided for his second laceration. The figure of this person was highly grotesque: he appeared to be an able tall man, in a grey coat, with a huge wig, and a large slouched hat; but his face was the most singular part of his appearance; it was completely covered with yellow ochre, strongly tattooed with deep lines of black. He, however, fully answered the purpose for which he was employed, cutting the unfortunate and misguided man's back at every stroke, which he bore with a firmness and stoicism worthy of a better cause. Quin chewed a bullet between his teeth the whole of the way, and did not suffer even a groan to escape him. When arrived at the Royal Exchange he smiled on the crowd with the air of a martyr; and the people set up a shout, mixed with hisses and execrations, against the magistrates and police; but the executioner was the principal object of their fury, and they manifested every disposition for riot, which was timely suppressed, and several of the ringleaders were taken into custody.

MAJOR J. G. SEMPLE, ALIAS LISLE,
SEVERAL TIMES CONVICTED OF SWINDLING AND THEFT.

THIS notorious character was born in Scotland, of a respectable family, in 1759. In 1775 he entered the army, and went to America, being then only sixteen years old. The following year he was taken prisoner, but was soon released, and shortly afterwards sent home, in consequence of being wounded.

Being afterwards on the Continent, he entered the army of Frederic the Great, at the time when that monarch was marching against the Empress Queen Maria Theresa. In 1779, however, he quitted the Prussian army, and returned to England, but immediately repaired to the Continent again. At Harwich he became acquainted with an English lady of great respectability, whom he soon married. Being a short time after in France, his wife introduced him to the Duchess of Kingston, who persuaded him to accompany her to Russia, where he was soon appointed by Prince Potemkin a captain in the Russian army. His conduct was such as gained him various honours from Potemkin; but, being dissatisfied with the service, he quitted it in 1784, and retired to Copenhagen, from whence, after visiting the King of Prussia, he returned to England.

We wish the after-occurrences of Major Semple's life were as free from censure as those we have already enumerated; but our narrative is unfortunately interrupted by a circumstance, which appears to justify various assertions derogatory to his character that were afloat previous to this period.

On the 1st of September, 1785, the major was indicted at the Old Bailey, on a charge of feloniously stealing a post-chaise, value fifty pounds, the property of John Lycett, a coachmaker in Whitechapel. The indictment charged him with hiring a post-chaise for a limited period, which he never returned; the defendant, however, protested that the chaise was regularly ordered and sent home, and therefore the transaction could be only looked upon as a debt. The judge, however, thought otherwise, and the prisoner was found Guilty.

Semple, in his own Memoirs, speaking of this occurrence, says:—'The case stood thus with me: I had bespoke a travelling post-chaise of a coachmaker, Mr. Lycett. It was ordered to be finished on a particular day, and on that day he sent it home. My then situation rendered such a carriage necessary for me, and I was at that time able to pay for it; but my fatal turn fo extravagance soon put that out of my power. After remaining some time in town, I went again to the Continent, and, during twelve months, passed and repassed very frequently; on which occasions several attempts were made to arrest me for the debt: nor was there any idea of calling it a fraud till a year after the carriage was delivered to me at my lodgings at Knightsbridge. I am far from vindicating the nonpayment of a just debt, but I solemnly declare that I had not the smallest idea of defrauding the coachmaker.'

After sentence Semple was of course committed to the charge of the keeper of Newgate, by whom he was lodged in the state apartments, where he remained a considerable time, until he was sent to Woolwich, where, by the intercession of his friends, he received his majesty's pardon, on condition of going abroad.

While in Newgate he invented a new saddle and accoutrement for cavalry, a model of which he sent to the King of Prussia.

From Woolwich Semple went to France, where he became acquainted with Bernyer, Pethion, Roland, and several of the then leaders. He was present at the trial of Louis XVI. and shortly after resolved on returning to England, in consequence of the irruption with this country, which he then saw was inevitable. He therefore obtained a passport, which he had scarcely done when he was denounced to the Committee of Public Safety as a spy, and going to join the enemy. Being, however, secretly apprized of what was going forward, he was able to effect his escape, although with some difficulty, before the arrest was issued.

On his escape Semple joined the allied army against France, and distinguished himself on various occasions, particularly in the battle of St. Fronde, which lasted three days. On the retirement of the King of Prussia from this campaign, Semple lost his best friend, and, being shortly after wounded, he found himself incapacitated from service, and almost destitute of the means of existence. After a short retirement, however, he recovered sufficiently to remove to Augsburgh; on his arrival at which place he was suddenly arrested by order of the Baron d'Ompteda, in the name of his Britannic Majesty; no reason, however, was assigned for the arrest, and he was liberated in a short time.

Considering he had been ill used on the Continent, Semple again returned to England; and in 1795 we again find him at the bar of the Old Bailey, on a charge of stealing in the shop of Mr. Wattleworth, in Wigmore Street, one yard of muslin, two yards of calico, and one linen shirt.

It was proved that the prisoner came into the shop of Mr. Wattleworth, about noon, on the 10th of November, 1794, and, showing two patterns, one of muslin, and the other of calico, said he wanted them matched for Mrs. Coningham, of Egham Green. They could not find an exact match in the shop to the muslin; but he chose one; and a yard being cut off, and two yards of calico, he said he would give them to the lady's servant, then at the door, and, calling in a man, gave them to him. He then said that he had just arrived from the Continent, and should want a quantity of shirts, and wished to take one with him to consult his sister, who, he thought, would be a better judge of the linen than he was; that he would bring it back in the morning, and then give his order. This sister he called Coningham; and, as the witness had a customer of that name, he made no hesitation, but gave him the shirt under those conditions. This happened in November; but the prosecutor never saw the prisoner again until January, when he was in custody in Bow Street.

The counsel for the prisoner contended that they had not made out the charge of the felony, the evidence, if true, amounting only to that of obtaining money under false pretences. Mr. Justice Buller, who tried the cause, admitted the counsel was perfectly right as to the calico and muslin; but he did not agree with him in respect to the shirt, and therefore should leave it to the jury.

Semple, being called upon for his defence, begged permission to read a few words which he had put to paper, fearful his embarrassed situation might otherwise prevent him from saying what he wished. This paper stated that he did not mean to deny he had unfortunately been in that place before; but some of the public prints had so misrepresented facts, that he had reason to fear the minds of the public might be so far prejudiced against him as to suppose he had spent his whole life in committing depredations: to prove that this was not true, he begged to show how his latter time had passed.

On going abroad, he found the French engaged in a war, fighting, as he thought, for freedom; he entered their service, and was soon honoured with rank in their army.

This, however, at much hazard, he quitted, on their declaring war against this country, and went over to the Austrians, with whom he for some time served as a volunteer.

The commander, noticing his exertions, gave him a commission of no small rank, in which he continued until he was recognised by some British officers, and it was instantly circulated through the army that he was the convicted Semple, he having taken upon himself the name of Lisle.

On this he was obliged to quit that service; but, still willing and desirous to serve, he went towards the Rhine, and obtained a commission under the hereditary prince.

He had not, however, been long here, when a British officer sent to the commandant, that he had been condemned to transportation, without stating that the time had expired.

Being thus suspected of being a runaway felon, he was taken into custody by the police, and confined in a prison for more than five weeks, without even the permission of pen and ink.

The fact being cleared up, he was set at liberty, but not without losing his situation; he again, however, went into the field, and was twice wounded.

This induced him to return home, and he sent a letter to Mr. Dundas, a copy of which he desired might be read; but the Court thinking it irrelevant, it was not admitted.

He then concluded, that he had been thus persecuted because he was Major Semple, and which had also brought him to that bar on that day, upon a charge of which he was totally innocent.

The jury, however, found him Guilty of stealing the shirt, but Not Guilty upon the charge of the muslin and calico; and he was accordingly transported.

Had this action failed, several other indictments were out against him, on various charges of swindling; notwithstanding which, such was the mixture of Semple's character, that various persons of the greatest respectability interested themselves in his behalf, among whom were Burke and Boswell, who both wrote to the under secretary of state, interceding for the royal mercy.

After remaining in Newgate, on the state side, for two years, in a state of uncertainty as to his future destiny, he was at length removed to Portsmouth, and from thence proceeded to New South Wales. On his passage a mutiny took place on board the vessel, and twenty-nine persons were sent adrift in an open boat, among whom was Semple, who had contrived to conceal a quantity of gold in some soap, by which stratagem he succeeded in taking it with him. After a dangerous passage they landed in safety at Fort St. Pedro, in the province of Rio Grande.

The governor of the fort received them with great hospitality, and Semple was introduced as a Dutch officer and passenger. In consequence of a quarrel, however, with an ensign, the latter exposed Semple's character, which so irritated him that he would have murdered him with his sword, if he had not been prevented. After remaining some time in the Brazils, he left it in 1798, and arrived at Lisbon, where he was arrested in consequence of his Brazilian quarrels. By an order, however, from the British minister at Lisbon, he was sent on board an English vessel, and conveyed to Gibraltar. While here he was arrested on account of the discovery of a conspiracy; nothing, however, appearing against him, he was conveyed to Tangier, where he remained some time.

In December, 1798, an order arrived from England, ordering him home in custody; and he was accordingly sent on board a ship, and arrived at Portsmouth the following April. He was immediately conveyed to Tothillfields' Bridewell, where he remained till he was again sent out of the country.

From this period nothing particular occurred in the major's life until his return from Botany Bay in 1810, when he resorted to his former evil practices; but as he became more notorious he became less successful, until at length he was reduced to the utmost distress, and had recourse to the basest means of supporting a miserable existence.

In 1814 he went into a cheesemonger's shop in Devonshire Street, Queen Square, and ordered a small quantity of bacon and butter to be sent to No. 42, Cross Street. He met the messenger at the door, and, taking the articles from him, sent him back for six pennyworth of eggs. When the boy returned he knocked at the door, and was informed that the person he inquired for did not live there, and that they knew nothing about him. This was true, for the major had only made a feint of going in to deceive the boy, and had made off when the lad was out of sight.

For this offence he was apprehended, and brought to trial at the Middlesex sessions, December the 3d, 1814, and found Guilty, when, for the third time, sentence of transportation for seven years was passed on him.

It must be lamented that a man possessing the courage and ability which Semple certainly did would not pursue the path of honour, which he might have done so profitably to himself and so serviceably to others. As an additional proof of his talent, we insert the following lines, which were written by him to a young lady at Richmond, in Yorkshire, to whom he was to have been married, but fortunately his character was timely discovered:—

' For ever, O merciless fair!
  Will that cruel indifference endure?
Can those eyes look me into despair,
  And that heart be unwilling to cure?

How oft what I felt to disguise
  Has my reason imperiously strove,
Till my soul almost fell from my eyes,
  In the tears of the tenderest love!

Then, Delia, determine my fate,
  Nor let me to madness be drove;
But, oh! do not tell me you hate,
  If you even resolve not to love.'

CHARLES WELLER,
CONVICTED OF STEALING NOTES AND BILLS.

This malefactor was paid to protect the property he stole, being guard of the Swansea mail-coach, out of a parcel sent by which he purloined notes and bills to the amount of two thousand three hundred pounds.

In the month of October, 1813

the above parcel was forwarded from the bank of Newport, in Monmouthshire, to Down and Co. bankers, in London; and, for the better disguising its value, the property was put into a box, and the box packed in a coarse canvass bag, and directed to Mr. Fothergill, a relation of one of the partners in the bank.

The box and bag arrived as directed, but without the property, and every exertion was made to detect the robber. In the course of his inquiries, Vickery, the Bow-Street officer, learned that some bank-notes had been concealed at a place called Totterdown Hill, near Bristol, by a woman named Hickman, with whose daughter the prisoner was particularly intimate, and who absconded soon after; but being apprehended, as was Weller also, she was admitted evidence against him. The notes were traced in various directions, some even to Paris.

On Saturday, January the 14th, 1815, Weller was indicted for this robbery; and, the facts being proved, he was found Guilty; but, the offence not being capital, he was only sentenced to fourteen years' transportation. Many men have been hanged for a crime of much less magnitude.

SARAH STONE,
TRANSPORTED FOR STEALING A CHILD.

THE public attention was so much excited by the case of Mrs. Magnis, who stole the little boy in 1811, that an express act of parliament was passed, making child-stealing felony, thereby subjecting the offender to transportation—a punishment by no means too severe for this species of crime, by which families are thrown into the greatest confusion and distress.

The following curious case was the first which occurred after the passing of the act; and, though we rejoice at the conviction of the woman, we cannot but smile at the simplicity of the ignorant tar, whose credulity seems extraordinary, though his paternal affection was amiable.

At the Old Bailey sessions, January the 19th, 1815, Sarah Stone was indicted for feloniously stealing, on the 14th of October, 1814, a female child, seven weeks old. The following was the evidence against her:—

Catharine Kreemer, the prosecutrix, deposed that she was a poor woman, residing at No. 3, Swan's Court, Cowheel Alley, Golden Lane: her husband was a labourer; she had had six children, two of them twins, and was occasionally obliged to solicit charity in the streets for their support. On the 14th of October the twins were about seven weeks old, on which day she went out with one of her children, five years old, having her twins in her arms; and, whilst she was sitting on the steps in St. Paul's Churchyard, the prisoner accosted her—gave her a penny, saying she had fine babies in her arms—and observed that, if she would go with her she would introduce her to a fine lady, who would give her half a guinea. She accordingly set off with the prisoner, carrying her twins, and followed by her other child. In Cheapside her cloak fell from off her babes, when she requested the prisoner to put it over them, to prevent them from catching cold, who offered to carry one of them. She delivered the largest of them into her arms, and they proceeded together to the Commercial Road, where, at the corner of a public house, the prisoner gave her threepence, to get something to drink. The prosecutrix thanked her for the money, but said she did not want either beer or gin, but wished to see the fine lady. The prisoner said she would go and show the lady her fine twin, and immediately return to her. She followed the prisoner up a court, not choosing to part from her child, when her little girl, who was walking by her side, fell over some bricks. She assisted her to get up, and then turned round to look for the prisoner, who was gone out of sight. The prosecutrix immediately screamed out, being unable to pursue the prisoner, from the incumbrance of her two children. Her cries collected a number of people about her, some of whom were going to take her into custody, on account of the clamour she raised. This was about three o'clock in the afternoon; she ran about in search of the prisoner and her child until half past seven o'clock. She particularly noticed the prisoner's person, who had a tooth broken out in her right upper jaw, was of a swarthy complexion, had dark eyes, and was much pitted with the small-pox: she was dressed in a reddish spotted gown, a light shawl, and a black straw bonnet. Poor as she was, the prosecutrix immediately had advertisements and hand-bills published, with this description of the prisoner, for which she paid seventeen shillings. The same night she gave information at Lambeth Street police office. Six weeks afterwards she was taken on board a ship in the Thames, when the prisoner was pointed out to her, and she immediately recognised her, and found her lost child in the prisoner's arms. As she ascended the side of the ship she heard a child cry, and knew it was the voice of her infant. The moment she perceived it she asked the prisoner to let her have a kiss of her baby, when a sailor, who was standing by, said 'No, not if you were the Queen of England,' and took the child out of the prisoner's arms. Her child appeared thinner than it was when she lost it. The prisoner was not suckling the child. She never entertained a doubt of the prisoner being the woman who stole her child. Dalton then took the prisoner into custody, and went ashore with her, the prosecutrix, and child. When she undressed the child she found the piece of blanket it had on when she lost it round its body. The prisoner said it was very silly of the prosecutrix to think the child was hers, it being her own, and seemed very unwilling to part with it. The twins were females, and greatly resembled each other. The sailor said he was the father of the child, and acted as if he thought so.

Elizabeth Murray, a widow, deposed that she lived next door to the prosecutrix: had known her for fifteen years: remembered her being delivered of twins: saw her in Golden Lane about six or seven o'clock in the evening of the day on which she lost one of them; saw a child that was found on board of a ship by the prosecutrix, which she believed was the same that was lost, though it was much wasted. It died last Friday. The mother had plenty of milk, and kept them in 'good case.'

Ebenezer Dalton, the officer, deposed that he went with the prosecutrix on board the Hugh Inglis East Indiaman, where he saw the prisoner, and, from the description he had had of her from the prosecutrix, immediately knew her: she had a child in her arms, which she fed with pap. He told the prisoner he had come about the child, which she said was her own, and she would show him the room where she was delivered: that she was taken in labour in the Minories, and named the very day on which the child was lost, when she stated a young woman took her to her apartments, where she was immediately delivered, in White Horse Court, Rosemary Lane: the young woman's name, she said, was Mary Brown. When there, she could show the officer where the man-midwife lived who was fetched to attend upon her, as it must be near the place, the young woman who went for him having been absent only a very short time; that she was delivered at three o'clock, and returned to her home in Blythe's Buildings, Sun Street, Bishopsgate, at five o'clock, in a coach, where she lived with her mother, though in a separate apartment; and Swaine (the sailor who refused to let the prosecutrix kiss the child) was its father. When the prosecutrix first saw the prisoner with the child in her arms, she flew towards her, and would have struck her if he had not interfered, exclaiming, 'That is my child, and that is the woman who stole her from me.' The prosecutrix's description of the prisoner's person was correct, except with regard to her age. He brought the prisoner to London, accompanied by the prosecutrix, who refused to be again separated from her child, and it was restored to her by the order of the magistrate. He then inquired ineffectually, at every house in White Hart Court, for a person named Mary Brown; and, on telling the prisoner of his ill success, she said she must have mistaken the name of the court; but, if she were to go herself, she could find the place. He went with her by desire of the magistrate, and she led him to Johnson's Chain, Rosemary Lane, and pointed out a house, in which she said she was delivered in the front room, up one pair of stairs. Miller, another officer, who was along with them, went into the house, and returned with Elizabeth Fisher, who inhabited the room described by the prisoner, who, when she saw her, appeared much confused, and said she did not know her, though she was sure of the house; and Elizabeth Fisher professed herself unacquainted with the prisoner. He went to the only man-midwife near, who said he had never delivered a woman in the house they mentioned, and the prisoner said he was not the person. Swaine gave up his voyage, and accompanied the witness and prisoner in a post-chaise to London, to assert his right to the child. There were other women with children in their arms besides the prisoner on the deck of the ship, when the prosecutrix, without hesitation, fixed upon her as the woman who stole her child.

Isabella Gray deposed that she lived at No. 3, Blythe's Buildings, in Sun Street. The prisoner and Swaine lodged in her house as man and wife. Saw the prisoner go out about one o'clock on the 14th October: remembers her dress, which she described to have been the same as that the prosecutrix swore was worn by the woman who stole her child. Prisoner had lodged in her house about three months. The witness went out in the afternoon, and on her return was told by the prisoner's mother that she was delivered. Saw the child, and remarked it was a very large one, appearing like a child of a month old more than like a new-born infant. The prisoner heard her say this, but made no reply. Swaine was in the room at the time: witness asked him if that was his child. He said 'So they told him: he had just come into the house.' Prisoner had previously appeared like a woman who was pregnant: never saw any medical man or other person attending the prisoner on account of her lying-in.

Grace Brown deposed that she lived opposite to the prisoner in Blythe's Buildings: saw her come into the court about five o'clock in the afternoon of the 14th of October. The prisoner did not appear as if she had been just delivered: she had had children herself, and did not believe that any woman who had been only delivered that afternoon could have walked up the court as prisoner did. Prisoner had been 'big six months:' she had jumped out of a two pair of stairs' window whilst she was said to be pregnant: never spoke to the prisoner.

The prisoner, in her defence, told the same story to the Court which she had related to Dalton, and pointed out Elizabeth Fisher as the person who took her into her room, where she persisted she was delivered, and that Elizabeth Fisher called herself Mary Brown, to which name she said she answered before the magistrate.

Elizabeth Fisher was called, and declared she never saw the prisoner before she was brought to her house by the officer; that, when before the magistrate, she had answered to the name of Brown, on some person's addressing her by that appellation, being greatly alarmed by the circumstance of appearing before a magistrate.

The mother of the prisoner, Swaine, the reputed father of the child, and two other persons, ineffectually endeavoured to establish the prisoner's innocence, and to prove that the child was her own.

The jury unhesitatingly found her Guilty; sentence, seven years' transportation. A sum of money, for the relief of the prosecutrix, was subscribed by the jury.

ANNE RADFORD,
TRANSPORTED FOR PERJURY.

FEW subjects have excited greater complaint than the inconsistency of the English criminal code. A man is hanged for cutting or maiming, with intent to kill, because, say the commentators on the law, though the wounded man recovers, that is no palliation of the crime, for the offender deserves the same punishment as if the object of his attack had actually expired, the intention being the same. By analogy, this argument applies to those who falsely endeavour to swear away the life of a man; yet the most aggravated perjury is only punished with transportation, and in most cases with only fine and imprisonment, though an artful perjurer may as much endanger the life of an innocent man as the infuriated assassin, for circumstances may be such, in either case, as to preclude the possibility of defence. The case we are going to narrate will illustrate the foregoing remarks.

In the latter end of the year 1814, Anne Radford, a poor man's daughter, aged nineteen, accused her sweetheart, John Bird, a farmer's servant, of having murdered a rival of his, one Buckhill, a gentleman's servant, two years before. Bird was accordingly apprehended, and his accuser deposed as follows:—That one evening, in the month of June, she and Bird were walking along the road, about eight o'clock, when they met Buckhill, whom Bird immediately attacked, knocked him down, cut his throat, and then dragged him into a neighbouring corn-field, where he buried him. The particulars she described with such apparent candour and minuteness, that it was impossible to suspect her story to be fabricated.

Bird was committed to Exeter gaol; and Anne Radford, not being able to procure bail to prosecute, was also sent to prison, there to be taken care of until the ensuing assizes.

The momentary wonder which this extraordinary charge excited having somewhat subsided, the sober part of the people began to reflect on its improbability. The publicity of the place where the alleged murder was committed, the early hour at which it took place, and the silence which attended the transaction, no one having ever heard of any such murder in the neighbourhood, seemed to attach falsehood to the charge, and throw discredit on the accuser's story. But then the circumstantial manner in which she described the deed, and the absence of any inducement to prompt her to fabricate so atrocious a statement, as well as the fact of Buckhill not having been since seen in the neighbourhood, were considered corroborating proofs of the truth of her charge, which she alleged having made to rid her conscience of an intolerable burden that pressed heavily upon it during the last two years.

The magistrates had her brought to the field where she stated Buckhill to have been buried, and had the place dug up where she described the body to have been deposited; but, though the utmost diligence was used, nothing was found to lead to a supposition that any such interment had taken place.

In the mean time it was confidently reported that Buckhill was still alive; and Bird's master, whose humane and praiseworthy exertions merit the highest eulogium, went in search of him. Having travelled seven hundred miles, he at length found the object of his pursuit, who had just returned from France, where he had been with Lord Beauchamp's family during the two years preceding.

To save a fellow-creature from ignominy and death, Buckhill hastened to Exeter, where the assizes were about to be held; and, on Radford hearing of his presence, she declared her whole story was a falsehood, though up to that moment she persisted in 'her wicked allegations.

When Bird was arraigned at Exeter, January the 16th, 1815, in a most crowded court, the Recorder asked Radford what she had to say: she replied, 'Nothing, sir; I am guilty:' upon which Bird was discharged, and a bill of indictment was then presented to the grand jury, and found against Anne Radford, for wilful and corrupt perjury. She was immediately put upon her trial, and said, 'Though I know I am guilty, I am advised to plead Not Guilty.'

Her affidavit having been read, Buckhill, the man stated to have been murdered, was called. He deposed that he never knew Bird, and consequently that he could not have had any quarrel with him. About two years before he was in the habit of privately visiting the prisoner in her father's garden, during the eleven days which he stopped in the country, since which time he knew nothing of her.

Bird having also been called, and his evidence gone through, the jury, without hesitation, found the prisoner Guilty, and she was sentenced to seven years' transportation.

Were it not for the zeal of Bird's master in finding Buckhill, the circumstantial and minute evidence of this wicked girl would in all probability have convicted him of murder. What a lesson for jurors!

WILLIAM SAWYER,
EXECUTED FOR THE MURDER OF HARRIET GASKETT.

WILLIAM SAWYER was a young man in the commissariat department of the British army, and the circumstances of his case are of a most extraordinary and singular nature. In the month of February, 1814, he went out to Portugal, where he lived in the same house in the Campo Major, at Lisbon, with a friend, Mr. Riccord, who had a female, named Harriet Gaskett, under his protection. An attachment grew up between this unfortunate woman and Sawyer, though he had a wife at the time in England; and his attentions were so apparent that they excited jealousy in his brother officer, who appears to have remonstrated with his friend and mistress, which occasioned much infelicity.

On the 27th of April they met at dinner, with two or three other officers; but such was the agitation of their feelings, that Riccord, Harriet, and Sawyer, ate no dinner. The latter appeared greatly dejected; and, as well as Harriet, withdrew as soon as possible.

In the evening the party heard the report of three pistol-shots; and, on going into the garden, Harriet and Sawyer were found both lying on the ground. Harriet was quite dead, but Sawyer had not been mortally wounded. On being removed into the house, he was left in the care of a brother officer, while the others went in search of a physician; and during their absence he contrived to get a razor, with which he cut his throat in a dreadful manner, but not mortally.

Next day the officers met, and reduced the facts to writing, which Sawyer signed. When he was sufficiently recovered he was removed to England, where, shortly after his arrival, he was indicted at the Old Bailey, April the 7th, 1815, for the above murder. His case excited great interest, and the court was filled long before the arrival of the judges.

The above facts being deposed to—

Mr. Tobin was called.—Was at Lisbon at the time of this unfortunate transaction. Knew the parties before the 27th of April, and saw them together the evening before. Mr. Riccord seemed indisposed. Witness called to see him the next morning; saw the prisoner on that occasion: he requested him, the witness, to accompany him to view a house which he wished to take. Witness did so, and advised him not to take the house; he, however, said he would take it. In the evening, about eight o'clock, Mr. Riccord and Mr. Green called at his house: they were much agitated. They stated that the prisoner and the deceased had murdered each other, or something to that effect, and requested witness to go and render what assistance he could. Witness went to Mr. Riccord's house, and found the prisoner lying on the floor, with his throat cut, and a wound in his temple. Remained some time with him, and assisted in washing his wounds. There was a paper on the table, on which the prisoner appeared to have been writing. Witness inquired where Harriet was; and, handing that paper, the prisoner wrote that she lay in the garden in the first lane from the house. Witness went in consequence of this information, and found the deceased. She was quite dead. There was a wound in her temple. The prisoner was finally removed from the floor on which he lay to a sofa in an adjoining room. About eleven o'clock the doctor came. Saw nothing more that night: went to the prisoner the next morning at eleven, and found him in bed. Several gentlemen were assembled to inquire into the facts of the case, who judged it advisable that the prisoner should be called upon to give some account of the fatal transaction. In consequence of this opinion witness wrote down on a paper such facts as had come to his knowledge respecting the calamitous circumstance. This paper was read over to the prisoner distinctly; he afterwards read it himself, and subscribed to the correctness of its contents: he also signed his name to it. Upon this paper having been read over, they saw that it was not sufficiently clear for the want of the word 'my.' Witness, therefore, went once more to the prisoner the next day, and requested permission to amend it. He pointed out that the paper, as it existed, left room to doubt whether Harriet had not murdered herself: he therefore requested the prisoner to say who had fired the pistol-shot by which she had been killed. The prisoner said he fired it, and desired the necessary correction to be made to the paper, which was accordingly done. There was also another memorandum written, to which he likewise signed his name. To these papers there were four subscribing witnesses.

The papers in question were now put in and read. The first was dated 28th April, 1814, and was, in substance, as follows:—

'Having laid violent hands upon myself, in consequence of the death of Harriet, I think it but justice to mankind and the world, being of sound mind, solemnly to attest that her death was occasioned by her having taken part of a phial of laudanum, and "my" discharging a pistol at her head, provided for the occasion. I took the residue of the laudanum myself, and discharged two pistols at my head. They failing in their effect, I then retired to the house, and endeavoured to put an end to my life, leaving myself the unfortunate object you now behold me.

(Signed) 'WILLIAM SAWYER,'
And three witnesses.

The word 'my,' in the above paper, was interlined, as stated in Mr. Tobin's evidence.

The second paper was dated seven o'clock, Saturday evening, the 30th of April. It was nearly as follows:—'The word "my," interlined in the above paper, was inserted with my full concurrence. I have heard the contents of that paper deliberately read, and entirely agree to them. We mutually agreed to destroy each other; and then she requested me to destroy her previous to my destroying myself.'

Captain Thomas Tyrrell witnessed the signing of the second paper by the prisoner, and, at Mr. Riccord's request, produced to him another paper for him (the prisoner) to sign. This was for the purpose of removing any imputation against Mr. Riccord's character. Witness then read over a paper of considerable length, which was signed by the prisoner: it was, in substance, as follows:—

'On my arrival in Lisbon I called upon Mr. Riccord, who, in consequence of some attention which I had shown him, when ill, on a former occasion, received me with great kindness, and invited me to his house. I lived there with Harriet and him for some time, with great happiness, till about three months back, when Mr. Riccord manifested some displeasure, in consequence of some civilities, of more than a common description, which I paid to Harriet. This, however, was soon forgotten, as I assured him there was no ground for his suspicion. On or about ——, Harriet gave way to my solicitations, and agreed to live with me, provided Mr. Riccord went to England, and was restored to his family.'

Here the witness stated, that, in addition to the declarations, he had put several questions to the prisoner, which he had answered. They were as follow:—

Q. Harriet having declared, in the most solemn manner, to Mr. Riccord, that she never had any connexion of an intimate nature with you, it is but just that you should state whether you had such connexion, and when and where that connexion took place.—A. I had connexion with Harriet, and slept with her three times, during the time that Mr. Riccord was obliged to sleep at the Convent.

Q. When Harriet ran towards the well, did not Mr. Riccord tell you you might live together, and that he would go to an hotel, and only waited for Harriet to hand him some things?—A. He did.

Q. Then, if you had this permission, why did Harriet require you to shoot her, when you had a full opportunity of living together?—A. Harriet assigned as a reason for asking me to shoot her, that, if she lived with me, she was sure Riccord would shoot himself; and, although she had promised not to live with me, she had not promised not to die with me.

Q. Was it not Harriet's request that you should destroy her, because you said you would destroy yourself if she did not live with you?—A. No, so help me, God! I declare that she entreated me to shoot her, without any such declaration on my part.

The prisoner was then called upon for his defence, and put in a written paper, in which he stated that, in consequence of his being unable to articulate, from the wound in his throat, he had committed to paper all he had to say in his defence. The paper then went on to state that the prisoner had felt the sincerest affection for the unfortunate individual in question, towards whom he had never meditated the slightest injury. He perfectly recollected her having entreated him to shoot her, but had no idea of what passed subsequently, till some time afterwards, when he was told he had signed papers, of the contents of which he had no recollection. He then expressed acknowledgments for the efforts made by his prosecutors to bring forward Mr. Riccord, who would have been a material witness in his behalf; and had only to lament that these efforts had not been attended with success.

Several persons were then called to speak to the general humane character of the prisoner, among whom were General Sir Edward Howard, Colonel Sir William Robe, W. Stacey, Esq. E. Weaver, Esq. Mr. Wells, and Mr. Guy.

A Mrs. Nicholls proved that the deceased had lodged with her from June, 1813, to February, 1814. She was of a most violent and tyrannical disposition, and had a pistol, which she kept constantly in her room.

Lord Ellenborough summed up the evidence, when the jury retired, and, after an absence of two hours, returned with the verdict of Guilty; but recommended the prisoner strongly to mercy, on the ground that there was no malice on his part towards the deceased, further than the act itself imported.

Lord Ellenborough now desired to hear whether any thing was to be submitted as a ground for respiting the sentence of the prisoner.

Mr. Alley repeated his former arguments, and contended that the prisoner could not legally receive sentence for a crime committed in another kingdom, where there were laws to which he was distinctly amenable.

Lord Ellenborough considered this point as decided, and therefore did not think it proper to reserve it. He was induced to believe, however, that there were other grounds upon which a motion for a respite of sentence might have been claimed. He desired the counsel for the prisoner to look to the indictment, and see whether that did not present some points which it would be proper to reserve for discussion.

Mr. Alley and Mr. Curwood having looked, in compliance with his lordship's intimation, to the indictment, but not immediately discovering any points of the nature alluded to, his lordship, to save the time of the Court, stated there were two points which had presented themselves to him, on the face of that indictment, as sufficient under the act to warrant him respiting the judgment of the prisoner:—The first was, that the prisoner was said to have committed the murder in question 'against the form of the statute,' but the particular statute infringed was not specified, as it ought to have been; and, next, it was not stated that the prisoner was a 'British subject;' and therefore the Court adjudged that the sentence should be respited accordingly.

On the 12th of May Mr. Sawyer was brought up to receive the decision of the judges, which Sir Simon Le Blanc delivered as follows:—

'William Sawyer was tried and convicted, under the authority of a special commission, appointed for that purpose, for the wilful murder of Harriet Gaskell, in the kingdom of Portugal, a subject of our lord the king, and in the peace of the king.

'Upon this conviction, three objections were taken upon the indictment, in arrest of judgment. The first of these was, that the jurisdiction of this country had no power whatever to try the offence of an individual committed in a country beyond the seas, and under the dominion of a foreign power; second, that the indictment did not, upon the face of it, show that the parties were British subjects; and, third, that the indictment did not conclude, as being agreeable to the form of the statute, &c. With respect to the first point of objection, namely, that which related to the 33d of Henry VIII. the words and construction of that statute must be taken as implying that the offender must be tried by a jury where the offence is committed; but it also appeared, from that statute, that, if a murder is committed upon a British subject, it may be lawful, upon information of such murder being given, for any of his majesty's counsel to bring the offender to justice, whether the offence be committed within or without the kingdom, or any of his majesty's shires. That such offender shall be tried under a special commission of the great seal, either within or without the kingdom, or any of his majesty's shires, for such offence, the words were sufficiently clear, and admitted of the construction which had, since the passing of the act, been put upon them.' [He then cited three cases where convictions had taken place pursuant to this statute. The first was the case of one Chambers, who had committed a murder in Barcelona, in the kingdom of Spain, in 1709, when the law took its course: the next was the case of one Ealing, who was convicted of a murder committed in Sweden in 1720: and the third was that in which Captain Roche was convicted of the murder of one Ferguson, at the Cape of Good Hope, in 1775.] —' In all these cases the construction of the act quoted applied, and the law had taken its regular course. They were all cases, too, where the offence had been committed beyond the seas, and out of the dominions of his majesty. With regard to the second objection, the words of the statute are, "that if any person shall commit such offence of murder against any subject, in the peace of the king," &c. and sufficient appeared upon the face of the indictment to show that the subject so murdered was a British subject, and in the peace of the king. As to the last objection, stating that the indictment did not conclude "under the form of the statute," &c. it did not appear of so much importance, being interwoven with the other arguments, and sufficient appearing on the face of the indictment to make the case clear, agreeably to the statute.'

The learned judge concluded by saying, that, after the fullest consideration that could be given to the case, the judges were unanimously of opinion that there was no ground whatever for arrest of judgment.

The recorder then proceeded to pronounce the awful sentence of the law.

The prisoner appeared deeply affected throughout, and, upon hearing the awful decision and sentence, remained motionless for some time, when at length he faintly requested one of the officers to entreat the Court to recommend him to the royal clemency. He was then taken from the dock.

Monday, May the 22d, 1815, being the day appointed for the execution of this infatuated man, at an early hour an immense number of spectators assembled in the Old Bailey, to witness the awful scene. Since the sentence of death was passed on him he assumed a degree of sullenness; and the only declaration he was heard to make was 'that he would not be executed:' this was considered to import that he was resolved on self-destruction. His intentions, however, if such they were, were defeated by the constant attendance of two officers night and day. On Sunday he received the sacrament, after which he appeared more composed. About three o'clock on Sunday his wife went to the prison, for the purpose of taking a farewell: she was announced by an officer; but the unhappy man gave a peremptory order that she should not be admitted, and all that could be urged could not induce him to see her. When he went to his cell he was much depressed, and refused any kind of sustenance: about two o'clock he laid down, and soon after became very sick, and vomited copiously. he continued restless until half past six o'clock, at which time he was visited by the Rev. Mr. Cotton, who prayed to him fervently. A little before eight o'clock Mr. Sheriff Reay, attended by the usual officers, proceeded from Justice

Hall towards the cell. The unfortunate gentleman was introduced into the Press-yard by the Ordinary: he was very dejected, and did not utter a word during his being conveyed to the platform. At eight o'clock precisely, every necessary arrangement being complete, the fatal signal was given, and the unhappy man was launched into eternity. During the ceremony a profound silence prevailed throughout the populace. He died under evident symptoms of paroxysm, and a quantity of blood gushed from his mouth, from the cut in his throat. At nine o'clock the body was taken to Bartholomew's Hospital in a cart, attended by the under-sheriff and officers. He was dressed in a suit of black, and was not ironed.

THOMAS JESSON,
EXECUTED FOR THE MURDER OF A CHILD.

THE man who has no self-respect, or principles of honour, is seldom virtuous; and, though reason may conduce to good conduct, yet ninety-nine men out of every hundred are influenced by feeling only; and, happily for society, the general feeling of mankind is on the side of virtue and morality.

In the case before us we have a deplorable instance of the bad consequences which uniformly proceed from conduct in opposition to what the world approves. Jesson married a woman with an illegitimate child, the daughter of a wealthy seducer, at her breast; and, though he promised to protect, and apparently did caress the infant, yet he privately hated and detested the innocent cause of his anger; for he was aware of the circumstances attending its birth and filiation before he married its imprudent mother.

Whoever reads the history of delinquents (and we know not one more copious than the 'Newgate Calendar') must be struck with the obvious advantages which, even in this world, attend a life of propriety and virtue. Scarcely a case of atrocity, horror, or dishonesty occurs, but we find the parties concerned immersed in sin and crime. If men, they are the companions of prostitutes, whose extravagance and dissipation are to be supported by illegal means; and, if women, we find them either abandoned to shame and infamy, or living in secret or open defiance of the laws of God and society. The parties before us, though not exactly of this class, were nevertheless far from being models of propriety: the woman was a mother before she was married; and the man undertook to father her child begotten in shame. From such a connexion little good was to be expected, though what followed could not possibly be anticipated.

Thomas Jesson, a nailer, aged twenty-five, was indicted at the Salop assizes, March the 24th, 1816, for the wilful murder of his wife's child, in the parish of Hale's Owen, on the night of Saturday, the 28th of the preceding January. By the evidence of a surgeon it appeared that the right cheek and temple were bruised very much, the skin was ruptured on the right side of the child, and the lower jaw was broken exactly in the centre. He observed a large fracture on the back part of the head: after removing the scalp two large portions of the bone were entirely detached, and pressed upon the brain. A single blow would not have caused the fracture of both the jaw and the head.

The prisoner stated that he was in a fit when it was done; and that he knew not how it happened. This, however, did not appear from the evidence to be the fact; and the jury brought in a verdict of Guilty, in the propriety of which the judge fully concurred, and immediately passed sentence of death upon him.

JOHN MURDOCH,
EXECUTED FOR THE MURDER OF JAMES MURDOCH.

PHILIP, King of Macedon, derived less glory from all his victories than from one single act of justice. One of his veterans had been billetted on a poor peasant, who treated him with great hospitality; but the base soldier, in return for such kindness, resolved to ruin his host: he fabricated a tale for the ear of his commander, injurious to the character of the peasant, and solicited for himself the home and field of his benefactor. His villainy was detected, and the indignant monarch ordered to be branded, on his forehead, 'The ungrateful guest'—a stigma which, in Christian times, is, we are sorry to say, often merited by modern soldiers, as the following case will show:—

John Murdoch was a discharged soldier, who, in the beginning of the year 1815, visited a namesake of his, with whom he was formerly acquainted, at Langrig, a small village near Whitburn, Scotland. Although of the same name, there was no relationship between them; but, on the strength of nominal connexion, the veteran received a hearty welcome from his friend, James Murdoch, who lived in a house by himself, and kept a little shop.

For eight days the old soldier was hospitably entertained; but, like the 'ungrateful guest,' he wished to possess himself of the property of his host, and, horrid to relate, he one night took up a carpenter's adze, and clove the poor man's head in two! after which he concealed the body in a corner.

Next day, the shop not being opened as usual, the neighbours became alarmed, and, going to inquire, they were told by the murderer that the old man had gone to Whitburn, and would not return until the evening. This not satisfying the people, they rushed forward, and soon discovered the mangled corpse of the deceased.

The 'ungrateful guest' attempted to escape; but he was pursued, and quickly overtaken. When examined, the money of the poor shopkeeper, as well as his watch, was found upon the wretch, who was fully committed for trial.

On Monday, February the 18th, 1815, he was indicted for this murder in the High Court of Justiciary, Edinburgh, and found Guilty. The execution of a murderer does not take place in Scotland so soon after conviction as in this country; and this malefactor did not suffer until the 29th of the following March.

JOHN EILEM,
EXECUTED FOR RAVISHING A YOUNG GIRL.

THIS brutal and unmanly villain richly deserved the fate he earned for himself; for he that forcibly violates the person of an unprotected female is unfit to fill any station in civilized society, and commits a private injury which nothing on earth can recompense, as his unfortunate victim may be said to walk through life an animated corpse, shunned by the living, and insulted by the wicked and the thoughtless, while the commiseration of the humane only renews those tortures which nothing but death can assuage. The man who subjects a female, otherwise innocent and lovely, to such a life as this, deserves more tortures than are found in physical death.

John Ellem, a wealthy ropemaker, at Barking, was indicted at Chelmsford, July the 14th, 1815, for ravishing Anne Pearson, on the 24th of March.

Anne Pearson, the prosecutrix, stated that she was sixteen last Christmas. On the 24th, her master, his wife, and the servant boy, went out to go to London, but her master returned in about half an hour; it was about six o'clock: he asked her if the kettle boiled, and told her to get the things; there was no person in the house but themselves; having placed the tea-things, he desired her to go up stairs and fetch his pocket-book; she went, but could not find it; she called down stairs to say it was not there; he again called up to look into his waistcoat pocket; she did, it was not there; she told him so, and he desired her to look into his jacket pocket; it was not there: she then heard him coming up stairs, and she, having a suspicion of his intention to take improper liberties with her, shut the door and locked it; he knocked at the door, and desired her to open it; she refused, unless he would go down stairs; he said if she did not open the door he would break it open, adding, what the hell do you think I want with you? She then opened the door; he immediately threw her upon the bed: she got up once, and had reached the door, but he again caught her and accomplished his purpose; he then went down stairs, and she followed in about two minutes; he walked about the room whistling; she left the house in less than half an hour, and went to her mother's. On her way she met a young friend, who asked her what she was crying about. She said her master had behaved rude to her; she told her mother the same, but did not then tell her the whole. Her friend came in shortly afterwards, and she told her the particulars, desiring that she would tell her mother, as she did not like to do it herself. In the evening, when she went to bed, disclosed the whole to her mother, who (on the Monday), this being Good Friday, sent for Mr. Desormeaux, the doctor.—She was subjected to a very severe cross-examination. She said she could not have been heard to cry out; she could not get to the window; she denied having had any loose conversation with a milkman on that same day; she knew a Mr. Smith, a doctor, at Barking, but she had never applied to him for any medicines, or had ever spoken to him. Her mother, Mr. Desormeaux, and Caroline Walker, were called, who confirmed her as to her immediate disclosure of the facts, except that Mr. Desormeaux said, that, in stating the mode of perpetration, she had described it differently with respect to confining her hands. The prisoner, being called upon for his defence, said he left it to his counsel. They called witnesses to show a contradiction in parts of her testimony. The washerwoman's girl said, that, when she had brought the waistcoat, she had another girl with her, and that she came in a laughing manner, as though nothing had happened; but the principal witness was Richard Baker Smith, who described himself as a surgeon and apothecary, now residing at Ilford, then at Barking. He said the girl came to his house about ten o'clock on the night of the 1st of April. When he opened the door, he supposed she came about a certain disorder, and he asked her if it was so. She said no; but some young men had been playing tricks with her, and she wanted some physic. A woman was with her, wrapped in a red cloak. He told her to come in the morning. He was sure it was her, as he knew her and her family. Upon cross-examination he proved a most ignorant man; so much so, that he spelt dropsy, *dropsee*, and fistula, *festerly*. He insisted, however, that he was a regular-bred medical man, and had two hundred venereal patients from Barking alone, and produced a certificate, which, upon examination, proved to be a certificate written by himself. The girl, who was confronted with him, most solemnly denied ever having spoken to him. He named also the mother's brother as his patient. He happened to be in court, and denied the fact. The witness said, 'If not him, he had had his wife under his care.' His lordship expressed great indignation at the conduct of this witness. The foreman of the prisoner was called to prove a conversation between the girl and a milkman on the day of the transaction, which she denied. He said two other persons heard it, but they were not present. The noble and learned judge having detailed all the evidence on both sides, the jury, after a very short deliberation, found the prisoner Guilty. His lordship immediately passed sentence of death upon him, assuring him that he need not hope for mercy in this world.

ELIZABETH DREW,
TRIED FOR ROBBERY.

THIS singular trial took place at Cornwall, July the 26th, 1815, and occupied the Court for a considerable time, during which the spectators, the Bar, and the Bench, were convulsed with laughter.

Elizabeth Drew was indicted for robbing Thomas Martin of a watch, some wearing apparel, &c. &c.

The prosecutor, who was an Irish seaman, with his arms folded, in an erect though careless attitude, a smile of apparently invincible good humour on his countenance, and every minute casting a significant glance on the prisoner, answered the interrogatories of the Bench in a language which his lordship declared to be wholly incomprehensible but which was composed of technical phrases, delivered with a rather slight brogue. In vain was it that he was desired to cut short his prolix narrative: honest Tom Martin knew how to keep, but not to abridge, a log-book; every interruption caused him to lose his reckoning, and he found it easier to begin anew than to splice a broken story. He had marked down every course he had steered, and every variation of wind and weather he had experienced—every port he had made, and every harbour in which he had anchored—from the time he had embarked with the prisoner to the hour of his appearance in court; and he would relate the whole. He said he was armourer of the Severn frigate, and was in

Hamoaze in the beginning of the present month, when he got his *long* liberty. He knew the prisoner; and why should he not? She washed for him, and was a country girl of his own. He was surprised that the judge did not know that *long* liberty lasted a month. The prisoner was on board the Severn for four or five days before he got his *long* liberty, and he told her he was going to spend it in Ireland. On her expressing a wish also to visit her dear country, which she had not seen for three years, he said he would pay her passage. This offer she accepted on condition that one bed should serve them during their voyage; to which, of course, he made no objection. Some smugglers coming on board, he resolved to have a parting jollification with his messmates, and bought half a gallon of rum. He had a hearty booze before he left the ship, so that, when he came on shore, he was rather top-heavy. On coming to North Corner he gave his companion two pounds to take her clothes out of pawn; after which they shortened sail, and came-to at the second public house on the right hand as you go up. Here they drank some beer, and Tom got intoxicated, so that he determined to cast anchor, and take a nap. However, having the same confidence in his country-girl as if she had been his real wife, he gave her charge of his money, which amounted to twenty-seven pounds, before he turned in to sleep. A canvass bag, containing five white shirts, four pair of stockings, and sundry other articles of wearing apparel, with a prayer-book, called the 'Key of Paradise,' a pocket-book, and a green book that he used to keep his accounts in, he left in the bar. He had his watch in his pocket when he fell asleep.

The prisoner took the bag from the bar, his watch from his pocket, and the *lady* even took his handkerchief from his neck, and put an old rag in its place, not worth a penny. The watch was as good a watch as ever went; she was worth ten guineas of any man's money. The seal and key were gold; the chain was what is called composition, and he could not tell what it was worth. But, after all, he wished his country-girl should have fair play: he was sorry to come against a woman; he would rather come against a man by ten degrees. Finding himself plundered, he made inquiry for his companion, and he just got a sight of her in the public house; but she gave him the double, and he saw her no more till, after a long chase, he made her out at Callington. When he saw her he clapped his hand on her shoulder this way (giving a specimen of his mode of salutation by a smart slap on a gentleman's shoulder who sat near the witnesses' box); 'but,' said he, 'madam knew nothing about me; she did not know me at all.' The manner in which he pronounced this, with an arch smile on his countenance, pointing to the prisoner, and casting a significant glance first on her, and then on the judge, would have done honour to the most celebrated of the Thespian votaries; it was one of the best pieces of comic acting we ever saw, and completely overturned the gravity of the Bench, drawing a peal of laughter and applause from a crowded Court. Order being restored, Tom Martin proceeded with the same degree of *sang froid*. Having once got sight of the chase, he was not to be baffled, but kept her close on board until the constable, whom he had hailed on reaching Callington had procured a warrant. His ungrateful countrywoman, finding she could not give him the double a second time, resolved to adopt another manœuvre, and, desiring to be left alone with him, gave up the watch as a peace-offering.

Being desired to produce the watch, Tom first hesitated, and then owned that he had pawned it for two guineas, in order to prevent the necessity of his going on board before his long liberty was expired; a circumstance that he appeared most seriously to deprecate. His lordship then asked what he had done with the *double* he said the prisoner had given him. 'What did I do with it?' replied the witness, evidently much amused at the misconception of the Bench; (his lordship supposed that by *double* was meant a *duplicate* given by a pawnbroker;) 'why I could do nothing; she gave it to me *entirely*. But, as it is going as it is, I'll out with the whole on her. This waistcoat on me, my lord'——

Judge.—' No matter about this waistcoat; it is not mentioned in the indictment.'

Witness.—' Ay; but I'll tell all about it.'

His lordship, however, would hear nothing about the waistcoat, and told the witness he knew not what to make of his story; on which Tom replied—' I believe, my lord, I've told it very fair; it is very fair doctrine, and there is no Englishman but will understand what it means.' His canvass bag, he said, was found at the prisoner's lodgings; but the ' Key of Paradise,' and the rest of its contents, except a pair of stockings, were gone.

His lordship summed up the evidence, as well as he could collect it from the prosecutor; and the jury, not thinking that the things produced were sufficiently identified, acquitted the prisoner.

WILLIAM BRADFORD,
EXECUTED FOR FORGERY.

THIS unfortunate culprit was a young man, twenty-three years of age, of most respectable connexions, and held a situation as clerk in the Victualling Office, where he had various opportunities of becoming acquainted with the forms of bills, as well as a correct knowledge of the handwriting of those by whom they were usually signed.

Thoughtless extravagance plunged him into pecuniary difficulties, from which he resolved to relieve himself by committing forgery. Desperate and criminal as the resolution was, he carried it into effect by fabricating a bill for eight hundred and sixty-eight pounds, nine shillings, and sixpence, purporting to be drawn on the commissioners of his majesty's Victualling Office by Robert Tieverton, purser of the Acasto, and certified by Alexander Robert Kerr, the captain.

Bradford then procured an unsuspecting friend, named Williams, to carry the bill for acceptance to the Victualling Office; and so well was it executed, and every thing managed with such adroitness, that it passed through all the necessary offices without exciting the least suspicion. He next sent it to the Bank of England, and got it discounted.

Suspicion was, however, subsequently excited, and Bradford was taken into custody. A fifty-pound note was found in his lodging, which turned out to be one of those paid for the bill at the Bank: and eventually every one of the notes was traced to his possession; even a ten-pound note, with which he redeemed his watch, proved to have been one of these.

The trial of this miserable young man came on at the Old Bailey, October the 26th, 1815, and lasted for five hours. The evidence was conclusive, and he was accordingly found Guilty. When he was removing from the bar he fainted, so great was the impression made upon him by the verdict.

The efforts of his friends to procure a commutation of his sentence proved unavailing, and the law was left to take its course. On Monday, December the 8th, he was visited by his two younger brothers, for the purpose of taking leave of him; but, when the hour of parting came, their feelings were wound up to such a pitch, that the keepers with difficulty separated them from the unhappy sufferer; and, even after they had been taken from the cell, the younger brother clung to every object in his way, exclaiming, in a dreadful paroxysm of grief, 'My brother! oh, my unhappy brother!' At length they were tranquillized, but did not quit the mansion of misery for some time.

During Tuesday night Bradford was attended by the Rev. Mr. Rudge, and he appeared tranquil, joining most fervently in prayer with his friend. In the course of the night he took a little negus, but it did not remain on his stomach. He slept for about two hours, and afterwards partook of some toast and water. The next morning, Wednesday, December the 10th, 1815, being the time appointed for his execution, he was brought, at eight o'clock, to the Press-yard, and disencumbered of his irons: after which he walked with a firm step to the scaffold; and his last words were—'O Lord, spare my soul; for I am a miserable sinner!'

ELIZABETH FENNING,
EXECUTED FOR ATTEMPTING TO POISON A FAMILY.

THE extraordinary interest taken by the public in this very peculiar and affecting case is at least an honourable proof that, however lax may be the practice of virtue, the principle still continues to be our national character. A more striking evidence of this can hardly be adduced than the spontaneous movement excited by the prosecution, condemnation, and execution of Eliza Fenning, in whose lamentable fate all classes and descriptions of persons seemed to be animated by a common feeling.

The reflection that all institutions of men are liable to abuse operates as a standing lesson to make us watchful over the forms of law and the proceedings of Courts, that what was established by the integrity and wisdom of our ancestors might not be injured by our folly or perverted by our remissness. Men should be aware of that blind confidence which induces them to rely upon the intrinsic excellence of legal institutions and the solemnity of judicial proceedings; for experience shows that, though they may be secure from corruption, they are still liable to erroneous administration. 'Better,' says the legal maxim, 'that ten guilty escape, than that one innocent person should suffer;' and, as jurors are the great arbitrators of life and death, they cannot hesitate too long before they consign a fellow-creature to a premature grave. But, where guilt is only *presumptive*, they should not only reflect well upon the motives of human action, and the prejudice of prosecutors, but give the accused the whole benefit of every possible doubt.

As the case of this unfortunate young woman is pregnant with instruction, both in a legal and individual point of view, we have used every diligence in preparing an unbiassed statement of facts, free from error and misrepresentation.

Elizabeth Fenning was born in the island of Dominica, in the West Indies, on the 10th of June, 1793. Her father, William Fenning, was a native of Suffolk, and belonged to the first battalion of the 15th regiment of infantry. Her mother was a native of Cork, in Ireland: her parents were respectable, and she was married to Fenning in 1787, in her native town, where the regiment had been quartered. In 1790 they sailed from the Cove of Cork for the island of Barbadoes, and from thence to Dominica, where the subject of this narrative was born. Both her parents were Protestants, and she was baptized by a minister of the same religion.

In 1796 or 1797 the regiment came home, having suffered great mortality, and were quartered in Dublin. In 1802 Fenning solicited and obtained his discharge, with a certificate of his good character, which it appears he merited, as he rose to the rank of a non-commissioned officer. He then came to London, and entered the service of his brother, a potatoe-dealer in Red Lion Street, Holborn, with whom he continued for three years, and afterwards lived as servant in a potatoe-warehouse in Red Lion Passage, where his correct conduct gave satisfaction to three successive proprietors. His wife, for five years, worked for one upholsterer—a sufficient proof of her good conduct. They had ten children, all of whom died young except Eliza, who was the darling of her parents, who, being industrious themselves, did not rear their daughter up in idleness. From the age of fourteen she lived in servitude, and, in the latter end of January, 1815, was hired as cook in the family of a Mr. Orlibar Turner, at No. 68, Chancery Lane, where she had not been above seven weeks when circumstances unhappily arose which led to the poor creature's being charged with an attempt to poison Turner's family.

The facts of the case will be best explained by the following report of the trial, taken in short-hand by Mr. Sibly, short-hand writer to the corporation of London, which differs materially from the 'Sessions' Paper' report.

Eliza Fenning was indicted at the Old Bailey, April the 11th, 1815, for that she, on the 21st of March, feloniously and unlawfully, did administer to, and caused to be administered to, Orlibar Turner, Robert Gregson Turner, and Charlotte Turner, his wife, certain deadly poison, (to wit, arsenic,) with intent the said persons to kill and murder.

The case was stated by Mr. Gurney; after which—

Mrs. Charlotte Turner deposed— I am the wife of Mr. Robert Gregson Turner, who is a law-stationer in Chancery Lane, in partnership with his father, Mr. Orlibar Turner, who lives at Lambeth. About seven weeks before the accident the prisoner came into my service as cook; and about three weeks after I had occasion to reprove her, for I observed her, one night, go into the young men's room partly undressed. It was very indecent of her to go into the young men's room thus undressed. There were two young men, about seventeen or eighteen years old. I reproved her severely next morning for her conduct; the excuse was, that she was going to fetch the candle. I threatened to discharge her, and gave her warning to quit; but she showed contrition; I forgave her for it, and retained her. That passed over. For the remaining month I observed that she failed in the respect that she before paid me, and appeared extremely sullen. About a fortnight before the transaction she requested me to let her make some yeast dumplings, professing herself to be a capital hand. That request was frequently repeated. On Monday, the 20th of March, she came up into the dining-room, and said the brewer had brought some yeast. I had given no orders to the brewer to bring any yeast: I told her I did not wish to trouble the man; that was not the way I had them made; I generally had the dough from the baker's, which saved the cook a great deal of trouble, and was also considered the best. Having this yeast, I said it was of no consequence; as the man had brought a little, the next day she might make some. On Tuesday morning, I, as usual, went into the kitchen. I told her she might make some; but, before she made the dumplings, to make a beef-steak pie for dinner for the young men. As she would have to leave the kitchen to get the steaks, I did not wish her to do so after the dumplings were made. I told her I should wish the dough to be mixed with milk and water. She said she would do them as I desired her: this was about half past eleven. She carried the pie to the baker's before kneading the dough commenced: I told her I wished her not to leave the dough that she might carry the pie to the baker's. I suppose she carried the pie to the baker's near twelve. I gave her directions about making the dough. I said, I suppose there was no occasion for me stopping. She said, Oh no, she knew very well how to do it; and then I went up stairs. In not more than half an hour I went again into the kitchen: I then found the dough made, and set before the fire to rise. We have one more servant, a house-maid, Sarah Peer I had given Sarah orders to go into the bed-room, to repair a counterpane, at the time the dough was made. During the time the dough was made I am certain there could be nobody in the kitchen but the prisoner: I suppose this might be half past twelve. We dine at three—the young men at two. In the interval between half past twelve and three I was in the kitchen two or three times, until the dough was made into dumplings. The dough remained in a pan before the fire, for the purpose of rising; but I observed the dough never did rise. I took off the cloth, to look at it: my observation was, that it did not rise and it was in a very singular position, in which position it remained until it was divided into dumplings. It was not put into the pan, as I have observed dough: its shape was singular; it retained the shape till the last; it remained heavy all the time, not rising at all. I am confident it never was meddled with after it was put there. The dumplings were divided, to put into the pot, about twenty minutes before twelve. I was not in the kitchen at the time, but I was in it about half an hour before that time.

By a Juror.—I did not remark to her the singular appearance of the dough. I told her it had never risen: the prisoner said it would rise before she wanted it. There were six dumplings brought upon the table about three o'clock, when I sat down to dinner. I observed to the other servant that they were black and heavy instead of being white and light. My husband, Robert Gregson Turner, and his father, Orlibar Turner, sat down to dinner with me: I helped them to some dumplings, and took a small piece myself. I found myself affected in a few minutes after I had eaten. I did not eat a quarter of a dumpling. I felt myself very faint—an excruciating pain, an extreme violent pain, which increased every minute: it came so bad, I was obliged to leave the table—I went up stairs. I ate, beside the dumpling, a piece of rump steak, cooked by Eliza. When I was up stairs I perceived my sickness increased, and I observed my head was swollen extremely. I retched very violently: I was half an hour alone, and wondered they did not come to my assistance. I found my husband and father very ill—both of them. I was very ill from half past three until about nine: the violence abated, but did not cease. My head was swollen, and my tongue and chest were swollen. We called in a gentleman who was near, and afterwards Mr. Marshall, the surgeon. We applied for the nearest assistance we could get.

Cross-examined by Mr. Alley.—This happened about six weeks after the girl came to live with me. I had no other cause of complaint except that. I forgave her. I do not think it was that day the coals had been delivered: the girl is here who received them: it could not be that day. She had no occasion to receive the coals.* I have heard the prisoner herself was taken very ill.

Orlibar Turner deposed—I believe I am the father of Robert Gregson Turner. On Tuesday, the 21st day of March, I was at my son's house in Chancery Lane: I dined there. The dinner consisted of yeast dumplings, beef-steaks, and potatoes. After some time Mrs. Turner left the room indisposed. At the time she left the room I did not know she was ill. Some time after my son left the room, and went down stairs. I followed him very shortly. I had gone into my parlour below: I came into the passage. I met my son in the passage, at the foot of the stairs: he told me that he had been very sick, and had brought up his dinner. I found his eyes exceedingly swollen—very much indeed. I said I thought it very extraordinary. I was taken ill myself in less than three minutes afterwards. The effect was so violent, I had hardly time to go into my back yard before my dinner came up. I felt considerable heat across my stomach and chest, and pain: I never experienced any vomiting before like it, for violence; it was terrible indeed. It was not more than a quarter of an hour when my apprentice, Roger Gadsden, was very ill, in a similar way to myself. My son was also sick. While we were sick I was repeatedly in the parlour and the back yard. My son was up and down stairs at intervals; Gadsden, I believe, was in the kitchen below. The prisoner gave not the smallest assistance. We were all together alarmed: it was discovered that she did not appear concerned at our situation; our appearance was most distressing—more so than ever I witnessed in my life. I did not observe the prisoner eat any of the dumplings.† I had a suspicion of arsenic: I made a search the next morning.

* It is a serious and confirmed fact that the coals were delivered on that day, and received by Eliza Fenning; consequently both Mrs. Turner and Sarah Peer were mistaken in their evidence. After the poor girl's condemnation this was found to be the case, on application to the coal-merchant and the men who delivered the coals.

† How could he, when he did not go into the kitchen, or she come out of it?

By the Court.—I suspected it was poison. I observed, the next morning, in the pan in which the dumplings had been mixed, the leavings of the dumplings: they stuck round the pan. I put some water into the pan, and stirred it up with a spoon, with a view to form a liquid of the whole. Upon the pan being set down for a moment or two, or half a minute, and taking it up slowly, and in a slanting direction, I discovered a white powder at the bottom of it. I showed it to several persons in the house: I kept it in my custody until Mr. Marshall came; no person had access to it. Arsenic had been kept in a drawer in the office, fronting the fire-place, in two wrappers, tied up very tight, the words 'Arsenic, deadly poison,' written upon it. I believe the prisoner can both read and write.

Mrs. Turner was here asked 'Is that so?' and she replied 'Yes, she can read and write very well.'

Orlibar Turner resumed—The drawer always remained open; any person might have access to it. It was the prisoner's duty to light the fire: she might resort to that drawer for loose paper that was kept in it; she might resort to it to light a fire. I had seen the parcel of arsenic there on the 7th of March; not since that time. Before the 21st of March I heard of its being missed about a fortnight. I made observation on the appearance of the knives and forks which I ate the dumplings with: I have two of them in my pocket now to show; they have been in my custody ever since. I saw them with the blackness upon them the next day: it appeared upon them then; there is some little rust upon them now. The next day I spoke to the prisoner about these yeast dumplings: I asked her how she came to introduce ingredients that had been so prejudicial to us. She replied it was not in the dumplings, but in the milk that Sarah Peer brought in. I had several discourses with her that day upon this subject, during the whole of which she persisted it was in the milk, as before described. That milk had been used for the sauce only: the prisoner made the dumplings with the refuse of the milk that had been left for breakfast. The prisoner did not tell me what use had been made of the milk that had been fetched by Sarah Peer. I asked her if any person but herself had mingled, or had any thing to do with, the dumplings. She expressly said 'No.'

Cross-examined by Mr. Alley.—In the conversation I had with the prisoner I did not tell her that, two months before, I had missed the poison. I do not know if the clerks keep the door of the office locked when they are not there.

Roger Gadsden sworn.—I am an apprentice to Mr. Turner. I remember seeing, in a drawer in the office, a paper, with 'Arsenic, deadly poison,' written upon it. The last day I saw it was on the 7th of March: I missed it in a day or two after; I mentioned in the office that I missed it. On Tuesday, the 21st of March, between three and four, I went into the kitchen: I had dined at two. In the kitchen I observed a plate: in it was a dumpling and a half. I took a knife and fork up, and was going to cut it, to eat of it. The prisoner exclaimed, 'Gadsden, do not eat of that; it is cold and heavy; it will do you no good!' I ate a piece about as big as a walnut, or bigger. There was a small quantity of sauce in the boat: I took a bit of bread, and sopped it in it, and ate that. This might be twenty minutes after three. I went into the office: Mr. Robert Turner came into the office about ten minutes after, and said he was very ill. They were all up stairs in the parlour:—not the least alarm of any body being ill then. About ten minutes after that I was taken ill, but not so ill as to vomit. I was sent off for Mr. Turner's mother. I was very sick going and coming—I thought I should die. The prisoner had made yeast dumplings for supper the night before: I and the other maid, and herself, partook of them: they were quite different from these dumplings in point of colour and weight, and very good. When the poison was missed I made no inquiry about it of the prisoner.

Cross-examined by Mr. Alley.—We don't keep the door of the office locked when we are out of it. The prisoner made the fire. No person could go into the office until I did. Any person might go in and out in the day. At night it was locked. Paper was kept in the drawer where the poison had been. If the prisoner went to that drawer I should not watch her, to see what she did there.

Margaret Turner sworn.—I was sent for. When I arrived I found my husband, son, and daughter, extremely ill. The prisoner, very soon after I was there, was ill, and vomiting. I exclaimed to her, 'Oh, these devilish dumplings!' supposing they had done the mischief. She said, ' Not the dumplings, but the milk, madam.' I asked her 'What milk?' She said ' The halfpenny-worth of milk that Sally had fetched, to make the sauce.' She said my daughter made the sauce. I said 'That cannot be; it could not be the sauce.' She said 'Yes; Gadsden ate a very little bit of dumpling, not bigger than a nut; but licked up three parts of a boat of sauce with a bit of bread.'

Mrs. Turner, jun. being called, said—' The sauce was made with the milk brought by Sarah Peer. I mixed it, and left it for her to make.'

Robert Gregson Turner sworn.—I partook of the dumplings at dinner; I ate none of the sauce whatever. Soon after dinner I was taken ill: I first felt an inclination to be sick; I then felt a strong heat across my chest. I was extremely sick: I was exactly as my father and wife were, except stronger symptoms. I had eaten a dumpling and a half. I suffered more than any person. I should presume that the symptoms were such as would be produced by poison:—all taken in the same way, and pretty near the same time.

Sarah Peer sworn.—I have been servant to Mrs. Turner near eleven months. I recollect the warning given to the prisoner some time after she came. After that I heard her say she should not like Mr. or Mrs. Robert Turner any more. On the 21st of March I went for some milk after two o'clock, after I had dined with the prisoner on beef-steak pie. I had no concern whatever in making the dough for the dumplings, or in making the sauce. I was not in the kitchen when the dough was made: I never meddled with it, or put any thing to it; I never was in the kitchen until I went up to make the beds, a quarter after eleven, until I came down again. I had permission to go out that afternoon, directly after I took up the dumplings. I went out directly. I came home at nine o'clock exactly. I ate none of the dumplings myself. In eating the beef-steak pie, I ate some of the crust. I was not at all ill. I had eaten some dumplings she had made the night before: I never tasted any better. They were all made out of the same flour. I had no difference with my mistress at any time.

Cross-examined by Mr. Alley.—

The coals were not delivered on that day. It is not true that I was set to watch the coals coming in. As the dumplings were taken out of the pot I went out. The prisoner and I were on good terms by times: our last quarrel was two or three days before. She had taken something out of my drawer for a duster: I said I did not like to lead that life without she altered her temper. About a week or a week and a half before we had another quarrel: I don't know what it was about. It was the habit of the house for the servants to take it turn about to go out of a Sunday. On Tuesday I visited my sister at Hackney: I had been to my sister's about a month before that: it was my turn to go out before this Tuesday. The prisoner lived seventeen weeks in my master's house. Never went to visit my sister but on a Sunday, except on that day. I went very seldom into the office where the young men were. I knew the waste paper was kept in the office; but my mistress always kept it up stairs in the dining-room for my use. I did not know there was waste paper in the office; I never touched any there. I did not know it for certainty: there might be waste paper there, but I never touched it. Did not know there was poison kept there. I never went to the drawer in the office, nor never knew there was poison kept there to kill rats and mice.

Mr. Orlibar Turner re-examined. —This poison was kept to destroy mice, and for no other purpose. It had not been used before for a year and a half.

William Thiselton sworn.—I am an officer of Hatton Garden office. I took the prisoner into custody on the 23d of March, the day before Good Friday. She said she had made a beef-steak pie of the flour she had made the dumplings with; that she and her fellow-servants, and one of the apprentices, had dined off the pie. She said she thought it was in the yeast; she saw a red settlement in the yeast after she had used it.

The brewer's man was then called. He deposed that the yeast was the same as bakers use. He gave the yeast to the house-maid, not to the prisoner.

John Marshall sworn.—I am a surgeon. On the evening of the 21st of March I was sent for to Mr. Turner's family; I got there about a quarter before nine o'clock. All the symptoms attending the family were produced by arsenic; I have no doubt of it by the symptoms. The prisoner was also ill, by the same, I have no doubt. Mr. Orlibar Turner showed me a dish the next morning: I examined it; I washed it with a tea-kettle of warm water; I first stirred it, and then let it subside; I decanted it off; I found half a tea-spoonful of white powder; I washed it the second time; I decidedly found it to be arsenic. Arsenic cut with a knife will produce the appearance of blackness on the knife; I have no doubt of it. There was not a grain of arsenic in the yeast: I examined the flour-tub; there was no arsenic there.

The case for the prosecution closed here, and the poor girl made the following defence:—

' I am truly innocent of the whole charge: I am innocent; indeed I am; I liked my place, I was very comfortable.

' Gadsden behaved improperly to me; my mistress came and saw me undressed: she said she did not like it; I said, " Ma'am, it is Gadsden that has taken liberty with me." The next morning I said " I hope you don't think any thing of what passed last night." She was in a great passion, and said she would not put up with it; I was to go away directly. I did not look upon Mrs. Turner as my mistress, but upon the old lady. In the evening the old lady came to town; I said, "I am going away to-night." Mrs. Turner said "Do not think any more about it; I don't." She asked Mrs. Robert Turner if she was willing for me to go. She said "No, she thought no more about it.'

'As to my master saying I did not assist him, I was too ill. I had no concern with that drawer at all; when I wanted a piece of paper I always asked for it."

The prisoner called five witnesses, who gave her an excellent character for integrity, sobriety, cheerfulness, and humanity. One of these was proceeding to state an accidental conversation he had with the prisoner two days after she had ordered the yeast, wherein she declared herself happy and contented with her situation, and pleased with her master and mistress; but the recorder stopped him, saying it was not evidence.

Whilst the trial was proceeding, William Fenning, the father of the prisoner, went to a public house, and got a person (for he was too agitated himself) to write on a slip of paper, that on the 21st of March he went to Mr. Turner's, his daughter having sent for him in the morning, and that Sarah Peer told him Eliza had gone of a message for her mistress, whilst, at the same time, she was in agonies below stairs from the effect of having eaten of the dumplings. He then went home, and thought no more about it.

When this note was written, it was handed to Mr. Alley, who, standing upon tip-toe, showed it to the recorder, who leaned over and looked at it.

No further notice was taken of this paper, either by the recorder or Mr. Alley; and, soon afterwards, upon the prisoner requesting the apprentice to be brought forward, Gadsden went up into the witnesses' box; whereon the prisoner energetically exclaimed, 'No, my lord, it's not that apprentice boy—it's not the younger apprentice that I want —it's Thomas King that I want— the elder apprentice, who knows that I never went to the drawer in my life; for when I asked for paper he always gave it me; and if he was here he dare not deny the truth to my face, and I wish him to be sent for.'

The recorder said 'You should have had him here before.'

The prisoner replied, 'My lord, I desired him to be brought, and I wish him to be sent for now.'

The recorder said 'No, it's too late now—I cannot hear you.'

The recorder then asked Roger Gadsden 'Who lit the fire in the office?' He replied 'The prisoner; I and my fellow-apprentice have seen her go to that drawer many times.'

William Fenning, the prisoner's father, greatly agitated, stepped up into the witnesses' box, and said, 'I am the father of the unfortunate girl, my lord: if you won't hear her, I hope you will hear me.'

He was then proceeding to relate, amongst other circumstances, his having been denied access to his daughter, in the manner mentioned in the note delivered to Mr. Alley, and shown to the recorder; and to state that his daughter, when he was denied, was lying in great agony below stairs, from the effects of the poisoned dumplings.

The recorder would not suffer the prisoner's father to go on—he put his hand out, and motioned him to leave the witnesses' box—he told him 'he could not hear him—it was too late—he must go down.'

Finding that the recorder would not hear him, and being ordered down, the father left the witnesses' box.

The recorder proceeded to sum up the evidence, and charge the jury.

Before the summing up, Mr. Alley, the prisoner's counsel, left the Court.

The recorder, in summing up the evidence, made remarks as he went on, and dwelt particularly on the prisoner's declaration to Sarah Peer, that she should not like Mr. and Mrs. Turner any more—on her repeatedly requesting her mistress to let her make yeast dumplings; particularly her telling her mistress, when she complained they did not rise, that they 'would rise time enough;' and on her telling Gadsden not to eat of the dumplings that had come down stairs—that they were cold and heavy, and would do him no good.

The recorder observed that, vellum and parchment being very valuable, arsenic was kept to preserve these valuable things from the vermin called rats and mice; and that it was evident that the prisoner at the bar could not be ignorant of the poison, because it was written on 'Arsenic, deadly poison;' and as this girl had an education, and could read and write, she could not be ignorant of the poison.

The recorder concluded his charge in the following words, or words to the like effect :—

'Gentlemen, you have now heard the evidence on this trial, and the case lies in a very narrow compass. There are but two questions for your consideration; and these are, the fact of poison having been administered, in all, to four persons, and by what hand such poison was given. That these persons were poisoned appears certain from the evidence of Mrs. Charlotte Turner, Orlibar Turner, Roger Gadsden the apprentice, and Robert Turner; for each of these persons ate of the dumplings, and were all more or less affected; that is, they were every one poisoned. That the poison was in the dough of which these dumplings were composed has been fully proved, I think, by the testimony of the surgeon who examined the remains of the dough left in the dish in which the dumplings had been mixed and divided; and he deposes that the powder which had subsided at the bottom of the dish was arsenic. That the arsenic was not in the flour, I think appears plain from the circumstance that the crust of a pie had been made that very morning with some of the flour of which the dumplings were made, and that the persons who dined off the pie felt no inconvenience whatever: that it was not in the yeast, nor in the milk, has been proved; neither could it be in the sauce, for two of the persons who were ill never touched a particle of the sauce, and yet were violently affected with retching and sickness. From all these circumstances it must follow that the poisonous ingredient was in the dough alone; for, besides that the persons who partook of the dumplings at dinner were all more or less affected from what they had eaten, it was observed, by one of the witnesses, that the dough retained the same shape it had when first put into the dish to rise; and that it appeared dark and was heavy, and in fact never did rise. The other question for your consideration is, by what hand the poison was administered? and, although we have nothing before us but circumstantial evidence, yet it often happens that circumstances are more conclusive than the most positive testimony.

'The prisoner, when taxed with poisoning the dumplings, threw the blame first on the milk, next on the yeast, and then on the sauce; but it has been proved, most satisfactorily, that none of these contained it, and that it was in the dumplings alone, which no person but the prisoner had made. Gentlemen, if poison had been given even to a dog, one would suppose that common humanity would have prompted us to assist it in its agonies: here is the case of a master and mistress being both poisoned, and no assistance was offered. Gentlemen, I have now stated all the facts as they have arisen, and I leave the case in your hands, being fully persuaded that, whatever your verdict may be, you will conscientiously discharge your duty both to your God and to your country.'

After the charge, the jury in a few minutes brought in a verdict of Guilty, and the miserable girl was carried from the bar convulsed with agony, and uttering frightful screams.

The recorder passed sentence of death upon her.

In the foregoing trial there is no proof that the prisoner took the arsenic out of the drawer, or that she had ever seen it there; it was not seen with her, neither was there any indication of her having had it, when she and her box were searched after the fatal accident. There was no proof that arsenic was in the dumplings; and, what is more, in all probability, it was not arsenic that caused the sickness in Turner's family. A moment's reflection must lead to this opinion. Gadsden ate only the size of a walnut of the dumpling, and was ill in a way similar to old Mr. Turner; Mrs. Robert Turner did not eat a quarter of a dumpling, and was first ill, and continued longest indisposed; while Robert Gregson Turner ate a dumpling and a half,* and does not appear to have been more ill than his wife, who did not eat more than one-fifth of that quantity. Arsenic does not operate in this way; one grain will not have the effect of five.

Mr. Marshall swore that he found next morning, in the dish in which the dumplings were made, half a tea-spoonful of arsenic. If the arsenic had been mixed in the dough, no doubt it would have been equally diffused throughout the whole mass, for, though it had not been done so with the kneading, it has that property in itself. Now every one in the habit of going into a kitchen knows that the dough which adheres to a dish wherein dumplings had been made is very small, and, if collected, would certainly not exceed the size of a walnut, or one-eighth of a dumpling. If, therefore, there was in that quantity half a tea-spoonful of arsenic, which it has been ascertained would weigh fifty grains, there would have been in the four dumplings and a half, eaten by the five persons, a quantity of arsenic weighing one thousand eight hundred grains. Now as five grains of arsenic would destroy any human being who swallowed it, the quantity in Mrs. Turner's quarter of a dumpling was equal to the death of ten persons; that in her husband's dumpling

---

* There were but six dumplings in all; and if Robert Turner and his wife ate one and three-fourths, and there remained, when the liquorish Gadsden went down to the kitchen, only a dumpling and a half, then Eliza and the old man must have eaten two dumplings and three-quarters between them, which clearly demonstrates that Eliza Fenning ate nearly as much as any one in the house.—Would she have done this had she put poison in them?

and a half would have killed one hundred and twenty; and in that eaten by the five persons would have destroyed three hundred and sixty people!!!

It is probable, therefore, that arsenic was not in the dumplings; and, if the illness of the family arose from having swallowed arsenic, it must have been shaken upon the dumplings after they were made, and this supposition accounts for the large quantity found in the dish out of which the dumplings were taken. But, after all, may not the deleterious ingredient have been some other mineral less fatal in its effects than arsenic, though capable of exciting similar symptoms? and might not this have been introduced by some mischievous or malignant person who might have gone into the kitchen while Eliza was absent?

It is true, indeed, that Mr. Marshall, the apothecary, swore positively that it was arsenic he found in the dish; but he was evidently a man of little science, for his evidence was in part untrue; and, coming from a medical man, though erroneous, might have had a fatal influence on the decision of a jury. He swore that arsenic being cut with a knife would blacken the knife; and, as this is not the case, it is not very unreasonable to suppose that he was also mistaken in respect to the powder which he found in the dish.

Of all the criminal cases which can come before a jury, that of poisoning is the easiest accomplished, the hardest to guard against, and the most detestable, and most difficult of proof. There can be no punishment too severe for such an enormity. When it is committed in a family, every individual of that family is seized with horror of the crime—anger and abhorrence of whoever is accused—and a proportionate dread of being each suspected and sacrificed. Until some individual is apprehended, suspicion attaches upon all the inmates, and the master, mistress, and servants, are equally objects of arrest and imprisonment; but the moment any one of these is committed, the united detestation of the others collects upon that individual; and facts which, otherwise, would be proofs of innocence, are then arrested to their disadvantage, and are brought in as corroborating evidence of guilt. A jury ought, therefore, with generous manliness, to stand upon the forlorn hope of the accused, and not for a single moment to forget that every one of those who deposed against the prisoner at the bar came that morning from one house, had conferred together upon the evidence they were to give, and were knit together by the ties of blood, the interest of family character, and the bonds of domestic dependency and servitude. They ought to recollect that all the deponents partake of the same prejudices, horror, and alarm for themselves, and have an absolute interest in the conviction and execution of the unfortunate accused, as they are thereby secured from future suspicion of the horrid crime. Proper weight is to be given to the testimony of consistent witnesses, substantiating the whole of their presumptive evidence by some one act of evil in itself; but an intelligent juror will not permit inconsistency, improbability, and outrageous impossibility, to pass on him for evidence, merely because they are sworn to in his presence. It is worthy of remark that the whole of the witnesses against Eliza Fenning were in Court, listening to each other, during the unfortunate girl's trial.

We make no apology for the length of this case, because it is one of vital importance to every individual, since it may possibly fall to the lot of any person, in whatever walk of life, to become accidentally an object of suspicion, and to be charged with an offence of the greatest enormity on mere surmise. The discussion, therefore, of a subject so momentous, and which comes home to the bosom of every man, cannot surely be reprehended as useless or uncalled for.

Few cases ever excited greater interest than that of Eliza Fenning; and as some men—through inadvertency, to say no worse of it—maligned her character, we are happy in being able to state that her religious principles were correct, and her professions sincere: through life she was distinguished by a superiority of intellect, and a propriety of deportment, which could hardly be reconciled with the depravity of which she was accused. Her person was short of stature, but of the most perfect symmetry; while her countenance evinced a heart at ease, and a mind at once intellectual and lively. She had been, before the fatal transaction, betrothed to a young man, to whom she appears to have been sincerely attached — a circumstance which must have added to her sufferings.

After the unfortunate girl's conviction she was induced to apply to the fountain of mercy for remission of the sentence of death, and sent a petition to the prince regent. She next addressed the lord chancellor, to whom she mentioned the remarkable fact that Mrs. Turner swore at one time that she (Eliza) carried the pie to the baker's about twelve o'clock, while in an another place she states that the dough was divided into dumplings twenty minutes before twelve. She also sent a letter to Lord Sidmouth, and another to her late master, requesting him to sign a petition in her favour, with which he refused to comply.

Several gentlemen now interested themselves in the fate of the poor girl, and Mr. Montagu, of Lincoln's Inn, waited on the recorder, offering to produce evidence of a member of Mr. Turner's family, who was insane, having declared that he would poison the family; but the recorder assured him that the production of such evidence would be wholly useless.

The night before her execution a meeting of gentlemen took place in Mr. Newman's apartments, in Newgate, at which Mr. Gibson, of the house of Corbyn and Co. chymists, No. 300, Holborn, stated that Robert Gregson Turner, in the month of September or October, called at their house in a wild and deranged state, requesting to be put under restraint, otherwise he declared he should destroy himself and wife. Mr. Gibson also stated that it was well known in the family that Robert Turner was occasionally subject to such violent and strange conduct.

With this information Mr. Gibson, accompanied by a clerk from the secretary of state's office, waited on the recorder, requesting that the unfortunate girl might be respited, to admit of investigation:—in twelve hours after, Eliza Fenning was executed!

From the moment the poor girl was first charged with the poisoning, however or by whomsoever questioned, she never faltered in her denial of the crime, and rather courted than shunned an investigation of her case. So many circumstances, which had developed themselves subsequently to the trial, had been communicated to the secretary of state by the gentlemen who interested themselves in her favour (among whom were some of great respectability), that a reprieve was confidently expected to the last: and the order for her execution, four months after her conviction, was received with very great surprise.

On Tuesday morning, the 25th, she took her last farewell of her father, who, by the firmness of his manner, exemplified the courage he wished his child to sustain upon the scaffold: but with her mother the parting scene was heartrending.

On the fatal morning, the 26th July, 1815, she slept till four o'clock, when she arose, and, after carefully washing herself, and spending some time in prayer, she dressed herself neatly in a white muslin gown and cap. About eight o'clock she walked steadily to the spot where criminals are bound; and, whilst the executioner tied her hands—even whilst he wound the halter round her waist—she stood erect and unmoved, with astonishing fortitude. At this moment a gentleman who had greatly interested himself in her behalf adjured her, in the name of that God in whose presence she was about to appear, if she knew any thing of the crime for which she was about to suffer, to make it known; when she replied, distinctly and clearly, 'Before God, then, I die innocent!' The question was again put by the Rev. Mr. Vazie, as well as by the Ordinary, and finally by Oldfield, who suffered with her, and to each she repeated 'I am innocent.' These were her last words; and she died, without a struggle, at the age of twenty-one.

Her miserable parents, on application for her body, were not prepared to pay the executioner's fees of fourteen shillings and sixpence: they, however, borrowed the money, and were then permitted to remove it. On Monday, the 31st, the corpse was interred in the burial-ground of St. George the Martyr, near Brunswick Square, in the presence of an immense concourse of spectators.

Thousands of people, deeming the poor girl innocent, vented all their indignation on her prosecutors: vast numbers assembled before Turner's door, in Chancery Lane, hooting and hissing, inflamed by all sorts of exaggerations. This state of things continued for several days, notwithstanding the active interference of the police to avert the public anger. Davis, a turnkey in Newgate, made an affidavit that Eliza Fenning's father conjured his daughter, when she came out on the scaffold, to declare that she was innocent. This affidavit was printed, and industriously circulated; but old Fenning, after his daughter's funeral, replied to it in a counter affidavit, which, with Davis's explanation, showed that the assertion was utterly false. The public sympathized with the unhappy parents of Eliza Fenning, and a subscription was entered into for their benefit.

ELIZABETH WOOLLERTON,
EXECUTED FOR POISONING.

This wicked woman, unlike the unfortunate Eliza Fenning, had the crime brought home to her, which she aggravated by attempting to throw the charge upon her daughter.

Elizabeth Woollerton, the wife of a farmer, residing at Denton, in Norfolk, and the mother of nine children, was tried on a charge of having mixed a certain quantity of arsenic in a cake, which cake she sent as a present to her uncle,

Tifford Clarke, Esq. on the 2d day of July, 1816, thereby intending to kill him; and part of the said cake being eaten by Robert Sparkes, son of Benjamin Sparkes, occasioned his death.

Mr. Benjamin Long, apothecary at Bungay, said that the prisoner had purchased from him a quantity of arsenic on the 22d of June; also on a prior occasion.

It was proved by the prisoner's daughters, who were admitted evidence against her, that she had made the cake in question, and sent it to her uncle. It further appeared that she stood indebted to her uncle in the sum of two hundred pounds, and who intimated leaving her by his will a further sum of five hundred pounds.

Mr. Clarke proved the having received cakes from the prisoner on a former occasion, the eating of which had made him extremely ill, and in consequence he desired her not to send him such cakes in future; and for the reason alluded to he refused to eat of the cake in question. The housekeeper of Mr. Clarke, upon this, unknowingly sent the poisoned cake to her son-in-law, Sparkes, who had a family of five children. Upon receipt of it, the mother of the deceased divided the cake into equal portions for the children's breakfast next morning, previous to their departure for school at an early hour. The youngest of these, a boy six years old, was the first to eat his portion, which ultimately proved fatal to him; the other four were dangerously ill, but by means of timely assistance recovered, not having ate their full proportions: owing to this circumstance, the eldest, a girl about twelve years old, perceiving an acrid taste, took from her brothers and sisters that which remained uneaten.

The surgeons who opened the body of the deceased proved, by means of analyzation, that that part of the cake found in the stomach contained arsenic, occasioning the death of the boy; and, in like manner, that part of the cake which had not been eaten.

The prisoner, in her defence, persisted in her innocence, after an attempt to throw it upon her daughter, an interesting girl fourteen years of age! She was found Guilty —Death; and pursuant to her sentence was executed on Monday, July 17, 1815, at Ipswich, amidst an immense crowd of spectators.

ELIZABETH HUNTER AND REBECCA JARVIS,
CONVICTED OF ROASTING A CHILD.

These were worthy descendants of Mother Brownrigg, of notorious memory; and, had not their wicked proceedings been fortunately interrupted, no doubt they would have earned for themselves the fate of their infamous predecessor in this unnatural species of cruelty.

Elizabeth Hunter, aged forty-six, resided in the parish of Barking, and was in the habit of receiving parish children to nurse. Rebecca Jarvis, aged twenty-one, was a servant in Hunter's employ.

Catherine Evans stated on the trial that she was in the habit of washing and ironing clothes for the prisoner, and that on the morning of the 24th of May she went at an early hour to look for work, when she found Hunter chastising one of the children she had under her care, whom she told to strip. The child did so, when Hunter and Jarvis bound it hand and foot. Evans asked the former what she was going to do with the child, when she replied that she was going to roast it. Evans instantly apprized a neighbour, and they went together to Mrs. Hunter's, whom they found with her servant holding the child stripped before the fire. The child was very close, and cried out greatly. They were so shocked at the sight that they ran out of the house; but returned again, when the child was gone. Not being able to get a sight of it, they went to the parish officers, and informed them of the circumstance. An officer was in consequence sent to take away the child, who being found in a dangerous state, the perpetrators of the cruel act were apprehended, and indicted at the Chelmsford assizes on the 3d of August, 1816, when they were found Guilty, and Mrs. Hunter was sentenced to eighteen months' imprisonment, and Rebecca Jarvis to six, in the county gaol.

Grant and his Companions attacked by the Military.

JEREMIAH GRANT,
EXECUTED FOR BURGLARY.

THE exploits of this celebrated Irish freebooter were fully equal to those of the accomplished robber Duvell. *Captain* Grant was the son of a poor peasant in the Queen's County, and early evinced a predilection for the bread of idleness. His progress in literature was very trifling; indeed it has been stated that he could neither read nor write. His fertile genius, however, obviated this misfortune, and his daring spirit triumphed over minor obstacles. He sallied out, before the age of twenty, to levy contributions on the highway, and before he was twenty-one a chosen band of followers hailed him Captain.

His depredations for several years were confined to his native county, where his improvident liberality secured him the esteem and blessings of the lower orders, while the terror of his name, and dread of his vengeance, kept those of a higher rank in complete subjection to his authority.

Like Rob Roy, he levied an annual tax on the farmers, which they cheerfully paid, as it secured them from the nocturnal visits of his followers; for Grant was a man of strict honour and a rigid disciplinarian, who punished with severity any dereliction of duty in his band.

Notwithstanding the offer of reward for his apprehension, Captain Grant, as the country people called him, was to be seen at every fair and pattern in the country, and had a more numerous acquaintance than the village doctor. At every farmer's table he was welcome, and the cottages that gave him shelter were sure of reward; for he freely shared the contributions he obtained with danger.

With the ladies he was a second Macheath, and more wives than one claimed him for their husband; and no wonder, for he was frequently complimented, on his person and manner, by the mistresses of those houses which he visited without the formality of an invitation. But it must be observed that Grant never forgot his accustomed humanity and politeness; and, unless when attacked by the police, he never did an individual a personal injury. His behaviour always evinced a degree of refinement above his education and birth; so much so, that even those who suffered from his depredations never spoke of him but as an accomplished villain.

His person was of the most elegant symmetry, and his agility surprising. At rural games he had no rival; and he danced with so much grace, that the country girls were often heard to wish he had not been a robber.

His character at length grew so notorious in the Queen's County, that a consultation of magistrates was held for the purpose of devising means for his apprehension. In consequence of the measures they adopted several of Grant's followers were brought to justice, and they died, as their Captain expressed it, of the 'gallows fever.' For some time his knowledge of the country and the partiality of the peasantry towards him, aided him in evading the pursuit which was made after him; but a traitor was found, and Grant was delivered into the hands of the Philistines.

The gentry of the country, and ladies of the first rank, crowded to the gaol of Maryborough to see the 'bold outlaw,' which, it was supposed, so much affected his sensibility, that he took his departure, one night, from prison, through a window, having first contrived to cut the bars that guarded it.

Dreading another specimen of the rudeness of the Irish aristocracy, he prudently resolved to leave the Slieve-bloom mountains, and, with the remnant of his banditti, he removed to the wood of Killoughram, in the county of Wexford, within four miles of the town of Enniscorthy. Here he continued for some time, and made frequent visits to the neighbouring towns, where he was known by the name of Cooney.

In the March of 1816 he made a journey to his native county, where he robbed the house of Thom

Cambie, Esq. of money and plate to a large amount. Mrs. Cambie was at home, and he behaved with so much politeness, that she ordered him supper and wine. The captain, being impatient of delay, applied his teeth to extract a cork from a bottle; upon which the mistress observed 'it was a pity to spoil his fine white teeth,' and immediately stood up and procured him a cork-screw. Grant, on his departure, took the liberty to borrow Mr. Cambie's horse and gig, in which he rode to his retreat in the wood of Killoughram.

The captain's occasional depredations in the county of Wexford excited great alarm, for a robbery there then was a thing of very rare occurrence. Notice was given of the banditti retreat, and Archibald Jacob marched the military out of Enniscorthy and surrounded the wood. Some of the soldiers and yeomanry penetrated the fastness, and in the thickest part of the shade they discovered the 'Robber Chief,' and five of his followers, on a bed of straw, situated in a romantic cave. The freebooters defended themselves with desperate valour, and, ere they surrendered, wounded five of the military. In the cave were found all the utensils of housebreaking, and abundance of arms.

The captain was committed to Wexford gaol by the name of Cooney; but the evidence against him being doubtful, it was apprehended he would be acquitted, when fortunately it was discovered that he was the celebrated Captain Grant. The gaoler of Maryborough now claimed his body, and he was forthwith transmitted to his former abode. This was fortunate for the ends of justice; for it was discovered that on the night of his removal he had matured a scheme of escape from the Wexford gaol.

His trial came on at Maryborough August the 16th, 1816, when he was found Guilty of the burglary in Mr. Cambie's house. To the question 'What reason he had why judgment and sentence of death should not be passed on him?' he replied in the most firm, collected, and, indeed, feeling manner,—' My lord, I only beg of the Court some short time to arrange things before my departure for another place; not in the idle hope of escape or pardon, but to make restitution to the persons who have suffered by my bad line of life. I have been visited in my cell by some blessed people, who have, thank God, given this turn to my mind, and to which I implore your lordship's attention.'

Grant's conduct throughout the trial was firm and collected, and was spoken of by the judge in terms of melancholy approbation.

Sufficient time was allowed him to make the arrangements he wished, after which he met his fate with decent fortitude and pious resignation, at Maryborough, August the 29th, 1816.

JAMES MARSH,
EXECUTED FOR MURDER.

THIS was a most hardened and deliberate murderer, and had the audacity as well as wickedness to face his God with 'all his sins upon his head,' and no 'preparation made.'

James Marsh and a man named Parsons lived in the employ of Mr. Metford, of Glastonbury, in Somersetshire. One Saturday morning, Parsons was going, as usual, for the purpose of paying the spinners of Mr. Metford their wages, and carrying in his cart a supply of work for the ensuing week. He was assisted in loading the cart by Marsh, who afterwards followed him on the road towards Wells. On his way he provided himself with the bone of a horse's leg, and got permission of Parsons to ride with him in the cart.

At a moment when Parsons was offering him a pinch of snuff, he knocked him down with the bone, repeated his blows and afterwards cut his throat. He was immediately after detected in endeavouring to hide the body. He fled instantly, but, being closely pursued, was apprehended, and confessed the murder.

The deceased had twelve pounds of his master's money; and this sum, it was supposed, tempted the wretch Marsh to take away his life, as he was in want of money to provide for his wedding, which was appointed to take place the ensuing week. This money was found on him.

For this dreadful deed he was brought to trial at the Spring assizes for Somersetshire, in 1816, when he was found Guilty, and ordered for execution.

From the time of his apprehension Marsh appeared quite insensible to the enormity of his crime, and behaved in the most hardened and audacious manner. He confessed his crime to the chaplain; but assigned no reason for it. On arriving at the fatal spot, finding the chaplain about to call him to prayers, he said 'No, I shall say no more—where is the man? (meaning the executioner;) I am ready.' He was, however, prevailed on to join in prayer, after which he again called for 'the man,' and frequently repeated 'Make haste, I am ready.'

Thus perished this desperate murderer, in the 26th year of his age. He was a good-looking man, and of a mild countenance; not at all indicating the dreadful depravity of his mind.

THOMAS CARSON,
CONDEMNED FOR THE MURDER OF C. CASSIDY.

THE Irish, though seldom successful on the stage, are nevertheless capital actors, but generally give to tragic parts a comic effect. The following case of successful adroitness is only one out of many such tricks played off through the prisons of that country. Similar cases have frequently occurred, and a few years before this period two convicts made their escape the same day, unknown to each other, out of Wexford gaol.

Thomas Carson, and his brother John, were tried at the Meath assizes in the spring of 1816, for the wilful murder of a man named Cassidy. The Carsons belonged to a corps of yeomen, that is, a kind of local militia, and, being Protestants, were thus privileged to carry arms. Of these, however, they made a bad use, and turned them against one of his majesty's subjects, named Cassidy, whose life they took away, through wanton cruelty, in 1800, in Kilmainham Wood, in the county of Meath. John was acquitted; but Thomas Carson was found Guilty, and ordered for execution on the following Friday morning, at one o'clock.

At five o'clock on Friday morning a brother of the prisoner went to see the unhappy culprit, and informed the gaoler that Mr. Wainwright, the clergyman would attend in a short time to pray with, and administer the sacrament to, his brother. The judge had, from humanity, directed that his relations should have free access to the prisoner, so that his brother was permitted to go into the condemned cell to him. Some time after the gaoler entered the cell, and said that the time was very short, and, if the clergyman was expected, they had better send for him. The brother offered to go for him, and accordingly did. Shortly after Mr. Wainwright came; and being shewn into the cell, continued a long time in prayer with the prisoner. The time of execution approaching the gaoler came in accompanied by the prisoner's uncle. The clergyman told the prisoner he had no time to lose—that his uncle had come, and would communicate with him in the administration of the sacrament. The prisoner entreated to be allowed to pray a little longer, and appeared absorbed in devotion. At length the gaoler becoming quite impatient, he rose from the straw on which he was kneeling, and welcomed his uncle. The latter instantly exclaimed, 'Good God! how grief has altered him!—this cannot be Tommy!'

and, looking nearer—'No,' said he 'this is Anthony Carson!' The clergyman was amazed—the gaoler ran down stairs, and discovered that the person whom he had sent for the clergyman was no other than the convict himself, who had not thought proper to return.

Coming back into his cell, the gaoler cried out in a rage, 'Your brother is gone off! what shall I do? I am ruined!' 'Gone off!' cried Anthony, with great surprise; 'Oh! he has taken away my big coat!'

The two brothers served in the same corps, and were so alike in appearance that Anthony came to the prison in a frize great coat, which he gave to the convict, who, thus disguised, passed all the doors of the prison, and walked deliberately into the street, from whence, in great apparent affliction, he looked up at the preparation for execution, and passed on as if to Mr. Wainwright's house.

Diligent search was made for the fugitive, but without effect. The brother was detained, but the extent of his crime was a misdemeanour.

CAPTAIN GEORGE HARROWER,
CONVICTED OF BIGAMY.

ALTHOUGH the conduct of Captain Harrower was far from blameless, yet we have no hesitation in pronouncing him a 'man more sinned against than sinning.' He met treachery, in more instances than one, where he had a right to expect gratitude; and was prosecuted by him who should, for many considerations, have been his friend.

The captain's conduct, even from the most fastidious, admits of many palliations. His first wife might be said to be, though not physically, morally dead, and his treatment of his second seems to have been honourable, kind, and tender; for she reprobated his prosecution, and continued to perform towards him, even after accusation, all the offices of an affectionate wife. But, whatever censure may be cast upon him, it was not for the ungrateful father of his second wife to drag him to a court of justice, in the hope of transporting him from his country, for the base purpose of revenge or lucre, at the expense of his daughter's happiness.

At the Old Bailey sessions, February the 17th, 1816, Captain George Harrower was indicted for having married one Susannah Anne Giblett, on the 12th of October,

1812, his former wife, Mary Usher; being then living.

It appeared in evidence that the captain was married at Bombay, in 1794, to Mary Usher, who afterwards becoming a lunatic, he was obliged, on leaving that country, to leave behind him.

After residing some years in this country, and feeling conscious that the unfortunate state in which his wife remained at Bombay precluded the possibility of his ever seeing her again, he resolved on marrying Miss Susannah Giblett, the daughter of a butcher in Bond Street, which he did on the 12th of October, 1813, with whom he lived in perfect happiness.

The circumstance of his former marriage, however, coming to the ears of his father-in-law, Giblett, the latter took advantage of it to obtain money from Harrower, who, in his defence, adverted to the period when he had the misfortune to become known to the prosecutor, Giblett, who, in draining him of his purse, and instituting proceedings against his liberty and character, had left him but one consolation, an amiable and beloved wife, unfortunately the daughter of the worst of men. The prosecution, he said, was the result of a foul and infamous conspiracy, and not that of a desire to support the laws of the country, or to punish those who transgressed them. He had been introduced to Giblett in an unguarded way, and, feeling a consciousness of his own integrity, did not suspect a contrary principle to prevail in him. After the acquaintance between them was matured, he married his daughter, upon whom he settled a jointure of ten thousand pounds. He afterwards lent Gibbett sums of money amounting to seventeen thousand pounds; and further sums, which raised the whole of what Giblett had succeeded in drawing from him to more than thirty thousand pounds. In fact, he had not only deprived him (Capt. Harrower) of all the money he could by possibility extract, but he had robbed his own daughter of the ten thousand pounds which had been settled upon her. Every means was used by Giblett to cause his wife to leave him, and live at home with himself, when he offered to give up certain apartments in his house for her accommodation; adding, that they would be able to get the whole of the money to themselves, and he (Captain Harrower) 'might go and starve.' These proposals, however, were always uniformly and indignantly refused by his wife. He alluded to the commission of bankruptcy which had been issued against Giblett, by which he had contrived to defraud him of his money, and mentioned a circumstance which that person had been heard to declare, namely, 'that he would try and get the money into Chancery, if other designs failed of depriving him of the property.' He went into a variety of other statements, the object of which was to represent Giblett to be a character of the worst description; a character such as he never thought existed in England, and as he trusted never would be found in it again. He concluded by protesting his innocence, and trusting that the Court would rescue him from the infamous plot which had been laid against him, and restore him to the arms of a beloved and only partner.

The jury, after retiring half an hour, brought in a verdict of Guilty, but strongly recommended the prisoner to mercy.

The laudable recommendation of the jury was subsequently attended to, and Captain Harrower, after a short confinement, was restored to society, and the arms of her who at least deserved to be his wife.

In less than two years afterwards Giblett was committed to Newgate, and confined to the apartment which Captain Harrower had occupied, for not giving satisfactory answers to the commissioners, on his bankruptcy.

SUSANNAH HOLROYD,
EXECUTED FOR POISONING HER HUSBAND AND TWO CHILDREN.

THIS is a most shocking case, and shows to what an extent human depravity may be carried. Susannah Holroyd was the wife of a weaver, named Matthew Holroyd, who had the misfortune not to live on good terms with her, though they had three children. She was in the habit of nursing illegitimate children, and at the time of poisoning had one of these in the house, as well as its mother. About a fortnight previous to the horrid deed she had a very extraordinary conversation with this woman, whose name was Mary Newton. She told her that she had had her fortune read, and that in the course of one week, and within the period of the ensuing six weeks, three funerals would go from her door.

She did not delay her destined purpose, however, until the six weeks of the fortune-teller had expired; for in about a month afterwards she went to the shop of a chymist, and purchased an ounce and a half of arsenic, to fulfil the prophecy.

This happened on Saturday, the 13th of April, 1816, being Easter-Eve. Next morning her husband had some coffee for his breakfast, and soon after became ill. The children were likewise affected. To restore them she prepared some water-gruel, and in it she mixed the poison. The wretched man felt that the gruel had an uncommon taste, and at first refused to take it; but she urged him so strongly, by telling him that 'it was the last gruel she ever would prepare for him,' that he complied with her entreaties, not knowing the enigma hid under these words.

As he grew worse, she called in a doctor, the better to allay suspicion, and was intrusted by the physician with the remedies to be administered; but she refused to apply them, saying her 'husband would die.'

The wretched man died on the 18th following, and his son, a boy of eight years old, survived him only six hours, and the child of Mary Newton died the Tuesday following, in great agony.

This wicked woman was now apprehended, and, on being brought before a magistrate, made an unreserved confession of her guilt.

Her trial came on at the Lancaster assizes, September the 13th, 1816, when she was found Guilty on the clearest evidence, and the judge pronounced on her the awful sentence of the law, ordering her for execution on the following Monday. She evinced throughout her trial the greatest indifference to her situation; but on hearing her sentence she appeared somewhat affected.

In addition to the horror felt at her crime, there was a pretty general belief that, in her occupation of nursing illegitimate children, she had murdered, at different times, several infants in the same manner that she had taken away the life of her husband and the other two victims of her unprovoked malice.

THOMAS BROCK, JOHN PELHAM, AND MICHAEL POWER.
CONVICTED OF COINING.

In the year 1816, when Matthew Wood, Esq. was lord-mayor of London, several conspiracies of a most diabolical nature were detected, and some of the conspirators punished. The conduct of the chief magistrate was such as to do honour not only to his understanding and ability, but to his disinterestedness and humanity; and, when he retired from office, the benedictions of thousands followed him into private life, while he had the consciousness of leaving behind him a public character from which envy could not detract, nor friendship make more exalted in the opinion of all good men.

The legislature, with the intention of stimulating the exertions of police-officers, and inducing others to give information, had awarded certain rewards to the parties who should contribute to the conviction of offenders against the laws. This, though laudable, was capable of great perversion, and in a country of freedom is liable to many objections; one in particular—it gives the prosecutor an interest in the conviction of the prosecuted, and on that account tends to impress the public with the belief that the condemnation, and not the acquittal of the accused, is the object of our criminal laws. Too true, the 'blood money,' as this species of remuneration was emphatically denominated, did contribute in reality to the evil we allude to. But had not a development of unparalleled villainy put scepticism to flight, we could not have brought ourselves to believe that those who were paid to detect crime should be found the most active in seducing innocence and youth to its commission. Yet it is an indubitable fact that, for ten years preceding 1816, victims were brought up, session after session, to be convicted of crimes to which they were seduced by the very men who gave evidence against them; and for what?—that they might revel on the ' blood money,' or make use of it to provide other victims for the insatiate law. Several of those connected with the police-offices, particularly the patroles, were detected in this traffic of blood;* but only one officer of

---

* The following are the parliamentary rewards for the conviction of felons:—
1. By 4 W. and Mary, cap. 8. forty pounds on the conviction of every highwayman.
2. By 6 and 7 Will. III. cap. 17. forty pounds upon the conviction of every person who has counterfeited the coin, or clipped, &c. the same, or has brought into the kingdom clipped coin, &c.
3. By 5 Anne, cap. 31. forty pounds on conviction of every burglar or housebreaker.
4. By 14 Geo. II. cap. 6. ten pounds on the conviction of every sheep-stealer, &c.
5. By 15 Geo. II. cap. 28. forty pounds for conviction of any person of treason or felony, relating to the coin upon this act; and ten pounds upon the conviction of counterfeiting copper money.
6. By 16 Geo. II. cap. 15. twenty pounds upon conviction of a person returning from transportation before the expiration of his term.

Mr. Philip Holdsworth, city-marshal, when examined before a committee of the House of Commons, was asked ' Did he think these parliamentary rewards a good or bad mode of paying the officers of police?' His reply was, ' Infamously bad. I wish M'Coul was here; he would name the men, and tell you the *supposed crimes* for which they *suffered*, and would give you *proofs* that they were *not guilty* of the things they suffered for; but he would tell you the *confession* of men who afterwards suffered; particularly I remember a man of the name of Arthur Connelly, *who committed a highway robbery, and another man was executed for it!*'

any consequence, named Vaughan, was found sporting with the lives of his fellow creatures.

The modes by which these inhuman villains proceeded were an aggravation of their crime; the hungry, the idle, and the industrious, were alike their victims; and when the wretched child of sorrow was receiving what he thought their bounty, he was only closing his hand upon what would ultimately lead to his conviction. The principal victims were poor distressed objects who were met in the streets, to whom these traders in blood, under the mask of pity and charity, gave base money, with which the starving creatures hastened to procure something to eat. The minions of the law watched their movements, and generally contrived to apprehend them in the act of passing the bad money; conviction followed as a thing of course.

But this was only one resource of their iniquity; others were supplied with forged notes under different pretences, and apprehended when they dreamed not of improper or illegal conduct; others were seduced to break into private houses, by wretches whose business it is to mature youth in crime, and who had previously arranged with the officers the mode of apprehension. To detail the ingenuity and extent of these iniquitous practices would be impossible; for though the worthy lord-mayor discovered upwards of thirty cases, he declared that the ramifications of the system extended beyond any thing he at first imagined; and no doubt many modes by which 'blood money' was procured remained unknown to his lordship.

The case which led to the detection of these men of blood was that of three poor illiterate labouring Irishmen, of the names of Quin, Riorton, and Connolly. These men were detected in fabricating base shillings and Bank tokens, brought to trial, and convicted; but, fortunately for them, something occurred during their trial which induced the lord-mayor to suspect the guilt of their prosecutors rather than the prosecuted. An investigation took place; but the convicted men, when confronted with their employers, refused to disclose the particulars which led to their supposed guilt, because they had been sworn by the 'men of blood' to secrecy. Their religious veneration for their oath declares at once their innocence and their ignorance; but a Catholic priest being sent for, he succeeded, with some difficulty, in convincing them that there was no obligation due to an illegal oath. Thus relieved in their conscience, they disclosed the whole particulars, through which Brock, Pelham, and Power were brought to justice.

These malefactors, though the seducers of the three poor 'Irishmen' into an offence against the law, were obliged to be indicted for a similar crime, for which they were convicted, namely, high treason, in traitorously, feloniously, and deceitfully counterfeiting the current coin of the realm. There was a second count in the indictment, with having aided and abetted Dennis Riorton, James Quin, and Thomas Connolly, who were convicted at a former sessions.

Upon the motion of the attorney-general, at the Old Bailey, September the 25th, 1816, the three Irishmen were called to the bar, to receive his majesty's pardon, which was necessary previous to the commencement of the present trial.

It appeared from the evidence of a man named Barry, that Pelham applied to him to get some men to make bad shillings, which Power could colour. Barry said they must go to the market for them, which was in Cheapside, at the corner of King Street, where poor Irishmen were waiting for employment. Some days after, he went with Brock and Power to the market, when Quin and Riorton were engaged by them. Being told they could not be employed unless they would be sworn to secrecy, they took an oath on a piece of paper. A room was hired, and tools procured by the prisoners, and the poor Irishmen were set to work to cut brass into the form of shillings, &c. under the superintendence of Power. Connolly was sent for to assist. He said to Barry, in Irish, 'We are doing a job that will hang us all.' Barry replied that if he thought so he would not work another day at it. The Irishmen were then employed in colouring the metal, and every thing being in readiness, notice was given, the officers entered, and the Irishmen were seized, tried, and found guilty.

Power and Pelham's landlady proved that the scissars used by the Irishmen in cutting through brass had been procured by her at Pelham's request; another woman also swore that the hammer and files taken in the coining room had been sold by her to Brock and Pelham.

Quin, one of the entrapped Irishmen, used to go to the city market to find employment. One morning he was hired, with Riorton, by Barry, who brought them to the room where they were apprehended, with Connolly, while they were rubbing pieces of copper with sand-paper. Power coloured the pieces.

Brock, in his defence, declared his innocence. Power denied either going to the market or the room; and Pelham said the Barrys were noted perjurers, and the women were false witnesses.

The jury, without hesitation, brought in a verdict of Guilty—Death.

The cause of the three unfortunate Irishmen was taken up by the lord-mayor, and others, who opened a subscription, through which they were enabled to return to their own country, and purchase small farms; after which they wrote to the lord-mayor, expressive of their happiness and gratitude.

GEORGE VAUGHAN, ROBERT MACKEY, AND GEORGE BROWN,

CONVICTED OF A CONSPIRACY.

WHILE the lord-mayor was detecting the 'men of blood' in the city the magistrates at Bow Street were not less meritoriously employed in tracing similar crimes to a police-officer, named Vaughan, and several others not immediately employed by the magistrates, but who were well known as loungers about the different offices. Several of these atrocious wretches were apprehended, and many revolting circumstances disclosed.

George Vaughan, Robert Mackey, and George Brown, were tried at the Middlesex sessions, on the 21st of September, 1816, on a charge of conspiring to induce William Hurley, Michael Hurley, William Sanderson, William Wood, aged thirteen, and Dennis Hurley, to commit a burglary in the house of Mrs. M'Donald, at Hoxton; and, by having them convicted of the fact, thereby procure for themselves the rewards given by parliament for the conviction of housebreakers.

It appeared on the trial that

Drake,* who had been an acting lieutenant in the navy, had been introduced by Mackey to Vaughan, when the latter proposed that Sanderson and the others should commit a burglary at the house of a friend of his in Gray's Inn Lane. Drake accordingly spoke to Sanderson and the others, who agreed to do it. This he communicated to Vaughan and Mackey, and they went to Brown's house to talk over the matter. About eleven at night Drake went with the men to the house which was to be robbed, but which they could not effect in consequence of the watchman. Some time after, the burglary in Mrs. M'Donald's house was planned, for which Vaughan found the money. Brown kept Mrs. M'Donald out of the way, and Drake took the five men to the house, when Vaughan and Mackey came up, and took the men into custody. Vaughan had promised Drake part of the rewards.

Various witnesses were examined, who proved the facts against the prisoners, and Mackey made a full confession, which exposed the nefarious conduct of the conspirators, and stated that Vaughan furnished the skeleton-keys and crow-bar which was used at Mrs. M'Donald's.

The prisoners being found guilty, the Court sentenced them to five years' imprisonment in the House of Correction, and at the expiration of that time to find security for three years, themselves in eighty pounds, and two sureties in forty pounds each. Vaughan was tried two days afterwards, with John Donnelly. The latter for burglariously breaking into the house of James Poole, and stealing therein thirty yards of cloth; and the former for counselling, aiding, and abetting him in the same, on the 16th of December, 1815. On which charge both prisoners were found Guilty.

* William Drake, the accomplice and evidence against Vaughan in one of his exploits, is a person whom the town loungers and treasurers of electioneering anecdotes will recognise as an accuser of the late Mr. Sheridan, whose natural daughter he married. It seemed that Drake forged a certificate from that gentleman, while Treasurer of the Navy, recommending a Jew slopseller to the captains of ships of war, for which he obtained five guineas, or thereabouts. This affair Drake made known to Mr. Paull; and by means of a petition of the latter to the House of Commons against Mr. Sheridan's return for Westminster, an investigation took place, when it plainly appeared that Drake had taken advantage of his known connexion with Mr. Sheridan to sell a forged recommendation, and afterwards, in revenge for merited neglect, had attempted to prove him corrupt, by means of his own forgery, offering his services to Mr. Paull, who was his dupe, for that express purpose. The extreme contemptibility of this man, and that of another reptile with whom he was connected, were so apparent to the house, that Drake was, by unanimous vote, committed to Newgate, and the whole business fell to the ground. He said he had lost his leg at Camperdown—it was not true: that he had half a dozen pensions for services—he had only one from the Greenwich chest. His time, place, and circumstances, with respect to the immediate subject of his evidence, were nearly all proved false; and, in short, he was altogether disregarded as a dissolute and abandoned character. His real history proved him to be a young man whom an unfortunate accident injured in his professional career, and who had consequently fallen into idleness and bad company. His utter degradation at present it is unnecessary to dwell upon, presenting, as he does, the horrible picture of superior address and cunning prostituted to the vilest purposes. And hence another feature of the blood-money system; the friends it creates are all of the specious Belial kind—creatures who possess talents to concert means and ends with exceeding plausability. The necessity of making such men as Drake witnesses, too, grows out of it; for though it fortunately happens in the present case that his evidence is fully supported, the indecency of this exhibition, combined with impunity to so much wickedness, produces a sensation of moral loathing, which saps the foundation of general philanthropy and good will to mankind.—*W. Hone.*

JOHN CASHMAN,

EXECUTED FOR FELONY COMMITTED ON THE DAY OF THE SPAFIELDS RIOT.

THE city of London had not exhibited, since 1780, so great a scene of riot and outrage as that which occured on Monday, December the 2d, 1816. Happily the prompt and constitutional conduct of the civil power prevented any of those atrocious excesses which distinguished the infuriated followers of the fanatic Lord George Gordon.

On the cessation of that protracted war which consigned Buonaparte to St. Helena, Great Britain found herself subject to those temporary difficulties which always succeed a sudden return from hostility to peace. The revulsion was felt by nearly every individual in the kingdom; agriculture, trade, and commerce became, for the instant, almost torpid, and thousands of the labouring classes were thrown out of employment.

In this moment of paramount distress, the evil-minded and the designing, taking advantage of the disposition of the people, commenced disseminating their specious political principles. The multitude could not be persuaded that the difficulties were only temporary, and ought to be borne with patience. They attributed them to defects in the representative system, which they considered the *root* of the evil, and hence they were denominated '*Radicals*.'

The oracles of these misguided men were those whom dissipation and improvidence had rendered vicious and desperate. Their names, having nothing of immortality or veneration about them, are sinking fast into oblivion, and we certainly shall not retard the acceleration of decay by any attempt at resuscitation. A few of them, however, cannot be passed over in silence; for the base and the worthless sometimes acquire a lasting notoriety; and we doubt not but that posterity will read the deeds of Thistlewood, Watson, and Hunt, with much the same feelings.

Englishmen have the undoubted privilege of assembling for the purpose of expressing their grievances and soliciting redress, whether from the sovereign or his parliament. This liberty afforded the demagogues a good opportunity for inflaming the passions of the deluded, and disseminating their own pernicious opinions. Meetings were held in various parts of the kingdom for the ostensible purpose of petitioning for parliamentary reform, and the metropolis followed the example. When we come to the case of Watson and Thistlewood, we shall enter fully into the atrocious scheme of those who devised many of these meetings, but at present it is necessary to confine ourselves to a detail of facts, which will serve as an illustration of what is to follow.

The first meeting, which may be called the prologue to the riot, took place November the 15th, 1816, in the Spafields, then a wild uninclosed space. A flag was unfurled bearing the following words, " Nature to feed the hungry—truth to protect the oppressed—justice to punish offenders." Orator Hunt had attended in consequence of an invitation, and was deputed to carry a petition to the Prince Regent. This meeting dissolved, after having passed a resolution to meet at the same place on the 2nd of December, to receive the answer to their petition. This meeting professed to be exclusively composed of distressed artisans.

Previous to the 2d of December hand bills of a very inflammatory nature were industriously distributed, and well-calculated to draw together a vast concourse of people; for it was designed, no doubt, for the curious, the idle, and the vicious. Accordingly, on the day above-mentioned the meeting took place.

Shortly after twelve o'clock, a crowd was seen entering the fields, surrounding two tri-coloured flags and a banner; the largest of the two first mentioned was that which was so triumphantly waved in presence of Mr. Hunt on the former occasion. The latter was new and much swollen. The banner contained the inscription already alluded to—'The brave soldiers are our brothers; treat them kindly.' Part of the crowd in front of the public houses were attracted, with others, who had been straggling about the fields, towards the flags, which became stationary; and, in a short time not less than four or five thousand persons were congregated within about thirty yards of the corner of the field next the Cold Bathfields prison. Here a waggon was placed very opportunely; a fellow, dressed in sailor's attire, bearing the larger flag, mounted amidst loud huzzas, and asked if the people wanted a leader? He received an answer in the affirmative, and suddenly Dr. Watson, his son, and a Mr. Hooper, all distinguished with tri-coloured cockades in their hats, jumped into the waggon to his support; and being recognized as having been present at the former meeting, were hailed with loud cheers. Dr. Watson now took off his hat, and waving his hand in all directions, craved silence while he addressed the meeting.

The doctor was followed by his son, who, in a most inflammatory speech, called upon the people to follow him. On their crying out that they would, he jumped from the cart and proceeded towards Clerkenwell.

The enfuriated mob followed their desperate leader, under the idea that he was going to the lord-mayor, at the Mansion-house; but a cry of 'arms' being set up in Smithfield, they rushed down Snow Hill, where young Watson, with a pistol in his hand, followed by five others, entered the shop of Mr. Beckwith, gunsmith, crying out, 'Arms! arms! I want arms!' At this moment a gentleman, named Mr. Platt, who was quitting the shop, attempted to seize his arm, but failed, on which the desperate youth fired and wounded Mr. Platt, after which he attempted to strike him with the butt-end, but was prevented, and the pistol fell in the struggle. The assassin was then pushed into the counting-house, when Mr. Platt said to him, 'You have shot me.'—'Oh!' he exclaimed, 'I am a misled young man—I have been at Spafields —send for a surgeon—I am a surgeon myself;' and he was about proceeding in a manner that clearly shewed he spoke the truth; his profered service was, however, rejected, and another surgeon was procured. During a quarter of an hour, which they continued in the counting-house, Watson frequently exclaimed, ' I am a misled young man!' but being allowed by the thoughtless constable to shew himself at the window, the mob, who had at first fled on the firing of the pistol, under the impression that their leader had been shot, became riotous, and demanded his liberation. Furious at his detention they proceeded to demolish the shop-windows, and carried him off with nearly all the fire-arms in the place. Mr. Platt and the constable were obliged to seek their safety in climbing over a wall at the back of the house; this gentleman, though dangerously wounded, we are happy to state recovered under the skilful care of Mr. Astley Cooper.

Young Watson, feeling himself secure amid his desperate plunderers, thought proper to give them a proof of his courage and coolness before he left the scene of blood and devastation. He accordingly took up a brace of pistols, and loaded them with great care and deliberation, an example which his comrades followed, after which they set off for the Tower, the rampart of which Watson mounted, and harangued the soldiers, telling them that the people were their friends; and that if they abandoned their allegiance they should have one hundred guineas a man; as might be expected, the orator was heard with indignation.

In the mean time the Minories were one scene of devastation; gun-smith-shops were the objects of general attack, and arms were supplied in abundance. The rioters, for the most part, consisted of sailors—some black, some tawny, some English, some foreign—some boys, and some men.—A sweep took a fancy to a dress-sword, and gave much satisfaction by a display of those antics which the sooty gentlemen are in the habit of performing every May-day.

The irruption of the mob was sudden and unexpected. The lord-mayor, Matthew Wood, Esq. was proceeding to the public business of the mansion-house, when he first heard of their proceedings; his immediately went to Guildhall, where he was joined by several magistrates and a large party of police; but before they could act, the mob had arrived at the Royal Exchange, which they entered in military order; as soon as the greater part of the rioters had passed through the north side, directions were given to close the gates, by which means three men, with arms, were taken into custody by Sir James Shaw and the lord-mayor.

The remainder of the insurgents, on learning the capture of their comrades, became exceedingly furious; and not being able to force the Exchange, they raised each other upon their shoulders, and fired over and under the gates, upon the lord-mayor and his party. A fresh force, however, arriving, the ruffians departed, taking the direction of the Minories, where they committed numerous depredations.

Another portion of the mob took the direction of St. Giles's, and then towards the Strand, robbing bakers shops as they went along. Holywell Street, St. Clement's, held out more invitations than one: the Dog tavern supplied them with delacies for their palates, and the shops of the *honest* Israelites afforded clothes for all sizes; with these they made quite familiar, and stripped the shelves of the Jews, without the formality of trying if the clothes would fit.

Such scenes, in a well-regulated city, could not last long, though it is alarming to think of the destruction of life and property that must have taken place had the rioters commenced proceedings during the night, or even after dark. Lamentable as the case was, it must have been then deplorable indeed, for though the riot occurred early in the day, several hours had elapsed before the mob was dispersed. A few of the military was sufficient for this purpose, as the incendiaries fled in all directions on the appearance of opposition, having first thrown away their arms. The military patroled the streets and suburbs during the day and night, but, fortunately, no disposition to riot manifested itself.

These disgraceful scenes being ended, the next object of importance was to bring those who had been taken into custody to justice. Private and public examinations took place, and several of the most active were committed to prison: but the leader evaded pursuit with an ingenuousness unparalleled. Watson, the elder, of whom we shall speak more hereafter, was apprehended; but of the son nothing positive could be ascertained.

At first it was not known to the magistrates that young Watson was the man who shot Mr. Platt, but no sooner was this fact ascertained than officers were instantly dispatched in search of the assassin in every direction; and the lord-mayor was daily annoyed by the arrival of hundreds of letters pretending to give information; but which were, in fact, for the purpose of misleading him.

Young Watson, notwithstanding that a reward of several thousand pounds was offered by government and numerous corporate bodies, for his apprehension, evaded the officers of justice, and got clear off to America, where he continued to reside.* He was described in the proclamation as follows:—A young man, about 23 years of age, five feet four inches high, rather slender made, has a scar or mole under his right eye; had on a brown great coat, blue under coat, black waistcoat, dirty drab breeches, and long gaiters—appearance, shabby-genteel."

In justice to this misled youth we must state, that it appears he was the victim of an enthusiastic temperament and some designing villains, who made him an instrument to forward their own base purposes. He declared that the pistol which unfortunately wounded Mr. Platt went off by accident in the scuffle, and that he deplored the event which cast such a stigma on his character.

As the circumstances which attended his escape are of a singular and extraordinary nature, we shall give those best authenticated: after his foolish and insane attempt on the soldiers at the Tower, he returned hastily to his lodgings, and possessed himself of some papers and other trifling articles. after which he went to a public house in Fetter-lane, where he fell in with his father and the notorious Thistlewood, afterwards decapitated for high-treason.

This trio, considering themselves in danger of arrest, thought it advisable to leave London immediately, and proceeded, after nightfall, for Northampton. At Highgate, however, they were intercepted by the patrole, who took them for highwaymen, and a desperate scuffle ensued, which ended in the arrest of the elder Watson, and the escape of the other two; young Watson had the good fortune to get safe to London, where he continued until his friends provided him with the means of escaping.

The Spafields riot, so formidable on its first appearance, terminated with the loss of one life, and that one according to the laws of the

* In 1821 we learn, from American newspapers, that young Watson was convicted of a burglary, and received twenty lashes as his punishment.

country. Several men were apprehended and brought to trial, but John Cashman only was capitally convicted. In the justice of this man's sentence we must acquiesce, but there appears so many palliations of his crime, that we could almost wish mercy had been extended to the culprit, particularly as numbers were evidently guilty of the crime for which he suffered, without being able to allege, as he could, that they were goaded by hunger, and precipitated on the offence without being aware of its culpability; for it is not to be forgotten that Cashman was a thoughtless sailor, who had been, through life, actively engaged, and, of course, knew but little of the duties of a landsman.

It appears that Cashman was one of the most active of the rioters who attacked and demolished Mr. Beckwith's shop in Skinner Street. Several persons deposed that he frequently brought out bundles of firearms and distributed them among the mob in the street, and he was actually apprehended with one of Mr. Beckwith's guns in his hand, at the Royal Exchange, being one of those seized by the lord-mayor.

For this offence Cashman, with four others, were brought to trial at the Old Bailey, January 20th, 1817. The indictment did not charge them with any species of treason, being confined to capital felony only, for stealing the fire-arms, &c. stated to be considerably above the value of two hundred and fifty pounds. The names of the four others were,—John Hooper, R. Gamble, William Gunnell, and John Carpenter. Two of these were apprehended at the same time as Cashman, and under similar circumstances, and the evidence against them all went to implicate them in the crime of felony; but the jury, to the apparent astonishment of the court, acquitted all but Cashman, who was found Guilty—Death.

When asked what he had to say why sentence of death should not be passed on him, he addressed the Court as follows:—

'My lord—I hope you will excuse a poor friendless sailor for occupying your time. Had I died fighting the battles of my country, I should have gloried in it; but I confess that it grieves me to think of suffering like a robber, when I call God to witness that I have passed days together without a bit of bread rather than violate the laws. I have served my king for many years, and often fought for my country; I have received nine wounds in the service, and never before been charged with any offence. I have been at sea all my life, and my father was killed on board the Diana frigate. I came to London, my lord, to endeavour to recover my pay and prize-money, but being unsuccessful I was reduced to the greatest distress; and being poor and pennyless, I have not been able to bring witnesses to prove my innocence, or to acquaint my brave officers, or I am sure they would all have come forward on my behalf. The gentlemen who have sworn against me must have mistaken me for some other person, there being many sailors in the mob; but I freely forgive them, and I hope God will also forgive them, for I solemnly declare that I committed no act of violence.'

Wednesday morning, March the 12th, 1817, was the time appointed for the execution of this unfortunate man, and to make the dreadful ceremony as awfully impressive as possible, it was ordered that he should suffer in front of Mr. Beckwith's shop, where the crime, for which his life was forfeited, had been committed.

When the ordinary of Newgate stated to Cashman the short time he had to remain in this world, and exhorted him to devote that period to making his peace with God, the unhappy man received the information with much calmness, exclaiming, 'Well, if it must be so I am ready to die!' He was visited by a Romish priest; and, during the condemned sermon, the Rev. Mr. Cotton addressed him as follows:

'How lamentable is it to behold a British sailor, who has fought nobly against foreign foes, traitorously seduced by domestic ones—enlisting himself under their banners, to wield the sword against the authority of the laws; plundering and devastating in the very bosom of his country, and in one fatal moment making shipwreck of his duty and allegiance! Let us, however, hope charitably that the crime originated in inflamed and misguided passion—not in the heart: and may your sad end operate as a warning to all your fellow-mariners, to guard against the arts of designing men, who, while they promise liberty, make use of that liberty as a cloak of maliciousness!'

Previous to the fatal moment, Cashman was visited by several friends, among whom was an Irish gentleman named Upton, who had been the landlord of his father. To this person he spoke freely, and said he was entitled to two hundred pounds wages and prize money, about the disposition of which he was very anxious, and dictated a will, which Mr. Upton, to gratify his feelings, drew up. In this he left the property chiefly to purchase a boat for his brother, who had been a fisherman on the coast of Ireland; to his mother, and for the payment of his debts, about which he appeared particularly solicitous.

He spoke freely to his fellow-prisoners, and admitted that he had been in Beckwith's shop, but denied that he was at all privy to the firing at Mr. Platt, or even aware of the circumstance. He said he had been down to the Admiralty with a letter, and that on his way back he met with a brother sailor, by whom he was persuaded to go to Spafields. In their way they drank a great quantity of rum, gin, and beer; and having had but little food for two days before, it had a great effect upon him. He spoke much of his bravery on various occasions, and that he had received several wounds, to which some of his officers bore testimony.

On the morning of execution great precautions were taken to guard against any disturbance, by stationing constables and soldiers in various parts of the metropolis. At eight o'clock Cashman was brought from his cell; he seemed perfectly composed, but exhibited a good deal of levity. In alluding to his approaching death, he said, 'he had often faced the enemy amidst a shower of balls, and with the devil before him, without shrinking, and did not now fear to face his God.'

As he passed through the Press-yard, he exclaimed with an oath, ' I wish a 44-pounder would now come and cut me in two, rather than that I should go into the hands of Jack Ketch!' He made several other observations with levity, in which he was checked by Mr. Devereux, the Catholic priest.

On quitting the prison he bid good-bye to all he met, and evinced great levity on the way to the dreadful spot. On arriving at the fatal scene the mob expressed great indignation, groans and hisses burst from all quarters, in which the unfortunate man joined. In a short time the executioner had concluded his awful task, during which Cashman made repeated mad expressions until the drop fell, and this world closed on him for ever.

Such was the fate of a man who had fought honourably against the enemies of his country; and we hope that the crime for which he suffered was not deliberate or premeditated, but rather the result of momentary frenzy and thoughtless desperation. May his example operate as a warning in deterring others from mixing with or aiding in the pursuit of a mob, who are always as cowardly in the face of legal force as they are audacious in the absence of opposition!

Several rioters were tried and convicted of minor offences; but the capital charge, as we have already stated, was substantiated against no person engaged in the transaction of the memorable 2d of December, but the unfortunate John Cashman. We shall, therefore, close the account of the Spafields riot with the trial of Watson, Thistlewood, &c. for though these men were acquitted, the evidence on the part of the prosecution throws a new and fearful light on the whole affair, and serves to develop circumstances which otherwise would appear mysterious and unaccountable.

JAMES WATSON THE ELDER, JAMES WATSON THE YOUNGER, ARTHUR THISTLEWOOD, THOMAS PRESTON, AND JOHN HOOPER,

INDICTED FOR HIGH TREASON.

After the military had dispersed the rioters on the 2d of December, 1816, Dr. Watson, his son, and Thistlewood, quitted London in haste, and were pursuing their journey into the country when the patrole stopped them at Highgate on suspicion of their being highwaymen; what helped to confirm this opinion was, the circumstance of a pistol protruding itself from Dr. Watson's breast, in consequence of which he made him prisoner, but with considerable difficulty; and in the squabble which ensued, the younger Watson and Thistlewood made their escape. Some people coming out of a public house at this instant, the doctor was given in charge to them, while the patrole went in pursuit of the fugitives. During his absence the doctor made an unsuccessful effort to regain his freedom, and in the struggle stabbed one of his detainers with a cane-sword.

For this offence or accident, Dr. Watson was indicted at the Old Bailey on Tuesday, January the 21st, 1817, charged under the cutting and maiming act; but the counsel for the prosecution having stated the case, the judge who presided suggested the necessity of stopping it, as the indictment could not be supported.

The doctor was acquitted, but not liberated, for a charge of great magnitude was suspended over his head, which, at length, descended in the form of an accusation for high-treason.

The government had received information of a formidable, or at least a dangerous, conspiracy, in which Dr. Watson and others were stated to be deeply implicated. The parties were, in consequence, apprehended; and, along with the doctor, were committed, being state prisoners, to the Tower.

A bill being found by the grand jury, Watson, Thistlewood, Preston, and Hooper, were brought up from the Tower to the Court of

King's Bench, on the 17th of May, 1817. They severally pleaded not guilty, and the privilege of choosing their counsel being granted them, they were carried back to the Tower until the 9th of June, when they were put upon their trial for high-treason.

Doctor Watson was the first arraigned, and the others were removed from the dock, as they were to be tried separately. We shall give only the testimony of the principal witnesses and the charge of the judge, as these combine all the particulars of the case. The trial occupied the court for seven days, and excited a degree of interest seldom known in this country, where, thank God, the number accused of high treason is small indeed.

A number of witnesses were examined to prove the active part taken by Dr. Watson in procuring the Spafields meeting, as well as his conduct on the 2nd of December. The evidence given amounted only to the facts we have already stated, and part of the circumstances hereafter detailed by John Castles, whose testimony we shall give :—

The statement of this man is the more worthy of record, inasmuch as it exhibits an instance of the most extraordinary and frightful innate depravity. He confesses that early in life, abandoning all pursuits of humble and honest industry, he had subsisted by shuffling and dishonest means, and had scarcely set foot on the threshold of manhood, before he was twice apprehended for passing forged bank-notes, and on each occasion escaped the punishment due to his crimes, by turning evidence against his associates, whereby two of them were brought to the gibbet, and another transported for life,—that he was afterwards concerned in a base and treacherous transaction with a French prisoner of war, and, continuing his career of crime, deserted his lawful wife, and became the bully of a brothel, and the paramour of its mistress. On joining the revolutionary committee, he gloried in being the most sanguinary and blood-thirsty amongst them, and in urging them forward to the enlargement and commission of those crimes which, again to screen himself from well-merited punishment, he afterwards denounced.

On contemplating the evidence of this worthless man, the feelings that naturally force themselves upon the mind, are horror and disgust at the individual, and regret that the ends of public justice could not be obtained without recourse to so criminal and contemptible an agent.

John Castles being sworn, was examined by Mr. Gurney, and deposed to the following effect :—

'He knew the prisoner Watson perfectly well. Had not any promise of pardon for giving his evidence. Also knew Thistlewood, Preston, and Hooper, perfectly well. That he became acquainted with the prisoner Watson about three weeks or a month before the first meeting at Spafields took place; in the month of October. Had seen him at the Cock in Grafton Street, where he went frequently to meet a society called the Spenceans. Never saw him at any other place but at those meetings. Watson introduced himself by saying, it was a very easy matter to upset government, supposing it was handled in a proper manner. Met Watson and Preston by appointment the night following, at the Mulberry Arms, Moorfields, at a meeting of a society of Spenceans, of the same kind as those who met at the Cock. There were other persons present, and among them young Watson, Hooper, Thistlewood, the two

Evans, father and son, and one John Harrison. He (Castle) after the meeting broke up, walked away with the elder Watson, who again observed, that it was a very easy matter to upset government, provided a few good fellows would act together. He then said, that he had drawn out a plan that would debar the cavalry from acting, by interrupting the horses, and that he had got several people who had solicited at different houses, and that they had formed a committee which was sitting, to devise the best modes and plans. He inquired where Castles lived, and promised to call the next morning, and show him the plan.

'In pursuance of this appointment, he called at the lodging of Castles on the following Sunday morning, and produced several papers, one of which was a plan of the Tower, and another a plan of the machine, which he had described on the Thursday before, for obstructing the cavalry. It was to run upon four wheels, with sharp knives, which were to be on each side, and spikes in the middle. The knives were to be something like scythes, and placed horizontally. There were also several other drawings of the Tower-bridge, and different places and entrances about the Tower. He then,' continued Castles, 'asked me how many men I could bring; and how many I knew? I told him I knew a great many, but I did not know whether they would act when put to the test; he begged I would exert myself as much as I could. I told him that I was a smith, and that I had nothing but my little business to live on; but he said never mind that, they would find something better for me than that; they had plenty of money for every thing. We then made another appointment, and I met him at one Newton's. Similar conversation took place there, and he said they had got a committee, consisting of five; namely Harrison, Preston, Thistlewood, and his son, and himself; and that I should be made one of the generals, and head a party of pikemen, and other men, and that I should hear further in a few days, and might consider myself as one of the committee from that time; that I should make the sixth, and they would not have any more.

'Shortly afterwards I met the elder Watson, and we went to King Street barracks, and across the Park, to a small magazine in Hyde Park, where the powder is kept, to examine the whole of the avenues, and determine which was the best place for setting fire to the barracks. There was also one Skinner with us, but he left us in the Park, and Watson said he thought that Skinner had been a cleverer man than he was; that he intended to have made an officer of him, but he found him not at all calculated, as he had not any cultivated idea whatever.

'About this time I was introduced to Thistlewood by one John Harrison. Thistlewood asked me how much money it would take to make a few hundred pikes, and how long it would take me. I told him it would entirely depend on their size, and the steel or iron they should be made of. He said they should be about nine or ten inches long, and I told him they would come to about fourpence, or fourpence halfpenny a pound. He wished me to make one as a pattern, and I told him I would; but that I had no place to make them in, and Harrison replied that he knew a person who would lend me the use of his forge. Hooper and Harrison went with me to a little shop in a cellar, kept by a man of the name of Bentley, in Hart Street. I asked him to allow me to make use of this forge to make a pike, to put round a rabbit-warren or fishpond. He told me, if I would look out a piece of iron, he would make it himself; and, when done, it was given me, and I brought it away. I took that pike in the course of the day to one Randall's, where I met the two Watsons, Thistlewood, Harrison, and Hooper, and Watson said it was a famous instrument. He afterwards wrote upon a paper the name of the house, No. 9, Greystoke Place, where the committee met. I had been to Paddington with Thistlewood the night before, among the navigators, for the purpose of seeing how many men we could get together out of employ, and the spirit of them. We found a great number of them, and treated them with some beer; and they said that they were out of employ, and wished for a good row, that they would rather be killed, as they had nothing to do; we intimated to them that we wanted them for a job, and wished to know how many we could collect together, and whether they wanted for any thing in particular. They said they could get five hundred or six hundred in the course of a very few hours any morning they chose, there were such a number of them out of employ.

'After this, we called at a public house in Long Acre, and another in Vinegar Yard, which the soldiers who attend the theatres use, and we treated them with beer. We asked them how they were treated by their officers, and what their pay was. One of them, a Yorkshireman, spoke rather violently against the government. The conversation was about their pay, and the number of them being very ill-treated, from being discharged without pensions, after fighting so many years for their country.

'Thistlewood and I afterwards went to a house called the Fox-under-the-Hill, in the Adelphi, and found three great quantities of coalheavers and people who work upon the Thames. We got into conversation with twenty or thirty who were out of employ, said we wanted them in the course of a few days, and asked how many we could get together; they said that every morning we could see fifty or sixty of them at the different wharfs and stairs.

'When we separated, I went to other places, to see how many I could get together that were out of employ, and if I could get any one more violent than another, I took down his name, and communicated it to Thistlewood.

'A day or two afterwards, the committee, namely, the two Watsons, Thistlewood, Preston, and myself, met at the house in Greystoke Place, to deliberate upon the best mode of setting fire to the barracks, and getting all the men we possibly could together. A pike was produced, and Thistlewood said that it was a famous weapon, and gave orders to have two hundred and fifty made immediately by Bentley. Dr. Watson and I reported that we had been to inspect the barracks, to see how many avenues could be set on fire at one time, and that we had thoroughly inspected both the Portman Street and the King Street barracks. The object of our going there was to see how many avenues there were, so that there could be a regular calculation made when we met on Sunday, how much combustibles would be necessary to set the whole on fire, to prevent the soldiers getting out. A general meeting was appointed of the whole six of the committee, at Greystoke

Place, to arrange the whole of the business, and how it was to be conducted in each way; and we met on Sunday, previous to which I paid part of the money to Bentley for the 250 pikes, and ordered them to be made off-hand as soon as possible. When we met, Thistlewood produced a map of London. It was marked out which were the best roads to take; the men who were to be collected together at the different barracks and places to be attacked. The whole of the committee were to act as generals; to have their several stations; and were to attack the separate barracks at one given time and moment. Watson proposed Thistlewood as the head general. Thistlewood and young Watson were to take the guns and two field-pieces that were in the artillery-ground in Gray's Inn Lane; Preston was to attack the Tower; Harrison the artillery-barracks near the Regent's Park; and I was to set fire to the King Street Barracks, and either to take the men prisoners, or kill those that might attempt to escape; the elder Watson was to set fire to the Portland Street barracks. We were to attack the whole of those places at a given hour, and set them on fire at one in the morning; any person we met we were to take them, and make them join us—such as gentlemen's servants; and coachmen were to be taken from their carriages, and those who could ride were to have the horses, which were to form a cavalry, and the coaches and carriages were to be used to barricade the entrances. After I had set fire to the King Street barracks, and after we had seen that all were in flames, and that none had made their escape, I was to meet the elder Watson at the top of Oxford Street. Harrison was to join us with the artillery, which he was to bring from the barracks by the Regency Park, and as soon as that was done, there was to be a volley fired, to let the remainder know we had got possession of the artillery. Piccadilly gate was to be fastened and chained, and a party stationed there to fire upon the horse if they attempted to come from the barracks, and then to proceed towards Charing Cross and Westminster Bridge, and barricade there all the avenues upon that side, to prevent them coming round by Chelsea and that way, and then young Watson and Thistlewood, after getting possession of the guns, were to break open all the oil-shops and gunsmiths'-shops, in which they could find either combustibles or arms. They were then to blockade Chancery Lane and Gray's Inn Lane to St. Giles's, where Thistlewood was to make his grand stand. One gun was to be pointed up Tottenham Court Road, and the other up Oxford Street.

' Preston, if he had not succeeded in taking the Tower, was to barricade London Bridge, to prevent the artillery coming from Woolwich. He was then to barricade Whitechapel, to prevent any troops coming from the country that way; and then, when he had a body sufficient, the main body was to have met at the Bank.

' After this arrangement had been made, Watson calculated how much combustibles it would take for every avenue, such as sulphur and spirits of wine, and how much they would cost. He said they would come to one hundred pounds. Thistlewood said, " Let us not spare a hundred pounds; let us roast them well." Watson replied, that it would burn so rapidly, and the stench would be so strong, that it would stifle them in a few minutes. Young Watson and I were appointed to look after a house between the King Street and the Portman Street barracks, to lodge the combustibles and arms in. We were to take it as an oil and colour-shop, so that there should be no suspicion but that it was for a shop, when we were taking in the combustibles.

'The attack upon the barracks was to have been on the Saturday night or Sunday morning, between the 9th and 10th day of the month, as upon Saturday night there would be a great number of people going about drunk. It was then arranged that we should have a committee of common safety, to be called together if we had got the better of the soldiers. If the soldiers joined us, we were to be called together, and to form a new parliament; the greatest part of the names were mentioned by Watson and Thistlewood. These were Sir Francis Burdett, the lord-mayor, Lord Cochrane, Mr. Hunt, Major Cartwright, Gale Jones, Roger O'Connor, Fawkes, of Bainbridge, Yorkshire, a person of the name of Brookes, Thompson, of Holborn Hill, the two Evans's, and Watson the elder, and Thistlewood. A proclamation was to be issued immediately we had got the better, announcing that the new government was to be established, and a bounty of one hundred pounds was to be offered to the soldiers, or double pay for life, as they chose, if they would join us.

'Things being so far settled, and several meetings having been held at public houses in Spitalfields, and other places, it was at length finally determined to call a public meeting, to see how many people could be called together. The place talked of was Spafields; and young Watson and Thistlewood went out to look at the ground, leaving us (the committee) sitting. They reported that it was a famous place, being so near to the Tower and the Bank that they could get into the town, and take them by surprise. A placard was to be stuck up upon the walls, and hand-bills were to be distributed about, amongst the mechanics and the lower orders of the people, such as those at Paddington, Spitalfields, Petty France, and in the Borough, amongst all the factories. The bill was drawn up, read, and unanimously agreed to, and it was to be put into the Statesman newspaper as soon as we could, as the meeting was to be called on Friday, the 15th of November. Thistlewood produced a ten-pound note to get the bill printed, and to pay me as much out of the remainder as would pay for the pikes. Thistlewood asked who would undertake to get a waggon to speak from; he did not address himself particularly to me, but I undertook to get it. We were to have a flag of three colours, green, red, and white, with the motto, "*Nature, Truth, and Justice;*" and I undertook to carry it. I also went to Paddington to engage half a dozen navigators to have placards fastened on their backs on pasteboard, and I met the two Watsons next morning at a coffee-shop in Kingsgate Street, High Holborn, to receive the money, to fetch away the pikes, and to buy two nail-bags to put them in. Watson gave his son five one-pound notes for the purpose. When Watson and I went to the printer for the bills, he said that he was afraid it was dangerous to print them, that he was afraid he might get himself into trouble, and therefore he would rather have nothing to do with them: he had got nearly two hundred finished, and he would destroy them. His wife, and several of us, and a gentleman who was with him, and another who came in afterwards, all wanted to persuade him to let us have them, and we should cut his name off so that he should not get into any harm. He said "No," he would have nothing to do with them, and that he should destroy them. It was then resolved that Watson the elder should go to one of the name of Seale, a printer in Tottenham Court Road, to see if he would print the bills, and he returned, and reported that there would be two hundred and fifty copies ready by eight o'clock on Wednesday morning. Letters were then written to Sir Francis Burdett and Mr. Hunt, to invite them to attend the meeting.

'By this time we found it necessary to give up our plan of burning the barracks, in consequence of having met with more difficulty than was anticipated in getting possession of the house intended for the depository of the combustibles, but having obtained a promise from Mr. Hunt that he would preside at the ensuing meeting, it was settled that we (the committee) should be on the spot previous to his arrival, and that the two Watsons and Preston should address the mob, and if we saw the spirit of the people was ready to act, we were to jump down, and head them into the town. There were six cockades, and some flags prepared, and those cockades were to be placed in our hats or bosoms, and if the mob called out for weapons, we were to tell them that we should soon find them weapons: for, at that time, there was scarcely a gun-smith's shop in London which had not been inspected, to see what number of guns it contained. We were to proceed to the Bank, and take it by surprise, and to place men upon the roof to destroy the soldiers if they should attempt to retake it: they were not only to get to the top of the Bank, but also upon the tops of the surrounding houses, and to get glass bottles, and every thing that would kill or hurt; the whole of the Bank books were to be brought out, and burnt, in order to do away with the national debt.

'On the morning of Friday, the 15th of November, being the day of the first Spafields' meeting, I went to Thistlewood's lodgings, in Southampton Buildings, and received the colours and six cockades from Thistlewood, in the presence of Mrs. Thistlewood and her son, and I went off to the meeting, carrying the colours in my bosom, and the staff to fix them on, in my hand. When the business of the meeting had commenced, and Hunt had got on the top of a coach to address the mob, Thistlewood desired me to hoist the colours; I took them out of my bosom, and tied them on to the staff, as I stood upon the box of the carriage. A motion was afterwards made for us to remove to the house, and I then handed them to some person in the one pair of stairs room. Several speeches having been addressed to the populace, the meeting was adjourned to the Monday fortnight; and we got into a hackney-coach to return. I shewed the colours out of the window, and the horses were taken out by the populace, and we were drawn along, but had not proceeded many yards, till by some means or other we were near a wall, and we all got

'Preparations were for the second the 2d of D Watson and collect the expe pose of and t munit Th

wharfs and gun-wharfs, and those gentlemen who serve the ships, such as ship-chandlers and ship-brokers, to ascertain where balls, canister, and grape-shot, might be found, and what quantity there was. We also examined the oil-shops where there were any combustibles, such as oil, turpentine, and such things, and regularly reported to the committee every night what was done.

'Among other things, it was proposed, at one of the meetings of the committee, that we would get a couple of hundred young women together, and dress them in white, to carry small flags and cockades, or, if we had money sufficient, to dress them all alike, for the purpose of walking first, in order to take off the attention of the soldiers.

'We were all actively employed in distributing bills, announcing the meeting for the 2d of December, and in going from one public house to another among the soldiers and labouring men, to prevail on them to come in large bodies to the meeting, that we might calculate on their assistance in any active measures we might take, and I hired a waggon to be taken to Spafields, for the purpose of forming a stage from which we could conveniently address the meeting. Young Watson and myself were also sent out in different directions to purchase pistols and other arms for our own use, and I succeeded in procuring some at a very low price. Flags and cockades to be exhibited at the meeting were prepared, and delivered into my care.

'On the morning of the day of meeting, we assembled at the Black Dog, in Drury Lane, and among other arrangements then made, it was settled, that I should give the colours to Hooper to tie them on the staff, and if any of the civil power inquired what they were, we were immediately to shoot them, as we did not care for the civil power, if we could only keep the soldiers off; if any officers or magistrates were to interfere, we were to shoot them or run them through. There were a number of slugs and bullets put into an old stocking, and tied in an old dirty white handkerchief, and put in the possession of Keens to take to the waggon. I tied the flag on the staff, and deposited it in the waggon myself, and, giving it in charge to Hooper, proceeded to Dean Street, where I found Keens wrapping up a banner, bearing the inscription, "*The brave Soldiers are our Friends, treat them kindly*," in a couple of old blankets; I left him to take it to the waggon, and saw no more of him. I then went to the place where I was ordered, viz, to London Bridge, to meet the smiths, but I found every thing perfectly quiet, and no person that I knew. I then proceeded to Tower Hill, where I found the Tower gates shut, and an extra sentry on. I went up to a soldier, and asked why the gates were shut up, and he said it was on account of the meeting. I proceeded towards the Bank, and there found some difficulty in getting in, as the gates were shut, and then went on to Little Britain, where I heard a shouting, and met a great mob, and the first persons I saw were Dr. Watson, with his dirk-stick, undrawn, and Thistlewood. I asked Watson where his son James and the rest of them was. He said, "To the Tower, first to the Tower, make haste, otherwise we shall be too late." They went on, and I soon lost sight of them; in a short time afterwards I saw Keens, and he told me what had taken place in Spafields, and that he had been in the waggon, and that he was afraid he had left the blankets and balls in the waggon. We afterwards overtook Mr. Hunt going towards Spafields; he was in a landau; and I stopped him and asked him why he was so late; he inquired what was the matter; I answered, that Dr. Watson had gone to attack the Tower. Keens and myself went afterwards towards the Tower, and stepped into a gunsmith's shop, and stopped some time. After that, I saw young Watson close by the Bank, at the back of the Exchange; he had in his hand a drawn sword, and was encouraging the mob to follow him. A great many were firing in the air: there were about two hundred men and boys.

'I then left young Watson, and went to Tower Hill, where I saw old Watson and Thistlewood; they went up close to the Tower rails, and seemed to be addressing themselves to the soldiers without the walls of the Tower, or across the walls of the Tower, but I was not nigh enough to hear what was said. They then turned up the Minories to go to Spafields, to get a greater force, as the soldiers did not seem to take any notice of them. On proceeding up the Minories with the mob, Watson called upon them to stop, for when near the top, thirty or forty soldiers met them, and the mob threw down their arms, and ran away. I walked forward with the soldiers as if I had nothing to do with it, till the soldiers had passed me, and then returned back again, and went down towards Tower Hill. At the corner of Mark Lane, I went into a little public house, and stopped until nearly dark, when I went to No. 1, Dean Street, where I arrived about six or half past six o'clock. I found there the two Watsons, Preston, and Thistlewood: the elder Watson and Thistlewood began to pack up their linen, as if going away. I inquired where they were going to, and Thistlewood said, they were going a little way in the country, as he had got a house in the country, and we should hear from him in the course of a day or two. I inquired what had become of Hooper, and he said, Hooper was taken with the colours, and that some of us must expect to be taken. He asked me if I had shot my pistols off. He said he was going into the country, and we should hear of him at the Red Hart in Shoe Lane, by the name of John Williams. I asked him if young Watson had shot any body, and he said they did not know, but that he was perfectly well satisfied that the people were not ripe enough to act. We parted a little after; he and the two Watsons went away together about seven o'clock, but I stopped at the public house until near dark.'

On his cross-examination it appeared that this wretch was a government spy, and that his morals admirably fitted him for such an employment. There were few crimes, short of murder, with which he was not made to charge himself.

On the close of the case for the prosecution Mr. Wetherell proceeded to comment on the evidence which had been given, in a strain of argumentative eloquence which evinced at once the deep lawyer and brilliant advocate.

On the 6th day Mr. Hunt and several other witnesses were called, whose testimony went to impeach the credit of Castles and others for the prosecution, after which counsel was heard for the prisoner, and the attorney-general spoke in reply.

Watson having declined to make any defence after the ability displayed by his counsel, the Lord Chief Justice Ellenborough proceeded to charge the jury, who, after a short consultation, returned a verdict of acquittal—a verdict which must have proceeded from the very natural suspicion the jury entertained of Castles' testimony.

As the two Watsons, father and son, made a notorious figure at this period, we make the following extract from a cotemporary, who seems to have been well informed:

'Dr. Watson had much reason to complain of the frowns of fortune. He was born near Boston in Lincolnshire, and married in early life a woman of respectable family, by whom he had sixteen children. He was a man whose professional character stood rather high among his patients; but the expenses of so large a family operated as a bar to his advancement in life. Having failed of establishing himself in the country, he removed to London, determined to push his fortune there, and commenced in Newcastle Street in the Strand, where he resided a few years, much respected by his neighbours, but where he failed through the pressure of the times and the poverty of the neighbourhood. In the midst of his distress, his goods were seized for debt, and a miserable bed torn from under a favourite daughter, who lay expiring in the arms of death, and who shortly after, surrounded by starvation and misery, yielded up this life of sorrow and of trouble for one, we trust, of eternal happiness and peace.

'During the above period, Dr. Watson's eldest son was with a Mr. M'Phinn, an apothecary at Bath, from whence he went to Marlborough, where his wild and unmanageable temper induced a belief that his mind was rather disordered.

'After quitting Newcastle Street, Dr. Watson and his family became wanderers from lodging to lodging. The excess of domestic affliction, combined with poverty and distress, had rendered him desperate; and, abandoning his professional pursuits, he gave himself up wholly to his wild political theories, became a thorough *Spencean*, agreed with the *cobbler* Preston, and all the radical desperadoes of the age.'

ROGER O'CONNOR, ESQ.
INDICTED FOR ROBBING THE MAIL.

This gentleman, though of retired habits, has had the misfortune to be almost perpetually before the public, and sometimes in situations and under circumstances very inconsistent with his rank or fortune. Although Mr. O'Connor has been most honourably acquitted on more occasions than one, we shall make no apology for introducing his case here; for, as all men are liable to be accused of mal-practices, it is satisfactory to know, that there is but one legal ordeal for the high and the low, through which they may expect to come off honourably, if not guilty.

Mr. O'Connor traces his ancestry to the last king of Ireland, and has uniformly evinced an extraordinary attachment to his native country. Whether the links of genealogy are unbroken or not is of little consequence; for the individual must be judged by his actions, and not by his name or pretensions. Mr. O'Connor, though not an Irish monarch, which some of his countrymen say he ought to be,* is certainly an independent Irishman. His education was that of a gentleman; his profession that of the law; and his fortune ample, being at least four thousand pounds a year.

The reader may recollect the case of Arthur O'Connor, which we have already given. That gentleman was brother to the subject of this sketch; and the principles for which Arthur was prosecuted were supposed to be those of his elder brother, Roger. Accordingly we find him apprehended, on the suspicion of treason, at his seat of *Connor-ville*, in the county of Cork, in 1796, and from that year to 1803 he may be said to have been a state prisoner; for he was no sooner liberated than he was again arrested, and passed, a state shuttlecock, several times between the Irish and English ministers.

During these peregrinations he displayed great firmness, and, on the coast of Ireland, actually saved the lives of the officers in whose custody he was. Refusing the terms accepted by his brother, and the other state prisoners, in 1798 he was transmitted to Fort George, in Scotland, and, at length, was liberated from prison, on condition that he should reside in Middlesex, for the absurd timidity of the government apprehended his influence in Ireland too much to permit his return; and when they did comply with his earnest solicitations, it was on condition that he should not visit the south, where his name was supposed to be a tower of strength.

In consequence of this prohibition Mr. O'Connor had to dispose of his family mansion, and choose another place of residence. He became the purchaser of Dangan, in the county of Meath, the estate of the Marquis of Wellesley, where he continued to live engaged in agriculture and literary pursuits, never mixing in politics; and, although the intimate friend of Sir Francis Burdett, he has never appeared to give either the baronet or his friends any support, though possessed of large property in England.

O'Connor was what is called in Ireland a *marked man;* that is, he was one whose movements the minions of power watched closely, and, consequently, in a country where the gentry are all connected with the powers that be, he was not regarded with much respect. Almost every assizes exhibited a case in which O'Connor was either a witness, a plaintiff, or a defendant; and wherever his name appeared, angry discussion was sure to follow, though his fearless independence, and well-known courage, kept it within proper bounds.

For several years his name, except when introduced at the assizes, was almost forgotten, until the year 1817, when a most extraordinary charge was exhibited against him; nothing less than an accusation of having robbed the Galway mail five years before.

Two notorious characters, named *Owen* and *Waring*, were apprehended for a robbery in 1817, tried in Dublin, and found guilty. They received sentence of death, and the day of execution was appointed; but before the fatal hour arrived they charged Mr. O'Connor with

* In a humorous little work, lately published by Mr. Moore, entitled, 'Memoirs of Captain Rock,' the etymology of the name is thus accounted for: R for Roger, O C for O'Connor, and K for King, i. e. Roger, O'Connor King. This is a double-edged satire, for it ridicules at once the supposed pretensions of the individual, and the folly of etymologists.

being the captain of the banditti who had robbed the Galway mail. The circumstances which they detailed were so minute, that O'Connor was apprehended, and the two approvers received the royal pardon, to qualify them as witnesses against the persons accused, for O'Connor's steward, named M'Keon, was also included in the charge.

The robbery of the Galway mail had taken place in 1812, ten miles from O'Connor's residence at Dangan; but the mail-bags, and some of the fire-arms, were subsequently found in the demesne; a circumstance which, when combined with others,* served to give a probability to the charge of Owen and Waring.

The arrest of O'Connor upon such a base charge produced an extraordinary sensation, not only in Ireland, but in England, which was considerably heightened by an address from that gentleman, then in Newgate, entitled "*Third Attempt upon the Life of O'Connor.*" In this pamphlet he attributes, perhaps justly, the prosecution to a conspiracy against his life; but when he insinuates that government, from political motives, brought all their power and influence to give effect to the charge, we can hardly suppose it possible, though we are ready to admit that the gentlemen of the post-office, as they were bound to do, supposing him guilty, did all in their power to convict him.

Mr. O'Connor's trial came on at Trim, August the 5th, 1817, the prisoner having been removed thither, by *habeas corpus*, from Newgate. The court was crowded to excess, and O'Connor, with his friend Sir Francis Burdett, were allowed to sit within the bar.

---

* An extraordinary robbery took place at Dangan in 1815. We extract the particulars from the Irish papers, and can vouch for their authenticity; for they were afterwards fully proved in evidence when an action was brought to recover the sum lost from the county:—

'Mr. Roger O'Connor, of Dangan, in the county of Meath, for which place he pays an annual rent of one thousand five hundred pounds to Colonel Burrowes, who resides in London, has been in the habit of refusing to pay his rent at any place but on the premises. A Mr. Francis Gregory, agent to Colonel Burrowes, after some preliminary discussion with Mr. O'Connor, employed Mr. Doyle, postmaster of Trim, to receive the latter half-year's rent. On the 28th ult. Mr. Doyle went to Dangan for this purpose: at the gate he was accosted by a person, who said he was stationed there to give Mr. O'Connor immediate notice of his approach; and Mr. Doyle followed him into the house, where he found Mr. O'Connor and his son Roderick; when Mr. Doyle entered, O'Connor desired his son to withdraw. He then proceeded to pay Mr. Doyle the rent, amounting to seven hundred and fifty pounds, and which was chiefly in one-pound notes. Mr. Doyle observed upon the inconvenience of that mode of payment, and requested the use of pen and ink to mark the notes. This was refused: Mr. Doyle, after counting the notes, left the house—and within thirty yards of it, and before he had got to the stable, he was attacked from behind by two persons in disguise, whose faces were masked; they knocked him down, tied a handkerchief over his face, robbed him of the money he had just received, and some silver of his own; and having bound his legs with a cord, and forced a sack over his head, they left him. During the whole transaction, the robbers never uttered a word. No person whatever having come to his assistance, Mr. Doyle remained for some time before he was able to extricate himself. On his return to the house he saw a lady, to whom he mentioned how he had been treated. Shortly after Mr. O'Connor arrived, who expressed great surprise at the robbery. Mr. Doyle then took his departure. The robbery having been committed at eleven o'clock in the day, the necessary steps are in progress to levy the money upon the county of Meath. We have every reliance that the gentlemen of that vicinity will use their best exertions to discover the persons engaged in this most mysterious transaction.'

Several witnesses having proved the robbery of the mail on the 2d of October, 1812, and the conviction of Richard Waring for the said robbery, Michael Owen, the chief informer, was called.

He stated that he had been a labourer in the employ of Mr. O'Conner, at Dangan, and that previous to the robbery he was asked by his master if he would join in robbing the Galway mail; he said that he would; and that Mr. O'Conner procured him and others arms; that they repaired to the turnpike gate at Cappagh Hill, stopped the mail, shot the guards, and robbed the coach and passengers; that on their arrival at Dangan Mr. O'Connor met them—hoped they had had 'good luck,' and then in a private part of the demesne proceeded to divide the booty, which amounted to three hundred and fifty pounds each—that O'Connor took his portion, and obtained two hundred pounds more from two of the robbers, to whom he had afforded previous protection.

Owen further stated he had been twice tried for the robbery—once on the capital charge, and at another time for passing some of the stolen notes; that he had been recently found guilty of a robbery in the county of Dublin, and sentenced to death, and that he obtained his pardon for having given information against Mr. O'Connor. On his cross-examination he admitted that he could not tell the number of robberies he had committed, they were so many.

After the examination of other witnesses, Sir Francis Burdett deposed to his knowledge of the prisoner, to whom he gave a high character for honour, principle, and integrity. The jury, without retiring, gave a verdict of—Not Guilty, and the court rang with approbation.

'I have suffered much,' said O'Connor, 'but what would I not suffer for a day like this?'

Mr. O'Connor, being thus triumphantly acquitted, commenced a prosecution of Waring for perjury. Waring's trial came on at Green Street, Dublin, October the 30th, 1817; and the post-office, as if still believing in his statement, employed the most eminent counsel to defend him. From Mr. O'Connor's evidence it appeared that he had more than once given Owen and Waring good characters, when on their trial for robberies; and it was proved that he had evinced great solicitude for them at one of the Trim assizes. This suspicious attachment of Mr. O'Connor for such abandoned ruffians as murderers and mail-coach robbers produced its effect upon the jury; but what helped to throw complete discredit on Mr. O'Connor's evidence was the fact, elicited on his cross-examination, that he did *not* believe in the Jewish dispensation, or the Christian atonement. This acknowledgment of his infidel opinions created a buzz of disapprobation; and, when the acquittal of the prisoner was announced, it seemed to give great satisfaction: so fickle is the opinion of the multitude, that a *word* will convert their applause into condemnation!

In this case there appears something very strange and unsatisfactory; but, as we are unable to penetrate the mystery which must for ever environ it, we leave our readers to draw their own conclusions. One word, however, is necessary. Mr. O'Connor was acquitted by a jury, and is therefore to be considered innocent; while it is very possible that his apparent solicitude for such wretches as Owen and Waring might have arisen from the purest humanity, and active friendship for the unfortunate portion of his countrymen, with whose destiny he boasts to have connected himself. At all events, let it not be supposed that we 'set down aught in malice,' either in respect to Mr. O'Connor or his prosecutors.

Since 1817 Mr. O'Connor has published the 'Chronicles of Eri,' and, if we believe himself, he was, at the time of his trial, engaged on a work on the Bible. It has not yet appeared, and, it is to be hoped, never will.

JAMES ASHCROFT THE ELDER, JAMES ASHCROFT THE YOUNGER, DAVID ASHCROFT, & WILLIAM HOLDEN,
EXECUTED FOR MURDER.

SINCE the murder of the Marr family the public mind had not been so shocked by any dreadful atrocity as that for which these malefactors so deservedly suffered.

These men had for several years subsisted by plunder and gaming; for although brought up to the trade of weavers, they had long declined seeking their livelihood by an honest pursuit of that business. James Ashcroft the elder, father of James Ashcroft the younger, and brother of David Ashcroft, had formerly been in the Methodist connexion, but had been expelled by the members of that persuasion for immoral conduct. He was quite a fanatic, and was fully persuaded that his faith was such that he could work miracles, and that, having once attained the perfection of grace, he never could again fall; consequently, he imagined that he could offend Heaven with impunity—a doctrine at once extravagant and ridiculous, and seems, in this instance, to have operated on the disturbed intellects of this man, in a way which doubtless contributed to his crimes. He once, to illustrate the fanatic doctrine of *faith* only, thrust his hand and arm into the fire, to show that they would not burn; but the experiment did not succeed, and the effect of the scorching was such that he lost a joint.

James Ashcroft, the son, was worthy of such a father, but appears the greater villain, for he added hypocrisy to his other crimes. He was the principal of a society that met for religious edification; and so imposing was his affected piety, that his *instructions* were preferred, by a respectable family, to those of a sincere clergyman of the Established Church. David Ashcroft, and Holden, held similar tenets, and, no doubt, were influenced by the doctrines acted upon by the father and son.

It was necessary that we should have stated these particulars, because they serve to explain the infatuated wickedness of these men, in denying to the last the justice of that sentence which followed the verdict of twelve honest men; and, indeed, there was not a man in the country who read the evidence against them who did not rejoice in their conviction and punishment.

These atrocious monsters became, from long acquaintance with iniquity, so familiari ed to crime, that they, at length, committed, in the very face of day, a deed which is without a parallel for cool and deliberate turpitude. They resolved to rob the house of Mr. Littlewood, at Pendleton, near Manchester; and as this gentleman and his wife spent every Saturday in Salford, where they had a grocer's shop, the ruffians chose Saturday, April the 26th, 1817, to effect their purpose.

About the hour of two o'clock in

the day they gained an entrance, when, horrid to relate! they butchered two defenceless females—one a Mrs. Marsden, aged seventy-five, and the other an interesting girl, not more than twenty, the only persons in the house. After this atrocious and unprovoked deed, they robbed the house of one hundred and sixty pounds in money, and some few valuables.

When a discovery of the murder took place in the evening, nothing could surpass the sensation it excited; and as the apprehension of the monsters who perpetrated it was desired by all, some individuals came forward, and deposed to having seen the Ashcrofts, and two other men, lurking about Pendleton on the day of the murder. In consequence of this information, the three Ashcrofts, Holden, and a man named John Robinson, were taken into custody, and brought to trial at Manchester, September the 5th, 1817. Against Robinson nothing criminatory appeared, and, of course, he was acquitted.

After the jury were sworn, the elder Ashcroft flung up his hand, with a theatrical air, and exclaimed, 'Not Guilty!' The others followed his example, and a number of witnesses were sworn.

William Mortimer saw the prisoners on Friday morning, April the 25th, at the Crown and Anchor public house; and Martha Bake, the hostess, observed them in secret conversation, as if plotting about something of importance.

Several witnesses corroborated each other as to their having seen the prisoners together, and separate, on Saturday, in the neighbourhood of Pendleton.

Hannah Tatterson lives with Mr. Watkins, the Quaker, next door neighbour of Mr. Littlewood. She saw Hannah Partington at half past twelve on the 26th of April; the shutters of the kitchen window were then open, but at two o'clock she observed they had been shut.

Mary Hallows was passing by the kitchen window between one and two o'clock, as she was going for water, and swears positively that she saw Holden sitting in the kitchen. She afterwards identified him among several others, when before the magistrate.

Harriet Towel, at half past four, went to Littlewood's, and seeing the kitchen shutters closed, she looked under them, and saw Mrs. Marsden sitting on a chair, with her head sunk on her breast, as if she had been dead. The dresser was sprinkled with blood. She returned at seven, and, seeing the old woman in the same position, she gave the alarm.

Mr. Littlewood returned home on the evening of the 26th of April, at eight o'clock. He gained access to his house through an upper window, by the help of a ladder, and, on going into the kitchen, found Mrs. Marsden dead in her chair, and Hannah Partington lying dead under the dresser. One hundred and sixty pounds that he had in the house were gone. The kitchen was covered with blood. Hannah Partington were a very handsome girl—she had no sweetheart; he was sure she had not.

A surgeon proved that the women came by their death in consequence of blows inflicted with a poker and a cleaver, which fractured the skull, and foered it in on the brain.

Ely Dyson, a weaver, was passing by Mr. Littlewood's house a little before four, and saw James Ashcroft the younger, David Ashcroft, and Holden, coming out of the gate, with bundles in their hands. He was certain these were the persons, because he looked very sharp at them, in consequence of their looking sharp at him. He afterwards pointed them out from among several others, in the gaol-yard.

Several other witnesses deposed to having seen them on the road, and others saw David Ashcroft coming out of the gate.

Two witnesses saw James Ashcroft, the younger, on the playground at Manchester, in the evening, when he exhibited one hand full of notes, and another full of gold and silver.

The officer who apprehended the whole party found nothing on the prisoners except a few notes and some small pieces. There was no attempt to prove these to have belonged to Mr. Littlewood.

William Collins, through misconception, had been confined on a charge respecting a horse and cart, in the *lock-up*. James Ashcroft the elder was also there. Collins told him his whole case, and Ashcroft, in return, made him acquainted with his. Ashcroft stated the whole particulars of their movements about Pendleton, previous to the robbery; he remained at the back of a hedge while the others went in, and was to give a signal if he saw any one approach the house.

Several witnesses were then called, who corroborated the statement made to Collins by the elder Ashcroft, respecting their different movements.

The case for the prosecution here closed, and the prisoners severally addressed the Court, protesting their innocence: after which a few witnesses for the defence were called; but their testimony was vague, and their own characters doubtful.

The Chief Baron summed up the evidence in a very luminous address of more than an hour and a half. Towards the conclusion of it, David Ashcroft begged to be allowed to say something farther. The Chief Baron said it was quite irregular, but he would certainly indulge him. He then threw out many incoherent charges against the evidence for the prosecution, and begged to have Mr. Wright, a magistrate, and Mr. Witherton, a constable, examined to contradict Mary Hallows.

The judge said he would allow it, but insisted that Mr. Williams, the counsel for the Ashcrofts, and Mr. Starkie, the counsel for Holden, should be sent for.

After a considerable interval Mr. Williams appeared without wig or gown, and after he had conversed for a considerable time with his lordship and with the prisoners, David Ashcroft said he would leave the case as it was to God Almighty, who he hoped would direct his lordship and the jury to do justice.

James Ashcroft, the elder, then ejaculated—'O! may God, by his Holy Spirit, inspire the jury to perceive the truth, and to give a true verdict, for we are all innocent of this murder.'

The Chief Baron—' I'll listen to any thing for which you can offer evidence; but you must not be allowed to make speeches of that kind.' His lordship then concluded by a very impartial and solemn peroration.

The jury in two minutes returned their verdict James Ashcroft the elder, David Ashcroft, James Ashcroft the younger, and William Holden —Guilty. John Robinson — Not Guilty.

James Ashcroft the elder.—' This is murdering us in cold blood. God will reveal this injustice. I pray earnestly that he would now send two angels to declare upon that table who committed this murder. We are innocent, and I will declare so to the last.'

David Ashcroft invoked God, and

protested his innocence in the same manner.

James Ashcroft the younger.—' If I must suffer death for a crime I never committed, I implore your honour to look in mercy on my poor wife and children. (Here a tremendous shriek burst from a female in the crowd, who, it was found, was his unfortunate wife.)

William Holden.—' Silence, silence! (flinging one arm towards heaven and the other towards his earthly judge)—There is a God yonder who knows that we are innocent, and who will make amends for this.'

The Chief Baron here directed the business of the Court to be proceeded with, and the prisoners again repeated their protestations of innocence, and declared all the evidence against them to be perjuries and lies.

The awful sentence of death was then pronounced. They were ordered for execution on the Monday following. The judge declared, that no sensible person, who had heard the evidence, could have a doubt of their guilt; that he owed it to justice to say, that he considered the verdict the only one an intelligent jury could have returned.

The moment sentence was pronounced, James Ashcroft, the elder, waved his right hand, with a white bundle in it, over his head, and exclaimed aloud, ' Glory to God!'

David Ashcroft said he hoped God would not allow the injustice done to them to be always unknown.

James Ashcroft, the younger, said he would meet a higher judge with a conscience clear of this guilt.

William Holden vociferated in a wild tone, ' There is Mr. Nadin, and there is Mr. Fox (attorney for the prosecution), and before they leave the earth God will punish them.'

Thus were these terrific culprits hurried away from the bar, while every person in Court was penetrated with a chilling horror at such a dreadful scene.

The trial lasted from eight in the morning till eight at night.

After their condemnation these wretched men still persisted in asserting their innocence, and every appeal to them to acknowledge their guilt, even with reference to the awful moment so fast approaching, the pangs of which might be mitigated by relieving their minds from the load of crime under which they laboured, was fruitless and ineffectual; they seemed influenced by the most determined feelings of unrelenting obduracy, which they reconciled to themselves by fanaticism and superstition.

On the 8th of September, pursuant to sentence, they were led to the fatal scaffold. Precisely at a quarter past twelve, the door, leading from the castle to the scaffold, opened, and William Holden, a strong-built, middle-sized, and grey-headed man, was led forth, with his hands pinioned both at the wrists and elbows: before the cap was placed on his head, he turned round to the immense multitude of spectators, and, with a firm and loud voice, said, ' I am innocent of the crime for which I am to suffer as the child unborn. May God take away all my sins as I am innocent of this murder.' The cap was then drawn over his face, and the rope tied about his neck.

David Ashcroft was stationed next him. He spoke to this effect, with frequent repetitions of the same observations—' I am glad to see so many persons now looking on, as I testify to them that we are all ignorant of this crime. I do protest to you all, before God, that we are all innocent. Every one that now sees me is as guilty as I am. I would not say so if we had any connexion in any way with the concern; but I declare before God that we are perfectly innocent, for which I bless God. My prayer to God is, that all our persecutors may be forgiven. May God bless the town of Manchester. I know that many thirsted for our blood, but they have sorer hearts than we have. We forgive them, and may God give his Holy Spirit to the town of Manchester. I pray earnestly that we may be the last innocent persons to suffer from this castle. May God find out the true murderers; and may you see them suffer in this place, and hear the confession of their guilt. I am now, I trust, going to glory, and I would not, for the whole world, die with a lie in my mouth. We are all innocent.'

Here Holden exclaimed, 'I can answer only for myself. I am innocent.'

James Ashcroft the younger, who had, in the mean time, been brought out, and on whom the cap and rope had been put, cried out, 'We are all innocent!'

David Ashcroft continued: 'And now may the grace of God be with you all, now and for ever. Amen.' The cap was now put on his face, and the rope was tied round his neck. He was a good-looking man.

James Ashcroft the elder, a tall, thin, grey-headed man, came out last; when in front of his son, he kissed him with much earnestness, then took his station by his side, but said not a word.

They were all pinioned at the wrists and elbows. They joined the clergyman afterwards in repeating the Lord's Prayer quite loud. David Ashcroft continued praying: —'Lord, take away my sins, and save my soul, for the merits of Jesus Christ.' Holden repeated the same expression. All four then began to sing, David Ashcroft repeating, line after line, as they sung:

'I'll praise my Maker with my breath;
And, when my voice is lost in death,
My days of praise shall ne'er be past,
While life and thought and——'

The drop fell, their voices instantly ceased, and they swung round in the same direction. David Ashcroft's mouth being uncovered, his tongue was seen swollen and thrust half out on the upper side of his mouth. Old Ashcroft never moved a limb. The young men quivered in the convulsions of death about a minute after they had been thrown off. There was scarcely a tearless eye among the crowd, while many of the women wept aloud.

PATRICK DEVAN,
EXECUTED FOR THE MURDER OF THE LYNCH FAMILY.

An extraordinary spirit of vindictiveness seems to be inherent in the lower orders of Ireland. Revenge has such charms for them, that an injury is remembered and retaliated after the absence of years; and, if of a religious or political nature, centuries are not sufficient to erase it. No doubt this arises from their former state of clanship,

which has not been yet altogether eradicated, and the disturbed state of the country, in which opposite parties take retributive justice into their own hands.

At the same time there appears in this sanguinary and vindictive spirit a strange principle of wild fidelity and barbarian honour. It is not a brother that revenges the death or wrongs of a brother; a father those of a son; or a son those of a father. The whole clan or association take that duty formally on themselves, and seldom desist until their ideas of justice are satisfied. We find the same principle acted upon in Scotland, when that country was less civilized than at present.

The case of Devan illustrates these remarks, and proves that religion has no influence over the baneful practice. All the parties concerned were Roman Catholics, and Devan was no way related to those whose deaths he was so desperate in revenging.

In 1816, a respectable farmer, named Lynch, in the county of Louth, had his house attacked by a band of ruffians, who carried off some arms. Lynch prosecuted them to conviction for a burglary and robbery, and they were executed accordingly. Lynch being a brave old man, the magistrates of the county gave him arms* to defend himself, in case his house should be again attacked.

The illegal association, to which the persons executed had belonged, now determined to revenge upon Lynch the death of their comrades. Their meetings were held in a little chapel at Stonestown, of which Devan had the key, as he always officiated as clerk, being a schoolmaster in the village. On this occasion he appears to have been very active, and zealously urged the necessity of sacrificing Lynch to the manes of their comrades. What stimulated these atrocious villains to a more speedy execution of their diabolical revenge, was the circumstance of Lynch, the Sunday before he was murdered, having stood up in chapel, after mass, to second the censure of the priest on those who joined in illegal associations. Lynch very honestly, but very imprudently, informed the priest that many who belonged to the association were then in the chapel; and made such significant allusions, that the congregation readily knew them, though no name was mentioned.

This was in the month of October, 1816, and in a few nights after Wild Goose Lodge, a most retired spot, the residence of Lynch, was burned to the ground, and, horrid to relate, the whole family, consisting of eight persons, perished in the ruins. The next Sunday the priest, in all the awe and ceremony of his church, proceeded to pass sentence of excommunication on the foul perpetrators of this horrid deed. The person who responded *Amen* to the heavy denunciation of the priest was Devan, who thus wilfully invoked maledictions on his own head.

Devan, being in apprehension of an arrest, quitted that part of the country, and travelled to the south. This movement increased the suspicion against him, and a reward was offered for his apprehension; but no discovery of his retreat took place until one of his letters to his father fell into the hands of a magistrate, from which he learned that Devan was working at the dock, in Dublin. Proper officers were now dispatched in pursuit of him, and in a few days he was taken into custody.

On the 19th of July, 1817, he was indicted at the Louth assizes, for the murder and burning of the Lynch family. The main points of the case were sworn to by Bernard M'Ilroy, who in his evidence acknowledged to his having been with Devan and Gubby at the burning of Lynch's house. The desperate gang assembled, to the number of forty, at Stonetown chapel, about half past nine at night, and proceeded from

* The Roman Catholics, in Ireland, are not allowed to carry arms.

thence to the scene of destruction. The party were joined on their way by about sixty other persons, and the whole spread themselves round the house to prevent Lynch or his family escaping. Other evidence proved the guilt of the prisoner, and the jury immediately found him Guilty.

Devan heard his sentence without being the least moved. He asserted his innocence to the very moment of his going to the place of execution, but then acknowledged his guilt. He was hung on a beam suspended from two chimneys of the house that were remaining in the ruins of Lynch's farm. He prayed very devoutly, and acknowledged his guilt to the last. The only thing which gave him concern was his being hung in chains opposite to his father's house.

JAMES HARRY, ALIAS HARRIS,
EXECUTED FOR THE MURDER OF HIS WIFE.

GUILT was brought home to this man by a succession of circumstances which at once established his crime, and showed the finger of Providence visibly pointing out the murderer, whose deep-laid schemes of secrecy could not shelter him from the punishment awarded by justice.

Harry, *alias* Harris, lived in the parish of Dixtone, in Monmouthshire. For fourteen years he had been from home, and during his absence his wife supported herself by attending women lying-in and by sewing. After his return they lived very unhappily; and it appeared that the wife had a most aggravating tongue, and Harry was not blessed with much patience.

On Sunday, the 30th of March, 1817, Mrs. Harry was seen, as usual, at church, and subsequently at her own cottage, dressed in her accustomed gown, shawl, &c.: but next morning she was missing. Harry said she had been called up during the night, and he expressed much surprise at her not appearing during the ensuing week. At length, the murdered remains of the unfortunate woman were found buried in an adjoining wood, and from attending circumstances suspicion fell upon Harry, who was apprehended, and brought to trial, August the 15th, 1817, at the Monmouth assizes, when it was satisfactorily proved that he had murdered his unfortunate wife; and, for concealment, had buried her in an adjoining wood.

On the following Monday this wretched man paid the forfeit of his existence on the gaol of Monmouth, in the presence of several thousand spectators. No sooner was the unhappy culprit convinced that he had no mode of escape, than he sunk into a sullen apathy. His brother, his son, and his friends, were alike regarded by him as obtrusive, and were forbade his presence. Avarice seemed to be his ruling passion, and the loss of the trifling property, in amassing which he had derived so much pleasure, seemed to have solely occupied his mind. At length, by the exertions of the chaplain, he was induced to confess his guilt. He admitted the justice of his sentence, and acknowledged the fact of his having murdered his hapless wife, under circumstances, however, he said, on her part, of great aggravation. It appeared, from his statement, that he killed her on the Sunday night by a blow on the temple with some heavy instrument, but not the stone produced on the trial; and when her spirit had fled for ever, he employed himself in cleaning up those traces of the deed which her flowing blood produced. Having at length partially accomplished this work, he secreted the body under the bed, and in the garden buried some of those clothes with which he had been performing his terrific labours.—Thus matters rested till the succeeding night, when he went forth to the Cross Wood side, and there dug the grave, in which he immediately deposited the remains of the deceased, hoping that by the course of conduct which he had adopted he should avert suspicion, until he should be enabled to depart from a spot which his conscience rendered peculiarly terrible.

JEREMIAH BRANDRETH, WILLIAM TURNER, AND ISAAC LUDLAM,

EXECUTED FOR HIGH TREASON.

IN an introductory paragraph to our account of the Spafields' riot we took occasion to mention the most prominent causes of public discontent; and though these had partially disappeared in 1817, still the impulse given to disaffection continued to operate for a considerable time, being protracted by the injudicious, if not unconstitutional, resort of government to the base system of spies and informers, who no doubt fanned that flame of disloyalty which had nearly caused a traitorous explosion in the county of Derby, more formidable and appalling than that for which Brandreth and his ill-fated companions suffered.

No doubt the seeds of disloyalty, at this period, had been sown through the kingdom with a strange industry, and that the infatuated populace were too accessible to opinions of a dangerous tendency; but was it wise, was it humane, to take advantage of their ignorance and delusion, to hurry them upon illegal proceedings, that their crimes might qualify a few of them for that punishment which was to be inflicted only for the purpose of warning others of their danger, and deterring the infatuated by exhibiting the decapitated victims of the law? The vile agent of government, in the northern districts, was a wretch named Oliver, for whose history and practices we refer the reader to the Parliamentary Reports of 1818.

Of Oliver, it is supposed, the three unfortunate men, who form the subjects of this case, were victims; for the contemptible insurrection which they headed originated among the peasantry of Pentridge, Southwingfield, and Wingfield Park, in Derbyshire, the last places in England that could be suspected of becoming the scene of treason and rebellion; and, therefore, it is rational to conclude that no ordinary deceptions were practised on them to cause a departure from their peaceful habits and contented homes. The country is fertile and picturesque; the population thin and scattered; and the inhabitants simple, industrious, and affectionate. How these became the willing instruments of villainy, we are unable to state; but it has been fully ascertained that they were deluded by those who were in correspondence with Oliver, and who consequently were his dupes.

Jeremiah Brandreth, better known by the name of the *Nottingham Captain*, was one of those original characters for which nature had done much, and education nothing. Of his parents, or early habits, we know nothing; for on these subjects he maintained a studied silence, and since his execution nothing ce!-

culated to remove our ignorance on these points has come to our knowledge. All we know with certainty is, that he had been in the army, and that his wife, and three children, resided at Nottingham, where he was compelled to apply to the parish officers for occasional support.

The figure and countenance of this man were subjects well adapted for the wild and impassioned pencil of Salvator Rosa, and would not have been unsuitable to stand prominent in a group of mountain banditti. His age was not more than six-and-twenty; yet he evidently possessed an influence of command, and resolution, irresistible to common men. His eye was black and piercing, and his whole face indicated a character of daring intrepidity, and decision of no ordinary kind. Those who had seen him declared that it was no wonder that ordinary men looked on him with a kind of awful respect, not unmixed with dread; for he might have sat for the picture Lord Byron has drawn of the 'Corsair.'

'But who that chief?—his name on every shore
Is famed and feared—they ask, and know no more.
With those he mingles not but to command,
Few are his words, but keen his eye and hand.

'His name appals the fiercest of his crew,
And tints each swarthy cheek with sallower hue;
Still sways their souls with that commanding art
That dazzles—leads—yet chills—the vulgar heart.
What is that spell, that this his lawless train
Confess and envy—yet oppose in vain?
What should it be that thus their faith can bind?
The power, the nerve, the magic of the mind!
Linked with success—assumed and kept with skill
That moulds another's weakness to its will—

Wields with their hands—but still to these unknown,
Makes even their mightiest deeds appear his own.

'Unlike the heroes of each ancient race,
Demons in act, but gods at least in face.
In Conrad's form seems little to admire,
Though his dark eye-brow shades a glance of fire.
Robust, but not Herculean—to the sight
No giant frame sets forth his common height;
Yet in the whole—who paused to look again,
Saw more than marks the crowd of vulgar men—
They gaze and marvel how—and still confess
That thus it is, but why they cannot guess.
Sun-burnt his cheek—his forehead high, and pale,
The sable curls in wild profusion veil.

'There breathe but few whose aspect could defy
The full encounter of his searching eye.

'There was a laughing devil in his sneer,
That roused emotions both of rage and fear;
And where his frown of hatred darkly fell,
Hope withering fled—and Mercy sigh'd farewell.'

Such was the man who might have done honour to a better cause, had fortune afforded him the opportunity. His companions, though not more fortunate, were less remarkable. William Turner lived in the village of Southwingfield, where he erected, with his own hands, a neat stone cottage for his parents; his character was unimpeachable until this insurrection, and his only fault was that of being too partial to drink, under the influence of which he lost all sense of prudence, and all power of control.

Isaac Ludlam had, until this event, also possessed the esteem of his neighbours. He inherited some property from his father, and had rented some farms; but, speculating too high, he became unfortunate, in consequence of which he assigned all his effects to his creditors. He then endeavoured to support himself and family, consisting of a wife and twelve children, by providing and carting stones for house-building. In the severe pressure of the times this resource failed him, and, in an evil hour, this grey-headed old man joined in Brandreth's desperate attempt. Ludlam regularly attended the Methodist meeting, and, in the absence of a preacher, conducted the prayers and praise of the people.

These unfortunate men acted under complete illusion. Formal statements of the number of the disaffected were given them, as well as the quantity of arms and ammunition, &c. accompanied with flattering pictures of the liberty, happiness, and wealth, which were to wait upon success.

On the 5th of June, Brandreth came from Nottingham to the neighbourhood of Pentridge, to take command of the rebel forces; and on the 9th, they proceeded on their march for Nottingham, where it was reported several thousand anxiously waited their coming, that they might unite in forwarding a revolution. Their numbers were truly contemptible, not exceeding forty or fifty; yet, small as they were, they committed several excesses, and Brandreth shot one harmless man. It was during the night they commenced operations; and next morning, on the approach of a score of cavalry, they precipitately fled, leaving their arms promiscuously scattered behind them. Several were then apprehended, and several more the two or three ensuing days, Brandreth among others.

To try these thoughtless rebels, a special commission was issued, which was opened at Derby, October the 15th, 1817. Brandreth was the first put on his trial; and as the evidence against him was conclusive, he was, of course, found Guilty. Turner and Ludlam were also convicted, as well as a young man named Weightman, whose sentence was afterwards commuted to transportation. Justice being now satisfied, twelve men pleaded Guilty, and the remainder were discharged. Those who pleaded guilty received sentence of death, but were afterwards respited.

The unfortunate Brandreth, on being removed to prison, after his conviction, although he exhibited a manly firmness, was, nevertheless, much affected. The other prisoners thronged around him in anxious suspense to hear his fate. He uttered the single and appalling word—Guilty; and, in a moment, a perfect change was visible in the countenances of those whose fate was undecided.

Brandreth throughout his confinement seemed to have entertained a confident expectation of acquittal, and this hope appears to have rested solely on the supposed impossibility of identifying him, as he was a total stranger in that part of the country, and had, from the time of his committal, allowed his beard to grow, which completely shaded his whole face. The singular cast of his features, however, aided by the peculiar and determined expression of his eye, rendered his identity unquestionable; and almost every one of the witnesses swore to the person of the 'Nottingham Captain.' This wretched man, both before and after his conviction, evinced the utmost propriety of conduct. He appeared calm and happy, and exhibited great firmness in the contemplation of his unhappy fate.

His companions in misfortune, however, evinced much less fortitude; for each appeared the very picture of despair. They attributed their melancholy situation to Brandreth, and a man, named Bacon, who seems to have evaded the punishment merited by his crime.

November the 7th, 1817, was the day appointed for the execution of Brandreth, Turner, and Ludlam. a quarter before twelve, the hurdle was drawn up at the door of the prison, into which Brandreth got; and proceeded immediately to the scaffold. He looked coolly round upon the immense multitude of spectators, and in a loud and firm voice said 'God bless you all, and Lord Castlereagh!' He stood resolute and silent, whilst the executioner adjusted the rope; and at twenty-five minutes before one the drop fell, and he was launched into eternity; after hanging half an hour, the body was cut down and laid on the bench. The cap was removed from the head; and the neck having been pressed close on the block, the executioner struck the blow, and the head was at once detached from the body. The head fell into the basket; and the hangman, seizing it by the hair, held up the ghastly countenance to the populace, exclaiming, 'Behold the head of the traitor, James Brandreth!'

ABRAHAM THORNTON,
TRIED FOR THE MURDER OF MARY ASHFORD.

THIS most extraordinary case, from the great interest it universally excited, and the strength of the evidence against the prisoner, though that evidence failed to convict him, added to the unparalleled heinousness of the crime which he, t can scarcely be doubted, committed, is almost unequalled by any of the atrocities which it has been our painful duty to record.

Abraham Thornton was a well-formed, powerful man, the son of a respectable builder, and by trade a bricklayer. He was indicted, at the Warwick assizes, in August, 1817, for the murder, after having violated the person, of Mary Ashford, a lovely and interesting girl, who fell a victim to the imprudence of going to a country dance unattended, and trusting herself to the protection of a stranger. Her character was unsullied, and the surgeon who opened her body bore evidence to her virgin innocence up to the period of the fatal event.

It appeared from the statement of the counsel for the prosecution, which was borne out by numerous witnesses, that the unfortunate deceased went, on the evening of the 26th of May, 1817, to a dance at Tyburn, a few miles from Birmingham. The prisoner, who was there, admired her figure and general appearance and was heard to say, 'I have been intimate with her sister, and I will have connexion with her, though it should cost me my life.' He accompanied her from the dancing-room, and was seen with her at a stile about three o'clock in the morning. At four she called at a friend's in good spirits. On her leaving Erdington, between four and five in the morning of the 27th, the fatal deed was done: the footsteps of a man and woman were traced from the path through a harrowed field, by which she was going towards Langley. These footmarks, which exhibited proofs of running and struggling, led to a spot where a distinct impression of the human figure, and a large quantity of coagulated blood, were discovered; in the same place were seen the marks of a man's knees and toes From that spot the blood was distinctly traced for a considerable space towards the pit where the body was found, and it appeared plainly as if a man had walked along the footway carrying a body, from the extremity of which the blood dropped. At the edge of the pit, her shoes, bonnet, and bundle, were found, but only one footstep could be seen there, and that was a man's. It was deeply impressed, and seemed to be that of a man who thrust one foot forward to heave the body he had in his arms into the pit. There were marks of laceration upon the body, and both her arms had the marks of hands, as if they had pressed them with violence to the ground.

By his own admission Thornton was with her at four o'clock, and the marks of the man's shoes in the running corresponded exactly to his. By his own admission, also, he was intimate with her; and this admission was made not before the magistrate, nor till the evident proofs were discovered on his clothes: her clothes too afforded most powerful evidence. At four in the morning she called at a friend's, Hannah Cox, and changed her dancing dress for that in which she had gone to Birmingham.

The clothes she put on there, and which she had on at the time of her death, were all over blood and dirtied. The surgeon stated that the coagulated blood could not have proceeded except from violence.

The case, therefore, appeared to be, that Thornton had paid attention to her during the night; shown, perhaps, those attentions which she might naturally have been pleased with; and afterwards waited for her on her return from Erdington, and, after forcibly violating her, threw her body into the pit.

The prisoner declined saying any thing in his defence, stating that he would leave every thing to his counsel, who called several witnesses to the fact of his having returned home at an hour which rendered it very improbable, if not impossible, that he could have committed the murder, and traversed the distance from the fatal spot to the places in which he was seen, in the very short time that appeared to have elapsed; but it was acknowledged that there was considerable variation in the different village clocks; and the case was involved in so much difficulty, from the nature of the defence, although the case for the prosecution appeared unanswerable, that the judge's charge to the jury occupied no less than two hours. 'It were better,' he said in conclusion, ' that the murderer, with all the weight of his crime upon his head, should escape punishment, than that another person should suffer death without being guilty;' and this consideration weighed so powerfully with the jury, that, to the surprise of all who had taken an interest in this awful case, they returned a verdict of Not Guilty, which the prisoner received with a smile of silent approbation, and an unsuccessful attempt at concealment of the violent apprehensions as to his fate by which he had been inwardly agitated.

He was then arraigned, *pro forma*, for the rape; but the counsel for the prosecution declined offering evidence on this indictment, and he was accordingly discharged.

Thus ended, for the present, the proceedings on this most brutal and ferocious violation and murder; but the public at large, and more particularly the inhabitants of the neighbourhood in which it had been committed, were far from considering Thornton innocent, and subscriptions to defray the expense of a new prosecution were entered into.

On an investigation of the circumstances, the secretary of state granted his warrant to the sheriff of Warwick to take him into custody on an *appeal of murder*, to be prosecuted by William Ashford, the brother and heir at law of the deceased. He was accordingly lodged in Warwick gaol, until removed to London by *habeas corpus*, the proceedings on the writ of appeal being held in the Court of King's Bench in Westminster Hall.

On the 6th November, the appellant, attended by four counsel, appeared in court, when the counsel for Thornton stating that they had not had time to prepare for a case of such importance and novelty, the proceedings were adjourned to the 17th, on which day the prisoner availing himself of a barbarous privilege extended to him by the antiquated and absurd law under which he stood appealed, demanded trial by *wager of battle*.* The folly of

* When the privilege of *trial by battle* is claimed by the appellee, the judges have to consider whether, under the circumstances, he is entitled to the exercise of such privilege; and his claim thereto having been admitted, they fix a day and place for the combat, which is conducted with the following solemnities:—

A piece of ground is set out, of sixty feet square, enclosed with lists, and on one side a court erected for the judges of the Court of Common Pleas, who attend there in their scarlet robes; and also a bar is prepared for the learned sergeants at law. When the Court is assembled, proclamation is made for the parties, who are accordingly introduced in the area by the proper officers, each armed with a *baton*, or staff of an ell long, tipped with horn, and bearing a four-cornered leather target for defence. The combatants are bare-headed and bare-footed, the appellee with his head shaved, the appellant as usual, but both dressed alike. The appellee pleads Not Guilty, and throws down his glove, and declares he will defend the same by his body; the appellant takes up the glove, and replies that he is ready to make good the appeal, body for body. And thereupon the appellee, taking the Bible in his right hand, and in his left the right hand of his antagonist, swears to this effect:—

"Hear this, O man, whom I hold by the hand, who callest thyself [John], by the name of baptism, that I, who call myself [Thomas], by the name of baptism, did not feloniously murder thy father, [William] by name, nor am any way guilty of the said felony. So help me God, and the saints; and this I will defend against thee by my body, as this Court shall award."

To which the appellant replies, holding the Bible and his antagonist's hand, in the same manner as the other:—

"Hear this, O man, whom I hold by the hand, who callest thyself [Thomas], by the name of baptism, that thou art perjured, because that thou feloniously didst murder my father, [William] by name. So help me God, and the saints; and this I will prove against thee by my body, as this Court shall award."

Next, an oath against sorcery and enchantment is taken by both the combatants, in this or a similar form. "Hear this, ye justices, that I have this day neither ate, drank, nor have upon me, neither bone, stone, nor grass; nor any enchantment, sorcery, or witchcraft, whereby the law of God may be abased, or the law of the devil exalted. So help me God and his saints."

The battle is thus begun, and the combatants are bound to fight till the stars appear in the evening.

If the appellee be so far vanquished that he cannot or will not fight any longer, he shall be adjudged to be hanged immediately: and then, as well as if he be killed in battle, Providence is deemed to have determined in favour of the truth, and his blood shall be attainted. But if he kills the appellant, or can maintain the fight from sun-rising till the stars appear in the evening, he shall be acquitted. So also, if the appellant becomes recreant, and pronounces the word *craven*, he shall lose his *liberam legem*, and become infamous; and the appellee shall recover his damages, and shall be for ever quit, not only of the appeal, but of all indictments likewise of the same offence. There are cases where the appellant may counterplead, and oust the appellee from his trial by battle: these are vehement presumption or sufficient proof that the appeal is true: or where the appellant is under fourteen, or above sixty years of age, or is a woman or a priest, or a peer, or, lastly, a citizen of London, because the peaceful habits of the citizens were supposed to unfit them for battle.

thus admitting that 'right should follow might' was particularly obvious in this case, for whilst the appellee was an athletic man of great muscular power, the appellant was of a delicate frame, and quite unequal to a personal combat with such an antagonist.

The revival of this obsolete law gave rise to repeated arguments of counsel on both sides, which were adjourned from time to time till the 16th April, 1818, when the judges delivered their opinions *seriatim*, the substance of which was, that sitting there to administer the law, not as they wished it to be, but as they found it, they considered the defendant entitled to claim trial by wager of battle, and the decision of the Court was, 'That there be trial by battle unless the appellant show reason why the defendant should not depart without day.'

On the 20th, time having been asked by the appellant's counsel, the matter was finally disposed of, the judgment of the Court being ' that the defendant be discharged from this appeal, and that he be allowed to go forth without bail.'

Though the rigid application of the letter of the law a second time saved this wretched man from punishment, nothing could remove from the public mind the conviction of his atrocity. Shunned by all who knew him—his very name become an object of terror—he, in a few months, attempted to proceed to America; but the sailors of the vessel in which he was about to embark refused to go to sea with such a character on board. He, however, succeeded in a subsequent attempt by disguising himself, and thus was his country relieved from the presence of one who was more than suspected of as large a load of moral crime as ever disgraced it in the form of a human being.

CHARLES HUSSEY,

EXECUTED FOR THE MURDER OF MR. BIRD AND HIS HOUSEKEEPER.

Two murders, similar in atrocity and mystery to that of the Marrs, were committed at Greenwich on the 8th of February, 1818, on the bodies of Mr. Bird, aged eighty-three, and his housekeeper, Mary Simmons, aged forty-four.

Mr. Bird had resided for many years in Greenwich, where he carried on the business of a tallow-chandler, in which he acquired sufficient property to enable him to retire, and live on his income, arising from houses, and money in the funds. His wife died in 1816, and from that time no person resided with him but his housekeeper. He had been a most constant attendant at Greenwich church, and was always in his place as soon as

---

Besides the folly which on the very face of this proceeding must be obvious to every reader, namely, that 'right should follow might,' there are other absurdities which must tend to make it equally unpalatable to an enlightened age. For instance, if the appellant be the widow of the murdered person, and in just indignation should proceed against his murderer, yet if she should marry before the appeal comes into court, then she can have no redress against the slayer of her first husband, because, in the eye of our old legislators, one man was as good as another; and as she was thus supposed to have taken compensation into her own hands, she was not entitled to receive any from the law. Again, though the appellee, if found guilty, would be out of the reach of pardon from the Crown, yet the appellant might sell his life to him for any sum which he chose to ask. This last mode of estimating a man's life like that of an ox or a sheep, was a remnant of the most barbarous ages, and is still to be found among many tribes of African and Indian savages.

service began, accompanied by his housekeeper. On Sunday morning, the 9th of February, it was noticed by the beadle of the parish, and others, that they were not in their seats in the church as usual. At the conclusion of the service this circumstance excited some alarm, which was considerably heightened when the neighbours discovered that Mr. Bird's house had not been opened, though it was then noon. The beadle and others knocked at the door, but, receiving no answer, they concluded that something dreadful must have taken place, and therefore forced an entrance through the back part of the premises.'

On entering the house a most shocking spectacle presented itself. The body of the housekeeper was lying in the passage on its face in a revolting state, her skull having been driven in, and fractured in a most inhuman manner; the horrid act had been perpetrated with a blunt instrument. On proceeding from this scene of blood, one equally horrible presented itself. In a parlour adjoining the passage, the body of Mr. Bird was lying on its back, with his arms stretched out, and his head more fractured than that of his housekeeper, evidently with the same instrument, employed by a powerful man.

As Mr. Bird had been in the regular habit of retiring to bed at ten o'clock every night, the murder must have been perpetrated before that hour; and, as the housekeeper always kept the hall-door chained, the murderer must have gained admittance under some false pretence, and, no doubt, the moment he entered the work of death commenced. The body of the unfortunate woman was literally swimming in blood, as well as that of her master, who, it was supposed, had been reading, as a book lay on the table, whilst one of his hands held his spectacles.

On proceeding up stairs it was found that plunder was the object of the murderer, for the keys of the drawers and boxes had been procured from the pockets of the deceased, as they were stained with blood, and the different apartments rifled. What property had been carried away could not be ascertained, as it was not known what amount of money Mr. Bird kept in his house. A secret drawer had remained untouched, where a sum of thirty-one pounds was found; but whatever other money had been in the house was carried off. Some silver spoons, a silver ladle, &c. were also missing.

Mr. Smith, the magistrate, was in attendance on the spot, to act with promptitude, in case any suspected person had been discovered, but there appeared no one to whom suspicion could attach. On the dreadful and distressing intelligence being communicated to Mr. Bird's son, he hastened to the house, when the overwhelming grief and distraction, with which he was agitated on viewing the mangled body of his deceased father, can be better imagined than described.

The horrid discovery created a very considerable degree of alarm, and Mr. Bicknell, a respectable solicitor, who resided at Greenwich, sent off an express to the public office, Bow Street, on receipt of which proper officers were sent down to examine the premises, and to endeavour to discover the murderer or murderers.

An inquest was held on the bodies of the deceased, without giving any clue to the perpetrator of the horrid deed; and on the following Saturday the remains of Mr. Bird and his housekeeper were deposited in the churchyard of Greenwich, amidst an immense concourse of spectators.

During the three succeeding weeks several persons were apprehended on suspicion, but nothing material could be alleged against them. At length a complete discovery took place, and the murderer was pointed out by his own sister, who showed, on this occasion, a Roman love of justice. This woman was married to a man named Godwin, and resided, with her husband, at Peckham. About a week after the murders had been committed, her brother, Charles Hussey, came to her house, and said he was going to see his brother, who resided at Basingstoke. He went to a box of his under a bed, and took something out; she supposed it was money, for he had sixty-seven pounds left him four days after the murders were committed, by a sister, who cut her throat, in Queen Street, Cheapside, where she had lived. Hussey told his sister he should return in a week, but he did not do so for nearly a fortnight. She then said to him, 'Oh, Charles! I have been so uneasy during your absence, I have had such frightful dreams, and could not think what detained you.' He replied, 'Why, what could cause you to dream?' and appeared greatly agitated. After he had gone away Mrs. Godwin said to her husband, 'I think there is something in Charles's box there should not be;' his behaviour caused her to say so; and with one of her own keys she opened the box, when the first things that met her eye were a pair of watches, which herself and husband suspected to have belonged to the late Mr. Bird. Their suspicion was confirmed by Hussey not returning according to promise, and, with a detestation of so black a crime which did them infinite honour, they repaired to Greenwich, and give information of the circumstance.

Another box of Hussey's was brought, soon after the murders, to a Mrs. Goddard, who resided at Deptford; and as this woman's suspicions were excited by some inquiries made after Hussey, she opened the box, and found in it property she supposed to have belonged to the late Mr. Bird. Officers were sent for, and on searching the trunk, they found a silver winestrainer, a soup-spoon, two shirts, three pair of sheets, a white jean jacket, stained with blood in several places, especially about the right hand pocket; a pair of gaiters, made of drab cloth, with blood upon the buttons of them; a piece of new shirting, which was very bloody, and a glazed hat. In the same trunk were found several articles of silver plate, which proved to have been Mr. Bird's property. It was remarkable that this trunk was only corded, not locked, and that Hussey never called to inquire after it from the time it had been deposited with Mrs. Goddard.

From Deptford the officers proceeded to Mrs. Godwin's house, at Peckham, where, in addition to the watches, they found, in the box, five one-pound Bank of England notes, and two two-pound notes, all marked with Mr. Bird's initials. In the same box they found Hussey's discharge from the East India Company's service, which contained a description of his person.

In consequence of these discoveries no doubt remained but that Hussey had been the principal, if not the only, perpetrator of the foul murders. Diligent inquiry was accordingly made after him; but it was found that he had, with the consciousness of guilt, absconded. More than twenty of the most active metropolitan officers were dispatched in every direction, and others sent to distant parts of the country. Advertisements were inserted in all the principal newspapers, describing his person, and offering large rewards for his apprehension.

The exertions of the regular police were not, however, crowned with their usual success; and the circumstances under which he was secured may almost be considered as accidental, being taken in Oxfordshire by a publican, who happened to have read the advertisement describing his person.

John Poulton, the man who apprehended the prisoner, stated that he kept a public house in Deddington, and was the constable. He read the Oxford newspaper, in which he saw the prisoner advertised. Soon after nine o'clock, he saw the prisoner pass his house; and his person answering the description given, he followed him. The witness asked a neighbour to accompany him; they followed the prisoner to a farm-yard, which he supposed was a thoroughfare, and, finding it was not so, returned again; he was then convinced the prisoner was a stranger, and he went up to him, and said he must go with him, as he had strong suspicion he was the man advertised. The prisoner, after some hesitation, confessed his name was Charles Hussey. On his taking him to his house, he proceeded to search him, and found a watch and a pocket-book, with a ring in it, part of the property stolen from the late Mr. Bird's house. The prisoner denied any knowledge of the murders or robbery, but admitted being in possession of the stolen property.

The magistrate told the prisoner it would be necessary for him to account for being possessed of the things which had been stolen.

The prisoner said, that between four and five o'clock on the Sunday afternoon after the murders, he saw a man get over a wall into Mr. Smith's grounds at Greenwich, and run; he followed him, and saw him put down a bundle against a large tree and leave it there, and then run again: curiosity led him to the spot, and he opened part of the bundle, and saw two watches, and the handle of a silver soup-ladle. He left the bundle then as he found it. On the Saturday afternoon following he went to the spot again, and found the bundle against the tree exactly in the same state as when he left it. The bundle consisted of three watches, a silver soup-ladle, a silver wine-strainer, four sheets, six or eight shirts, six rings, a quantity of old silver coins, two two-pound Bank of England notes, and three one-pound notes. The rings were wrapped up in rags. There was no wearing apparel in the bundle. His motive for absenting himself was, that he was ashamed to return back, after having such things in his possession, meaning Mr. Bird's stolen property, and not coming forward at the time to tell of it. He was asked if he had any thing to say respecting the charges that were made against him; he replied, 'No, he had nothing to say on the subject.' He was told witnesses would attend against him at the next examination, and it would be heard what they had to say against him; he replied, 'Very well, sir.'

Mr. Poulton was bound over to give evidence at the prisoner's trial, at the assizes for Kent.

The prisoner, during the whole of the examination, betrayed no particular emotion. After his examination he was ironed strongly, and conveyed to the House of Correction.

Hussey had been originally a sailor in the East India Company's service, from which he was discharged, when he became a servant, and lived in that capacity with a Mr. Stevens, at Greenwich, not far from the house of Mr. Bird. Previous, however, to the murders, Hussey had been discharged, and was, at the time, out of place.

In person, Hussey was tall, his hands and feet remarkably large, and his countenance pallid, mild, and humane. His appearance, when placed at the bar, was apparently that of a person above his rank in life.

July the 31st, 1818, Hussey was indicted at the Maidstone assizes for the wilful murder of Mr. Bird and his housekeeper. The dreadful deed was fully brought home by evidence, certainly circumstantial, but, at the same time, most satisfactory and conclusive. It was proved that the hammer with which the murders were committed had been taken from a cooper several days before, and that it was afterwards found in a pond, into which the assassin had thrown it. With this cooper Hussey had been intimate, and was almost daily at the house, where he kept his trunk until subsequent to the murders, when he had it removed to his cousin's, Mrs. Goddard, at Deptford. It was also proved that Hussey belonged to a 'Society of Odd Fellows,' and that he did not join them the night of the murders until near ten o'clock. The proprietor of the house where the Odd Fellows met, being asked whether Hussey appeared any way agitated when he saw him, replied, ' He might, but I did not observe him, for he is the last man in the world, from his general character and habits, whom I should suspect of either dishonesty or murder.' The remainder of the evidence only confirmed the facts we have already narrated, and the case for the prosecution having closed, Hussey was called on for his defence.

He declared his innocence, and gave a confused account of the manner in which he was employed the night of the murder; but his criminality was too plain to be doubted, and, accordingly, he was found Guilty.

He suffered August 3d, 1818, on Pennenden Heath, near Maidstone, the usual place of execution for the county of Kent. He made no confession, except that when asked by the Rev. Mr. Argles if he knew who did the deed, he replied with eagerness, ' I do, I do.'

Soon after Hussey's execution the Rev. Mr. Rudge published something like a confession of the wretched man, which, at first, served to unsettle the opinions of many respecting his guilt. A gentleman at Greenwich, however, soon showed the falsehoods and inconsistencies of this ' confession.'

DR. LAURENCE HYNES HALLORAN,
TRANSPORTED FOR FORGING A FRANK.

This unfortunate gentleman was a scholar and a clergyman. For many years he was head of a seminary where some of the brightest characters of the day had received the rudiments of a classical education. Yet this venerable preceptor, in the winter of life, was transported with felons to Botany Bay for seven years—a punishment which some of our readers will doubtless think disproportioned to his offence, when they hear that his crime was that of having forged the frank of a letter whereby he defrauded the Post-office of ten pence.

When placed at the bar of the Old Bailey, September the 9th, 1818, and asked the usual question by the clerk, he addressed the Court as follows:—

'My lord, owing to the long period of my confinement on this charge, upwards of twenty months, the death during that period of the only witness who could substantiate my innocence, the exhaustion of my pecuniary resources, and my consequent inability to employ counsel, or have the advantage of professional advice, I have no alternative left me but to plead guilty to the offence with which I am charged.'

Mr. Baron Graham advised him to consider well the effect of his plea.

He replied: 'My lord, I have no alternative; I stand here unarmed and defenceless against a phalanx of powerful opponents arrayed against me, and determined to prosecute. It would be a waste of your lordship's time to plead not guilty. I must persist in my plea.'

His plea was then recorded, and he was ordered from the bar.

September the 30th he was brought up to receive sentence, when he addressed the Court at conderable length, reflecting severely on the motives which influenced the prosecution, and urging the improbability that a man not in a state of actual infatuation would volantarily commit such an offence as that laid to his charge for the sake of tenpence, and that not to pass into his own pockets, but into that of the promoter of the prosecution.

He was then sentenced to seven years' transportation.

The Abduction of Miss Crockatt.

SAMUEL DICK,
CONVICTED OF AN ABDUCTION AND RAPE.

THE barbarous practice of forcibly carrying off females prevails in Ireland to a shameful extent. Dishonoured women are too often induced to bestow their hand on the ravisher, and thus the success of one villain stimulates the lust and avarice of twenty. The law, which visits this crime with death, has not been sufficient to abolish so base and abominable a practice, as the Irish newspapers are, from time to time, filled with details of cases of abduction.

The robber may plead necessity, and the murderer provocation; but the wretch who deliberately invades the chastity of a female whom he wishes to make his wife, is not only without any excuse whatever, but betrays such a total absence of manly feeling that we know not any offender whose crime deserves a more speedy and capital punishment. Such a monster should be hurried, with a fearful precipitancy, out of society; for he has given proof that he is unfit for the company of virtuous and honourable men, by deliberately attempting to debase what all the world regards as sanctified and pure. Among the lower orders in Ireland, and sometimes among those of a higher rank, this practice is not looked on in the light it deserves. Indelicate and gross minds can see no moral turpitude in an abduction which terminates in marriage; but, as female purity is the vital essence of morality in society, whoever invades that source of all our virtues, and all our happiness, should be hunted down as a monster that preyed upon the dearest interests of man. Besides, it is a crime fearful, not only in its consequences, but in its commission. Family anguish must proclaim its commencement; virgin screams announce its completion; and protracted grief seal its guilt; for how can that woman, though a wife, feel happy, who is liable to have the 'slow unmoving finger of scorn' pointed at her, as one that had been 'dishonoured among men?'

Samuel Dick was one of those contemptible wretches, who would arrive at wealth through the charnel-house of lust, where his own sister stood the officiating goddess. His case is one of revolting indelicacy and deep-laid villainy. We shall give it in the words of the counsel retained to prosecute him at the Carrickfergus assizes, March the 21st, 1818.

'The prisoner, Samuel Dick, stands indicted for the forcible abduction and subsequent defilement of Elizabeth Crockatt, the prosecutrix. She is a young woman of respectable family in Derry; and upon the death of her father she became possessed of about two thousand six hundred pounds: this property, her youth, being scarcely seventeen, and her personal attractions, had been the causes of two different atrocious outrages, for the purpose of obtaining possession of them. In August last, upon the Sabbath day, while returning from the meeting, she was forcibly carried off, and taken to Ballymena, where she was rescued by her brother and her uncle. On their return home, her mother, alarmed for her safety, sent her for some time to reside within a few miles of Stewartstown, with a Mr. Matthew Fairservice. On the night of the 3d of November, Mr. Fairservice's family were invited to spend the evening at Mr. Henry's, where the prosecutrix met Miss Jane Dick, sister to the prisoner, and who is related to the prosecutrix. The prosecutrix, with Mr. Robert Fairservice, his sister, and Miss Dick, then went from Mr. Henry's upon the car to a ball at a Mr. Park's, where she danced the greater part of the night. While at Mr. Park's, Miss Dick invited prosecutrix to Stewartstown, which she declined. When they had got on the car, Robert Fairservice drove rapidly towards Stewartstown, without paying any attention to the remonstrances of the prosecutrix; when in Stewartstown, they drove to the prisoner's house, where she saw the prisoner: after breakfast Miss Dick asked Miss Fairservice and the prosecutrix to go to Dungannon with her, as she wished to make some purchases. She was prevailed upon, and did go into Dungannon; remained shopping there until the evening; returned to Stewartstown, dined in the prisoner's house; and about nine or ten o'clock the prosecutrix was asked by Miss Dick to go out to the next door to assist her in purchasing some thread; and the distance being so trifling, she did not think even of putting on her bonnet. When out of the hall-door, she was forcibly seized by some person, and put into a chaise in which was the prisoner, who caught her by the arm; when in the carriage, she found her cloak and bonnet had been previously placed there, which was sufficient proof of the pre-concerted plan. The prosecutrix, the prisoner, with Miss Dick, and the other person, were driven to Lurgan, a distance of twenty miles, before day-light in the morning, the prisoner Dick guarding the prosecutrix with a pistol! After some time she was again put into the chaise, and driven to the house of a person named Swayne, where, after having wept and fasted the whole day, she was prevailed upon to go to bed with Miss Dick. From the fatigue she had suffered the two preceding nights, joined to, the anxiety of mind she had undergone, she fell asleep; and found, on awaking, that in place of Miss Dick being her bed-fellow, the prisoner at the bar was. The next morning the prisoner attempted to soothe the prosecutrix by promises of marriage, and went to Dr. Cupples, of Lisburn, to procure a license, leaving his sister and the other person to watch over her till his return: in spite of them, she contrived to escape to the house of a Mr. English, where she was protected until delivered into the hands of her uncle."

This statement being supported by the evidence, the jury without hesitation found the prisoner Guilty—Death.

JOHN DRISCOL, WILLIAM WELLER, & GEORGE CASHMAN,
EXECUTED FOR FORGERY.

THAT the punishment of death does not deter from the commission of crime is very evident in cases of forgery; for though an offence rarely pardoned, yet its progressive increase had now become an undoubted fact, at once alarming and melancholy. In 1814 the number of detected one-pound forged notes on the Bank of England was 10,342; in 1815, 14,085; in 1816, 21,860; in 1817, 21,421; and from the 1st of January to the 10th of April, 1818, 8,937. The facility of imitating the Bank of England notes at this period, and the ease with which they were put into circulation, were the inducement to hundreds who embarked in this dangerous trade; and though they knew the consequence of detection, yet each hoped he was the fortunate one who was to escape. This is the 'flattering unction' which every criminal lays to his soul, and no fact can more forcibly illustrate the impolicy of capital punishments.

At this period, 1818, the victims of forgery were more than ordinarily numerous. Days were occupied at the Old Bailey with their trials and convictions only; while Newgate was crowded to excess with those who waited, in horrid suspense, for the Recorder's report. The public mind, ever alive to sympathize with the unhappy, took the alarm, and felt great indignation at the conduct of the Bank, who, they thought, should have procured a bank-note, impossible to imitate by the ordinary process of engraving.

In consequence of this general complaint, a committee of scientific men sat to examine all specimens that might be submitted to them by artists. Many curious engravings from copper, wood, &c. were sent in, but none of these, it seems, though some of them were ingenious and beautifully executed, were of a nature that would warrant their adoption, as engravers were found who could exactly imitate them in a few days. From this it appears nothing could be fabricated, but what could be imitated by ingenious villainy.

At the same time, it must be observed that the public were too easily imposed upon; for most of the forgeries were so indifferently executed that the least attention would be sufficient to detect the counterfeit. It was a very erroneous, though very prevalent, opinion, that the Bank had a private mark by which they instantly detected a forgery. They had not, nor could not have, any such distinguishing mark.

Another complaint was, that the Bank had no right to assume the office of prosecutor, when they never sustained any loss. But it was necessary for them to protect the public, among whom their paper passed with as much facility as the current coin of the realm, and in discharging this duty they incurred incredible expense.*

* An account of the number of persons prosecuted by the Bank for forgery, or for uttering or possessing forged notes, from the 1st of January, 1798, to the 1st of January, 1819; stating where prosecuted, and the total expense incurred each year on account of such prosecutions up to the 1st of October, 1818, being the latest period to which the account could then be made up, was laid before parliament about this time, of which the following is a brief abstract.

In the year 1798 the prosecutions took place in four counties; the number amounted to twelve, and the expense was 4,130l. 16s.

Year.	Counties.	Prosecutions.	Expense.
1799	8	15	£5,705 0 10
1800	14	44	12,753 7 6
1801	12	54	11,349 18 7
1802	20	63	15,618 19 1
1803	7	9	3,861 1 6
1804	5	25	6,148 3 4
1805	15	28	9,873 1 7
1806	6	10	2,849 17 9
1807	15	45	11,844 12 3
1808	13	34	8,136 16 7
1809	16	68	16,414 9 3
1810	15	29	8,070 19 9
1811	9	33	7,236 12 6
1812	13	64	15,752 1 5
1813	16	65	15,306 17 1
1814	12	47	10,952 10 11
1815	17	63	13,818 13 3
1816	22	120	25,971 8 11
1817	25	142	29,910 4 1
1818	26	243	34,357 7 0

Next to Middlesex, Lancaster presents the greatest number of prosecutions: indeed, during the first half of the years here quoted, the number prosecuted at Lancaster considerably exceeded those tried at the Old Bailey.

From another paper presented, including the same period, from January, 1798, to

The public voice, in some measure, prevailed; the Bank was compelled to change its mode of proceeding, and allow the accused to plead guilty to a minor charge, which subjected them to transportation, whereas the evidence against them would have proved the capital charge. Numbers availed themselves of this privilege, and even those who traversed were tried only on the minor charge; a course rendered absolutely necessary from the number of convictions, as the public could not, at the time, have endured the spectacle of twenty or thirty persons suspended on the gallows for passing forged notes. In that case, indeed, the satirist might exclaim:—

'Scarce can our fields, such crowds at Tyburn die,
With hemp the gallows and the fleet supply.'

Driscol, Weller, and Cashman, were three of those, however, on whom the law was allowed to take its course. They were tried, on separate charges, at the Old Bailey, September the 12th, 1818, and were individually convicted of having sold forged notes. Driscol pleaded guilty at first, but was prevailed upon to alter his plea. The witnesses against them were two persons of bad character, but there was no doubt of their guilt. Whether they had been entrapped into the crime is not exactly known. Driscol was an illiterate Irish labourer, and likely to be operated on by a designing villain; but Weller and Cashman were old offenders, and could not be suspected for dupes. Cashman was a Jew, and had not long returned from the hulks.

The fate of these men was no sooner known with certainty, than a meeting was held in the 'Bread Street Ward,' where a petition in their behalf was agreed to. They were also induced to apply themselves to the fountain of mercy. These applications proved, however, unavailing, and the unhappy men were left to their fate. A man of the name of Williams was to suffer with them, and he and Weller received the sacrament on Sunday, when the Rev. Mr. Cotton preached a very appropriate sermon. Driscol, being a Roman Catholic, did not attend, and Cashman, being a Jew, was visited, in his cell, by members of his persuasion, who were constant in their attentions. It is a custom with the Jews to watch every motion of a brother, for some hours before the fatal moment arrives. Ten men sat up with Cashman the whole of the night. The visits during the day were all cheerfully received, with the exception of those from a wife or child, which sometimes broke in upon the train of meditation from which so much relief had been obtained.

On Tuesday morning, December the 15th, 1818, at five o'clock, the usual apparatus, preparatory to the execution of criminals, was moved to the front of the debtors'-door of Newgate. From this moment to the time of execution the crowd increased till the Old Bailey and all the avenues to it were completely

January, 1819, it appears, that Bank forgeries have increased in number from 1,102 to 30,476, and, in value, from 8,139l. to 36,301l. The account stands thus:—

	Total Number.	Total Net Value.
Year 1796	1,602	£ 8,139
1818	30,476	36,301

There is a curious disproportion here between the value, as compared with the number, in these two cases: which is explained by the fact, that in the first of the years quoted, there were 139 forged notes above 20l.; and in the last only one above that value.

filled. At half past seven the sheriff entered the inner yard, when the prisoners, Driscol, Weller, Williams, and Cashman, had their irons knocked off. At eight o'clock the bell tolled as usual, and the prisoners were brought out.

A Quaker lady (Mrs. Ripley) had been admitted to the prisoners, and had taken much pains to give them religious instruction; she was with them again by six o'clock on Tuesday morning, by their own desire. Driscol was the first who mounted the platform, which he did in a most hurried manner, and with great agitation. Having ascended it, he gazed wildly around upon the spectators, and once or twice pushed his cap from his mouth. Weller was the next ushered to the scaffold, and he exhibited a considerable portion of firmness. Williams followed. Cashman, alias Emanuel, followed: he was a Jew, and by the tenet of the Mosaic religion was not permitted to sleep during the night; he was attended by a priest of his own persuasion, and Mrs. Ripley, who manifested great anxiety for his future state. She accompanied him even to the scaffold, but there her feelings overcame her, and she burst into tears. The priest who attended him furnished the executioner with a peculiar kind of cap, which was substituted for the ordinary one used upon such occasions. By a quarter past eight, all the malefactors were arranged, Driscol labouring under great emotion and agitation. The Mosaic priest, the Rev. Mr. Devereux, and the Rev. Mr. Cotton, continued for a few minutes addressing prayers to the delinquents, when Mr. Cotton gave the signal, and thus they were launched into eternity.—Immediately upon the unfortunate culprits being launched off, some of the populace vociferated —'Shame! shame! Murder! murder!!'—After hanging the usual time, their bodies were cut down, and given over to their friends for interment.—The Rabbies who attended Cashman were permitted to cut him down. They took away the rope along with the body. Shortly after, a great crowd of Irish, men, women, and children, applied for the body of Driscol, which they bore away with the usual custom of howling. The bodies of the other two were taken into the prison, to be delivered to their friends.

So much had been apprehended from the public indignation on this occasion, that the Bank had a body of guards down lest an attack might be made, by the mob, upon that establishment. Within the walls of Newgate preparation had also been made to resist any attack, and similar precaution was manifested in other places. Happily no disturbance took place on the melancholy occasion.

JOHN KINNEAR, MOSELY WOOLF, AND LEWIS LEVY,
CONVICTED OF CONSPIRACY.

The commercial world affords great opportunities for knaves to practise their impositions in, but we are not aware that it has ever been subjected to a more extensive system of fraud than that effected by the trio whose names head the present article.

These dishonest sons of Israel were reputed merchants in London, and contrived for several years to keep up a tolerable character. They were in extensive trade, and kept separate concerns, turning each in business something like three hundred thousand pounds a year.

With the profits resulting from this trade they were, however, dissatisfied, and resolved to grow rich by speedier means. They originated three mercantile houses, and placed as proprietors in them three men, who were, in fact, merely paupers. The first was John Meyer, a Jew, who kept a house on Tower Hill, for the reception of sailors. This man they supplied with money, gave him a character, and reported him as a merchant of an inexhaustible capital. The next was Henry Weiller, a German Jew, who, having served under Napoleon, came, in 1816, to England, with ten francs in his pocket. This fellow they dressed up, and instructed him to represent himself as a foreign merchant. Weiller having been once in business in Paris, and being known to a respectable house there, he procured a letter of recommendation to a London banker. By this means he established his credit, and began to pass bills with amazing rapidity.

Having these two houses under their control, they wanted another, and in the formation of this they shewed the greatest skill; for they established it in such a manner, as to procure goods to a large amount, without creating suspicion. They took a Jew boy, named Joseph Leigh, who had been once or twice tried at the Old Bailey, and represented him as the son of a Dutch merchant. Levy then called upon a man named Reeves, who had been known in the Manchester trade, but who had been unfortunate in business, though his character stood yet high at Manchester. To him Levy represented Leigh as a youth well acquainted with the Continental trade, and stated that his father, being a wealthy man, proposed giving him a thousand pounds, provided he could get a person to join him who understood the country trade of England. Reeves consented to become his partner, and articles of partnership, with a great shew of candour, were drawn up between them. The one thousand pounds was then handed to Reeves, and lodged at a banker's. Levy also lent them five hundred pounds, and appeared a very good friend. He introduced Reeves to Meyer, as well as to Weiller, and recommended his dealing with them, as they generally traded on ready money. Reeves readily became their dupe. He made a circuit of the manufacturing countries, being supplied with the loan of one thousand pounds, and sent home goods to the amount of thirty-three thousand pounds, for which he paid by bills on Meyer. Before the conclusion of his business, however, he was informed that Meyer had absconded; and, on hastening to London, he found himself not possessed of a shilling, all the goods he had purchased having been sold, on their arrival, to Meyer.

A disclosure now took place, and it was found that these fictitious houses had practised the vilest impositions. Weiller was sent out of the way, but, being apprehended in Holland, he was brought back, and made a bankrupt of. On his examinations it was discovered that Kinnear, Woolf, and Levy, were the contrivers of the fraud, and, in consequence of this information, they, with several others, were indicted for a conspiracy Meyer and several others who were implicated escaped detection, but the three leaders in, and contrivers of, the scheme were brought to justice in the Court of King's Bench, April the 20th, 1819, before Lord Chief Justice Abbott and a special jury.

Reeves, Leigh, and Weiller, were the principal evidence against them, and after an investigation of two days they were found guilty. No sooner was the verdict made known, than the vast crowds who waited for the decision manifested the greatest satisfaction. A man named Le Vay, who was indicted with them, was acquitted. The trial disclosed the means by which they procured credit. One of the fictitious houses served to give a character to the others, while at the same time they played into each other's hands, by drawing and discounting bills, accepting and negotiating drafts, &c. &c. The goods thus dishonestly procured were shipped off to Holland, India, &c. on Levy's account.

On the 30th of April a motion was made for a new trial, on the ground of the jury having dispersed and slept at home, no officer being sworn to keep them together, or prevent their intermixing with the multitude. The Court, however, decided that the mere separation of the jury was no ground for setting aside the verdict, unless some improper tampering with them could be shown, the Court having a discretion to allow the jury to disperse. The application was, therefore, refused, though it was the opinion of some leading counsel that a new trial would have been granted in consequence of this irregularity.

On the 14th of May they were brought up to receive judgment, when two affidavits were put in on the part of the defendants, stating that the deponents had seen two of the jurymen, on the first night of the trial, conversing with Mr. Harmer and Mr. Adams, the solicitors for the prosecution. In answer to these, affidavits of the jury, the above gentlemen, &c. were put in, denying that any such intercourse had taken place; also two affidavits of the owners of the houses, where the deponents on the part of the defendants stated themselves to reside, stating that no such persons lived there; whence they were supposed to be fictitious names.

The sentence of the Court was, that John Kinnear should be imprisoned in the gaol of Ilchester for two years; that Lewis Levy should be imprisoned in the gaol of Gloucester for two years, and pay a fine of five thousand pounds; that Mosely Woolf should be imprisoned in the House of Correction, Cold-Bath Fields, for two years, and pay a fine of ten thousand pounds: and that Levy and Woolf should be farther imprisoned till those fines were paid. Levy had sent large quantities of goods to India, obtained by this conspiracy, and the Court considered that from the sale of those goods he might obtain remittances to pay his fine.

ROBERT JOHNSTON,
EXECUTED FOR ROBBERY.

THE extraordinary circumstances attending the execution of this unfortunate man give his case a melancholy interest. Our readers, doubtless, recollect the singular conduct of the Edinburgh mob, at the execution of Porteous. A scene, if possible, more disgraceful, occurred on the present occasion.

Robert Johnston was a native of Edinburgh, where he spent the first part of his life without reproach. His parents were poor, and Robert was employed as a carter. In his twenty-fourth year he got into bad company, and was engaged in the robbery of a chandler in Edinburgh. Being apprehended he was brought to trial, with two others, and found Guilty. His companions had their sentence commuted to transportation, but on Johnston the law was destined to be put in force.

December the 30th, 1818, was the day appointed for his execution, when it accordingly took place, but under circumstances of a very extraordinary nature. A platform was erected at one of the windows of the New North Church, in the Lawn Market. On the platform was a quadrangular table, on which the criminal was to stand, and which was to be lowered in order to leave him suspended. An immense crowd was assembled. The unfortunate culprit was brought from the lock-up-house to the place of execution about twenty minutes before three o'clock, attended by two of the magistrates, the Rev. Mr. Tait, Mr. Porteous, chaplain of the gaol, several city officers, and the public executioner. After spending some time in prayer with the clergyman, Johnston mounted the platform with alacrity, looked boldly round him, and gave the signal. But nearly a minute elapsed before the table could be forced down; and after it was got down, the perpendicular fall was so short, that the unhappy man's toes were still touching the surface, so that he remained half-standing, half-suspended, and struggling in the most dreadful manner. It is impossible to find words to express the horror which pervaded the crowd, while one or two persons were at work with axes beneath the scaffold, in the vain attempt to hew down a part of it beneath the feet of the criminal. The cries of horror from the populace continued to increase with indescribable vehemence; and it is hard to say how long this horrible scene might have lasted, had not a person near the scaffold, who was struck by a policeman, while pressing onward, cried out 'Murder!' Those who were not aware of the circumstance imagined that this cry proceeded from the unhappy Johnston. A shower of stones, taken from the loose pavement on the streets, compelled the magistrates and the police to retire in a moment. A cry of 'Cut him down—he is alive,' succeeded, and a person, genteelly dressed, sprung upon the platform, cut the rope, and the culprit fell down in a reclining position upon the scaffold, after having hung about five minutes.

A number of the crowd broke through the railing, and took possession of the platform, where they lifted up Johnston, took the ropes from his neck and arms, and the cap from off his face, which they threw among the multitude below; they then loosened a part of his clothes, and finding him alive, deliberately carried him off towards the High Street; while another party tore the coffin prepared for the criminal to pieces, and threw the fragments against the windows of the church, endeavouring also to demolish the fatal apparatus, which, however, was found too strong for them to accomplish their object. A lieutenant of police was severely cut on the head with a stone; about ten of the officers were more or less hurt by the mob; and the executioner, who was for some time in their hands, suffered severely. In the mean time the police-officers rallied in augmented force, and retook the criminal from the mob at the head of Advocates' Close. The unhappy man, half alive, stripped of part of his clothes, and his shirt turned up, so that the whole of his naked back and upper part of his body was exhibited, lay extended on the ground in the middle of the street, in front of the police-office. At last, after a considerable interval, some of the police-officers, laying hold of him, dragged him trailing along the ground, for about twenty paces, into the office, where he remained upwards of half an hour, while he was attended by a surgeon, bled in both arms, and in the temporal vein, by which suspended animation was restored; but the unfortunate man did not utter a word. In the mean time a military force arrived from the castle under the direction of a magistrate. The soldiers were drawn up in the street surrounding the police-office and place of execution.

Johnston was then carried again to the scaffold. His clothes were thrown about him in such a way, that he seemed half naked, and while a number of men were about him, holding him up on the table, and fastening the rope again about his neck, his clothes fell down, in a manner shocking to decency. While they were adjusting his clothes, the unhappy man was left vibrating, upheld partly by the rope about his neck, and partly by his feet on the table. At last the table was removed from beneath him, when, to the indescribable horror of every spectator, he was seen suspended, with his face uncovered, and one of his hands broke loose from the cords with which it should have been tied, and with his fingers convulsively twisting in the noose. Dreadful cries were then heard from every quarter. A chair was brought, and the executioner having mounted upon it, disengaged by force the hand of the dying man from the rope. He then descended, leaving the man's face still uncovered, and exhibiting a dreadful spectacle. At length a napkin was thrown over his face. Shouts of 'Murder,' and 'Shame, shame,' broke from the crowd: Johnston was observed to struggle very much; but his sufferings were at an end in a few minutes. The soldiers remained on the spot till the body was cut down; and, as it was then about dusk, the crowd gradually dispersed.

The bleeding of the unfortunate culprit by a surgeon, with the view of restoring animation, was, we apprehend, an illegal torture, as by it the poor wretch was made to suffer a double death. It is true the authorities did not call in the surgeon; but it is equally true that they did not prevent, when they might, the surgical process. The whole proceedings were afterwards properly investigated, and those to whom blame was attached were punished.

HENRY STENT,
CONVICTED OF STABBING HIS WIFE.

THIS is another of those melancholy cases, arising from the violation of the sacred duties of wedded life, which have furnished matter for our criminal courts.

Stent was a respectable butcher, residing at Pimlico, about twenty-eight years old, and at the time of his wife's guilty intercourse had been married about seven years. The destroyer of their peace was a fellow named Sweeting, who resided in the adjoining house, and was upon terms of family intimacy with them. By what means he first acquired an influence over the mind of the unhappy woman does not appear, but the following is a specimen of the arts which he used to induce her to desert the man whose confidence she had already abused.

A short time previous to the elopement, Mrs. Stent had been afflicted with an indisposition which rendered country air desirable. She was in consequence sent to the house of an uncle of her husband, a farmer within three miles of Uxbridge, where she was repeatedly visited by Sweeting, both publicly and privately, and from whence he endeavoured by every possible argument to induce her to elope, urging his illicit passion with unceasing violence. Still, however, she resisted his importunities. Whether he had at that time accomplished her seduction does not appear, but, in order to work upon her mind, and to incline her to place a more implicit belief in the strength of his unnatural affection, he went through the farce of hanging himself to a tree in the neighbourhood, as if in despair at her cruelty. From this perilous situation he took especial care to be providentially relieved; he next pretended to quench the flame by which he was devoured in the canal; but here, too, he contrived to be rescued from the crime of self-destruction.

These feats were performed anonymously; he would not disclose his name, or the cause of his contempt of life; but he took care that Mrs. Stent should not remain in ignorance of the ordeals through which he had passed; and at length the poor woman became so alarmed by these occurrences that she returned to town. In a few days afterwards she fled from her husband; and her fate remained involved in obscurity, except that Sweeting was suspected to be the partner of her flight, as he had disappeared from his home about the same time.

Sweeting had four children living, and his wife was far advanced in pregnancy with a fifth. On the evening previous to the elopement, Mr. and Mrs. Stent were invited to meet a party at Sweeting's house, who, after tea, engaged Stent in a game of cards, while his wife returned home, packed up all the moveables on which she could lay her hands, clothes, plate, and money, and removed them to another place; after which she returned and finished the evening in the most convivial manner. The next morning she eloped.

About three weeks after, Sweeting returned to his wife in the dead of night, and demanded what money she had in her possession. She denied that she had any; but he persisted that she had, and insisted upon having it. The poor woman urged the proximity of her confinement, and the calls of her other children. He was, however, deaf to these arguments; he shut the door, and with dreadful threats forced her to strip herself, and from her stays ripped sixty pounds, with which he went off. His unhappy wife was soon afterwards seized with the pains of child-birth, and was delivered; but Nature gave way to the full tide of misery which had burst upon her, and she became raving mad. Her neighbour Stent was sent for, to assist in clothing her in a strait waistcoat, and in an hour afterwards she died in his arms, her death being soon followed by that of her helpless infant. Another child died shortly after, and whatever property remained was soon dissipated in the necessary expenditure of the funerals, and the support of the surviving children, who were subsequently removed to the parish workhouse.

What were the sensations of the guilty father when this heart-rending tale reached his ears it is impossible to say; but if a shadow of feeling remained in his bosom, his misery could not be less than his crime; nor could the partner of his flight and the participator in his infamy be less exposed to the horrors of remorse.

The guilty woman, and her infamous paramour, fled to France, f om whence it appears they returned to England very soon afterwards, and then sailed to America. The unnatural bonds of licentious attachment have, however, but a very weak hold, either of the slaves or the victims of its lawless influence, and Mrs. Stent found full soon that she was fated to add to the list of dupes and outcasts. In a foreign country, far removed from the reach of help, cut off by her own act from protector or friend, she fatally felt the extent of her crime. He who had seduced her from home, from husband, and from fame, treated her as the wretch he had made her, while to the poignancy of her bodily sufferings were superadded the mental torments produced by a despairing consciousness of guilt.

At length remorse, mingled perhaps with somewhat of real penitence, induced the wretched woman to think of returning home, to throw herself at the feet of her injured husband, and to make some atonement by her future conduct for the deep and irreparable injuries she had committed. Her sated seducer gladly availed himself of the opportunity of getting rid of the degraded being who had now become a burden to him, and readily agreed to her return; first extorting from her a promise that she would for ever conceal the circumstance of his being the partner of her flight, and fiercely threatening that, if she ever disclosed the fact, he would return and cut her throat.

The ship in which she took her passage to England encountered severe storms, but Providence was pleased to save her from a watery grave, to endure sufferings more appalling. On her arrival at Liverpool she took the stage to London; and being set down at the Saracen's Head Inn, Snow Hill, retired to a room, from whence, in the wild frenzy of conscious guilt and hopeless despair, she addressed the following letter to her injured husband:—

'*August* 5, 1819.

'Henry—You, no doubt, will be offended at my writing to you, one that I have used so ill; but, believe me, I have considered of my crime, and will repent, if possible. Oh, Henry! I have suffered more than I can tell you in crossing the seas; there was nothing but storms and trouble, and the ship was lost. But you, perhaps, already know that I have put my trust in God for safety in crossing them again, and have got safe to England once more, to throw myself at your feet, and implore your pity, if you cannot pardon me; but oh! for one moment consider before my doom is fixed. Indeed, I am penitent, and sorry for my sins, and hope you will hear my prayer for mercy, as well as that God which I have offended. But if my story was told by any other than me, you would see what a villain he was. If you find you cannot forgive—but oh! that thought makes me tremble—do not let my dear father and mother know you have heard of me, for that would bring their trouble afresh to their minds (that is, if their lives are spared), and I hope I have not got that to answer for.

'All I wish is, to pass the remainder of my days in obscurity, or in the workhouse, if you think proper, or in any other place; do not desert me—for God's sake, do not. I have come from America, landed on Tuesday morning, and at night left Liverpool; and this morning got to the Saracen's Head, where I shall await your answer with the greatest distress. If you please to let me have some of the clothes I left, as I have not a gown to wear. Oh! Henry, think well before you say what shall be my fate; only ask your own heart. Do not tell any body that you know of my being in England, but think what a journey for a lone woman to take. I do not know when you will get this, but, if you can, let me know to-night what is to be my lot. Indeed, I will be content on bread and water, if I can but obtain your forgiveness. Oh! Henry, be not deaf to my prayers; I know it is a crime I have often heard you say you never would forgive; only write to say you will pardon me, and do what you like after; but do not let any of my friends know that I have wrote to you—grant me that request, if you cannot grant any more. Let me know, for I had only two pounds five shillings to bring me to London.

'MARIA STENT.

'One o'clock.'

The frightful part of our tale now advances. Stent had felt deeply the wound that had been inflicted on him; he had felt the desolation of his domestic fire-side; he had known the want of the anxious attendant, in those moments of worldly care from which no human being is exempt; and had vainly sought for repose upon his 'widowed bed of fire.' He had witnessed, too, the death-bed of the wife of his wife's seducer, and seen her helpless infants struggling in the last agonies of mortal disease, or stretching out their little hands in supplication for food, while their unnatural father was squandering in licentiousness that which should have placed them out of the reach of want. At length, unexpected and unannounced, the prime agent of all his sufferings was, as it were, at his feet, and full and ample means of vengeance within his grasp. In a state of frenzy, he hurried to the inn from whence his wretched wife had dispatched the letter which had newly lighted up the smothering embers of his fury; was shown into the room wherein she was sitting; and instantly commenced a fierce and bloody attack with a knife upon her person. Fortunately, her screams of terror and cries for mercy were heard by the attendants, who rushed into the room time enough to save her life, though dreadfully cut and mangled in the bloody encounter.

The fury of the unhappy man evaporated with the knowledge of his having punished the offender against the honour of his bed and his peace of mind; he calmly surrendered himself into the hands of justice, and was conveyed, without a struggle, to the Giltspur Street Compter, from whence he immediately dispatched a letter to his sister, acquainting her with what had passed.

The next morning he underwent an examination at Guildhall, previously to which a certificate was produced from the house-surgeon of St. Bartholomew's Hospital, stating that Mrs. Stent had passed a good night and was considered out of danger, but not able to undergo an examination at present.

Few particulars transpired on this examination beyond what we have already stated. On entering the room the waiter and porter of the inn found him stabbing her with great violence in the throat. He then said, 'I have accomplished my purpose; I wish for nothing but to suffer; I know I shall suffer.' The wife replied, 'Yes, you have, Henry, and I freely forgive you; come and kiss me.' The prisoner then knelt down and kissed her twice, which she returned, saying, 'I hope the law will not take hold of you; you are the best of husbands, and I am the very worst of wives, and I hope my fate will be a warning to all bad wives.' She was then taken on a shutter to the hospital, and in her way thither she was continually calling on her dear Henry, wishing him to kiss her, and begging him to give her his hand. The knife with which the bloody deed was committed was one of the common sticking-knives for killing calves, and was covered with blood up to the hilt; the point and the edge appeared turned, as if it had struck against a bone. Five stabs were inflicted; one on her arm, another on her hand, a third on her breast, a fourth on the right side, and a fifth in her neck.

The prisoner was remanded for further examination from time to time until his wife, whose recovery was very slow, was able to appear and give her evidence, as the mode of committal would have been different in case of her death.

Both Mrs. Stent and her father declared their intention not to prosecute. This, however, could make no difference as to the course of justice; for the king would become the prosecutor, and the evidence of Mrs. Stent might be altogether dispensed with. As, however, from the fact of the prisoner having been in the room with his wife ten minutes before an alarm was given, a doubt might arise as to the cause of the assault, which might operate favourably for the prisoner, the magistrate was bound to take cognizance of the offence, and it was indispensable that Mr. Stent should, at all events, be committed for trial.

Mrs. Stent being at length pronounced sufficiently recovered to be able to appear in public and give her evidence, the final examination took place at Guildhall, on Wednesday, the 18th of August. This being previously known, so great a concourse of persons collected that before eleven o'clock all the avenues to the justice-room were completely stopped up.

Mrs. Stent, accompanied by her father and sister, came from the hospital in a coach. Her appearance was by no means interesting; she was short of stature, had light blue eyes, small nose, and fair complexion. She looked remarkably pale, and was more annoyed than fatigued by the curiosity of the surrounding spectators; her voice and manners were remarkably mild and fascinating.

Henry Benwell, Esq. the house-surgeon at St. Bartholomew's Hospital, was first examined. He stated that Maria Stent was brought to the hospital between six and seven o'clock on the evening of Thursday the 5th of August inst.; he saw her directly; she was very faint and cold, but perfectly sensible. On examining her, he found she had received several wounds; there were three on her neck and right breast, one on her right arm, one on her right side, and one on her left thumb. One wound on the neck had penetrated the windpipe, and that on the side had penetrated the right lobe of the lungs; from this last-mentioned wound she bled most profusely. This wound, and that which had injured the windpipe, were the most serious; the others were small and of little consequence. He at first apprehended considerable danger; Mrs. Stent, however, continued getting better till the Sunday morning following, when he was called up at seven o'clock, in consequence of an attack of inflammation on his patient's lungs; from this, however, she had now recovered: the wounds were not yet perfectly healed, but he considered her now out of danger. He had not seen the knife with which the stabs were given, but from all appearances they must have been made by a sharp instrument.

Mrs. Stent next underwent examination. When the alderman informed her it was necessary she should be sworn, she replied mildly, but firmly, 'Very well, Sir.' After taking the oath, she stated, in answer to the different questions put to her, that she was the wife of the prisoner; that she arrived in London from Liverpool on the day in question; that she wrote a letter to her husband, and that he came to her at the Saracen's Head about six o'clock in the evening, that she was so agitated on seeing her husband that she could recollect nothing after she saw him, till she found herself undressed in the hospital. In giving this evidence, she was particularly guarded in not saying too much, making no extraneous observations, but confining her answers strictly to the questions, and frequently giving them in a single word; as, when asked how she found herself when she came to her recollection, she replied, 'Wounded.' When asked, 'Where?' she said, 'Principally in the neck.' She persisted, when re-questioned, that she had no recollection of any thing that passed in the interview with her husband.

Mr. Beecher, Mrs. Stent's father, declined to be bound over, and Hirdsfield, the officer who took the prisoner into custody, was then bound over as the prosecutor. Mr. Beecher agreed to be answerable for the appearance of his daughter. Stent was then finally committed for trial, but was permitted to remain in the Compter instead of being sent to Newgate.

During his confinement Mrs. Stent had several interviews with him in the Compter, in which he seemed carefully to avoid any thing like the appearance of returning affection. At neither of these visits did she venture the slightest allusion to her own misconduct, or her husband's severity; seeming aware that he still remained too much irritated against her.—On the 17th September, 1819, his trial took place at the Old Bailey, when the evidence confirmed what had transpired on the several examinations. Mrs. Stent was plainly dressed, wore a large Leghorn hat, which tended much to conceal her features, and appeared greatly agitated. On being questioned by Mr. Justice Best, she entreated that she might not be called on to give evidence against the best of husbands: he, however, told her that it was his duty to ask some questions which she was bound to answer. To these questions she replied as she had done on her examination, nearly in monosyllables, and persisted that she had no recollection of any thing that passed during the interview with her husband till she found herself in bed at St. Bartholomew's Hospital.

The prisoner left his case to his counsel, and a vast number of witnesses appeared to his character, who stated that they had known him for many years, and had always believed him to be a kind-hearted, humane, good-natured man as any in existence, and a particularly affectionate and indulgent husband.

Mr. Justice Best explained the law upon the subject. From the evidence detailed, and which he should again read over to them, no doubt could remain on the mind of any unprejudiced person that the crime charged upon the prisoner came within the provisions of that most excellent act of parliament introduced by the late lamented Chief Justice of the King's Bench, for the protection of the subject's life. Though it did not appear in evidence upon the present occasion, the fact, however, might be fairly assumed, that Mrs. Stent, the unhappy woman who appeared before them on that day, had forsaken her husband, and, by proving unfaithful to his bed, had inflicted upon him the most poignant anguish, the most acute suffering, that a man devoted to a wife could possibly endure. This, however, could by no means be admitted as a justification of his crime. The law of the land upon this subject proceeded upon the same principles as the religion of the country, which was Christianity. If a husband detected his wife in the very fact, *in flagrante delicto*, as it were, and that at the moment he plunged some deadly weapon into her bosom, so as to occasion death, it would not be considered murder. The law, like the religion of the country, making fair allowance for the frailties of human nature, considered the husband, with such provocation immediately before his eyes, as no longer under the guidance of reason, and of course not accountable for his acts. Here, however, the circumstances were quite different. A considerable time had elapsed since the elopement of the first witness, and on her return he manifested those symptoms of repentance—that appearance of returning affection—which might well be supposed to disarm vengeance, and prevent that ferocious purpose which the prisoner appeared to have deliberately contemplated. Even while her blood was flowing from the wounds he had inflicted, she still entreated him to kiss her, and in that kiss conveyed a pardon to her assailant. Under circumstances such as these, the law did not admit of the same excuse as when a husband detected his wife in the very fact. Sufficient time having been given for cool reflection on one side, and for repentance on the other, the law, proceeding on the same principle as the benign religion which it imitated, did not allow vengeance to be inflicted with impunity. After some further observations, which the learned judge delivered with great talent and feeling, he summed up the evidence at length.

The jury then retired, and, after consulting for about half an hour, returned with a verdict of Guilty, but recommended the prisoner strongly to mercy, on account of his good character.

Mr. Justice Best.—The recommendation shall certainly be forwarded.

A petition, most numerously and respectably signed was presented to the Prince Regent, on behalf of Stent, who, in consideration of all the circumstances, was graciously pleased to commute the sentence of death for two years' imprisonment.

HENRY HUNT,
IMPRISONED FOR A HIGH MISDEMEANOUR.

HENRY HUNT was the most popular demagogue that appeared in England during the reign of George the Third, except Wilkes; and, like his prototype, he appears to have been totally undeserving the confidence or the applause of the people. Like Wilkes, too, he was the occasion of several deluded people losing their lives, while he himself escaped with a comparatively trifling punishment.

Hunt was born at Widdington, in the parish of Upavon, near Salisbury Plain, on the 6th of November, 1773. His father was a very respectable farmer, and the family was of ancient standing Young Henry was sent to school, where he learned the rudiments of a classical education, being intended for the church; but at sixteen he altered his mind, and became a farmer; in the business of which he soon obtained a great proficiency. Being the eldest of six children, he was treated with great confidence by his father, whose principles he imbibed; and, as these were church and state, young Hunt was a violent loyalist, and mortally hated that party whose politics he subsequently embraced.

A threatened invasion being then talked of, Hunt enrolled himself in the Everly corps, of the commanders of which he tells some ridiculous anecdotes, not very creditable to either their honour or their courage. In 1796 this corps refused to leave their own county in case of an invasion, and Hunt, being a stout loyalist, and indignant at their baseness, flung his sword, &c. at his commander's feet, having first made his maiden speech, in the hope of inducing his comrades to volunteer; but his eloquence failed to inspire cowards with courage.

His conduct on this occasion being highly applauded, he was solicited by several corps to join them, and he accepted the offer of Lord Bruce, into whose corps he entered. The next year, however, he was dismissed, this body of cavalry having happened to give offence to the noble commander, by shooting some pheasants on his estate. Hunt, being at this time a man of property, his father having died, took the letter of dismissal in high dudgeon, and, riding to the place of parade, challenged Lord Bruce to fight a duel. His lordship, not expecting such a rencontre, put spurs to his horse, and fairly run away; but, in a few days, moved, in the Court of King's Bench, for a criminal information against Hunt, who, in consequence, was fined one hundred pounds, and imprisoned six weeks in the King's Bench. During his confinement he associated with some of those who had imbibed the principles of the French Revolution, and Hunt, on his return home, found himself a complete democrat.

Previous to this time he had got married, against his father's wishes, to an inn-keeper's daughter, for whom he had formed a most romantic and violent attachment. With this lady, however, he lived only five years; for, in 1802, he seduced another man's wife, with whom he eloped from Brighton. In praise of this unfortunate woman Hunt is grossly fulsome, and impudently avows, in his 'Memoirs,' the love he bore her; and dwells, with rapture, on the happiness he found in her society, for she was living with him in 1824. His indignant and insulted wife refused to live any longer with him, and he made on her, if we believe himself, a settlement of three hundred pounds a year, allowing her to keep her two daughters, the son remaining with the father, under the tuition, of course, of the kept mistress. Hunt, in extenuation of his conduct, alleged his love, his infatuation, &c. and while he unblushingly avowed his unprincipled baseness, he wished his countrymen to believe that in their cause he was inflexible,— that he, who could not be just to his own family, would be just to the public—*Proh pudor!*

The high prices of farming produce enabled Hunt, about this time, to keep a splendid establishment. He had several hunters, and a kennel full of dogs, and pursued with eagerness all the sports of the field, living in the style of a country gentleman, and kept a private house in Bath, where he resided during the winter months.

While in Bath he formed an acquaintance with the son of a brewer, who deluded him into a partnership, and Hunt absolutely lost eight thousand pounds in a brewing concern at Bristol, and this was the first occasion of his becoming acquainted with the people of that city.

In 1804 he first attended a public meeting, which was held at Devizes, respecting the conduct of Lord Melville; and, in the next year, he first affixed his name to a public address, calling on the inhabitants of Wiltshire to oppose the corn laws. Having once embarked in politics, he was ever restless, and on every possible occasion he forced himself upon public notice with officious zeal. In 1807 he thrust himself forward at Bristol, to propose an Irishman, named Sir John Jarvis, as a fit representative for that city.

About this time his noisy interference on all public questions drew upon him a host of enemies, particularly among his own neighbours, who forbade him to sport upon their grounds; and, as no gentleman would hunt with him, he was obliged to dispose of his stud of horses. On one occasion he committed a trifling trespass, on which an action was brought against him, when he effectually pleaded his own cause, and, encouraged by success, he determined from that day forward to dispense with the assistance of counsel.

In 1809 he held the first meeting for reform, for by this time he had become a disciple of Cobbett. In 1811 he took a large farm in Sussex, called Rowfant, where he continued to reside for one year, a expiration of which he sold it, went to live at Middleton Cottage, which is situated on the Western Road, three miles from Andover.

In 1812 he stood twice candidate for Bristol, but was defeated by a large majority. On each occasion he was opposed by the venerated Sir Samuel Romilly; and that he failed each time excited no regret among the friends of the country. This year he also became a liveryman of London, and from that time Guildhall has been often favoured with his presence. He now attended almost every public meeting throughout the country, and gradually became the idol of the mob, to whose comprehension his speeches were admirably adapted. His patriotism, however, proved injurious to his private affairs, for we find, in 1815, he had overdrawn his account with his bankers, who refused to advance him any more money.

In 1816 he attended the notorious meeting in Spafields, where he acted as chairman; and it is but justice to say that he held no previous communication with Thistlewood and his colleagues, except for the purpose of expunging the offensive matter contained in their resolutions.

Hunt, having several times entertained the mob in Palace Yard, thought himself quite popular enough in Westminster to oppose Sir Francis Burdett, at the general election in 1818. The experiment did not, however, succeed, as, at the termination of the poll, he counted only forty-one votes.

The principles of radicalism, in 1819, had reached their zenith, and the sober part of the community began to have apprehensions of the levelling spirit which was abroad. At this crisis Hunt stood conspicuous as a leader, and officiated as chairman at a meeting held in Smithfield, more numerously attended than had ever been known before. His conduct on this occasion was without reproach, and the reformers regarded him as their best and firmest champion.

An event, however, soon occurred, which gave him still greater notoriety. The Manchester reformers, who had posted up notices of a meeting to be holden on the 9th of August, for the purpose of proceeding to the election of a representative, as at Birmingham,* were informed by the magistrates that, as the object of the proposed assemblage was unquestionably illegal, it would not be suffered to take place. In consequence of this determination, they relinquished the design; and issued notices of a meeting, for the avowedly legal object of petitioning for a reform in parliament, on the 16th of August. An open space in the town, called St. Peter's Field, was selected as the place of assembly; and never, upon any former occasion of a similar nature, was so great a number of persons known to be present. Some hours before the proceedings were to commence, large bodies began to march in from the neighbouring towns and villages, formed five deep, many of them armed with stout staves, and preserving a military regularity of step. Each body had its own banner, bearing a motto; and, under a white silk flag, two clubs of female reformers appeared. The numbers collected were estimated at sixty thousand. A band of special constables, stationed on the ground, disposed themselves so as to form a line of communication from a house where the magistrates were sitting to the stage or waggon fixed for the orators. Soon after the business of the meeting had been opened, a body of yeomanry cavalry entered the ground, and advanced with drawn swords to the stage; their commanding officer called to Mr. Hunt, who was speaking, and told him that he was his prisoner. Mr. Hunt, after enjoining the people to be tranquil, said that he would readily surrender to any civil officer who should exhibit his warrant; and he was taken into custody by a constable. Several other persons were apprehended. Some of the yeomanry now cried out, 'Have at their flags!' and they began to strike down the banners in the waggon, as well as others which were raised in various parts of the field. A scene of dreadful confusion arose; numbers were trampled under the feet of men and horses; many persons, even females, were cut down by sabres; some were killed, and the number of maimed and wounded amounted to between three and four hundred. In a very short time the ground was cleared of its former occupants, and military patroles were stationed in the principal streets of the town to preserve tranquillity.

Much difference of opinion has ever since prevailed on this subject; and, perhaps, the Manchester meeting is one of those events, upon which, in all its variety of details, historians will never be found to agree. Whether the Riot Act were actually read is still a moot point: the reformers and their friends insist that it was not; the magistrates and their adherents contend that it was. Probability seems to favour the latter opinion; and certainly the affirmative of a proposition is more easily established than its negative. The whole appears to have taken place within ten minutes, by which time the field was entirely

* The people of Birmingham had some time before elected Sir Charles Wolseley as their legislatorial attorney, or representative.

cleared of its recent occupiers, and filled with different corps of infantry and cavalry. Hunt and his colleagues were, after a short examination before the magistrates, conducted to solitary cells, on a charge of high treason. On the following day notices were issued by the magistrates, by which the practice of military training, alleged to have been carried on in secret, by large bodies of men, for treasonable purposes, was declared to be illegal. Public thanks were, by the same authority, returned to the officers and men of the respective corps engaged in the attack; and, on the arrival in London of a dispatch from the local authorities, a cabinet council was held, the result of which was the return of official letters of thanks to the magistrates, for their prompt, decisive, and efficient measures for the preservation of the public tranquillity; and to all the military engaged, for the support and assistance afforded by them to the civil power.

The circumstances of the Manchester case turned out to be such, that government, by the advice of the law officers of the crown, found it expedient to abandon the threatened prosecution of Mr. Hunt and his colleagues for high treason. Those persons were accordingly informed that they would be proceeded against for a conspiracy only, which might be bailed; but Mr. Hunt refused to give bail, even, as he said, to the amount of a single farthing: some of his friends, however, liberated him. On his return from Lancaster to Manchester, Hunt was drawn about two miles by women, and ten by men. In fact, his return was one long triumphal procession, waited upon by thousands, on horse, on foot, and in carriages, who hailed him with continued shouts of applause.

The sensation produced throughout the country by this fatal business was intense. Hunt's conduct was universally applauded, and he received the thanks of nearly every county in England. Those who opposed him on principle now forgot their enmity, and hailed him as the uncompromising champion of Liberty. His entry into London was public, and some of the first characters of the day honoured him with their presence, whilst hundreds of thousands welcomed him with deafening applause.

The agitation had hardly subsided when true bills were found against Hunt and others, and their trials came on at York, and continued, without intermission, for fourteen days, during which time Hunt displayed powers of intellect and acuteness of perception which even his friends did not suspect him to be possessed of. He was found Guilty, however, and ordered to be brought up to the Court of King's Bench for sentence, before the passing of which he moved, in person, for a new trial. Although he argued with all the tact and ability of the most experienced lawyer, his motion was refused, and he was sentenced to two years and a half imprisonment in Ilchester gaol.

He had not been long incarcerated when he brought to light a system of the most infamous cruelty which had been practised on the unfortunate inmates of that dreadful Bastile by the barbarous gaoler. Mr. Hunt himself, being treated with great cruelty, addressed a letter to Mr. Justice Bayley, detailing cases of atrocious cruelty.

The question was, at length, brought before the House of Commons, and an inquiry followed. Hunt substantiated all his charges, and the inhuman gaoler was dismissed and punished, while the country rung with the praise of his accuser's manly conduct.

The two years and a half having expired, Mr. Hunt was liberated, and once more made his public entry into London. But the times had changed; the public prosperity had banished discontent, and he was attended on this occasion by none of that popular enthusiasm which accompanied him on his former visit. He made several attempts to arouse the lethargy of his partisans, but failing, he very wisely betook himself to his private duty.

In 1819 he had introduced roasted corn as a substitute for coffee, and his son superintended the manufactory during his imprisonment. On his liberation he opened several houses for the sale of this economical article; and, in 1824, he added to his business of roasting corn by commencing a manufactory of blacking. The name of the once-popular demagogue might then be seen 'rubric on the walls;' and, from being an opponent of the Whigs and Tories, he became the humble rival of Day and Martin.

ARTHUR THISTLEWOOD, RICHARD TIDD, JAMES INGS, WILLIAM DAVIDSON, AND JOHN THOMAS BRUNT,

EXECUTED FOR HIGH TREASON.

On the morning of Thursday the 24th of February, 1820, the metropolis was thrown into the greatest consternation by the fearful intelligence that a conspiracy to assassinate the whole of his majesty's ministers, and overturn the government, had been discovered and frustrated the preceding evening. In all the leading places in and about London, a proclamation was exhibited, offering a reward of one thousand pounds for the apprehension of the notorious Arthur Thistlewood, who had been formerly indicted with Dr. Watson on a charge of high treason. On the present occasion, in addition to the crime of high treason, he was charged, with that of murder, and the heaviest penalties were denounced against all who should either harbour or conceal him.

It had been known to ministers, for some time previous, that an attempt at their assassination was meditating, and that Thistlewood was at the bottom of it. After weighing various plans, the conspirators determined on accomplishing their object when the ministers were assembled at a cabinet dinner; and a meeting of this kind, at Lord Harrowby's, in Grosvenor Square, being announced in the newspaper for Wednesday, the 23d of February, Thistlewood resolved to avail himself of this opportunity for the execution of his purpose. Contemptible as his means were for effecting any political change in the government, they do not appear to have been so totally inadequate to the consummation of his immediate object as to render its success altogether improbable. The plan, as detailed in the confession of one of the conspirators, seems to have been, that a man should proceed to Lord Harrowby's residence with a letter, and when the door was opened, his companions should rush in, bind, or, in case of resistance, kill the servants, and occupy all the avenues of the house, whilst a select band were to proceed to the chamber where the ministers were assembled, and massacre the whole indiscriminately. To increase the confusion, hand-grenades were prepared, which it was intended should be thrown lighted into the several rooms; and one of the party engaged to bring away the heads of Lord Castlereagh and Sidmouth in a bag which he had provided for that purpose.

Thus far the conspirators might probably have carried their plans into effect; but of the scheme for a general revolution, which these men, whose number never exceeded thirty, appear seriously to have considered themselves capable of accomplishing, we cannot seriously speak. Among other arrangements the Mansion House, selected, we suppose, for its proximity to the Bank, was fixed upon for the 'palace of the provisional government.'

The place chosen for the final organization of their proceedings, and for collecting their force previous to immediate action, was a half dilapidated tenement in an obscure street called Cato Street, near the Edgware road. The premises were composed of a stable, with a loft above, and had been some time unoccupied. The people in the neighbourhood were ignorant that the stable was let, till the day fixed upon for the perpetration of their atrocious purpose, when several persons, some of whom carried sacks and other packages, were seen to go in and out, and carefully to lock the door after them.

The information upon which ministers proceeded, in frustrating the schemes of the conspirators, was derived from a man named Edwards, who pretended to enter into their views, for the purpose of betraying them. Odious as is the name of a spy, ministers only did that, in listening to this man's testimony, which any individual would have done under similar circumstances, for we cannot for one moment suppose them capable of hiring this man to destroy a few poor wretches, without resources of any kind, and from whom nothing could have been apprehended. It is more than probable, however, that such a man would overact his part, and create much of the mischief he was employed to prevent: indeed it was affirmed by Thistlewood that Edwards first suggested the attempt to him, and had supplied him with small sums of money for the purchase of arms.

Thus accurately informed of the intentions of the conspirators, measures were promptly taken for their apprehension. A strong body of constables and police-officers, supported by a detachment of the guards, were ordered to proceed to Cato Street, under the direction of Mr. Birnie, the magistrate. On arriving at the spot they found that the conspirators had taken the precaution to place a sentinel below, and that the only approach to the loft was by passing up a ladder, and through a trap-door so narrow as not to admit more than one at a time. Ruthven led the way, followed by Ellis, Smithers, and others, of the Bow Street patrole, and on the door being opened they discovered the whole gang, in number between twenty and thirty, hastily arming themselves. There was a carpenter's bench in the room, on which lay a number of cutlasses, bayonets, pistols, swordbelts, and a considerable quantity of ammunition. Ruthven, upon bursting into the loft, announced himself as a peace-officer, and called upon them to lay down their arms. Thistlewood stood near the door with a drawn sword, and Smithers advanced upon him, when the former made a lunge, and the unfortunate officer received the blade in his breast, and almost immediately expired.

About this time the guards, who had been delayed in consequence of entering the street at the wrong end, arrived under Captain Fitzclarence, and mounted the ladder; but as the conspirators had extinguished the light, fourteen or fifteen of them, among whom was Thistlewood, succeeded in making their escape. After a desperate conflict, in which peace-officers and military had to contend with a band of assassins, in their obscure den, and in utter darkness, nine were secured, viz. Ings, Wilson, Bradburn, Gilchrist, Cooper, Tidd, Monument, Shaw, and Davidson, and conveyed to Bow Street, with a great number of pistols, blunderbusses, swords, and pikes, a large quantity of ammunition, and a sack full of hand-grenades.

The same sources of information which led to the detection of the conspiracy disclosed the hiding-place of Thistlewood. Instead of returning to his own lodgings in Stanhope Street, Clare Market, he proceeded to an obscure house, No. 8, White Street, Little Moorfields. Thither, at nine o'clock on Thursday morning, the 24th of February, Lavender, and others of the patrol, were dispatched, and after planting a guard at the back and front, to prevent escape, they entered a room on the ground floor, in which Thistlewood was discovered in bed, with his breeches and stockings on. In his pockets were found some ball-cartridges and flints, the black girdle, or belt, which he was seen to wear in Cato Street, and a sort of military silk sash.

He was conveyed to Bow Street in a hackney-coach, where a short examination was taken by Mr. Birnie, who then sent him to Whitehall, to be examined by the privy council, before whom he was conducted at two o'clock. He was still handcuffed, but mounted the stairs with alacrity. On entering the council-chamber he was placed at the foot of the table, when the Lord Chancellor informed him that he stood charged with the twofold crime of treason and murder; and asked him whether he had any thing to say for himself. He answered, that he should decline saying any thing on that occasion.

Thistlewood was then remanded to prison, and several arrests having been made in the course of the week, the whole of the prisoners were brought to Whitehall on the 3d of March, when Thistlewood, Monument, Brunt, Ings, Wilson, Harrison, Davidson, and Tidd, were committed to the Tower as state prisoners. The other persons charged were remanded to Cold Bath Fields.

A special commission having been issued for the trial of the Cato Street conspirators, they were arraigned at the Old Bailey on Saturday, April the 15th, 1820. The following were their names, Arthur Thistlewood, William Davidson (a man of colour), James Ings, John Thomas Brunt, Richard Tidd, James Wilson, John Harrison, Richard Bradburn, John Shaw Strange, James Gilchrist, and Charles Cooper, making eleven in the whole.

These were indicted, first, for high treason, and, subsequently, for the murder of the unfortunate Smithers. The indictment contained many counts, and the whole of the prisoners pleaded Not Guilty.

Counsel having been appointed for the prisoners, according to the statute, and the other necessary forms having been gone through, Thistlewood received intimation that his trial would be proceeded with on Monday morning, the prisoners having agreed to be tried separately.

On Monday morning, April the 17th, at nine o'clock, Arthur Thistlewood was accordingly placed at the bar. He looked pale, but evinced his usual firmness. The jury having been sworn, and the indictment read, the attorney-general stated the case at great length, and twenty-five witnesses were examined in support of the prosecution, among whom were several accomplices, whose testimony was satisfactorily corroborated. Some of those who appeared to give evidence had been apprehended on the fatal night in Cato Street, but were now admitted witnesses for the crown. After a trial which occupied the Court four days, Thistlewood was found Guilty of high treason. He heard the verdict with his wonted composure, seeming to have anticipated it; for when it was pronounced he appeared quite indifferent to what so fatally concerned him.

The evidence against Tidd, Ings, Davidson, and Brunt, differed little from that upon which Thistlewood was convicted, and they were of course found Guilty. Their trials, being separate, occupied the Court six days. On the evening of the tenth day the six remaining prisoners, on the suggestion of their counsel, pleaded Guilty, having been permitted to withdraw their former plea, by which they escaped capital punishment.

On Friday, April the 28th, the eleven prisoners were brought up to receive sentence. When the usual question was put to Thistlewood by the clerk of arraigns, he pulled a paper from his pocket, and read as follows:—

'I am asked, my lord, what I have to say that judgment of death should not be passed upon me according to law. This to me is mockery—for were the reasons I could offer incontrovertible, and were they enforced even by the eloquence of a Cicero, still would the vengeance of my Lords Castlereagh and Sidmouth be satiated only in the purple stream which circulates through a heart more enthusiastically vibrating to every impulse of patriotism and honour, than that of any of those privileged traitors to their country, who lord it over the lives and property of the sovereign people with barefaced impunity. The reasons which I have, however, I will now state—not that I entertain the slightest hope from your sense of justice or from your pity.—The former is swallowed up in your ambition, or rather by the servility you descend to, to obtain the object of that ambition — the latter I despise; justice I demand; if I am denied it, your pity is no equivalent. In the first place,

' I protest against the proceedings upon my trial, which I conceive to be grossly partial, and contrary to the very spirit of justice; but, alas! the judges, who have heretofore been considered the counsel of the accused, are now, without exception, in all cases between the crown and the people, the most implacable enemies of the latter —In every instance, the judges charge the jury to find the subject guilty, nay, in one instance, the jury received a reprimand, and that not in the genteelest terms, for not strictly obeying the imperious mandate from the bench.

' The Court decided, upon my trial to commit murder rather than depart in the slightest degree from its usual forms; nay, it is with me a question, if the form is usual which precluded me from examining witnesses to prove the infamy of Adams, of Hieden, and of Dwyer. Ere the solicitor-general replied to the address of my counsel, I applied to the Court to hear my witnesses: the court inhumanly refused, and I am in consequence to be consigned to the scaffold. Numerous have been the instances in which this rule of court has been infringed, but to have infringed in my case, would have been to incur the displeasure of the court and to forfeit every aspiring hope of promotion—A few hours hence, and I will be no more —but the nightly breeze which will whistle over the silent grave that shall protect me from its keenness, will bear to your restless pillow the memory of one who lived but for his country, and died when liberty and justice had been driven from its confines, by a set of villains, whose thirst for blood is only to be equalled by their activity in plunder.

'For life, as it respects myself, I care not—but while yet I may, I would rescue my memory from the calumny which I doubt not will be industriously heaped upon it, when it will be no longer in my power to protect it.

'I would explain the motives which induced me to conspire against the ministers of his majesty, and I would contrast them with those which these very ministers have acted upon in leading me to my ruin.—To do this, it will be necessary to take a short review of my life for a few months, prior to my arrest for the offence for which I am to be executed, without a trial, or at least, without an impartial one by a jury of my peers.

' 'Tis true the form, the etiquette, of a trial has been gone through, but I challenge any of the judges on the bench to tell me, to tell my country that justice was not denied me in the very place where justice only should be administered.—I challenge them to say that I was fairly tried—I challenge to say if I am not murdered—according to the etiquette of a court (falsely denominated) of justice I had witnesses in court to prove that Dwyer was a villian beyond all example of atrocity.—I had witnesses in court to prove that Adams was a notorious swindler, and that Hieden was no better; these were the three witnesses; indeed almost the only ones against me, but the form and rules of court must not be infringed upon to save an unfortunate individual from the scaffold.

'I called those witnesses at the close of Mr. Adolphus's address to the jury, and before the solicitor-general commenced his reply, but the court decided, that they could not be heard.—Some good men have thought, and I have thought so too—that before the jury retired, all evidence was in time for either the prosecutor or the accused, and more particularly for the latter— nay, even before the verdict was given, that evidence could not be considered too late—Alas! such people draw their conclusion from principles of justice only—they never canvassed the rules of court which have finally sealed my unhappy doom.

'Many people who are acquainted with the bare-faced manner which I was plundered by my Lord Sidmouth, will perhaps, imagine that personal motives instigated me to the deed—but I disclaim them. My every principle was for the prosperity of my country—my every feeling—the height of my ambition was the welfare of my starving country. I keenly felt for their miseries —but when their miseries were laughed at, and when because they dared to express those miseries, they were cut down by hundreds, inhumanly massacred and trampled upon, when infant babes were sabred in their mothers' arms, nay when the breast from whence they drew the tide of life, was severed from the body, which supplied that tide —My feelings became too intense, too excessive for endurance, and I resolved on vengeance—I resolved that the lives of the instigators should be the requiem to the souls of the murdered innocents.

'In this mood I met with George Edwards, and if any doubt should remain upon the minds of the public whether the deed I meditated was virtuous or contrary, the tale I will now relate will convince them, that in attempting to exercise a power which the law had ceased to have—I was only wreaking national vengeance on a set of wretches unworthy of the name or character of men.

'This Edwards, poor and penyless, lived near Picket Street, in the Strand, some time ago, without a bed to lie upon, or a chair to sit in. Straw was his resting-place; his only covering a blanket. Owing to his bad character, and his swindling conduct, he was driven from thence by his landlord. It is not my intention to trace him through his immorality: suffice it to say, that he was, in every sense of the word, a villain of the deepest atrocity. His landlord refused to give him a character: some short time after this, he called upon his landlord again, but mark the change in his appearance, dressed like a lord, in all the folly of the reigning fashion. He now described himself as the right heir to a German Baron, who had been some time dead; that Lords Castlereagh and Sidmouth had acknowledged his claims to the title and property, had interfered in his behalf with the German government, and supplied him with money to support his rank in society. From this period I date his career as a government spy.

'He got himself an introduction to the Spenceans, by what means I am not aware of; and thus he became acquainted with the reformers a general. When I met with Edwards, after the massacre at Manchester, he described himself as very poor; and after several interviews, he proposed a plan for blowing up the House of Commons. This was not my view: I wished to punish the guilty only, and therefore I declined it. He next proposed that we should attack the ministers at the fête given by the Spanish ambassador. This I resolutely opposed; because the innocent would perish with the guilty: besides, there were ladies invited to the entertainment, and I, who am shortly to ascend the scaffold, shuddered with horror at the idea of that, a sample of which had previously been given by the agents of government at Manchester, and which the ministers of his majesty applauded. Edwards was ever at invention; and at length he proposed attacking them at a cabinet dinner. I asked where were the means to carry his project into effect? He replied, if I would accede, we should not want for means. He was as good as his word: from him, notwithstanding his apparent penury, the money was provided for purchasing the stores which your lordships has seen produced in court upon my trial. He, who was never possessed of money to pay for a pint of beer, had always plenty to purchase arms or ammunition. Amongst the conspirators, he was ever the most active; ever inducing people to join him, up to the last hour ere the undertaking was discovered.

'I had witnesses in court, who could prove they went to Cato Street by appointment with Edwards, with no other knowledge or motive than that of passing an evening amongst his friends. I could also have proved, that subsequent to the fatal transaction, when we met in Holborn, he endeavoured to induce two or three of my companions to set fire to houses and buildings in various parts of the metropolis. I could prove that, subsequent to that again, he endeavoured to induce men to throw hand-grenades into the carriages of ministers, as they passed through the streets; and yet this man, the contriver, the instigator, the entrapper, is secured from justice and from exposure by those very men who seek vengeance against the victims of his and their villainy.—To the attorney and solicitor-general I cannot impute the clearest motives; their object seems to me to have been rather to obtain a verdict against me than to obtain a full and fair exposition of the whole affair, since its commencement. If their object was justice alone, why not bring him forward as a witness, if not as an accomplice; but no, they knew that by keeping Edwards in the back ground, my proofs, aye, my incontrovertible proofs of his being a hired spy, the suggestor and promoter must, according to the rules of court, also be excluded.

'Edwards and his accomplices arranged matters in such a manner as that his services might be dispensed with on the trial, and thus were the jury cut off from every chance of ascertaining the real truth.—Adams, Hieden, and Dwyer were the agents of Edwards, and truly he made a most admirable choice, for their invention seems to be inexhaustible. With respect to the immorality of our project, I will just observe, that the assassination of a tyrant has always been deemed a meritorious action. Brutus and Cassius were lauded to the very skies for slaying Cæsar; indeed, when any man, or any set of men place themselves above the laws of their country, there is no other means of bringing them to justice than through the arm of a private individual. If the laws are not strong enough to prevent them from murdering the community, it becomes the duty of every member of that community to rid his country of its oppressors.

'High treason was committed against the people at Manchester, but justice was closed against the mutilated, the maimed, and the friends of those who were, upon that occasion, indiscriminately massacred. The prince, by the advice of his ministers, thanked the murderers, still reeking in the gore of their hapless victims. If one spark of honour, if one spark of independence still glimmered in the breasts of Englishmen, they would have rose to a man. Insurrection then became a public duty; and the blood of the victims should have been the watch-word to vengeance on their murderers. The banner of independence should have floated in the gale that brought their wrongs and their sufferings to the metropolis. Such, however, was not the case—Albion is still in the chains of slavery. I quit it without regret—I shall soon be consigned to the grave—My body will be immured beneath the soil whereon I first drew breath—My only sorrow is, that the soil should be a theatre for slaves, for cowards, for despots. My motives, I doubt not, will hereafter be justly appreciated.—I will therefore now conclude, by stating that I shall consider myself as murdered, if I am to be executed on the verdict obtained against me by the refusal of the court to hear my evidence.

'I could have proved Dwyer to be a villain of the blackest dye—for since my trial, an accomplice of his, named Arnold, has been capitally convicted at this very bar, for obtaining money under circumstances of an infamous nature.

'I seek not pity; I demand but

justice. I have not had a fair trial, and upon that ground I protest that judgment ought not to be passed against me.'

The lord chief justice, during the reading of this address, more than once interposed, to prevent the prisoner from either seeking to justify assassination, or slandering the characters of witnesses who had appeared to give evidence in that court. The prisoner, however, proceeded to read till he had finished what had been written on the paper in his hand. His manner was rapid and confused; and the mode in which he pronounced several words, gave abundant evidence that this paper was not his own composition.

Mr. Shelton then put the same question to Davidson, who spoke, and with great vehemence, and much gesticulation, nearly as follows:—

'My lords, you ask me what I have to say why I should not receive judgment to die for what has been said against me? I answer that I protest against the proceedings in this trial in toto. In the first place, I always thought that in a court of justice, the balance of justice was held with an even hand. But this has not been the case with me; I stand here helpless and friendless. I endeavour to shew that the evidence against me was contradictory and incredible, and I hoped I had made an impression on the gentlemen in the box; but the moment I was done, the attorney-general got up and told them, that the evidence was pure and uncontaminated, and to this I may add, that Baron Garrow almost insisted that they should pronounce me guilty. I would ask, has any person identified me but the officers? who, every one knows, have at all times been instrumental in the death of innocent persons. I do not now plead for my life; I know I must fall a victim to the vengeance of my enemies. But in what manner have I been guilty of high treason? It would seem I was a silent spectator; none of the witnesses impute to me a single observation. Now is this probable? I had always got a great deal to say for myself, consequently I was not the person who would stand by without uttering a word; and yet such has been the testimony of Adams. Then, with regard to the blunderbuss, I have already explained that this was not mine, and that I acted in that affair entirely as the agent of Edwards. I have also declared how I came by the sword, and I now declare upon my soul which will shortly appear before its Maker, that I never made any blow at any man, or discharged any carbine. As for Munday, the man who swore that I had a long sword, with a pair of pistols in my girdle, who is he? He is a poor labouring man who comes here for his day's pay and his victuals, to swear away the life of a fellow-creature, and to suport the unfounded charge against me that I meant to assassinate his majesty's ministers. I appeal to any man, whether it is upon such evidence the life of an innocent man is to be sacrificed? But even supposing, for the sake of argument, that the lives of his majesty's ministers were threatened, it did not follow that this was to extend to the king himself. In a passage of Magna Charta, it was ordained, that twenty-five barons should be nominated to see that the terms of the charter were not infringed; and if it was found his majesty's ministers were guilty of such infringement, then four barons were to call upon them for redress. If this were not granted, then the four barons were to return to their brethren, by whom the people were to be called together to take up arms, and assert their rights. Such an act was not considered, in old times, as an act of treason towards the king, however hostile it might be towards his ministers. But this does not apply to me. I had no intention of joining in any scheme whatever, either to put down my king, or to murder his ministers. I was entrapped by Goldworthy and Edwards, in order, for some private purposes of their own, that they might have my life sworn away. I have no objection to tender my life in the service of my country; but let me at least, for the sake of my children, save my character from the disgrace of dying a traitor. For my children only do I feel, and when I think of them I am deprived of utterance—I can say no more."

Mr. Shelton, having put the same questions to Ings, he said:—

'My lords,—I have very little to say. My abilities will not allow me to speak. If Mr. Edwards had not got acquainted with me, I should not be here; he came to me, unfortunately, when I had no business, nor no means of getting a living for my family. I entered into the conspiracy only through him, and it was only necessity, and the want of the means to support my wife and family, that brought me here. It is only through Edwards that I shall lose my life. I do not mind dying, if you will let that man come forward, and die with me on the scaffold. It was through him I was going to do that which, I must allow, was of a most disgraceful and inhuman nature. On the other hand, his majesty's ministers conspire together and impose laws to starve me and my family and fellow-countrymen; and if I was going to assassinate these ministers, I do not see that it is so bad as starvation, in my opinion, my lord.'

Here Mr. Shelton began to address the prisoner Brunt but Ings said:

'I am not done. And there is another thing, my lord; a meeting was called at Manchester, under the protection of the law of England, for which our forefathers died, and which King John signed in the open air. This meeting was called under the protection of that law, for the people to petition parliament to give them their rights; but, previous to the business of the meeting, the Manchester yeomanry rode in among them, and cut down men, women, and children, in a manner that was a disgrace to the very name of Englishmen. These yeomen had their swords ground beforehand, and I had a sword ground also, but I do not see any harm in that. I shall suffer, no doubt; but I hope my children will live to see justice done to their bleeding country. I would rather die like a man than live like a slave. I am sorry I have not the power to say more; I shall therefore withdraw.'

John Thomas Brunt was next called upon, and spoke as follows:—

'My lords and gentlemen,—I am precluded from saying much: I had intended to have committed to writing my defence, but I have been denied pen, ink, and paper—as such, what I have to state will be very short. In the first place, whatever impression I made on the jury yesterday was knocked down by the solicitor-general, who appears to me, by his sophistical eloquence, to be capable of making the worst of crimes appear a virtue. And next, with regard to Edwards, to whom I alluded before, and to whose machinations I have at last fallen a dupe: he once before nearly entrapped me when a cabinet dinner was given, I believe, at the Earl of Westmoreland's. He said he had part of the men mustered, but there was not sufficient. He had like to have hooked me in then, but I happened not to go to the house. No doubt that Hieden was in that plot for me; it was held at the Scotch Arms. Of all the infamous characters on earth, Edwards is the worst; and yet he has been kept altogether out of the view of the Court. I protest against the verdict which has been pronounced against me. For my life, if it was sacrificed in the cause of liberty, I care not a farthing; but it is galling to have it sworn away by a set of villains who thirst after blood, merely for the sake of personal gain. Edwards is far more worthy of punishment than any of us. He it was that furnished the arms—and he it was that goaded us on to our own ruin. He always spoke well of me, and said, if he had a hundred such men as me, he would be satisfied. He knew I was not a shuttle-cock, to be bandied about at pleasure. He knew he could put confidence in my word, and that I would perish before I shrunk from what I undertook. (The prisoner then went on in a strain of strong invective against the witness Adams. After which he referred to the two Monuments. These two persons had been described by the solicitor-general, as having had no communication with each other, and yet having agreed 'n all respects in their testimony. Was this the fact? No, for three weeks previous to the trials, they met twice a day at the Tower, rehearsed their story, and thus were enabled to come forward quite perfect in their respective parts. He next adverted to the character of his apprentice Hale, and was casting strong reflections on his conduct)—when

The chief justice said he could not suffer such observations to be made under such circumstances.

Brunt begged pardon, but said he stated nothing but facts. He next adverted to the conduct of Lords Castlereagh and Sidmouth; 'They,' he said, 'had been the cause of the death of millions, and although he admitted he had conspired to put such men out of the world, still he did not think that amounted to high treason. He was one of those who would have been satisfied with taking off the cabinet ministers; but the verdict against him, of intending to depose his majesty, he contended, was utterly at variance with truth and justice. He had never contemplated any such consequence. He was neither a traitor to his king nor to his country; nor would he suffer any man, in his presence, to speak irreverently of his sovereign. In undertaking to kill Lord Castlereagh, Lord Sidmouth, and their fellow ministers, he did not expect to save his life—he was determined to die a martyr in his country's cause, and to avenge the innocent blood shed at Manchester.

In conclusion, he said, 'he was willing to suffer for the acts which he had contemplated; but it grieved him to think that he was to suffer for a crime of which he was innocent, namely, High Treason. On these grounds, he protested against the verdict of the jury, as contrary to law and justice.'

Richard Tidd was the next called upon. He spoke as follows:—

'My lords and gentlemen, being only found guilty so late last night, I have not had an opportunity to make up any defence. All I can say is, and I positively swear it, that the evidence that has come before you, with the exception of that of Captain Fitzclarence, is utterly false.'

James Wilson said, 'I am not gifted with the power of talking much, but I mean to say, that I was certainly drawn into this by Edwards.'

John Harrison.—'I likewise say I was brought into it by Edwards.'

John Shaw Strange.—'I have this much to say to the evidence of Brunt's apprentice, likewise that of Adams, I declare solemnly to God they are both perjured villains.'

James Gilchrist.—'What I shall say in the presence of my God and you is, that till the Wednesday evening at four o'clock I knew nothing about this business. I was going to look for work, and I had neither money nor bread. So I went to what I was told was to be a supper of the radicals. (Here the prisoner was overcome by his feelings.) At six o'clock I met C. Cooper, who was the only man I knew, and I borrowed an half-penny of him, which, with another, enabled me to get a pennyworth of bread, and this I eat very sweet. I wish I may never come out of this place if I tell false. We then went into the stable and up stairs, where there was some bread and cheese. I took an old sword and hewed down the loaf, of which others who were as hungry as me, partook. I then asked what all these arms were about, and when I heard, I was so shocked that I determined to get away as fast as I could. Soon after the officers and soldiers came, and I thought it my duty to surrender. I now stand here convicted of high treason, after I served my king and country for twelve years, and this is the recompence. Oh, God!—I have nothing more to say.'

Charles Cooper said, he had much to say, but his friends thought it would be imprudent. He said, 'he could only declare that he was not guilty of the crime imputed to him.'

Gilchrist again came forward, and said, 'he was very willing to give up his life if it could save that of a fellow-creature. He had already tendered it to save one of the poor men by his side. He never thought of such a thing as to take any man's life.'

The crier of the court now proclaimed silence in the usual manner, while sentence of Death was passing upon the prisoners:—

The Lord Chief Justice then proceeded to address the prisoners severally by their respective names, making a distinction between those who had withdrawn their pleas of 'Not Guilty,' and pleaded 'Guilty,' and those who had been convicted by juries of their country. If any of them should ultimately have their lives spared, which he trusted would be the case, he hoped they would always bear in mind that they owed that life to the benignity and merciful disposition of their sovereign, aided and seconded also by the merciful dispositions of those very persons upon whom they had contemplated the foul crime of assassination. One of them, Arthur Thistlewood, had upon his trial proposed to call certain witnesses, whom the Court had refused to hear. This refusal was according to the due course of justice, as it was administered in this country. The witnesses whom he proposed to call, were for the purpose of impugning the testimony of a man of the name of Dwyer, and no other. His learned counsel had previously called witnesses to the same effect. It could not be allowed to him, according to the ordinary course of proceeding, to do more. Indeed, even if he had been allowed so to do, it could have been productive of no advantage, because his case did not depend upon the evidence of that witness alone. This observation was confirmed by the fact, that in subsequent cases, where the evidence of Dwyer was altogether omitted, a similar verdict of guilty was returned. Some of them had thought fit to say much of the character of a person who had not appeared as a witness upon this occasion. The Court could proceed only upon the evidence which was brought before it. Of the person, therefore, to whom they alluded, or of the practices of which he had been guilty, they could have no knowledge. Upon the testimony, however, which had been adduced against them, there was abundantly sufficient to induce a jury of their country to come to a conclusion that the whole of them had taken an active part in the crimes imputed to them in the indictment. From all that had appeared in the course of these trials, as well as from much of that which they had then heard, it was plain to see, that they did not embark in their wicked designs until they had first suffered their minds to be corrupted and inflamed by those seditious and irreligious publications, with which, unhappily for this country, the press had but too long teemed. He did not make these remarks to aggravate their guilt, or to enhance the sufferings of persons in their situation. He made them as a warning to all who might hear of their unfortunate fate, that they might benefit by their example, and avoid those dangerous instruments of sedition, by which their hearts and minds were inflamed, and by which they were drawn from every feeling of morality,—from every sense of obligation towards their Creator, and of justice towards society. The treason of which they were charged and found Guilty, was that of compassing and imagining to levy war against his majesty, for the purpose of inducing him to change his measures and ministers; the first step towards effecting which, was to have been the assassination of the cabinet ministers. They had endeavoured now to complain of the testimony of those persons who had been examined as witnesses on the part of the prosecution. Some of them were accomplices in their guilt. It had here happened, as it had upon other occasions, that the principal instruments in the hands of justice, were the partners of their wickedness; and he trusted that circumstance would have its due weight and consideration with all those who became acquainted with their situation, and with the circumstances of their trial. He hoped, that for the sake of their own personal safety, if they could not be restrained by any other consideration, that they would abstain from evil communications, and from evil connexions, such as had brought the prisoners to the unhappy position in which they stood. Some of them had avowed their intention to have taken away the lives, and to have steeped their hands in the blood of fourteen persons, to many of them unknown—a crime of a character so black, that it was hitherto without parallel in the history of this country, and he hoped it would remain unparalleled hereafter. (His lordship here seemed considerably agitated.) It now, he said, only remained for him to pass upon them the awful sentence of the law; but before he did so, he exhorted them, he implored them, to employ the time yet left to them in this life, in endeavouring, by prayer, to obtain mercy from that Almighty Power, before whom they would shortly appear. The mercy of Heaven might be obtained by all those who would unfeignedly and with humility express contrition for their offences, and seek that mercy through the merits of their blessed Redeemer.

His lordship having once more solemnly exhorted the prisoners to repentance, pronounced the awful sentence of the law in the following words:—

'That you, and each of you, be taken from hence to the gaol from whence you came, and from thence that you be drawn upon a hurdle to a place of execution, and be there hanged by the neck until you be dead; and that afterwards your heads shall be severed from your bodies, and your bodies be divided into four quarters, to be disposed of as his majesty shall think fit. And may God of his infinite goodness have mercy upon your souls!'

The Crier said aloud 'Amen!'

On the following Monday the execution of Thistlewood, Ings, Brunt, Davidson, and Tidd took place opposite the debtors' door, Newgate. With the exception of Davidson, they refused all religious consolation, and when on the scaffold, Thistlewood, who was the first brought out, turned away with marked indifference from the ordinary.

Tidd was next summoned. He proceeded to shake hands with all but Davidson, who had removed himself at a small distance from the rest.

At the moment Tidd was going out, Ings seized him by the hand, crying out with loud laughter, 'Come, give us your hand!—Good by!' Nature began to assert her claims in Tidd's bosom: a tear glistened in his eye; and he faintly murmured something about his 'Wife and daughter,' as some understood. Ings, with the most alarming levity of manner, said, 'Come, my old cock-o'-wax, keep up your spirits: it will all be over soon!' Tidd appeared to squeeze his hand, and then actually attempted to run up the steps to the scaffold. In his haste or agitation he stumbled; but speedily recovered himself, and ran upon the scaffold in the most hurried manner; and when there, he appeared as if he actually stamped his feet, as if in the act of affecting to run with eagerness to his grave! He was received by the surrounding multitude with loud cheers, which he returned by repeated bows; and with some apparent wish to return them in the same manner in which they were given; but this wish, if he really entertained it, he repressed.

Whilst the executioner was tying the rope round his neck, he appeared to recognize some friend in an adjoining window; and he nodded to him, with an appearance of great familiarity and ease. He repeatedly turned round and surveyed the multitude on every band. He then looked down upon the coffins behind him, and attempted to smile with indifference and contempt of them. He repeatedly sucked at an orange he held in his hand; as also did Thistlewood to one in his. He also requested that his eyes might yet be uncovered, and whilst the executioner was adjusting the rope round his neck, he assisted him, and told him to place the knot in a certain direction, as if thereby better calculated to hasten the termination of his dying pains. It is almost needless to remark, that Mr. Cotton's tender of service was rejected by Tidd, as they had been by Thistlewood before.

Ings was the next summoned. From his first leaving the Press Yard he manifested the most determined obduracy. He laughed without the least apparent thought of what he was going to suffer; and whilst in the lodge he sucked an orange, and sang, or rather screamed,

'Oh! give me Death or Liberty!'

to which Brunt, who stood near him, rejoined, 'Aye, to be sure: it is better to die free than to live like slaves.'

On being earnestly and charitably desired to turn their attention to more serious subjects, and to recollect the existence of a God, into whose presence they would soon be ushered, Brunt said, 'I know there is a God,' and Ings, agreeing to this, added, 'that he hoped he would be more merciful to them than they were then.'

Just as the hatch was opening to admit him to the steps of the scaffold, he turned round to Brunt, and smiling, shook him by the hand, and then with a loud voice cried out, 'Remember me to King George the Fourth; God bless him, and may he have a long reign!' Then recollecting that he had left off the suit of clothes in which he had been tried; but which, after his conviction he had exchanged for his old slaughtering jacket, because, as he said, he was resolved that Jack Ketch should have no coat of his, he desired his wife might have what clothes he had thrown off. He then said to Mr. Davies, one of the turnkey's, "Well, Mr. Davies, I am going to find out this great secret.'

He was again proceeding to sing

'Oh! give me Death or Liberty!'

when he was called to the platform, upon which he leaped and bounded in the most frantic manner. Then turning himself round towards Smithfield, and facing the very coffin that was soon to receive his mutilated body, he raised his pinioned hands, as well as he could, and leaning forward with savage energy roared out three distinct cheers to the people, in a voice of the most frightful and discordant hoarseness. But, it was pleasing to remark, that these unnatural yells of desperation, which were evidently nothing more than the ravings of a disordered mind, or the ebullitions of an assumed courage, were not returned by the motley mass of people who heard them.

Turning his face towards Ludgate Hill, he bowed, and cried out, 'Here's the last remains of James Ings!' And again sung aloud, preserving the well known tune of that song as much as possible,

'Oh! Give me Death or Liberty!
'Oh! Give me Death or Liberty!"

Observing some persons near him, and amongst them one who was taking notes, he said, 'Mind, I die an enemy to all tyrants. Mind, and put that down!' Upon viewing the coffins, he laughed, and said 'he would turn his back on death. Those coffins are for us, I suppose.'

At this time Tidd, who had been just spoken to by Thistlewood, was heard to remonstrate with Ings, and to tell him not to make such a noise; adding, 'we can die without making a noise,' upon which Ings for a moment was silent; but soon burst out afresh, asking the executioner not to cover his eyes, as he wished to see as long as he could. At another time he said, 'Mind you do it well—pull it tight;' or, as some heard it. 'Do it tidy.' He also requested to have a greater length of rope to fall; and that at last his eyes should be tightly bandaged round, with a handkerchief which he held in his hand.

Upon the approach of Mr. Cotton to this poor hardened man, he rejected his pious services; but cried out, as if sarcastically, 'I hope you'll give me a good character, won't you, Mr. Cotton?'

Davidson was the next summoned; and it is truly gratifying to state the difference that marked the character and conduct of him who had derived his fortitude to face death, and all its awful preparations, from other principles and sources than those from whence the rest appeared to have borrowed their wild courage and daring.

Davidson's whole soul had been absorbed in reflections respecting a future state, and his own condition in that 'unknown country' which he was now going to enter; and he was remarked to walk with a firm and steady step from the lodge to the platform, which he ascended without the least apparent emotion of fear; but with all that respectful humiliation which such a condition to which he had reduced himself was calculated to inspire. His lips moved in prayer, yet he gently bowed to the people before him. He joined with great fervour in the prayers with Mr. Cotton, and made no request to have his eyes uncovered; but was evidently labouring to prepare himself for bidding an eternal adieu to a world of which he had ceased to be an inhabitant; and to hasten to one into which he had hope and confidence he should be received with comfort.

The last summoned to the fatal platform was Brunt; and when the proper arrangements had been made the fatal signal was given, and the wretched men were launched into eternity. After hanging half an hour the disgusting ceremony of decapitation took place.

Five of those who pleaded Guilty were transported for life, and Gilchrist, who though taken amongst the rest in the loft in Cato Street, had, it appeared, been induced to go there in total ignorance of the atrocious purpose for which the assemblage took place, received his majesty's pardon.

Having thus acquainted the reader with the particulars of the horrid Cato Street plot, we shall proceed to give a brief biographical sketch of the principal performers in the revolting drama.

Arthur Thistlewood was a native of Horncastle, in Lincolnshire, and was born in 1770. His father was a land-steward to an ancient family in that neighbourhood, and maintained through life an unblemished character. Arthur was placed early in life under an eminent schoolmaster, to be educated as a land-surveyor. This pursuit he subsequently abandoned, and evinced a great predilection for indolence and pleasure. Through the interests of his friends, at the age of twenty-one, he obtained a lieutenancy in the militia, which he subsequently exchanged for one in a marching regiment.

Soon after this he married a young lady of property, her fortune being ten thousand pounds. This step, so promising in the outset, was pregnant with future troubles. Thistlewood imagined her fortune to be at her own disposal; but it was, in fact, so settled that she was entitled to the interest only during her life, and at her death the principal reverted to her relations. Sixteen months after marriage this lady died in childbed, and Thistlewood was left without a shilling of her property.

At the commencement of the revolutionary war, Thistlewood accompanied his regiment to the West Indies, where he soon gave up his commission, and proceeded to America. From America he sailed for France, and arrived there soon after the fall of the tyrant Robespierre. In Paris he became initiated in all the doctrines of the revolutionists, and actually entered the French service, and was at several battles. Although a man of but middling talent, he had a considerable knowledge of military tactics; was a good swordsman, and possessed undeniable courage. His habitual hatred of oppression involved him in many disputes, and it is but justice to say that most of these redound to his credit. After the peace of Amiens he returned to England, and found himself possessed of a considerable estate, which accrued to him on the death of a relative; but his evil genius still accompanied him. He sold this property to a person at Durham for ten thousand pounds, who becoming a bankrupt before the money was paid, Thistlewood found himself again reduced to comparative poverty.

Thistlewood's father and brother, both of whom resided in Lincolnshire, now took a farm, and stocked it for him; but, in consequence of high rent and taxes, he found himself an annual loser by the speculation, and of course abandoned agriculture.

Previous to this, however, he had been married to his second wife, Miss Wilkinson, of Horncastle, a woman who perfectly coincided in the political opinions of her husband.

Driven from the country, he repaired to London with his wife, and contracted an acquaintance with the Spenceans. A propensity to gaming seems to have been the first step to his ruin. In early life he lost considerable sums at the *hells* of London, and this vicious habit did not abandon him in his later years, as it was well known the gaming-table was his only resource against the pressing demands of his family; and precarious indeed must have been the subsistence derived from such a vile pursuit.

In London his constant companions were the Watsons, Evans's, &c.; and the consequence of this connexion the reader may learn by a reference to the case of Dr. Watson. His acquittal at that time, on the charge of high treason, seems not to have taught him more prudence. He had been scarcely released from incarceration when he sent a challenge, to fight a duel, to Lord Sidmouth; the consequence of which was a motion in the Court of King's Bench, and Thistlewood was sentenced to six months' imprisonment in Horsham Gaol.

Before this last confinement his dress was genteel, and his air that of a military man; but, after his release from Horsham Gaol, his dress indicated extreme poverty. His coat was threadbare, and his shoes broken. Of this he appeared sensible; for, in passing through the streets, he either walked very quickly or ran in haste, apparently with the design of avoiding observation.

Oppressed by poverty, and instigated by revenge and want, he forgot the lessons misfortune should have taught him; he listened to the sanguinary suggestions of the villain Edwards, and entered but too eagerly into the trap that was laid for him. The police watched his movements, and his every word and action were known to the secretary of state. Strange, indeed, was the infatuation he laboured under; and, if we look upon him as perfectly sane, his conduct must appear unaccountable. He had already been the dupe of a government spy, and might easily have seen a second edition of Castles in Edwards. But the wretched man was occasionally supplied with money, and his case being desperate, danger, in his eyes, lost its forbidding aspect. The jaws of destruction were extended before him, and he rushed upon his fate with all its horrors staring him in the face. A man of such a sanguinary disposition was not fit to live; and, though we may depre-

-cate the means used to draw him into treason, we must rejoice that his punishment purged society of one of its most dangerous members.

Thistlewood was in his person tall and thin; his countenance was dark, but by no means expressive, unless when impressed with that gloomy malignity in which he too often indulged. He had no issue by either of his wives, but a natural son took leave of him the day before execution.

The following lines are said to have been written by him while under sentence of death in Newgate:—
'Oh! what a twine of mischief is a statesman!
Ye furies! whirlwinds! and ye treach'rous rocks!
Ye ministers of death! devouring fires!
Convulsive earthquakes! and plague-tainted air!
Ye are all mild and merciful to him!!'

Richard Tidd was born at Grantham, in Lincolnshire, in 1775. He was apprenticed to Mr. Cante, of Grantham, but quitted his situation at sixteen years of age. He then went to Nottingham, where he lived two years and a half; from thence he came to London, where he resided till 1803; when, having voted for Sir Francis Burdett, at the Middlesex election, without being a freeholder, he fled to Scotland to avoid prosecution for perjury, a reward of one hundred pounds being at the time offered for his apprehension. In that country he remained five years.

On his return from the north he went to live at Rochester, where for some time he worked at his trade of shoemaker. Having again returned to London, he was engaged in the conspiracy for which Colonel Despard suffered; but a temporary absence from town preserved him from sharing the same fate.

His last stay in town commenced on the 10th of March, 1818. From that time he attended all Mr. Hunt's meetings, public and private, and was present at all the subsequent radical meetings. He was introduced to Edwards by Brunt, at his own residence, Hole-in-the-Wall Passage, Baldwin's Gardens. Edwards's assumed violence suited his disposition, and he eagerly closed with every proposition, however desperate.

It was a most extraordinary circumstance that he had constantly an impression on his mind, for the last twenty years, that he was to be hanged, as he frequently expressed to his wife that he should die on the gallows. He was, unhappily, too good a prophet; and thus a life of irregularity terminated in the most ignominious manner.

Tidd, during the war, enlisted into more than half of the regiments under the crown, and received the different bounties. It is astonishing how he escaped detection; he was always in disguise when he enlisted, and as soon as he had obtained the bounty he deserted. When he had spent the money he enlisted into another regiment.

It will be evident from this account, that the statements of his uniform good character and conduct published at the period of his first arrest, for the crime of which he was ultimately found guilty, were put forth by some zealous friend, to produce a favourable impression on the public mind in his behalf.

Tidd was forty-five years of age at the time of his execution, and left a wife, a daughter, and a brother, to deplore his fate.

James Ings was the son of a respectable tradesman in Hampshire. He commenced business as a butcher at Portsmouth, where he married; at which time he had a handsome property, consisting of several houses, and some money in the funds.

Trade growing bad at the termination of the war, and his property having decreased, some of his tenements were sold, and he came up to London in 1818, with a little ready money, produced by the sale of a house, and opened a butcher's shop at the west end of the town. He could, however, get no business, and in a few months gave up the shop; and, with a few pounds he had left, he opened a coffee-shop in Whitechapel.

Business becoming dull there, he was involved in great distress, and at last was compelled to pawn his watch to enable him to send his wife and children down to Portsmouth to her friends, to prevent their starving in London.

At the coffee-house in Whitechapel he sold, besides coffee, political pamphlets. Having given up the shop, and finding that there was no prospect of supporting himself and his family with credit, he gave himself up to despair. He had read the different Deistical publications during the time he sold pamphlets, and, from being a churchman became a confirmed Deist.

He was a most affectionate husband and father; and his desperate situation, no doubt, was a principal cause of his joining the Cato Street plot.

Edwards, Adams, Thistlewood, and Brunt, had frequently visited Ings during the time he kept the coffee and pamphlet shop; and, when he was in more desperate circumstances, he became a fitter companion for persons engaged in such an atrocious crime as the one for which he suffered the sentence of the law.

For some weeks before the Cato Street discovery, Ings was in the utmost distress, quite pennyless, and the money he was supplied with to subsist upon was given him by George Edwards. Ings was also supplied with money by the same person to take an apartment, where arms and ammunition could be safely placed. He took a room in the house where Brunt lodged, and thither the greater part of the ammunition and arms was conveyed by Edwards, Adams, and himself; indeed it was the depôt of the conspirators.

This unfortunate man left a wife and four children to deplore his ignominious death.

William Davidson was born in the year 1786, at Kingston, in Jamaica, and was the second son of Mr. Attorney-General Davidson, a man of considerable legal knowledge and talent. His mother was a native of the West Indies, and a woman of colour.

He was sent to England when very young, for the purpose of receiving an education suitable to the rank of his father, and his own prospects.

Having learned the first rudiments of education, he was sent to an academy, where he studied mathematics; and after some time he was apprenticed to a respectable attorney at Liverpool, at whose office he remained near three years, when he became tired of confinement, and ran away from his master. He entered on board a merchantman, and on the first voyage was impressed. He arrived in England about six months afterwards, and wrote to his father's friend a supplicatory letter. His father's friend sent for him, and, at his own particular desire, apprenticed him to a cabinet-maker in Liverpool.

Davidson, though a man of colour, had a prepossessing person, and was upon the point of marriage to the daughter of a respectable tradesman at Liverpool; but her friends prevented the match. Being somewhat disappointed, he determined to leave England, and visit his relatives at Kingston, in Jamaica.

He took a passage on board of a West-India merchantman, and on his voyage again experienced the misfortune of being impressed into the king's service. He took the first opportunity of running away from the vessel on its arrival in port; and, having obtained some money from his friends, he got work at his trade as a journeyman.

About twelve months after his mother allowed him two guineas a week, which was paid him regularly through her agent. Davidson was employed by Mr. Bullock, a cabinet-maker, at Litchfield, and was a most excellent workman.

With his mother's allowance he was able to live and dress very genteelly; and the company he kept was highly respectable. By some accident he met at Litchfield a young lady of the name of Salt, who had at her own disposal, when of age, the sum of seven thousand pounds. He paid his addresses to her with her mother's permission, but her father disapproving of the intercourse, the match was broken off, and the young lady subsequently married another; an event which filled Davidson with great affliction.

Having received twelve hundred pounds from his mother, he entered into an extensive way of business at Birmingham; but being, from the disappointment in his marriage with Miss Salt, rendered quite unsettled in his mind, he did not attend to his business, and in a short time the whole of his money was expended.

After his failure he came to London, and was employed as a journeyman by a cabinet-maker. He affected a great deal of sanctity; attended a Methodist meeting-house, and became a teacher in a Sunday school; but his conduct towards one of the female scholars being far from decorous he fell into disrepute.

He subsequently entered into business for himself at Walworth, and then married a Mrs. Lane, the widow of a respectable man, who had left her with four small children. For a short time he appeared to be doing well; at length, trade falling off, he was obliged to remove to London, and take a lodging in Mary-le-bone.

On the Sunday night, when Davidson parted, for the last time, with his distressed wife, he expressed himself very strong against Lord Sidmouth.

After he had kissed her, he said, 'If I should betray a weakness when I come out on the scaffold, I hope the world will not attribute it to cowardice, but to my intense feelings for you and my dear children. Farewell, love! pray that God will take mercy on me, and receive my soul!' Mrs. Davidson then left him.

This unfortunate woman was left with six children; four by her former husband, and two fine boys by Davidson, both under four years of age.

John Thomas Brunt was born in Union Street, Oxford Street, London. His father, a tailor, apprenticed him at the age of fourteen to Mr. Brooke's, a lady's shoemaker, in Union Street He served Mr. Brookes till he was eighteen years of age, when, his father dying, his mother purchased the remainder of his time, and his indentures were given up to her; and he supported his mother for some years by his labour.

At the age of twenty-one years he articled himself to learn the boot-closing; and, in a short time, became an excellent workman. A prize-boot once exhibited in the shop of a tradesman in the Strand was made by him. When he was twenty-three years of age he married a respectable young woman, named Welch. On the 1st of May, 1806, she brought him a boy, who was fourteen years of age on the day his unfortunate father suffered the sentence of the law. Brunt was thirty-eight years of age.

Edwards, whose name so frequently occurs in the foregoing pages, had been originally a modeller, and kept a little shop in Fleet Street, where he sold plaister of Paris images. His poverty had been always apparent until a few months previous to the Cato Street plot, when there is no doubt he accepted the wages of sin, and became a government spy. For this office he appears to have been admirably adapted, being shrewd, artful, and unprincipled. His former acquaintance with the Spenceans procured him the confidence of some of its deluded members; and through them he got acquainted with Thistlewood and the others. These desperate men he occasionally supplied with money, often to purchase the means of supporting life, and more frequently to procure instruments of death.

There is no doubt that the Cato Street business was got up by Edwards; he furnished the means of providing the destructive instruments, and actually made the grenades himself; and when Thistlewood had escaped from Cato Street, Edwards conducted him to the lodgings where he was next day apprehended.

Immediately after the execution of the unfortunate traitors, several persons made depositions before Alderman Wood, stating the many attempts of Edwards to seduce them from their allegiance. The worthy alderman applied to the secretary of state to have the villain apprehended, but he refused to interfere. A motion was made in the House of Commons a few nights afterwards by the same alderman, but nothing was done. Recourse was next had to the civil power, and the grand jury of Middlesex returned a true bill against Edwards, upon which a reward of one hundred pounds was offered for his apprehension; but he could not be found, having been sent, as was supposed, to our colony of New Brunswick.

However our indignation may be excited by the conduct of that infamous wretch, Edwards, the events with which he was connected furnish us with an useful lesson— Never to trust the man who attempts to instil principles contrary to *religion, virtue, peace, or loyalty*; for such a man cannot have our interests at heart. But, above all, the reader henceforth should recollect that the violent demagogue or factious friend of liberty may *be* a Castles or an Edwards, and therefore should avoid them.

JACOB MAGENNIS,
EXECUTED FOR SHOOTING A CONSTABLE,

This culprit was a native of Ireland, and by trade a weaver. In 1816 he came to England, and worked at his business at Stockport, where his restless disposition led him to associate with the reformers, who at this period were extremely violent. Magennis seems to have been an enthusiast in the cause, and constantly attended the sermons of a disaffected man named Harrison, who was subsequently tried, convicted, and punished, for having preached sedition. The pulpit should never be converted into a rostrum for popular declamations; for religion and politics have no necessary connexion. This Harrison kept a school at Stockport, and officiated on Sundays as a dissenting clergyman, in which capacity, it is to be apprehended, he did much mischief.

The magistrates of Stockport became alarmed at the doctrines publicly preached by this reverend demagogue, and issued a warrant for his apprehension; but, being aware of their design, Harrison left Stockport. A bench warrant was then procured, and a constable named Birch was sent to execute it. He did so, and on the 23d of July, 1819, brought the divine a prisoner to Stockport; and, for security, kept him confined in his (Birch's) house.

t was no sooner known that the idol of the mob was in custody, than a number of people collected in a very tumultuous manner about the constable's house. Alarmed for his safety, Birch went out by a back door, with the determination of consulting a magistrate concerning his duty, but had not proceeded far when a man named Bruce accosted him. Having known this man before, Birch stopped to speak with him; and, while in conversation, he received the contents of a pistol, fired over Bruce's shoulder by Jacob Magennis.

In the confusion that ensued Magennis made his escape, and passed over to Ireland, where he was apprehended, and brought to Chester gaol. Bruce was also taken into custody on the charge of aiding and assisting, as it was supposed he acted in concert with Magennis and another man, who could not be identified, though only the three were by at the transaction. Bruce was a stranger at Stockport, not having lived in it more than a few months, during part of which time he acted as usher in Harrison's school, and latterly had taken a school on his own account. He also kept a nightly school, where people were taught to make speeches. His manners and address were, however, far above that of his noisy pupils.

Birch's wound happily did not prove mortal; and on the trial, which took place on the 8th of April, he was able to give his evidence. The Jury found both Guilty, and when the verdict was pronounced, Magennis declared that Bruce was innocent; for it was he (Magennis) who fired the pistol.

Bruce was afterwards respited, and finally received the royal pardon, for it appeared he was not guilty; but Magennis underwent the awful sentence of the law at the time appointed. He was a man of strong capacity, but uneducated. He employed his few last days in writing his life, which he desired to be published; but it never was. He met his fate with fortitude, and was sincerely penitent.'

JOHN SCANLAN, ESQ. AND STEPHEN SULLIVAN,
EXECUTED FOR THE MURDER OF MRS. SCANLAN.

This is a most affecting case, and displays the utmost depravity of heart, as well as the most barbarous atrocity. John Scanlan was of a highly respectable family in the county of Limerick, Ireland, and allied to persons of the first distinction. Soon after the peace he was discharged, on half-pay, from the army, in which he had held the commission of a lieutenant. Sullivan had been a soldier under him, and having been also discharged, he accompanied Scanlan in the capacity of a servant. He was also a native of Limerick, and though not more than thirty-two years of age, was much older than his master, who had not attained twenty-five.

Young Scanlan, on his way to Limerick, where he proposed residing, stopped for some time in Dublin, where he found an opportunity of ingratiating himself into the favour of a thoughtless but lovely girl of fifteen years of age, the niece of a Mr. Conery, a ropemaker.

The gentlemanly appearance and polished address of Scanlan, when aided by his protestations of love and tenderness, flattered the vanity of the poor girl; but still she would not listen to him on any but honourable terms. She acknowledged her partiality, and charged him, if he was sincere, to make her his wife. To this proposal he affected to consent, after some conditions had been agreed on: these were that she was to keep her marriage a secret from her uncle, lest his friends should hear of it—an event which he seemed to regard as pregnant with ruin to him.

The foolish girl consented to all he chose to enjoin, and in an evil hour quitted the roof of her kind uncle, carrying off with her one hundred pounds in notes, and twelve guineas in gold. He pretended to act honourably, and carried her before an excommunicated priest, who joined their hands in wedlock. Scanlan resorted to this man, thinking the ceremony, when performed by him, not obligatory; but in this he was mistaken, for he soon after learned that, according to the laws of Ireland, a marriage so celebrated is valid.

The fugitive lovers quitted Dublin, and took up their abode in the romantic village of Glin, situated on the banks of the river Shannon, on the Limerick side. Scarcely, however, had the honeymoon passed over their heads, when it appears Scanlan formed the dreadful resolution of getting rid of his wife. Her beauty, her love, her innocence, appealed to him in vain; he persisted in his resolution, and too fatally carried it into effect.

It appears he was prompted to the dreadful deed by avarice and ambition: his sister, who had been married to a nobleman in the county of Limerick, apprized him of a match she was forming for him with an heiress of wealth and beauty, and requested his acquiescence. Knowing that he could not avail himself of the proposed advantage while his wife (for she was legally his wife) was alive, he determined that she should not long remain an obstacle to his advancement to rank and opulence.

Sullivan was his confidant throughout the whole affair, and to him was intrusted the execution of his atrocious plan. Scanlan had purchased a pleasure-boat, in which they used to take excursions on the Shannon. Of this amusement his wife was very fond, and it was during one of these moments of recreation, while she should be impressed with the beauty of the scenery, that the monsters resolved to rob her of that life which bloomed so exquisitely on her youthful and animated cheek.

One evening in the July of 1819, Scanlan affected to be called from home on business, but desired his wife to make Sullivan amuse her for an hour on the river in the boat. With this request she complied; and Sullivan, by his master's directions, got ready to execute their horrid purpose. Having provided a club to knock out her brains, and a rope and stone to tie to the body to sink it, he proceeded down the river. This man was treated by his master and mistress with great familiarity, so that he was not obliged to keep that distance so necessary to good order, but used every freedom consistent with respect. When the boat had drifted to a secluded inlet, Sullivan prepared to execute his purpose: he raised the club in a menacing position, and was about to strike, when the lovely creature, thinking he only intended to frighten her, gave him a smile of such innocent sweetness and simplicity, that the assassin was disarmed. He dropped the instrument of destruction, conducted his mistress home, and told his unfeeling master that he had not strength to execute his commands.

The horrid resolution was postponed, but not abandoned. A few evenings after, Scanlan, accompanied by his wife and Sullivan, went out in the boat as usual; but the unfortunate woman was never seen alive after. Scanlan returned to his lodgings, and said that for misbehaving he had shipped Ellen (his wife's name) on board some vessel, the captain of which had taken her under his protection. This story was disbelieved, and a few days discovered their guilt—the corpse of the murdered Ellen was washed ashore, mutilated in a most shocking manner. The legs were broken in several places, one arm had been knocked off entirely, and a rope was tied round her neck. Her skull was fractured in a thousand pieces, her eyes knocked out of her head, and nearly all her teeth forced from her mouth. Horrid and deformed as was her once-lovely person, still it was instantly recognised, when the murderers endeavoured to fly from justice. Of their guilt there could be no doubt; they were seen together in the boat; Sullivan had sold the murdered girl's clothes, and he and his master had quarrelled about some money, in which quarrel Scanlan had been accused of the murder.

Sullivan escaped for twelve months the pursuit of justice; but Scanlan was almost immediately apprehended, though he had resolved never to be taken alive. The following August he was tried at the assizes; and, being found Guilty, Baron Smith, to his immortal honour, ordered him for almost instant execution, lest the powerful interest of his family should procure a respite, if he left him even the period usually allowed to criminals convicted of murder. The time allotted Scanlan to live was too short to admit a messenger going to Dublin and back again, and consequently he was executed, to the satisfaction of all lovers of justice.

Twelve months after, his guilty servant met a similar fate. Before his execution he made a full confession, from which the above particulars are partly taken. Such was the powerful influence of Scanlan's family, that, though they could not avert his fate, they succeeded in keeping it a secret from a large portion of the community, for they had influence enough to prevent an insertion of his case in all the Limerick newspapers; and consequently it remained unknown, except in the immediate neighbourhood of the transaction.

The trial of Sullivan, however, revealed his own and his master's guilt, and proved that, in this country, neither wealth nor power can turn aside the sword of justice, or make the criminal less abhorrent, though he should have great and wealthy friends.

The circumstances of this case, we are persuaded, furnished the author of the 'Tales of Irish Life' with the idea of 'The Poor Man's Daughter.'

JAMES LIGHTFOOT,
EXECUTED FOR THE MURDER OF THOMAS MAXWELL.

THE guilt of this young man was established with irresistible certainty, and other circumstances which transpired after his execution leave no doubt of his having perpetrated the crime for which he suffered. Yet, untainted with either sedition or infidelity, which are often forced to account for moral phenomena, independent of their influence, Lightfoot solemnly protested his innocence with his last breath, and surrendered his life on the scaffold with a coolness and fortitude that would be celebrated in a martyr.

This malefactor's case shows that a man conscious of a deadly crime can die with all the appearance of innocence, apparently pious, and seemingly impressed with the truth of Christianity, which excludes the liar and the impenitent from the joys of Heaven. We cannot find, even in the full view of dissolution, a refutation or confirmation of any system of opinions, so contradictory are the operations of the human mind.

James Lightfoot was one of nineteen children by the same parents, thirteen of whom were living at the time of his execution. His father, who had been accidentally killed in 1816, was a poor man, and his children had all to earn their bread by laborious industry, and were generally employed as servants by farmers in Cumberland, in which county they all resided.

James, in 1820, lived with a farmer, named Leach, at Cumwhitton, and had got married about twelve months before, his age not being quite twenty-one. In the neighbourhood of Cumwhitton lived a tailor, named Maxwell, who, with his son, Thomas Maxwell, an amiable youth of eighteen, worked for all the people in the place. Thomas and Lightfoot were inseparable companions, whenever leisure permitted their being together; yet this youth, generally beloved and esteemed by all who knew him, was treacherously assassinated by Lightfoot, for no other discoverable motive but that of robbing him of fifteen shillings, four of which he had himself paid him a few minutes before.

Country tailors generally go from house to house to work, and are frequently obliged to give servants and poor people credit until such time as they can get money. The 20th of May, in Cumberland, is the day for hiring and paying servants their wages; and this too is the time when country tradesmen expect to get their money. On the eve of this day, in 1820, Thomas Maxwell, being going his annual round to his customers, called at Mr. Leach's, where he was kindly received, as indeed he was everywhere. Having smoked a pipe, he went to the barn where Lightfoot was threshing, to give him a smoke. While in the barn Lightfoot asked his master for four shillings, which he gave to Maxwell, being that sum in his debt. After a little time the youth took his departure, signifying his intention to cross a ford, which was situated a few hundred yards from Mr. Leach's house. His way lay through a plantation, and here it was that he was murdered.

Immediately after his departure Lightfoot entered the kitchen, and took out a loaded gun, although he had been repeatedly told not to touch it. Shortly after, a report of a gun was heard in the plantation through which Maxwell had to pass, and Lightfoot, who had been missed from the barn, was seen running towards the house in a crouching manner, as if he wished not to be seen. His master had entered the house before him, and, though angry at seeing the gun in his hand, he forbore to speak, as Lightfoot was to leave his service the next day.

The father of the murdered youth, alarmed for his son's absence, was inquiring next morning for him; and apprehensive, as the river was much swoln, that he might have been drowned, he had it dragged for the body. Notwithstanding all the poor man's exertions and anxiety, the deceased was not found for a week, so secluded was the place where the mangled remains had been deposited. Suspicion immediately fell upon Lightfoot, and when taken into custody his exclamation betrayed his guilt; for when the constable arrested him his first words were—'What! me murder Tom Maxwell on Friday!' The reply of the officer was pointed—'You know the day better than I do.' When taken before the coroner he said to the father of the deceased, 'Do you think I would murder your son for fifteen shillings?' Fifteen shillings was the exact sum the poor boy had about him; for before he left his father's house his sister saw him put eleven shillings into his purse, which, with the four received from Lightfoot, made the fifteen shillings. The purse was found empty, lying beside the mangled remains of the unfortunate boy.

On the 16th of August, 1820, Lightfoot was brought to trial at Carlisle, and was found Guilty, after a protracted inquiry into his case. The evidence against him was conclusive, though circumstantial; and the learned judge (Bayley) concurred in the verdict of the jury, though in his charge he had mentioned every thing that bore in favour of the prisoner, saying that a verdict of acquittal would not establish the innocence of the accused, but imply that the evidence was not sufficient to convict him.

Lightfoot, on being removed from the bar, declared that he was a murdered man, being perfectly innocent of the charge imputed to him. An idea that the denial of his guilt would diminish the disgrace brought upon his family was probably the motive of his obstinate protestations of innocence. His mother visited him the day before execution, and indirectly encouraged him to deny his crime, by saying, 'You are innocent, James; keep up a good heart.' Yet this woman was well aware of his guilt; for the Sunday after the murder had been committed, and before any one had been accused, she was heard to exclaim, in a fainting fit, 'My son has murdered a man!' Lightfoot's wife brought forth her first child about the time he perpetrated the murder, and so shocked was the poor woman on hearing the charge against her husband, that she had not recovered at the time when he was ignominiously launched into eternity.

JAMES NESBETT,

EXECUTED FOR THE MURDER OF MR. PARKER AND HIS HOUSEKEEPER.

A MURDER was committed in the town of Woolwich, on Friday night, March the 3d, 1820, not exceeded, in point of atrocity, by any which stain the calendar of crimes in this country. It bears a striking resemblance to that perpetrated by Hussey; for the victims were an old gentleman and his housekeeper, a Mr. Thomas Parker, aged seventy, and Sarah Brown, about forty-five years old.

Mr. Parker had been a working jeweller in London, where he made a fortune sufficient to enable him to retire to Woolwich, where he had resided for twenty-three years. His house was situated in Mulgrave Place, Red Lion Street, at a short distance from the Artillery Barracks.

Mr. Parker was an inoffensive gentlemanly man, very much respected by the whole neighbourhood. At one o'clock on Saturday morning, the sentinel on duty at the north arch of the Artillery Barracks observed a dense smoke rising from Mr. Parker's house. He gave an alarm; several of the artillerymen rushed forth, and found the flames bursting from the parlour window. The men rapped at the door with great violence, but no answer was returned. The cry of 'Fire' spread; two engines arrived on the spot, and commenced playing into the window. The men then forced the street door, and rushed into the passage. From thence they went up stairs into the front room on the first floor; here the ravages of the fire were perceptible; the furniture of a bed had been partly consumed. In the bed itself there was no vestige of a human being. The men then ran into the bed-room on the second floor, which was found in flames; they were soon extinguished. Neither Mr. Parker nor his servant could be found. Every exertion was now turned towards suppressing the flames in the parlour, which were extending to the room above. A hole was cut in the floor of the bedchamber, through which water was poured; and by this means, added to the incessant playing of the engines without, the danger was subdued. In a short time the parlour door was thrown open, a man belonging to the artillery entered, and perceived a heap of something lying behind the door; he attempted to lift it up, when he found it to be part of a human body. A second body, which proved to be that of a female, was found stretched in the same place, although not so much burnt. A further investigation of the premises now took place, when it was perceived that blankets had been nailed up against every window, as if to conceal the appearance of the flames within. Fire had been communicated in three different places—the parlour, on the ground floor, the bed-chamber on the first floor; and the bed-chamber on the second floor. The drawers about the house were found standing open, and articles of apparel were lying about. In the kitchen, some silver utensils were strewed on the floor. At break of day the bodies of Mr. Parker and his servant were examined. The former was burnt nearly to a cinder; the left leg and foot, on which there was a black silk stocking and a shoe, only remained entire. The skull, however, although the flesh was burnt off, remained whole, and afforded convincing testimony of murder: on the left side, towards the back, there was a terrific fracture. The woman lay stretched upon her face; her apparel was partly consumed; and her hair, which was long, was spread in dishevelled locks about her. A horrible wound, inflicted apparently with a blunt instrument, appeared over her eye, and at the back of her head were three deep fractures.

Several suspicious persons were taken up, but nothing appearing to criminate them, they were discharged. At length the real murderer was apprehended at Portsmouth, and several articles of Mr. Parker's property were found in his possession, particularly two watches, some silver spoons, a silver ladle, &c.

The person apprehended went at Portsmouth by the name of James Watson, but his real name was James Nesbett. This malefactor had been in the artillery for twenty-three years, and after his discharge lived in Woolwich, where his wife kept a chandler's shop. They had five children; the eldest eighteen, and the youngest at this time only sixteen months old. Nesbett himself followed that vicious and dangerous occupation — smuggling; bringing lace, silk, &c. from France, and carrying back other contraband goods from this country. In pursuit of this traffic he stopped some time at Portsmouth, where he cohabited with a girl of the town, who was afterwards the principal witness against him.

While sleeping with this girl she observed him to be very much troubled in his mind, as he frequently started in his sleep, and sometimes terrified her; so much so, that she left him on that account only. He, however, allured her back by presents; and, to account for the unnatural agitation in his sleep, he told her that he had killed two men in a duel, and one woman with a blow; and also promised to communicate another important secret to her.

The life of this man seems to have been composed of a succession of crimes, but the amount of his guilt will never be known. During his last trip to France, a short time before he committed the treble crime of murder, arson, and burglary, he seduced a young girl of a respectable family; and, having brought her to this country, he abandoned her to all the horrors of her situation. She had the virtue, however, to acknowledge her error, and seek protection from her friends.

Nesbett, when he first visited Portsmouth, appeared to have good sight; but after the murder he wore, whenever he appeared abroad, spectacles—the identical pair he had taken from Mr. Parker. In addition to the spectacles, he wore different dresses to disguise himself; but, notwithstanding all his caution, he was known, and apprehended; not, however, without much difficulty, for he attempted to shoot the officers, having a case of pistols loaded to the muzzle. Fortunately he was prevented from firing, and thus was preserved from having an additional murder to answer for.

When brought to Woolwich the people received him with a shout of exultation—a circumstance which affected him very much; it quite overcame him, and he was obliged to be carried before the justices, who were then sitting. He denied the crime with which he was charged; but after his committal to Maidstone, he confessed that he had been privy to it, having stood sentinel at the door while the work of destruction was going on inside. His accomplices he stated to have been old soldiers, whom he did not know—a tale as improbable as untrue; for most likely he was himself the only person implicated.

Nesbett's trial came on July the 28th, 1820, when his guilt was established by a chain of circumstantial evidence so conclusive, that the jury did not hesitate many minutes about their verdict. Nesbett's countenance indicated great firmness of purpose, but nothing of atrocity. During his trial he showed great fortitude and self-possession, which was not disturbed by his hearing the awful sentence of the law, which consigned him to an ignominious death.

This wretched criminal was executed according to his sentence on Pennenden Heath, July the 31st, 1820. It is gratifying to know that, in the interval which elapsed between his condemnation and execution, he acknowledged the justice of his sentence.

ROSALIE CURCHOD,
INDICTED FOR CHILD-MURDER.

This lovely but ill-fated girl was a native of Switzerland. Her father resided at Lausanne, and a young gentleman of that town had paid his addresses to her, contrary to the wishes of her family, who had forbad him the house. His attentions, however, were clandestinely continued for a considerable length of time, until Mademoiselle Curchod's health becoming seriously affected, her friends, guessing the secret, determined to remove her far from the cause of her indisposition, hoping that, by change of scene, her health would be restored, and that she would forget the object of her attachment. England was resolved upon as the place of her sojournment. The prospect of so painful a separation produced the strongest sensation in the minds of the lovers. An opportunity for a stolen interview was found, and in the tumult of ardent passion that event occurred which, in the end, plunged the unhappy object of ill-fated love into the deepest affliction. She reached England; and the friends to whom she was recommended thought that, by employing her mind, the purpose of her friends might be more effectually accomplished, and they therefore placed her at the boarding-school of a lady named Siffkin, at Barking, in the capacity of French teacher. There she continued until the month of December, 1819. In the unhappy interval she experienced the progressive symptoms of approaching child-birth. On the 20th of December she was delivered of a male infant unknown to the family. In three days afterwards the dead body of the infant was found in a pan in her bed-chamber, and in the result, after a coroner's inquest, she was consigned, in the prime of youth, beauty, and finished accomplishments, to the horrors of a dungeon. The author of her sufferings had been informed of the consequences of their illicit intercourse (but before they became exposed), and had set out for England with slender means, intending at all hazards to unite his hand to hers in marriage. He had arrived at Paris in pursuit of his journey: but his pecuniary funds being exhausted, he was detained so long, that he did not reach England until three days after the victim of his attachment had been committed.

At the ensuing spring assizes she was indicted for the murder of her child, and at the hour appointed for her trial she was conducted into court with the assistance of some female attendants. Agitated in every limb, and overwhelmed with grief, she was almost carried into the dock, and seated on a chair. She was attired in deep mourning, and her face was completely concealed with a veil, which, if even removed, would not have been enough to satisfy the brutal curiosity of some individuals in court, whose unfeeling anxiety to behold the beauty of her countenance called forth the indignant animadversion of the judge, who checked the inhuman indifference to her awful situation. Her head, during the whole time, was bowed on her bosom. Nothing but the contour of her elegant person confirmed the opinion entertained of her charms. With great difficulty she sobbed aloud, in French, that she was not guilty.

Fortunately for her, the surgeon who attended her during her illness could not swear that the child had been born alive, and, consequently, she was acquitted.

Mackcoull robbing the Minister of his Watch on quitting the Pulpit.

JAMES MACKCOULL, *alias* MOFFAT,
CONVICTED OF ROBBERY.

THIS was the most extraordinary offender of the age in which he lived; and, from the variety and extent of his depredations, might be called the robber of the world; for while his associate, the notorious Huffey White, was unlocking the doors of his majesty's subjects, Mackcoull was defrauding the natives of Holland and Germany. In his nefarious schemes he was too successful; he frequently possessed such sums of money as, under other circumstances, might have kept him independent—nay, in affluence—during his life; but the curse of dishonesty pursued him, and he frequently was master of thousands without being able to enjoy them. Heaven seems only to have prolonged his loathsome life, for the wise purpose of demonstrating to the world that ill-gotten wealth will ruin the possessor's peace of mind, and, ultimately, bring him to shame, infamy, and destruction.

James Mackcoull, though he had an honest father, was educated a thief, and from infancy was initiated into all the mysteries of picking pockets, shop-lifting, and house-breaking. He was born in the parish of St. Sepulchre, London, in the year 1763. His father, Benjamin Mackcoull, a man of unblemished character, was a pocket-book maker; but, being unfortunate in business, he was appointed a city officer, in which situation he continued until his death. This poor man did all in his power to bring his children up in honesty; but, unfortunately, his praiseworthy exertions proved abortive in consequence of his wife being a base unprincipled woman, who might be said to have educated her offspring for the gallows; for though they all, except one, singularly escaped such an ignominious death, they are allowed to have richly merited it.

James had three sisters and two brothers. The daughters emulated the example of the mother, and were, with her, frequently convicted of petty crimes, being the most expert and notorious thieves in London. They all lived till within a few years of James's death, notwithstanding their abandoned and vicious lives. The younger brother, Benjamin, was executed in 1786 for street-robbery; but the eldest, John, was always fortunate in eluding justice, though well known as a notorious character. He was frequently tried for various offences, but uniformly escaped conviction. This extraordinary villain received a more liberal education than any other of the family, and served his apprenticeship to a law-stationer. He possessed some talents, and gave proofs of them on various occasions. In 1810 he published a volume, entitled 'Abuses of Justice,' in which he very freely speaks of himself; indirectly acknowledges his previous crimes; but resolves to abandon his evil ways in future. His contrition, however, may be doubted; for, in 1820, he was the proprietor of two brothels in London, and of the Apollo circulating library in Worthing, Sussex.

James Mackcoull received a very limited education, and could just read and write. At school he was frequently detected purloining the play-things of other boys, and at a very tender age robbed a poor man who sold cats' meat through the streets. The young villain saw the vender of offal put his money, as he received it, into a bag which hung on the handle of his barrow, and, watching his opportunity, when the owner's back was turned he cut the cord, and carried off the booty. Emboldened by success he ventured again and again, and soon associated with gangs who are known to infest the entrances to theatres and places of amusement, where they are on the alert to snatch or steal hats, bonnets, umbrellas, &c. &c.

The father, ignorant of the vicious habits of the son, bound him apprentice to a leather-stainer, in Clerkenwell; but James, encouraged by the mother, adhered to his former comrades, and soon gave occasion to his master to discharge him.

He now became a notorious thief, and, by shifting his quarters, continued to elude detection; but, having been engaged with another in snatching the seals of a gentleman's watch in St. James's Park, they were pursued, Mackcoull's companion was apprehended, and himself only escaped detection by going at night on board the tender, at Tower Hill, and entering as a volunteer.

For two years he remained on board the Apollo frigate, in the character of an officer's servant, and afterwards on board the Centurion, in the same capacity. In the absence of temptation even a rogue may be honest. Mackcoull acquired so good a character in the navy, that he was in a few years appointed purser's steward, and in the course of nine years saved a considerable sum of money. In 1785 he returned to London, where, in a short time, he dissipated all his earnings in the society of the dissolute and abandoned, and to repair his finances had recourse to his former habits of dishonesty. Mackcoull soon eclipsed all his companions in iniquity, and shone pre-eminent as a pugilist, horse-racer, cock-fighter, gambler, swindler, and pickpocket. To carry on his depredations with success he assumed various characters, and succeeded in all. Not even the sanctuary of religion was free from his desperate villany; for he frequently went there to pick pockets, and on one occasion deprived the preacher of his watch, on his way from the pulpit. The knowledge and acuteness he displayed, as well as the successful manner in which he obviated discovery, procured him among his vile associates the appellation of 'The Heathen Philosopher.'

Being at Brentford during an election, Mackcoull saw a self-important baker very busy among the electors, and observed him put a bundle of notes into his side pocket. Desirous of possessing the notes, Mackcoull made various attempts, but failed until the evening, when, learning the baker's extreme passion for the science of astronomy,

he went into his shop and invited him out to view a strange alternating star. The baker declared he would not lose the sight for fifty pounds, and accordingly hastened into the street, and, while he was busy with his telescope viewing the starry heavens, Mackcoull contrived to ease him of the notes in his breast pocket, after which he quitted the spot and hastened to London.

A thief, to use a vulgar adage, throws out with a shovel what he brings in with a spoon; or, in other words, his improvidence is greater than his precarious gains, and, in addition to a thousand other apprehensions, he lives in continual dread of want and poverty. Mackcoull, notwithstanding all his address, was in continual pecuniary embarrassments, and when unsuccessful as a pickpocket at the theatre, or a fair, had to go to bed supperless. His particular misfortunes seem to have consoled, on various occasions, his less notorious brethren, for it has passed as a remarkable saying among the thieving tribe, 'That the best hand will miss at times, like Jem Mackcoull.'

Mackcoull, in his twenty-eighth year, married the mistress of a brothel, and assisted her in furnishing her house in Clifford's Inn Passage, which, in addition to its being a receptacle for unfortunate women, he made a depot for stolen property. He planned several burglaries, but was an actor in none. The stolen property he always deposited in a recess, formed by the shutting up of a window, which he called Pitt's picture, in allusion to the window-tax. This secret recess was, however, detected by the ferrets of the law, and Mackcoull was obliged to take a trip to the West Indies, a phrase he made use of to signify a removal from London. His friends endeavoured to hush the business, but their efforts failed, and Mackcoull was compelled to quit the country.

In 1802 he arrived at Hamburg, and took the name of Moffat. In company with two others he affected the air of a merchant, and pretended to have large consignments from England and Scotland. Of the latter country he said he was a native. He had recourse here to his former practices, and supported himself by gaming, picking pockets, and shop-lifting. He was no sooner suspected in one town than he removed to another, but had to make a precipitate retreat in 1805, and came home. In London he found it not prudent to stop, and therefore went to Edinburgh, where he arrived the 10th of September, and called himself Moffat.

In Scotland he followed his usual practices, and, the better to conceal his real character, pretended to follow the business of a dyer of leather, and took premises for the purpose, into which skins were seen to be taken, but no one ever saw any coming out. A gentleman pickpocket was then a character unknown north of the Tweed; and Mackcoull had so plentiful a harvest, that he brought his wife from London, and she passed in Edinburgh for a genteel proper woman. Being of a facetious turn, full of anecdote, and not deficient in low wit, Mackcoull was regarded as an agreeable companion, and was known in the different taverns and coffee-houses as the good-humoured red-faced Englishman.

In the beginning of November, 1806, William Begbie, porter to the British Linen Company, was assassinated in the entry leading to the bank at Edinburgh, and robbed of a bag containing five thousand pounds. Though this daring murder took place in clear day-light, the perpetrator was never discovered; but subsequent events lead to the presumption of Mackcoull being the ruthless assassin. The large notes, payment of which was stopped, were afterwards found in a spot frequented by Mackcoull, who no doubt purposely left them there.

Until 1808 Mackcoull committed his depredations with impunity; but about this period he was detected picking a gentleman's pocket in the theatre; for which offence he was committed to prison; but, strange to say, he was liberated without being prosecuted. He now returned to London, and concealed himself for some time in the neighbourhood of Somers Town, but again visited Scotland the following year. On his arrival he was apprehended for passing forged notes; but having artfully got change of a five-pound note on his journey in presence of a fellow-passenger, the latter, a respectable man, came forward and procured Mackcoull's liberation. After this he visited Glasgow, Perth, Dundee, and Montrose, and during his migrations met with a notorious character named French, with whom he agreed to rob one of the Scotch banks, and they hastened to London to procure the necessary implements. On their arrival French was apprehended on a charge of burglary, tried, and sentenced to transportation for life, in accordance with which he was sent to the hulks. In consequence of this event the robbery of the Scotch banks was deferred.

Meeting with the notorious Huffey White, whose case we have already given, Mackcoull agreed with this expert housebreaker to rob the Chester bank. White, having just escaped from the hulks, was very poor, so that Mackcoull had to provide for the expenses of the journey,

&c. White at the time lodged with a blacksmith, named Scoltock, who lived in Tottenham Court Road, and who supplied him with the implements of housebreaking. Arrangements having been made with this descendant of Vulcan, the villains set off for Chester, to reconnoitre, desiring that the keys, &c. should be forwarded to them on a certain day, directed to James Wilson.

Scoltock executed his order with punctuality; but on the way the box, in which the implements were sent, yielded to the friction of the coach, and one of the skeleton keys protruded through an opening. An officer being sent for, he concealed himself in the office until Mackcoull and White called, and then took them into custody. When taken before the magistrate, Mackcoull said his name was James Martin, and White said his was Evans. Not being able to give an account of themselves, they were committed, May the 17th, 1810, to the House of Correction, as rogues and vagabonds.

Information of the transaction being given at Bow Street, an officer was dispatched to Chester, who soon recognised this pair of notorious villains. White was tried the ensuing assizes for being at large before the expiration of his sentence, and was condemned to death, but had his sentence commuted to transportation for life. On the 10th of January, 1811, Mackcoull was discharged from Chester Castle, and on his arrival in London he met French, who had made his escape from the hulks, and they agreed to go and put their former determination of robbing a Scotch bank into execution. But as neither of them were very expert at the business, they resolved to release Huffey White from the hulks, whose abilities in this way were of a superior order.

They soon effected the escape of White, and all three set off for Glasgow, Scoltock, as usual, promising to send the necessary implements of housebreaking after them; for which he was to be paid when the job was done; indeed, so poor were the parties, that French had to sell his furniture to meet the expenses of the journey.

On their arrival in Glasgow they took lodgings in the house of a Mrs. Stewart, and gave their names as Moffat, Stone, and Down, and spent their time chiefly in smoking and drinking, occasionally going out to adjust their keys, &c. under the pretence of fishing. The Paisley, Union Bank, in Ingram Street, was the object of their attack; but on the arrival of the implements they found they could not open it. White, *alias* Down, thought to obviate this difficulty by making a pewter key, but neither would this answer, and Mackcoull had to set off to London to give Scoltock the necessary instructions. On his return they were too successful, and robbed, one Saturday night, the bank of Scotch notes to the amount of twenty thousand pounds, after which they posted to London, changing a twenty-pound note at every stage.

As the thieves had, on leaving the Bank, locked the doors, the robbery was not discovered until Monday morning, when a person went in pursuit of the fugitives, and traced them to London. An officer from Bow Street was then dispatched in search of the robbers, and that evening White was apprehended in Scoltock's house, where Mackcoull had only a few minutes left him, to provide some wine. The implements of housebreaking were found on the prisoner, but no money: for on their arrival in London Mackcoull had deposited the whole with the noted pugilist, Bill Gibbons, who acted as *flash* banker to such characters. There is no honour among thieves. Mackcoull assured his companions that the booty amounted only to sixteen thousand pounds, thus pocketing four thousand pounds for himself. On the apprehension of White, Mackcoull went into concealment, and French, who dreaded the ferrets of the law, sent for Mrs. Mackcoull, and proposed, as the only way to save their lives, to return the money to the bank, and thus hush the business. To this she consented, and her husband also acquiesced with the view of making his own fortune. His wife had been an acquaintance of Sayer, an officer who attended on the king, and through him she procured a pardon for her husband as well as for White and French for escaping from the hulks, on giving up the money to the bank. To this proposal the agents readily agreed; but, when Mrs. Mackcoull brought the notes, they were found only to amount to eleven thousand nine hundred and forty-one pounds, with which the gulled agents were obliged to return to Scotland.

The pardon obtained for White and French did not relieve them from their former sentence of transportation, and, accordingly, White was once more transmitted to the hulks. French for a while kept out of the way; but, meditating revenge on Mackcoull for the part he had acted, the latter contrived to have him apprehended, and sent to New South Wales.

Mackcoull, being now in possession of eight thousand pounds, had it reported that he was gone to the West Indies, when, in fact, he was passing the notes in Scotland, in the purchase of English bills. In 1812 he was arrested in a brothel in London, having abandoned his own wife for the charms of one Mary Reynolds, who had turned housekeeper, *alias* mistress, of a brothel. Mackcoull was now transmitted to Glasgow, where he arrived the 8th of April, 1812, and was committed to gaol. While here he did not seriously deny the robbery, but offered to make restitution to the bank, and promised their agent one thousand pounds, and gave them a bill for four hundred pounds. The bank not being at this time prepared to substantiate his guilt, he was discharged the following July, and the agent of the bankers absolutely received from Mr. Harmer, of London, the one thousand pounds, which, however, Mackcoull subsequently recovered by suit at law from that able solicitor, he having paid it without sufficient authority.

Mackcoull now considered himself beyond all danger, and in company with one Harrison, a brother of Mary Reynolds, made several trips to Scotland, and purchased commercial bills in the name of James Martin, a merchant, and everywhere introduced his friend Harrison as a most respectable merchant. In 1812 he opened a deposit account with Messrs. Marsh and Co. bankers, in the name of James Ibel, and had in their hands at one period above two thousand pounds.

In March, 1813, he again visited Scotland to vend more of the stolen notes, but was taken into custody, and bills and drafts, in favour of James Martin, to the amount of one thousand pounds, which he had purchased, taken from him. Owing, however, to Mackcoull having run his letters against his Majesty's advocate, he could not again be committed for the same offence, and consequently he was discharged out of custody, the bank, however, holding the bills.

On his return to London he paid a visit to his wife: but an altercation ensuing, he struck her; for which he was, after being tried at the Quarter Session, sentenced to six months' imprisonment. While in 'durance vile,' Huffey White 'died in his calling,' an event which gave Mackcoull much satisfaction, as he apprehended great danger when he heard of his old associate being at large.

In 1815 he resolved to recover the bills and drafts detained by the magistrates at Edinburgh, and, as they refused compliance with his request by letters, he visited that city in person, and demanded, in the most insolent manner, the restitution of what he called his property. This being refused, he commenced an action against them, which, more than any other case that ever came before a court of justice, proves the glorious uncertainty of the law; for it continued to be litigated for five years, and the country, for the first time, witnessed the singular fact of an acknowledged thief contending with persons about the property he had actually stolen from them.

During the progress of this protracted case, Mackcoull attended the courts of law in person, and gave instructions to his agent. He always conducted himself with the greatest *sang froid*, and treated with contempt and derision the allusions made by counsel to his character. At length it was ruled that Mackcoull should be interrogated in person before the Court, and after some hesitation he consented. This circumstance was no sooner known, than crowds flocked to hear his examination, which lasted for several days. He behaved in the most cool and determined manner; and when his absurd replies elicited a laugh in court, he always smiled with seeming self-approbation. The account he gave of himself was that he traded as a merchant, and that he chiefly transacted business with one James Martin, whose residence he could not tell. He objected to many questions put to him with the acuteness of a lawyer, and replied to others with that sarcastic grin which was peculiar only to Cooke, in Richard III. This was in 1819, and the session rose without having come to any decision. Mackcoull returned to London in great spirits, to arrange with his brother John about some letters he had, on his examination, promised to write to Mr. James Martin, who was obviously a fictitious character. The following letter and answer were then prepared by John, and both, as was afterwards proved, in his handwriting:—

'*Edinburgh*, 10*th May*, 1819.

'Dear Sir—I am still detained here with that infernal suit against the partners of the Paisley Union Bank, whose agents here, while in the act of themselves robbing that bank with both hands, have made myself a most unwilling instrument in their hands, and art and part guilty with them. The Lord Ordinary, when I complain to him of this, tells me, that they must not be obstructed in their lawful avocations; and how long I am to be stuck up between the bank and their agents, or, in other words, placed between the hammer and the anvil, will depend upon the ability of the bank or of myself to continue the litigation. For six years has this process been most actively carried on before Lord Gillies, Ordinary, who they say is among the best of the Scottish judges, without one relevant averment, and without a definitive judgment. Though his lordship sees the most pointed charge of forgery made by me against one of the bank agents, and has the admission of all of them distinctly stated upon his record, of their having robbed me by a prostitution of the police law, he, nevertheless, refuses judgment:—he has not energy to direct them to return my money, which the defender admits was forcibly taken from my person.

'His lordship, after six years' litigation, is going to send the bank defence to the Jury Court, namely, that I and one White robbed with false keys their bank; and this pretty little defence, which the rhetoric of Mr. Erskine, the celebrated Scotch counsel, who wrote on Black of Inverkeithing's case, has spun out in two thousand folio pages, embraces all that they have been speaking about for the last six years. Lord Gillies, fatigued with this nonsense, has at last obliged them to plead issuably, and to confine their pleas to the fact of the robbery; but, ere the bank can enter the Jury Court, it has occurred to them as proper, after so long an acquaintance, to discover, from myself, *who I am? where I come from?* what business I follow? and whether my conduct through life has been, like theirs, honest and moral?—It has pleased the Scottish judges to indulge their curiosity in all this, so that the bank agents, as one of the honourable judges expressed himself from the bench, might have an opportunity, from "his biographical sketch," to trammel me before the jury, in case the history of my life, 'taken by surprise, and upon their interrogatories, shall be incorrect. This, you must know, is Scotch law, and Scotch practice, and, I may add, Scotch breeding; and I have, of course, submitted to three several examinations before this inquisitorial court. These honourables have now got my life and travels for these last sixteen years, together with some account of yourself; for they have made, of necessity, the discovery that you and I have been most deeply connected in business together. What this biographical account may suggest to the fertile mind of our modern Cicero, whose grimaces in pleading are really frightful, I know not; but, if you come to this country soon, you had better empty your pockets ere you cross the Tweed, for greater ruffians never infested Hounslow Heath than those who have robbed me with impunity. I have myself expended eight hundred pounds in my attempts to get my money from them, of which, without the least dread or fear for the consequences, they openly confess in a court of law that they robbed me! I want a judgment in terms of their own confession, and that I cannot get. I never knew what a court of inquisition was till I came to Scotland. In my judicial declaration, I was asked if I made any entry, in any memorandum book, of the money I received from your cousin and Harrison? "declare, I dare say I did." Interrogated, What book I referred to, and where it now is? "declare, I think it was a memorandum book for the year 1815, which, I think, is now in the hands of Mr. James Martin, but that I am not sure." Being requested to write Mr. James Martin to transmit all his books, for the purpose of being put into the hands of the clerk of the process, " declare, that he has no objection to write to Mr. Martin, as desired, but he is sure Mr. Martin will not pass the books out of his hands." So you see what has passed; and it lies with you to say what I shall report to the Lord Ordinary. The session has risen, and will not again sit till May, when I shall then use every exertion in my power to get away with my property and with my character from that court and that country where I now am, through the medium of a jury. I have sacrificed eight hundred pounds of law expences. I have lost six years of my time, together with the fatigue and trouble of going and returning to London, and hitherto for no other purpose than to hear myself abused. For these six years my life has been made a burden to me. Mr. Jamieson, who conducts my suit, often tells me, what I believe to be true, that not a person in the whole United Kingdom could have manifested so much resolution and firmness; and he tells me that not one case could so opportunely occur to show *the general distress of the nation*. God only knows whether the practice is general: if so, I sincerely pity those who shall run the hundredth part of the gauntlet I have done; for it is a general robbery. The Scots live like fishes — the large devour the small!

'If there is any truth in the story about the bank being at all robbed with false keys, it may, as I am told, happen that this man White, who is said to be my accomplice, may turn out to be some *Edinburgh deacon* or *magistrate*, with a *gold chain* and *cocked hat*; for it was by them, along with the procurator-fiscal, that my money was first of all taken forcibly from my person, under the pretence of a crime, but for the covered purpose of taking my money. They have dropped the charge, *but detained my property!*

'You can have no conception to what length corruption and oppression is gone in this part of the United Kingdom; and what is most lamentable, the higher orders of society are chiefly implicated in it: this you will see from the advocation. In short, my good sir, all I can tell is, that, after the most active research which, during the course of six years, could be made after *roguery*, all that is hitherto made out *is, that, of all of us concerned in that fraudulent inquiry*, there is but one honest man among us, and that is *myself*: they are all of them chargeable, from the face of the records, *but one*. But, put jests aside, I have been shockingly used; and, if you can make a step down this way, as a witness for me at the jury trial, I shall be well enough pleased. I am,' &c.

[The reading of this letter occasioned a great deal of amusement in court, from the grave folly in which it is couched, particularly its reflections on the Scotch courts.] 'And this,' continued the learned counsel, 'is from an honest man, demanding the surrender of his own books!' He would now read the answer of Mr. Martin, which was of a piece with the foregoing, and was written according to the instructions of Mackcoull, by Mackcoull's own brother. The jury would perceive what a fraternal correspondence it was:—

'*April* 13, 1819.

'Sir,—Your application to me, relative to the books in my possession, is so very strange and absurd, that I am really at a loss to account for it. *In the name of reason*, what can the books have to do with the bills taken or stolen from your person? It is but a short period since you informed me that Sir William Forbes and the Commercial Bank had declared they cancelled the bills—and I am now told they are not cancelled. What Iam I to think of this juggling? If you report truly, I do not only think, but am justified in saying, Sir William

Forbes and the Commercial Bankers are a set of scoundrels, and the greatest villains in existence; and certainly not deserving any credit whatever. I shall, most assuredly, report their conduct, not only to the bank directors of England, but post them in every commercial town in Europe.

'Let these fellows have any books belonging to me, or in my possession! Certainly not. Pray let me ask, how am I to know, when they are in such villainous hands, what use they may make of them to answer their own ends and purposes? Afterwards I may then be told by some of the gang, "O, they are honourable men, and would not do so bad an action!" and so to be cozened by their honourableships. Although I am but a plain, blunt Englishman, I know these sort of honourables too well to trust them with any thing they can construe to make subservient to their purpose. I would not, after such swearing, lying quirks, tricks, and subterfuges as these honourables have been guilty of, trust them with the piece of tobacco paper now before me. I therefore decidedly decline having any thing to do with such honourables, and wish to have no other communication with them but in a court of justice, where I could scarcely even there think myself safe (particularly in a Scotch court, where they are permitted to say and swear what they please through their agency.)

'I shall be away from here in a day or two, *either for Berne or the Italian States*. I am exceedingly ill, and have been for a long time; indeed my health is daily declining. Your agent, Mr. Jamieson, certainly knows what is best to be done with these honourables; and, therefore, as there is no other alternative, you must wait with patience the issue. Trusting you are better in health than I am, I remain

'Your very sincere friend,
(Signed) 'JAMES MARTIN.'

At the close of every session, during the progress of the case, Mackcoull went regularly to London by sea; and returned in the same manner, when the courts met. On these occasions he was to be seen in Edinburgh every evening at a low public house, surrounded by journeymen and apprentices, whom he amused with his humorous description of Scotch bailies, lawyers, and bankers, applying to them the most ludicrous names and epithets that could be devised, denouncing against them vengeance and public exposure. He was extremely generous, and was looked on by this low company as a little king.

During the summer sessions he produced the letters supposed to be to and from Martin, and, as if now confident of success, he urged his counsel to accelerate the business; but, as before, the court rose without coming to any decision. The bank was at this time in a critical situation; unless they proved Mackcoull's participation in the robbery, and that the bills, &c. were purchased with notes stolen from the bank, they would have to deliver up to Mackcoull not only the bills, &c. but pay all attendant expenses, besides the disgrace of losing the action—an action unparalleled in the annals of any court of Europe: a public depredator—a convicted rogue and vagabond—going at large in the metropolis, without any lawful employment, denouncing courts, magistrates, and individuals, and prosecuting with their own money a respectable banking company, for attempting to keep part of the property of which he had robbed them. But this was not all. Mackcoull's intention, if successful, was to follow the decision with an action of damages, in which it was the opinion of many that he would also succeed.

In December, 1819, Mackcoull and his agent urged the matter so strenuously, that the trial was fixed for the 20th of February, 1820; and the issue to be tried was, whether Mackcoull was concerned in the robbery.

To prepare for the trial, the bank sent Mr. Donovan, an intelligent officer in Edinburgh, from Glasgow to London, to trace the route the robbers had taken nine years before, and to procure witnesses. Donovan was successful, and brought down with him Scoltop, Mrs. Huffey White, several waiters at inns, and even Mrs. Mackcoull, who consented to give evidence against her husband. The most eminent lawyers at the Scotch bar were engaged on each side; and on the morning of the trial, May the 11th, 1820, every avenue to the court was crowded to excess, so intense was the interest excited by the case. The result was against Mackcoull, for the witnesses completely established his guilt; and so unexpected was the appearance of some of them to him, that he frequently ran out of court, and on seeing Scoltop actually swooned away.

Mackcoull's career of villainy was now near its end. On the 19th of June he was indicted for the robbery, in the High Court of Justiciary; and the same witnesses being again examined, the jury returned a verdict of Guilty—Death. Towards the conclusion of the trial Mackcoull often looked about him with a kind of vacant stare, and was observed frequently to mutter and grind his teeth. When the verdict was announced he gave a malignant grin: and, when sentence was passed, he bowed respectfully to the Court. On being carried back to gaol his fortitude forsook him, and he appeared overwhelmed with despair. At this moment he said with emotion, ' Had not the eye of God been upon me, such a connected chain of evidence never could have been brought forward!' His spirits, however, soon returned, and he received the number of visitors, who were led by curiosity to see him, with great cheerfulness.

Although he had treated his wife with great unkindness, she now came forward, and supplied him, during his imprisonment, with every necessary in profusion. She also made application for a reprieve; and whether from her exertion or not, on the 14th of July, a respite arrived, and in three weeks after a reprieve during his majesty's pleasure.

All who visited Mackcoull did not do so from mere curiosity. One man went for the laudable purpose of awakening in his mind some sentiments of religion, and to induce him to repent of his manifold crimes, as a necessary means of salvation. This person was attached to the Methodists, and one day brought with him a friend, a missionary, whom he introduced to Mackcoull. The convict received his guests with great politeness, and soon began to question the missionary so closely concerning his travels in Germany, that he was glad to fly to Poland and Silesia; when, finding that Mackcoull had not been there, he began to expatiate on the ignorance and barbarism of the people, whom he represented as eating jackasses. ' Hold! hold!' said Mackcoull, ' I do not believe you; for, if they eat *asses*, how the devil did you escape being devoured?'

After the month of August Mackcoull fell into a natural decline, which affected his mental faculties so much that he became altogether silly and childish. He was haunted in his sleep by frightful dreams and visions, and frequently started up with such dreadful cries, and horrible expressions and imprecations, that none of the other felons could remain in the cell with him. He was visited occasionally, not only by the regular ordinary of the gaol, but also by several eminent divines, to all of whom he behaved with becoming respect, but generally refused or declined to enter with them on religious subjects. Sometimes, however, it is said, he attributed this obduracy to the want of a religious education, and the very slight acquaintance he had with the Bible. Previous to his death he was so much emaciated that those who saw him at the trial could not again recognize him; while, from the time of his conviction, it was remarked that his hair began to change colour. At that period it was jet black, but in the course of three months it became silver grey. He died in the county gaol of Edinburgh, on the 22d day of December, 1820, and was decently interred, at the expense of his wife, in the Calton burying-ground.

Thus terminated the mortal existence of a man who seemed destined by Nature for a better fate. That he possessed abilities which, with honest and industrious application, might have rendered him a useful member of society, cannot be denied: but it is difficult to overcome the effect of early impressions—he was reared and nurtured in a hot-bed of vice. He felt no spur, no incentive, to virtue; and he implicitly followed the impulse of a polluted conception. His whole life may thus be considered as one uninterrupted career of villany, almost without a parallel. That he did not expiate his crimes on a gibbet, was merely owing to circumstances which are not worth explaining; but, during the period of his imprisonment, he suffered many deaths. Of the fatal tree he spoke without fear; but the dread of a future tribunal paralized his understanding. He saw and trembled at the approach of that unerring shaft which no earthly ruler could control; while the horrors of his mind, by affecting the nervous system, accelerated his dissolution. The retrospect of his life often obtruded itself with new modifications of insupportable reflection—the prospect of futurity he could only contemplate with fearful apprehension. He felt the wakening of a seared conscience, from which there was no retreat. He crawled about, grinding his teeth; his intervals of slumber were broken and interrupted with the most frightful visions, and he saw the hairs of his head become grey with anguish! The picture is too horrible to finish. To Religion he was a stranger, a total stranger, in this hour of need: he felt not her soothing influence — he cherished not the hope of forgiveness or mercy. Unhappy man! he looked to God as to a cruel and vindictive ruler, at whose hands he could only expect the full punishment of his crimes: his resignation was despair!

FREDERICK WHITE,
CONVICTED OF HIGHWAY ROBBERY.

THE extraordinary escape of this young man from an ignominious death demands a notice, of which the circumstances of his conviction would otherwise be unworthy. It appeared on his trial that he was present at a fire in Wardour Street, Soho, on the 30th of November,

1820, when a gang of pickpockets, the usual attendants at such scenes, among other depredations made an attack upon an individual in the crowd, and succeeded in robbing him of his chain and seals. White, who was near enough to witness the transaction, was seized by the person robbed, charged with the theft, and taken in custody to the watch-house. As he was entirely alone, he could do no more than declare his innocence, which was attested at the time by a stranger, who followed him to the watch-house. The complainant and the guardians of the night naturally enough suspected this voluntary witness for an accomplice, and discredited his testimony: White, however, who knew its truth, begged of him ' to come to-morrow for him.' He accordingly attended at the police-office in the morning, and obtained precisely the same credit he had gained the previous evening. White was, therefore, fully committed: the grand jury found the bill against him on Wednesday, December the 5th; and on the Friday following he was brought to his trial, and capitally convicted. The only evidence of importance against him was that of the prosecutor, who swore to his person, and that he kept pulling, and made a screw to get the watch out at the time he (the prosecutor) had hold of him. Two persons who had accompanied the prosecutor to the fire did not see the robbery, being then at some distance, but assisted in securing and conveying the prisoner to the watch-house. The stranger who had previously appeared as the prisoner's witness, made it his business to examine the list at the Old Bailey; and without any communication with, or solicitation from, White or his friends, again tendered his evidence on his behalf. His testimony was, that the prosecutor, after declaring his loss, seemed much confused, and stood two minutes or more before he laid hold of any body: that presently after there was a great rush of all the mob; the prisoner was seized, and he followed him to the watch-house to say he did not think the prosecutor could swear to the man, as he was greatly confused, and appeared much intoxicated. The prosecutor being again called, declared he was sober at the time; and this testimony being corroborated by his two companions, who both declared he was perfectly sober, the stranger of course was discredited, and the conviction of the prisoner necessarily followed.

The unhappy youth concealed his actual situation from his friends, in the delusive hope that some chance would save both him and them the exposure, till it was too late; for, strange as it may appear, his first communication to his mother of his awful situation was not made until the morning on which the grand jury found the bill against him; and so little acquainted were his friends and himself of his danger, or the common means of averting it, that a learned gentleman, a relation of the family, and who might have rendered him great assistance, was left wholly unacquainted with the facts of the case till the trial was over.

Such was the situation of the youth when his unhappy fate attracted the attention of Mr. Sheriff Waithman, who ascertained, from undoubted testimony, the previous good character and conduct of the prisoner himself, and the respectability of his parents, with whom he resided, in the neighbourhood of the fire, to which his curiosity unfortunately led him.

That he was unconnected with the gang by whom the robbery was committed is obvious, from the circumstance that, although there were ten or twelve of them together, the prisoner used no endeavours to escape; not the slightest attempt was made to rescue him; nor had he been visited during the whole of his imprisonment by any persons but those of his family, or their immediate friends. The fact, however, was put beyond doubt by the affidavit of a respectable gentleman, who was wholly ignorant of White's unfortunate situation, but who, when referred to, deposed (in corroboration of a statement previously made by the prisoner) that he was passing near the spot on the night of the fire, and within a few minutes of the time of the robbery; that he there saw and spoke to White; that he was entirely alone, and no person whatever in company or conversation with him.

The stranger, who so perseveringly appeared on the prisoner's behalf was proved, by evidence most satisfactory, to be a young man of character residing with his mother, and in no way acquainted with White or any of his family; and the veracity of his testimony was established by the voluntary declarations of eight or ten respectable individuals, all of whom agreed as to the intoxication of the prosecutor on the evening in question; which, added to the state of confusion such an attack was likely to occasion, left no doubt but that he must have been mistaken in the person of the prisoner.

In the prosecution of his inquiries Sheriff Waithman judged it important to ascertain the grounds upon which the verdict of the jury was founded; and in answer to a letter on that subject, addressed by him to the foreman, he received a declaration, signed by all the jury, that their verdict was given upon the conviction that the prosecutor and his companions were sober at the time of the robbery, and their disbelief of the evidence of the witness to the contrary, whom they viewed in the light of an accomplice rather than a disinterested person, as he stated himself to be.

These concurrent testimonies in the youth's favour were communicated to Lord Sidmouth as they were obtained; but, to the great surprise of the sheriff, an obstacle of a serious nature presented itself at the outset of his exertions. A petition had been delivered at the office of the secretary of state for the home department, purporting to be signed by the prisoner, in which he confessed his guilt, and acknowledged the justice of his sentence. It has, however, been subsequently established, by the most indubitable testimony, that, although this petition had been drawn up under an impression generally entertained in the prison that a denial of guilt would be considered as an imputation upon the court and the jury, and render all applications for mercy unavailing, the prisoner, fully aware of this circumstance, could by no entreaty be prevailed upon to acknowledge guilt, even for the chance of saving his life. A pious fraud was therefore committed, and the prisoner's name affixed to the petition by his brother, without his knowledge or consent.

Lord Sidmouth, the home secretary, received these communications with caution, not giving the sheriff any hope of a pardon, but determined to submit the whole to the consideration of Mr. Baron Garrow, before whom the prisoner was tried; who gave it as his decided opinion that if such evidence had been brought forward at the trial, the jury would have found the prisoner not guilty. Lord Sidmouth had now no hesitation in recommending him as a fit object for the royal clemency, and he was of course discharged.

At the same time with White a youth named Harley, was liberated from Newgate on his majesty's free pardon. The circumstances of his case are singular and remarkable.

Harley was convicted at the January sessions, 1821, of a street robbery near Northumberland House, on Monday, the 11th of December, 1820. The prosecutor was surrounded and hustled by fifteen or twenty fellows, and had his watch forcibly taken from him. He seized one of the gang, but the others fell upon him directly, rescued their companion, and then beat the prosecutor unmercifully.

He subsequently described the dress and person of the man who robbed him; and, upon that description, Harley was taken into custody. He was put into a room with ten or twelve others, and the prosecutor, when sent by the officers, recognized him immediately. The evidence of the prosecutor, on the trial, was positive and direct. He saw the prisoner pull the watch from him, and hand it to another. When asked if he was sure of his person, he replied, 'If he was tarred and feathered all over, except his face, I could swear to him.'

Harley, in his defence, attempted to prove an *alibi*; but as his witnesses were the inmates of a brothel, where he had actually been at the time, they received no credit, and he was found Guilty, and received sentence of death.

Fortunately for him the prosecutor swore that he knew his person previous to the time of the robbery, having had Harley pointed out to him as a notorious thief on a certain Saturday; on which day, it afterwards appeared, Harley had been in custody on another charge. This fact was brought under the cognizance of the secretary of state, and it appeared that another person, exactly resembling Harley, both in person and dress, was known as a *hustler*, a respite followed of course; and the prosecutor stating that he swore to him on the presumption of his being the person so pointed out, a free pardon was obtained.

Between White and Harley there was no similarity, further than their innocence of the crime for which they had been convicted. White was a youth of correct morals and virtuous habits, but Harley was known as a bad character; and, on his hair-breadth escape, he returned to his former vicious companions.

JOHN THOMPSON AND JOHN BARNICOAT,
EXECUTED FOR THE MURDER OF WILLIAM HANCOCK.

There is every reason to believe that the latter of these unfortunate men died innocent of the crime for which he suffered. In proof of this opinion we have, in addition to his own dying declaration, the testimony of his guilty companion on the fatal gallows. Jurymen should always bear in mind that the accused is entitled to the benefit of every possible doubt which the case admits of, and we do not know why the witnesses for this unhappy man, who proved a complete *alibi*, were considered unworthy of credit. They differed certainly from each other in immaterial facts; but when have two men, without previous communication, given precisely the same account of a trivial occurrence?

On the night of the 12th of August, 1820, several robberies, and one murder took place, on the highway, near Helston, in Cornwall. A man named Jose, and his wife, were robbed and wounded, and another man, named William Hancock, was shot, and treated so unmercifully that he died a few days after. Previous to his death, however, Barnicoat was brought before him, when he declared that he was one of the men who robbed him, and identified him as the man who struck him with a long pole after he had been shot. Barnicoat denied this, upon which the dying man asked him, 'How he could say so, as he stood over him, and threatened to knock his brains out.' Hancock also identified John Thompson as one of the villains who had attacked him.

In consequence of Hancock's dying declaration, Barnicoat, John Thompson, and his brother, Thomas Thompson, were committed to gaol, and brought to trial, March the 30th, 1821. Barnicoat produced witnesses to prove an *alibi*, but as they contradicted each other in parts of their testimony, they were disbelieved, and a verdict of guilty was pronounced against Barnicoat and John Thompson. Thomas Thompson was acquitted, the declaration of the murdered Hancock not having included him. Barnicoat was in his twenty-fourth year, and Thompson only in his seventeenth.

On Monday, April 2, 1821, these two miserable youths underwent the awful sentence of the law at Launceston. About half past nine they were lead to the scaffold, which was erected in the Castle Green, adjoining to the gaol. Barnicoat manifested a considerable degree of firmness; but it was found necessary to support Thompson, who was placed on a chair on the drop. Whilst standing on the fatal platform, the chaplain asked Barnicoat if he still persisted in his declaration of being innocent of the offences for which he was about to suffer. He replied, with much earnestness, that he did; adding, that he knew no more about the attack on Jose, or the murder of Hancock, except what he had heard of them, than the child unborn, and that he was at home in bed during the whole of the night on which the attacks took place. For the truth of his assertions respecting his innocence he solemnly appealed to Thompson, who was now beside him, and about to suffer with him. Thompson confirmed the declaration of Barnicoat, as far as came under his own knowledge. He declared that Barnicoat was not present at either the attack on Jose or the murder of Hancock, nor did he know any thing of them; the persons concerned were himself, his brother William, and Thomas Dawe; that Dawe was the person who shot both Mrs. Jose and Hancock; and that it was he himself who carried the pole, and who beat Hancock after he fell: the pole he had was the handle of a pike. The necessary preparations being completed, the chaplain spent a few minutes in prayer with the culprits, and then withdrew; almost immediately after, Barnicoat gave the signal previously agreed on, and with his companion was launched into eternity, in presence of a great concourse of spectators.

BRIDGET BUTTERLY AND BRIDGET ENNIS,
EXECUTED FOR THE MURDER OF MISS THOMPSON.

Murder becomes doubly revolting when perpetrated by a female, and receives its last hue of enormity when committed without provocation. These malefactors were natives of Dublin, and Butterly had been servant with Captain Peck, who resided at Portland Place on the banks of the canal, north of the city. The captain's wife, Mrs. Peck, author of several novels, did not live with her husband, but he kept under his protection a young lady named Thompson, *alias* Bailis, a native of England. Butterley states that while in Captain Peck's service she had improper connexion with her master, and on being turned out of his service she became jealous of Miss Thompson, and consequently wished to do her some harm.

It is but justice to state that Captain Peck denied having had any improper connexion with Butterly, but she declared to the contrary a few minutes before her execution, and it is not likely that on the verge of the grave she would persist in a falsehood, which served no purpose but to add to the infamy of her own memory.

After leaving the service of Captain Peck she went to lodge with one O'Brien, in Summer Place, where she had Ennis for a fellow lodger. The latter, after some time, proposed visiting England — the common resource of all the vagabond Irish, from the Giants' Causeway to Cape Clear. Butterly consented, and offered to provide funds for the journey by robbing the house of Captain Peck. This was agreed to, and on the 28th of March, 1821, they watched the house until they saw the captain go into town, when Butterly went up and knocked at the door. Miss Thompson received her with great kindness, shook her by the hand, and took her into the parlour, where Butterly took up a child of two years old, and began to caress it. In a few minutes Ennis knocked at the door, and on gaining admission she desired Butterly to put a handkerchief round Miss Thompson's mouth, to prevent her from giving alarm. Butterly immediately did as desired, and dragged the poor young lady down stairs into the kitchen, where she kept her until Ennis had procured the trunk and writing desk, in which was money to a considerable amount.

Ennis on going away cried out from the top of the kitchen stairs, 'Butterly, don't injure the young lady on your life.' But she had no sooner closed the door after her, than jealous fury took possession of the atrocious wretch, and she took up the poker, with which she struck Miss Thompson on the head, and repeated her blow until life was extinguished. The sight of death seems to have softened the savage barbarity of her heart; for, with an unaccountable impulse, she took up the mangled body in her arms, and wished that she could again infuse life into that once beauteous form. But as this was now impossible she thought of her own safety, and ran up stairs. In the hall she met Miss Thompson's child; kissed it, and carried it into the parlour, after which she took her departure. On going to her lodgings she was alarmed by not finding Ennis at home, and suspecting that all was not right she became dreadfully agitated.

In the mean time, Captain Peck's servant, who had followed her master to the market, returned, and not gaining immediate admission looked down the kitchen window, where she saw her mistress lying on the floor. Giving the alarm, the door was forced open, when the robbery and murder were quickly made known, and thousands flocked to Portland Place, to inform themselves of a fact which at first appeared too atrocious for belief without ocular demonstration.

The sensation produced in Dublin by this mid-day murder was intense; the youth and beauty of the deceased deeply affected all who saw her mangled remains; and, fortunately for the ends of justice, the culprits did not long enjoy their ill-acquired wealth. Ennis went to a grocer in Great Britain Street, and having ordered some tea tendered a note, which she called a pound-note, for payment. The grocer, whose name was M'Gloin, seeing that it was a ten pound-note, questioned her, and finding that she became alarmed he sent for a peace-officer, and had her taken into custody. The note was soon identified by Captain Peck, and Ennis having mentioned her lodgings, the officers proceeded thither, when they found Butterly, with part of the money, as well as the trunk and writing-desk; for Ennis had returned soon after Butterly, and deposited these things in her room.

These wretched women were no sooner committed to prison than they acknowledged their guilt, and, through the influence of the priest who attended them, Captain Peck was put in possession of the remainder of his money. On the first of the following May they were tried and convicted, and on Monday the 4th were executed in front of Kilmainham gaol, amidst an immense concourse of spectators. Soon after they had been turned off, a butcher's dog got into the circle kept clear about the fatal drop by the dragoons, who attended for that purpose. One of these men made a cut of his sword at the dog, who immediately attacked his horse, and in the confusion which ensued the people imagined that the soldiers had charged the people. The consequence was a simultaneous movement to get away, and in the hurry a young man was trampled to death, and several persons were dangerously hurt. The wretched culprits on the morning of execution confessed the crime for which they were about to die, and appeared truly penitent.

DAVID HAGGART, ALIAS JOHN WILSON, ALIAS JOHN MORRISON, ALIAS BARNEY M'COUL, ALIAS JOHN M'COLGAN ALIAS DANIEL O'BRIEN, ALIAS THE SWITCHER,

EXECUTED FOR MURDER.

DAVID HAGGART was born at a farm-town called the Golden Acre, near Cannon Mills, in the county of Edinburgh, on the 24th of June, 1801. His father was a gamekeeper; but as his family increased, he followed the occupation of a dog-trainer, and was much taken up in accompanying gentlemen on shooting and coursing excursions. On these occasions David was employed to assist in keeping the kennel, and the gentlemen who had their dogs in training took great notice of him, and never failed giving him a few shillings for paying particular attention to their dogs.

He was also, when very young, taken to the Highlands for two seasons to carry the bag during the shooting time, and as he was always a merry boy, the sportsmen took a liking to him, and sent him home with plenty, so that he never wanted the means of indulging himself in childish follies.—In these habits and these indulgencies an intelligent observer of human nature at once discovers, not the seeds of his vices, for they had their deep-rooted origin in human depravity, but the soil that pushed them forward to such an early and awful maturity. Perhaps there is nothing in every point of view more injurious to young persons, than a profuse supply of pocket money in proportion to their circumstances and stations in life. It takes off every stimulus to industry, and every incentive to frugality; promotes a spirit of selfishness, pride, and contempt of authority; exposes to the snares of evil company; multiplies the wants, and consequently enhances the privations of future life, or leads to unjust means of avoiding them.

David Haggart acknowledged, that although he was so much employed in assisting his father in his business, his education was not neglected. His father early instructed him in religion;—but while pursuing a course of life so replete with temptations to vice, it seemed only like building with one hand and pulling down with the other. Children are not merely to be told the way in which they should go—but 'trained up' to go in it;—they should not only be brought up in the *nurture*, but in the *admonition* of the Lord. Discipline must be carefully exercised, as well as instruction diligently imparted. In addition to domestic instruction, David was sent to school, where he acquired considerable knowledge of English grammar, writing, and arithmetic. He appears to have been a sharp active lad, and was always the leader of his schoolmates, both in learning and in sports. He did not recollect ever losing his place in the class for deficiency in acquiring his lessons, but was often punished for playing truant.—This is an offence which boys at school too seldom look upon in the light of a crime. Many a boy, who would feel ashamed of being detected in what he considered a mean dishonourable action, will speak with great self-approbation of the adroitness with which he managed an enterprise of this nature; and too often parents are found thoughtless enough to encourage such conduct by making a laugh of it, and even relating their own feats of childhood. A little consideration of the bad principles thus called into exercise, and the exposure of bad company incurred, would certainly check such erroneous conduct.

At about ten years of age, the subject of this narrative was seized with a fever, and on his recovery did not return to school, but staid to assist his father in his business, and thus terminated his education for a considerable time. A trifling accident having occurred at home, through fear of punishment from his father, he came to the resolution of quitting his house; and from that fatal hour he dated the commencement of his sinful career. Perhaps he might, with great propriety, have gone back to that in which he first slily staid away from school, and spent the hours with sinful companions in forbidden sports. A boy who had never been guilty of disobedience and artifice at school, would scarcely, on account of a small accident at home, have taken at once the rash step of forsaking a father's house. Young people!— the distinction is not unimportant; if you wish always to shudder, as you now shudder at the thought of the second step in vice, take care to shrink from the first.

At this time David observes he had formed no wicked acquaintances; perhaps he confined this epithet to those who had taken the same flagrant steps in vice to which he afterwards attained. A well-taught youth will apply it to all who are capable of disobedience to parents, artfulness, and irreligion. Being of a bold and fearless disposition, even at this early period of life, he committed several depredations. The first of these was stealing a bantam cock, the property of a poor woman: young Haggart took a fancy to it on account of its great beauty, and offered to buy it, but the owner would not part with it; so he got another cock, set the two a fighting, and ran off with his ill-gotten prize. He also tried shop-lifting, and carried off the till of a poor woman. He knew and felt all this was wrong: but fully employed in vice, he took no time to be sorry or repent; beside, he falsely and wickedly argued that it was of no use for him to repent, for he must fulfil his fate. There is not a more dreadful delusion, nor one perhaps that the great enemy of souls more frequently imposes upon wicked men, than that of charging their sins and miseries on fate. Often have these dangerous sentiments been uttered, and still oftener indulged:—'It was my lot to get among bad companions, and so fall into wicked ways.' 'If I am doomed to go on to my ruin, it is in vain to strive against it.' 'If I am to be saved at last, something will turn up for my conversion.' What can have a stronger tendency than sentiments like these to harden men in their sins?

Haggart's next adventure was in accompanying a lad, with whom he had been very intimate, on a visit to a relation, six miles from Edinburgh. They saw a pony grazing on the road side, when Haggart, feeling himself tired, proposed to mount the beast, and return home; his companion did not object, and they set off at full gallop. The animal was very restive, and threw them several times. On reaching home they lodged him in a donkey hut, and kept him there several days, until traced by the owner, who threatened to have them both punished, but was appeased by the neighbours. Haggart declared that he had no intention of stealing the pony, but having once taken the notion of getting a ride home, he was determined to avail himself of the opportunity, and was afterwards at a loss how to return the beast.

Shortly after this adventure, he went to attend Leith Races, in July, 1813; he had no previous intention of committing depredations, but merely to idle a few days, and amuse himself. But 'Satan finds some mischief still for idle hands to do;' and David Haggart was not the first, who on a race ground was led into vices and follies of which he had no previous intention or idea. In the close of the week, being in a state of intoxication, he fell in with a recruiting party at the races, and got enlisted in the Norfolk militia.

He soon learnt to beat the drum, and afterwards to blow the bugle horn; he liked the red coat and the soldiering well enough for a while, but soon became tired of it; he found the confinement disagreeable, and the pay too small for his extravagant ideas. In about a year the regiment was ordered to England to be disbanded; and having made interest with his commanding officer, he got his discharge in Edinburgh, and returned to the house of his father, who again kindly put him to school, where he continued about nine months, and obtained a farther knowledge of arithmetic and book-keeping. He was then bound apprentice to Cockburn and Baird, millwrights and engineers, for the period of six years. 'I had now,' said Haggart, 'reflected on my past follies, and formed a resolution of following my new business with honesty and zeal.' He applied himself closely to work for about two years, and acquired the good opinion of his masters, and perhaps inspired his afflicted parents with hopes of his permanent reformation. At this time he was entrusted to pay in and draw considerable sums of money at the bank, and appears to have acted with fidelity towards his masters; but at length he contracted an intimacy with several very loose characters, and was often engaged in disgraceful adventures in the streets at night; but they were in some degree limited, by his parents imposing on him the salutary restriction of keeping early hours, as also by his ignorance of houses for the reception of stolen goods. The affairs of his employers becoming involved, David was thrown on his parents; idleness exposed him afresh to temptation, and he pursued his former ill-habits with wretched proficiency and success. He was very fond of company, and having now greater opportunities of gratifying his propensities, he continually frequented dances and raffles, where he mingled in the society of both sexes of the most dissolute character. In less than three months from the time that young Haggart obtained unrestricted liberty to attend his sinful pleasures, he found himself, at the early age of sixteen, plunged into such a state of vice and wretchedness, that his mind could not endure reflection. He spent whole nights in the streets, or in worse places: every thing he saw, or heard, or did, was wicked; his nights and his days were evil; he could not bear to look at his relations, and growing at last impatient of the restraint of living in his father's house, he formed the resolution of shifting his scene of action. Among his wretched associates, he had formed a great intimacy with Barney M'Guire, an Irishman, considerably older than himself; of a bold, enterprising spirit, of great bodily strength, and a most dexterous pick-pocket. Instructed by this veteran in the arts of wickedness, they agreed to travel to England together, and share the fruits of their unlawful occupation. It was when in company with, and encouraged by the daring acts of this man, that he first attempted to pick a pocket in open day-light; and be it observed, this attempt was made on a race ground, and on the person of a gentleman who had been very successful in his bets. Haggart was so eager on his prey as to pull out the pocket along with the money, and nearly upset the gentleman, who turned quickly round and examined his hands; but the booty was already passed to his companion in wickedness, and the gentleman appeared satisfied of his innocence, but said some one had picked his pocket. The produce of this achievement was eleven pounds.

From Portobello, Haggart and his wicked companion proceeded to Jedburgh, and thence to Kelso to attend St. James's fair. They repaired to the ground soon after breakfast, where they continued until dark. Having observed a man who had some horses for sale, and who had a bulk, apparently notes, in his breast pocket, Haggart came up to price a good looking horse, while Barney acted as his assistant. A discussion arising respecting the animal's age, the jockey, eager to satisfy them, held the jaws of the animal and shewed his teeth, and while his arms were raised, Barney contrived to ease him of the contents of his pocket, which, however, contained only nine pounds. Haggart immediately requested to see the horse's paces, and on the jockey complying they made off when his back was turned. During the day they committed other depredations, particularly on a gentleman whom Haggart watched all day.

Soon after Dumfries fair invited the attention of the young plunderers: here they remained three weeks; but M'Guire being already known there as an old offender, kept in close, and the prosecution of their schemes of plunder was committed to Haggart and a brother of M'Guire, and as he also was a well-known pickpocket, Haggart kept at a distance from him, and never spoke to him in the streets. What a wretched thing must it be, that regard to personal safety compels these chosen companions in vice, these partners in the gains of iniquity, to disavow and avoid each other in the presence of their fellow-creatures!

Beside collecting about seven pounds in silver, (perhaps much of it from persons whom the loss might sink into deep distress,) Haggart, observing a person going about in quest of change for a ten-pound note, followed him into the shop of a hosier, under pretence of purchasing goods, but in fact for the purpose of plundering the unsuspecting stranger. He secured his booty, and decamped; and the day following started with his companions to Annan, and thence to Lockerby, where a fair was about to be held.

Here, at an inn, they got themselves into company with a farmer and drover, both pretty much in liquor, and in consequence inclined to quarrel. Of these circumstances the villains took advantage. Haggart fanned the flame of contention, and urged them on to fight; at length they rose and stripped; M'Guire, under pretence of dissuading and separating, irritated them the more, and involved them in a general scuffle, during which Haggart got from the farmer's coat his pocket-book, containing twenty-three pounds; then rang the bell in a violent passion, paid the reckoning, abused the waiter for putting them into a room with such company, and decamped. Well did the wise man observe, ' Who hath woe? Who hath sorrow? Who hath contentions? Who hath babbling? Who hath wounds without cause? Who hath redness of eyes?—They that tarry long at the wine—they that go to seek mixed wine.'

The plunderers next proceeded on foot to Langholm, again to the fair. There a gentleman, apparently a dealer in cattle, whom young M'Guire had seen with a pocket-book containing a large quantity of bank-notes, was fixed on as the object of their attack. They watched an opportunity, and while Haggart, apparently by accident, turned over the left breast of his coat on his arm, Barney M'Guire diverted his attention by a question relative to some sheep just by, and young M'Guire took from him his pocket-book. This was passed to Barney, who immediately made off; the others remained a minute or two, and afterwards walked slowly away to avoid suspicion.

On joining Barney, he showed them the pocket-book, stuffed with cambric paper, and laughed at his brother for giving them so much trouble about nothing; but on getting alone with Haggart, he showed him the prize, which amounted to two hundred and one pounds. This is not the first instance in which Haggart and M'Guire conspired to cheat the younger M'Guire of his share of the booty; such meanness and treachery in persons of their character cannot excite much surprise; but it must be exceedingly humiliating to these sharks of the earth, thus to be made a prey to each other, and it is a contradiction of the foolish boast of 'honour among thieves.' Haggart observes, that he never was happier in his life than when he fingered all this money; but adds, he thought sore about it afterwards, when he was ill and likely to die.—Ah, the pleasures of sin are but for a season! at the last they bite like a serpent, and sting like an adder. About half an hour after the above adventure, they saw, to their great surprise and terror, a police-officer running about, but he did not see them; they immediately took a post chaise, and set forward on the road to Annan, leaving word with their landlord that they were gone to Dumfries.

Next day they went on to Carlisle, and remained there about a month, amusing themselves by riding about through the days, and passing the evenings in gambling houses and dancing rooms. Here Haggart acquired great proficiency in the use of cards, dice, and billiards, beside a number of legerdemain tricks. Oh! had this ingenuity and application been directed to the pursuit of some rational and innocent science, in all probability a youth of Haggart's abilities would have insured to himself an honest independence, and become a useful and honourable member of the community, instead of its pest and disgrace.

During their stay in Carlisle, they attempted to pick a gentleman's pocket of a gold watch and seals, but the watch being secured in the pocket, disappointed them; the gentleman accused them of their intention, but they overpowered him with abuse, and he left them. He, however, watched them into their lodging, and the same evening their trunk and portmanteau were secured by constables. To avoid being taken themselves, they shifted their abode to the house of one who appears to have been a comrade in iniquity. Next morning, finding their stock of clothes reduced to what they had on, they went to a respectable merchant tailor, and were measured for suits of superfine clothes. He had them ready in two days, when they called for them; and under pretence of wanting some other articles, while the master left the room a moment to fetch them, the sharpers took up their new clothes and made off, taking the next stage for Kendal. At this place is held one of the finest horse markets in England: here, under pretence of dealing for horses, they robbed a gentleman of forty-three pounds, and hastened next day to Morpeth, where a fair was shortly to be held. Here they fell in company with some others of their own profession, and strengthened each other's hands in sin; they engaged in two hazardous adventures — picking one gentleman's pocket of fifteen pounds, and snatching seventeen pounds out of the hands of another, who was bargaining for a horse. It is painful to observe, that at this place they fell in with a constable or police-officer, who had formerly been acquainted with Barney; they renewed their acquaintance with a familiarity and confidence which too clearly proved the connexion that often subsists between characters of these descriptions. They next proceeded to Newcastle, where they obtained lodgings in the house of a respectable private family, and remained there a month, assuming the false names of Wilson and Arkison, and passing for gentlemen travelling on pleasure. It appears they were admitted to the intimate society of this family, and were allowed to attend the young ladies to the theatre, and other places of public amusement. Who but must shudder at the perilous situation in which these young females were placed? and what a lesson of caution is conveyed both to young persons and those who have the charge of them, against forming habits of intimacy with persons whose character they are not thoroughly acquainted with! While their thoughtless companions supposed them intent only on amusement, these adepts in iniquity, like him to whose service they had devoted themselves, were in reality 'going about, seeking whom they might devour.' On one occasion, observing a gentleman whom they supposed might afford them a considerable booty, Barney, under pretence of indisposition, left his companions, attacked the stranger, and robbed him of thirty-three pounds. Other similar adventures put them in possession of about seventy pounds, yet this sum did not defray their expences by fourteen pounds: no, for he that worketh iniquity 'earneth wages to put into a bag with holes.'

One circumstance that occurred at Newcastle must not be wholly unnoticed, because it proves that the society of gamblers is often that of swindlers, cheats, profane and quarrelsome persons; and that gambling not unfrequently leads to the commission of these crimes. Haggart and his companions were at a house for receiving stolen goods, gambling with the bully of the house, from whom they gained about three pounds; he became enraged, and swore an oath that they should not leave the house with his money; on which a severe scuffle ensued, which had well nigh ended in bloodshed and murder.

In January, 1818, on their way to Durham, to attend a fair, they came to a house in a lonely place, and determined to break into it. They entered it by a window, and met a strong resistance from the master of the house; but, having knocked him down, they succeeded in binding him hand and foot, and gagging him with a handkerchief. The rest of the family, being females, were too much terrified to interrupt them, and they proceeded to rifle the property. Having taken about thirty pounds, they went to Durham, where Haggart was apprehended the next day; but having changed his clothes, and considerably disguised himself, the man whose house they entered could not identify him: he was accordingly liberated, and returned to Newcastle.

In two or three days they were both apprehended, and carried back to Durham; having on the same clothes in which they had committed the burglary, the man whom they had robbed immediately recognised them, and was bound over to prosecute. They were tried under the feigned names of Morrison and Arkison, and were found guilty, and sent back to prison, in order to be brought up for sentence of death at the end of the assizes.

They lost no time in contriving their escape, and after long deliberation with their fellow-prisoners, resolved on the attempt. They set to work on the wall of their cell, and got out to the back passage, when the turnkey made his appearance. They seized him, took his keys, bound and gagged him: having gained the back yard they scaled the wall, but Barney and another prisoner fell, after gaining the top: by this time the alarm was given, and they were both secured.

Haggart having made his escape, returned to Newcastle, in company with a Yorkshireman (most probably one who had escaped from prison with him), where he obtained a tool with which to assist M'Guire in making his escape; and they were returning to Durham when they were pursued by two officers, who got close to them on a wild part of the road unobserved. Just as they were springing on Haggart, he laid one of them low with his pistol, and left him, uncertain whether he had his murder to answer for, but believing that his aim was but too true; and that was indeed the case. The Yorkshireman knocked down the other, and they then proceeded to Durham; where, in the night time, Haggart, by means of a rope ladder, got over the back wall of the gaol, and conveyed the spring saw to M'Guire, who made his escape that same night, by cutting the iron bars of his cell window, and followed Haggart to Newcastle, and thence accompanied him to Berwick-on-Tweed, Dunse, and Coldstream, where they lodged at a house for receiving stolen goods; in the evening they stripped a drover of nine pounds, and removed next day to Kelso. It is mentioned in this and in several other instances, that the persons they attacked were more or less in a state of intoxication: let this be a warning against that common, but disgraceful and ruinous vice;—intoxication renders a person an easy prey both to ill-designing men and to the great tempter, who is ever on the watch to catch unwary souls.

At Kelso they made a similar attack on the person of a farmer, but he had his eyes about him, and, detecting Barney in the act of bringing his money out of his pocket, he seized him by the collar, and a terrible scuffle ensued. The farmer, who was very powerful, still retained his grasp; a mob soon gathered; Haggart escaped by flight, but M'Guire was secured, and imprisoned for three months.

Being now left without an associate, Haggart returned to Newcastle, where he resided four months, in the house of his old friend, Mrs. A——: during his stay there, one of the young ladies was married to a respectable shopkeeper, on which occasion Haggart took the lead in conducting the festivities of the wedding. About two months of the time Haggart supported himself by gambling, in the same low and vicious society he had before frequented. One evening, having accompanied one of the Miss A——'s to the theatre, on their return, a gentleman much in liquor attempted to insult the young lady; struggling in her defence, Haggart contrived to pick the pocket of his antagonist of nineteen guineas. On another occasion he observed a person at the gambling-house also much intoxicated, whom he watched out of the house; affected accidently to jostle him, and stripped him of thirty-three pounds. Soon after, attempting to take a gentleman's gold watch, he was detected and pursued, but made his escape by back ways home. He attempted nothing farther in Newcastle; but in the month of June took leave of his hostess and her daughters, with much regret on both sides. For the kindness and friendship manifested towards him by the family, Haggart expressed great gratitude, and observed, 'Little did they know the person whom they had so long harboured in their house, and introduced to most of their acquaintances and relations, under the name of Mr. John Wilson.'

On returning to Edinburgh Haggart employed himself, in connexion with a new associate, in shoplifting. The goods thus obtained were disposed of for a quarter of their value, and the servant of iniquity experienced the pinchings of poverty—so expensive is vice, and so insatiable the desire of forbidden goods. With his new companion (Henry) Haggart next visited Perth, where they accosted a Highland farmer, already intoxicated—invited him to take some more liquor, and robbed him of nine pounds.

A day or two after this Haggart was seized with violent illness, and returned to Edinburgh: after a few days, finding himself somewhat recovered, he strolled out at dusk, and assisted some old companions in their iniquitous pursuits; he was accidentally seen by George M'Conner, an old apprentice of his father's, who had faithfully promised if ever he met with him to bring him home. He succeeded in inducing him to return to his father, by whom he was gladly and kindly received; and he promised faithfully to remain with his parents, and apply himself to his old business of a mill-wright; but when asked where he had been, or how employed, would give no satisfactory answer. He remained at home two or three days, and then resolving to pass the night at a house of ill-fame, which he had before frequented, he took two guineas from the collar of his coat, where he was in the habit of concealing his ill-gotten treasures, and was proceeding on his guilty purpose, when he was seized with such a shock of sickness as obliged him to take to his bed. During his illness, which lasted four weeks, feelings of remorse operated greatly upon him; he trembled at the thought of being cut off in the midst of such wickedness, and called to give an account of all his crimes; to use his own words, ' I felt that I was such a sinner, that I was ashamed to ask forgiveness either from God or man, and such a stranger of late to religious instruction, that I had no words for prayer; I was altogether without hope.' Oh! that these feelings had been deep and abiding enough to drive the sinner to seek mercy, pardon, and purity from the blessed Jesus, who is exalted at God's right hand, a Prince and a Saviour, to give repentance and remission of sins! but without his grace softening and changing the heart, terrors alone will not prevail to work an abiding change in the character. ' Can the Ethiopian change his skin, or the leopard his spots? No more can they that are accustomed to do evil, learn to do good.' When Haggart recovered, the thoughts of repentance soon left his mind, and even while in a weak and feeble state he recommenced shop-lifting. Let sinners beware of stifling their convictions and breaking off their purposes of repentance, lest (according to our Lord's awful and expressive words) the evil spirit that seemed to withdraw for a while should return, bringing with him other spirits more wicked than himself; and so the last state of that man should be worse than the first.

Though Haggart returned to his old practices, he so far kept up appearances at home, by never being out after eight o'clock in the evening, and seldom more than half an hour at a time, that his parents thought he could not be doing any thing wrong, and pleased themselves with the hope of his reformation.

One evening he accompanied a lad, named John Steel, to Leith, and went into a shop to buy some tobacco, not intending at that time to practise his profession; when, to his surprise, Steel snatched the roll of tobacco from the woman's hand who was serving it, and ran off. Haggart was taken so unawares by this trick, that he made no attempt to run away till seized by the woman's son, to whom he dealt a violent blow, sent him reeling on the ground, and ran off. The pursuit soon became general; he was overtaken, and conveyed to the police-office; he was examined for this and for some other offences before the sheriff; there was not sufficient proof against him, but he was detained in gaol till he could obtain bail for his appearance at any time within six months. On being released he went to his father's, where he was kindly received; he put such a good face upon his projects, that his too partial parents could not credit his guilty intentions. His next adventure was at shop-lifting, in company with two infamous female companions; he disposed of his booty at the house of an acquaintance, and hastened home to bed soon after seven o'clock in the evening. His father and mother, who had been out, came in shortly afterwards, and asked of his sister where he was, and whether he had been out? She replied that he had not, and that he was in bed. This was very mistaken, as well as sinful kindness: she was indeed quite ignorant of what he had been about, and concealed what she did know to prevent any reproof from his parents for going out contrary to their orders; but the watchfulness and reproofs of kind and careful parents were far rather to be desired than a continuance in sin undetected and unreproved. However, he was next morning taken up, and one of those hardened wretches who invited him to the commission of the crime, appeared as evidence against him. He stoutly denied any knowledge of the affair, and offered to prove an *alibi*; his parents were called, who proved his being in bed at a quarter past seven, and who believed he had not been out all the preceding evening: thus was their veracity exposed to be called in question by the improper means used by their daughter to conceal her brother's disobedience. The magistrates released him on the word of his father, whom they knew to be an honest man, but expressed their fear that his son was a rogue.

He remained very quietly at his father's for about three weeks, when he was again taken up; his other female companion, having been secured, had divulged every thing. However, on cross-questioning her, he so puzzled her that the judge put no faith in her evidence, and he was only ordered to find bail. He then remained at his father's till February, 1819, when one night he met a former companion in vice, who enticed him to his old trade of a pick-pocket. Next day they started in company for Musselburgh, and the same evening plundered the shop of a merchant tailor of two pieces of superfine cloth, and some other articles; this valuable prize they exchanged, when in liquor, for a small sum.

Having now again deserted his father's house, and involved himself in the society of the most vicious and abandoned of both sexes, Haggart became very careless and shabby in his dress and appearance, and was engaged in various petty, disgraceful scuffles: at length he was taken up, and brought before the same magistrates from whom, in the former instance, he had escaped so easily. One of them thus addressed him—'Haggart, you are a great scoundrel, and the best thing I can do for you, to make a good boy, is to send you to Bridewell for sixty days:—bread and water, and solitary confinement.' He was immediately removed from the bar, and conducted to his doleful cell; whence, about ten days after, he was again brought before the magistrates on another charge. For this he was sentenced to other sixty days' imprisonment. Although fully conscious of his guilt, he stiffly denied the charge; and, with the most hardened impudence, told the judge, that if he died in Bridewell they would be at the expense of burying him.

After four months' imprisonment he was released, in July, and returned to his father's, where he lived quietly a few weeks, and recruited his strength.

The time of his confinement had been spent, not in penitent reflections on his past sinful course, and humble resolutions of amendment, but in projecting new schemes of vice with an associate in prison. In the month of September they set out together on their unlawful enterprises, and were soon joined by two more abandoned characters of each sex, and pursued their trade in company. At Aberdeen races, among other offences, Haggart stole a watch, and passed it to one of his companions (Graham), who took it to his lodgings, and hid it in the draught hole at the back of the grate. That very night a mason was employed to put in another grate, when the watch was discovered, and taken to an officer of justice, who went immediately in search of them. They were all sentenced to imprisonments of different lengths; the magistrate expressing his regret at seeing so many good-looking lads going on in the ways of vice and ruin.

After two months, Haggart and one of his companions, named (or nick-named) Doctor Black, were released, when they immediately recommenced their courses of vice, especially in the shop-lifting way. Having stolen a pedlar's pack, and several other articles of linen drapery and hosiery, Haggart assumed the character of a pedlar, and travelled the country to dispose of his ill-gotten goods. After this he returned to Edinburgh, where he remained till January, 1820, committing depredations of every description, both there and at Leith; especially robbing private houses of large quantities of plate. On the 1st of March he was arrested at Leith, in company with an accomplice named Forest. The offenders made a desperate resistance, but were at length secured and committed for trial. On the evening of the 27th of March, having obtained a small file, Haggart cut the irons from his legs, then forced up the door of his cell, and got into the passage. He then set to work upon a very thick stone wall, through which he at length made a hole, and got on the staircase just as the clock struck twelve. He had still the outer wall to penetrate, on which he fell to work with great caution, lest he should be heard by the person who was appointed to watch him all night. Whilst he was working at the wall this person came several times to the door of his cell, which was just below. Having made considerable progress, he returned to the room where his companion Forest was, and brought him to his assistance; he also awoke one of the debtors whom he knew, and obtained his assistance in removing his hand-cuffs, having all along been working with them upon him. After great labour and violent pain they succeeded in wrenching the chain in two pieces. He then renewed his operations on the outer wall, and, having removed a large stone, got out a few minutes before five o'clock in the morning. When he gained the outside stair he saw a man coming towards him, and, supposing him to be an officer in pursuit of him, he leaped over the back of the stair; but recollecting that Forest had yet to get out, he prepared to give the man battle, lest he should attempt to seize Forest; but the man said to him, 'Run, Haggart, run; I wont touch you.' Forest came out, he took hold of his hand, and ran off at full speed, pulling him along with him. Here one cannot but pause, to regret that such abilities, industry, perseverance, and self-denial, had not been exerted in obtaining an honest livelihood, rather than in escaping a just punishment.

It is distressing to relate, that the very evening of their escape, they returned to their detestable trade. But indeed they had reduced themselves to a sort of wilful necessity, having no other means of subsistence. Let no one flatter himself that in the ways of vice, he may say to himself, 'Thus far shalt thou go, and no farther;' no! the first step in vice almost necessarily draws on an hundred more, and impels the sinner on to destruction. At Dumfries they were joined by two Irishmen of their own guilty profession, T. M'Colgan, and Felix Donnelly, the former of whom suffered the awful sentence of the law at Glasgow, for housebreaking, a few months before Haggart. How short is the course of vice! and how truly has it been said, 'Vice has had more martyrs than godliness.'

These companions in guilt attended at Dalbeattie fair, where they gained fourteen pounds, and on their return to Dumfries took several purses and watches from the door of the circuit court, which was then sitting; and one evening about eight o'clock, Haggart entered the house of a Mrs. Graham, and took thence a very large quantity of plate, which he disposed of to a wretch of the same name (though of course not connected) with the lady from whom they were stolen. At Dumfries he met with his old associate, Barney M'Guire, whom he had not seen for two years. The remainder of the party were taken a few days afterward; so Haggart and M'Guire resolved to leave Dumfries for Carlisle; but going into a shop, M'Guire was seized by an officer in mistake for Haggart, whose great coat he had on: by this mistake he escaped for a short time, but had not gone above six miles on the road, when he was pursued and taken, after a stout resistance. Haggart was brought back to Leith, where he was fully committed to the gaol, and indicted to stand trial before the High Court of Justiciary on the 12th of July, for one act of housebreaking, eleven acts of theft, and one act of prisonbreaking. Of the house-breaking he was acquitted, it appearing that he got in at an open window; but was brought in guilty of theft, and remanded to gaol without getting any sentence. After lying there some time, he was indicted to stand his trial at Dumfries, for the affair in which he had been there concerned with Graham.

M'Guire was sentenced to fourteen years transportation, and they parted with great regret.

On the 6th of September, Haggart was removed in a chaise, attended by two officers, from Edinburgh to Peebles, where he was kept two days in the gaol: this was long enough for him to form a plan of escape; which had nearly succeeded. The iron frame of his window was only fixed with lime; he tore up one of his blankets, tied one end to the window bars, and the other to the door of his cell; he then got a short wooden spoke off part of his bedstead, and began twisting the centre of the blanket; by this means he would soon have pulled out the window, but the blanket was so rotten, that it broke as soon as he laid any stress upon it. Being disappointed in his plan, he plastered up the lime which he had removed so neatly, that it was not observed by the turnkey. A part of the torn blanket he wrapped round his body for future use, little anticipating the awful purpose it would be afterwards turned to. He proceeded to Dumfries, and on the 11th of September was taken into court for trial. For some cause his trial did not go on, and he was sent back to prison; there he became acquainted with a youth named John Dunbar, who was just sentenced to seven years' transportation, and after some caution they entered into a scheme for making their escape.

During the short time that Haggart was in the gaol at Dumfries, several respectable persons noticed him, and kindly interested themselves in his behalf. One of these amiable and excellent females, who delight to mitigate the horrors of imprisonment, and to attempt the instruction and reformation of the guilty, frequently called at the prison, and behaved very kindly to him; but her kindness appears to have had no beneficial effect on his callous heart.

With one person, whom he styles 'a very respectable man,' Haggart was allowed to tamper in order to his escape; he gave him the plans of four keys, as there were four doors between him and his liberty, and expected from him such assistance as should enable him to regain it. Certainly the epithet was grossly misapplied; no one can be respectable who does not honour justice; and no one who respects the laws of God, can wilfully violate, or aid another to violate, those of his country. Having also a spring-saw, by means of which he could cut away any iron that opposed his progress, Haggart felt himself secure of liberty, but was drawn into another scheme with Dunbar, careless whether or not it succeeded; the prosecution of which however led to the horrid deed for which he suffered.

His cell was opposite to that of Edward M'Grory, who was then under sentence of death for robbery, and was afterwards executed; another prisoner, named Laurie, under sentence of transportation, was in the cell adjoining. One night he asked Haggart through the wall, 'You that have been at gaol-breaking before, how do you think this could be broke?' Unwilling to trust him, Haggart replied, 'I don't think it could be broke at all;' although at the same time he knew to the contrary. Laurie then stated his plan of getting a stone tied in a handkerchief, and some morning when they were all in the passage together, to knock down Hunter, the head-gaoler, and take the keys from him. To this Haggart objected, saying, if he never should get his liberty, he never should strike the serjeant for it, because he thought he could accomplish it in a better and easier way:—this was, in the absence of Hunter, to gag Thomas Morrin the turnkey, in a closet, at the head of the stairs, just opposite the cage door, take the keys from him, and let all the prisoners out. Laurie still insisted on getting a stone, saying that although they could gag Morrin, they had still all the debtors to get through. Haggart refused to get the stone, but told him to try Dunbar, who agreed; and next day when John Reid, a prisoner, was passing along the yard, he asked him for a stone to break a flint. As soon as Dunbar got the stone, he gave it to Laurie, who fixed it at the bottom of a bag made for pulling up things out of the yard, out of the piece of blanket that Haggart had brought from Peebles. The next thing was to cut off the irons of M'Grory and Laurie; the spring-saw would soon have accomplished this, but Haggart was determined to keep it secret for his own purposes, in case of failure. He, therefore, with the assistance of a file, made a small saw out of a table-knife, which he had procured from a prisoner lately released. This he passed to Laurie, and then to M'Grory, and on the morning of the 10th of October, which Haggart denominated the blackest day of his life, he spoke through to both of them, and the attempt was agreed upon. About ten o'clock, Robert Simpson, another prisoner, was put into the cage with Dunbar and Haggart; they told him their plans, and although he was to be dismissed the next day, he said he would join them, and accompany Haggart; who however, made no reply, determining, if he escaped, to be off alone. He afterwards observed Simpson and Dunbar whispering in a corner of the cage, and suspected some plan to betray him. About twelve o'clock they saw Hunter leave the prison, and heard that he was gone to the races. Soon after, Morrin brought in two ministers to visit M'Grory, and they were locked into the cell with him. When one o'clock came, although the ministers were not gone away, the culprits resolved to delay no longer, but proceed in their criminal enterprise. Haggart concealed himself in the closet at the head of the stairs, where he had previously placed the bag with the stone. Dunbar then called Morrin to come up, and let out the ministers; he came up the stairs with a plate of soup for M'Grory. When he got to the top, he shut the cage door, and Haggart burst upon him from the closet; the pushing open of the door knocked the plate out of his hand. Haggart struck him one blow with the stone, dashed him down stairs, and without the loss of a moment, took the key of the outer door from his pocket. Haggart declares that he gave but one blow with the stone, and immediately threw it down; Dunbar picked it up, but it appears that no more blows were given, and that Morrin must have received his other wounds in falling.

Dunbar was standing over him, apparently rifling for the key which Haggart had already secured. Simpson had hold of Morrin's shoulders, and was beating his back upon the stairs, when Haggart rushed past them, crossed the yard as steadily as he could, took out the key, and opened the door. On getting out he ran round great part of the town; Dunbar overtook him, and at that moment they saw an officer coming directly up to them. They wheeled round, and ran, but in a moment Haggart had the mortification of seeing his fellow-adventurer secured. He at first thought of rushing in among them to rescue him, but the crowd was too great to make the attempt; so he consulted only his own safety, and ran nearly ten miles in less than an hour. He then got on the high road to Annan, when he saw a post-chaise at full gallop almost within twenty yards of him; upon this he threw off his coat, and leaped a hedge into a field where some persons were employed in digging potatoes. They all joined the officers who had got out of the chaise in pursuit of him; he fled across the field with amazing speed, and made for Cumlangan wood. The pursuers followed him into the wood, but he kept concealed close to the edge, and although they were very near him, he thus eluded their pursuit.

He then made for Annan, got through it before the alarm spread, and concealed himself in a hay stack a mile or two on the Carlisle road. There he remained all night, and most of the day following, when he heard a woman ask a boy if the lad was taken that had broken out of Dumfries gaol. He replied, 'No; but the gaoler died at ten o'clock last night.' These words struck him to the soul—his heart died within him, and he lay a good while in a state of insensibility. On coming to himself, he could scarcely believe that he had heard them, for the possibility of poor Morrin's death had never entered into his mind. He came out of the stack, and resolved to proceed, whatever should be the consequence. Seeing a scare-crow in the field, he stripped it, put on the clothes, and thus proceeded. That night he slept in a hay-loft; in the morning a man came in to fill the horserack, and was within a foot of him, but did not observe him, he being concealed amongst the hay. He overheard the man converse with another in the stable about him, observing that he was one of the most awful characters that ever lived; he had before broken all the gaols in Scotland except Dumfries, and had broken that at last; the other replied, he wished he might keep away, for it would not bring back the poor man's life, and he felt much for Haggart's father, whom he knew.

About eight o'clock he started unnoticed from his place of confinement, and pursued his weary way to Carlisle, where he found the whole town in an uproar about him. He assumed the name of Barney M'Coul, by which he had formerly been known there, and obtained a lodging and some food, the first he had tasted since leaving Dumfries; next day he procured a change of dress, and some women's garments, in which he determined to prosecute his journey. He travelled by night, lurking in wild places or in plantations during the day time, till he arrived at Newcastle, where he remained about twelve days, dressed in woman's clothes, and fell in with a former associate, whom he joined in new acts of robbery.

One evening he came out for the purpose of going to the theatre—and was it possible that a guilty wretch like him, his conscience corroded with blood, should feel any disposition or power to seek amusement?—Oh, yes!—diversion is the world's universal recipe for drowning both remorse and apprehension; it is recommended in every case of mental distress and depression. Under the slighter wounds of conscience, the sinner resorts to amusement, and cannot do without its delusive exhiliration; and when at the borders of despair, he still flies to his old remedy, which seldom fails to stupify the feelings, and harden the heart, though it can never, never effect a cure.

As Haggart came out, he espied John Richardson, the police-officer before mentioned; and so close was he upon him, that the cape of Haggart's coat touched his shoulder; however, he passed on without observing him. He had no hesitation in telling his companion how closely he was pursued, for he himself had several times escaped from prison, and was one whom Haggart had assisted in releasing from the Lock-up-house in Edinburgh. He immediately determined to return to Scotland, as he knew they would not suspect him of going where he was so well known. He walked out of the town with a bundle containing his different suits of clothes. The Berwick coach soon overtook him; he got outside, and arrived at Berwick without molestation; there he remained about a week, watching the arrival of the coaches, both to observe the movements of the police respecting himself, and also occasionally to pick the pockets of the passengers. After this he returned to Edinburgh in the coach, with another inside passenger, whom he intended to rob, but falling into conversation, they became so intimate that he had not the heart to do it.

Haggart professed himself quite a stranger to Edinburgh, and at a loss where to put up. His new friend recommended him to a tavern, at the door of which he had stolen many a watch. There they remained together several days, Haggart, under pretence of indisposition, declined to accompany his friend in walking out, or to places of public amusement; in private visits to houses of disgrace and iniquity, he was less scrupulous. After a few days, he said he was obliged to proceed to Glasgow, and took leave of his friend, who had known him by the name of Mr. John Wilson. He took his portmanteau, and marched along the street in open day-light, and remained some days longer concealed in the city with an acquaintance, keeping close within doors all day, and walking out at dusk disguised in woman's clothes. He visited several of his acquaintance, and among the rest saw his poor father, but did not let him know his plans or his residence. One night, venturing out in his own clothes, he saw an officer of the police, their eyes met each other; Haggart's heart shrunk for a moment, and but a moment. He plunged his hand into his breast pocket as if for a pistol. The officer, who knew him too well to engage him alone, ran away, as did also Haggart, but in another direction. He then got some plate and other articles which he had concealed in a garret where he formerly lodged, and having exchanged them into money, determined first to go to the north of Scotland, then take a tour to the west, and to go to Ireland. During his stay in and about Edinburgh, he picked up an acquaintance, with whom he went in company to Anstruther, St. Andrews, Cupar-Fife, and Dundee. There he gave Thomson the slip, took lodgings, and procured a suit of sailor's clothes, determining to do something in the way of his business.

Passing by a jeweller's shop, he observed two gold watches hanging among many other metal ones; he thrust his hand and took them. He soon outran the crowd that pursued him, threw on his white great coat over his sailor's clothes, and returned to the spot, where several persons who came together to lament the jeweller's loss, soon had good reason to lament their own; for in a few minutes he picked their pockets to the amount of eighteen pounds, besides a watch, &c. After this he took a circuitous return to Edinburgh. There he began to reflect why he had come back again to a place which was the scene of all his earliest bad habits, and where also danger was most to be apprehended, as he knew there was a price upon his head; he resolved to pursue his guilty traffic that night, and leave the town for ever, early the next morning. Accordingly, he went back to Newhaven, and stopped within doors all day; but still hankering after the scene of his vices, his gains, and his pleasures, he returned to Edinburgh in the afternoon. The first thing that struck his eye was a bill posted up, offering a reward of seventy guineas for his apprehension. The folly of haunting a place where he was so well known, struck him afresh; he walked to Leith, and got into a boat which was setting sail for Kinghorn; then went on to Perth. During his stay there, the illuminations and other rejoicings for the Queen's acquittal, afforded him an opportunity of exercising his trade. He got four silver watches, and a gold one, besides a considerable sum of money. Next day he started for Dunkeld, to attend a fair with two associates, where he robbed a farmer of about nine pounds. At Dundee he stole from a gentleman's house three dozen of table spoons; and at Kenmore fair, thirty-nine pounds from a Highland farmer. After practising also at Cupar-Fife fair, he parted with his companion, and went alone to Arbroath fair, where he took a purse containing twenty-two guineas, but having seen an Edinburgh officer, he did not think it safe to remain in Arbroath all night, so started inside the first coach to Perth; cheated the guard of his fare, and joined an old acquaintance, James Edgy, at his lodgings. Next evening, as he was sitting in his lodgings with Edgy and a female companion, two constables came in upon them; 'Gentlemen,' said Haggart, 'you are in a mistake,' and ringing the bell, desired the landlord to show the gentlemen into a room. One of them said, 'Oh no, it is you we want;' he then very unconcernedly asked them their business; they in reply asked his name, and he theirs, which they refused to give. The landlord observed to Haggart that they were police men; on which he told them he would call and acquaint the magistrate of their conduct, and in the mean time if they did not make off, threatened them with a horse-whipping; thus intimidated, they left the room: Haggart conveyed his female companion out of the house, and in a few minutes the officers returned with their staves of office, which they presented, and required Haggart and Edgy to go before a magistrate. To this Haggart made no objection, and rang for his great coat; but just as the landlord was retiring to fetch it, he bounced up, saying, 'Oh, I believe it is in my own bedroom, I'll get it myself;' and retiring by the back door, he made off as fast as he could, to the mortification of the policemen, and the astonishment of his landlord, who had often trusted him with the keys of his drawers, and every thing in his house. Being thus deprived of his lodgings, he went to one of the most profligate houses in the town, where he remained a day or two, and then went with Edgy and another to Glanmis fair. Seeing a farmer with a considerable sum of money about him, they determined on attacking him; but as two other persons joined him, Edgy and Smith shrunk off, and persuaded Haggart also to relinquish the attempt; but he was determined to persevere, and ultimately succeeded in his design. He took twenty-eight pounds from the farmer, for which two other persons were taken up and lodged in Forfar gaol, whom Haggart declared were truly innocent of it. He then returned to Perth, paid his reckoning to Mr. Taylor, his unsuspecting landlord, whom he found with his wife in tears on his account. He told them he was immediately going to leave town, but remained some days, during which he got forty-five pounds at one adventure in the market, and saw several pickpockets taken close by his side. Next day he went with Edgy to Glasgow; they made up their minds to go to Ireland, and went on board, when Haggart saw a person who had been confined for debt in Edinburgh gaol when he was there. However, he concealed himself in one of the sailor's cribs, and passed unnoticed. On one occasion, when he was sitting in the fore cabin, a gentleman came below, looked closely at all the passengers, and fixed his eye particularly on Haggart. He soon after went on shore at Lamlash. Haggart suspected something bad, and was inclined to leap overboard, it being a dark night, thinking that the best way of escape. The gentleman was left behind at Lamlash, and Haggart afterwards learned who he was, and that he wrote about him to Dumfries. ' It was well,' he observed, ' that his suspicions were unknown to him at the time, for he went on shore at black night, and he could but too easily have put him overboard.' On landing in Ireland, Haggart and Edgy rambled over the town of Belfast for two days in one continued state of intoxication. Edgy being well known in Belfast, was soon taken for some old offence, but Haggart pursued his guilty trade from place to place. When he first arrived at Belfast from Scotland, he saw Robert Platt, who had been confined in Dumfries gaol while he was there. Platt was taken for stealing in Drumore market, on a day that Haggart also was there, and with a view of getting his liberty, gave information that he had seen Haggart the murderer there. The officers, dazzled with the information of reward for taking him, seized every one of whom they had the slightest suspicion; while he was in a public-house, two lads were taken sitting close beside him. Little did he suspect what they were after, when in a few minutes Platt peeped in at the door, and instantly four officers sprang in, seized him, and carried him before a magistrate. On being asked his name, he replied in a rich brogue, ' Why sure, and it's John M'Colgan.' The officers began to suspect themselves mistaken. Haggart kept up the deception by his broad Irish brogue, professing himself a native of Armagh, and as never having been in Scotland. However, the magistrate ordered three yeomen to sit up with him all night, together with the officers, in the court room; and retired, having witnessed a strict search of his person, on which nothing was found but a thirty-shilling note, and some silver.

He now thought it was all over with him, and determined to make a desperate struggle to gain his liberty, or perish in the attempt. He plied his attendants with plenty of drink, and they were very civil to him. About eleven o'clock, he prevailed upon them to allow an acquaintance to bring him some supper. When the person came, he asked leave to speak to her a minute behind the boxes in the court, where there was a large window. They granted his request, and taking a sudden leap, he sprang through the window, and alighted upon the street, without being either cut by the glass, or hurt by the fall. He crossed the street to an opposite entry, and immediately saw the whole of his keepers below the window staring at each other, not knowing what to do. They all went off to follow him; he took the road for Belfast, and soon got there, having run fifteen Irish miles in two hours and a quarter. He travelled from place to place, taxing each as he went for his dishonourable and unjust maintenance. After remaining a week or two in Dublin, he paid three pounds ten shillings for his passage to America, but afterwards changed his mind,

'The judge, in a violent rage, said that he would make oath, if necessary; and the jury in a moment returned a verdict of "Guilty of felony at large." I was then sentenced to seven years' transportation; but the judge at the same time telling me, that if I would produce my father, and show to him that he had mistaken me, he would change the sentence to twelve months' imprisonment. I told him I would rather go abroad than let my friends know any thing about the matter; that he was sending me among pick-pockets, where I would likely learn the art myself; and the first man's pocket I would pick on my return would be his.

'I have been twice tried for my life in Scotland. The first time I got more than justice, for I was acquitted; the second time I got justice, for I was convicted. But in Ireland I got no justice at all; for at Downpatrick there was none to speak for me but the judge, and he spoke against me.'

If this statement be correct, it is a striking and singular circumstance, that he who had by his own artifices, or by the mistakes of others, escaped his just punishment, should at last be reserved to it by a sentence which bore the appearance of mistake, if not of injustice. However man may be mistaken or deceived, 'verily there is a God that judgeth in the earth—and though hand join in hand, the wicked shall not always go unpunished.'

Haggart was removed to the gaol, and in the afternoon the magistrate of Drumnore, who had formerly examined him, came into the press yard, where he was walking among the other prisoners. He instantly distinguished him, and asked him if he ever was in Drumnore? Haggart replied, 'Yes, twenty times; he then asked if he recollected him, or bribing a constable, and breaking away?' 'No!' replied the hardened liar, 'I have never seen you, or been in custody in Drumnore in my life.' 'Did you ever take the name of John M'Colgan?' 'No, nor do I know what you mean,' was the reply. The gentleman then told the turnkey that if they did not iron him, he would be off in half an hour. He was accordingly loaded with irons, and remained in that state three days, when he was removed to Kilmainham gaol, where he was put among the convicts of every description.

He soon thought of making his escape by digging through the back wall, with the assistance of several others, having first secured the entrance of their apartment; but some of the prisoners gave information, and Haggart being the first man who made his appearance through the hole, got a severe blow; the others rushed after him, but having still a high wall to get over, they were all secured by a party of soldiers, and locked up in their cells. A few hours after this, Haggart called out of his cell window to two young women* accused of murder, in Dublin. He felt much for their situation, and shivered when he looked at them, his own hands having been stained with blood. He gave them (as he expresses it) such serious advice, as a poor guilty wretch could. They were afterwards condemned and executed. While in conversation with them, the cell door opened, and the turnkey found fault with him for interfering with them, and bade him be silent. Haggart replied he would not be silent, as he was saying nothing improper, and he felt much interested for these poor creatures, whose situation was so much like

* Bridget Butterly and Bridget Ennis.

his own. Some insolence succeeded on the one part, and perhaps some ill-nature on the other, and it resulted in his being handcuffed and confined with a horrible iron instrument fitted on his head, from the front bar of which an iron tongue entered his mouth and prevented his speaking. This, which Haggart considered an arbitrary and cruel exercise of power, excited only opposition, and the moment it was removed, he resumed his seat on the window of his cell, and remained there the rest of the day, singing the most profane songs he could think of. Even the fear of the iron helmet of Kilmainham could not keep him quiet.

But something awaited him far worse, and which, had he known, would have made his heart tremble, hard and wicked as it was. Next morning the prisoners, consisting of some hundreds, were taken down into a yard, and ranked in companies of twenty each. In a few minutes, John Richardson, the police-officer from Scotland, made his appearance, accompanied by the two gaolers and turnkey; a terrific sight to Haggart! He passed through all the ranks, and the second time stopped, and, taking Haggart's hand, said, 'Do you know me, David?'— 'What does the man say?' asked Haggart, in a master-piece of Irish brogue, turning at the same time to the gaoler, who said 'Don't you know him?' 'Troth and by my sowl,' replied Haggart, 'I know nothing at all, at all, about him.' The officer persisted that he knew him; and he was conveyed to the condemned yard; the gaoler telling him, if he was a Scotchman, he was greatly mistaken; for that he had the brogue as well as any boy in Ireland. He was then taken to the police-office, and heavily loaded with irons. An iron belt was fixed round his waist, with his wrists pinioned to each side of it; a chain passed from the front of the belt and joined the centre of a chain, each end of which was padlocked round his ancles, and a chain passed from each wrist to each ancle. In this dreadful (but by his own hardened and daring conduct necessary) state of torture and confinement, he was conducted to Dumfries. The officers treated him with the utmost tenderness and humanity, but he obstinately kept up his pretended ignorance for a considerable time.

On their approach towards Dumfries, which was in the dark, there were many thousands of people on the road, many of them with torches in their hands, waiting his arrival; and at the gaol it was scarcely possible to get him out of the coach for the multitude, all crowding for a sight of HAGGART THE MURDERER. —Some discovered sorrow, and some terror; but whose could equal his own? He plunged through them all, rattling his chains, and making a great show of courage, but owned that his heart was shaken at the thought of poor Morrin. As he went up the stairs to the cells, he had to pass the very spot where he struck him; and oh! confessed the guilty murderer, 'it was like fire to my feet!' Oh! that sinners would remember this when tempted to commit sin; though at the moment it may be sweet and pleasant, yet at the last it shall sting as a serpent, and bite like an adder. It has been well observed, 'if we had as much fore-sight as we have after-wit, we should not easily be drawn into sin.' And why have we not? Because the love of sin blinds our eyes and hearts, that they should not discern its natural tendency.

After remaining at Dumfries three weeks, where the greater part of his Irish irons were removed, and he was twice examined by the sheriff, he was removed to Edinburgh, and indicted to stand his trial for the murder of Thomas Morrin. His trial came on June 11th: many witnesses were examined against him; some of them gave an incorrect testimony, but Haggart freely allowed that perhaps they were only mistaken, and that he was fully as wicked as they represented him; but there was one witness by whom he felt himself injured. This man knew the whole of their plans, and ought to have testified that their object was liberty, not murder. 'However,' said Haggart, 'this would have made no difference, for it was the pleasure of God Almighty that I should come to an end.'—We will again use his own words:

'All that man could do, was done for me at my trial, and I had good hopes till the judge began to speak; but then my spirits fell, for his speaking was sore against me. I did not altogether despair when I saw the jury talking together; but, oh! when they said GUILTY, my very heart broke; but I was even then too proud to show my feelings, and I almost bit my lip through in hiding them. When the judge was passing the awful sentence, I turned dizzy, and gasped for breath. They say I looked careless; but they could not see within me. I did not know what happened or where I was. I thought of every thing in a minute; I thought of my father— I thought of my mother, who had died of a broken heart;—I thought of escape, and very near made a plunge over the heads of the crowd; then I could have cried out.'

The judge adverted to some particular circumstances in his case, which pointed out especially for a ... le. Not only, he observed ... impossible he should escape the common penalty due to the unnatural crime of murder; but that all Scotland might know that the law would most decidedly avenge the violence done to keepers of his Majesty's prisons, the Court had doomed the prisoner to expiate the crime in the city of Edinburgh. His lordship earnestly exhorted him to call in the assistance of the ministers of religion: solemnly warning him that if he did not seek pardon at the footstool of divine mercy, in deep repentance for all his sins, there was another and more terrible day of reckoning reserved for him, in that state upon which he was about to enter. It is most distressing to add, that, under warnings so solemn, and in circumstances so awful, he still discovered the most depraved insensibility and contempt. He adds, 'When the sentence was over, I gathered my thoughts, and my heart was as hard as ever, for I said, "Well! the man that is born to be hanged, will not be drowned;" this was very wicked'—wicked indeed, but, alas! too common, and little thought of; as though his destiny impelled him to a course of life that should terminate in this dreadful end. Such a necessity, the God of Justice, Holiness, and Mercy, never put on any of his creatures. No; the voice of his word and of his dispensations ever is—(oh, that sinners would regard it!)—'As I live, saith the Lord, I have no pleasure in the death of a sinner, but rather that he should turn from his wickedness and live; turn ye, turn ye, for why will ye die?'

But to return to Haggart's account of his feelings. After being brought back to the gaol, the wickedness of his heart was still great, and he had so little thought of his awful situation, that he made the following foolish verses, expressive of his hardened and unsubdued spirit:—

'Able and willing, you will find,
Though bound in chains, still free in mind;
For with these things I will never be grieved,
Although of freedom I am bereaved.

'In this vain world there is no rest,
And life is but a span at best;
The rich, the poor, the old, the young,
Shall all lie low before its long.

'I am a rogue, I don't deny,
But never lived by treachery;
And to rob a poor man, I disown,
But them that are of high renown.

'Now, for the crime that I am condemned,
The same I never did intend;
Only my liberty to take,
As I thought my life did lie at stake.

'My life, by perjury was sworn away,
I will say that to my dying day.
Oh, treacherous S———, you did me betray,
For all I wanted was liberty.

'No malice in my heart is found,
To any man above the ground.
Now, all good people, that speak of me,
You may say, I died for liberty.

'Although in chains you see me fast,
No frown upon my friends you'll cast,
For my relations were not to blame,
And I brought my parents to grief and shame.

'Now, all you ramblers in mourning go,
For the prince of ramblers is lying low;
And all you maidens, who love the game,
Put on your mourning veils again.

'And all your powers of music chaunt
To the memory of my dying rant;
A song of melancholy sing,
Till you make the very rafters ring.

'Farewell, relations, and friends also,
The time is nigh that I must go;
As for foes, I have but one,
But to the same I have done no wrong.'

'These wild and wicked thoughts,' he afterwards said, 'soon left me. Every body was kind to me. How this happens I cannot tell, for from my infancy my hand has been against every man, and I never saw a human being without trying to do them a harm. This kindness is an awful lesson to me now; but it has done me great good, for it is the sorest punishment I have met with yet in this world. I have been visited by several clergymen; they have prayed much with me and for me. I told them I had no words to pray, but they taught me, made me read my Bible, and gave me hopes of mercy in heaven—at least such hopes as a poor miserable wretch like me can have, for my sins stick close to me.

A clergyman, who visited him says—'For nearly a fortnight after his condemnation he appeared to be in the most hardened and unfeeling state of mind; but the pious admonitions he received roused him at last from his insensibility. When asked how he felt with respect to his soul and eternity, the answer he gave was, that he was sure he did not feel as he ought to feel, and he complained that his heart was like a stone. He then inquired if there were any instances in the Scripture of persons who had committed a crime similar to his; and he was directed to the case of David, of Manasseh, of Peter who denied Christ, of the dying thief, and the persecuting Saul, who thought that, by putting people to death, he was verily doing God service. That passage in Ezekiel was also mentioned to him, "I will take away the heart of stone, and give him a heart of flesh." These passages had a wonderful effect on him, and seemed to make a deep impression. He began to consult his Bible, and from that time his conviction became powerful, strong, and permanent, and his mind was very evidently much enlightened.

'He was particularly exhorted to examine himself whether his repentance was sincere, and not to rely on false hopes; or suppose, because the thief was pardoned in his dying moments, that therefore he might expect the same. When he was asked whether his repentance did not arise more from the unhappy circumstances in which he was placed, than from a sense of having offended God, and transgressed his holy law, he candidly acknowledged that he was afraid he was more influenced by the former than the latter.

' He desired a friend to go to his father, and to tell him that he died in the faith of Christ, his Redeemer. Indeed, he frequently exclaimed, "Why should I complain of my sufferings when I consider what Christ has undergone for me?" And he declared on the morning of his execution that he would not wish to escape, if the prison doors were open, as his death was the only atonement he could make in this world for the violated laws of God and man.

' Early on the morning of his execution, David Haggart joined earnestly in devotional exercise with his ministerial attendant. After the chaplain of the gaol had prayed, one of the officers of justice appeared, and requested all the persons present to retire, as he had something to communicate to the unhappy prisoner. Haggart immediately exclaimed, in a hurried tone, "Oh! I suppose it is the executioner." His firmness for a moment abandoned him, and he walked rapidly across the cell, with his arms folded, and with deep despair strongly painted on his countenance. He speedily, however, regained his composure; and when the executioner did appear, at once allowed his arms to be bound. He was then removed to a hall in the lower part of the lock-up-house, where he was received by two of the clergymen of Edinburgh and the magistrates. After prayers the procession proceeded to the scaffold. The conduct of the unfortunate youth there was in the highest degree becoming. While the beneficial influence of religion was apparent in his whole demeanour, his natural firmness of character never for a moment forsook him. He kneeled down, and uttered an earnest prayer; and, after addressing a few words of deep and anxious exhortation to the great multitude by whom he was surrounded, he met his fate with the same intrepidity which distinguished all the actions of his short, but guilty and eventful life, having just completed his twentieth year.' He was executed at Edinburgh, July the 18th, 1821.

Haggart, after his condemnation, wrote the history of his short and wicked life, which was subsequently published for the benefit of his father, who he requested might receive any profit arising from it, for the purpose of educating his younger brothers and sisters. The foregoing particulars are taken from this singular piece of auto-biography, which evinced a strong, though uncultivated mind; which, if it had been directed to laudable pursuits, could not fail to have placed the writer in an honourable station in society.

JOHN M'NAMARA AND THOMAS MALONY,
EXECUTED FOR THE MURDER OF MRS. TORRENS.

In 1821, and for one or two years before it, the south of Ireland was in a very disturbed state. Bands of lawless banditti roved through the country by night, dictating laws to the peaceable inhabitants, and inflicting summary vengeance on all who refused obedience to their arbitrary mandates. Among those who opposed their proceedings was a gentleman named Torrens, who resided at Mondella, in the county of Limerick, not far from the city. In March, 1821, his house was attacked by a band of nocturnal marauders, whom he beat off in a most gallant manner, killing several of the party.

Mr. Torrens's bravery on this occasion made him obnoxious to the Whiteboys; and apprehending danger from their known vindictive spirit, he removed to Adare, where he held a farm, which, after his removal, he frequently visited. On Sunday, the 10th of June, 1821, Mr. Torrens and his amiable and heroic wife dined at the farm-house, and were returning in the evening to Limerick, by a well-known and frequented path, but had not proceeded far, when a man crossed a stile and presented a letter to Mr. Torrens, who was about to read it, when he received a blow of a stone, and at the instant another ruffian leaped over the wall and attacked him. Mr. Torrens was unarmed, and must have fallen under the ruffians, had not Mrs. Torrens rushed to his assistance and extricated him, exclaiming, 'Come off my husband's body, you villains!' Mr. Torrens was for a while stunned; and on looking about he saw his heroic wife engaged in a personal contest with one of the assassins, who had a stick which she rescued from him, and ran with it to her husband. The battle was then renewed, and Mr. Torrens was immediately engaged with the man who first attacked his wife, and both came to the ground, Mr. Torrens making such good use of the stick that it broke with the force of his blows. At this time Mr. Torrens saw the other assassin engaged with his wife, and heard him cry out to his comrade, 'Tom, come away!' Tom obeyed with some difficulty; and as the other fellow was going from Mrs. Torrens, her husband saw him wipe something like a knife or dagger.

The unfortunate lady immediately ran to her husband, but said little; her bosom was streaming with blood; and, in a few minutes she became convulsed and expired, for the cowardly assassin had stabbed her to the heart. Mr. Torrens, though bathed in blood, from the effect of fifteen wounds, contrived to crawl to a cottage, where he fell senseless on a bed; so dreadful was one of the wounds in his neck, that his breath came through the incision it made.

The cottager, whose name was Switzer, found Mrs. Torrens a corpse; and, by strict medical care, her surviving husband was gradually restored to partial health; but his constitution was seriously affected by the wounds he had received.

To discover and apprehend the assassins was now the business of justice, and in a short time, Malony and M'Namara were taken into custody. These men were labourers, and perpetrated the foul deed in conformity with that baneful system of confederacy which had, at this time, bound the deluded peasantry together. Against Mr. or Mrs. Torrens these assassins had no individual cause of enmity, but had, in obedience to their bandit laws, attempted the life of both, and had too fatally succeeded as to one of them. The fate of Mrs. Torrens excited universal regret. Her amiable conduct in private life had endeared to her a number of friends, while her heroic fidelity to her husband, and the manner of her death, secured respect for her memory.

When Malony and M'Namara

were brought before Mr. Torrens, that gentleman immediately recognized M'Namara as the man who had handed him the letter, and Malony as the murderer. They were consequently committed to prison, and, a short time before the assizes, Maloney made a full confession of his guilt. Their trial came on at Limerick, December the 17th, 1821, when they were convicted by an impartial jury; and on the next day but one, were executed, when they behaved as became their awful situation.

Hayward Waltzing with a Lady of Quality.

SAMUEL DENMORE HAYWARD,
EXECUTED FOR BURGLARY.

Few men better deserved the appellation of the 'Modern Macheath' than the unfortunate Hayward, the incidents of whose short life deserve to be recorded, as affording not only a view of his own character, but a powerful lesson to youth.

Samuel Denmore Hayward was born in October, 1797. His father was an industrious journeyman currier, who resided in the Borough of Southwark; and, being very poor, he allowed his son to deliver messages for the prisoners in the King's Bench, who regarded him as a boy of great promise. Indeed, it was a general remark in the whole neighbourhood that Samuel had all the appearance of a 'gentleman's child.'

Flattered by the early notice thus shown him, he indulged higher notions than could possibly be gratified by following the humble business of his father, and, accordingly, he procured himself to be bound an apprentice to a tailor. But business was not his *forte*; he disliked the confined ideas of trade, and aspired to a higher station in society than that usually attained by a tailor. At the expiration of the first year his master was glad to cancel his indentures; and, thus freed from further restraint, young Hayward became waiter in the New York Coffee House, near the Royal Exchange.

This situation did not exactly accord with his ambition, but it answered his purpose; it afforded him an opportunity of exhibiting his fine person and mixing with gentlemen, though in the humble capacity of an attendant. In dress, too, he could partially indulge his vanity, and this was not the least inducement to his entering this menial occupation. While here his address and pleasing deportment gained him universal esteem, and attracted the observation of Dr. Hughson, who was then compiling his celebrated 'History of London,' and residing in Furnival's Inn. The doctor admired his politeness and attention, and, convinced that he was a lad of parts, took him home to assist him in collecting materials for works on which he was then engaged.

The road to an honourable career in life was now opened to his ambition, and he seems to have laudably availed himself of the opportunity; for he not only acquitted himself reputably in his new engagement, but applied industriously to the cultivation of his mind. He acquired a complete knowledge of the French and Italian languages, both of which he spoke with great fluency; and also became a proficient in music, for which he had a natural taste. He played on several instruments with elegance and skill, and, in short, was deficient in none of those polite accomplishments so necessary to a man of fashion. He remained with the doctor about five years, and then entered the service of Captain Blanchard, with whom he travelled over the greater part of Europe. His new master was too indulgent, looking upon Hayward rather in the light of a companion, until the genteel lacquey, tired of being an attendant, sighed to exhibit himself as a principal in the gay and frivolous scenes he had witnessed at a respectful distance.

Buoyed up with inflated notions of his own personal importance, he quitted the service of Captain Blanchard, and made his first step towards ruin, by returning to London, where he assumed the character of a gentleman, and trusted to his wit and abilities for the means of supporting his apparent rank in society. Apprehensive that his origin might be discovered, he entirely cast off all his former acquaintances and relatives, and pretended to be a young man of family and consequence. The better to disguise himself, he assumed a military appearance, and having the air of a dashing young officer, easily imposed himself on fashionable society as belonging to the Commissariat Department.

Hayward, though now only twenty-one years of age, had read much, and was an acute observer of character. He had remarked that very superficial qualifications, when aided by appearance, were sufficient passports to the fashionable world, who are 'still deceived by ornament,' and determined to make a progress in the fluttering and heartless scene, he set about the necessary preparations. Nature had been prodigal to this vain young man; his person was elegant; his features animated, intelligent, and handsome; and his dress, being in the first style, fully accorded with the form it clothed.

Thus qualified by nature and art, he had only to present himself at the door of the Temple of Fashion to secure a ready admission. His polished manners, superior address, and handsome person, soon secured him the esteem of the ladies, while his military air, sporting phrases, and unblushing confidence, procured him the friendship of the gentlemen. In a very short period he was regarded as one whose society was worth courting, and whose presence could add to the attractions of a drawing-room. The 'voluptuous melodies of Moore,' he sang with rich and tasteful sweetness, while his execution on the flute was little, if at all, inferior to the performance of the celebrated Drouet. Such an addition to a fashionable party was not to be dispensed with. Hayward was invited by the dowager and the duke, the lord and the baronet, the dissipated and the wealthy, and, in a few months, he had run the complete circuit of fashionable life. In the morning he was to be seen paying a visit to one of the squares in the west end; in the middle of the day escorting ladies of the first distinction, to the Exhibition; and, in the evening, encompassed by elegance and beauty at the Opera.

The doors of respectable families were thrown open to him; and it is a melancholy truth that innocent and lovely females were introduced to this unprincipled scoundrel by their unsuspecting fathers and brothers. Is it, therefore, to be wondered at, that so many distressing and immoral scenes take place in high life, since so little caution is shown? Whatever is most estimable mankind guards with most care; but fashion reverses this as well as most other things, and thoughtlessly exposes the purity and innocence of unthinking females to the polluting contact of every villain who has art enough to worm himself into what is called polished society.

The amatory epistles received by Hayward from the fair sex, during his short career, amounted to upwards of three hundred. These were found in his trunk on his apprehension, but, from a proper feeling of delicacy, were not made public. The frail writers, no doubt, on hearing of the circumstance, were sufficiently punished for their indiscretion and credulity. We shall give one of these *billet-doux*, which 'wafts a sigh from Indus to the Pole,' as a specimen; and we can assure the reader it is one of the least objectionable:

'Mrs. ———'s compliments to Mr. Hayward, and if he will have the politeness to accompany her to the Royal Academy, it will not only prove his attention and kindness, but she will possess the advantages resulting from his good taste and knowledge of the works of the first artists of the day. A corner of her carriage is also at his service. Mr. H. must not refuse.

'S. Hayward, Esq.

But Hayward was a general lover—a perfect man of gallantry. The lady, the courtezan, and the servant maid, by turns, claimed his attention, as his roving eye fastened on their charms. He was to be seen at Almack's joining in the voluptuous waltz with some honourable miss of the west end, or sporting a toe in a quadrille with a woman of the town at places of inferior note. Hayward danced with ease and elegance, and wherever he exhibited himself was sure to elicit applause; and, as the man was egregiously vain, most probably he did not care much whether the commendations came from elegant females or vicious prostitutes.

To support this gay and dissipated life required means, and as Hayward was without any, he had resource to the gaming table. The profits of play proving inadequate to his necessities, he made the gambling-house subservient to his wants by imposing forged notes on the frequenters of those scenes of vice. He was soon, however, detected and literally kicked out; when, finding himself excluded, he became the visitor of smaller hells, where less notorious wretches play for shillings instead of pounds. The gradations of the vicious are regular and rapid; from the gaming table to the brothel, and from the brothel to the gallows. Hayward, in less than a twelvemonth, found himself obliged to resort to the basest means for support; and as his character began to develop itself, he found himself shut out from families which he had lately visited. In his best day he was a passer of forged notes, was known to have stolen the money out of several tills, having insinuated himself into the bars for that purpose; and was suspected of having picked pockets! To what base means will not the man resort who sets out in life with an assumed character!

Hayward, whilst running his career of fashionable life, attracted the notice of a beautiful young creature, who was the mistress of a superannuated, but wealthy, general. Such an opportunity was not to be lost. He paid her the most marked attention, and she acknowledged his gallantry; he became a petticoat pensioner; indeed, he might be said to be in keeping, as he lived for several months upon the purse of this woman, who evinced for him the most extravagant affection. By her he had one child, unknown, of course, to the amorous veteran; but, neglecting her charms for some other unfortunate woman, she became jealous, and banished him from her presence.

It is a melancholy truth that, in this modern Babylon, thousands are found, in the shape of men, who subsist on the prostitution of unfortunate females, whose nocturnal and vile earnings are spent by these wretches, known by the name of 'fancy-men.' Hayward became one of these, and shared the sinful gains of more than one prostitute. What a degradation! A young man of such talents and acquirements as those possessed by Hayward, need never descend to vice or meanness. In this country, abilities like his are sure to be appreciated, and fair industry is certain of reward. Laudable endeavours seldom fail to procure, at least, the necessaries of life, while all the arts and schemes of the swindler are insufficient to keep him from starving. He may, indeed, be momentarily successful; but his career is always short. Hayward, with all his address, was driven, in less than three years, to the utmost distress; and a little before he committed the crime for which he suffered, he had no means of raising the price of his bed but by forcibly snatching the shawl from off a girl of the town, and running away with it.

A sharper is compelled to be always on the alert, and avail himself of every opportunity to augment his finances. While Hayward was immersed in pleasure, he did not omit to profit by the consequence derived from his associating with men of rank; and tradesmen, seeing him in company with their wealthy customers, could not refuse him credit. Jewellers supplied him with trinkets for his girls, and tailors dressed him out in the first style of fashion. It is needless to say that he owed hundreds and never paid a halfpenny. An anecdote or two will illustrate at once his address and assurance.

Passing one day by the shop of a Mr. Sperling, jeweller, 42. Judd Street, Brunswick Square, Hayward's eye was attracted by a flute with silver keys. He went in and asked the price; finding it six guineas, he lamented that he had only four pounds and ten shillings in change about him, which he laid on the counter, and desired the instrument to be sent to his lodgings, when he would pay the remainder. Before taking his leave, he astonished the jeweller by producing on the flute some of the finest notes he ever heard; and, having thus secured his ear, he took occasion to mention some noblemen whom he should recommend to Mr. Sperling's shop. The jeweller, believing him to be a man of fashion, was flattered by his patronage, and instantly sent home the flute; and, when Hayward called the next day, let him have a gold watch worth forty guineas.

At another time Hayward was detected in attempting to pass a forged ten pound note. The shop-keeper took him before the sitting alderman at Guildhall, when he expressed himself hurt at the suspicion, and assuring the magistrate that being a gentleman a little addicted to play, the note in question came into his possession that way the preceding night, at one of the gambling-houses in St. James's, where the worthy alderman must know such notes are sometimes improperly and dishonourably imposed upon gentlemen, he told this plausible story with so much polished ease and unembarrassed countenance, that the magistrate dismissed the complaint, and the shopkeeper, ...ng himself wrong, apologised ...conduct.

Hayward had not been on the town more than a twelvemonth when he found a short absence from London necessary, as his character had got wind. On learning that some of his acquaintance, in the neighbourhood of Russell Square, had gone to the Isle of Wight on an excursion of pleasure, he resolved to follow them. The difficulty of an introduction was no obstacle to one whose life was artifice, and who rather depended on accident than design. He started for the Isle of Wight in the style of a first rate man of fashion, and was received with warmth on his arrival, as one who could contribute to the amusement and pleasure of those circles in which he had been before the delight. He was now upon a new scene, which afforded ample scope for the exercise of his talents, and he did not allow them to lie dormant. He entered with spirit into every party; was esteemed the best shot among the sportsmen; and acknowledged the most accomplished suitor by the ladies. His talents astonished the islanders; for he seemed as much at home in remarking on the scenery of the place as in commenting on a piece of Mozart's music.

Such an agreeable and accomplished companion as Hayward must have been interesting, had he possessed true notions of honour and integrity; and if he had not been led away by his vanity and dissipation, he might now have formed an advantageous connexion among the circles he visited. But pleasure and dissipation left him no time for reflection; and thus his want of thought prevented him from securing his own independence, and saved some elegant female from having to deplore an unfortunate alliance.

While he remained here he be

came the intimate friend of a gentleman who, with his son and daughter, were making a tour of the island. Hayward's conversation was so agreeable, that they solicited his company on the excursion. He agreed, and during their progress the young lady gave him marked encouragement, which he probably might have availed himself of, were it not for one of those fortunate circumstances which sometimes preserves innocence and discomfits the wicked. While he was one day engaged in pointing out the beauties of some local scenery, several strangers passed by, and among them Hayward espied one of the gamblers who had formerly detected him in the act of imposing forged notes on the *blacklegs* of St. James's. The unexpected appearance of this person, at such a moment and in such a place, acted on Hayward like an electric shock, and completely overpowered him. Dreading exposure, he became much agitated, made a hasty apology, and, abruptly quitting his companions, returned to London. The upright man is never surprised; but the guilty one is, like the timorous hare, alarmed at even the 'rustling of the brake.'

On his return to the metropolis he entered once more on his vicious course, and was to be seen nightly in the saloons of the theatres accompanied by dashing cyprians, or found at some *free and-easy*, surrounded by dishonest characters, with whom he now began to associate. He was no longer a welcome visitor at the fashionable squares, as his deceptions had been in most instances discovered, and in one or two places he was treated rather unceremoniously.

Soon after his return from the Isle of Wight he became acquainted with a lady, who, living separately from her husband, had an allowance of twelve hundred pounds a year. Hayward soon insinuated himself into her favour, and for a time found her a most convenient banker. This absurd woman had long passed the 'hey-day of her youth,' yet she was so vain that her purse was at Hayward's command in return for the encomiums he bestowed on her person; for no further impropriety took place between them than a kind of ridiculous coquetry. This lady recommended her sentimental admirer to lodgings in her neighbourhood; but his landlady not getting her rent in due time, she took the advantage of Hayward's absence to inspect his wardrobe. Not meeting with any thing but a few collars, a pair of false ancles, and some paint for his cheeks, she concluded that all was not right, and that if her lodger was a captain, as he pretended to be, he must have been long on half pay, for he appeared nearly as distressed as the lieutenant who so much interested my uncle Toby and Corporal Trim. Accordingly on his return, she intimated a wish to be paid her rent; but the mock captain replied in terms so disagreeable that she locked him out that night, and refused him further admission into her house. His friend, the liquorish old lady, paid the rent next morning, to avoid an application to her husband on the business.

His landlady had more causes than one for lamenting having let Hayward into her house, for he endeavoured to seduce her daughter; and, failing in his object, he spread reports so injurious to the young lady's character, that a gentleman who had been paying his addresses to her declined to persevere in his suit. Hayward was but too successful in deluding young women. At this time he seduced a girl of a respectable family, who had some money in the funds, and when her little property had been spent he abandoned her, leaving her pregnant and pennyless; an act which, in a moral point of view, deserved death more than the crime for which he suffered. This transaction coming to the ears of his female friend, she, either from jealousy or indignation, shut the door in his face, and desired her servants to admit him no more.

Hayward had by this time become too well known at all the places of fashionable resort to attempt practising his impositions there any more, and, in consequence, he was obliged to resort to the lowest and basest means of procuring the means of subsistence. At one time he ran away with a bundle of gloves off the counter of a hosier, and subsisted for some time by disposing of articles, made of a newly-discovered metal, for gold. Some hinted, after his death, that they suspected him of a crime of disgusting atrocity; but of this there appears no proof.

Disowned and degraded, his career was rapidly drawing to a close, and, as he began to descend, he became more vile and infamous. One night he took a dashing cyprian to one of the hotels which abound near Leicester Fields, and having treated her to supper, wine, &c. she considered him a perfect gentleman, until the next morning, when, under pretence of stepping out to his agent, he forgot to return, and left the unfortunate creature in pawn for the bill, which she discharged by pledging her watch, &c. A few nights after she met him in the saloon of Covent Garden Theatre, and among other reproaches told him he was well known as a passer of forged notes, and that she would have the pleasure of seeing him hanged,— a prognostication which even then deeply affected him.

In the spring of 1821, Hayward accidentally fell into company with a young lady, to whom he represented himself as a young man of family and fortune; and the credulous girl believing him, he obtained permission to visit her, at the house of her mother, in Somers' Town. This lady, whose name was Stebbings, imprudently admitted Hayward to pay his addresses to her daughter; and while he affected the utmost attachment, he was only making his observation on her house and premises, that he might give information to a desperate gang of housebreakers, with whom he had now connected himself.

Having observed where the valuables and money were placed, Hayward and his companions met and concerted the plan of operation. In addition to the regular organized housebreakers, there was a young man, named Elkins, an artist, who had become acquainted with Hayward, and who at the time lodged with him.

On the night of the robbery they met at a public-house, in Somers' Town, and after twelve o'clock proceeded to the back of Mrs. Stebbings's house. Hayward then gave the housebreakers, five in number, the necessary directions; and he and Elkins remained in the brickfield behind, while the others went to work. The robbers succeeded but too well, and brought out their booty without having excited any alarm; but Hayward discovering that they had left a valuable article behind them, he re-entered the house with them, and brought it away. His avarice on this occasion was the cause of his apprehension; for, by the time they had returned, after the second visit, a watchman had, in his rounds, come near the place where they were, and, seeing bundles with them, resolved to bring them to an account. On his approach they fled, and Hayward threw away a parcel, in which several articles of plate were tied up; but the watchman being nearer to him than the others, he succeeded in apprehending him. On being taken to the watch-house, several articles of Mrs. Stebbings's property were found on his person. Next morning this lady identified the property, and went away without knowing who was the robber—a circumstance which seemed to disappoint Hayward; as he expected, had she seen him, she would have declined to prosecute.

A female, named Mary, who lived with Hayward as mistress, having called at the lock-up-house, was traced back to her lodgings, where Elkins was found sitting at the fire, and he was immediately taken into custody. This young man soon turned king's evidence to save himself, but as he only knew Hayward, an offer of pardon was held out also to the latter, if he would deliver up his more guilty companions to justice; this he indignantly refused, and was accordingly fully committed; Mrs. Stebbings resolving to prosecute, though two hundred pounds had been offered, by a secret agent, if she would forbear.

A report of the transaction having appeared in the newspapers, the young lady who lived with the general, commiserating Hayward's unfortunate situation, applied for permission to see him; but being in the first instance refused, she contrived to let him know that she forgave him, and, during the remainder of his short life, supplied him with money to meet all his demands.

In prison he manifested the same minute regard to his appearance that he had done through life, and dressed every day with as much exactness as if he was about to figure in Bond-street. Again he was advised to deliver up his guilty companions to justice, but he positively refused. In Newgate, he assumed all his former consequence; and, lest his origin should be known, he told Mr. Brown, the governor, that he had no relation living. His composure never for a moment forsook him; and, though he knew he had a very narrow chance of escape, he seemed but little affected.

Various endeavours were made to induce Mrs. Stebbings to forbear prosecuting, but all was unavailing; and the indictment having been found, Hayward was put upon his trial at the Old Bailey. His appearance in court excited the greatest surprise; his dress was rich and elegant, and he appeared more like a man about to enter the drawing-room than one going to be tried for his life. He affected all the ease and grace of a polished gentleman, and every thing about him bespoke inordinate vanity and self love, which predominated over the terrors of approaching infamy and destruction. He seemed, during the trial, to have but one apprehension—lest it should come out that he was of mean origin; and took an indirect way to establish a belief that he was the character he had assumed, by lamenting, on his defence, that he did not then see in court some of the officers who had known him in the Commissariat department. He had subpœnaed several characters of distinction; but knowing how little they could say in his behalf, he had not the assurance to call them.

The principal witness against him was Elkins. This young man was a sculptor, and possessed great intelligence. He gave a clear account of the burglary, and of course established Hayward's guilt, against whom a verdict was delivered. A coachman was tried along with him, on the charge of having aided the robbers in removing the goods, the housebreakers having got into his coach and drove off, leaving Elkins to shift for himself. This man was acquitted, as the uncorroborated evidence of an accomplice is not sufficient to convict.

The verdict, when first pronounced, appeared to have affected Hayward very much; but he immediately recovered his self-possession, and on retiring from the bar made a graceful bow to the court.

On being brought up, at the end of the sessions, to receive sentence, his appearance and demeanour rendered him peculiarly distinguishable from his fellow-culprits; and by the attention he paid to the unhappy females who were among the number, he seemed to forget his own wretched situation.

After condemnation, this unfortunate young man laboured to keep up the delusion as to his respectability and high connexions, but he was stripped of his borrowed plumage; for his poor father, having seen the name of his son in the public papers, became alarmed, and repaired to Newgate to ascertain whether his fears 'forebode him right.' He sent in his name, but Hayward refused to see him, saying that he must be under a mistake, as his father was not living. The governor of Newgate, however, was struck with the anguish of the miserable parent; and desiring him and his wife to come on a certain day, he introduced them into the press-room, where Hayward was walking, without communicating his intention to either party. On catching each other's view, they, for a moment, stood transfixed with surprize and horror; then wild exclamations of emotion burst from each, as they rushed to embrace; while convulsive sobs expressed the anguish of their feelings. Hayward beat his forehead, exclaiming, 'Oh! father, forgive your wicked and undutiful son. I have abandoned and disowned you, but you have not forgotten me in my afflictions;' and he repeatedly prayed to God to spare his life, to afford him the opportunity of showing his gratitude to his father, and atone for his past transgressions.

The interview lasted for a considerable time, and it was with difficulty they were separated; when the wretched father set about making every possible exertion to save the life of his unhappy son. Indeed Hayward, from the strong solicitations in his favour, indulged in the hope of a commutation of his sentence to transportation until the Saturday before his execution, when he learned the dreadful fact that he was included in the number that was doomed to suffer, every application in his behalf having failed.

From the moment of his awful fate being communicated to him he evinced a proper spirit of resignation, and attended the chapel on Sunday, to hear his condemned sermon, in a suit of full mourning; his hair was tastefully arranged, and his irons were kept up by a black leather belt and buckle. He received the sacrament with great devotion, after which he returned to his cell. The next day he was visited by about forty gentlemen, whose houses he had been in the habit of frequenting, and who could not believe, without ocular demonstration, that it was Sam Hayward who was about to suffer the ignominious sentence of the law. On Tuesday morning, November the 27th, 1821, he entered the press-yard in the most gentlemanly manner; and, though he looked pale and feverish, advanced to the block to have his irons knocked off with a firm step. During this operation he was supported by the sheriff and the ordinary, to the former of whom he returned thanks for the interest he expressed in his fate. On being asked how he felt, he replied, 'As a man ought to feel who had violated the laws of God and his country.' Hayward evinced a sincere spirit of contrition, and appeared grateful for the pious attention of the ordinary. In a few minutes the prison bell announced that he had but a few minutes to live, when, casting his eyes around, he asked, 'Is there not a poor female to suffer?' Being answered in the affirmative, he exclaimed, 'Oh! gracious God, have mercy upon her!' He then advanced towards the place of execution with a firm tread, and, while his miserable companions were tying up, he leaned his head upon his hand. From the dreadful agony of this moment he was aroused by the executioner, when, having bowed to all around, he mounted the scaffold with astonishing firmness: his youth and gentlemanly appearance excited universal commiseration from an immense crowd of spectators. His dreadful situation seemed to penetrate his soul, and, as if willing to escape from the anxious gaze of the multitude, he requested the executioner to pull the cap over his eyes. He prayed most fervently until the drop descended, when he was launched into eternity.

Joseph South, for uttering a forged ten pound note, and Anne Norris, for robbing a man at a house of ill-fame, suffered with Hayward.

Such was, and ever will be, the termination of an ill-spent life. Hayward possessed talents that might, with laudable exertion, have placed him in a situation of honourable independence; but, as all the gifts of nature were perverted by him, he reaped the consequence—a short and miserable life, which ended ignominiously, but without securing oblivion; for the infamy of his memory has survived his breath, and casts back its stigma upon his name and family. Let not unthinking youth be led from the even and peaceable paths of integrity and virtue by the alluring invitations of the vicious, who draw so pleasing a picture of gay and fashionable life; for be it remembered that, according to Mr. Colquhoun, twenty thousand individuals awake every morning in this vast metropolis, without knowing where they shall lay their heads at night, or where they are to procure the necessaries of the day. These are not the children of virtuous poverty, whose misfortunes arise from circumstances beyond their own control, but deluded and mistaken beings, most of whom probably are the victims of vanity and dissipation; and who, rejected by society, have no means of supporting an infamous and miserable existence, but by preying upon the honest and industrious part of the community.

We must here repeat, what we have frequently said before, that virtue and rectitude have the advantage of deceit and villainy, even as regards the happiness of this world; and, in support of this remark, we can refer to the case before us. The reader may estimate the abilities of Hayward, and can picture the miseries of his short career of vice; and then say what would have been the reverse had he followed an opposite line of conduct. We have no doubt but the conclusion will be in accordance with the old adage, which says, 'Honesty is the best policy.' In that vile pursuit, where the talents of Hayward failed to prosper, let no unthinking young man flatter himself that he shall succeed.

WILLIAM WELSH, EDWARD DOOHERTY, LAURENCE WELSH, AND WILLIAM MARTIN,
EXECUTED FOR THE MURDER OF MR. HOSKINS.

THE trial of these atrocious offenders disclosed such a scene of unparalleled iniquity, that we shall give it in full. Thomas Hoskins, Esq., for whose murder these malefactors suffered, was a young man, of a most respectable family in the county of Limerick. In resisting a party of Whiteboys, in 1821, who had beset his father's house, he brought upon himself the vengeance of these illegal banditti; and on the 27th of July, in the same year, he was barbarously murdered, in the face of day-light, on his return from Newcastle, in the county of Limerick.

For twelve months, the savage assassins escaped the pursuit of justice; and some of them never have been apprehended. The two Welshes, Dooherty, and Martin were taken into custody in the summer of 1822, and brought to trial at Limerick, on the 1st day of August. The case for the prosecution being stated, Patrick Dillane, an informer, was called and examined:—

Witness saw Mr. Thomas Hoskins once; believes that he is now dead; saw him this time twelvemonth at the west of Barna-Hill; he was on horseback; knows where Mr. Patrick Hayles lives at Cragg, right well; he rode a mule, and a little boy accompanied him, who ran away when he heard the shots fired; heard the boy's name was Crowly; William Welsh, Laurence Welsh, Edward Dooherty, Patrick Neil, not as yet taken, James Welsh, not taken, and William Martin, were with the witness; on seeing Mr. Hoskins the party divided; Martin, Dooherty, William Welsh, and witness, stationed themselves at the sand-pit; the others were under the bridge, which was forty paces from his party; Mr. Thomas Hoskins was coming in the direction of Newcastle; Drohedeena Solus is the Irish name of the bridge; Mr. Hoskins was near the bridge when first the witness saw him, and from where witness was stationed he heard the shots fired from under the bridge; two shots were fired, but they did not take place; James and Laurence Welsh fired first at Mr. Hoskins; witness was in front of him.

Mr. O'Connell.—Did you see them fire; how do you know that?

Witness.—No other men were at the bridge, but those spoken of; Mr. Hoskins was half way in the direction of the sand-pit, when witness ran out with his gun when he heard the shots from the bridge; witness then fired at young Mr. Hoskins, and desired a man named Hartnett to be off; witness's shot took place when he fired at Mr. Hoskins; Hartnett made off; he shot Mr. Hoskins in the arm and breast; they were small slugs in the gun, and the mule fled; the slugs were lead; he had beat into a rod, and then cut it with a chisel into small slugs; Mr. Hoskins fell; after which he ran up a mountain at the right hand side, in the direction of Newcastle; he then went on his knees to where there was gravel, and begged his life.

Court.—Who was it pursued him?—All of us.

Witness and party then overtook Mr. Hoskins; he was on his knees begging his life; there was a hole with gravel near it; that precise spot he showed to Mr. Percy, chief constable, and to Mr. Vokes; it was on this spot that Bill Welsh struck him with the but-end of a gun, which was broke near the head from the blow.

[Mr. Hoskins, father to the late unhappy young gentleman, placed his head on his hands, and seemed to be in the most acute agony—an awful stillness pervaded the Court.]

The gun was a peculiar one; witness lent the gun to one Jack Murphy, which, when he saw it with Welsh on the mountain, he asked him where he got the gun; it was a left-handed gun, as the lock was at this side. Edward Dooherty, one of the prisoners, fired a pistol down through the body of Mr. Hoskins as he lay on his face and hands; it was about the loins he shot him; he had received no other wound but the one witness fired; it was the third shot; witness then took his watch and five tenpennies from his pocket; thinks he would know the watch; saw chains, &c., belonging to it; a ring was on the seals.

[Here the watch was handed to the witness. It was a small watch, chased on the back, gold, a plain curved chain, one seal and a ring. The witness viewed the watch closely.]

Witness.—To the best of his belief it is the same watch he took from Mr. Hoskins; sold it about a month afterwards to one Hanlon for ten shillings; shewed it first to Daniel Doody, who was also present when it was sold; the ring was not to it when sold; gave the ring to Peggy Clifford, wife to George Reidy; shewed her the watch; the party separated after the murder, and went towards Fournavulla; after separating, Bill and Laurence Welsh went with the witness: the others faced to Rathcahill; Martin Dooherty, otherwise Sladdy, and James Welsh, not on his trial, Neill, not on his trial, went to Fournavulla; witness and family went to Kelly's to drink whiskey; witness heard the police and army; went off, and no one with him; but met William Welsh before break of day, and they both went into one Curtin's house.

To the Court.—Curtin was in bed when he went there.

Witness put his gun into a rick of turf on the mountain; saw no one else hide his arms; Laurence Welsh lives near Fournavulla; Kelly lives near the Strand; the distance between the two houses is twenty paces only; witness never since saw the left-handed gun; left Curtin's house after breakfast, and left the house first; it was about four o'clock in the evening when first he saw Mr. Hoskins; knows one James Fitzmaurice; knows Martin Sheehan; saw Sheehan the same day of the murder; Sheehan's wife and children were within; no one else was along with witness at the interview; left the party on the hill while he was at Sheehan's; Laurence Welsh told witness that Sheehan would direct him to Fitzmaurice; the latter could tell whether Mr. Hoskins was coming on or returning to Newcastle that day; he could not see the prisoners from Sheehan's house, but could by going about forty yards from the house see the men on the hill; saw Fitzmaurice; was at Sheehan's about an hour and a half before the murder took place; Fitzmaurice lived round the hill; went back again to the party; they questioned him as to his seeing Fitzmaurice and what he said; witness said he saw him, and Mr. Hoskins was returning home; saw Mr. Hoskins coming along; he was a mile and a half distant; as soon as witness met him, he fired on him from the sand-pit . heard Mr. Haye's son was along with Mr. Hoskins; saw the white trowsers; ran down to meet him; saw a boy with a bundle of rushes facing Sullivan's house ·before he fired the shot; whistled to a man digging to go in quickly—he did so, and was working in his shirt, and left his spade; don't know the man's name, and never saw him; a rick of turf was between him and his view before the shot was fired: witness showed the place, but did not go to the spot; it was to Mr. Percy and Mr. Vokes he showed the situation where he called out to the man; heard the horsemen coming in the direction of Furnavulla a little after nightfall, when he threw himself into a ditch.

Cross-examined by Mr. O'Connell.—Did you live three or four years with Walter Fitzmaurice, Captain Rock?—I was the first that was called Captain Rock at that time. I was christened so by a schoolmaster.

I should be glad to know who that worthy disciple is?—His name is Morgan: it was he christened me; was once or twice examined about the murder; was not examined yesterday, nor the day before; it was Mr. Vokes who brought him into court.

Was he hander and feeder? Witness swears he don't know whether he told it yesterday or the day before, nor the last week, nor the last fortnight, nor the last month, nor the last two months, but told it when he gave his information; told it within the last three months; did a month ago, when giving information: knew Walter Fitzmaurice was in the house where he was; witness was carried to Newcastle in a hack; he showed the spot where the murder was committed; on the way he told every word of it; it is not a fortnight ago since he told every word of it.

Mr. O'Connell.—What harm did the young gentleman you murdered ever do you?—He was a nice young gentleman, and he never owed him any rent.

Was it not you that *set him?*—Yes.

Was it not you that went in order to find when he was coming home, when you coolly and deliberately murdered him?—I was at the murdering him.

Would you not have fired at the man in the garden whom you desired to go in, if he refused doing so?—I might fire at him, and would make him go in if he did not.

Were you not the first who shed the blood of this young gentleman? —Yes.

Did you then believe that there was a God?—I am sure of it: sorry for it. Sorry for it?—Sorry that there is a God.

Witness was brought up the last assizes to be arraigned at the dock behind him, and postponed his trial.

Don't you think if you were tried for the offence you were arraigned for last assizes, that you deserved to be hanged for it? How long after you postponed your trial was it you gave information?—Two months. So then you gave information with the rope about your neck?—I did it with a pious view for what I had done—I love piety. Didn't you know Galvin, who was tried for Mr. Hoskins's murder, was innocent?—I did. And Mr. Vokes fed the witness, and paid them for that prosecution; didn't you hear he had a narrow escape, and that one Anglim swore also against him?—I heard he had a narrow escape. Didn't you hear that Galvin was sworn to particularly, by having a mark on his cheek?—Knew Galvin was innocent. Witness gave the gun to Murphy; had often two guns, but had only one that time; forced these guns from other people. Did Mr. Vokes tell you you would be examined?—He told me to tell nothing but the truth. And if you didn't swear, Vokes would hang you?—I deserved to be hanged. Is there a greater villain in the creation than you are; were you not the first to draw his blood? didn't grant him mercy, when he implored it from your hands! Yet you knew Galvin was innocent, why not come forward then? Did you think, if Galvin was hanged, it would be murder?—At that time he intended to give himself up. But you let the trial go on; and only for Mr. Ashe's testimony, he would have been hanged, notwithstanding the cross-examination that gentleman underwent. It was after Galvin's trial he was christened Captain Rock; and never at that period told Mr. Vokes he had a notion of giving information; he thought nothing of spilling blood! Heard there was a large reward for giving information. About how many times did you deserve to be hanged?—Several times. You are a pious man! Now give me in a lump how many times?—Often; don't know how often; if that which he fired at Mr. Hoskins was the shot, did not take effect so as to kill him. Give me no if or and—give me yes or no—do you think you are a murderer? If you stop there until midnight, you must give an answer: I ask you, in your own mind, don't you think you are a murderer?—I went there with that intent—the shot I fired didn't kill. Well, that is one answer. Remember you are sworn—sworn with blood upon your hands! Do you think you are a murderer?

Court.—Do you think or not whether you are a murderer?—I think I am.

Mr. O'Connell.—I should not have got the answer had the Court not interfered.

How much money did you get?—I got fifty shillings.

What for?—I was hired to commit the murder!—was put up!

Mr. O'Connell.—Oh, go down, go down; I'll not ask you another question.

The indignation and awful feeling which prevaded the court lasted a considerable time.

Alexander Hoskins, Esq. examined by Mr. White.—The watch was handed him, and asked whether he ever saw it; said the last time he saw it was in his son's possession; his son occasionally wore a ring, which sometimes he attached to the seal.

Several other witnesses were examined, whose evidence was conclusive against the prisoners. For the defence two witnesses vainly endeavoured to prove an *alibi* in favour of Martin. The other three had no evidence to offer.

His lordship charged the jury in this important case at very great length. The jury retired for half an hour, when they returned and brought in a verdict of Guilty against all the prisoners.

After the clerk of the crown asked the prisoners, in the usual way, why judgment of death should not be pronounced, &c. Martin declared to God he was not guilty.—Laurence Welsh, in an emphatic manner, and lifting his hands in a declamatory style, said, ' he who swore against them committed the murder, and brought them into it.'

His lordship, in a most feeling and impressive manner, passed the awful sentence of death. In his charge he particularly alluded to the enormity of the offence, and trusted that the prisoners would occupy the few hours they had to live in prayer and devotion. His lordship ordered them for execution on Saturday, their bodies to be given for dissection.

The awful sentence of the law was carried into effect on the appointed day; and it is to be lamented that justice could not be administered without releasing the wretch Dillane from a similar fate, which he appears to have richly merited.

DANIEL DOODY, JOHN CUSSEN, *alias* WALSH, JAMES LEAHY, MAURICE LEAHY, WILLIAM DOODY, DAVID LEAHY, DANIEL RIEDY, WILLIAM COSTELLO, AND WALTER FITZMAURICE, *alias* CAPTAIN ROCK,

CONVICTED OF ABDUCTION.

It was the opinion of Dr. Johnson that many of the romantic tales of the middle ages had their origin in truth, and that the absolute distress of females might, in all probability, have called for the institution of ' knight errantry.' To protect the defenceless is a natural impulse, which has its foundation in the sympathies of our nature; but when a female, young, beautiful, and innocent, is the victim of oppression, there is no man, with common feelings, who would not risk his life to snatch her from despair and misery. In this happy country there are few instances of abduction; but in Ireland this unmanly crime, as we have already noticed, is too prevalent. The distracted state of certain parts of the country gives aid to the schemes of unprincipled ruffians, acting on the presumption that injured females, when degraded and dishonoured, would of necessity save the violators of their innocence from ignominy by a marriage—the only means, they suppose, left them to escape from unmerited shame. The persons thus forcibly carried away are generally the daughters of opulent farmers—a fact which clearly shows the mercenary views of those who commit so base and cowardly an outrage on the most defenceless part of the creation.

Among the many outrages of this nature was one on the person of Miss Honora Goold, a young lady remarkable for her personal beauty. She lived in the house of her mother, at Glangurt, in the county of Cork, 'and had two sisters older than herself, she being scarcely sixteen, and a brother. On the 4th of March, 1822, about twelve o'clock at night, their dwelling was attacked by an armed banditti, who, on threatening to burn the house, were admitted. One of the ferocious ruffians burst into Miss Honora's apartment, and asked if she was the eldest Miss Goold. She replied in the negative, and said that her sister was on a visit in Cork. The inquirer then withdrew, and, having searched several other apartments, returned, followed by five or six others, and repeated his interrogation, which he, however, answered himself in the affirmative; and then desired her to arise and dress herself. At the suggestion of one of the party they withdrew outside the door, to allow a compliance with their orders.

The young lady had no hesitation in obeying their mandate; for she very naturally preferred being up and dressed in the presence of such ruffians. She had scarcely put on her clothes, however, when one of them re-entered, seized the screaming girl in his arms, and bore her out of the house, where a horseman was waiting to receive her. Before this stranger she was placed, in spite of all her cries for mercy; and the party, having obtained their prize, set off at full speed, bending their course towards the Galties, a range of mountains between the counties of Cork and Limerick. At the distance of several miles they halted and procured a pillion, and then compelled her to ride behind the unknown leader of this atrocious band. In her eagerness to escape she fell several times during their progress; and having continued her screams all the time, one of the ruffians threatened to murder her unless she desisted.

By day light they had entered the recesses of the Galties, and several of the party having occasionally dropped off, she was conducted by the few that remained to the house of David Leahy, a substantial farmer.

The leader of this outrage was a young man named Brown, of a respectable family, and who had received an education which should have rendered him incapable of such base and unmanly conduct. The elder Miss Goold was entitled, on her marriage, to a large fortune; and Brown, hoping to possess himself of it, resolved to carry off the young lady. Being disappointed by the precipitancy and mistake of his assistants, he determined to make sure of the lovely victim who had fallen into his power, knowing that the opulence of her family could make him independent, provided he could insure the consent of the astonished girl he had forcibly carried off. With virtuous indignation she repulsed his fulsome advances, and begged the protection of Mrs. Leahy, in whose parlour she now was; but, strange to say, this mother of children connived at the ruin of her unprotected guest.

Foiled in his direct attack, Brown had recourse to an expedient, which, for the honour of human nature, we would wish never to record, did not impartial justice demand an honest discharge of our duty as faithful narrators of criminal occurrences. It was proposed, immediately after breakfast, that Miss Goold should take some rest. A bed was in the parlour, and she was directed to repose upon it. This, indeed, after the fatigue of the night, was most desirable; but to her utter astonishment, the family, in which were two females, left the room, at the same time locking the door upon herself and Brown. The monster, in spite of her intreaties and screams, proceeded to undress her, and insisted on sleeping beside her. The reader need not be told the rest—the purity of female innocence was grossly violated in the person of this young and lovely creature; and her destroyer arose from his bed of lust the polluter of one whose peace of mind neither the world's sympathy nor the world's wealth could restore.

The friends of Miss Goold, who comprised the wealth and respectability of the county of Cork, set instantly about recovering the injured lady. The pursuit was continued from day to day for three weeks, and the vigilance of her friends was only evaded by removing the poor afflicted creature from cabin to cabin, and from the house of one farmer to that of another. One day she was kept on the bleak mountain, and had the anguish to see her friends at a distance, while she was prevented from flying to them by a ruffian who stood sentinel over her with a loaded pistol.

Abused, insulted, and almost exhausted with fatigue, this delicate female resolutely refused to sanction the presumption of her destroyer; and at the conclusion of three weeks she was placed, by her ferocious guards, in a poor cabin on the road side, where her friends might find her. When discovered, she was in a most deplorable condition, being literally unable to walk, stand, or sit. It took seventeen hours to remove her thirteen miles, the distance from her mother's house; but, when once restored to home and its enjoyments, her recovery was rapid, and in a short time her health was established as well as it was possible to be, under all the circumstances of her affecting case.

From the description of the banditti received from Miss Goold, several of the party were apprehended. Brown, the guilty contriver of the whole, escaped out of the country; and Walter Fitzmaurice, *alias* Captain Rock, evaded the pursuit of justice for a considerable time, but at length surrendered himself to a magistrate. The men whose names are mentioned above, with the exception of Costello and Fitzmaurice, were brought to trial at Limerick, on the 29th of July, 1822. Miss Goold appeared to give evidence, dressed in deep mourning, and her narrative, which she delivered with modest dignity, procured her the willing sympathy of a crowded court. The prisoners were found guilty—Death; but the three Leahys and Cussen were subsequently discharged, on a point of law operating in their favour.

On the 23d of August following, Walter Fitzmaurice, better known at the time as Captain Rock, pleaded Guilty at the Cork assizes, and, along with Costello, who was found Guilty on the solitary evidence of Miss Goold's brother, who swore to having seen him on the night of the abduction, received sentence of Death.

On the ensuing Saturday, Costello underwent the awful sentence of the law, but Fitzmaurice was respited, something having arisen in his favour, principally on the ground of his having pleaded guilty in consequence of the judge refusing to put off his trial in the absence of a material witness. Costello, to the last, declared his innocence, not only of the crime for which he was convicted, but of any connexion whatever with the White Boys.

The history he gave of his misfortune to persons who conversed with him in the gaol, previous to going out to execution, was this:—He was a relative of Brown's, and was workman to him for five years, up to September, 1821; when he left him for the purpose of assisting his brother, whose wife then died, leaving a large family. He continued in the practice of habits of industry, and, as he declared on the scaffold, knew nothing of Miss Goold's abduction till the morning after. He slept, he asserted, on that night, and it was endeavoured to be established on the trial, with his brother; and Fitzmaurice, who pleaded guilty, was frequently afterwards heard to declare the innocence of this unfortumate man. Before going out to execution, he observed to a person in the gaol—'Are not these queer laws that make a man's life depend on the oath of one witness?' He also asked this person whether he thought there was much pain in the punishment he had to undergo, but being assured there was not, and that it was only instantaneous, it afforded him great consolation. The only thing that he seemed to apprehend was the first sight of the hangman, and the tying up of his arms; but being reasoned with on these points, he acquiesced in their propriety, and assumed his usual firmness; and when the executioner came to tie his arms, he put them so far back that the tightness became extremely painful to him in his progress to the gallows. His manner of going to and at the place of execution was such as to awaken the sympathy and to excite the astonishment of all, even of those who guarded him, some of whom were observed to shed tears. He was firm to the last; and in him was observable that unpresuming confidence which could arise from no other source but the innocence of his heart, and his conscious freedom from the crime for which he suffered. His attention to the clergymen who accompanied him showed him to be deeply impressed with feelings of true piety: he died blessing his prosecutors, and begging the prayers of the people. He was a well-looking man, with rather a soft and open countenance, and had nothing daring or determined in his appearance.

JOHN SMITH,
EXECUTED FOR THE MURDER OF A FEMALE.

THIS offender was a native of Ireland; and had been, as he himself expressed it, 'a roving blade.' In 1822 he resided at Greenwich, where he cohabited with a woman of loose character; and suspecting her of infidelity, in a fit of jealousy he stabbed her in the throat. She died of the wound, and he was convicted of murder at the next Maidstone assizes.

Immediately after sentence had been pronounced on him he sent for a gentleman of Maidstone, and with a vehement injunction, desired him to make public what he called a history of his life, at the same time putting into his hand a scrap of paper. The surprise of the gentleman may be conceived, when, on examining the paper, he found it to contain a precise history of the place of Smith's birth—his propensities—and, finally, his motive for committing the murder, described in doggrel verse, which exhibit an extraordinary instance of mental abstraction, in a man of seventy-eight years of age, under the awful sentence of death. Although the production of an illiterate mind, it is truly astonishing how Smith could abstract himself from his situation so as to produce them. They may be regarded as a *literary* curiosity, and the levity of the concluding lines is not the least remarkable of the whole.

The following is copied from the original *literatim et verbatim.*

' In the County of Wicklow I was born'd
but now in Maidstone die in scorn
I once was counted a roving blade
but to my misfortune had no trade
women was always my downfall
but still I liked and loved them all
a hundred I have had in my time
when I was young and in my prime
women was always my delight
but when I got old they did me slight
a woman from London to me came
she said with You I would fain remain
if you will be constant Ill be true
I never want no Man but You—

and on her own Bible a Oath did take
that she never would me forsake
and during the time that I had Life
she would always prove a loving Wife
and by that means we did agree
to live together she and Me—
but soon her vows and Oath did break
and to another Man did take
Which she fetch'd home with her to lay
and that proved her own destiny
So as Jack Smith lay on his bed
this notion strongly run in his Head
then he got up with that intent.
to find her out was fully bent [broke
swearing if he found out her Oath she'd
be stick a knife into her throat
then to the Cricketers he did go
to see if he could find it out or no
not long been there before she come in
with this same fellow to fetch some Gin
then with A Knife himself brought in
immediately stab'd her under the Chin
and in five minutes she was no more
but there laid in her purple gore
Now to conclude and end my song
they are both dead dead and gone
they are both gone I do declare
gone they are but God knows where—'

On Monday, December the 23d, 1822, Smith was executed on Pennenden Heath. He appeared truly penitent, and attributed the misfortunes of his life to his licentious propensities. He prayed aloud and very fervently until the drop fell about twelve o'clock.

ROBERT HARTLEY,
EXECUTED FOR WILFULLY STABBING.

THE ruthless deeds of this young offender almost rival those of the notorious Avershaw. Robert Hartley was convicted at the Maidstone Assizes, on the 16th of December, 1822, of wilfully stabbing Captain Owen, of the Bellerophon convict ship, lying at Sheerness, on the 29th of the preceding August, where Hartley was confined as a transport.

Some days before his execution he confessed to the Rev. Mr. Winter that he had been concerned in upwards of two hundred burglaries in Kent, Essex, Surrey, Middlesex, Hampshire, Hertfordshire, Yorkshire, Westmorland, Durham, Lincoln, and Norfolk. He had been confined in sixteen different prisons, besides undergoing several examinations at the different police-offices; and had gone by the following names:—Robt. Stainton, Alexander Rombollen, George Grimes, Robert Wood, William Smith, George Croggington, and Robert Hartley.

Hartley's father formerly kept an inn (the Sir John Falstaff) at Hull, in Yorkshire. He was put to school in that neighbourhood; but his conduct there was so marked with depravity, and so frequently did he play the truant, that he was dismissed as unmanageable. He then, although only nine years of age, began with pilfering and robbing gardens and orchards, till at length his friends were obliged to send him to sea. He soon contrived to run away from the vessel in which he had been placed, and, having regained the land, pursued his old habits, and got connected with many of the principal thieves in London, with whom he commenced business regularly as a housebreaker, which was almost always his line of robbery.

Hartley acknowledged that, from his earliest days, he was of a most vindictive and revengeful spirit. He had been punished when at school, and in revenge contrived to get from his bed in the night, and destroy the whole of the fruit trees, and every plant and shrub in his master's garden. At another time, having robbed a neighbour's garden, he was detected and punished, when, in order to wreak his vengeance, he set fire to the house in the night, which was nearly destroyed, together with its inmates. He had adopted a plan to escape from his father's house in the night time without detection, which was done by means of a rope ladder that he let down from his bed-room window; and, after effecting his robberies, he used to return to his room in the same way.

Hartley had once before received sentence of death, and was not respited till within a few hours of the usual time of execution; he was then sent to Botany Bay, from whence he contrived to make his escape, and afterwards entered on board one of his Majesty's ships in the East Indies. Whilst at this station he was removed to the hospital on shore at Bombay, on account of sickness; but even in this state he could not refrain from thieving. His practice was to scale the walls of the hospital in the evening, and way-lay the natives, whom he contrived to rob by knocking them down with a short stick, and then seizing their turbans, in which their wealth was usually deposited.

While on this station a gentleman on board the ship missed a box of pearls, and suspicion falling on a native Indian, he was put on shore and dreadfully tortured, his fingers and toe-nails being torn out to make him confess. A few days before Hartley's execution he confessed that he stole the pearls, and secreted them in a crevice in the ship's side, whence they had slipped to the bottom, and he could not recover them. He wrote an account of this circumstance to the commander of the ship, who came to Maidstone immediately, and recognised him as having been engaged as an officer's servant on board, and Hartley assured him that the pearls still remained in the place where he had secreted them.

Hartley acknowledged that he was an accomplice in the murder of Mr. Bird and his housekeeper, at Greenwich, for which murder Hussey was executed in 1818, but that neither himself nor Hussey were the actual murderers. Hartley obtained admission into the house by presenting a note at the door, when himself, with Hussey and another person, whom he named, ——, rushed into the house and shut the door. Hartley instantly ran up stairs to plunder the drawers, and whilst there he heard a loud cry for mercy. He went to the top of the stairs, and saw Hussey pull Mr. Bird's housekeeper to the floor, whilst —— struck her repeatedly with a hammer. Hartley ran down stairs, and saw Mr. Bird lying dead on his back. The sight so affected him, that he immediately threw on the table two watches which he had secured, and ran out of the house, and never saw Hussey afterwards, nor had he any share in the plunder.

Happy would it have been had his hands always been as free from blood, as he confessed that he afterwards met a gentleman on the highway, and shot him dead; after which he took from his person a watch and seventy-five pounds.

Hartley was also witness to another scene of murder which occurred in one of his midnight robberies. Himself and a companion had entered the house of a gentleman, who, being alarmed, seized the poker, and made towards Hartley, who snapped a pistol, which missed fire. The gentleman seized him by the collar, and dragged him to the floor, when Hartley's companion plunged a knife into his heart, and he fell dead upon Hartley. Two ladies had followed the gentleman into the room, and, at the horrid sight, they instantly fainted, whilst

Hartley and his companion made their escape. He has also frequently confessed that the murderer of Mrs. Donatty was the abovementioned ———, whom he represented to be a most blood-thirsty villain.

In one of his midnight excursions with two of his companions, he had a narrow escape of his life. They had packed up the principal part of the plate in the lower rooms, when one of his companions with horrid oaths, declared that he would proceed up stairs; in attempting which he was shot dead at the side of Hartley, who, with his other companion, made a hasty retreat. This circumstance only served to harden him in iniquity, as he acknowledged that he was totally devoid of fear or natural affection. Feelings of remorse were, however, awakened a few days before his trial, by an affectionate letter from his sister, imprisoned for debt, whom he had robbed of two hundred pounds, by forging a power of attorney; by which he obtained possession of a legacy of that amount, which had been bequeathed to her by a distant relation.

He looked forward to the time of his execution with astonishing coolness; and, in order that he might have the day continually before him, he had drawn a circle on paper, to form a kind of dial, with an index pointing to the number of days yet remaining; and this index he moved daily, as the days of life decreased. This monitor he fastened against the wall of his cell, where it was constantly in view. He was twenty-five years of age, and about five feet six inches high.

On Thursday morning, January the 2d, 1823, this hardened offender underwent the awful sentence of the law, on Pennenden Heath, near Maidstone. From the time of his condemnation to the evening preceding his execution he behaved in the most impenitent manner, stating his disbelief in a future state, and disregarding the pious exhortations of the chaplain. He was wont to speak of his wicked deeds with exultation, and appeared to be totally lost to all sense of moral rectitude and religious feeling.

JOHN KEYS,
EXECUTED FOR PARRICIDE.

HAPPILY a crime of this enormity occurs but seldom; too many are wicked, but few, thank God, are found unnatural enough to destroy the source of their own being, by imbruing their hands in the blood of a parent.

John Keys lived with his father, a poor farmer, in Enniskillen, Ireland. His eldest brother was absent in the army, and John had received a part of the little farm as his inheritance, it being a common thing there to divide the land among the children. On the 23d of April, 1822, John and his father went out in the fields to make a ditch. They appeared in great harmony; came home, dined together, and afterwards went again to their work.

In the evening John returned without his father, and being asked where he was, said he had gone to the mountain to look after the goats. The old man not having appeared that night, the same question was repeated by his sister next morning, when he prevaricated, and said that his father had gone to look for his brother, who was in the army.

Suspicion was now excited. A brother of the deceased came and commenced a search, when the body was found buried in a ditch. The skull exhibited marks of violence, and no doubt remained but the son had murdered his father with the spade, and afterwards buried him. The parricide was at this moment seen walking by the side of a neighbouring lake, and the people ran to apprehend him. With conscious guilt, when he saw them approach he ran into the water up to his neck, saying, 'You want to accuse me of murdering my father—I will not endure to be pointed at as the murderer of my father.' At this time no one had accused him. His uncle entreated him to come out of the water, and surrender himself, but he refused. When the people would withdraw a little he came out, but the moment they attempted to close upon him he ran in again, leaving nothing visible but his head. In this posture he was proceeding to make his will, determined to drown himself sooner than surrender, when a man arrived who could swim, and who quickly brought him out of his watery position. Being taken to the house of a magistrate, he told the constable that his brother had come to him the day before the parricide, and persuaded him to join him in murdering their father, that they might share the farm between them.

Keys was brought to trial at Enniskillen on the 21st of March, 1823, and found guilty on the clearest evidence. After sentence had been pronounced he acknowledged his guilt, and completely exonerated his brother, and all other persons, from any participation in his crime. He committed the dreadful act in consequence of a trifling dispute with his father, and had accused his brother in the vain hope of being admitted as king's evidence.

At the place of execution he repeated the confession of his guilt, and exculpated all others from any participation. He was little more than twenty years of age, and had been brought up in total ignorance of all religious duties. During his confinement he had profited by the school opened in the gaol, and had listened attentively to the pious instructions of the chaplain. Keys, being a Protestant, was attended by a minister of the established church.

JOHN NEWTON,
EXECUTED FOR THE MURDER OF HIS WIFE.

'Be master of thy anger,' said the sage of Corinth; and certainly a more important advice was never given to individuals; for how much of domestic misery is attributable to the violent and brutal passions of masters of families, who exercise in their own houses the most despotic and cruel conduct. It is a melancholy truth, that too many females have their lives made miserable by the unfeeling conduct of those who had pledged themselves, in the eyes of Heaven, to 'love, cherish, and protect,' these sweeteners of life. But humanity is not to be outraged with impunity; she avenges herself on her insulters, by making their homes miserable; and that which would otherwise be the scene of gladness and affection, becomes the seat of anger and unremitted contention.

John Newton was an opulent farmer, who resided at Severn Hall, near Bridgenorth. He had been married for several years to an amiable woman, who had brought him a smiling and youthful progeny. His unfortunate consort was in the habit of experiencing great violence from her unfeeling husband; and, if we may judge from his last act, he was a mere brute in a human form.

On the 12th of January, 1823, a man named Edwards, a tinman at Bridgenorth, brought in his account to Mr. Newton, for whom he was in the habit of working. There was an article charged for which Mrs. Newton had received money to pay, and being called into the parlour by her husband, she did not deny the fact, but stated having disposed of the money in the purchase of something else for the use of the house. He got into a great passion, blustered, and swore that he would give her a complete threshing. Mr. Edwards, with a view of pacifying him, offered to erase the item, which was for a mere trifle, sooner than have any thing unpleasant occur about it; but he still persisted in his determination of beating his unfortunate wife, who had been all day busied in baking and brewing, and who was at the time five months gone with child.

About eight o'clock in the evening Mr. Edwards went away: before doing so he passed through the kitchen and shook hands with Mrs. Newton, who appeared dejected, but not ill. Newton stopped him for a few minutes at the door, and as he was about to depart he turned round to bid her good night, but she had quitted the kitchen. 'Oh! she's gone to hide herself,' said the husband, 'as she knows what she has to expect.' On this Edwards remonstrated with him, and told him that, if he beat his wife, he would never speak to him again.

The counsel of his friend had no effect on the brutal wretch; for immediately on Edwards leaving the house, he proceeded to put his threats into execution, and beat and kicked the unfortunate woman in an unmerciful manner. The children made such a dreadful outcry, that the servant-maid heard them, at four fields distance, exclaiming, 'Oh! dear, dad, do not!' This girl then hastened home, and found her mistress lying in her blood across the hearth-stone. The carter came in about the same time, and the poor woman took him by the hand, saying, 'God bless you! I take my leave of you!' Newton all this time did not attempt to send for a doctor, but kept teazing his miserable wife, by asking her, 'Who is the greater rogue, you or I?'

The wretched woman was then carried to bed, and the carter went to fetch a doctor, who, on arriving, gave her some laudanum, and then went away, without having clearly ascertained the extent of her injuries. This man's conduct was really very culpable, as physicians afterwards gave it as their opinion that, with proper treatment, she might have recovered.

Newton, before he went to bed, came into his wife's room, and began to teaze her anew; when the woman, who was taking care of her, very properly desired him to go to bed, and defer what he had to say until a fitter opportunity. At one o'clock the wretched woman expired; and on this being communicated to her husband he jumped out of bed, and set off for a doctor. The suddenness of his wife's death seems to have brought him to a proper feeling, for he was heard to exclaim that he would give the whole world to have her back again.

In a few days a coroner's inquest was held on the body; and, as he dreaded inquiry, he manifested great anxiety to suppress the most material evidence. The coroner, whose name was Whitcomb, seems to have culpably entered into his views, and corruptly endeavoured to procure a verdict which would acquit Newton of the murder. But the jury were dissatisfied with the coroner's explanation; and being unjustly prevented from seeing the body, returned the following verdict:—' Died by bleeding; but how caused is to us unknown.' ' That is,' said the coroner,* ' by the visitation of God.' ' No,' replied the jury, ' that is not what we mean ;' and the verdict was recorded as given in.

The neighbours were, however, dissatisfied with this verdict ; they applied to a magistrate, and Newton was committed. His trial came on at Shrewsbury on the 22d of March, 1823, and the foregoing facts being substantiated, he was found Guilty.

Newton, who was a robust man, about forty, seemed little affected during his trial ; but when the judge proceeded to pass on him the awful sentence of the law, he appeared bewildered—looked wildly about—moved, as if involuntarily, up and down the dock, and once or twice attempted to turn away. When the learned judge had concluded, he remained at the bar, as if in expectation of something being done for him, and resisted the attempts to take him away. When they began to force him away, he cried out wildly; and after being carried out, it was some time before his lamentations ceased to appal the court.

He suffered at Shrewsbury next day but one, and manifested on the platform a proper feeling of piety and resignation.

JONATHAN COOK,
EXECUTED FOR A RAPE ON A CHILD.

WE are a loss to reconcile the credulity of a great bulk of the people with the dissemination of knowledge which is admitted to have latterly taken place. Every ignorant empiric who proclaims the virtue of his nostrums through the country seems to procure abundant customers, *alias* dupes; for, to the disgrace of modern times, the sale of quack medicines has increased, as appears from the return of stamp duties in 1823, to the House of Commons. In London, we have hundreds of these base men, called quacks; but every village in the country is cursed with one of these wretches, who publishes, with unblushing effrontery, forged testimonials of his healing powers. The harm done by these vile impostors is incalculable ; they kill hundreds of their miserable patients through absolute ignorance, and corrupt others by the scandalous debauchery of their lives. To the credulous who have been duped, and the incredulous who think these remarks overstrained, we recommend the perusal of the following case.

* The conduct of Whitcomb on this important occasion was so glaring a dereliction of duty, that the county determined to prosecute him ; and accordingly, on the 29th of the ensuing July, he was found Guilty, at the Shrewsbury Assizes, of the following charges :—' That, disregarding the duties of his office, and seeking to pervert the course of justice for his private gain, did, before the swearing of the jury, take a secret examination of several witnesses—that he had an interview with Newton, whom he knew to be suspected of the murder of his wife, and corruptly agreed with him to persuade the jury that he was not the cause of his wife's death—that, contrary to the evidence of the surgeon, he endeavoured to persuade the jury that Mrs. Newton's death proceeded from a natural cause—that he dismissed, in furtherance of his design, thirteen of the jurors—that he corruptly returned an erroneous verdict—and, finally, that he neglected calling certain witnesses, whose evidence he knew was of the utmost importance ; at the same time refused to let the jurors see the body of the deceased, well knowing that it exhibited great marks of violence.' These charges were fully proved, and Whitcomb was dismissed from his office, fined, and imprisoned.

Jonathan Cook lived at Calne, near Salisbury, and practised among the country people as a quack doctor. On the 14th of May, 1823, he went to the house of a labouring man named Lawrence, who had a son under his care. After inquiring about his patient, Lawrence's wife showed him a swelling under the chin of her little girl, aged nine years. Cook said he could cure it, but it was necessary that he should provide some herbs, and requested to have the assistance of the little girls, the eldest of whom was only twelve years old. The unsuspecting mother readily gave her consent, and the villain led the poor children to a solitary field, at a mile distance, where he forcibly violated the person of the eldest, having first made a similar attempt, which proved abortive, on the youngest.

The poor children on their return appeared agitated and ill, and being questioned by their mother, communicated what had taken place. What added to the diabolical crime was the circumstance of the wretch having communicated to his victim a certain abominable disease, of which she had not been cured when she gave evidence against her violator.

With the greatest effrontery the villain called next day on the distracted mother, and being accused of the fact, flatly denied it; but on the poor woman going out to call her husband, he made off, and was not apprehended for a month after.

Cook was brought to trial at Salisbury on the 15th of July, 1823, when the victim of his abominable passion appeared against him. She seemed an intelligent modest child, and excited a general sympathy throughout the court. The wretch had the impudence to cross-examine her, with a view to show that she consented, but her evidence was direct and conclusive, and the jury found him Guilty, on which the judge immediately passed on him the awful sentence of the law, advising him to apply for mercy in another world, for none could be extended to him here.

He was a man of about twenty-eight years of age, of robust make, and dressed like a creditable farmer. He heard his sentence with composure, and bowed to the court on leaving the bar. He underwent, in a few days, the awful sentence of the law.

PHILIP STOFFEL AND CHARLES KEPPEL,
EXECUTED FOR THE MURDER OF MRS. RICHARDS.

On Tuesday night, April the 8th, 1823, a most inhuman murder was committed at Clapham, on the body of Mrs. Elizabeth Richards, a widow of seventy-five years of age. The unfortunate lady had resided for thirty years in the same house at the above town, where she was greatly respected by the neighbours. She kept no servant, and had no inmate but an elderly lady named Bell. The latter was in the habit of going out in the evening to attend a place of religious worship, and had done so on the one in question. A few minutes after eight o'clock, a neighbouring woman coming to see Mrs. Richards found her dead, lying on her back in the parlour, with an apron stuffed into her mouth. On examination it was found that robbers had perpetrated the dreadful deed, as the pockets of the deceased had been violently torn from her side, her watch and some money taken, as well as several articles of wearing apparel. The villains, however, had missed the principal object of their attack, for a large sum of money had escaped their search, being concealed in a room up stairs. The poor old woman had been left, by age, only two teeth, and one of these was forced down her throat by the violence with which the wretches had thrust the apron into her mouth, with the view, no doubt, of preventing her from giving alarm. A paper parcel was found in the hall, on which was written 'Mrs. Bell, *hat* Mrs. Richards, Clapham'

The sensation produced by this unprovoked murder was so great, that a public meeting was called in a day or two at Clapham, and a reward of two hundred guineas offered for a discovery of the murderers. The active officers of Union Hall police-office in the course of a week apprehended a suspicious character, Philip Stoffel, nephew to Mrs. Richards, a ruffianly-looking fellow of about twenty years of age. When brought to the police office he denied all knowledge of the crime with which he was accused; but, being requested to write 'Mrs. Bell at Mrs. Richards,' &c. he wrote the word *hat* for at, in a hand precisely the same as the superscription on the parcel found after the murder. Seeing himself detected he exclaimed, 'It is of no use—I was at the murder!' He then, unsolicited, gave a full account of the whole transaction, and acknowledged who were with him at the time. Previously, however, to this confession, another of the gang, named Thomas Scott, a rat-catcher, was in custody, and had been admitted king's evidence. In his confession, which gave a minute account of the whole transaction, he stated that the robbery was planned by Stoffel, who called in the aid of himself, Keppel, and Pritchard, but that the murder was the act of Keppel alone, Stoffel particularly desiring that they would not hurt her. Whilst Scott was giving the parcel to Mrs. Richards, who went into the room to read the direction, Stoffel walked in gently, and said, 'My good old lady, we don't want to hurt you; we only wish for you to be quiet.' She exclaimed 'Oh Lord! oh dear!' when Stoffel put his hand upon her mouth, and the other two men coming in, he desired Keppel to hold her whilst he went up stairs, as he knew best where the money was, but not to hurt her. They then proceeded to rifle the house of all they could get at, but did not break any locks, for fear of alarming the people in the next house. Though Mrs. Richards did not move, Scott declared that he did not think that she was dead, but only that she had fainted.

In consequence of the information contained in Scott's confession, the officers went in pursuit of Keppel and Pritchard; and, after having travelled from Gravesend to Portsmouth, they succeeded in apprehending Keppel, who was disguised in a smock-frock, &c. Keppel and Pritchard were by trade bricklayers, but had led a most abandoned life among the lowest prostitutes about Westminster. Pritchard, we are sorry to say, escaped the pursuit of justice, as he was never apprehended. Keppel denied all knowledge of the murder, and behaved in the most hardened manner.

Stoffel had every expectation of being admitted a king's evidence; but he was not so fortunate, being arraigned along with Keppel at the Croydon assizes, July the 25th, for the murder of Mrs. Richards. The evidence against them was conclusive; for the confession of Stoffel, and the corroborated testimony of the accomplice, Scott, left no doubt whatever of their guilt.

The verdict having been recorded, Mr. Serjeant Onslow put on the black cap, and proceeded to pass the awful sentence.

Stoffel, though his appearance was more savage than that of Keppel, did not exhibit the same careless hardihood. The latter, on leaving the bar, had the audacity to apostrophise the judge as a bloody old rogue, and damned him and his bloody laws together. Such conduct, under such circumstances, exhibits a depravity which we are almost ashamed to record.

On Monday morning, July the 28th, these desperate young men underwent the sentence of the law, on the top of Horsemonger Lane gaol. The tragic scene was witnessed by a prodigious crowd of people, eager to get a glance of the miserable culprits. Until the preceding evening they manifested the utmost indifference; and employed themselves on Saturday with tossing halfpence. Keppel was the most hardened; and when brought into the chapel on Sunday morning he appeared still inexorable; rolled his eyes from one side to the other, and kept picking his fingers, until he brought blood through the quick. The pious exhortations of the worthy chaplain, however, brought them to a sense of duty, and they behaved afterwards with that decorum which became their unhappy situation.

The mother of Stoffel was left, by the will of Mrs. Richards, two hundred pounds, and the remainder of seven hundred pounds, her whole property, was divided among other relatives. The fate of Stoffel holds out an awful warning to vicious young men, who are not yet irrecoverably lost to virtue, as it shows the dangers to be apprehended from abandoned associates, for whose crimes and deeds the law justly makes their companions accountable. Though Stoffel suffered for a crime of which he did not contemplate the commission, for he particularly requested that no injury should be done to his aunt, he did not less deserve death for putting her in danger.

JAMES WILSON,

CONVICTED OF AN ATTEMPT TO COMMIT INCEST.

It was a maxim amongst the Romans, that no law should exist against persons guilty of parricide, upon the principle that such a crime could not exist. It might also be a maxim in the English law that no punishment should be assigned to those who were guilty of incest, upon the presumption that nature could not be so grievously violated. Some persons, however, in the shape of human beings, have been found so depraved and infamous as to trample upon the laws of God and nature. But we don't know if the long catalogue of crime exhibits a more abominable wretch than James Wilson, who, at the age of sixty, was convicted of attempting to commit a rape on his own daughter.

This hoary sinner was a watch-case maker, and resided in Northampton Row, Clerkenwell. In 1819 his wife died, leaving two daughter and a son, the age of the eldest girl, named Sarah, not being, at the time, more than fifteen years. She was a most interesting girl, and was serving her apprenticeship to the dress-making business. The unnatural father, abandoning the powerful suggestions of nature, began, soon after his wife's death, to take indecent liberties with his daughters, but particularly the eldest, who was four years older than her sister. In the room where they slept were two beds, and it was the constant practice of the incestuous brute to get into the bed of his children and strive to accomplish his revolting purpose. Happily they were successful in resisting the base attack; and he only desisted from persecuting them when they threatened to expose him. At such times he would protest most solemnly to annoy them no more; but, notwithstanding, in a few days he would repeat the offence, soliciting Sarah, like a lover, to submit to his embraces. The villain seemed as anxious to pervert their minds as to debase their bodies; for when his eldest girl used to reproach him for his unnatural conduct, he told her it was the tyrant laws of custom, and not those of nature, which bound her to resist. When repelled, as he always was, his conduct was most cruel. Sometimes, in resisting his violence, she had swooned away; but always succeeded in thwarting his revolting designs. Frequently did the poor girl implore him, on her knees, to desist, remonstrating with him, that his conduct was unnatural, but he only laughed, telling her the Almighty saw no harm in it, and to obey his inclinations was no crime.

As the eldest girl grew up, not liking to ruin her father by an exposure, she quitted him and went to service, leaving him ignorant of her place of residence. He found her out, however, and prevailed on her to return home, invoking Heaven that his arms might drop off if ever he would attempt to molest her again. The poor girl suffered herself to be prevailed on, and she went home, but had not been long there, when he renewed his base attempts. On the 17th of December, 1823, he threw her on the floor, and was proceeding to the most indecent liberties, when she resisted, scratched his face, and cried out for help, on which he desisted for that time; but in a day or two resorted again to the same offence.

By this time Mr. and Mrs. Smith, in whose house Wilson lodged, became acquainted with his conduct, they questioned the poor girls, for both had been similarly prosecuted; and, having heard the tale of their sufferings, took lodgings for them, unknown to their father, and when they got Wilson out of their house brought them back, and treated them with the utmost kindness; for their situation and virtues had endeared them to all who knew them.

The enraged monster of a parent, dreading the consequence of exposure, which it was natural for him now to expect, issued the following hand-bill, evidently for the purpose of cloaking his infamy:—

'Left their home, two girls, the eldest between eighteen and nineteen, and the youngest about fourteen. There is little doubt but that they have been enticed away from their home and duty by wicked advisers, the eldest having absented herself once before to associate with the basest of mankind, who spend their time in wickedness and drunkenness. She is capable of the basest insinuations, even to disgrace her father, who has from her infancy worked hard to support her.' The bill then went on to describe the dress of the fugitives, and threatened to punish whoever should harbour them after this notification.

Mr. Smith, under whose protection the girls were, now recommended an application to the magistrates. Wilson was accordingly brought up to Hatton Garden police-office, where his two daughters exhibited charges against him. Being asked what he had to say to the appalling narrative delivered by his indignant children, he threw himself into a theatrical posture, and exclaimed, "It's as false as hell—that elder girl is a felon and a prostitute, and capable of the worst action.'— Finding that these accusations availed him nothing, he turned round with an air of defiance, and said, with great emphasis, ' They are not my daughters, they are only my children by adoption.'

The magistrates, apprized that this assertion was as false as the other part of his defence, rose from their seats with disgust, and declared that they had heard enough to satisfy them of the infamy of his disposition. He was accordingly ordered to find bail.

Wilson was indicted at the Middlesex sessions, September the 18th, 1823, charged with having repeatedly attempted to ravish his own daughter. The prosecutrix was greatly affected during the trial; she sobbed aloud frequently, and appeared an object of general compassion. She was an interesting looking girl, and gave her evidence with natural and becoming modesty. Her revolting narrative was substantiated by several other witnesses, who had long been aware of Wilson's conduct, some of whom had seen the poor girl struggling in the embraces of her father.

Wilson, being called on for his defence, said the whole was a base story to ruin him; that his daughter had robbed him, and that she had been turned away from her situation for being a thief and a whore.

This accusation was instantly repelled. Her master came forward and gave her the highest possible character, saying that neither himself or her mistress would ever have parted with her, had she not gone away herself on the suggestion of her father. Several other persons gave her the highest character for modesty and proper deportment. It was proved that she was Wilson's daughter.

The jury instantly found the wretch Guilty, and he was sentenced to twelve months' imprisonment—a punishment by no means proportioned to his crime. By our laws an attempt to commit murder is punished in the same manner as if the deed had been perpetrated; surely, then, by analogy, an attempt to commit a rape should be visited in the same way as if the offence had been actually committed.

THOMAS CHARLES FITZHUE SANDON, ESQ.
TRANSPORTED FOR FRAUD.

Had this offender possessed as many virtues as he claimed Christian names, we should not have to state his villanies in the 'Newgate Calendar.' We are at a loss which to estimate most, the extreme credulity of the prosecutor or the impudent frauds of Sandon.

In April, 1822, Edward Putland, who had been a timber and coal merchant, was committed to the King's Bench prison, being indebted to sundry creditors in the sum of five or six hundred pounds. In the same prison was kept, in 'durance vile,' Mr. Sandon, whose polite address and easy confidence procured him a speedy admission to the friendship of Mr. Putland, who, 'good easy man,' quickly unbosomed himself to his new acquaintance. Sandon affected the utmost kindness, and frequently conversed with Mr. Putland respecting the hardships of his confinement. Seeing him so desirous of being restored to his family, Sandon called him into his room, on the 13th of June, and said, that, commiserating his situation, he had applied, in his behalf, to a worthy friend named Green, who had such influence in the commercial world that he could get his, Putland's, business immediately settled for thirty pounds, and added, that he expected Green that very evening to call on him.

Mr. Putland expressed his surprise that Mr. Green could get his business settled for so trifling a sum.

'Aye,' replied Sandon, 'if it were as many thousands it would make no difference, so peculiar and extensive is his influence.' Putland having no money, Sandon said his acceptance would do, and a bill of exchange was soon after drawn for the thirty pounds.

Under various pretences Sandon artfully contrived, from time to time, to defraud his credulous dupe of different sums of six pounds, nine pounds, fourteen pounds, and seventeen pounds, which were chiefly furnished by Mrs. Putland, who, anxious for her husband's discharge, put herself to the greatest distress to raise the money.

On the full disclosure of Sandon's villany he was tried at the Surrey Sessions, and found guilty on the 29th of July, 1823. The chairman declared it the most atrocious fraud he had ever met with, and sentenced him to seven years' transportation.

Sandon was a man of education and polished address, but such was his propensity to wickedness, that he had been frequently tried for the most petty frauds, and had once stood in the pillory.

Thurtell, when nearly overpowered, cutting Weare's throat.

JOHN THURTELL AND JOSEPH HUNT,
CONVICTED OF MURDER.

For cold-blooded villany in the mode of its conception and planning, and in the cool ferocity of its perpetration, this murder stands almost alone; and the sensation it created throughout the country was such, that no recent atrocity can be at all compared with it.

To the vice of gaming, and its associations with boxers and blacklegs, this tragical event owed its origin. John Thurtell, the principal actor, was the son of a respectable and worthy man, Alderman Thurtell, of Norwich. Early in life he went to sea, and on his return obtained a lieutenant's commission in the German Legion, then serving in Portugal. He also served in Spain, and was at the storming of St. Sebastian's. In 1821 he was residing at Norwich as a bombasin manufacturer, and came to London to receive four hundred pounds for goods which he had sold to a respectable house, and which, on his return, he was to pay among his creditors. Instead of doing so, however, he propagated a story that, as he was walking along a lonely spot, near Norwich, he was stopped by footpads, and robbed of it; but his creditors did not hesitate to tell him that he had invented this tale for the purpose of defrauding them; and, to avoid their importunities, he set off for London, in company with a girl, with whom he lived for some time. Here he commenced business, in conjunction with his brother Thomas, but soon failed. On the 26th of January, 1823, their premises in Watling Street were burnt down, which they were accused of doing wilfully, for the purpose of defrauding the fire-office, being insured for two thousand pounds, when their loss was not more than one hundred pounds.*

John Thurtell's first introduction to what is called 'the London ring' was at the Brown Bear public-house, in Bow Street, in 1820, at which time that house was much frequented by the boxing fraternity and their patrons; several fights were *made* there, and the money deposited. Dinners to celebrate victories, and to pay and receive bets, were also held there; and it was therefore considered in a great measure as the focus of pugilistic intelligence. At the time spoken of, John Thurtell one day accosted the landlord at his door in Bow Street, and said he knew that he was better acquainted than most people with fighting men, and had therefore waited upon him to ask if he could recommend two men who could be depended upon to fight a cross. The landlord told him i was an odd question from a stranger and he could give him no information upon such a subject, even if h knew him intimately.

From this time Thurtell becam a constant visitor at the house, an was introduced to several 'sporting men,' who were in the habit of meeting there. There was a room at the back of the premises, detached from the house, where high play was frequent; and here Thurtell lost three hundred pounds; but Weare was not present. The game was blind hookey, or hazard—a game, perhaps, which affords a better opportunity for the dexterous to play upon the unwary than almost any other. The whole three hundred pounds were won in a very short space of time. Thurtell was extremely angry at his loss, but his new friends contrived to conciliate him.

It happened that about that time matches were on the tapis between Hickman (the Gas Man) and Oliver, and Randall, and Martin. Hickman and Martin were under training at Wade's Mill, in Hertfordshire; and John Thurtell was found to be so good a flat, that it was determined to get him down to that place, gratify his vanity, by allowing him to assist in the training, and fleece him of whatever

* On the 3d of June, 1824, after the execution of John Thurtell, Thomas was found guilty of having set fire to these premises.

cash he might have left. Weare was appointed as the *plant* upon this occasion—that is, he was to come down as a stranger to all parties, and so to conduct himself as to appear to be a good subject for fleecing. The plan answered completely. Weare was pitted at play against Thurtell, who was suffered to win at first, but finally lost another three hundred pounds. He was afterwards played upon again in London; and these repeated losses irritated him so much, that he made use of threats which alarmed the fraternity, and it was thought best to adopt some mode of conciliation. After some consultation it was agreed upon that a cross should be fought between two of the pugilists then matched—namely, Randall and Martin—and that Thurtell should share in the profits. An attempt was at first made to buy over Randall, but that pugilist was proof against all their offers; and their attention was next turned to Martin, with whom, it is well known, they succeeded. One bet of eleven hundred pounds to six hundred guineas was made at a masquerade at the Opera House with a celebrated sporting character, and Thurtell had his share of the six hundred guineas.

From this time he became abandoned to all the vices of gaming, and was known as the constant companion of unprincipled gamblers, who live only by the folly and simplicity of their dupes.

The circumstances attending the horrible murder of Mr. Weare are so fully detailed in the speech of Mr. Gurney, who stated the case for the prosecution on the trial, which took place on the 5th of January, 1824, that it is unnecessary to do more than give it at length.

The deceased, said Mr. Gurney, whose murder was the subject of the present inquiry, was the late Mr. William Weare—a man, it was said, addicted to play, and connected with gaming-houses.—The prisoner at the bar, John Thurtell, had been his acquaintance, and in some practices of play had, it was said, been wronged by him, and deprived of a large sum of money. The other prisoner, Hunt, was described as being a public singer, and also known to Mr. Weare, but not in habits of friendship with him. Probert had been in trade as a spirit-dealer, and rented a cottage in Gill's Hill Lane, two or three miles from Elstree. The cottage of Probert was selected, from its seclusion, as a fit spot for the perpetration of the murder. Probert was himself much engaged in London, and his wife generally resided at the cottage, which was a small one, and fully occupied in the accommodation of Mrs. Probert, her sister (Miss Noyes), some children of Thomas Thurtell's (the prisoner's brother), and a maid-servant and boy. The deceased having been invited by John Thurtell to this place to enjoy a day or two's shooting, the prisoner Thurtell met the deceased at a billiard-room, kept by one Rexworthy, on the Thursday night previous to the murder; where they were joined by Hunt. On the forenoon of the Friday, the deceased was with Rexworthy at the same place, and said he was going for a day's shooting into the country. Weare went from the billiard-rooms between three and four o'clock to his chambers in Lyon's Inn, where he eat a chop dinner, and afterwards packed up, in a green carpet bag, some clothes, and a change of linen, such as a journey for the time he had specified might require. He also took with him, when he left his chambers, in a hackney-coach, which the laundress had called, a double-barrelled gun, and a backgammon box, dice, &c. He left his chambers in this manner before four o'clock, and drove first to Charing Cross, and afterwards to Maddox Street, Hanover Square; thence he proceeded to the New Road, where he got out of the coach, but returned after some time, accompanied by another person, and took his things away. At this time, Thomas and John Thurtell had need of temporary concealment, owing to their inability to provide the bail requisite to meet a charge of misdemeanour; and Probert had procured for them a retreat at Tetsall's, at the sign of the Coach and Horses, in Conduit Street, where they remained for two or three weeks previous to the murder. On the morning of Friday, the 24th of October, two men, answering in every respect to the description of John Thurtell and Hunt, went to a pawnbroker's in Marylebone, and purchased a pair of pocket-pistols. In the middle of the same day, Hunt hired a gig, and afterwards a horse, under the pretence of going to Dartford, in Kent: he also inquired where he could purchase a sack and a rope, and was directed to a place over Westminster Bridge, which, he was told, was on his road into Kent. Somewhere, however, it would be found that he did procure a sack and cord; and, the same afternoon, he met at Tetsall's Thomas Thurtell and Noyes. Some conversation took place at the time between the parties, and Hunt was heard to ask Probert if he 'would be in it,'—meaning what they (Hunt and John Thurtell) were about. Thurtell drove off from Tetsall's between four and five o'clock to take up a friend, as he said to Probert, 'to be killed as he travelled with him:' an expression which Probert said at the time he believed to have been a piece of idle bravado. He requested Probert to bring down Hunt in his own gig. In the course of that evening the prisoner Thurtell was seen in a gig, with a horse of an iron-grey colour, with a white face and white legs. He was first seen by a patrol, near Edgeware; beyond that part of the road he was seen by the landlord of a public-house; but from that time of the evening, until his arrival at Probert's cottage on the same night, they had no direct evidence to trace him. Probert, according to Thurtell's request, drove Hunt down in his gig, and, having a better horse, on the road they overtook Thurtell and Weare in the gig, and passed them without notice. They stopped afterwards at some public-house on the road to drink grog, where they believed Thurtell must have passed them unperceived. Probert drove Hunt until they reached Phillimore Lodge, where he (Hunt) got out, as he said by Thurtell's desire, to wait for him. Probert from thence drove alone to Gill's Hill cottage, in the lane near which he met Thurtell on foot, and alone. Thurtell inquired — Where was Hunt, had he been left behind? and added, that he had done the business without his assistance, and had killed his man. At his desire, Probert returned to bring Hunt to the spot, and went to Hunt for that purpose. When they met, he told Hunt what had happened. 'Why, it was to be done here!' said Hunt (pointing to a spot nearer Phillimore Lodge), admitting his privity, and that he had got out to assist in the commission of the deed. When Thurtell rebuked Hunt for his absence, 'Why,' said the latter, 'you had the tools.' 'They were no good,' replied Thurtell: 'the pistols were no better than pop-guns: I fired at his cheek, and it glanced off.' Weare then ran out of the gig, cried for mercy, and offered to return the money he had robbed him of. Thurtell pursued him up the lane, and, finding the pistol unavailing, attempted to cut his throat with a penknife; and ultimately killed him by driving the barrel of the pistol into his head, and turning it in his brains, after he had penetrated the forehead. Such was the manner in which Thurtell described himself to have disposed of the deceased. A gig was about that time heard to drive very quickly past Probert's cottage. The servant-lad expected his master, and thought he had arrived; but he did not make his appearance. Five minutes after that period certain persons, who happened to be in the road, distinctly heard the report of a gun or pistol, which was followed by voices, as if in contention. Groans were next heard, which became fainter and fainter, and then died away altogether.—The spot where the report of the pistol and the sound of the groans were heard was Gill's Hill Lane, near the cottage of Probert. Thurtell arrived at about nine o'clock in the evening at Probert's cottage, having set off from Conduit Street at five o'clock; and though he had been seen on the road in company with another person in the gig, yet it appeared that he arrived at the cottage alone, having in his possession the double-barrelled gun, the green carpet bag, and the backgammon-board, which Mr. Weare took away with him. He gave his horse to the boy, and the horse appeared to have sweated, but to be then in a cool state, which corroborated the fact that he had stopped a good while on his way. The boy inquired after Probert and Hunt, and was told that they would soon be at the cottage. At length a second gig arrived, with those two persons in it. They rode, while Thurtell, who went to meet them, walked with them. Probert went into the house. Neither Thurtell nor Hunt was expected by Mrs. Probert. With Thurtell she was acquainted; but Hunt was a stranger, and was formally introduced to her. Having supped on some pork chops, which Hunt had brought down with him from London, they went out, as Probert said, to visit Mr. Nicholls, a neighbour of his; but their real object was to go to the place where the body of Weare was deposited. Thurtell took them to the spot down the lane, and the body was dragged through the hedge into the adjoining field, where they effectually rifled the deceased man,—Thurtell having informed his companions that he had, in the first instance, taken part of his property. They then went back to the cottage. Thurtell, before he went out, placed a large sponge in the gig; when he returned he went to the stable, and sponged himself with great care, and endeavoured to remove the spots of blood, many of which were distinctly seen by Probert's boy. In the course of the evening Thurtell produced a gold watch, without a chain. He also displayed a gold curb chain, which might be used for a watch, when doubled; or, when single, might be worn round a lady's neck. On producing the chain, it was remarked that it was more fit for a lady than a gentleman; on which Thurtell pressed it on Mrs. Probert, and made her accept it. An offer was afterwards made, that a bed should be given to Thurtell and Hunt, which was to be accomplished by Miss Noyes' resigning her bed, and sleeping with the children. This was refused, Thurtell and Hunt observing that they would rather sit up; Miss Noyes, therefore, retired to her own bed. Something, however, had raised suspicion in the mind of Mrs. Probert; in consequence of which she did not go to bed, or undress herself. She went to the window, and, looking out, saw that Probert, Hunt, and Thurtell, were in the garden. It would be proved that they went down to the body, and, finding it too heavy to be removed, one of the horses was taken from the stable. The body, enclosed in a sack, was then placed across the horse; and stones having been put into the sack, the body, with the sack, was thrown into the pond. Mrs. Probert distinctly saw something heavy drawn across the garden where Thurtell was. The parties then returned to the house; and Mrs. Probert, whose fears and suspicions were now most powerfully excited, went down stairs, and listened behind the parlour door. The parties proceeded to share the booty and Thurtell divided with them to the amount of six pounds each. The purse, the pocket-book, and certain papers which might lead to detection, were carefully burned. They remained up late; and Probert, when he went to bed, was surprised to find that his wife was not asleep. Hunt and Thurtell still continued to sit up in the parlour. The next morning, as early as six o'clock, Hunt and Thurtell were seen in the lane together. Some men who were at work there observed them, as they called it, 'grabbling' for something in the hedge. Being spoken to by these men, Thurtell observed, 'that it was a very bad road, and that he had nearly been capsized there last night.' The men said, 'I hope you were not hurt.' Thurtell answered, 'Oh! no, the gig was not upset,' and then went away. These men, thinking something might have been lost on the spot, searched, after Thurtell and Hunt were gone. In one place they found a quantity of blood, further on they discovered a bloody knife, and next they found a bloody pistol —one of the pair which were purchased by Hunt. That pistol bore upon it the marks of blood and of human brains. The spot was afterwards still further examined, and more blood was discovered, which had been concealed by branches and leaves; so that no doubt could be entertained that the murder had been committed in this particular place. On the following morning, Saturday, the 25th of October, Thurtell and Hunt left Probert's cottage in the gig which Hunt had come down in, carrying away with them the gun, the carpet bag, and the back-gammon board, belonging to Mr. Weare. These articles were taken to Hunt's lodgings, where they were afterwards found. When Hunt arrived in town on Saturday he appeared to be unusually gay: he said, 'We Turpin lads can do the trick. I am able to drink wine now, and I will drink nothing but wine.' He seemed to be very much elevated at the recollection of some successful exploit. It was observed that Thurtell's hands were very much scratched; and some remark having been made on the subject, he stated that they had been out netting partridges, and that his hands got scratched in that occupation. On some other points he gave similarly evasive answers. On the Saturday, Hunt had a new spade sent to his lodgings, which he took down to the cottage on Sunday: When he got near Probert's garden, he told that individual that he had brought it down to dig a hole to bury the body in. On that evening Probert visited Mr. Nicholls, and the latter said to him that some persons had heard the report of a gun or pistol in the lane on Friday evening, but he supposed it was some foolish joke. Probert, on his return, stated this to Thurtell and Hunt, and the information appeared to alarm the former, who said, he feared he should be hanged. The intelligence, however inspired them all with a strong desire to conceal the body effectually. Probert wished it to be removed from his pond; and Thurtell and Hunt promised to come down on the Monday, and remove it. On Monday, Thurtell and Hunt went out in the gig, and took with them Probert's boy, whom they carried to various places, and finally lodged the boy at Mr. Tetsall's, in Conduit Street. On the evening of that same Monday, Hunt and Thurtell went down to the cottage. Hunt engaged Mrs. Probert in conversation, while Thurtell and Probert took the body out of the pond, put it into Thurtell's gig, and then gave notice to Hunt that the gig was ready. In this manner they carried away the body that night; but where they took it to Probert did not know. It appeared, however, that the body was carried to a pond near Elstree, at a considerable distance from Probert's cottage, and there sunk, as it had before been in Probert's pond, in a sack containing a considerable quantity of stones. Hunt and Thurtell then went to London. The report of the pistol in the lane on the Friday evening, and the discovery of the blood in the field, had led to great alarm among the magistracy. Inquiry was set on foot, and Thurtell, Hunt, and Probert were apprehended. It was found that Hunt had adopted a peculiar mode of concealing his identity; for when he was hiring the gig, and doing various other acts connected with this atrocious proceeding, he wore very long whiskers, which, on the Monday after the murder, he had shaven off. Strict inquiries were made by the magistrates, but nothing was ascertained to prove to a certainty who was murdered. The body was, however, found on the Thursday, in consequence of Hunt having given information as to the place where it was deposited. Some of these circumstances, Mr. Gurney observed, would depend on the evidence of an accomplice; for Probert, though not an accomplice before the murder, was confessedly privy to a certain part of the transaction—to the concealment of the body, and consequently of the murder: but he would so confirm him in every point, as to build up his testimony with a degree of strength and consistency which could not be shaken, much less overturned. He would prove by other witnesses besides Probert, that Thurtell set out with a companion from London, who did not arrive at the ostensible end of his journey; that he had brought the property of that companion to Probert's house, the double-barrelled gun, the back-gammon board, and the green carpet bag; that some time before he arrived at the cottage the report of a gun or pistol was heard in Gill's Hill Lane, not far from the cottage; that his clothes were in a bloody state; and that, when he was apprehended, even on the Wednesday after the murder, he had not been able to efface all the marks from his apparel. Besides all this, the jury would find that in his pocket, when apprehended, there was a penknife which was positively sworn to as having belonged to Mr. Weare, and also the fellow pistol of that which was found adjoining the place where the murder was committed — the pair having been purchased in Marylebone Street by Hunt. These circumstances brought the case clearly home to Thurtell. Next as to Hunt. He was charged as an accomplice before the fact. He hired the gig, and he procured the sack. The gun, travelling-bag and backgammon-board, were found in his lodging. These constituted a part of the plunder of Mr. Weare, and could be possessed only by a person participating in this crime. Besides, there was placed about the neck of Probert's wife, a chain, which had belonged to Mr. Weare, and round the neck of the murdered man there was found a shawl, which belonged to Thurtell, but which had been seen in the hands of Hunt.

The collateral circumstances were proved by a variety of witnesses.

Ruthven the officer, in the course of his examination, deposited on the table a pistol, and a pistol key, a knife, a muslin handkerchief spotted with blood, a shirt, similarly stained, and a waistcoat, into the pockets of which bloody hands had been thrust. A coat and a hat marked with blood were also produced. These all belonged to Thurtell, and he looked at them with an eye of perfect indifference. Ruthven then produced several articles belonging to the deceased—the gun, the carpet-bag, and his clothes.

Symmonds the constable, when sworn, took from his pocket a white folded paper, which he carefully undid, and produced to the court the pistol with which the murder had been committed. It was a blue steel-barrelled pistol, with brass about the handle; the pan was open, as the firing had left it and was smeared with the black of gunpowder and the dingy stain of blood. The barrel was bloody, and in the muzzle a piece of tow was thrust, to keep in the horrid contents, the murdered man's brains. Against the back of the pan were the short curled hairs, of a silver hue, which had been dug from the man's head, and were glued to the pan firmly with crusted blood.

Probert's evidence was as follows:

'I occupied a cottage in Gill's Hill Lane six months before October last; my family consisted of Mrs. Probert, a servant maid, and a boy; in the month of October, Miss Noyes lived with us, and two children of Thomas Thurtell, a brother of the prisoner's. I have been for some time past acquainted with the prisoner John Thurtell; he had often been down to my cottage sporting with me; he knew the road to my cottage, and all the roads thereabouts well. Gill's Hill Lane, in which my cottage stood, was out of the high road to St. Alban's, at Radlett; my cottage was about a quarter of a mile from the high road, and fourteen miles and a quarter from Tyburn turnpike. In the latter end of October, the prisoner, John Thurtell, lodged at Tetsall's, the Coach and Horses, in Conduit Street; Thomas Thurtell lodged there also. They were there every day that week. On Friday the 24th, I dined at Tetsall's with John Thurtell and Hunt; Thomas Thurtell and Noyes were there also. After dinner, Thurtell said something to me about money. Four days previous to the 24th, I borrowed ten pounds from John Thurtell; he then said, you must let me have it back on the Thursday or Friday; on the Thursday I saw him at Mr. Tetsall's, and he asked me if I had got the ten pounds; I told him I had not; I had not collected any money. He said, "I told you I should want it to-day or to-morrow, else it will be three hundred pounds out of my pocket; but if you will let me have it to-morrow, it will answer the same purpose." On the same day (Friday) I paid him five pounds. I borrowed five pounds of Mr. Tetsall; that was after dinner. He then said, "I think I shall go down to your cottage to-night; are you going down?" and asked me if I could drive Hunt down. I said "yes." He said, "I expect a friend to meet me this evening a little after five, and if he comes I shall go down. If I have an opportunity I mean to do him; for he is a man that has robbed me of several hundreds." He added, "I have told Hunt where to stop; I shall want him about a mile and a half beyond Elstree. If I should not go down give Hunt a pound," which I did. Hunt had just come in, and Thurtell said, "There, Joe, there's a pound; if Probert don't come, hire a horse; you know where to stop for me." I do not know that Hunt made any answer; I gave him twenty shillings in silver. Thurtell left the Coach and Horses a little after five in a horse and chaise; it was a grey horse; I afterwards set off in my own gig, and took Hunt with me. When I came to the middle of Oxford Street, Hunt, by my request, got out of the gig to purchase a loin of pork for supper. When we came to the top of Oxford Street, Hunt said, "This is the place Jack is to take up his friend at." In our way down we overtook Thurtell, about four miles from London. Hunt said to me, "There they are; drive by, and take no notice." He added, "It's all right; Jack has got him." There were two persons in the gig; Thurtell and another; I passed them and said nothing. I stopped at a public-house called the Baldfaced Stag, about seven miles from London, two miles short of Edgeware. It was then, perhaps, a quarter to seven. When Hunt said "It's all right," I asked him what was the name of the man? Hunt replied, "You are not to know his name; you never saw him; you know nothing of him." I got out at the Bald-faced Stag; I supplied the house with spirits. Hunt walked on, and said, "I'll not go in, because I have not returned the horsecloths I borrowed." I stopped about twenty minutes; I then drove on, and overtook Hunt about a quarter of a mile from Edgeware. I took him up, and we drove to Mr. Clarke's, at Edgeware, where we had a glass of brandy and water. A little further on, in Edgeware, we bought half a bushel of corn, and put it in the gig. Hunt then said, "I wonder where Thurtell is; he can't have passed us?" We drove on to the Artichoke, kept by Mr. Field, and got there within about eight minutes of eight. Neither I nor Hunt got out. We had four or five glasses of brandy and water, while we waited for the express purpose of Thurtell coming up; we stopped more than three quarters of an hour at Elstree. We went about a mile and a half, to Mr. Phillimore's Lodge, to wait for Thurtell. Hunt said, "I shall wait here for John Thurtell;" and he got out on the road. I drove on through Radlett, towards my own cottage; when I came near my own cottage, within about a hundred yards, I met John Thurtell; he was on foot; he says, "Hallo! where's Hunt?" I said I had left him waiting near Phillimore's Lodge for him; John Thurtell replied, "Oh! I don't want him now, for I have done the trick." He said he had killed his friend that he had brought down with him; he had ridded the country of a villain, who had robbed him of three or four hundred pounds!" I said, "Good God! I hope you have not killed the man?" and he said, "It's of no consequence to you, you don't know him; you never saw him, do you go back and fetch Hunt, you know best where you left him!" I returned to the place where I left Hunt, and found him near the spot where I left him. Thurtell did not go. I said to Hunt, when I took him up, "John Thurtell is at my house—he has killed his friend;" and Hunt said, "Thank God, I am out of it; I am glad he has done it without me; I can't think where the devil he could pass; I never saw him pass any where, but I'm glad I'm out of it." He said, "This is the place where we were to have done it" (meaning near Phillimore's Lodge). I asked him who the man was, and he said, "You don't know him, and I shall not tell you:" he said it was a man that had robbed Jack of several hundred pounds, and they meant to have it back again. By that time I had reached my own house; John Thurtell stood at the gate; we drove into the yard. Hunt said, "Thurtell, where could you pass me?" Thurtell replied, "It don't matter where I passed you, I've done the trick—I have done it." Thurtell said, "What the devil did you let Probert stop drinking at his d—d public-houses for, when you knew what was to be done?" Hunt said, "I made sure you were behind, or else we should not have stopped." Having taken the loin of pork into the kitchen, and given it to the servant to cook for supper, I went into the parlour and introduced Hunt to Mrs. Probert; he had never been there before. Thurtell followed immediately; we had stopped in the yard a little time before we went in. I returned to the parlour, and told Mrs. Probert we were going to Mr. Nicholls's to get leave for a day's shooting; before we went out, Thurtell took a sack and a cord with him. We then went down the lane, I carried the lantern; as we went along Thurtell said, "I began to think, Hunt, you would not come." Hunt said, "We made sure you were behind." I walked foremost; and Thurtell said, "Probert, he is just beyond the second turning." When he came to the second turning he said, "It's a little further on." He at length said, "This is the place." We then looked about for a pistol and knife, but could not find either; we got over the hedge and there found the body lying; the head was bound up in a shawl, I think a red one (here the shawl, already produced, was shown to witness), I can't say that is the shawl. Thurtell searched the deceased's pockets, and found a pocket book containing three five pound notes, a memorandum book, and some silver. John Thurtell said, "This is all he has got, I took the watch and purse when I killed him." The body was then put into a sack head foremost; the sack came to the knees, and was tied with a cord; it was the sack John Thurtell had taken out of the gig; we then left the body there, and went towards home. Thurtell said, "When I first shot him he jumped out of the gig and ran like the devil, singing out that he would deliver all he had, if I'd only spare his life." John Thurtell said, "I jumped out of the gig and ran after him; I got him down, and began to cut his throat, as I thought, close to the jugular vein, but I could not stop his singing out; I then jammed the pistol into his head; I gave it a turn round, and then I knew I had done him." He then said to Hunt, " Joe, you ought to have been with me, for I thought at one time he would have got the better of me. These d—d pistols are like spits, they are of no use." Hunt said, " I should have thought one of those pistols would have killed him dead, but you had plenty of tools with you;" we then returned to the house and supped. In the course of the evening, after supper, John Thurtell produced a handsome gold watch, with a gold chain attached to it. He took off the chain and offered to make Mrs. Probert a present of it, saying it was more fit for a lady than a gentleman. Mrs. Probert refused for some time, but at length accepted of it. He put the watch and seals in his pocket. As we had no spare bed that night, I said that my sister would sleep with Thomas Thurtell's children, and that Thurtell and Hunt could have her bed. They answered, they would sleep on the sofa. Hunt, who is a professional singer, sang two or three songs after supper. Mrs. Probert and Miss Noyes went to bed between twelve and one. When they were gone, John Thurtell took out a pocket book, a purse, and a memorandum-book, the purse contained sovereigns; I can't say how many. He took 15*l*. in notes from the pocket-book, and gave Hunt and myself a 5*l*. note and a sovereign each, saying—" that's your share of the blunt." There were several papers in the books; they and the purse and books were burnt; a carpet bag was opened. Thurtell said it had belonged to the man he had murdered; it contained wearing apparel and shooting materials; there was also a backgammon-board, containing dice and cards, and a double-barrelled gun in a case. All the things were taken away next day in a gig, by Thurtell and Hunt. After this, Thurtell said, " I mean to have Barber Beaumont and Woods;" Barber Beaumont is a director of a fire-office with which John Thurtell had some dispute; Woods is a young man in London who keeps company with Miss Noyes. It was a general conversation, and I cannot recollect the particulars; he might have mentioned other names, but I can't recollect them. Thurtell said to Hunt, " We must now go out and fetch the body, and put it in the pond." I said, " By G-d, you shan't put it in the pond, you'll be my ruin else." Thurtell said, " Had it not been for the mistake of Hunt, I should have killed him in the other lane, and returned to town and inquired of his friends why he had not come." First, only Thurtell and Hunt went out; when they came back, Hunt said, " Probert, he is too heavy, we can't carry him; we have only brought him a little way." Thurtell said, " Will you go with us? I'll put the bridle on my horse and fetch him." I went out to the stable with him, and left Hunt waiting near the gate. Thurtell's horse was brought out, and Thurtell and I went down and brought the body on the horse; Hunt did not go with us. We took the body to Mr. Wardle's field, near my gate. Hunt took the horse back to the stable, and came back to the garden: we dragged the body down the garden to the pond, put some stones in the sack, and threw the body into the pond. The man's feet were perhaps half a foot above the water; John Thurtell got a cord, threw it round the feet, and gave me the other end, and I dragged it into the centre of the pond, and it sunk. We all three returned to the cottage, and I went to bed almost immediately. I found my wife up; next morning, I came down about nine o'clock. Thurtell said, in presence of Hunt, that they had been down the lane, to look for the pistol and knife, but neither could be found. They asked me to go down the lane and seek them in the course of the day, which I promised to do: but when I went down the lane, I saw a man at work near the spot. That morning they went away after breakfast. On Sunday they came down again; and Thomas Thurtell and Mr. Noyes came also. Hunt brought a new spade with him. He said it was to dig a grave for the deceased that he brought it. Hunt returned with the gig after setting down Thomas Thurtell, and brought out John Thurtell and Noyes. Hunt was very dirtily dressed when he came down, and went up stairs to change. When he came back, he was well dressed—in almost new clothes. Hunt said the clothes belonged to the deceased; he told me he had thrown a new spade over the hedge into my garden; I saw it afterwards. John Thurtell and I walked to the pond. He asked me, if the body had risen. I said no; and he said it would lay there for a month. In the afternoon, Hewart called, and I went with him to Mr. Nicholls's. On my return, I told Thurtell and Hunt that Mr. Nicholls had told me, that some one had fired a pistol or gun off in Gill's Hill Lane on Friday night, and that there were cries of murder, as though some one had been killed. He said it was about eight o'clock, and added, " I suppose it was done by some of your friends to frighten each other." John Thurtell said, " then I am baked." I said, " I am afraid it's a bad job, as Mr. Nicholls seems to know all about it; I am very sorry it ever happened here, as I fear it will be my ruin." Thurtell said, " Never mind, Probert, they can do nothing with you." I said the body must be immediately taken out of my pond again. Thurtell said, " I'll tell you what I'll do, Probert; after you are all gone to bed, Joe and I will take the body up and bury it." Hunt was present at this. I told them that would be as bad, if they buried it in the garden. John Thurtell said, " I'll bury him where you nor no one else can find him." As John Thurtell was going into the parlour, Hunt said, " Probert, they can do nothing with you or me, even if they do find it out, as we were neither of us at the murder." Thurtell and Hunt sat up all that night; I, Noyes, and Thomas Thurtell, went to bed. Thomas Thurtell slept with his children. In the morning, John Thurtell and Hunt said they went to dig a grave, but the dogs were barking all night, and they thought some one was about the ground. John Thurtell said, " Joe and I will come down to-night and take him quite away, and that will be better for you altogether." Thomas Thurtell and Hunt, and my boy, Addis, went away in one chaise after breakfast, and John Thurtell, Thomas Noyes, and Miss Noyes in another. The boy was sent to town to be out of the way. That evening John Thurtell and Hunt came again in a gig about nine; they took supper; after supper, John Thurtell and I went to the stable, leaving Hunt talking to Mrs. Probert. Thurtell said, " Come, let's get the body up; while Hunt is talking to Mrs. Probert, she will not suspect." We went to the pond, and got the body up; we took it out of the sack, and cut the clothes all off it. We left the body naked on the grass, and returned to the parlour; we then went to the stables, and John Thurtell went to his gig, and took out a new sack, and some cord; we all three returned to the pond, put the body headforemost into the sack, and carried it to the lower garden-gate, and put it into the gig. I refused to assist them in settling the body in the gig. They went away. I next morning burnt some of the clothes, and threw the rest away in different places. I was taken into custody on the Tuesday evening after they went away.

The following was the substance of Mrs. Probert's evidence:—

'I remember the night of the 24th of October, when Mr. John Thurtell and Mr. Hunt came to Gill's Hill cottage, to have heard the sound of a gig passing my cottage. It was about eight o'clock, I think. The bell of our cottage was rung nearly an hour after; but, at that ringing, nobody came into our house. My husband came home that night nearly at ten. I came down stairs, and found in the parlour Mr. Probert, John Thurtell, and a stranger, whom my husband introduced to me as Mr. Hunt. I saw John Thurtell take out a gold chain, which he showed to me. It was a gold watch chain with a great deal of work about it; it was such a chain as this, I think (the chain was shown her). He offered to make me a present of it; I refused it for some time, and at last accepted it (she was shown the box and chain produced by the constable at Watford). I recollect giving that box and the chain to the constable, in the presence of the magistrates. When I and Miss Noyes went up stairs, we left John Thurtell, Hunt, and Mr. Probert in the room. I did not go to bed immediately: I went from my room to the stairs to listen; I leaned over the banisters. What I heard in leaning over the banisters, was all in a whisper. What I heard at first was, I thought, about trying on clothes. The first I heard was "This, I think, will fit you very well." I heard a noise like a rustling of papers on the table; I heard also something like the noise of papers thrown into the fire. I afterwards went up to my own chamber. Out of doors I saw something; I looked from my window, and saw two gentlemen go from the parlour to the stable; they led a horse out of the stable, and opened the yard gate and let the horse out. Some time after that I heard something in the garden; I heard something dragged, as it seemed, very heavily; it appeared to me to come from the stable to the garden; the garden is near the back gate; it was dragged along the dark walk; I had a view of it, when they dragged it out of the dark walk; it seemed very large and heavy; it was in a sack. It was after this I heard the rustling of papers, and the conversation I have described. After the sack was dragged out of the dark walk, I had a view of it until it was half way down the walk to the pond. I had a good view of it so far. After this I heard a noise like a heap of stones thrown into a pit, I can't describe it any other way; it was a hollow sound. I heard, besides what I have before mentioned, some further conversation. The first I heard was, I think, Hunt's voice; he said, " Let us take a 5l. note each." I did not hear Thurtell say any thing; then I heard another voice say, " We must say there was a hare thrown up in the gig on the cushion—we must tell the boy so in the morning." I next heard a voice, I can't exactly say whose, "We had better be off to town by four or five o'clock in the morning;" and then, I think, John Thurtell it was, who said, "We had better not go before eight or nine o'clock; and the parlour door then shut. I heard John Thurtell say also (I think it was his voice), "Holding shall be next." I rather think it was Hunt who next spoke: he asked, "Has he (Holding) got money?" John Thurtell replied, "It is not money I want, it is revenge; it is," said John Thurtell, "Holding who has ruined my friend here." I did not at first understand who this friend was; I believe it meant Mr. Probert, by husband. I cannot say whether Holding had any thing to do in the transactions of my husband's bankruptcy. "It was Holding," said John Thurtell, "who ruined my friend here, and destroyed my peace of mind." My husband came to bed about half-past one or two o'clock; I believe it was; I did not know the hour exactly.'

At the close of the evidence for the crown, although, in answer to his Lordship's inquiry, the jury decided on going through the case, they revoked that decision at the desire of John Thurtell; who respectfully pressed on their attention the long and harassing time he had stood at that bar; and begged for a night's cessation to recruit his strength previous to making his defence. The Court therefore adjourned.

On the following morning, the trial proceeded.

Ruthven and Thomas Thurtell were recalled to be examined on some trifling points; and in a short time, Mr. Justice Park informed John Thurtell, that he was ready to hear any observations he had to make. Thurtell, through the gaoler, intimated, that he wished his witnesses to be examined first; but this was refused, as being contrary to the practice.

Thurtell then commenced his defence;—speaking in a deep, measured, and unshaken tone, and using a studied and theatrical action.

'My Lord, and Gentlemen of the Jury.— Under greater difficulties than ever man encountered, I now rise to vindicate my character and defend my life. I have been supported in this hour of trial, by the knowledge that my cause is heard before an enlightened tribunal, and that the free institutions of my country have placed my destiny in the hands of twelve men, who are uninfluenced by prejudice, and unawed by power. I have been represented by the press, which carries its benefits or curses on rapid wings from one extremity of the kingdom to the other, as a man more depraved, more gratuitously and habitually profligate and cruel, than has ever appeared in modern times. I have been held up to the world as the perpetrator of a murder, under circumstances of greater aggravation, of more cruel and premeditated atrocity, than it ever before fell to the lot of man to have seen or heard of. I have been held forth to the world as a depraved, heartless, remorseless, prayerless villain, who had seduced my friend into a sequestered path, merely in order to despatch him with the greater security—as a snake who had crept into his bosom only to strike a sure blow—as a monster, who, after the perpetration of a deed from which the hardest heart recoils with horror, and at which humanity stands aghast, washed away the remembrance of my guilt in the midst of riot and debauchery. You, gentlemen, must have read the details which have been daily, I may say hourly, published regarding me. It would be requiring more than the usual virtue of our nature to expect that you should entirely divest your minds of those feelings, I may say those creditable feelings, which such relations must have excited; but I am satisfied, that as far as it is possible for men to enter into a grave investigation with minds unbiassed, and judgments unimpaired, after the calumnies with which the public mind has been deluged—I say, I am satisfied, that with such minds and such judgments, you have this day assumed your sacred office. The horrible guilt which has been attributed to me is such as could not have resulted from custom, but must have been the innate principle of my infant mind, and have "grown with my growth, and strengthened with my strength." But I will call before you gentlemen whose characters are unimpeachable, and whose testimony must be above suspicion, who will tell you, that the time was when my bosom overflowed with all the kindly feelings; and even my failings were those of an improvident generosity and unsuspecting friendship. Beware, then, gentlemen, of an anticipated verdict. Do not suffer the reports which you have heard to influence your determination. Do not believe that a few short years can have reversed the course of nature, and converted the good feelings which I possessed into that spirit of malignant cruelty to which only demons can attain. A kind, affectionate, and religious mother directed the tender steps of my infancy, in the paths of piety and virtue. My rising youth was guided in the way that it should go by a father whose piety was universally known and believed—whose kindness and charity extended to all who came within the sphere of its influence. After leaving my paternal roof, I entered into the service of our late revered monarch, who was justly entitled the "father of his people." You will learn from some of my honourable companions, that, while I served under his colours, I never tarnished their lustre. The country which is dear to me I have served. I have fought for her. I have shed my blood for her. I feared not in the open field to shed the blood of her declared foes. But oh! to suppose that on that account I was ready to raise the assassin's arm against my friend, and with that view to draw him into secret places for his destruction—it is monstrous, horrible, incredible. I have been represented to you as a man who was given to gambling, and the constant companion of gamblers. To this accusation, in some part, my heart with feeling penitence pleads guilty. I have gambled. I have been a gambler, but not for the last three years. During that time I have not attended or betted upon a horse-race, or a fight, or any public exhibition of that nature. If I have erred in these things, half of the nobility of the land have been my examples; some of the most enlightened statesmen of the country have been my companions in them. I have indeed been a gambler—I have been an unfortunate one. But whose fortune have I ruined?—whom undone?—My own family have I ruined—I have undone myself! At this moment I feel the distress of my situation. But, gentlemen, let not this misfortune entice your verdict against me. Beware of your own feelings, when you are told by the highest authority, that the heart of man is deceitful above all things. Beware, gentlemen, of an anticipated verdict. It is the remark of a very sage and experienced writer of antiquity, that no man becomes wicked all at once. And with this, which I earnestly request you to bear in mind, I proceed to lay before you the whole career of my life. I will not tire you with tedious repetitions, but I will disclose enough of my past life to inform your judgments; leaving it to your clemency to supply whatever little defects you may observe. You will consider my misfortunes, and the situation in which I stand—the deep anxiety that I must feel—the object for which I have to strive. You may suppose something of all this; but oh! no pencil, though dipped in the lines of heaven, can portray my feelings at this crisis. Recollect, I again entreat you, my situation, and allow something for the workings of a mind little at ease; and pity and forgive the faults of my address. The conclusion of the late war, which threw its lustre upon the fortunes of the nation generally, threw a gloomy shadow over mine. I entered into a mercantile life with feelings as kind, and with a heart as warm, as I had carried with me in the service. I took the commercial world as if it had been governed by the same regulations as the army. I looked upon merchants as if they had been my mess companions. In the transactions I had with them, my purse was as open, my heart as warm, to answer their demands, as they had been to my former associates. I need not say that any fortune, however ample, would have been insufficient to meet such a course of conduct. I, of course, became the subject of a commission of bankruptcy. My solicitor, in whom I had foolishly confided as my most particular friend, I discovered, too late, to have been a traitor—a man who was foremost in the ranks of my bitterest enemies. But for this man, I should still have been enabled to regain a station in society, and I should have yet preserved the esteem of my friends, and above all, my own self-respect. But how often is it seen that the avarice of one creditor destroys the clemency of all the rest, and for ever dissipates the fair prospects of the unfortunate debtor. With the kind assistance of Mr. Thomas Oliver Springfield, I obtained the signature of all my creditors to a petition for superseding my bankruptcy. But just then, when I flattered myself that my ill fortune was about to close—that my blossoms were ripening—there came "a frost—a nipping frost." My chief creditor refused to sign, unless he was paid a bonus of 300*l.* upon his debt beyond all the other creditors. This demand was backed by the man who was at the time his and my solicitor. I spurned the offer—I awakened his resentment. I was cast upon the world—my all disposed of—in the deepest distress. My brother afterwards availed himself of my misfortune, and entered into business. His warehouses were destroyed by the accident of a fire, as has been proved by the verdict of a jury on a trial at which the venerable judge now present presided. But that accident, unfortunate as it was, has been taken advantage of in order to insinuate that he was guilty of crime, because his property was destroyed by it, as will be proved by the verdict of an honest and upright jury in an action for conspiracy, which will be tried ere long before the chief justice of the King's Bench. A conspiracy there was — but where? Why, in the acts of the prosecutor himself, Mr. Barber Beaumont, who was guilty of suborning witnesses, and who will be proved to have paid for false testimony. Yes; this professed friend of the aggrieved—this pretended prosecutor of public abuses—this self-appointed supporter of the laws, who panders to rebellion, and has had the audacity to raise its standard in the front of the royal palace—this man, who has just head enough to contrive crime, but not heart enough to feel its consequences—this is the real author of the conspiracy which will shortly undergo legal investigation. To these particulars I have thought it necessary to call your attention, in language which you may think perhaps too warm —in terms not so measured, but that they may incur your reproof. But—

'The flesh will quiver where the pincers tear,
'The blood will follow where the knife is driven.'

You have been told that I intended to decoy Woods to his destruction; and he has said that he saw me in the passage of the house. I can prove, by honest witnesses, fellow-citizens of my native city of Norwich, that I was there at that time; but, for the sake of an amiable and innocent female, who might be injured, I grant to Mr. Woods the mercy of my silence. When, before this, did it ever fall to the lot of any subject to be borne down by the weight of calumny and obloquy which now oppresses me? The press, which ought to be the shield of public-liberty, the avenger of public wrongs—which, above all, should have exerted itself to preserve the purity of its favourite institution, the trial by jury—has directed its whole force to my injury and prejudice; it has heaped slander upon slander, and whetted the public appetite for slanders more atrocious; nay more, what in other men would serve to refute and repel the shaft of calumny, is made to stain with a deeper die the villanies ascribed to me. One would have thought, that some time spent in the service of my country would have entitled me to some favour from the public under a charge of this nature. But no; in my case the order of things is changed — nature is reversed. The acts of times long since past have been made to cast a deeper shadow over the acts attributed to me within the last few days; and the pursuit of a profession, hitherto held honourable among honourable men, has been turned to the advantage of the accusation against me. You have been told that after the battle, I boasted of my inhumanity to a vanquished, yielding, wounded enemy—that I made a wanton sacrifice of my bleeding and supplicating foe, by striking him to the earth with my cowardly steel; and that, after this deed of blood, I coldly sat down to plunder my unhappy victim. Nay, more —that with folly indescribable and incredible, I boasted of my barbarity as of a victory. Is there an English officer, is there an English soldier, or an Englishman, whose heart would not have revolted with hatred against such baseness and folly? Far better, gentlemen, would it have been for me, rather than have seen this day, to have fallen with my honourable companions, stemming and opposing the tide of battle upon the field of my country's glory. Then my father and my family, though they would have mourned my loss, would have blessed my name, and shame would not have rolled its burning fires over my memory! Before I recur to the evidence brought against my life, I wish to return my most sincere thanks to the high sheriff and the magistrates for their kindness shown to me. I cannot but express my unfeigned regret at a slight misunderstanding which has occurred between the Rev. Mr. Lloyd, the visiting magistrate, and my solicitor. As it was nothing more than a misunderstanding, I trust the bonds of friendship are again ratified between us all. My most particular gratitude is due to the Rev. Mr. Franklin, whose kind visits and pious consolations have inspired me with a deeper sense of the awful truths of religion, and have trebly armed my breast with fortitude to serve me on this day. Though last, not least—let me not forget Mr. Wilson; the governor of the prison, and the fatherly treatment which he has shown me throughout. My memory must perish ere I can forget his kindness. My heart must be cold ere it can cease to beat with gratitude to him, and wishes for the prosperity of his family.'

Here the prisoner read, first, a long written comment on the weaker parts of the evidence; indeed the decisive parts he left untouched. This paper was either so ill-written, or Thurtell was so imperfect a reader, that the effect was quite fatal to the previous flowery appeal to the jury: he stammered, blundered, and seemed confused. He read next, from the Percy Anecdotes, some very tedious instances of the fallibility of circumstantial evidence. Then came the peroration:—

'And now, gentlemen, having read these cases to you, am not I justified in saying, that, unless you are thoroughly convinced that the circumstances before you are absolutely inconsistent with my innocence, I have a claim to your verdict of acquittal? Am I not justified in saying, that you might come to the conclusion that all the circumstances stated might be true, and yet I be innocent? I am sure, gentlemen, you will banish from your minds any prejudice which may have been excited against me, and act upon the principle that every man is to be deemed innocent until he is proved guilty. Judge of my case, gentlemen, with mature consideration, and remember that my existence depends upon your breath. If you bring in a verdict of guilty, the law afterwards allows no mercy. If upon a due consideration of all the circumstances you shall have a doubt, the law orders, and your own consciences will teach you to give me the benefit of it. Cut me not off in the summer of my life! I implore you, gentlemen, to give my case your utmost attention. I ask not so much for myself as for those respectable parents whose name I bear, and who must suffer in my fate. I ask it for the sake of that home which will be rendered cheerless and desolate by my death. Gentlemen, I am incapable of any dishonourable action. Those who know me best, know that I am utterly incapable of an unjust and dishonourable action, much less of the horrid crime with which I am now charged. There is not, I think, one in this court who does not think me innocent of the charge. If there be—to him or them I say, in the language of the Apostle, "Would to God ye were altogether such as I am, save these bonds." Gentlemen, I have now done. I look with confidence to your decision, I repose in your hands all that is dear to the gentleman and the man! I have poured my heart before you as to my God! I hope your verdict this day will be such as you may ever after be able to think upon with a composed conscience; and that you will also reflect upon the solemn declaration which I now make—I am innocent! —So help me God!'

Hunt was next called upon for his defence. His feeble voice and shrinking manner were doubly apparent, from the overwrought energy which his companion had manifested. He complained of his agitation and fatigue, and requested that a paper, which he held in his hand, might be read for him; and accordingly the clerk of the arraigns read it in a very feeling manner. It was prudently and advisedly composed; and insisted strongly on the magistrates' promise, when he first gave information on the subject.

When the paper was concluded, Hunt read a few words on a part of Probert's evidence, in a dejected voice, and then leant his head upon his hand. He was evidently wasting away minute by minute.

Mr. Justice Park summed up at great length. The charge to the jury occupied several hours—and the jury then requested leave to withdraw. Hunt, at this period, became much agitated, and as he saw them about to quit the box, he intreated leave to address them—but on his counsel learning and communicating to the judge what the prisoner had to say, the jury were directed to proceed to the consideration of their verdict.

After an absence of twenty minutes, the jury returned, and their foreman delivered a verdict of Guilty.

The officer of the court then said —What have you, or either of you, to say why sentence of death should not pass on you?

Thurtell—My Lord, before you pass sentence, I pray you to take into your serious consideration what I say. I now, for the last time, assert that I am innocent. I entreat a short delay in the execution of the sentence you may pass, as I have friends now at a distance, with whom it is necessary that I should transact some business. It is for the sake of some friends that are dear to me, that I ask this indulgence (here the prisoner seemed affected, and shed a tear), not for myself, for I am at this moment ready; my request, I hope your Lordship will take into consideration; and beyond Sunday next is all I ask.

This request could not be acceded to, and sentence was accordingly passed in the usual form; after which the two prisoners shook hands, and were removed to their respective cells. Hopes were held out to Hunt that, in consequence of the information which he had given, his sentence would be commuted into transportation for life.

During Thursday afternoon, persons of all ranks were seen driving into Hertford, by the desire of being present at the execution; and influenced by an expectation that some extraordinary declaration would be made by Thurtell in his dying moments. All the inns were completely filled, and many were incapable of procuring beds.

At ten o'clock on Thursday night, Thurtell intimated an earnest wish that Hunt might pass the night in his apartment. Hunt was introduced; he was received by Thurtell with a strong manifestation of cordiality. Thurtell took him by the hand, and said 'Joe, the past is forgotten. I stand on the brink of eternity, and we meet now only as friends: It may be your fate to lose your life as ignominiously as myself; but I hope the royal mercy will be extended to you, and that you will live to repent of your past errors. Although you have been my enemy, I freely forgive you.' Hunt, who had entered the room with feelings bordering on apprehension that some unfortunate turn had taken place in his affairs, and that he was himself to suffer, was suddenly relieved by this address, and, squeezing Thurtell's hand most vehemently, burst into tears; he then sat down by the fire, and Thurtell and he continued to pray and to read until one o'clock. Soon after one, he shewed symptoms of fatigue, and, laying himself on the bed, uttered a fervent prayer to the Almighty, for strength to meet his approaching execution with the firmness of a man, and the resignation of a Christian. In a few moments afterwards he dropped into a profound sleep.

On Friday morning, at daybreak, every road leading to Hertford was thronged with travellers. At half-past six, Mr. Wilson, the jailor, entered Thurtell's room and found him fast asleep. The prisoner Hunt was also in a deep slumber. Mr. Wilson, unwilling to disturb their repose, retired, and at seven o'clock returned again; but the wretched men were still asleep. Mr. Wilson approached the bed of Thurtell, and called him by name. Thurtell started up, and for a moment seemed lost to his situation, not even knowing where he was, but his recollection quickly returned. His breakfast was then brought in: it consisted of some tea and bread and butter, but he partook only of the former, and that but slightly.

At half-past eleven Thurtell and Hunt were conducted into the chapel. The Rev. Mr. Franklin then administered the sacrament to them. Thurtell read the appropriate prayers in a distinct and audible voice, and seemed fully impressed with the importance of this solemn rite. At its conclusion, Thurtell turned round to the prisoner Hunt, and grasped his hand repeatedly, and renewed, in the most forcible terms, the assurance of his perfect forgiveness of the past, and of his being about to die in peace and charity with all the world. The chaplain and Mr. Nicholson retired from the chapel, leaving Mr. Wilson and the prisoner Thurtell alone: Hunt had previously been reconducted to his cell, overpowered by his feelings. Mr. Wilson then turning to Thurtell, said, ' Now, Thurtell, as there is no eye to witness what is passing between us but that of God, you must not be surprised if I ask you a question.' Thurtell turned round, and regarded him with a look of surprise. Mr. Wilson continued—' if you intend to make any confession, I think you cannot do it at a better period than the present.' Thurtell paused for a few moments. Mr. Wilson then went on to say, ' I ask you if you acknowledge the justice of your sentence.' Thurtell immediately seized both Mr. Wilson's hands, and pressed them with great fervour within his own, and said, ' I am quite satisfied. I forgive the world; I die in peace and charity with all mankind, and that is all I wish to go forth upon this occasion.'

The chaplain then returned to the prisoner, and offered him some further words of comfort, asking him, whether there was any thing he could do to ease his mind with respect to his family and friends. Thurtell replied that he was anxious the Rev. gentleman would write to his father, and inform him of his extreme contrition, resignation, and penitence, which Mr. Franklin promised faithfully to do. The unfortunate man then uttered a short prayer, that the minds of his family might be strengthened under the deep affliction they must feel, and of which he had been the unhappy author.

At twelve o'clock precisely, Mr. Nicholson tapped at the door with his wand, as the signal that the hour of execution had arrived. Thurtell then seized Mr. Franklin's hands, and thanked him, not alone for all the personal kindnesses for which he was indebted to him, but for that Christian spirit with which he was about to depart this world. The chapel-door was then thrown open, and the prisoner went forth with a steady and assured step. He looked round with perfect calmness. The distance from the chapel-door to the door leading to the scaffold was not more than ten yards, and thither he was accompanied by the chaplain, the under sheriff, Mr. Wilson, an assistant of Mr. Wilson's, and the upper turnkey. The church-bell mournfully tolled as he advanced. On their arrival at the door, Thurtell again squeezed Mr. Franklin's hand, and again exclaimed ' God bless you, sir ; God bless you.' He then mounted the steps, preceded by the under-sheriff and the executioner, and followed by Mr. Wilson and the head turnkey.

Thurtell, on taking his station under the gallows, looked round with a countenance unchanged by the awfulness of his situation. His manner was firm and undaunted, at the same time that it betrayed no unbecoming levity. After regarding the crowd for a moment, he appeared to recognize an individual beneath him, to whom he bowed in a friendly manner. Previously to his mounting the scaffold, he had begged that as little delay as possible might take place in his execution after his appearance upon the platform.

His hands were confined with handcuffs, instead of being tied with cord, as is usually the case on such occasions, and, at his own request, his arms were not pinioned. He wore a pair of black kid gloves. The irons, which were very heavy, and consisted of a succession of chain links, were still on his legs, and were held up in the middle by a Belcher handkerchief tied round his waist.

The moment he placed himself under the beam, the executioner commenced by taking off his cravat. He stood perfectly calm and unmoved, holding out his neck in order to facilitate the hangman's duty. A white cap was then put upon his head and drawn over his eyes; this cap was so thin, as still to afford the wretched man a view of those about him, and he continued to look round in various directions. At that moment the clock sounded the last stroke of twelve. The rope was then placed round his neck, and while the executioner was attaching the other end to the beam above, Thurtell looked up, and, turning to him, said, ' give me fall enough.' The hangman replied, that he might be assured he should have plenty of fall, and that all would be right. Thurtell next turned to Mr. Wilson, and repeated the same request, and that gentleman assured him, that his wishes had been fully attended to. All being now in readiness, Mr. Wilson drew close to the prisoner, and, squeezing his hands, exclaimed, ' Thurtell, God Almighty bless you ;' the prisoner, pressing his hands in return, responded, ' God bless you, sir.'

Mr. Wilson then stood back upon some boards placed immediately behind the drop, and the executioner having previously retired, the under sheriff, with his wand, gave the last fatal signal, the drop suddenly fell, and the unhappy man was in an instant launched into eternity. His sufferings were but momentary, for, with the exception of a few convulsive motions of his hands and legs, he seemed to be deprived of all sensation. Thus perished, in an untimely manner, a man, who, but for untoward circumstances and the violence of his passions, might have been the pride of his family.

During the whole of this appalling ceremony there was not the slightest symptom of emotion discernable in his features; his demeanour was perfectly calm and tranquil, and he behaved like a man acquainted with the dreadful ordeal he was about to pass, but not unprepared to meet it. Though his fortitude was thus conspicuous, it was evident, from the alteration in his appearance, that in the interval between his conviction and his execution, he must have suffered much. He looked careworn; his countenance had assumed a cadaverous hue, and there was a haggardness and lankness about his cheeks and mouth, which could not fail to attract the notice of every spectator.

The different accounts of this execution given at the time agreed in stating that the crowd present showed more than an ordinary degree of sympathy on the occasion, as if there was something in Thurtell's case, that entitled him to peculiar commiseration. It is difficult to account for such extraordinary sensibility, for never was there so foul a deed committed. Some of the public prints joined in the strange lamentations for his fate, as if he was hardly dealt with, and had a claim on public compassion. He was compassioned by some, because he was a man of talent and education, but this was an aggravation of his guilt; because, from the respectability of his connexions, he might have mixed in respectable company. Every moment of Thurtell was commented upon, as if he had in fact been a martyr to some good cause; and he was spoken of, as if he were a hero, and not a great delinquent. These observations arise from the evil effects which such morbid sensibility may have on society at large, and young minds in particular; as if the more horrible the crime, the more entitled to compassion is the person by whom it was committed, when he becomes an object of public example, and falls by the hand of retributive justice.

Hunt, in consequence of the promise made him by the magistrates, had his sentence commuted to transportation for life, and was immediately sent to Botany Bay.

JOHN HILL WAGSTAFF,
EXECUTED FOR FORGERY.

THIS young man belonged to a highly respectable family, and for some years carried on an extensive trade, as a carpet-dealer, in Skinner Street, Snow Hill. Being young, thoughtless, and extravagant, he soon dissipated property to some amount, and in the beginning of 1823 his name appeared in the Gazette. At the same time it was discovered that he had endeavoured to sustain his sinking credit by fictitious bills, and apprehending a prosecution for forgery, he sought concealment. Not having surrendered as a bankrupt before the commissioners, he was outlawed, and one hundred pounds offered as a reward for his apprehension.

For eighteen months he remained

undetected; but, such was his desperation and folly, that he again repeated his first offence, and deliberately forged a draft for two hundred and fifty pounds. On Friday night, March the 19th, 1824, Wagstaff slept at the Old Hummums, in Covent Garden, and on Saturday morning sent for a ticket porter, who was accordingly brought him. He first sent the porter for a two-shilling stamp to a shop in Long Acre, and on his return gave him a check for two hundred and fifty pounds, purporting to be drawn by William Ridley upon John Bond, Sons, and Pattisall, bankers, in 'Change Alley, Cornhill, together with a piece of paper, on which were written directions for the porter to go to the Bull Inn, in Aldgate, and secure an inside place for him, in the two o'clock coach, for Brighton.

Mr. Ridley, the supposed drawer of the check, was the head of the firm of Ridley and Co. carpet manufacturers, in Castle Street, Holborn; and these gentlemen had a private mark on their checks, known only to themselves and their bankers; consequently, when the porter presented the check received from Wagstaff, the forgery was discovered, though the signature was an extremely close imitation.

Mr. Pattisall, one of the partners in the bank, now proceeded to the Old Hummums, but found Wagstaff had gone out. An explanation took place with the proprietor, and proper directions were given throughout the house, respecting Wagstaff, if he should return.

In the evening a hackney coachman called at the hotel, and inquired if the porter had brought back any message. He was answered in the affirmative, and that the parcel was in the possession of the proprietor until the gentleman should call for it. In about half an hour afterwards Wagstaff drove up in a coach to the door, and, as had been previously arranged, was shewn into a room where Bishop, the officer, was waiting for him. The latter asked him his name as soon as he entered, and the other replied, Samuel Tomkins, and said he lived next door to the White Hart, at Reigate. Bishop then informed him of his situation, and took him into custody. When secured, the officer saw him endeavouring to put something into his glove, which, upon examination, proved to be a parcel of oxalic acid. A phial filled with a solution of the same destructive poison was taken out of his pocket, from which it would appear that the wretched man had meditated suicide in case of detection. To guard against such an event proper precaution was taken.

Although several other charges of forgery were made against him, he was indicted only for this one, it being deemed sufficient for the ends of justice. On the 12th of the following April he was arraigned at the Old Bailey, and the fact of the forgery being proved, he was found Guilty—Death.

On Tuesday morning, June the 1st, 1824, this unfortunate man underwent the awful sentence of the law in the Old Bailey, in the presence of an unusual concourse of spectators, by whom his fate appeared to be universally commiserated.

AMY GEORGE,

INDICTED FOR THE MURDER OF HER BROTHER.

RELIGIOUS fanaticism has led, in all ages, to much mischief both private and public. In the early times of Christianity there arose a sect, the members of which went about murdering children, who had not obtained the age of seven years, believing it meritorious to send them to Heaven before they became responsible for their own actions. Doctrines so repugnant to human nature did not long find supporters; though fanaticism ever since has caused, in various ways, the shedding of blood. There seldom has occurred, however, an instance of religious delusion more gloomy than the one we are about to narrate.

Amy George, a young woman, nineteen years of age, resided in the house of her parents, at Redruth, in Cornwall. They were in humble circumstances, and of a religious turn. They belonged to the Methodist persuasion; and Amy, having attended one of their meetings called 'Revivals,' became considerably disturbed, and under the idea of securing the eternal happiness of her little brother, a boy under seven years of age, hanged him behind the door with a silk handkerchief, on the 4th of March, 1824. She did not attempt to conceal her crime; but went up stairs to the apartment of a fellow-lodger, and disclosed what she had done. She was instantly taken into custody, and brought to trial at the ensuing assizes, which took place at Launceston on the 1st of April. Several witnesses having deposed to the fact of the strangulation of the child, John Cocking, the constable of Redruth, gave the following testimony: 'I sat up with the prisoner at the bar on the night of the 4th of March. She told me her mind had been impressed, for some time, that she ought to commit a murder; and that on the Monday and Tuesday before she committed the act, her intention was to have murdered her mother, but she endeavoured to banish that idea from her mind, and prayed to the Lord to take the temptation from her; but that on the Thursday morning, while she was at work at the mine, the idea came upon her again with greater force than before. In the middle of the day, she went to get her dinner at the boiling house, where the girls generally dine. After she got to the boiling house, she recollected that she had seen a boy, a stranger, standing by the engine-house, near the shaft, or mouth of a pit, and she then regretted that she had not pushed that boy into the shaft. Returning home in the evening, a little before she came to a Methodist meeting, which stood in a back lane she saw two children before her at play, near another shaft alongside the road, but she could not get an opportunity of throwing one of them into the mine, as she had designed. She went to her own house, and found her mother was going to the meeting. On going in, her mother said, "Your supper is ready for you, Amy; you can take it, for I am going to the meeting, and little Benny will remain at home with you." The prisoner then told me she felt glad that she was going to be left alone with her brother, as she would thus be able to do the deed. She gave the child part of her supper, and said to him, "Should you like to go to heaven, dear?" She then rose from the place where she was sitting, and went to a line that was hanging across the room, and took from it a black silk handkerchief, and coming towards the child, put it round his neck, tying it, as she thought, in a running knot. She said to her brother "Is it too tight, dear?" The child looked up in her face and smiled, and said "No." She left the handkerchief round his neck, and said, "Go for a drop of water for me, dear!" intending, while the child was gone to a pail in the room, and while his back was towards her, to take him up and hang him to a crook behind the door. The boy was rather quicker than she expected, and she meeting him took the water from him, drank a little of it, and put the cup on the table. She then took her brother up with one arm, and with the other hand put the handkerchief over the crook, looked him full in the face, and left the room. I know there are the several shafts which the prisoner spoke of. I am not a member of the Methodist Society, but I have attended a Revival meeting at Redruth, which commenced about three months since. A Revival is termed an "out-pouring of the spirit," and causes the congregation to cry aloud to the Lord for mercy. The Revival continued at Redruth for a month or six weeks. The Revivals are held in the stated places of worship of particular congregations, and sometimes continue open for three nights and days in succession. I have been at Revival; those who are "convinced of sin," as it is called, fall on their knees, and with uplifted hands, and their bodies working to and fro, call as loud as they are able to the Lord for help. Their ejaculations are such as, "Oh! Christ, pardon me my sins—Oh! Lord, give me grace!" and a variety of other expressions, adopted as the zeal of the moment may suggest. Their conduct was wild and extravagant, and altogether out of the mild and decent course of addressing the Almighty, usually observed in places of worship. It is generally called screeching for mercy. There was usually a preacher at the meetings, but not always. The Revival is open by night as well as day. There is no appointment when the Revival is to be held; a congregation may be met, and at prayers, when, perhaps, some member will fall on his knees and call aloud to heaven for mercy; when this happens, the other members are generally moved by the same spirit, and the Revival commences. This is called the "out-pouring of the spirit," and continues till the preacher pronounces a benediction, and tells his flock, "the moment of conversion" is come, and they may expect "a ray of hope, of comfort, and joy." The moment of the coming of the "ray of hope" is uncertain, and the congregation continue their extravagant devotions till they are "convinced" or "converted." It is about ten years since there was a Revival at Redruth before the late one. The prisoner, in speaking of the child, generally called him the dear little Benny.

The unfortunate girl said nothing in her defence, but in proof of the aberration of her mind at the time she committed the miserable deed for which she stood indicted; her unhappy mother was called, and gave the following evidence :—

'My daughter attended a Methodist meeting at Redruth for about seven weeks before the death of my boy; she also attended the Revival. I went for her one night, about half-past ten o'clock, she having been there from two o'clock in the day. On going into the chapel, I found it extremely crowded. My daughter caught a sight of me, and immediately she lifted up both her arms, and called on her dear mother and father to pray to the Lord to help them, for that they could not see the danger they were in. I got her out of the meeting as soon as I could, but she had lost her cloak, bonnet, handkerchief, and pattens, and was extremely disordered in her dress. She had been moving from one part of the meeting to the other, and, in her unbounded zeal, had dropped her clothes, and they were trodden under foot. My daughter's conduct, after attending the Revival, was quite different to what it had usually been. This was about seven weeks before the dreadful act was done. On another occasion, she came home praying in a horrible manner for the conversion of her father and mother. She was then violently agitated. From the commencement of the Revival she never missed but one meeting. See also attended prayer meetings and class meetings. Before the death of my son, I apprehended my daughter would do me some violence. On the Monday preceding, she came home and sat by the fire, in a melancholy way, and said "Mother, I am going out of my mind." I spoke a few words to pacify her, and she went to bed. The next night she said she was better, but she appeared very low. On Wednesday night, on coming home, she said to me, "I am tempted to murder my mother!" I said I was surprised she should think of murdering me; and she said, "I do." After she had said this, she went to the Revival, and returned between nine and ten. From what she had said, I took the knives and hid them, to prevent her doing mischief to herself, me, or the family.

"These symptoms I observed on Monday, Tuesday, and Wednesday, and on the Thursday the child was killed."

At the close of the evidence the prisoner fainted, and was removed into the air. Being in strong convulsions her screams were heard for nearly a quarter of an hour. When she was re-conducted into court, the judge charged the jury, who immediately returned a verdict of—Not Guilty, believing her to have been insane at the time of the murder. The Court ordered her to be detained in custody, but assured her friends that she would not be kept long from them.

THE REV. JOHN CARROLL,

INDICTED FOR THE MURDER OF A CHILD.

The Roman Catholic Clergy among other absurdities, arrogate to themselves the power of working miracles; and about the period at which we are now arrived, there appeared in Germany a Reverend prince Hohonlohe, who, it was said, had performed some astonishing wonders by the force of his prayers. In England a Miss O'Connor, a nun, had been cured of a swelling in her arms, by the spiritual assistance of the prince, and some enthusiastic women in Ireland fancied that they were relieved by a similar process. One young lady was restored to her speech, having been previously dumb; and another literally took up her bed and walked.

This German prince was either a fanatic or an impostor, but the Irish Catholics regarded him as a saint, and accordingly solicited the aid of his prayers on all possib'e occasions. Hundreds, who imagined themselves ill, were cured, and many even swore to the truth of the pretended miracles. The effect of all this might have been more deplorable, had not a melancholy event helped to open the eyes of the people. A priest named Carroll, who resided in the barony of Forth, County of Wexford, undertook to rival Hohenlohe, and was supposed to be endowed with the power of working miracles. The delusive doctrine of his church, operating on a predisposition to insanity, produced a diseased mind, and when in this state he killed a child name Catherine Sinnott, on the 9th of July, 1824, while performing what he called a miracle. For this offence he was indicted, at the Wexford assizes, on the 4th of the following August. A Catholic barrister, who acted as his counsel on the occasion, has inserted the following particulars of this man's case in one of the periodicals.

'This unfortunate man (Carroll), for he deserves no harsher appellation, had from his childhood a strong predisposition to insanity. It was with great difficulty that he succeeded in obtaining ordination. His abberrations from reason, before they amounted to actual madness, were connected with the subject of exorcism; and although every person to whom he addressed his arguments in favour of the expulsion of devils, smiled at his extravagance, they still could not help acknowledging that he argued with subtlety upon wrong premises, and confessed that his applications on various passages in the holy writings were ingenious, however mistaken. It was in vain that Father Carroll was told that the power of Satan to possess himself of human bodies ceased with the revelation of Christian truth. He appealed to the Acts of the Apostles, and to incidents subsequent to the death of our Saviour, to establish his favourite speculation. A medical man, with whom he was intimate, perceived that the subject had laid such a hold upon his naturally excitable imagination, that he resorted to sedative medicines to avert the progress of an incipient malady, to which he had an organical predisposition. As long as he followed his physician's advice, he abstained from any acts of a very extravagant nature; but unhappily before the events took place, which formed the ground of a capital prosecution, he neglected to take his usual preventitives, and became utterly deranged. He suddenly fancied himself endowed with supernatural authority. This fantastic notion seized upon him in the midst of divine service; after the wild performance of which, he rushed into the public road that led from the chapel to his house, in search of an object for the manifestation of his miraculous powers. He was informed that a labourer of the name of Neill was confined by illness to his bed; and being convinced that he was possessed by an evil spirit, proceeded to effect the removal of the enemy. His singular demeanour attracted the attention of the passengers, who followed him to Neill's cottage; which he had no sooner entered, than he precipitated himself upon the sick man, and began his miraculous operations with marvellous vigour. A severe pommelling was the process of exorcism, which he regarded as most effectual. This he put into immediate and effectual practice. Neill did not attempt to resist this athletic antagonist of the devil. The unhappy gentleman had determined to take Beelzebub by storm. After a long assault, he succeeded in this strange achievement, and having informed the astonished by-standers that he had taken the enemy prisoner, announced that he should give him no quarter, but plunge him into the Red Sea. The manner of this aquatic ceremony was described by one of the witnesses, who endeavoured to illustrate it by his gesture. After uttering various cabalistic words, he whirled himself in a rapid rotation, with his arms outstretched, and then, suddenly pausing and raising himself into an attitude of importance befitting his new authority, advanced with one arm a-kimbo, and with the other extended, looking, as the witness expressed it, "as if he held the devil by the tail," and marched with a measured pace and a mysterious aspect to a bridge upon the river Slaney, where he buried the captive demon in what he took for the Red Sea.

'Not contented with this exploit, he exclaimed that Neill had seven more devils, which he was determined to expel from this peculiar object of diabolical predeliction. The operation was accordingly repeated with such success, that Neill, after much strenuous expostulation, leaped out of his bed, and exclaimed that he was quite well. This circumstance produced a deep impression upon the crowd, amongst whom there were some Protestants; and two of the latter, a Mrs. Winter and her daughter, knelt down and called upon the Lord to assist Father Carroll in the perpetration of the next miracle, which, encouraged by their pious sympathies, he almost immediately proceeded to commit. A poor woman happened to pass along the road, whom he had no sooner observed, than he knocked her down, and pursued a mode of exorcism similar to that which I have described, with such effect, that one of the spectators cried out for the people to make way, "as he saw the devil coming out." This achievement only served to excite the wretched maniac, and impel him to another undertaking of the same kind. He insisted "that the devil had taken possession of Sinnott's child." The circumstances which I have detailed, and by no means endeavoured to exaggerate, would be merely ridiculous if they were not the result of a malady which humbles human nature: the incident by which they were succeeded ought to make Democritus shed tears. Sinnott had a child who had been affected by fits, and over whom the priest had been requested by its mother to say prayers. This was not only a natural, but I will add a reasonable application. It is not supposed by Roman Catholics that the prayers of a clergyman are endowed with any preternatural efficacy; but it is considered that praying over the sick is a pious and religious act. The recollection of this fatal request passed across the distempered mind of the madman, who hurried with an insane alacrity to Sinnott's cabin. It was composed of two rooms upon the ground-floor, in the smaller of which lay the little victim. It was indeed so contracted that it could not contain more than two or three persons. The crowd who followed the priest remained outside, and were utterly unconscious of what he was about to do. The father of the child was not in the house when Father Carroll entered it, and was prevented by the pressure in the exterior room from approaching him; and for some time after the death of the child was wholly unconscious of what had taken place.

'No efforts whatever were made

to prevent his interference. He was produced as a witness upon the trial, and swore that it did not enter his thoughts that Father Carroll intended to do the child the least harm. He could not, he said, even see the priest. It is enough to say, that after uttering a few feeble cries, and calling upon its "mammy," every sound became extinct. The madman had placed the child under a tub, and life was extinguished. It may well be imagined that the trial of this case excited a strong sensation in the county where the rebellion had raged with its most dangerous fury, and from which it will be long before its recollections will have entirely passed away. The Protestant party, forgetting that many of their own sect had taken a partial share in the proceedings, of which they had been at all events the passive witnesses, exhibited a proud and disdainful exultation, and effected a deep scorn for the intellectual debasement of which they alleged this event to be a manifest proof; while the Catholics disclosed a festered soreness upon an incident which, they could not fail to tell, was likely to expose them to much plausible imputation.'

As these particulars, though somewhat extenuated, are pretty accurate, we shall only give the evidence of two of the witnesses on the trial.

Philip Walsh, examined by Mr. Fox.—Knows Sinnott; knew Catherine Sinnott the child; recollects seeing Father Carroll at Sinnott's house; went to the house after night-fall; thinks it might have been eleven o'clock when he went; went there and heard a noise inside, and then went in; the house was full of people; saw Father Carroll in the bed; did not see the child at that time; Carroll was sitting in the bed and was saying something; he then got up on his feet, and stood on the tub; heard the child cry, 'Mammy, mammy,' save me; saw the child, for the first time, next morning; the child was then dead; saw a tub in the room; was there before the tub was brought in; could not at that time get near the bed, the crowd was so great, but heard the people say the child was in it; heard Father Carroll call for some water; a bowl of water was then brought in, but the priest desired it to be taken away, and a tub of water to be brought. The tub was brought in by witness and James Devereux, one of the prisoners at the bar. Witness carried the tub close to where Father Carroll was, when the priest desired him to lift it on the bed. The priest was at this time standing on the bed; when the tub was settled on the bed, Father Carroll said some words over it, and threw some salt into the water; the priest then put his foot on the near handle of the tub, and upset the water, some part of it on his own feet, and the rest on the bed; the tub was turned upside down; the priest then said with a loud voice, 'Bury him, Jesus, in the depth of the Red Sea,' meaning, as witness believed, the devil; he said this, while he was overturning the tub; then the priest sat upon it, and afterwards stood and danced on it; the child all this time was under it; the priest stayed in the house till day-light. The priest ordered the people out of the room, and he, the witness, immediately went out; the priest desiring them in a loud voice not to touch his clothes, on which the people rushed out frightened, as they thought the devil was then escaping; saw the child's leg, and supposes the body was under the tub: saw the child dead in the morning; it was Sinnott's child; looked into the room after the priest turned the people out, and saw the priest sitting on the bed.

Thomas Sinnott, the father of the child.—Had a daughter named Catherine; she is dead; cannot recollect precisely the day on which she died; it was on the night that Father Carroll came to the house; the child was alive when Father Carroll arrived. When witness came into the house, he heard an unusual noise; he stopped and listened for a while, and heard the child crying. He made up to the child but was stopped; cannot say by whom he was stopped. Saw Father Carroll at the time; saw the head of the child; does not know at what hour the child's decease took place; did not see it but once; saw it dead in the bed. When he first came into the room, he saw the head of the child; thought the child was frightened by the noise. Some people desired him to kneel down, which he did; all the people knelt down and prayed; saw the priest in the room after the people had departed. The child was then dead; he took the child in his arms and showed it to the priest. Father Carroll desired him to lay it down on the bed. Did not ask the priest why he killed his child, as he thought he would return and bring it to life. At four o'clock in the morning the priest called him into the room, and he remained sitting with him on the bed for about five minutes. Father Carroll made no observation to him on the death of the child; but, said the witness, when I asked him what I was to do, he said, resign it to the will of God.

Two physicians were examined for the defence, and it appearing that Carroll was insane at the time he committed the direful act, he was of course acquitted.

Carroll's figure was tall and dignified. A large black cloak with a scarlet collar was fastened with a clasp round his neck, but not so closely as to conceal the ample chest, across which his arms were loosely and resignedly folded. His strong black hair was bound with a velvet band, to conceal the recent incisions made by the surgeon in his head. His countenance was smooth and finely chiseled; and it was observed by many that his features, which, though small, were marked, bore a minature resemblance to Napoleon. His colour was dead and chalky, and it was impossible to perceive the least play or variety of emotion about the mouth, which continued open, and of the colour of ashes. On being called to plead, he remained silent. The Court was about to make an inquiry whether he was 'mute of malice,' when it was seen by a glance of his eye, that he was conscious of the purport of the question; and by the directions of his counsel he pleaded Not guilty. During the trial, which was conducted with the most exemplary moderation by the counsel for the crown, he retained his petrified and statute-like demeanour; and although the heat was most intense, the hue of his face and lips did not undergo the slightest change.

ALEXANDER PIERCE.
EXECUTED FOR MURDER.

Our preceding pages furnish rather too many proofs of the depravity of human nature, but the present case 'out-Herods-Herod'—it is in fact monstrous; and though the occurrence, we are happy to say, did not take place in these kingdoms, yet, as the offender was a British subject, the particulars of the diabolical deed may not be considered out of place here.

In the November of 1823, Thomas Smith, coxswain to the commandant at Macquaire harbour, Van Dieman's land, saw a signal-fire on the beach near King's River, and on going thither found Pierce, who had some time before absconded from a gang of convicts. He requested to be taken back, and on his arrival at the harbour, confessed that he had murdered a convict, named Cox, who had accompanied him in his flight, for the purpose of devouring his flesh. Being brought to trial for the murder, he was convicted, and sentenced to be hanged, on Monday, June 21, 1824. The evening before his execution he made the following voluntary confession:—

'I was born in the county of Fermanagh, in the north of Ireland. In the twenty-sixth year of my age I was convicted of stealing six pair of shoes, and received sentence to be transported for seven years; I arrived in Van Dieman's Land, on board the ship Castle Forbes, from Sydney; was assigned as servant to John Bellenger, with whom I remained about nine months; and was then, from misconduct returned to the government superintendant. A few months after, I was assigned to a man named Cane, a constable, and staid with him only sixteen weeks, when an occasion obliged him to take me before the magistrates, who ordered that I should receive fifty lashes, in the usual way, and again he returned to Crown labour. Afterwards I was placed to serve a Mr. Scattergood, of New Norfolk, from whom I absconded into the woods, and joined Laughton, Saunders, Latton, and Atkinson, who were then at large; after ranging with them three months, I surrendered myself, upon a proclamation issued by the lieutenant-governor, and was pardoned. Shortly afterwards I forged several orders, upon which I obtained property. On hearing that the fraud was discovered, I was again induced to return into the woods. But, within three or four months, I was taken by a party of the 48th regiment, brought to Hobart Town, tried for the forgeries, found guilty, and sent to the Penal settlement at Macquarie harbour for the remained of my sentence. I was not there more than a month before I made my escape with seven others, namely — Dalton, Traverse, Badman, Matthews, Greenhill, Brown, and Cornelius. We all kept together for ten days, during which time we had no food except our kangaroo skin jackets, which we ate, being nearly exhausted with hunger and fatigue. On the eleventh night, we began to consult what was best to be done for our preservation, and made up our minds to a dreadful result.

'In the morning we missed three of our companions—Dalton, Cornelius, and Brown, who, we concluded, had left us with the intention of going back, if possible. We then drew lots which of us five should die; it fell to Badman's lot:

I went with one of the others to collect dry wood, to make a fire, during which time Traverse had succeeded in killing Badman, and had begun to cut him up. We dressed part of the flesh immediately, and continued to use it as long as it lasted. We then drew lots again, and it fell to the fate of Matthews. Traverse and Greenhill killed him with an axe; we cut the flesh from his bones, carried it on and lived upon it as long as it lasted. By the time it was all eat, Traverse, through fatigue, fell lame in his knees—so much so, that he could not proceed; Greenhill proposed that I should kill him, which I agreed to. We then made the best of our way, carrying the flesh of Traverse between us, in the hope of reaching the Eastern settlements while it lasted. We did not, however, succeed, and I perceived Greenhill always carried the axe, and thought watched an opportunity to kill me. I was always on my guard, and succeeded, when he fell asleep, in getting the axe, with which I immediately dispatched him, made a meal, and carried all the remaining flesh with me to feed upon. To my great disappointment, I was afterwards many days without food, and subsisted solely upon grass and nettle-tops, which I boiled in a tin pot that I brought with me from the settlement. At length I fell in with some natives' huts, which, from their appearance, the inmates had just left, where I collected some entrail, and bits of kangaroo, which afforded me a meal. Two days afterwards, when nearly exhausted, I came in sight of a hut, which proved to be M'Guire's, near the High Plains. I staid there a fortnight, and made up my mind to surrender myself to Captain Wood, a magistrate on the river Clyde, but on my way thither, I met Davis and Churton, who were then desperadoes, and living at the Shannon hut. They wished me to join them, to which I agreed. In a few weeks we were all taken, near Jericho, by a party of the 48th regiment, and brought into Hobart town gaol: Churton and Davis were tried, found guilty of capital offences, and suffered death. It was my fate to be returned to the penal settlement. I again made my escape with Thomas Cox, who eagerly pressed my departure. I had irons on at the time: when we had proceeded some distance, Cox knocked them off with an axe he had brought with him, and we made the best of our way through a thicket, which was very wet. At night we tried to make a fire but could not. We travelled on several days without food, except the tops of trees and shrubs, until we came upon King's river; I asked Cox, if he could swim; he replied he could not; I remarked, that had I been aware of that, he should not have been my companion; we were enabled to make a fire; the arrangement for crossing the river created words, and I killed Cox with the axe: I ate part of him that night, and cut the greatest part of his flesh up in order to take on with me. I swam the river with the intention of keeping the coast round to Port Dalrymple, my heart failed me, and I resolved to return and give myself up to the commandant. I threw most of the flesh away; one piece I carried in my pocket, to shew the commandant that Cox was dead. I confessed that I had killed him, and accompanied a party in a boat to bring up his remains, which was done.'

HENRY FAUNTLEROY,
EXECUTED FOR FORGERY.

The station in society of this unfortunate man, and the long-established respectability of the banking-house in which he was the most active partner, with the vast extent of the forgeries committed, gave to his case an intensity of interest which has scarcely ever been equalled.

On the 10th of September, 1824, Henry Fauntleroy, of the firm of Marsh, Stracey, Fauntleroy, and Graham, bankers, in Berner's Street, was apprehended in consequence of its being discovered that in September, 1820, 10,000*l.* 3 per cent. stock, — standing in the names of himself, J. D. Hume, and John Goodchild, as trustees of Francis William Bellis,—had been sold out under a power of attorney, to which the names of his co-trustees, and of some of the subscribing witnesses, were forged. It was soon ascertained that the extent to which this practice had been carried was enormous, no less than 170,000*l.* stock having been sold out in 1814, and 1815, by the same fraudulent means.

The payments of the banking-house were immediately suspended, and a commission of bankruptcy was the result.

Mr. Fauntleroy's private conduct became now the subject of general conversation, and the newspapers were daily filled with exaggerated statements of the depravity of his habits. He was said to be a licentious libertine, a deep gamester, and most profusely extravagant; but much of what was thus stated was afterwards refuted. He married a young lady, of a respectable, but not opulent, family, named Young, who previously bore him a child; but though he was persuaded thus far to redeem her character, he did not live with her after the day of their union; and to this unhappy circumstance is probably to be attributed much of that occasional excess which was magnified into the grossest libertinism.

It was for defrauding his wife's family that he was executed, the case selected by the bank for prosecution, being that of having forged the name of Frances Young, spinster, to a power of attorney, under which was sold the sum of 5000*l.* 3 per cent consols.

The trial took place on the 30th of October. At seven o'clock, the doors leading to the Court House of the Old Bailey were beset. The jury being sworn, the clerk read the first indictment, which charged Henry Fauntleroy with forging a deed, with intent to defraud Frances Young of 5,000*l.* stock, and with forging a power of attorney with intent to defraud the Bank. The Attorney-General, in his address to the jury, described the prisoner as the acting partner in the house of Marsh and Co. in Berner's Street. Mr. Fauntleroy, the father of the prisoner, became a partner at its establishment, and continued such till his death in 1807. At that period the prisoner was admitted into the concern, and became the most active member of it. In 1815, Frances Young of Chichester, a customer of the house, lodged in their hands a power of attorney to receive the dividends on 5,450*l.* 3 per cent. consols. The dividends were regularly received, but soon afterwards another power of attorney, authorizing the prisoner to sell that stock, was presented to the Bank, and the sale was effected by him;

to this power the prisoner had forged the names of Frances Young, and of two witnesses to it. But the most extraordinary part of the case was, that among the prisoner's private papers, contained in a tin box, there had been found one in which he acknowledged his guilt, and adduced a reason for his conduct. The Attorney-general then read the paper, which presented the following items, &c.: De la Place, 11,150*l.* 3 per cent. consols; E. W. Young, 5,000*l.* consols; General Young, 6,000*l.* consols; Frances Young, 5,000*l.* consols; H. Kelly, 6,000*l.* consols; Lady Nelson, 11,995*l.* consols; Earl of Ossory, 7,000*l.* 4 per cents.; W. Bowen, 9,400*l.* 4 per cents.; — Parkins, 4000*l.* consols. Sums were also placed to the names of Mrs. Pelham, Lady Aboyne, W. R. and H. Fauntleroy, and Elizabeth Fauntleroy; and the learned gentleman observed, that all the sums were added together, and the sum total, 120,000*l.* appeared at the foot of this list in the prisoner's handwriting. The statement was followed by this declaration :

"In order to keep up the credit of our house, I have forged powers of attorney for the above sums and parties, and sold out to the amount here stated, and without the knowledge of my partners. I kept up the payment of the dividends, but made no entries of such payments in our books. The Bank began first to refuse to discount our acceptances, and to destroy the credit of our house: the Bank shall smart for it."

The Attorney-General then called his witnesses, who confirmed in every point his statement of the case.

On being asked what he had to say in his defence, the prisoner read from a paper as follows:—

'My Lord, and Gentlemen of the Jury—Overwhelmed as I am by the situation in which I am placed, and being uninformed in what manner I should answer the charges which have been alleged against me, I will endeavour to explain, so well as the poignancy of my feelings will enable me, the embarrassments of the Banking-house in which I have been for many years the active and only responsible partner, and which have alone led to the present investigation; and although I am aware I cannot expect to free myself from the obloquy brought upon me by my anxiety to preserve the credit and respectability of the firm, still I trust that an impartial narrative of the occurrences will obtain for me the commiseration of the well-disposed part of the community.

'Anticipating the Court will extend its indulgence to me, I will respectfully submit such observavations as I think will tend to remove from influenced minds those impressions, which, with sorrow I say, must have been made upon them by the cruel and illiberal manner in which the public prints have untruly detailed an history of my life and conduct; hoping therefrom I may deserve your compassion, although I may be unable to justify my proceedings, and secure my liberation, by a verdict of the Jury, yet they may be considered, in the mercy of the Court and a discerning public, as some extenuation of the crimes with which I stand arraigned.

'My father established the banking-house in 1792, in conjunction with Mr. Marsh, and other gentlemen. Some of the partners retired in 1794, about which time a loss of 20,000*l.* was sustained. Here commenced the difficulties of the house. In 1796, Mr. Stracey and another gentleman came into the firm, with little or no augmentation of capital.—In 1800, I became a clerk in the house, and continued so six years, and although during that time I received no salary, the firm were so well satisfied with my attention and zeal for the interest and welfare of the establishment, that I was handsomely rewarded by them. In 1807 my father died; I then succeeded him; at this time I was only twenty-two years of age, and the whole weight of an extensive but needy banking establishment at once devolved upon me, and I found the concern deeply involved in advances to builders and others, which had rendered a system of discounting necessary, and which we were obliged to continue in consequence of the scarcity of money at that time, and the necessity of making further advances to those persons to secure the sums in which they stood indebted.

'In this perplexed state the house continued until 1810, when its embarrassments were greatly increased, owing to the bankruptcies of Brickwood and others, which brought upon it a sudden demand for no less a sum than 170,000*l.* the greater part being for the amount of bills which our house had either accepted or discounted for those parties, since become bankrupts.

'About 1814, 1815, and 1816, from the speculations with builders, brickmakers, &c. in which the house was engaged, it was called upon to provide funds to near 100,000*l.* to avert the losses which would otherwise have visited it from those speculations. In 1819, the most responsible of our partners died, and we were called upon to pay over the amount of his capital, although the substantial resources of the house were wholly inadequate to meet so large a payment.

' During these numerous and trying difficulties, the house was nearly without resources, and the whole burthen of management falling upon me, I was driven to a state of distraction, in which I could meet with no relief from my partners, and, almost broken-hearted, I sought resources where I could, and so long as they were provided, and the credit of the house supported, no inquiries were made, either as to the manner in which they were procured, or as to the sources from whence they were derived.

' In the midst of these calamities, not unknown to Mr. Stracey, he quitted England, and continued in France, on his own private business, for two years, leaving me to struggle as well as I could with difficulties almost insurmountable.

' Having thus exposed all the necessities of the house, I declare that all the monies temporarily raised by me, were applied, not in one instance, for my own separate purposes or expenses, but in every case they were immediately placed to the credit of the house in Berner's Street, and applied to the payment of the pressing demands upon it. This fact does not rest on my assertion, as the transactions referred to are entered in the books now in the possession of the assignees, and to which I have had no access since my apprehension. These books, I understood, are now in court, and will confirm the truth of my statement; and to whatever account all the sums may be entered, whether to that of stock, or of Exchequer bills, or to my private account, the whole went to the general funds of the banking-house.

' I alone have been doomed to suffer the stigma of all the transactions; but, tortured as I have been, it now becomes an imperative duty to explain to you, Gentlemen, and through you to the world at large, that the vile accusations heaped upon me, known to be utterly false by all those who are best acquainted with my private life and habits, have been so heaped upon me for the purpose of loading me with the whole of the obloquy of those transactions, from which, and from which alone, my partners were preserved from bankruptcy. I have been accused of crimes I never even contemplated, and of acts of profligacy I never committed; and I appear at this bar with every prejudice against me, and almost prejudged. To suit the purposes of the persons to whom I allude, I have been represented as a man of prodigal extravagance: prodigal indeed I must have been, had I expended those large sums which will hereafter be proved to have gone exclusively to support the credit of a tottering firm, the miseries of which were greatly accelerated by the drafts of two of its members to the amount of near 100,000*l*.

'I maintained but two establishments, one at Brighton, where my mother and sister resided in the season—the expences of which to me, exclusive of my wine, were within 400*l*. per annum, and one at Lambeth, where my two children lived, from its very nature private and inexpensive, to which I resorted for retirement, after many a day passed in devising means to avert the embarrassments of the banking-house. The dwelling-house in Berner's Street, belonged solely to my mother, with the exception of a library and single bedroom. This was the extent of my expenditure, so far as domestic expenditure is concerned; I am next accused of being an habitual gambler, an accusation which, if true, might easily account for the diffusion of the property. I am indeed a member of two clubs, the Albion, and the Stratford, but never in my life did I play in either, at cards or dice, or any game of chance; this is well known to the gentlemen of these clubs—and my private friends with whom I more intimately associated, can equally assert my freedom from all habit or disposition to play. It has been as cruelly asserted, I fraudulently invested money in the funds to answer the payment of annuities, amounting to 2,200*l*. settled upon females. I never did make any such investmen: neither at home or abroad, in any funds whatever, have I any investment; nor is there one shilling secretly deposited by me in the hands of any human being. Equally ungenerous, and equally untrue it is, to charge me with having lent to loose and disorderly persons large sums which never have, and never will be repaid. I lent no sums but to a very trifling amount, and those were advanced to valued friends. I can, therefore, at this solemn moment, declare most fervently, that I never had any advantage beyond that in which all my partners participated in any of the transactions which are now questioned. They indeed have considered themselves as partners only in the profits, and I am to be burthened with the whole of the opprobium, that others may consider them as the victims of my extravagance. I make this statement not with a view to criminate others, or to exculpate myself; but borne down as I am by calamity, I will not consent to be held out to the world as a cold-blooded and abandoned profligate, ruining all around me for the selfish gratification of vice and sensuality, and involving even my confiding partners in the general destruction.

'Gentlemen, I have frailties and errors enough to account for. I have sufferings enough, past, present, and in prospect, and if my life were all that was required of me, I might endure in silence, though I will not endure the odium on my memory, of having sinned to pamper delinquencies to which I never was addicted. Thus much has been extorted from me by the fabrications which have been cruelly spread amongst the public; that very public, from whom the arbiters of my fate were to be selected. Perhaps, however, I ought to thank the enemy who besieged the prison with his slanders—that he did so whilst my life was spared to refute them, and that he waited not until the grave to which he would hurry me had closed at once on my answer and my forgiveness. There is one subject more connected with these charges to which I am compelled to advert, and I do so with great reluctance. It has added to the other charges made against me, lest the world should think there was any vice in which I was not an adept. I have been accused of acting treacherously towards the female who now bears my name, having refused to make reparation until threatened by her brother, and of having deserted her at a moment when she had the greatest claim on my protection. Delicacy forbids me entering into an explanation on this subject further than to declare, that the conduct I adopted on that occasion was uninfluenced by the interference of any individual, and arose, as I then considered, and do still consider, from a laudable and honourable feeling on my part, and the lady's brother, so far from coming forward at the time alluded to, was on service in the West Indies.

Could all the circumstances be exposed, I feel convinced that every liberal-minded man would applaud my determination, and I feel satisfaction in stating, that the lady in question has always been, and still is, actuated by the best of feelings towards me.

'I have now to apologize to the Court for having entered so much at length into the statement of my unfortunate case, and in conclusion I have to express my perfect confidence, that it will receive every favourable consideration at your hands; and I fully rely that you, Gentlemen of the Jury, will give an impartial and merciful decision.'

Having finished reading the paper, he sat down, and wept with much agitation. Whilst the witnesses to his character were under examination he leant his head on his hand, in which his handkerchief was so held as to cover his face, apparently unwilling to be seen by his former friends. Seventeen gentlemen, of the greatest respectability, attested their high opinion of his honor, integrity and goodness of disposition, and that he was the person whom, of all others, they would have supposed incapable of a dishonourable action.

In summing-up, the judge told the jury, that as the evidence did not shew the forgery to have been committed within their jurisdiction, they, being a London jury, would have to decide on the count for uttering, and after twenty minutes' consideration they returned a verdict—Guilty of Uttering—Death.

Every exertion was used by Mr. Fauntleroy's counsel, his case being twice argued before the judges, but both decisions were against him; and on the 30th of November, 1824, his execution took place. The number of persons assembled was estimated at nearly 100,000! every window and roof which could command a view of the dreadful ceremony, was occupied, and places from which it was impossible to catch a glimpse of the scaffold, were blocked up by those who were prevented by the dense crowd before them from advancing further.

At a quarter before eight o'clock, the sheriffs arrived at Newgate, and proceeded immediately to the prisoner's room. The prisoner gently bowed to them on perceiving that they were present; but made no observations. Besides the Ordinary of Newgate, the Rev. Mr. Cotton, there were the Rev. Mr. Springett and Mr. Baker with the prisoner. Mr. Springett had remained all night.

Mr. Fauntleroy was dressed in a black coat, waistcoat, and trowsers, with silk stockings, and shoes. The demeanour of the unhappy man was perfectly composed. His eyes continued closed, and no emotion was visible in his countenance. His appearance had undergone little or no change since the trial. The sheriffs moved forward, and Mr. Springett and Mr. Baker each took hold of one of the prisoner's arms, and, thus accompanied, he followed the sheriffs and the ordinary. The prisoner never turned his head to the right nor the left till he reached the foot of the steps leading to the scaffold. The moment he appeared on the scaffold the vast crowd took off their hats. In less than two minutes after the criminal ascended the scaffold, every thing was prepared for his execution. Mr. Cotton now placed himself before the prisoner, who stood with his face towards Ludgate Hill, and commenced reading the passage—'Yet, O Lord God, most Holy! O Lord, most Mighty! O holy and most merciful Saviour! deliver us not into the bitter pains of eternal death. Thou knowest, Lord, the secrets of our hearts;' towards the conclusion of which the trap-door fell.

CHARLES LYNN,
CONVICTED OF KILLING.

THIS murder, as it appeared to have been committed without any object or motive, excited a considerable degree of curiosity. The theatre of its perpetration was an extensive chase, between Shenley and Whaddon, in the county of Buckingham.

The prisoner and the deceased had for a considerable number of years worked together in a large distiller at Vauxhall, near London. They left their employment on the th of January, 1825, and on the 7th they arrived at Brick Hill, in the county of Bucks, and agreed to sleep at the White ——— the prisoner, who was a Brick Hill, was absent ——gings at the White ——hat night, though his unfortunate companion slept there. On the following morning the prisoner and the deceased got upon the Eclipse Birmingham coach, with their luggage, and were driven on the road towards Shenley Brook End, which is within the limits of Whaddon Chase.

On the trial, which took place at Aylesbury, the circumstances of the murder were proved by George Beecham, a labourer, who stated, that he was at work near Snellswell Copse, on the 7th of January last; two men passed, they were going towards Whaddon; witness was ditching up a hedge, and did not notice their faces; one had an umbrella, and the other a gun-case; in about half an hour after, he heard alarming cries, which were not repeated, the sound came from the copse. Witness immediately got out of the ditch, and saw a man striking with a gun something on the ground; the man held the muzzle end in both his hands; he struck several times violently, until the gun broke; he continued the blows, even after the gun broke; he then threw away the piece of the gun, and walked backwards and forwards, as if looking at something; he walked a short distance, and picked up a bundle, and came towards witness. He pulled off his clothes, and put on a large fustian jacket and a hairy cap; he had on before a black hat, and a black coat; taking his hat in his hand, he went towards Shenley Common. Witness then went to the spot, and there saw the deceased, the blood was running very fresh from his wounds. There was a gun broken in two, a kerchief, and umbrella lying by him. The witness gave the alarm, and the prisoner was taken running out of the copse; on witness running towards him, he cried out, 'What's your reward?' Witness asked him if he had got any fire-arms; the prisoner replied 'No, for if he had, he would not be taken by him or any man alive.' He again asked witness about the reward — 'the blood-money,' and said, 'You would take your own father's life for sixpence.' He then said, it would break his friends hearts, when they heard of this. A Mr. Tarry asked, was the man in the wood quite dead? Prisoner said he hoped he was. On the Saturday after the murder, he was guarding the prisoner, who was reading the Bible, when he jumped up on a chair, then on the table, and struck himself down with violence; his head was cut severely.

Mr. Justice Gazelee informed the prisoner, that if he had any thing to say to the jury, now was his time, as his counsel could not speak for him.

The prisoner, after standing mute for some time, addressed the jury in a very unconnected strain. He said he could not work longer at Burnett's, because his mind was uneasy. He agreed to go with Abraham Hogg to Liverpool. On the Monday night he went out with Abraham, and drank wine. They got on the Liverpool coach at the Saracen's Head, and a black man (a sailor) on the top of the coach gave him gin out of several bottles, and made him drink it, and threw the bottles away. Abraham and the sailor whispered and chattered together, and they spoke to another man in a very suspicious manner. One of them said, 'Oh, the job can be done;' and they intended to murder him, he was sure. He told Abraham that there was something afloat, as he heard the men talking together about some pit, and there was a plan to murder him. Just before he jumped off the coach he heard the man planning something, and he believed Abraham was concerned, and he jumped off the coach, as he had made up his mind to sleep at a farm-house, rather than go on and be murdered. Abraham followed him, and he again told him they intended to murder him; but Abraham said it was no such thing. When Abraham got on the hill, he said to him, 'what do you do there? you have entered into a plan to murder me; you shall die with me,' and he struck him over the head, and was afterwards taken. The rest of the prisoner's address was a tissue of incoherency, delivered without any appearance of being feigned.

The jury retired to consider their verdict, and on their return, the Foreman said, 'Guilty of killing the deceased, but we believe him insane at the time.'

CORNELIUS WOOD,

EXECUTED FOR A RAPE.

THE charge for which this offender underwent the awful sentence of death is so frequently made by abandoned females, either to extort money, or to force a man unwillingly into a marriage, added to which, the case so frequently rests on the evidence of the female alone, that the utmost caution is necessary in the investigation. But when clearly proved, there are few crimes more deserving of an exemplary punishment. In this case, the jury were an hour and a half in deliberation, and yet there was more corroborative testimony than is usually produced on similar investigations.

Cornelius Wood, aged 20, was put to the bar at the Old Bailey, on the 14th of January, 1825, charged with having violated the person of Mary Eyre, on the 7th of the preceding month of December.

Mary Eyre, a strong, coarse woman, and by no means of a prepossessing appearance, stated her age to be 28 years, and gave her evidence to the following effect:—I am a servant out of place, residing at No. 16, Cleveland-street, Fitzroy-square; Jane Green lodged in the same house with me. On the 7th of last month I asked her to accompany me to Finchley, where I had lived as a servant, and whither I was going to get a character from my former mistress. On our return, at about five o'clock in the evening, we called at the White Lion public-house, to inquire when a stage would pass to town. The landlord told me, there would be no stage going for some time, but said there was a cart at the door, in which we might get a ride. He spoke to the driver of the cart, James Day, and he agreed to take us. My friend and I got in, and sat on the seat. There was another man in the cart besides Day, but I could not see who he was at this time. I told the driver where I was going, and that I wished to be set down as near Tottenham-court-road as possible. We drove on till we came to the Wellington public-house, on the Highgate-road, where I had left a cloak in the morning. Having got my cloak, I took my seat again in the cart. The prisoner Wood then drove, and turned the horse off the Highgate-road. I asked why he did so, and he said it was to avoid the turnpike. He drove to a public-house, which I have since understood to be the Crown at Holloway. Day asked me to treat him there, which I refused. The other man got out of the cart soon after, and I did not see where he went. The cart then stopped at another public-house, the Cock, where Day again asked us to treat him to some gin. I gave him sixpence to get some, but he got half-a-pint, and I gave him sixpence more. The half pint was drank between Day, the ostler of the house, Mrs. Green, and myself. Soon after this, Day said that he lived close by, and was going no further. He told us to get out, and pointed out the road to London. I complained of his conduct as a gross imposition, but we got out, and proceeded towards town. Soon after, another cart, with a grey horse, came up, and I asked the man to take us to town, as my companion was very ill. While speaking to the carter, another man came up, and told him not to take us, for that we were not going his way. The man in the cart then drove away. We walked on a little way, when a man overtook us, and told us that the man in the cart had taken us the wrong way. I said, that as my friend was very ill, I was anxious to get to some place where I might find a stage. The man said, 'If you will go across a few fields here, you will get into the Highgate-road, and find a stage in a short time;' and, at the same time, he offered to accompany us, and show us the way. We thanked him, and accepted the offer. He led us up a little lane. At this time I did not suspect that he was the man who had been with us in the cart from Finchley. We went over a stile, and into the fields, and thence over a second stile. I complained that it was so wet and muddy that I should prefer returning. Mrs. Green was close by me when I said this. The man said, "Do not go back, there are the lamps at a short distance, they are the lamps of Tottenham-court-road.' I looked, but could see no light. While the man was thus speaking, I observed him, and then found he was one of those who had been with us in the cart. I am positive the prisoner is the man. We went on till we came to the third field, where there was a kind of gap or bog, and I could not get over it. The prisoner helped me over it, and left my friend behind. When I came into the field I said, 'My good man, are you going to show us the road or not? For God's sake show us the road.' He then made use of some very indecent expressions to me, and I said 'Oh, no!' and became very much alarmed. The man then struck me in the forehead, and I fell; he attempted to keep me on the ground, but I succeeded in getting again on my feet. He struck me again and again: I screamed and called 'murder,' and called Mrs. Green to assist me, but she cried out that she could not get through the place as she believed she had broken her leg. Prisoner struck me often, and at last my strength left me, and I could resist no longer. [Here the witness detailed the particulars of the violence which had been offered to her.] When the prisoner left me, I missed my basket and shawl; the basket contained two handkerchiefs, a purse, with half a sovereign and sixpence in it. I followed in the direction which the prisoner took, but could not get over the hedge. I then saw him with his hand in my basket. I called out to him to assist me in getting out, but he said he could not help me, as he himself was up to his knees in water. At last I extricated myself, and he then threw the basket to me, but my purse, shawl, and handkerchiefs were gone. I returned and assisted Mrs. Green to get out. She was very ill. We both called out 'murder!' until we could call no longer, in the hope that somebody would come to our assistance. Mrs. Green could not get out without my assistance: she was stuck in the mire. At last we got out of the field. I then turned round, not knowing which way to go; but we walked on till we saw something which turned out to be a cottage. We knocked at the door, and an old man came to the window, let us in, and afterwards showed us the road. We then met with a gentleman, who hearing us crying very much, asked us what was the matter. We told him we had been robbed, and very ill used. He then consented to see us home.

Jane Green gave nearly the same account of the transaction as that given by the prosecutrix.

William Carroll, the poor old man at whose cottage the prosecutrix and her friend, Mrs. Green, had called on the night of the robbery, corroborated their evidence as to their complaints of ill usage when they called on him, and as to their appearance on that occasion.

James Day.—The prisoner was in company with me the day we came from Finchley to Holloway. I took him up at his own house that morning, and he was with me all day. We took up two women at Finchley—that woman (pointing to the prosecutrix), and another, a smaller woman. We left the White Lion about five o'clock, and came on towards Highgate. We went afterwards to the Cock. I then said to the young women, that I was not going any further, and they went on towards town. I missed Wood; he did not say to me where he was going. I saw no more of him that night. It would have been in his way home to have gone with me, and by my house.

The ostlers at the Crown and Cock identified the prisoner, and other witnesses deposed to minor circumstances.

When called on for his defence, the prisoner strongly asserted his innocence; and his mother and sister, who appeared to be very decent persons, stated that he returned home about ten o'clock on the evening in question, and that they observed no change of appearance in his dress or manner.

The summing up by Mr. Justice Holroyd occupied an hour and a half, when the jury retired, and after being absent a similar time, they returned a verdict of Guilty, and the prisoner was executed.

GEORGE ALEXANDER WOOD, AND ALEXANDER WELLESLEY LEITH.

INDICTED FOR KILLING AND SLAYING.

It cannot argue much for the progress of knowledge and civilization, that of the upper classes of the existing generation so many are patrons of pugilism, and proficients in the slang and blackguardism of its professors; whilst pugnacity and disobedience prevail among the rising generation at all our great public schools At Haylebury College, those who are to take part in the future government of our immense empire in India, are themselves ungovernable; the village of Harrow is kept in constant alarm by the riotous conduct of the boys in the great school there; and at Eton we have now to notice a melancholy instance of young men of high connections adopting the worst practices of the lowest order of pugilists, by administering brandy to an exhausted combatant, a lad not fifteen, and, during a contest of nearly two hours with a school-fellow much older and taller than himself, most culpably urging him on till his death was the result; and yet there are some who call such scenes a fine display of English spirit!—the true John Bullism!! Fie on such brutes!

On the 9th of March, 1825, George Alexander Wood, son of Col. Wood, and nephew of the Marquis of Londonderry, and Alexander Wellesley Leith, were placed at the bar at Aylesbury, charged with killing and slaying the Hon. F. Ashley Cooper, son of the Earl of Shaftesbury. The circumstances will be best explained as they appeared in evidence before the Coroner.

On Sunday, the 27th of February, about two o'clock, two young gentlemen, scholars at Eton, the Hon. F. A. Cooper and Mr. Wood, were in the play-ground, when some words arose between them. From words they proceeded to blows, and had fought for several minutes, when the captain came up and separated them. It was subsequently determined that they should meet on the following afternoon, and terminate their differences by a pugilistic contest. Many of the scholars were present to witness the battle; the combatants stripped at four o'clock on Monday afternoon, and commenced fighting. Mr. Cooper was under fifteen years, and his opponent, who was half a head taller, was near seventeen, Mr. Wood had the advantage in point of strength, but the quickness and precision of Mr. Cooper was remarkable for one so young, and he declared that he would never give in. In the eighth, ninth, and tenth rounds, he became weak and exhausted, and it was then evident he was not a match for Mr. Wood, and he ought to have been taken away. Some of the 'backers' had brought a quantity of brandy in bottles into the field; and the second of Mr. Cooper having, in the eleventh round, poured a portion of it down Mr. C.'s throat, he recovered his wind and strength. The young men continued fighting from four till nearly six o'clock, and when they were in a state of exhaustion, they were plied between the rounds with brandy. They fought about sixty rounds; and at the end of the last round, Mr. Cooper fell very heavily upon his head, and never spoke afterwards. He was carried off the ground to his lodgings, at the house of the Rev. Mr. Knapp, by his brothers, who were present at the fight. He was put to bed; but no medical assistance was sent for till four hours had elapsed; shortly afterwards he expired.

At two o'clock on Tuesday, a jury assembled to hold an inquest on the body. The jury and coroner proceeded to the house of the Rev. Mr. Knapp, and viewed the body. The temples, eyes, and upper part of the cheek bones were very black, and there were other external marks of violence about the ribs, breast, &c. The following evidence was then taken:—

Christopher Teasdale.—I am a student at Eton college; I knew the deceased; he is the son of Lord Shaftesbury, and I know his antagonist, Mr. Wood, the son of Colonel Wood. I saw them set-to about the hour of four o'clock on Monday afternoon. I saw repeated blows, during the fight, given to Cooper, on different parts of the head; I remember, in one period of the fight, a severe blow being given on his temple; the deceased instantly fell, and lay on the ground about half a minute. There were loud shouts from Wood's party in consequence of his being the best. It was a fair fight; I saw no unfair advantage taken. A young gentleman named Leith seconded the deceased; the fight lasted above an hour; the deceased's spirits were kept up in a most extraordinary manner by Leith giving him brandy in the eleventh and subsequent rounds, I remember that before the last round, Wood said he wanted to go to his tutor, Mr. Ottery, to attend his private business (studies), and he would make it up afterwards. Mr. Leith, the second, said, that as Wood wanted to go, he would appeal to the deceased's party, and hear what they had to say. The deceased's party exclaimed, 'we will have another round, we are in no hurry.' The parties fought another round, and the deceased at the conclusion fell from a severe blow; Wood fell heavily on him. After this round, Wood said, 'he must go, and he would make it up.' Leith advised it to be made up on the spot, and directly the proposition was made to make it up, the deceased fell back senseless. Wood walked up to the deceased and lifted his hand. I did not hear Wood say any thing.

Mr. O'Reilly, surgeon, of Windsor.—I was called to see the deceased last night; he was dead before I arrived. There were several contusions on the head; the eyes were black: there must have been a rupture of some internal artery. I opened the head, and found, under the dura mater, a considerable extravasation of blood, covering the whole of the left hemisphere of the brain, which was the cause of his death. I believe it was not produced by any blow that his opponent gave him, but by a violent fall; and I am of this opinion from the extent of the rupture, and the great quantity of blood that issued therefrom.

Coroner.—Would his drinking a great quantity of brandy have caused such effects?

Witness.—Certainly not.

Dorothy Large.—I am servant to the Rev. Mr. Knapp, at whose house the deceased boarded and lodged; he was brought home by some of the young gentlemen last night, about ten minutes before six o'clock; he appeared as if he was asleep, and he was put to bed, and I asked his brother if I should send for a doctor, and he told me there was no occasion for it, as the deceased was fast asleep; I went into the room about seven o'clock, and he was still asleep; he was breathing. About nine o'clock I found him in the same state. His brother said he was very comfortable, and that I had no occasion to take any further trouble, as he would see him safe before he went to bed. The deceased had his trowsers on, but no shirt; he was wrapped in a blanket. A little after ten o'clock, the brother of the deceased came down stairs, and said he was worse; a surgeon was sent for. Mr. Moss, a surgeon, first arrived; the deceased had then ceased to breathe.

The verdict of the Coroner's jury being manslaughter, the prisoners were arraigned before Mr. Justice Gazelee, who directed the several witnesses to be called, but no one answering he ordered their recognizances to be estreated; and, there being no evidence, a verdict of not guilty was returned. The young gentlemen left the bar attended by Lord Nugent, Colonel Brown, Sir John Dashwood King, and other distinguished persons.

EDWARD M'ELROY,

INDICTED FOR SETTING FIRE TO A CAR-HOUSE.

This case presents one of the most extraordinary instances of cross swearing ever witnessed, and so positive was it on each side that the jury were unable to determine which party was entitled to credit, and actually separated without giving any verdict.

Edward M'Elroy, a coarse country lad, about twenty years of age, was capitally indicted, on the 12th of March, 1825, for setting fire to a car-house, belonging to David Woods, of Carduffkelly, near Carrickmacross, in the county of Monaghan, in the preceding month of February.

David Woods deposed to the circumstances attending the burning of his car-house, which took place about 12 o'clock at night, when the family were all in bed. Being awoke, he heard a noise outside his house, as of some persons stumbling, in consequence of which he was induced to rise out of bed; and on going down stairs and opening the hall-door, which he did quietly, he beheld his car-house on fire, and distinctly saw the prisoner (M'Elroy) urging the flames towards the dwelling-house.

Thomas Woods, son to the prosecutor, stated, that, on hearing his father call out that the car-house was on fire, he ran out naked, and saw the figure of a man at a distance, running from the flames. He could not say who that person was.

This was the case for the prosecution.

In defence, Charlotte Woods, aged 18, the daughter of the prosecutor, appeared. She denied that any attachment subsisted between her and the prisoner, and then gave the following account of the transaction, in coming forward to declare which, she said, she was actuated solely by a regard for truth, and a desire to save an innocent life. On the evening in question, all the family, excepting herself and a servant girl, whom she called Ellen, went to bed between 9 and 10 o'clock. She usually slept in a small bed-room on the ground floor, off the kitchen; the servant girl, who slept in the same room, having some articles of wearing apparel to mend, sat up for that purpose, unknown to her master and family, and she (the witness) remained in the kitchen assisting her, until about half-past 11 o'clock, when, hearing her father cough and make a noise as if rising, she and the servant hurried into their bed-room, extinguished the candle, and began to undress; for she was afraid of her father knowing that they had been sitting up, as he had expressly prohibited any of the family from doing so. She and the girl had just knelt down to their prayers, when she heard a stool fall, and her face being turned towards the kitchen, into which a small window looked, she observed her father approaching the fire, from which he took a lighted turf; she then beckoned the servant to watch her father, and the two followed him to the door, where they remained concealed, and actually saw him with his own hand set fire to the car-house, he having first carefully loosened the calf and pig, and set them at liberty. On witnessing such extraordinary conduct on the part of her father, she and the servant hastily returned to the room, and crept into bed. She then heard him close the kitchen door and go up stairs, where he remained about a quarter of an hour, and then came down and gave the alarm of fire. In addition, she related the particulars of a conversation between her two elder brothers, which she overheard a night or two after the burning. One of them remarked to the other—' It (speaking of the burning) was a good plan to put M'Elroy out of the way:' on which he replied, ' Yes, but I doubt my father will go too far—he must perjure himself.'—She also said, that, some days previous to the burning, her father accused her of being intimate with M'Elroy, and told her that he would not suffer any person of such condition to come near his house, or have any acquaintance with his daughter. Being cross-examined on this point, she declared that she had no particular regard for the prisoner; that there had been no intimacy between them, nor had he ever taken improper liberties with her; that she always addressed him as a servant, and looked on him only as her father's servant. She admitted that she now lived under the pretection of the prisoner's relations, having left her father's house about a fortnight previously, at which time she and the maid-servant, who accompanied her, gave information of the foregoing facts to a neighbouring magistrate.

The servant-girl corroborated, in every particular, the statement given by Miss Woods.

A tailor was examined to prove an *alibi* for the prisoner. He swore, that, on the night on which the burning was said to have taken place, the prisoner came to his house to get a pair of small-clothes mended; and that the prisoner remained in his house from sun-set to sun-rise.

After the examination of these witnesses, the counsel for the prosecution called

George Woods, son to the prosecutor, who said, he had heard what was stated by his sister, relative to a conversation between him and his brother Thomas; he swore positively that no such conversation, nor any such words, ever passed between them. Witness stated, that an intimacy had subsisted between his sister and the prisoner, whom he discovered together one day, in a back room of a house in Carrickmacross, in such a situation as left no doubt on his mind of their improper intimacy.

Thomas Woods was then examined, relative to a conversation sworn by his sister to have taken place between him and his brother George. He swore positively that no such conversation had ever taken place.

A girl, named Collins, also in the service of the prosecutor, was examined. She stated, that she was in the kitchen on the night in question, in company with Miss Woods and the servant Ellen, and swore positively, that they did not remain there more than half an hour after the family went to bed; that they merely washed their feet, and did not sew or mend any part of their clothes. She said, that Miss Woods, Ellen, and herself, then went into the bed-room off the kitchen; that they had all three undressed, and were in the act of praying, when the alarm of fire was given by her master. She denied all that the two others had sworn respecting the conduct of her master; nothing of the kind took place that she saw, nor could it have taken place without her seeing it.

Charlotte Woods and the girl Ellen were confronted with the last witness, and both adhered firmly to what they had previously sworn.

The judge proceeded to sum up the evidence.

The jury remained closeted during the night, and until the afternoon of Thursday, when, not having agreed on any verdict, they were conveyed to the verge of the county, and there discharged in the usual way.

HENRY SAVARY,

CONVICTED OF FORGERY.

THIS case, which was tried at Bristol before Lord Gifford on the 4th of April, 1825, had excited great attention in consequence of the respectability of the prisoner's connexions, his father having been for many years a banker of some consequence in that city. He was committed on the 23rd of December, and all who knew him declared that he was appalingly altered since his imprisonment. He looked pale and was evidently most feverishly agitated. His age was thirty-three.

The offence was, that he had affixed the name of William Pearson to a note for 500l. dated Birmingham, 7th of October, 1824, with intent to defraud the Bristol Copper Company, no such person as William Pearson being in existence.

When asked by the Clerk of the Arraigns, 'Henry Savary, how say you; are you guilty or not guilty?' the prisoner replied, 'Guilty.'

This answer was wholly unexpected by the Court, and it was delivered in a firm and deliberate tone.

Lord Gifford paused for some moments, appearing to be taken more by surprise than any body else. He changed colour, and was evidently much affected by the painful duty he had to perform. His lordship at last said, earnestly looking at the prisoner, ' Have you well considered your answer?'

Prisoner.—I have.

Lord Gifford.— I trust no false hopes have induced you to give that answer?

Prisoner replied something about having deliberately pleaded as he had; but he was not distinctly heard.

Lord Gifford again paused a few minutes, and then said, 'Prisoner, you had better consider a short time before you resolve to persevere in pleading guilty.'

The prisoner shook his head, reclined on his hand, and again covered his face, agitated by grief. It was intimated to the Court, that the prisoner had no other answer to give than what he had given.

Clerk of the Arraigns.—Shall I enter the verdict, my Lord?

The Recorder.—Wait a short time.

The prisoner was taken from the dock, and in about five minutes he was brought back by direction of the judge. The prisoner appeared to be much more collected, and looked partially round the Court.

Lord Gifford. — I understand, Henry Savary, you persist in pleading guilty.

Prisoner.—I do, my Lord. (He then again looked round the Court somewhat collectedly, as if he had relieved his mind.)

Lord Gifford, having put on the fatal black cap, then addressed the prisoner:—Henry Savary, you have pleaded guilty to the crime of forgery charged against you,—the forgery of a bill of exchange for 500l. and purporting to be the note of W. Pearson, of Birmingham, and with the intent to defraud the prosecutors in this case. You have, I trust, well considered the consequences of pleading guilty. I trust no false hopes or expectations, that by so pleading you should avert the dreadful sentence which it will be my painful duty to pronounce on you, have induced you to plead guilty. You were brought up in commercial pursuits, and you followed them for a considerable period in this respectable city, so that you must have been intimately acquainted with them; you therefore could not but know the calamitous consequences to commerce which the crime of forgery is calculated to produce, as well as the magnitude of the penal results to yourself. So essential is it to give security to the circulation of bills of exchange, so important is it in this country to give ground for confidence in such transactions, that it must have been impossible for you, in your own experience, not to have known and felt the importance of such matters, and the extent of injury calculated to be produced by the circulation of forged instruments, whether the names forged were those of existing or non-existing persons.

Prisoner.—My lord, I was not aware that to forge the names of persons not in existence was criminal.

Mr. Smith, the prosecutor, who was standing near the witness box, most agitatedly attempted to address the Court. 'My lord.'—

Mr. Palmer, one of the counsel,—My lord, I believe evidence can be adduced of some circumstances——

Lord Gifford.—All these interruptions are really very irregular. I must proceed, painful as is the duty. It was impossible that you should not know you were circulating fictitious and fraudulent paper, and that the intention was to deceive and defraud. You could not be ignorant of those facts. It is melancholy to think that you should have so destroyed your own character, and wounded the feelings of others; it is not, however, my wish to add anything to the grief that they must feel. But let me renew my entreaty that you suffer not yourself to be led away by any delusive hopes or expectations. The scene of this life must shortly close upon you. Let me implore you, then, to endeavour—not to atone to society, for that, I fear, is impossible, but — to secure your peace with your Maker. And let me again say to you, that this Court can hold out no expectations that the sentence which it is now my painful duty to pronounce on you will not be carried into effect. The sentence is—that you, Henry Savary, be taken from hence to the place from whence you came, and thence to the place of execution, and there be hanged by the neck till you are dead.

The prisoner, on hearing the latter words, seemed to lose all power of breathing, and dropped down his head.

Mr. Smith, one of the prosecutors, who had before attempted to address the Court, made way through the crowd by the witness-box towards the Bench, and very agitatedly exclaimed—'My lord, as the prosecutor, I recommend him to mercy. I, the prosecutor, my lord, recommend him to mercy, if mercy can be shown. The consequences of his crime were limited, the public have suffered nothing—hardly any thing.'

Lord Gifford leant back on his seat, greatly affected; but made no reply.

The prisoner was then removed from the dock, and his sentence was afterwards commuted into transportation for life.

WILLIAM PROBERT,

EXECUTED FOR HORSE STEALING.

IT would indeed appear, from this very singular case, that murder is not allowed, even in this world, to go unpunished. The reader will recollect that on the trial of Thurtell and Hunt, the principal witness against the prisoners was ———— —arover of the name of Probman who had participated under, and partially aided in the murder, of the unfortunate Weare, but who then saved his worthless life by turning king's evidence. That man was the identical William Probert, whose case we are now about to narrate.

On Friday night, February the 18th, 1825, long after the business of the office had been concluded, this notorious character was brought into Bow Street police-office, having been apprehended on a charge of horse stealing. It appeared that the guilty wretch, after his discharge from Hertford gaol, wandered through the country without an object or a name. Public execration every where pursued him, and his misery was no doubt great. At length he found an asylum in the house of his aged mother, who lived at Ruarden, in Gloucestershire. Within a few miles of this place resided a man of the name of Meredith, a miller, who was married to a distant relation of Probert's. While paying her a visit the unprincipled villain saw and admired a mare, the property of her husband, and brought the animal to London, where he disposed of her for twenty pounds. He assumed different names, but the miller having traced his mare to London, succeeded in having the thief apprehended.

For this offence Probert was put on his trial at the Old Bailey on the 7th of the following April, and the evidence being gone into, he read the following defence from a written paper.

'My Lord, and Gentlemen of the Jury,—If I have this day pleaded not guilty to the indictment preferred against me, it is not that I wish by subtleties to evade or screen myself from the verdict and sentence which my country may award against me, if convicted, but that I might have an opportunity to say something in this Court, to evince to the public, that whatever may have been the unhappy circumstances of the latter days of my life, I was not driven into my present crime from depravity of disposition, but from a species of fatal necessity, which had placed me far beyond the reach of all human assistance and charity. The appeal I now make is not with a view to lessen my past error that I unfortunately fell into, as there is a God on whom I alone rely for mercy; but I do beg of the jury to banish all former unfortunate circumstances from their minds. It cannot have escaped your notice, my lord and gentlemen of the jury, that immediately after, and ever since my discharge from Hertford, the public animosity has been kept alive against me by the public press, which has reached every part of England. Wherever I went, even to the remotest village throughout the kingdom, I was spurned as an outcast of society; and the chief instrument which prevented my obtaining employment, or indeed to effect a reformation, was the public press, which has not slackened to follow, and portray me to the world. As the victim of prejudice, I could scarcely move from one place to another without seeing myself noticed in the daily papers. Those of my former friends, who might otherwise have wished to continue their services towards me, shrunk back from an apprehension of public reprobation for being connected with one such as myself. Every door was shut against me, every hope of future support blasted. My country had spared my life, but individuals rendered that life of no value or utility to me. I was hunted down like a wild beast of the forest. With this desolation around me, and with these dreary prospects before me, I felt my fortitude forsaking me, and I knew not what course to pursue. Heaven and myself only know what I suffered. I was a prey to the most heart-rending care—I was a prey to a deep and intense feeling, the cause of which I trust it will not be necessary to refer to. I appeal to you, my lord, and gentlemen of the jury, whether my situation was not most deplorable;

INDEX.

Name	Page	Name	Page
Jemmet, William	61	Richardson, Joseph	128
Jenkins, William	59	Riedy, Daniel	338
Jesson, Thomas	165	Rowell, George Turner	112
Ings, James	253	Sandon, Thos. Chas. Fitzhue, Esq.	352
Joachim	70	Savary, Henry	397
Johnston, Robert	240	Sawyer, William	160
Ivey, John	70	Scanlan, John, Esq.	273
Kendall, Richard	99	Semple, Major J. G. alias Lisle	151
Kennett, Robert	115	Skene, George, Esq.	63
Keppel, Charles	348	Sligo, Marquis of	72
Keys, John	244	Smith, John	62
Kinnear, John	258	Smith, John	341
Lamb, John	96	Smith, Thomas	97
Leahy, David	338	Spreadbury, David	118
Leahy, James	ib.	Stent, Henry	241
Leahy, Maurice	ib.	Stoffel, Philip	348
Leary, James	128	Stone, Sarah	155
Levy, Lewis	238	Sullivan, John	1
Leith, Alexander Wellesley	394	Sullivan, Stephen	273
Lightfoot, James	276	Swallow, John	96
Lomas, John	74	Sweeny, James	1
Louth, Lord	39	Symons, James	123
Ludlam, Isaac	222	Symons, Nathan	3
Lumley, John	2	Tardit, Antonio	111
Lyon, Charles	390	Taylor, William	76
Mackcoull, James, alias Moffat	281	Thistlewood, Arthur	202, 253
Mackey, Robert	194	Thomas, C.	11
Magennis, Jacob	272	Thomas, Richard Valentine	6
Magnis, Harriet	42	Thompson, John	295
Malony, Thomas	322	Thornton, Abraham	223
Marsh, James	186	Thorp, William	97
Martin	70	Thurtell, John	353
Martin, William	334	Tidd, Richard	ib.
May, John Drew	159	Tilling, Samuel	78
M'Elroy, Edward	322	Towers, Robert	92
M'Ilvena, Michael	396	Townley, William	50
M'Namara, John	126	Tucker, John	49
Mellor, George	97	Turner, William	222
Millington	70	Vaughan, George	194
Milnes, Charles	98	Wagstaff, John Hill	374
Mitchell, James	143	Walker, John	48
Morrey, Edith	74	Walsh, Benjamin, Esq. M.P.	44
Morris, Henry	113	Watson, James, the elder	202
Moulds, William	4	Watson, James, the younger	ib.
Murdoch, John	166	Weller, Charles	154
Nesbett, James	278	Weller, William	255
Newton, John	345	Welsh, Laurence	336
Nicholson, Philip	108	Welsh, William	ib.
Nugent, Thomas	94	White, Frederic	292
O'Connor, Roger, Esq.	211	White, Huffum, alias Huffey	99
Ogden, John	98	Whiting, Michael	38
Palm, Charles Frederick	78	Whitmore, John, alias Old Dash	8
Pearce, Richard	1	Williams, John	58
Pelham, John	192	Williams, —	20
Pierce, Alexander	383	Wilson, James	250
Piper, Michael	192	Winter, Joseph Simmons	76
Preston, Thomas	202	Wood, Cornelius	398
Probert, William	400	Wood, Geo. Alex.	324
Quin, William	149	Woolf, Mosely	238
Radford, Anne	158	Woollerton, Elizabeth	183

PRINTED BY J. ROBINS AND CO. IVY LANE.

extraordinary amount of those on whom the awful sentence was passed, and the more so when we consider that the proportion of capital convictions would be still greater did not juries frequently find offenders guilty of stealing to the value of thirty-nine shillings only, when the property is proved to be worth ten or twenty times that sum; a pious fraud to which they are driven by the sanguinary character of our criminal code, even to the violation of their oaths.

The offences made capital by the laws of England amount to about 223. Of these six were so made in the course of the 150 years that elapsed from Edward III. to Henry VII.; thirty in the next 150 years, from Henry VIII. to Charles II.; and 187 in the last 150 years. Taking another view of these enactments, four offences were made capital under the Plantagenets, 27 under the Tudors, 36 under the Stuarts, and 156 under the family of Brunswick. More offences were made capital during the single reign of George III. than during the reigns of all the Plantagenets, Tudors, and Stuarts, put together. There are persons now living at whose birth the number of capital offences did not exceed 70, and during whose lives such offences have been multiplied more than threefold. If we inquire whether, with this increasing severity, crime has been kept under, the answer is very much the reverse. But the fact is, as we have already shown, that this severity is more nominal than real—that out of an average of 1110 on whom the awful sentence is annually passed in England and Wales, the number executed does not quite average 83. Among those who are thus solemnly exhorted to prepare for another world, a very large proportion *know* that their offence is one for which the awful punishment is *never* inflicted. What beneficial effect, then, can result from the mere ceremony? In the name of reason and common sense what purpose can be answered by keeping the statute book in this state? The punishment usually substituted is transportation for life, one which, by those who have neither character nor connexion in this country, is not unfrequently anticipated with delight: and thus, whilst the judge is most solemnly exhorting the criminal to prepare for an hereafter, his mind is perhaps employed in contemplating a voyage of pleasure. It is only the other day that an offender, on being sentenced to transportation, thanked the judge, with an appearance of sincerity, for sending him to a much better country than this!

We have already stated that the number executed in the seven years of 1819 to 1825 was 579: their offences were as follows.

Arson, and other wilful burning of property	10
Burglary	128
Cattle stealing	2
——— maliciously killing	1
Coining	5
Forgery, and uttering forged instruments	62
Horse stealing	21
Housebreaking in the day-time, and larceny	9
Larceny in dwelling-houses to the value of 40s.	27
Letters containing bank-notes, secreting and stealing	5
Murder	101
——— shooting at, stabbing, and administering poison, with intent to	30
Rape, &c.	31
Riot, &c. (remaining assembled with rioters one hour after the proclamation under the Riot Act had been read)	1
Robbery on the person, on the highway, and other places	95
Sacrilege	2
Sheep-stealing	29
Sodomy	15
Treason, high	5
Total number of persons executed	579

INDEX.

Adams, Agnes	9
Allen, Benjamin	76
Andrews, Richard	31
Armitage, Richard	11
Ashcroft, James, the elder	215
Ashcroft, James, the younger	ib.
Ashcroft, David	ib.
Ashton, John	242
Badcock, William	117
Baily, Arthur	16
Baines, John, the elder	98
Baines, John, the younger	ib.
Baines, Zachary	ib.
Bardie, Frederic, alias Peter Wood	15
Barnicoat, John	295
Batley, John	96
Beasley, Edward	10
Bellingham, John	81
Blakeborough, William	98
Booth, William	93
Bowler, Thomas	65
Bradford, William	170
Bradley, Admiral	148
Brady, R. alias Oxford Bob	117
Brandreth, Jeremiah	222
Brenwick, Maurice	1
Britain, John	121
Brock, Thomas	192
Brook, James	98
Brook, Thomas	ib.
Brown, George	194
Brown, William	80
Brunt, John Thomas	253
Buckley, Edmund	1
Butterly, Bridget	297
Cullaghan Charles	137
Cardoza, Antonio	29
Carroll, Rev. John	378
Carson, Thomas	188
Cashman, George	235
Cashman, John	196
Clayton, John	59
Cook, Jonathan	347
Cooper, Robert	76
Cornwell, William	119
Costello, William	338
Cox, June	14
Crowther, Joseph	99
Cundell, William	62
Curchod, Rosalie	280
Cussen, John, alias Walsh	338
Davidson, William	253
Davison, John, Esq.	95
Dawson, Daniel	67
Deane, Jonathan	98
Denton, John	136
Devan, Patrick	219
Dick, Samuel	933
Doody, Daniel	338
Doody, William	ib.
Doherty, Edward	334
Drew, Elizabeth	168
Driscol, John	235
Duckworth, George	98
Eadon, John	ib.
Ellem, John	166
Ennis, Bridget	297
Fallan, James	7
Fauntleroy, Henry	385
Fenning, Elizabeth	171
Fitzmaurice, Walter, alias Captain Rock	338
Fleming, Patrick	1
Fletcher, Joseph	96
Folkard, John	94
Folkard, William	ib.
Foss, Thomas	137
Fountain, Azubah	112
Gamage, Lieutenant	69
George, Amy	376
Grant, Jeremiah	185
Green, Mary	10
Haggart, David	298
Haigh, James	98
Hall, Alexander	31
Halloran, Dr. Lawrence Hynes	232
Hannah, John	125
Harrower, Captain George	189
Harry, James, alias Harris	221
Hartley, Robert	342
Hartley, William	99
Hay, James	ib.
Hay, Job	ib.
Hale, N.	ib.
Hayward, Samuel Denmore	314
Heath, Luke	123
Hebberfield, William	48
Hill, John	79
Hill, S.	891
Hirst, John	17
Hodge, Hon Arthur William	61
Holden, William	215
Hollings, W. H.	145
Holroyd, Susannah	190
Hooper, John	202
Howe, William, alias John Wood	110
Hunt, Henry	248
Hunt, Joseph	353
Hunter, Elizabeth	187
Hussey, Charles	224
James, John	144
Jarvis, Rebecca	188

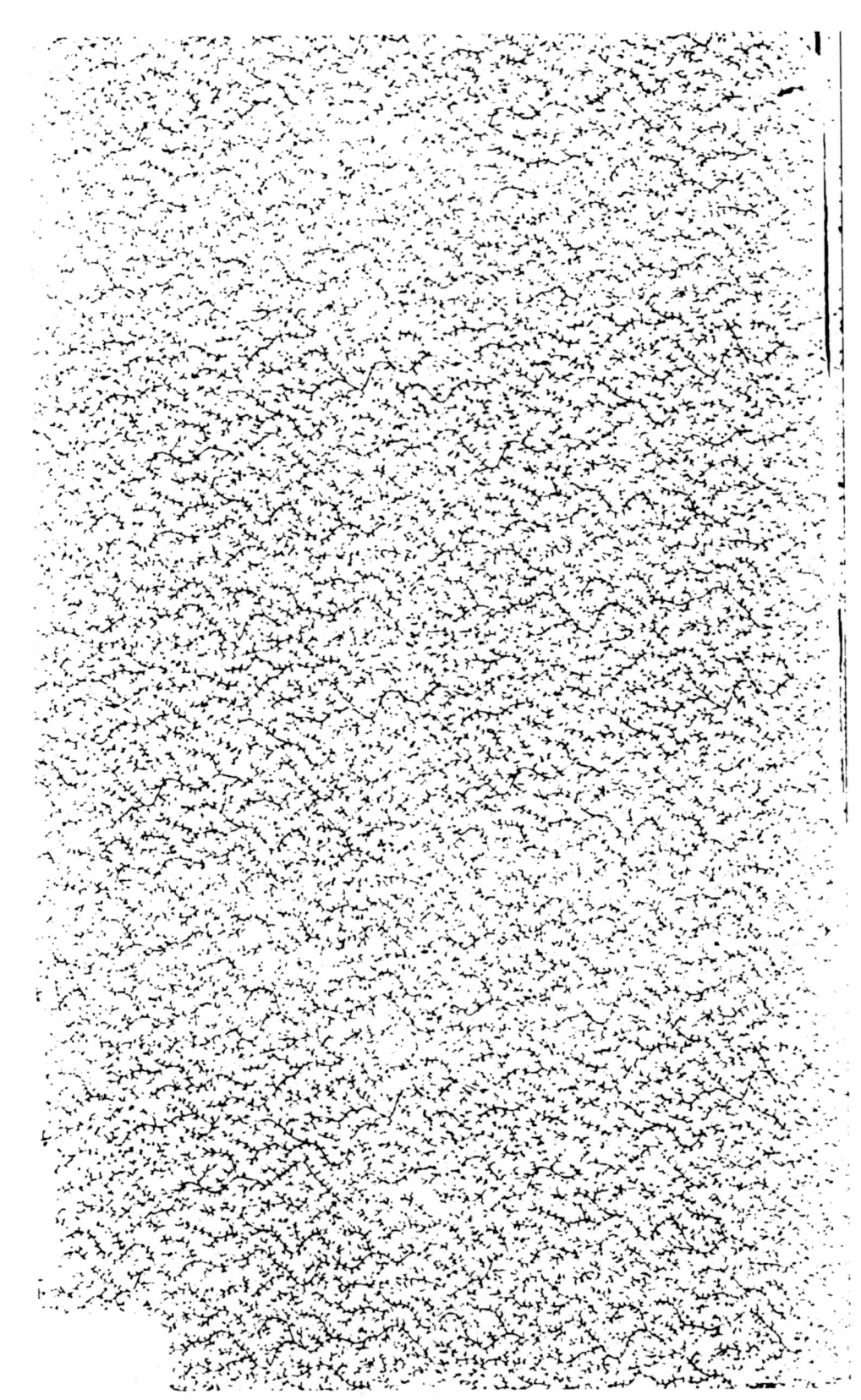

NOV 21 1973

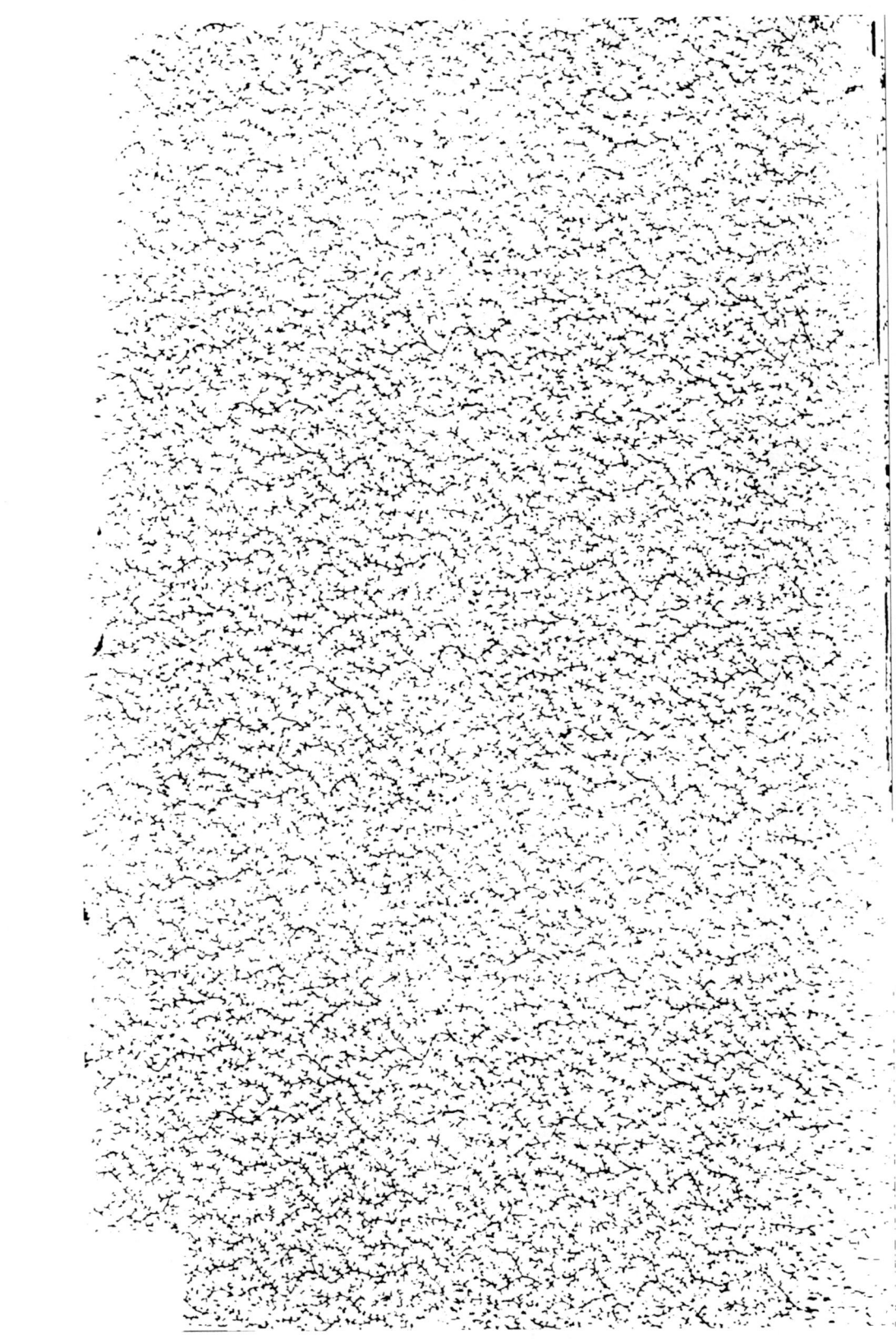

Lightning Source UK Ltd.
Milton Keynes UK
173134UK00005B/49/P